THE

PUBLICATIONS

OF THE

Lincoln Record Society

FOUNDED IN THE YEAR
1910

VOLUME 112

ISSN 0267–2634

THE MATERIAL WORLD OF A RESTORATION QUEEN CONSORT

THE PRIVY PURSE ACCOUNTS OF CATHERINE OF BRAGANZA

EDITED BY
MARIA HAYWARD

The Lincoln Record Society

The Boydell Press

First published 2024

A Lincoln Record Society publication
published by The Boydell Press
an imprint of Boydell & Brewer Ltd
PO Box 9, Woodbridge, Suffolk IP12 3DF, UK
and of Boydell & Brewer Inc.
668 Mt Hope Avenue, Rochester, NY 14620-2731, USA
website: www.boydellandbrewer.com

ISBN 978 1 910653 14 2

A CIP catalogue record for this book is available
from the British Library

Details of other Lincoln Record Society volumes are available
from Boydell & Brewer Ltd

Printed and bound in Great Britain by
TJ Books Limited, Padstow, Cornwall

CONTENTS

ILLUSTRATIONS

Figures

Maps

Tables

The editor and publisher are grateful to all the institutions and persons listed for permission to reproduce the materials in which they hold copyright. Every effort has been made to trace the copyright holders; apologies are offered for any omission, and the publisher will be pleased to add any necessary acknowledgement in subsequent editions.

ACKNOWLEDGEMENTS

This volume began as a lock-down project working from photographs taken several years earlier. I am very grateful to Dr Nicholas Bennett and the Lincoln Record Society for accepting my proposal to publish Catherine of Braganza's account books. I am especially grateful to Dr Bennett for his deft and very thorough editing of the text but any errors that remain are mine. Like all historical research, this edition owes a great debt to many archivists and librarians, including the wonderful people who work at the Lincolnshire Archives, the British Library, the National Archives, and Merton College, Oxford. I would like to thank the following colleagues who have helped with various aspects of this project: Jeanice Brooks, Alice Evans, Alasdair Hawkyard, Kendrick Oliver, Julian Reid, Ellie Woodacre and Chris Woolgar. This volume has benefited from conversations with the students who have taken modules on Charles II with me, and who have shared my interest in Catherine, including Tabitha Cook and Lucy Williams. It has also been shaped in other ways through discussion with Julie Gammon, Helen Spurling, and with Mark Stoyle, who very kindly read the text. Central to the completion of this book are Christy Beale and her team at Boydell, who have done a marvelous job with the text and have been a pleasure to work with. And finally, I would like to thank Mike for creating maps, photography, and welcoming Catherine as a temporary resident at home.

ABBREVIATIONS

Akerman, *Secret Services*	John Yonge Akerman (ed.), *Moneys Received and Paid for Secret Services of Charles II and James II*, Camden Old Series 52 (1851)
BL	British Library
Bucholz, Sainty and Wassmann, *Household of Queen*	Robert O. Bucholz, with John C. Sainty and Lydia Wassmann, *Household of Queen (from 1685 Queen Dowager) Catherine 1660–1705* [alphabetical list by office]
CSPD Charles II	*Calendar of State Papers Domestic, Charles II*
CSPD William III	*Calendar of State Papers Domestic, William III*
CSP Venetian	*Calendar of State Papers, Venetian*
CTB	*Calendar of Treasury Books*
DHC	Dorset History Centre
Evelyn, *Diary*	Esmond Samuel de Beer ed., *The Diary of John Evelyn* (London: Oxford University Press, 1959).
Exwood and Lehmann, *Journal of William Schellinks*	Maurice Exwood and H. L. Lehmann (eds.), *The Journal of William Schellink's Travels in England, 1661–1663,* Camden 5th Series 1 (1993)
Hamilton, *Memoirs*	Anthony Hamilton, *Memoirs of the Court de Grammont* (London: George Allen & Unwin Ltd, 1926)
HMSO	Her Majesty's Stationery Office
LAO	Lincolnshire Archives
MCR	Merton College Records
NS	New style, so dates using the Gregorian calendar
ODNB	*Oxford Dictionary of National Biography*
OED	*Oxford English Dictionary*
OS	Old Style, so dates using the Julian calendar
Pepys, *Diary*	Robert Latham and William Matthews (eds.), *The Diary of Samuel Pepys*, 11 vols (London: Harper Collins, 1978)

Sainty, Wassmann and Bucholz, *Household officers*	John C. Sainty, Lydia Wassmann and Robert O. Bucholz, *Household of Queen (from 1685 Queen Dowager) Catherine 1660–1705* [alphabetical list by name]
Statutes of the Realm	Alexander Luders, Thomas Edlyne Tomlins and John France (eds.), *Statutes of the Realm, 1235–1713*, 12 vols (London: G. Eyre and A. Strahan, 1810–28)
TNA	The National Archives, Kew

INTRODUCTION

ffor an Iron Cheest tto Keepe y^{r} Maties preuie purse Monnys in.[1]

The goods we buy, the services we pay for and the places we visit are highly revealing, which is why account books are such a rich source of information about people, groups and institutions. The four privy purse accounts under consideration here offer the reader a glimpse into Catherine of Braganza's (1638–1705) day to day activities and how these were closely linked to her role as queen consort to Charles II (1630–85), king of the three Stuart kingdoms of England, Scotland and Ireland. First and foremost, these volumes speak to aspects of Catherine's personality and what was important to her. Her Portuguese heritage and her Catholicism were ever present but understated, and situated alongside how she spent her leisure time, what she liked to eat and how she cared for her pets. The payments also reveal insights into Catherine's relationship with her husband, her integration into his family circle and the friendships that she developed with the women and men at court and amongst the wider social elite. Nestled around, and overlapping with, these familial and friendship connections was the queen's household, which she often referred to in letters as 'her family'. As a result, her household officers were ever present. Ultimately, the books are all about the queen's money: where it came from, how she spent it and, by implication, a commentary on her cash flow and liquidity. The accounts also reveal, as the opening quotation demonstrates, that her money was a precious resource that was kept securely in an iron chest.

Working with account books

Historians take various approaches when working with account books and the following offers a brief review of those most relevant to this edition. Jane Whittle and Elizabeth Griffiths have explored and rejected the idea that the consumption of goods, whether luxurious or everyday, was a predominantly female activity, in their study of the household accounts running from 1610 to

1 LAO, 1-Worsley 6, fo. 34r.

1654 of Lady Alice Le Strange of Hunstanton (1585–1656), in Norfolk.[2] Moving away from this focus on the gendered household, and indeed the gendered account book, there is a very strong cluster of work on the objects encountered in account books. A good place to start is with the work of Lorna Weatherill, who during the 1980s posed a series of insightful questions, including whether goods and consumables have the same value, and the same meaning, for everyone who encounters them.[3] In the following decade, Amanda Vickery's research focused on the lives and experiences of Georgian genteel women, and while she used account books, alongside diaries and letters, many of her conclusions about these women as consumers resonate with the experiences of Restoration women.[4]

As part of the material turn, Anne Gerritsen and Giorgio Riello, argued for the evaluation of material culture as 'not merely of "things", but also of the meanings they hold for people'.[5] Studies of specific types of material culture, such as Julia Marciari Alexander's work on the portraiture of Barbara Villiers, duchess of Cleveland (1640–1709), explored the many ways in which pictures could have value, ranging from the cultural and aesthetic to the political.[6] More recently, these sources have been used as a means of exploring attitudes towards, and engagement with, ideas of luxury, as seen in the work of Sophie Pitman and her analysis of the account books of Sir Edward Dering (1598–1644).[7] Dering described 1619, the year of his first marriage, as 'My prodigall year', with the first three months of this account period being 'my desperate quarter'.[8] His prodigality was closely aligned to spending on luxury items such as silk clothing.

2 Jane Whittle and Elizabeth Griffiths, *Consumption and Gender in the Early Seventeenth-Century Household: The World of Alice Le Strange* (Oxford: Oxford University Press, 2012).

3 Amanda Vickery, 'Women and the world of goods: a Lancashire consumer and her possessions, 1751–81' in John Brewer & Roy Porter (eds.), *Consumption and the World of Goods* (London: Routledge, 1993), 277. Also see Lorna Weatherill, *Consumer Behaviour and Material Culture in Britain, 1660–1760* (2nd edition) (London: Routledge, 1996).

4 Amanda Vickery, *The Gentleman's Daughter: Women's Lives in Georgian England* (New Haven and London: Yale University Press, 1998).

5 Anne Gerritsen & Giorgio Riello, *Writing Material Culture History* (London: Bloomsbury, 2015), 2.

6 Julia Marciari Alexander, 'Painting a Life: the case of Barbara Villiers, duchess of Cleveland', in Kevin Sharpe and Steven N. Zwicker (ed.), *Writing Lives: Biography and Textuality, Identity and Representation in Early Modern England* (Oxford: Oxford University Press, 2008), 163.

7 Sophie Pitman, 'Prodigal years? Negotiating luxury and fashioning identity in a seventeenth-century account book', *Luxury*, 3.1–2 (2016), 7–31.

8 Pitman, 'Prodigal years?', 7.

Yet the word accounting has other meanings beyond presenting a reckoning of debts and expenditure, including describing the process of answering for one's conduct. This is the sense in which the Quaker, William Penn (1644–1718), used the word when he asked if 'every poor Soul must Account for the Employment of the small Talent he has received from God'.[9] This notion of accounting for oneself is a theme that has been explored by Alexandra Shepard, and her analysis was based on witness depositions drawn from court records in which the witnesses were asked to assess their worth in relation to their moveable goods.[10]

Drawing on these approaches, this edition presents an exploration of what goods meant to Catherine of Braganza, a Portuguese Catholic woman, who was transplanted to Anglican England. The accounts can be seen as gendered in as much as they were kept by a woman for a woman, but many of Catherine's expenses would have had things in common with any member of the elite. The volumes also offer insights into a specific range of goods, luxurious and mundane, and services that fell within the remit of the privy purse. Underneath the detail is the presence of Catherine 'accounting' for herself as a woman and as queen consort.[11]

This edition

This edition of Catherine of Braganza's privy purse accounts aims to do two things. The first is to present full transcripts of the four account books, thereby allowing readers to consult these documents, either by reading them from cover to cover or by dipping into them. If the reader opts for the latter, there is a full glossary providing details of the people, places and things that were carefully noted in the accounts. The second aim of this book is to offer a brief analysis of what the accounts reveal about the 'material world' of Catherine of Braganza. Before going any further, what is meant by the phrase 'material world' needs unpacking and one way to do so is to consider what the diarist Samuel Pepys (1633–1703) revealed in his diary about his relationship with his possessions. Alongside discussions of his job, his health and his extra-marital affairs, Samuel recorded his love of music, the theatre, and books, as well as revealing a fervent wish for upward mobility, which he

9 William Penn, *An Address to Protestants upon the present conjunctive* (London: Sowle, 1679), I. sig. fo. 2v, https://www-oed-com.soton.idm.oclc.org/view/Entry/1195?rskey=QaSUZm&result=1&isAdvanced=false#eid [accessed 12/2/23].

10 Alexandra Shepard, *Accounting for Oneself: Worth, Status and the Social Order in Early Modern England* (Oxford: Oxford University Press, 2018), 1–2.

11 Catherine Richardson, 'Written texts and the performance of materiality', in Anne Gerritsen & Giorgi Riello, *Writing Material Culture History* (London: Bloomsbury, 2015), 43.

measured by what he owned, what he could afford and how his possessions and disposable income were perceived by others. In keeping with many men of the period, Samuel's clothes and appearance were hugely important to him.[12] So too were those of his wife. Indeed, throughout the diary, Elizabeth Pepys (1640–69) and her engagement with goods is presented though her husband's eyes with his judgements on how these might benefit him, her and the family economy. In contrast, the records of Catherine's privy purse expenditure record her purchases through the more factual and concise lens of the accounting process, and the eyes of her female accountant, Barbara Howard, countess of Suffolk (1622–81). While this adds a financial value to the goods and services the queen paid for, and so offers one way to assess their relative significance, the accounts do not offer, at first glance, the personal engagement with goods found within Pepys's *Diary*.

However, that first impression is deceptive and it is possible to tease out answers to questions about how Catherine engaged with what John Brewer and Roy Porter have described as 'the world of goods', a phrase that encompasses the moveable goods and personal possessions that were central to a consumer society.[13] One option, which is facilitated by the account books, is to consider, as Neil McKendrick has suggested, the ability of an individual to acquire goods.[14] This ability hinged on two things – having the opportunity to encounter particular commodities and the ability to pay for them. Catherine, as a queen consort, was part of the Stuart elite and so, by virtue of her status, encountered a range of desirable goods that were expensive, new, fashionable or exotic. However, she also experienced periodic constraints on her cash flow, while as Nancy Maguire has shown, the king's mistresses, most notably Louise de Kérouaille, duchess of Portsmouth (1649–1734), spent money freely and used goods to assert their position at court.[15]

Another way of approaching Catherine's accounts is to consider how she consumed goods and services, by type, such as flowers, food or the funerals that she provided for members of her queen's household who died while in service. This is essentially what the glossary does. A third approach is to focus on where Catherine acquired the items listed in the privy purse accounts, and except for the late summer months when she was often travelling on progress,

12 Kay Staniland, 'Samuel Pepys and his wardrobe', *Costume*, 37.1 (2003), 41–50.

13 Brewer and Porter, *Consumption*, 1.

14 Neil McKendrick, John Brewer and J. H. Plumb, *The Birth of a Consumer Society: The Commercialisation of Eighteenth-century England* (London: Hutchinson & Co, 2007), 1–3.

15 Nancy K. Maguire, 'The duchess of Portsmouth: English royal consort and French politician, 1670–85', in R. Malcolm Smutts (ed.), *The Stuart Court and Europe: Essays in Politics and Political Culture* (Cambridge: Cambridge University Press, 1996), 247–73.

the answer was in and around the city of London. The size of London, the significance of the shops and the fact of it being a port city as well as a court city and a capital, gave Catherine access to Portuguese goods, as well as a growing range of goods supplied by the East India Company, from India, China and Japan.[16] A fourth approach is a more qualitative one, which explores the balance between necessities and luxuries, between inexpensive goods or costly ones and between repeat and one-off purchases or which compares the familiar and quotidian with the exotic and rare.

In the spirit of this line of enquiry, the accounts have been analysed in two ways. First, I have set out to assess the distribution of Catherine's expenditure and the results of this analysis are interesting. As **Table 1** shows, Catherine spent her money on a cluster of identifiable things. Some fall into small but distinct categories relating to her extended household in the form of quarterly wages and one-off accommodations costs. Others only featured in certain accounts, such as money supplied to pay the queen's gambling debts and money into her hands. This last category of expenditure was very much a feature of the first account book and so coincides with Pepys comment on Catherine playing cards for money in February 1667, but such payments tailed off markedly after this.[17] In contrast, costs associated with travel were the single most frequent expense, although being most prominent in book 2, while rewards were given at a very consistent level across all four volumes. However, when the number of purchases, money laid out and rewards for gifts and service are put together, they represent just over fifty per cent (50.93) of the entries in the accounts.

The second way of exploring the accounts is to focus on the goods that are recorded in the privy purse as either purchases or as gifts. This is not a comprehensive list because in a significant number of entries the items bought or given were not identified. However, it does demonstrate that there is a marked difference in the type and range of items that were presented to Catherine as gifts as opposed to those that she bought or were bought for her. **Table 2** records gifts given to Catherine, which fall into six distinct groups with a cluster of miscellaneous items. Suitable small yet acceptable gifts to the queen were dominated by cut flowers, especially nosegays, fresh fruit and foodstuffs. They highlight the premium that was placed on fresh, seasonal, perishable goods, as luxuries, which made them suitable as gifts for a queen consort.[18] In contrast, **Table 3** summarises the range of good purchased for, or

16 See, for example, Mireille Galinou (ed.), *City merchants and the Arts, 1670–1720* (London: Oblong for the Corporation of London, 2004).

17 Pepys, *Diary*, 8, 70.

18 See, for example, Laura Giannetti, '"Taste of Luxury" in Renaissance Italy: In practice and in the literary imagination', in Catherine Kovesi (ed.), *Luxury and the Ethics of Greed in Early Modern Italy* (Turnhout: Brepols, 2018), 73–93.

Table 1 Distribution of Catherine of Braganza's expenditure in her privy purse accounts.

Account book	Gambling	Lodgings	Money 'laid out'	Music and musicians	Privy purse costs	Purchases	Rewards	Travel	Wages	Entries: total number
Book 6	124	3	6	77	41	155	343	293	5	1047
Book 7	13	1	19	91	52	208	383	650	12	1429
Book 8	0	6	136	113	68	256	395	373	13	1360
Book 9	0	9	81	63	40	87	309	234	10	833
Total	**137 (2.94%)**	**19 (0.4%)**	**242 (5.19%)**	**344 (7.37%)**	**201 (4.3%)**	**706 (15.12%)**	**1,430 (30.62%)**	**1,550 (33.2%)**	**40 (0.86%)**	**4,669 (100%)**

Key

Gambling – money to pay off gambling debts and money paid to the queen.

Lodgings – temporary accommodation provided for members of the household.

Money 'laid out' – a specific term referring to the acquisition of goods, often of an unspecified type, but by a core group of people who appear regularly, including Lady Cranmer, Mrs Hemden and Mr Stevens.

Music – payments for performances by the queen's musicians and the king's, as well as those associated with the household of the duke and duchess of York and various civic groups.

Privy purse costs – money spent by Barbara while keeping the accounts, including the exchange of money, raising warrants and buying account books.

Purchases – items bought for or by the queen, including items described as per bill and per acquittance.

Rewards – payments to individuals bringing small gifts on royal birthdays, at the New Year, etc. They were usually given to either members of her own household, or to the servants of the king, courtiers and others.

Travel – payments to footmen, coachmen, etc., and rewards to them, guides, and people lighting the way. Also including transport costs for stuff belonging to the queen.

Wages – paid quarterly, usually to women, including Mrs Hemden, Mrs More and Mrs Nun.

Table 2 Types of gifts given to the queen.

Accessories and perfume	**Animals and birds**	**Fishing and archery stuff**	**Flowers and plants**	**Food and beverages**	**Fruit and vegetables**	**Other**
Accessories: fans, feathers **Perfume**: essence, sweet powders, sweet waters	**Animals**: asses, dogs, horses **Bird**s: birds, chickens, fowl, hawks, hens from holland, ortolans, partridges, wheatears, wild fowl, woodcock	angle rods, arrows (cases of), hooks, worms	Flowers, flowers from guernsey, narcissi, nosegays, orange flowers, orange trees, tuberoses	Almond butter, biscuits, bucks, cake, caramel, carp, cheese, chocolate, cream, cream cheese, eel pie, fish, gingerbread (French), glasses of water, honey, jelly, lamprey pies, leaks, mullet, oysters, patties, pie, pigeon pie, panada, pudding, puffs, salmon, sturgeon salmon pie, stags, sweetmeats, sweets, tea, trout, venison, wafers, wine	**Fruit**: cherries, figs, fruit (baskets of), grapes, melons, mulberries, oranges, peaches, pears, pomegranates, pomecitrons, quinces, strawberries	Books, boxes, candlesticks, crosses, gazettes, gum, *The History of Portugal*, keys, leaches, linen, ninepins, pairs of stands, playbills, presents, statues, verses

Table 3 Types of goods purchased in the accounts.

Clothing, jewellery, and accessories	Food and drink	Household and garden items	Pets and animals	Recreational items	Stuff for the accounts/ printed material	Textiles and trimmings
Accessories: band-strings, coifs, cuffs, fans, hoods, gloves, handker-chiefs, muffs, scarves, shoes, tennis shoes **Clothing**: Colbertine sleeves and ruffles, half shirts, mantua (French, embroidered), masquerade clothes, mending linens, mourning, petticoat (silver), sleeves **Jewellery**: belt with gold buckles, Bristol stones, buttons (carnelian), diamond watch **Perfume/cosmetics/hair**: combs, curling tongues, essence, haircuts, patches, perfumed water, periwigs, powder, sponges, sweet powder, sweet water	**Drink**: tea **Food**: apricots, biscuits, cherries, cheesecake, fruit, ring o roots	**Carriages:** calash **Furnishings/textiles**: blankets, diaper, holland for sheets, linen for the chapel, Portugal mats, towels **Furniture**: standing screen, staircase, table, table and stands **Garden**: flowerpots, jonquils, turf **Household**: andirons, baskets, bathing tubs, bodkins (steel), box for handkerchiefs, brushes, candlesticks (crystal), looking glass and case, mousetrap, necessaries, needles, pictures, picture frames, pins, rat traps, shovels, sockets, sponges, tongues **Miscellaneous**: a marble piece **Plate**: mending the silver box in the standish, another silver box and gold bottles, plate, sugar trenchers, sweet water pot	**Animals/ birds**: barley, birds, a calf, hay **Pets**: balm for dogs, dog collars, monkey, oil for dogs, parrot's cage, silver chains for a monkey	**Archery:** arrows, bows, butts, press for bows and arrows **Fishing**: Angle rods (fishing rods), hooks, **Other**: billiard table, collations, ninepins, treats	**Accounts**: account books, Ink, paper, **Printed material**: Map of London, printed bills	**Textiles**: brown cloth, buckram for bands, calico (yellow), canvas, crape (white), crine, cut leather, embroidery, gauze, linen, stuff, stuff (French), tiffany, veil (double), velvet, wad **Trimmings**: Colbertine, filleting, lace, point, ribbon, scallop, silk for ribbon, silk (thread), tape, thread, trimmings

by, the queen. Three groups of items dominated: clothing, jewellery and accessories, household and garden items and textiles and trimmings. Prices ranged from Catherine's most expensive purchases, such as £400 on 21 September 1670 'to Mr Roch for a diamon watch as per aquitance', to the much more modest 2s 6d for 'a Ratt Trape'.[19] As we can see from this, the queen's privy purse embraced both the luxury and the everyday: purchases and gifts appear alongside records of payments facilitating her travel, providing music and keeping the accounts in order.

Catherine of Braganza: 'a fond and pleasant lady'

a) Becoming a queen

The woman at the heart of these account books is Catherine of Braganza, the second daughter of John IV of Portugal (1604–56) and Luisa de Guzman (1613–66). John was duke of Braganza from 1630.[20] He became king in 1640 when Portugal successfully rebelled against Philip IV (1605–65) of Spain. John's Spanish wife, Luisa, whom he married on 12 January 1634, is regarded as playing a central role in his seizing, and then securing, the Portuguese throne. Luisa was the daughter of Juan Manuel Péres de Guzman, duke of Medina Sidonia and a relative of Philip IV's chief minister, Gaspar de Guzman, the count-duke of Olivares (1587–1645). When John IV died in 1656, he was succeeded by his 10-year-old son Alphonso VI (1643–83), so placing Luisa in the role of regent, an office she held until 23 June 1662. During this time, Luisa worked to enhance Portugal's position in Europe and her plans included a marriage between Catherine and Louis XIV (1638–1715) to enlist French support for Portugal against Spain. However, in 1659 France signed the Peace of the Pyrenees with Spain and Louis married Marie Teresa of Spain (1638–83) to secure the alliance. When this plan failed Luiza turned her attention to England and an alliance with Charles II.

For many, the portrait of Catherine painted by the Dutch artist Dirck Stoop, typified their first impressions of the queen [**Figure 1**]: that she was young, petite and dressed in a style which looked alien to English eyes.[21] Just how distinctive Catherine's appearance was is very clear from the first impressions

19 LAO, 1-Worsley 7, fos. 3r, 20v.

20 Important older biographies of Catherine of Braganza include that by Lillias Campbell Davidson, *Catherine of Bragança: Infanta of Portugal & Queen-Consort of England* (London: John Murray, 1908) and key recent work such as Sonia Wynne, 'Catherine [Catherine of Braganza, Catarina Henriqueta de Bragança], (1638–1705), queen of England, Scotland and Ireland, consort of Charles II', *ODNB*, 3 January 2008, https://doi.org/10.1093/ref:odnb/4894 [accessed 25/11/22].

21 By or after Dirck Stoop, *Catherine of Braganza*, c.1660–61, oil on canvas, National Portrait Gallery, NPG 2563.

Figure 1 William Fairthorne the Elder, *Catherine of Braganza*, engraving after Dirck Stoop, 1662, Metropolitan Museum of Art, New York, accession number 22.42.3, Rogers Fund, 1922. Open Access. https://www.metmuseum.org/art/collection/search/826758.

of the diarist, John Evelyn (1620–1706), who saw her at Hampton Court on 30 May 1662: 'the Queene arrived, with a traine of Portugueze Ladys in their mo<n>strous fardingals or Guard-Infantas: Their complexions olivaster & sufficiently unagreable: Her majestie in the same habit, her foretop long & turned aside very strangely'.[22] Yet the new queen was rapidly transformed into a model Englishwoman, at least in terms of her hair and clothing, and on 11 August 1663, Pepys observed approvingly that Catherine 'is grown a very debonnaire lady and now hugs him [the king] and meets him galloping upon the road, and [performs] all the actions of a fond and pleasant lady that can be'.[23] This then is the Catherine whose account books are made accessible here from late 1662 to early 1681.

b) Catherine and the key events of Charles II's reign

This eighteen-year period represents a significant amount of Catherine's married life, and it is interesting to ask how far these account books can add extra detail to three specific events from her biography. This is a variant on the approach that Jason Scott Warren used when he teased out the purchases embedded in the journals of Richard Stonley (1519/20–1600), who was one of Elizabeth I's tellers of the Exchequer.[24] The first of these significant events is the great plague of 1665–66. The earliest possible link to that dark episode in Catherine's accounts is a payment for the funeral of a footman in March 1665. While this might be too early to attribute to plague, it highlights that the queen lived surrounded by people of many different social stations, anyone of whom might bring infectious disease into her orbit. More certain are the references to her movements, which are well known from other sources. From references in Pepys's *Diary* and other accounts, we can be sure that Catherine left London and travelled first to Salisbury,[25] then Wilton,[26] and finally to Oxford where she was greeted with 16 stanzas of verse by the poet Robert Whitehall.[27] On her return to the capital, she went first to Hampton Court before heading to Whitehall.[28]

While in Oxford, Catherine stayed at Merton College, the college that had welcomed two other queen consorts before her: Catherine of Aragon (1485–1536) and Henrietta Maria (1609–69). The College register indicates that Catherine

[22] Evelyn, *Diary*, 438.

[23] Pepys, *Diary*, 4, 272.

[24] Jason Scott-Warren, 'Early modern bookkeeping and life writing revisited: Accounting for Richard Stonley', *Past & Present*, 230, Supplement 11 (2016), 151–70.

[25] Pepys, *Diary*, 6, 172.

[26] Pepys, *Diary*, 6, 189.

[27] James Johnson, *A Profane Witt: The Life of John Wilmot, Earl of Rochester* (Rochester, NY: University of Rochester Press, 2004), 33.

[28] Pepys, *Diary*, 7, 46.

was in residence by 5 September 1665 when the Bachelors, Postmasters and Scholars were sent away to provide accommodation for the queen's retinue.[29] Her privy purse accounts reveal her contributions to the musical life of the city with 10s given 'To ye Ringers at Merten Colidge' to mark her birthday and 5s laid out for 'ye uniuerssity Mussique' on 1 January 1666.[30]

Not long after the plague, the Great Fire of London raged through the city and its suburbs from 2 to 5 September 1666. The immediate threat posed by the flames to Catherine's property resulted in a cluster of payments on 4 September in that year with several specifically referring to the fire: namely £3 given 'To yr Maties Barge Man yt wayted ye time of ye fiere', £1 1s spent 'ffor Loding & vnloding yr Maties goods ye time of ye fiere as per bill' and £1 paid 'To those yt feched in Liters tto lode your Majesties goods'.[31] These payments demonstrate the need to move the queen to safety in her barge at the height of the conflagration, alongside the actions taken to preserve the queen's possessions. Linked to these were the pound given to the soldiers who brought 'a Cristall Candellsticke ffrom Sumersett House' and £5 given to 'Lord Arlinton Seruants goieng tto St Jamesses'.[32] We know that other noble ladies were forced to take similar emergency measures at this time. The duchess of Monmouth's accounts also recorded the 'Hire of carts in ye time of Fire' at a cost of £20 18s.[33] While Whitehall, Somerset House and St James' palace all escaped the fire, many aspects of city life and government were severely disrupted and this was reflected in Catherine's accounts in two ways. First, there was a reduction in spending, with outgoings of only £158 7s 2d being recorded from 4 September to 24 December 1666. Second, this was the only accounting period when Barbara did not receive any money and had to rely on money still in hand to keep the privy purse afloat.[34]

In contrast, the accounts offer no direct references to the third great matter of Charles's reign: the so-called Popish plot which ran from 1678 to 1681 and the Exclusion crisis. This affair began in September 1678 with the deposition of the clergyman Israel Tonge (1621–80) and the informer Titus Oates (1649–1705) before a magistrate. Both men claimed to have information about a plot to kill the king. Shortly after a lavish celebration of her birthday, Catherine was implicated in this fictional plot, both as an active participant and indirectly, because key events were supposed to have involved members of her household and to have taken place at Somerset House. As Evelyn observed 'Oates…grew so presumptuous as to accuse the Queene for intending to Poyson the King:

29 MCR, 1.3, 453.
30 LAO, 1-Worsley 6, fos. 22r–22v.
31 LAO, 1-Worsley 6, fos. 29v–30r.
32 LAO, 1-Worsley 6, fo. 29v.
33 DHC, D/FSI, box 275, duchess of Monmouth's accounts 1665–67, p. 85.
34 LAO, 1-Worsley 6, fo. 32r.

which certainly that pious & vertuous Lady abhorred the thought of'.[35] On 18 July 1679 Evelyn noted that he 'went early to the old-Bailey Sessions-house to the famous Trial of Sir Geo: Wakeman (one of the Queenes Physitians)'.[36] The plotters believed that if Wakeman (1627–88) was convicted, the queen would be dangerously implicated, accused as she was of planning to kill the king with poison supplied by her physician. In the event, Wakeman was acquitted and Catherine survived.

c) Life as queen consort

The accounts provide a strong sense of Catherine as wife and a queen consort. There are regular references to her husband, 'the king', including celebrations of Charles' birthday, when she was attended by members of his household, or receiving gifts from him. There are glimpses of the less formal side of their relationship, including the time they spent fishing. For example, at Hampton Court in September 1669, Catherine paid 16s 'for anglerods hooks & lins to fishe' and 5s 'to on of yor Maties footmen for things he paid at fishing'.[37] These contrast with Catherine's more formal role as his queen consort, such as her interaction with various ambassadors.

As queen consort, Catherine enjoyed close links to other female members of the royal family, the most important of whom, in the early years, was Henrietta Maria, the king's mother, by now known as the queen dowager. She was Catherine's mother-in-law, a fellow Catholic and a fellow foreigner, and she features on a number of occasions in the accounts.[38] Henrietta was not well loved in England and she had attracted popular opprobrium from godly Protestants as a result of her active support of her husband's cause during the Civil War. In 1643, indeed, a Roundhead news-pamphlet *The Parliamentary Scout* had gone so far as to observe that 'three women ruined the kingdom: Eve, the Queen and the Countess of Derby [this is a reference to Charlotte de la Trémoïlle, who had garrisoned her great mansion of Lathom House for the king]'.[39] After the Restoration, Henrietta Maria returned to English soil on 2 November 1660 after many years of exile but she did not stay long. She travelled back to France on 2 January 1661. While she did not return to England again until 28 July 1662, she sent a fine wedding gift to Catherine, which Evelyn saw in her apartments and commented very

35 Evelyn, *Diary*, 661.

36 Evelyn, *Diary*, 668.

37 For example, LAO, 1-Worsley 7, fo. 12r.

38 See, for example, Susan Dunn-Hensley, *Anne of Denmark and Henrietta Maria: Virgins, Witches and Catholic Queens* (London: Palgrave Macmillan, 2017).

39 Quoted in Antonia Fraser, *The Weaker Vessel* (London: Phoenix Press, 1984), p. 199; Sandra Riley, *Charlotte de la Trémoïlle, the Notorious Countess of Derby* (Newcastle upon Tyne: Cambridge Scholars Publishing, 2017), 2.

favourably upon, referring to 'the greate looking-Glasse & Toilet of beaten & massive Gold [which] was given by the Q: Mother'.[40] In September of that year, Pepys described attending Henrietta Maria's presence chamber when she was hosting a Circle, or drawing room, at Somerset House, and seeing her seated with Catherine under the throne canopy, while the king's chief mistress, Barbara, countess of Castlemaine and later duchess of Cleveland (1640–1709), was also in attendance, along with the king's eldest natural son, James Croft (1649–85), later the duke of Monmouth.[41] She also played cards on some of these occasions, losing £5 on 20 April 1665 'att ombro att Sumersett house'.[42] Henrietta remained until July 1665, and then she returned to France where she died in August 1669. At this point Catherine took on her mother-in-law's mantle.

As noted above, Catherine could not avoid the king's mistresses and there are fleeting references to several of them in the accounts. For instance, £1 1s 7d is recorded as given on 18 June 1677 'to the dutchesse of portsmouths man [who] presented orange flowrs', while on 7 March 1678 she paid £5 8s 4d 'to Mr Metlans man w^{t} <a> present from the dutchesse of Cleueland from france'.[43] How Catherine responded to these gifts is impossible to tell, although the accounts do revel that she accepted them and that sums up well that, as her marriage continued, she learnt to live with these women and their children.

Barbara, countess of Suffolk

a) Early life

As all the account books that are reproduced in the present volume were kept by Barbara Howard (1622–81), countess of Suffolk, they make it possible to examine her handwriting, which was neat and regularly formed, but it is necessary to consider her portraits to gain an impression of her physical appearance. A miniature of a young woman said to be Barbara presents her as a brown-eyed brunette, with her hair arranged in fashionable small curls on her forehead and longer ringlets hanging down on either side of her face. However, it is a later portrait that reveals how she looked while in the queen's service. Several versions of this portrait survive, including a copy after a cutdown half-length portrait by Sir Peter Lely in the Royal Collection,[44] and

40 Evelyn, *Diary*, 439.

41 Pepys, *Diary*, 3, 191.

42 LAO, 1-Worsley 6, fo. 17v.

43 LAO, 1-Worsley 8, fos. 22v, 28v.

44 Att. to Remigius van Leemput, *Barbara Villiers, countess of Suffolk*, before 1675, oil on canvas, Royal Collection, RCIN 402555; https://www.rct.uk/collection/402555/barbara-villiers-countess-of-suffolk-1622-81 [accessed 24/11/22].

another half length of the same picture in an oval frame.[45] Dressed in a tawny satin gown, like so many of the women included in the sets of court beauties, Howard had clearly retained the key elements of the hairstyle that she had affected when younger and she wears a similar short necklace of matched pearls and drop pearl earrings.

Barbara Howard was the eldest daughter of Sir Edward Villiers (*c*.1585–1626) and Barbara St John (*c*.1590–1672).[46] Details of her early life are limited but she was possibly born at Brooksby Hall, Brooksby, Melton Mowbray, Leicestershire.[47] As keeper of the privy purse account books, it is possible to infer that Barbara learnt to read, and that she was literate and numerate, possibly benefitting from the tutors employed to teach her brothers. Her writing fits with the view that most women learning to write in the period 1550–1650 were taught the Roman or italic hand. One of the most famous seventeenth-century writing manuals, *The guide to pen-man-ship* (1664) by Edward Cocker, asserted that italic was 'of excellent use for Women, which they may imitate with facility, and write with dexterity'.[48]

She was one of ten Villiers children and her eldest brother, William Villiers, 2nd viscount Grandison (1614–43), was father of Barbara Villiers, mistress of Charles II.[49] Sir Edward's half siblings were John Villiers (1591–1658), viscount Purbeck, the royal favourite George Villiers (1592–1628), 1st duke of Buckingham, Christopher Villiers (*c*.1593–1630), 1st earl of Anglesey, and Susan Feilding (1583–1652), countess of Denbigh. Susan went on to be lady of the bedchamber to Henrietta Maria and Barbara was not the only member of the Villiers family to enter Catherine's household. Its ranks included Mary, duchess of Buckingham (1638–1704), the wife of George Villiers, 2nd duke of Buckingham (1628–87), and Lady Anne Douglas, who married William Keith,

45 Studio of Sir Peter Lely, *Barbara Villiers, countess of Suffolk*, oil on canvas, 1670s; sold Christie's 30 October 2014.

46 Andrew Thrush, 'Villiers, Sir Edward (c.1585–1626), government official and administrator', ODNB, 24 May 2008, https://doi-org.soton.idm.oclc.org/10.1093/ref:odnb/28288 [accessed 14/4/22].

47 https://wikitree.com/wiki/Villiers-95 [accessed 25/11/22]. She was baptised at Westminster Abbey, 1 June 1622: Joseph Lemuel Chester (ed.), *The Marriage, Baptismal and Burial Registers of the Collegiate Church or Abbey of St Peter, Westminster*, Harleian Society 10 (1876), 65.

48 Edward Cocker, *The guide to pen-man-ship* (London: printed and are to be sold by John Ruddiard, near the Royal Exchange, 1664), DIV, cited in Heather Wolfe, 'Women's handwriting', in Laura Lunger Knoppers (ed.), *The Cambridge Companion to Early Modern Women's Writing* (Cambridge: Cambridge University Press, 2009), 28.

49 Sonia Wynne, 'Palmer [*née* Villiers], Barbara, countess of Castlemaine, and *suo jure* duchess of Cleveland, (bap.1640–1709), royal mistress', ODNB, 24 October 2019, https://doi-org.soton.idm.oclc.org/10.1093/ref:odnb/28285 [accessed 14/4/22].

6th earl of Marischal. The significance of successive generations of Villiers is evident from their elaborate funerary monuments at Westminster Abbey. Barbara St John, for example, is buried in Westminster Abbey in the north ambulatory near St Paul's chapel.[50]

Barbara married three times: first, the Honourable Richard Wenman (d.1646), second, Sir Richard Wentworth (d. before 1651), and finally, James Howard, 3rd earl of Suffolk (1606/7–1688).[51] James also married three times: to Lady Susan Rich (d.1649), Lady Barbara Wentworth (d.1681) and Lady Anne Montagu (d.1720). Barbara and James married shortly after 19 February 1651 and were married for 30 years. After spending the 1650s at Audley End, the Restoration brought them both to court. James was Earl Marshal of England at Charles II's coronation on 23 April 1662, on which occasion Pepys noted that during the dinner 'above all was these three Lords, Northumberland, Suffolke and the Duke of Ormond, coming before the Courses on horseback and staying so all dinner-time; and at last, to bring up (Dymock) the King's Champion, all in armor on horseback'.[52]

Barbara was nominated as First Lady of the Bedchamber on 2 April 1662 but her appointment was delayed and not universally popular.[53] Lord Northumberland wrote to Robert Sidney, 2nd earl of Leicester, 'My Lady of Suffolk is declared first lady of the bed-chamber to Her Majesty, at which the Duchess of Richmond and Countess of Portland, both pretenders to the office, are displeased'.[54] These so-called pretenders – Margaret Banaster (*c*.1631–66), second wife of Charles Stewart, 3rd duke of Richmond (1639–72), and Frances Stewart, countess of Portland (1617–94), wife of Jerome Weston, 2nd earl of Portland (1605–63) – both had Stuart connections, either by blood or marriage, but they were denied this prized office by a Villiers – and Barbara was not the only Villiers at court.[55] Some joined it by marriage, as was the case on 18 December 1681, when Barbara Chiffinch, daughter of William Chiffinch, who was keeper of the king's closet, married Sir Edward Villiers, son of Colonel Edward Villiers, the Knight Marshal.[56] Others were born into the family, such as Katherine Villiers, a daughter of Colonel Edward Villiers and a maid of

50 Chester, *Registers of Westminster Abbey*, 178; https://findagrave.com/memorial/148319803/barbara-villiers [accessed 25/11/22].

51 Richard Minta Dunn, 'Howard, James, third earl of Suffolk, (1619–89), nobleman', ODNB online ed, 23 September 2004, https://doi-org.soton.idm.oclc.org/10.1093/ref:odnb/13919 [accessed 14/4/22].

52 Pepys, *Diary*, 2, 85.

53 *CSPD Charles II, 1661–62*, 329.

54 Quoted in Agnes Strickland, *Lives of the Queens of England*, vol. 8 (Philadelphia, PA: Lea and Blanchard, 1850), 214.

55 Wilson, *Court Satires*, pp. 289–91. There were two strands to the family – Grandison and Jersey.

56 Wilson, *Court Satires*, p. 66.

honour to the queen from 1681 to 1685.[57] And it was not just the Villiers women who enjoyed places at court. Sir William Villiers of Brooksby (1644–1711), Katherine's cousin, oversaw the king's stables.[58] The influence of the Villiers women would continue to persist at the royal court long after Charles II had gone to his grave, moreover. Elizabeth Villiers (*c*.1657–1733) – the daughter of Sir Edward Villiers (1620–89) and Frances Howard (*c*.1633–77) – would become both the countess of Orkney and Lady in Waiting to Queen Mary II (1662–94) and is often claimed to have been a mistress of King William III (1650–1702).[59]

b) Serving the queen

Barbara's role in the service of Queen Catherine began by guiding her on life at the English court, as indicated in a letter of 15 May 1662, which observed that 'The Queen as soon as she came to her lodgings, received my lady Suffolk and other ladies very kindly and appointed them this morning to come and put her in the habit they thought would be most pleasing to the King'.[60]

Barbara's cousin, Lady Castlemaine, and four others were appointed to the queen's household on 1 June 1663.[61] The following month, a private entertainment was held for Charles and Catherine on 22 July 1663, and Pepys reported that 'being at my Lady Suffolkes her aunts (where my Lady Jemimah and my Lord Sandwich dined) yesterday, she [Castlemaine] was heard to say, "Well, much good may [it] do them"'.[62] Just four days later, on 26 July, Pepys happily reported the latest court gossip: that Lady Castlemaine had recently had her son with the king, Charles Fitzroy, christened 'by a Minister' at St Margaret's, Westminster, even though her husband had already had the child christened by a Catholic priest. He also noted in passing that the king and the earl of Oxford were the boy's godfathers, while the countess of Suffolk was his godmother.[63] The countess was present in the same barge as the queen when she left Hampton Court on 23 August for her state entry into London. Four years later, on 16 September 1667, Pepys noted that 'the Duke of York's child is christened, the Duke of Albemarle and the Marquis of Worcester godfathers and my Lady Suffolk godmother'.[64]

57 Wilson, *Court Satires*, p. 66.

58 Wilson, *Court Satires*, p. 66.

59 Rachel Weil, 'Villiers [married name Hamilton], Elizabeth, countess of Orkney, (c.1657–1733), presumed mistress of William III', ODNB online ed., 3 October 2013 https://doi-org.soton.idm.oclc.org/10.1093/ref:odnb/28290 [accessed 10/2/23].

60 Quoted in Campbell Davidson, *Catherine*, 90.

61 *CSPD Charles II, 1663–64*, 160.

62 Pepys, *Diary*, 4, 238.

63 Pepys, *Diary*, 3, 146.

64 Pepys, *Diary*, 8, 438.

Alongside her involvement in court events, the Italian diplomat and poet Lorenzo Magalotti (1637–1712) reported a link between Barbara and the courtier, Baptist May (1628–98).[65] In particular, he observed that May had been promoted and now held office 'in the graces of the Countess of Suffolk, one of the Howard family, a lady now of some forty years or more, and first Lady of the Bedchamber to the queen'.[66] May was a close confidante of the king and keeper of his privy purse from 1665 to 1685. Magalotti also described the queen's household, listing five male officers: Lord Philip Howard, Grand Almoner (1629–94), Lord Cornbury, Chamberlain (1638–1709), Thomas Killigrew, groom of the bedchamber (1612–83), Ralph Montagu, Master of the Horse (1638–1709), and Sir Richard Bellings, secretary (1622–1716). He also described Barbara as the first lady in waiting and noted that 'she carries a golden key' as the symbol of her office. He added that under her were the ladies in waiting and the maids of honour. The former were married to high-ranking aristocrats while the latter were unmarried young women.[67] Barbara was one of only three office holders serving the queen to hold a golden key. The fact she was trusted with one put her on a par with the first gentleman of the king's chamber.

Barbara's offices required her to have apartments at Whitehall that were both appropriate to her status and her place in the household and close to the queen's apartments. According to Howard Colvin, in 1664 the countess of Suffolk's rooms were located next to Turk's gallery and at the east end of the privy gallery.[68] In 1671, the countess received new rooms next to the Volary, which were marked on a 1669–70 ground-plan of the palace, although by 1681 the queen herself was using some of them.[69]

Barbara received a variety of items from the Great Wardrobe that reflect the various offices that she held. These included regular deliveries of bare hides to cover carts transporting goods in Barbara's care and trunks with drawers to keep the queen's linen, as noted in an entry of 8 December 1669.[70] There are also references to specific items relating to her office as groom of the stool – in particular, close stool pans for the queen, although these were sometimes delivered to the servant known as the queen's necessary woman.[71] Barbara

[65] D. W. Hayton, 'May, Baptist (1628–97), of Jermyn Street, Westminster, Mdx, and Old Windsor, Berks', https://www.historyofparliamentonline.org/volume/1690-1715/member/may-baptist-1628-97 [accessed 14/4/23].

[66] W. E. Knowles Middleton (ed.), *Lorenzo Magalotti at the Court of Charles II: His Relazione d'Inghilterra of 1668* (Waterloo, ON: Wilfrid Laurier University Press, 1980), 76.

[67] Knowles Middleton, *Lorenzo Magalotti*, 109–10.

[68] Colvin, *History of the King's Works*, 5, 267.

[69] Colvin, *History of the King's Works*, 5, 274 and plate 36.

[70] For example, TNA LC5/61, pp. 33, 114, TNA LC5/63, p. 46.

[71] For example, see TNA LC5/62, fo. 93v, TNA LC5/63, p. 47.

had oversight over the queen's bed linen and was sent regular quantities of Holland, including 480 ells of linen on 28 November 1668 for sheets.[72] She was also given items linked directly to her service to the queen, including a side saddle and furniture for her own use, on 30 June 1664.[73]

Another of Barbara's key duties was keeping accounts as a means of providing oversight of the queen's household and its financial management. Household management was regarded as an important female task, whether a woman was looking after her own home, or in this instance, her employer's household. Indeed, as Rosemary Baird has observed, domesticity was a female virtue, which Louise, duchess of Portsmouth, was also keen to embrace, overseeing as she did the food served at her social events.[74] While this volume focuses on the privy purse accounts, Barbara also had oversight of several other sets of accounts, including those of the queen's wardrobe of the Robes. On 30 August 1663 Christopher Musgrave wrote to the politician Joseph Williamson reporting that, while the queen had made him clerk of the Robes, he was not able to return to London at that point. He hoped Williamson could persuade Lady Suffolk to allow a proxy to serve in his place for three or four months.[75] Whether his request was agreed or not, by mid-December, Musgrave had learnt that Lady Suffolk and Mr. Hinton 'complain that, through his absence, two quarters' accounts are not audited'.[76]

Barbara's offices and access to the queen brought her financial rewards. These included her salary and other financial benefits of office, even when other members of the royal households were not being paid, as in February 1666 when a warrant was issued for Barbara Countess of Suffolk to have board wages in lieu of her diet for a year, as groom of the stole to the queen, even though there was an 'order for stay of pensions'.[77] She also profited in other ways, as in February 1669, when she shared two thirds of the embezzled goods from the captured ship *Sancta Maria* with Henry, earl of Peterborough.[78]

Barbara lived much of her life alongside the queen, so when people commented on the queen's movements, she was often mentioned. A typical example can be found in a letter from John Swaddell to Williamson sent on 5 October 1670 reporting that:

72 For example, TNA LC5/61, pp. 259 (24 June 1665), 273 (14 December 1665), 310 (11 May 1666) and TNA LC5/63, p. 8.

73 TNA LC5/61, p. 159.

74 Rosemary Baird, *Mistress of the House: Great Ladies and Great Houses, 1670–1830* (London: Weidenfeld & Nicolson, 2003), 38.

75 *CSPD Charles II, 1663–64*, 260.

76 *CSPD Charles II, 1663–64*, 376.

77 *CSPD Charles II, 1665–66*, 271.

78 *CSPD Charles II, 1668–69*, 196.

> I delivered your letter to Lord Arlington, who arrived at Newmarket yesterday at 10 a.m., as did also the Queen, accompanied by the Duchesses of Buckingham and Monmouth, and Ladies Suffolk and Arlington, at 11; they all dined at one table with his Majesty and his Royal Highness, after which the Queen took coach with the ladies for Euston.[79]

Therefore, socialising with Barbara brought a degree of self-validation to her guests, as Evelyn experienced on 30 July 1673, when he subsequently noted that he 'dined at the Countesse of Suffolcks in her Lodging, groome of the stole to her Majestie, who used me with great respect'.[80] Barbara's support of Evelyn's close friend, Mrs Blagg, was evident at the court ball held on 22 December 1675. Mrs Blagg attended, having 'about her neere 20000 pounds worth of Jewells, of which one she lost, borrowed of the Countesse of Suffolck, worth about 80 pounds which the Duke [of York] made good'.[81]

Barbara appears in the pages of all the accounts books, when she repaid herself, but in the first book there is the suggestion that she either acted as banker to the queen when she was playing cards or that she played cards with Catherine and won. On 29 September 1664 Barbara paid £13 10s 'To My selfe and M^s^ Wells which y^r^ Matie Lostt att ombro att Somersett house in gold' and a further £20 on 3 December 1664 'To Lady Garrd & my self which y^r^ Matie Lostt att ombro in gold'.[82] She also exchanged gifts with the queen, recording £10 'To my owne woman' for delivering a New Year's gifts in 1662.[83] However, later in the accounts there is a switch and the countess is referred to in the third person. On 2 September 1675, it was noted that £5 8s 9d was 'paid by Lady suffolke at the forest', on 26 September 1676 that 'Lady Suffolkes seruants' had received £20, while on 15 February 1677, it was recorded that £1 1s 7d had been given 'to Lady Suffolkes page'.[84]

c) Married life

The earl and countess of Suffolk were a Restoration political and social 'power couple', holding offices in both royal households for almost twenty years. After serving at the king's coronation in 1662, Suffolk continued to mix in court circles and on 28 December 1663 Pepys went 'to the new Tenis Court and saw him [the king] and Sir Arthur Slingsby play against my Lord of Suffolke and my Lord Chesterfield'.[85] He was made a gentleman of the bedchamber in

79 *CSPD Charles II, 1670 with addenda*, 468.
80 Evelyn, *Diary*, 589.
81 Evelyn, *Diary*, 606.
82 LAO, 1-Worsley 6, fos. 13v, 15r.
83 LAO, 1-Worsley 6, fo. 3v.
84 LAO, 1-Worsley 8, fos. 8r, 16v, 19v.
85 Pepys, *Diary*, 4, 435.

1665 and the year after this Sandwich revealed to Pepys that Suffolk formed a key part of his social network:

> He tells me, my Lord of Suffolke – Lord Arlington – Archbishop of Canterbury – Lord Treasurer – Mr Atturny Montogu – (Sir Tho. Clifford in the House of Commons), Sir G Carteret, and some others I cannot presently remember, are friends that I may rely on for him.[86]

In the same year, Suffolk agreed to sell his home, Audley End, to Charles II for £50,000.[87] After the sale was completed in 1667, Howard became keeper (rather than owner) of Audley End. Howard's influence started to fail when Suffolk voted in favour of the second Exclusion Bill on 15 November 1680. The king took his revenge the following February when Suffolk lost his posts as gentleman of the bedchamber and as lord lieutenant of Cambridgeshire and Suffolk.[88]

James and Barbara had one child, a daughter called Elizabeth (1656–81), although she was usually called Betty. By the age of 15 she was mixing in the highest court circles. In February 1671, she carried the duke of York's daughter to her christening in James' private chapel, where the king and the prince of Orange were godfathers, and the queen (represented by the duchess of Buckingham) and the marchioness of Worcester were godmothers.[89] Two years later, she delivered the Prologue of the play, *The Empress of Morocco*, at Dorset Garden theatre, London. She was an engaging young woman, who Madame d'Aulnoy described as having 'a beauty and youth that were almost dazzling, and [which] won her the love of all who saw her, and being of a very gay disposition she seldom frightened her lovers away by her looks'.[90] The anonymous author of *Signior Dildo*, a scurrilous poem that circulated in December 1673 just after the arrival of Mary of Modena, suggested that Elizabeth welcomed these lovers. Early in the poem, which claimed that the Signior was part of Mary's Italian household, are several lines claiming that:

> The good Lady Suffolk, thinking no harm,
> Had got this poor stranger hid under her arm;
> Lady Betty by chance came the secret to know,
> And from her own mother stole Signior Dildo.[91]

86 Pepys, *Diary*, 7, 54.

87 Pepys, *Diary*, 7, 68.

88 Richard Minta Dunn, 'Howard, James, third earl of Suffolk, (1619–89), nobleman', ODNB, 23 September 2004, https://doi-org.soton.idm.oclc.org/10.1093/ref:odnb/13919 [accessed 14/4/22].

89 *CSPD Charles II, 1671*, 78.

90 *Memoirs*, 130; Wilson, *Court Satires*, 238.

91 Wilson, *Court Satires*, 15.

Barbara also looked to the interests of her step-daughter, Lady Essex Howard, who was the daughter of the earl of Suffolk and his first wife, Susan. For instance, Pepys recorded that Lady Essex Howard had been present at the queen's birthday ball in 1666, resplendent like the other ladies 'in rich peeticoats and gowns and Dyamonds – and pearl'.[92] Equally, Barbara ensured that neither of these two young women was appointed as a maid of honour: an office that Frances Harris has suggested appealed to families of some social standing but limited funds, such as Dorothy and Anne Howard, cousins of Lady Betty and Lady Essex Howard.[93]

Betty made a court marriage in 1677, when she wed Thomas Felton, 4th baronet (1649–1709). Felton was a page of Honour (1665–71) and then groom of the Bedchamber (1671–79) to Charles II.[94] Betty's beauty and her overt sexuality were evident in Benedetto Gennari's portrait of her painted in *c*.1679–80, which depicted her as Cleopatra, poised as if she was about to take a pearl from her ear and drop it into her goblet of wine.[95] In her last years Betty was the focus of further pointed written attacks. Written in 1680, for example, the lewd poem *Rochester's Farewell* described the duchess of Mazarin as the 'queen of lust', while 'Betty Felton' was disparaged as 'thy [whore] of honor, to attend thy throne'.[96] Similarly, the anonymous author of a verse satire entitled *The Ladies' March,* which circulated in early 1681, made reference to 'Betty Felton lewd and pocky' before going on to declare 'Lord have mercy on her jockey!'[97]

By the end of the year, Elizabeth was dead. A newsletter dated 15 December 1681 reported that 'The Countess of Suffolk died last Monday night (13 December 1681) and some say her death was much hastened by reason her daughter, Lady Elizabeth Felton, a great Court beauty, was lately at once struck blind, lame, deaf and dumb, and Lady Felton also is since dead'.[98] Eight days later, Barbara's body and that of her daughter 'were carried through the

92 Pepys, *Diary*, 7, 372. In 1667, she married Sir Edward Griffin (d.1710) of Braybrooke, Northamptonshire. He was made baron Griffin in 1688 but was later arrested as a Jacobite and imprisoned in the Tower of London.

93 Frances Harris, *Transformations of Love: The Friendship of John Evelyn and Margaret Godolphin* (Oxford: Oxford University Press, 2002), 109.

94 Catherine MacLeod and Julia Marciari Alexander, *Painted Ladies: Women at the Court of Charles II* (New Haven and London: National Portrait Gallery, London, in association with Yale Center for British Art, 2001), 179, 242.

95 Benedetto Gennari, *Lady Elizabeth Felton as Cleopatra*, c.1679–80, oil on canvas, National Trust, Kingston Lacy; see MacLeod, *Painted Ladies*, 178, fig. 79.

96 MacLeod, *Painted Ladies*, 179.

97 Wilson, *Court Satires*, 57.

98 *CSPD Charles II, 1680–81*, 622. Also see the Newsletter sent to Sir Francis Radcliffe, Dilston, dated 20 December 1681, *CSPD Charles II, 1680–81*, 636.

City... About 100 coaches with six horses accompanied them'.[99] They were buried on 26 December 1681 'in the vault under the Middle Chancell' at St Mary's church, Saffron Walden, in North-West Essex, which was close to Audley End.[100] Originally placed in the Howard vault, which was sealed in 1860, Barbara, her husband and daughter now rest in the lower vault.[101]

The queen's privy purse

As part of her series of *Lives of the Queens of England*, Agnes Strickland wrote her influential biography of Catherine of Braganza. In this work, she identified Sir Thomas Strickland (1621–94) as the keeper of the queen's privy purse, a post he was appointed to in 1671.[102] She based this on a reference to a 'bill for the privy purse' for £6 2s 6d in Sir Thomas's household accounts and a red silk velvet Lord Chancellor's burse embroidered with metal thread with the royal arms and CR, which was still held at his family home, of Sizergh castle, Cumbria, at the time Agnes was writing.[103] However, such a burse was not usually given to keepers of the privy purse; a payment of £6 2s 6d was not paid into the queen's privy purse in 1671 and there is no mention of him or his second wife, Winifred Trentham, whom he married in 1673, in the queen's accounts. Indeed, Sir Thomas's modern biographer, Leonard Naylor, notes of his court career only that he served Charles II as farmer of salt duties (1662–82), commissioner of the privy seal (1669–73) and a privy councillor (July to December 1688).[104] Naylor added that 'he is also said to have obtained a post in the Queen's household' but gives no further detail and neither Strickland nor his wife were listed in the standard work on Catherine's household officers by Sainty, Wassmann and Bucholz as being members of

99 *CSPD Charles II, 1680–81*, 651.

100 Essex Archives, Saffron Walden parish registers. For the church, see Nikolaus Pevsner, *The Buildings of England: Essex* (Harmondsworth: Penguin, 1976), 331.

101 Richard Griffin-Neville, Lord Braybrooke, *The History of Audley End and Saffron Walden* (London: Samuel Bentley, 1835), 204.

102 Agnes Strickland, *Lives of the Queens of England*, vol. 5 (London: Henry Colburn, 1854), 602, fn. 1.

103 National Trust, NT 998667 https://www.nationaltrustcollections.org.uk/object/998667 [accessed 11/4/23]. One possibility is that Sir Thomas was given it by Arlington, who he knew. Evelyn met him on 1 September 1671 'I dined with him [the Treasurer], my L: Arlington, Halifax, Sir Thomas Strickland', Evelyn, *Diary*, 558.

104 Leonard Naylor, 'Strickland, Sir Thomas, (1621–94), of Sizergh Castle, Westmld', https://www.historyofparliamentonline.org/volume/1660-1690/member/strickland-sir-thomas-1621-94 [11/04/23]. He was listed as keeper of the privy purse to Charles II in William Bray (ed.), *Diary and Correspondence of John Evelyn*, vol. 2 (London: Henry Colburn, 1850), 383.

Catherine's household.[105] While Agnes Strickland stated that her history was based on 'facts not opinions', Rosemary Mitchell has noted the 'romantic family tradition' linking them to the Stricklands of Sizergh castle.[106] Taken altogether, then, the evidence we have suggests that Sir Thomas did not keep Catherine's privy purse.

So what was the privy purse? It was essentially a pot of money used to cover relatively small, incidental expenses that were separate from the main household expenses, the royal furnishings (which were dealt with by the Great Wardrobe) or the royal clothes (which were paid for by the wardrobe of the robes). On occasion payments emanating from the privy purse could have a wider scope, as was the case with Henrietta Maria's privy purse when she was queen dowager. For instance, as Howard Colvin has noted, the Office of the King's Works paid for building work for the king and his consort but not for the king's mother. Consequently, work undertaken for Henrietta Maria at Somerset House between 1660 and 1665 was paid for from her privy purse accounts.[107] Privy purse accounts were not exclusively royal, as the papers of William Russell, 5th earl and 1st duke of Bedford, reveal. His accounts were kept by Dixy Taylor, one of the gentlemen of the duke's privy chamber, followed by a certain Mr Gregory in 1688.[108] The duke's privy purse paid for clothing, as well as gifts and gratuities.

As we have seen, Catherine's privy purse accounts were kept by Barbara, countess of Suffolk, keeper of the privy purse, in four volumes with payments running from 8 December 1662 to 8 March 1681. Her total income was £24,408 11s 4d, while her expenditure came to £25,133 13s 3d. Catherine did not sign each page – rather she usually signed the periodic summaries. By comparing Catherine's accounts with those of Elizabeth of York (1466–1503), queen consort of Henry VII (1457–1509) and the Lady Mary (1516–58), daughter of Henry VIII (1491–1547) and Catherine of Aragon (1485–1536), it becomes possible to arrive at some conclusions about how the privy purse was employed by royal women across the sixteenth and seventeenth centuries.

Elizabeth of York's accounts were kept by Richard Decouns, who was keeper of her privy purse, as well as the receiver of the revenue of her lands and a member of the signet office.[109] They cover a single year running from March 1502 to February 1503. Her income for that year was £3,585 19s 10½d

105 Sainty, Wassmann and Bucholz, *Household officers*.

106 Rosemary Mitchell, 'Strickland, Agnes, (1796–1874), historian', *ODNB*, 10 October 2019, https://doi.org/10.1093/ref:odnb/26663 [accessed 12/4/23].

107 Colvin, *History of the King's Works*, 254.

108 Gladys Scott Thomson, *Life in a Noble Household, 1641–1700* (London: Jonathan Cape, 1937), 328.

109 Nicholas Harris Nicolas (ed.), *Privy Purse Expenses of Elizabeth of York, Wardrobe Accounts of Edward the Fourth* (London: William Pickering, 1830), 1, 192.

and her expenditure came to £3,411 5s 9¼d, so leaving her with a small surplus.[110] However, during the year her accounts recorded several loans, including a loan of £206 13s 4d secured with 'certain plate in plegge' in May 1502.[111] Elizabeth signed each page of her accounts until 20 September 1502 and then stopped. Her payments, like Catherine's, fell into two main groups: rewards or gratuities for gifts, which were usually presents of food, and payments or disbursements for the wages of her household, as well as preparing her lodgings, distributing alms, hiring boats and paying her modest gambling debts.[112]

The keeper of Lady Mary's privy purse was not named at the start of the volume, but on folio 78v the following note can be found: 'Receyved of mr Hennage by thandes of mr Chechester and delyued to maistres Fynche to thuse of my lady Maries grace'.[113] This was Mary Finch, a member of her privy chamber, who was also listed as keeper of Mary's jewels in the inventory that accompanies the accounts.[114] The accounts run from December 1536 to June 1539 and then December 1542 to December 1544, thus spanning four years and seven months in all, with Mary's receipts totalling £1,784 11s and her expenditure coming to £2,118 5s 9½d.[115] Mary checked her accounts, making corrections and notes, and when satisfied, signed every page. Her pattern of spending was very similar to that of her grandmother, with payments being made for clothing, jewels, riding, hunting, music and dancing, as well as for celebrations associated with Valentine's Day, St David's Day, May Day and Christmas.

There are some interesting similarities and dissimilarities between the three accounts. Catherine and Elizabeth's money came from their own lands, while Mary's was from her father, yet all three women spent their money on very similar things. Chronologically, there was a shift from a male keeper of Elizabeth's privy purse to two female keepers, which may well reflect improving female literacy and numeracy rates from the early sixteenth century onwards. Most interesting of all was the disparity in how much money the three women had at their disposal and that it was not a linear increase across time.

110 Nicolas, *Privy Purse Expenses of Elizabeth of York*, 106–11.

111 Nicolas, *Privy Purse Expenses of Elizabeth of York*, 12.

112 Nicolas, *Privy Purse Expenses of Elizabeth of York*, ci-ciii.

113 Frederick Madden (ed.), *Privy Purse Expenses of the Princess Mary, Daughter of King Henry the Eighth* (London: William Pickering, 1831), 91.

114 Madden, *Privy Purse Expenses of the Princess Mary*, 233.

115 Madden, *Privy Purse Expenses of the Princess Mary*, clxxi-clxxii. These sums break down as follows: 1536–37: £390 received, £471 7s 3d spent; 1537–38: £200 received, £387 1s 4d spent; 1538–39: £206 13s 4d received, £223 13s 5½d spent; 1542–43: £478 2s 6d received, £470 12s 11d spent; 1543–44: £509 15s 2d received, £565 10s 10d.

Perhaps not surprisingly the Lady Mary received a modest allowance, ranging from £206 and £565 per annum, as a daughter rather than a queen consort, and one whose legitimacy and position was in flux. Next came Catherine of Braganza with her annual grant ranging from approximately £1,036 to £1,629. Finally, there was Elizabeth with a much more generous £3,585.

However, if the sums are adjusted to reflect their approximate equivalent value in 2017, then the impact of debasement, inflation and other factors reveals a different pattern:

- Elizabeth of York received a total of £3,585 19s 10½d = £2,388,116 in modern terms [using the valuation for 1500].
- Lady Mary received between £206 and £565 per annum = £90,903 to £249,321 in modern terms [using the valuation for 1530]
- Catherine of Braganza received between £1,036 and £1,629 per annum = £108,961 to £171,329 in modern terms [using the valuation for 1660].[116]

This evens out the gap between Mary and Catherine, while revealing the relatively modest sum given to Charles II's queen in comparison to that which was allotted to Elizabeth of York. Even so, as this volume will reveal, Catherine used her money in similar ways to her predecessors, striking a balance between luxuries and the necessities required to run her household.

Catherine of Braganza's privy purse accounts

The account books, which measure 14 by 9¼ inches (35.6 by 23.7 cm), are bound in brown leather and their acquisition was recorded within their own pages. Book one cost 11s, book two an undisclosed amount as part of a larger payment for £1 10s, while the last two books cost 16s each.[117] In addition, there were regular payments for paper, ink and pens, and while it is not possible to tell whether these were for Barbara or the queen, it was probably the countess, who wrote the entries themselves. Other areas of royal government used large quantities of stationery and there is no reason to think that the queen's privy purse would be any different. For instance, in January 1676, Treasurer Danby required the Customs cashier to pay £331 16s 8d and £37 9s 4d to Henry Ayloffe, the King's Remembrancer, for parchment to make the blank books of the Comptrollers of the outports and the port of London.[118]

Each of the four volumes begins with a list of money received by the countess of Suffolk from Thomas Wriothesely, 4th earl of Southampton (1607–67), the

[116] These figures come from the National Archive Currency converter, https://www.nationalarchives.gov.uk/currency-converter [accessed 9/2/23].

[117] LAO, 1-Worsley 6, fo.8v; LAO, 1-Worsley 6, fo. 40v; LAO, 1-Worsley 8, fo. 6r and LAO, 1-Worsley 9, fo. 3r.

[118] *CTB, 1676–79*, 107.

Lord High Treasurer, the queen and Mr John Hervey and Henry Hyde, 2nd earl of Clarendon (1638–1709), who were the queen's treasurer and receiver-general, from 1662–79 and 1680–88, respectively [**Table 4**]. Wriothesley only supplied money once: this was the first payment, made late in 1662, that started Catherine's privy purse. Catherine was married on 21 May 1662, but it took several months for her privy purse to be set up. On 18 November, a payment of £500 was authorised to be delivered to the Countess of Suffolk 'to be disposed of as the Queen Consort shall direct'.[119] Barbara made her first entries in the account book on 8 December recording a payment of £4 for 'Transportinge of Trunks from the wardrop to Hamton Court as ffees Payed in Receiving 500li and Expenses' and £45 for 'Changeinge 450li into Gold'.[120] After that, on five occasions between 12 April 1665 and 13 February 1666, Catherine supplied money totalling £1,139 10s 10d from another unspecified source to Barbara to pay for her own expenses. However, most of the payments were made by John Hervey, who was redistributing money derived from the queen's lands until the end of 1679, while a few additional payments were then made by the earl of Clarendon.

Regardless of where Catherine's income came from, she did not receive all of it, because various charges were imposed on it. In book 1, Barbara noted sixteen payments for exchanging gold coins, six for bags and charges and one for transporting the trunks of money, noted above, at a cost of £131 17s 7d. This represented 1.8% of the total income in this account book. Some of these payments were for the exchange of coins, including non-English coinage ('of Gene Gold') or 'of ould gold' or mixed coinage ('39 pices & an Angell of Gold').[121] This was also the only book where Barbara noted when she had made a payment in gold. Most of these payments were made to the queen when Catherine was playing cards such as £5 'To Quene Mouther which yr Matie Lostt in gold' on 23 December 1664, but occasionally others received payment this way, including £2 given to 'Lady Montagus Man yt braught venson in gold' on 1 April 1665.[122] In book 2, Barbara still paid fees and charges at the receipt of money but not for exchanging coins. More interesting, from October 1666 to May 1671, she paid quite small sums for variable amounts of money. Then from, August 1673, she paid at a standard rate of £3 15s per £100 coming to £100 15s 6d. This set a pattern, which continued in books 3 and 4. Sometimes, depending on where the queen and Barbara were, money was needed to transport the cash to them. This was the case on 6 September 1678 when Barbara paid 'fees & Charges at the Receit of one hundred pounds

119 *CTB, 1660–67*, 542.

120 LAO, 1-Worsley 6, fo. 2r.

121 LAO, 1-Worsley 6, fos. 8r, 12r, 14r.

122 LAO, 1-Worsley 6, fos. 15r, 17r.

for this present Month' plus 10s for 'Expenses to London for this mony'.[123] Barbara kept the queen's money in bags, in a coffer, until she used it to pay the queen's bills.[124]

After carefully recording the queen's income, Barbara drew up an itemised list of the money she had distributed with a running total from page to page. Catherine's expenditure fell into six main categories: first, money to the queen for unspecified purposes (mostly in book 1); second, money to the queen for gambling debts/others to pay of the queen's gambling debts (also mostly in book 1); third, payments for goods and services (the largest category); fourth, gifts including charitable gifts, rewards and New Year's Gifts; fifth, wages and arrears of wages; and sixth, repayment of money owing to Barbara herself.

Periodically, the accountant, as Barbara referred to herself, recorded the total of the money spent to date, listed this against money that had come in and then provided an assessment of whether the account was underspent, in which case money was owing to the queen, or overspent, in which case money was owing to Barbara. By implication Barbara either had enough money of her own to pay on the queen's behalf or had sufficient credit to cover the shortfall. The regular references to 'Repayd My selfe' suggest that Barbara kept the queen solvent out of her own pocket, and that she was keen to be repaid.[125] The accounts reveal other problems with royal cash flow relating to the payment of wages. In 1674, Book 2 recorded payments from Hervey for the arrears of the queen's footmen (£50), coachmen (£50) and grooms, littermen and sump[t]ermen (£57), along with the relevant fees and charges on this money, which came to £2, £1 17s 6d and £3, respectively.[126] These entries were indicative of a longstanding, bigger financial problem faced by the royal household staff. In 1666, Pepys noted that 'many of the [King's] musique are ready to starve, they being five years behind-hand for their wages'.[127]

The entries suggest two methods of payment – either goods and services were paid for at the time they were purchased in cash or bills and warrants were submitted by suppliers. Many of the sums, especially those given as small gifts or rewards are round figures, with payments of one or two pounds being very common. All the payments are dated, and it is evident that, while some dates correlate with the expenditure, in other cases there is a modest or quite sizeable lag between the queen receiving the item and Barbara paying for it.

123 LAO, 1-Worsley 8, fo. 33r.

124 For example, LAO, 1-Worsley fo. 38r.

125 For example, 20 November 1664, LAO, 1-Worsley 6, fo. 15r.

126 LAO, 1-Worsley 7, fos. 1v, 36v. However, this does not quite reflect the arrears paid in the accounts in 1674: £45 to the footmen, £48 to the coachmen, £21 to the grooms, £21 to the littermen, £15 to the sumptermen plus £9 each to the Portuguese baker and cook in March and September 1674, LAO, 1-Worsley 7, fos. 38v, 41v.

127 Pepys, *Diary*, 7, 414.

Table 4 Overview of Catherine of Braganza's privy purse income and expenditure, 1662–81.

This table was compiled using the figures from the accounts.

- *Income* – the total of the amounts listed at the start of each account book.
- *Income p.a.* – average figure based on the income over the time of the account book.
- *Disbursed [Dis]* – total of the amounts listed as spent in the interim summaries, which could include sums Barbara repaid to herself.
- *Received [Rec]* – total of the amounts listed by Barbara as 'received' in the interim summaries.
- *Money due/owing* – the amount listed by Barbara in the last summary account in each book as either owing to her or due to the queen.
- *Money carried over* – money listed as either due or owing and so listed twice in the accounts.
- *Receipts/expenditure minus money carried over* – book 1 to 3, receipts minus money repaid; book 4 receipts minus money in-hand brought forward.
- *Exchange costs/fees* – payments made at the delivery of money for the privy purse.
- *Book costs* – cost of the account books.
- *Sundries* – payments for paper, ink and pens.

	Book1 I-Worsley 6	**Book2 I-Worsley 7**	**Book3 I-Worsley 8**	**Book4 I-Worsley 9**
Dates	8 December 1662 to 28 February 1668	25 April 1668 to 3 April 1675	5 April 1675 to 1 April 1679	6 April 1679 to 9 March 1681
Income	£7,167 10s	£7,257	£6,316 10s	£3,667 11s 4d
Income p.a.	£1,365	£1,036	£1,579	£1,629
Disbursed	£7,168 5s 8d	£8,008 6s 8d	£6,380 3s	£3,576 17s 11d
Received by Barbara	£6,430[128]	£7,257	£6,316 10s	£4,841 17s 1d
Money due/owing at end of account	7s – owing to Barbara	£13 12s 3d – owing to Barbara	£16 08s 4d – owing to Barbara	~
	~	~	~	£93 13s 5d – due to the queen
Money carried over	£759 1s 4d – owing to Barbara	£796 14s 5d – owing to Barbara	£47 4s 8d – owing to Barbara	~
	£99 4s 10d – due to the Queen	£153 9s 4d – due to the Queen	~	£1,174 5s 9d – due to the queen

128 The difference comes about because the payment of £738 made on 1 January 1665 for New Year's Gifts did not go to Barbara to distribute via the privy purse.

Receipts/ expenditure minus money carried over	£6,409 4s 4d	£7,211 12s 3d	£6,332 18s 4d	~
	~	~	~	£3,667 11s 4d
Exchange costs/fees	£131 17s 7d	£100 15s 6d	£243 5s	£138
Book cost	11s	Part of £1 10s	16s	16s
Sundries	£2 10s	£8	£6 6s	£4 16s
Timespan/ no of payments	5¼ years 18 payments	7 years 13 payments	4 years 4 payments	2¼ years 5 payments
1	**8 Dec 62–23 Feb 63** Dis – £641 3s 6d Rec – £500 Owing – £141 3s 6d	**6 April–1 Oct 68** Dis – £477 5s 6d Rec – £500 Due Q – £22 14s 6s	**5 April 75–5 April 76** Dis – £1,206 3s 6d Rec – £1,200 Owing – £6 3s 6d	**6 April–31 Dec 79** Dis – £1,287 4s 8d Rec – £1,560 Due Q – £272 15s 4d
2	**27 Feb–1 July 63** Dis – £651 11s 9d Rec – £500 Owing – £151 11s 9d	**6 Oct–16 Nov 68** Dis – £266 10s 3d Rec – £200 From Q – £22 14s Owing – £43 15s 9d	**8 April 76–2 April 77** Dis – £1,532 8s 1d Rec – £1,500 Owing – £32 8s 1d	**31 Dec 79–29 Feb 80** Dis – £229 5s 5d Rec and from Q – £621 8s[129] Due Q – £392 2s 7d
3	**6 July–24 Aug 63** Dis – £381 11s 11d Rec – £350 Owing – £31 11s 11d	**16 Nov 68–12 May 69** Dis – £504 18s 5d Rec – £500 Owing – £4 18s 5d	**2 April 77–1 April 78** Dis – £1,925 3s 1d Rec – £1,916 10s Owing – £8 13 1d	**29 Feb–13 April 80** Dis – £226 3s 2d Rec and from Q – £592 2s 7d[130] Due Q – £365 19s 5d

129 £272 15s 4d + £350 13s 8d = £621 8s 0d.
130 £392 2s 7d + £200 = £597 2s 7d.

4	**25 Aug–1 Oct 63** Dis – £485 9s Rec – £500 Due Q – £14 11s	**12 May–15 Dec 69** Dis – £391 6s 11d Rec – £400 Due Q – £8 13s 1d	**1 April 78–1 April 79** Dis – £1,716 8s 4d Rec – £1,700 Owing – £16 8s 4d	**13 April 80–25 Jan 81** Dis – £1,781 9s 8d Rec and from Q – £1,924 18s 1d[131] Due Q – £143 8s 5d
5	**8 Oct 63–24 March 64**[132] Dis – £376 3s 2d Rec – £360 From Q – £14 11s Owing – £1 12s 2d	**20 Dec 69–4 June 70** Dis – £507 12s 5d Rec – £400 From Q – £8 13s 1d Owing – £98 19s 4d		**25 Jan–9 March 81** Dis – £49 15s From Q – £143 8s 5d Due Q – £93 13s 5d
6	**22 June–7 July 64** Dis – £208 17s 2d Rec – £200 Owing – £8 17s 2d	**7 June–17 Aug 70** Dis – £584 7s 6d Rec – £600 Due Q – £15 12s 6d		
7	**10 July–24 Aug 64** Dis – £199 16s 4d Rec – £200 Due Q – 3s 8d	**18 Aug–26 Sept 70** Dis – £726 12s 8d Rec – £700 From Q – £15 12s 6d Owing – £11 0s 2d		
8	**29 Aug–20 Nov 64** Dis – £241 13s 4d From Q – 3s 8d Received – £200 Owing – £41 9s 8d	**26 Sept –12 Nov 70** Dis – £403 8s 3d Rec – £400 Owing – £3 8s 3d		
9	**22 Nov 64–9 Feb 65** Dis – £290 4s Rec – £300 Due Q – £9 16s	**16 Nov 70–14 July 71** Dis – £638 10s 10d Rec – £500 Due – £138 10s 10d		

131 £365 19s 5d + £1,558 18s 8d = £1,924 18s 1d.

132 Gap in the accounts here between 24 March and 22 June 1664.

10	**16 Feb–31 May 65** Dis – £210 9s From Q – £9 16s Rec – £200 Owing – 13s	**14 July–20 Sept 71** Dis – £438 6s 1d Rec – £300 Owing – £138 6s 1d
11	**10 June 65–8 Jan 66** Dis – £578 16s 2d Rec – £510 Owing – £68 16s 2d	**22 Sept 71–1 March 73** Dis – £552 15s 7d Rec – £200 Owing – £357 15s 7d
12	**30 Jan–12 April 66** Dis – £548 8s 8d Rec – £540 Owing – £8 8s 8d	**25 March 73–9 April 74** Dis – £1,039 10s 9d Rec – £1,200 Due Q – £106 9s 3d
13	**19 April–9 July 66** Dis – £299 5s 2d Rec – £300 Owing – 14s 10d	**9 April 74–3 April 75** Dis – £1,477 1s 6d Rec – £1,357 From Q – £106 9s 3d Owing – £13 12s 3d
14	**10 July–27 Aug 66** Dis – £225 5s 10d Rec – £300 Due Q – £74 14s 2d	
15	**4 Sept–24 Dec 66** Dis – £158 7s 2d From Q – £74 14s 2d Owing – £83 13s	

16	**10 Dec 66[133]–13 May 67** Dis – £589 13s 1d Rec – £570 Owing – £19 13s 1d
17	**18 May–16 Dec 67** Dis – £681 3s 5d Rec – £500 Owing – £181 3s 5d
18	**30 Dec 67–28 Feb 68** Dis – £400 7s Rec – £400 Owing – 7s

Key:
Due – owing to Barbara – so the account is in deficit
Due Q – remaining with the queen – so the account is in credit
From Q – money remaining with the queen in the previous accounting period and carried forward to the next to offset money owed.

Catherine's expenditure was reviewed over different time periods between 1662 and 1681. It is clear that reviews were not held on a quarterly basis and that the timing of reviews changed over time [**Table 4**]. Account book 1 (1-Worsley 6) had twenty audit points over 5¼ years, of different lengths of time. Account book 2 (1-Worsley 7) had thirteen audit points over seven years, with the first eleven covering varying amounts of time ranging from just over a month to nine months, with the last two being a year each, so setting up the pattern found in account book 3 (1-Worsley 8). This was the most consistent accounting period, with four review periods, one for each year covered by the accounts, and all running from April to April. This neat pattern broke down somewhat in account book 4 (1-Worsley 9), having five review points over 2¼ years. The first was three quarters of a year ending at the end of 1679 and this probably coincided with the change from Hervey to Clarendon. There were then two very short intervals up to April 1680, then another three quarters of a year and finally a few months which were linked to Barbara's death and the end of the book.

It is helpful to place Catherine's privy purse into the context of her overall income. In 1681, the government drew up a 'View of Revenues and Expenses' for the queen. Catherine's projected income was then £41,000 per annum,

133 While the previous account period ended on 24 December 1666, the next began on 10 December.

but she was warned that 'y^r Maty cannot depend certainly upon a greater fond yearly than 38,000 lb'. The document then listed her outgoings, which included 'the expenses of ye Roabes', which came to approximately £2,500, her 'monethly money' of 300 guineas a month (£3,900 a year), so leaving her with £2,603 17s 2d, 'which your Maty may employ as you please, and out of which must be allowed what your Maty think fit for the Expences of your Privy Purse and other extraordinary Payments wch always doe and ever will happen.[134] The timing of this review coincided with the year of Barbara's death. Based on the average annual amount (£1,629) allocated to the privy purse in the final account book which ran from 1679 to 1682, Catherine would have been able to maintain this level of expenditure from the privy purse for the remaining years of her married life.

Glimpses of Catherine's world

The social cycle of the Restoration court was framed around the key liturgical feast days – most notably Christmas, Shrovetide and Easter – the dates of the legal and parliamentary sessions, the royal summer progress, trips to spa towns, and the increasingly fashionable spring and autumn races held at Newmarket.[135] People were keen to note where the royal couple were, as on 11 August 1663 when Pepys recalled that 'the King comes to town this day from Tunbrige to stay a day or two, and then fetch the Queen from thence….After the Queen come back, she goes to Bath and so to Oxford, where great entertainments are making for her'.[136] Catherine's travel will be explored further in the section dealing with her itinerary, so the focus here is upon what Catherine spent her privy purse money on. While most of her purchases were quite modest or were generous tips to servants delivering gifts of fresh fruit and vegetables, bunches of flowers or play bills and copies of the *London Gazette*, they were also very revealing about how she spent her time, as well as her money.

a) The queen's household

While not as informative as the queen's Establishment Lists, which recorded the membership of her household, the privy purse accounts contain many fleeting references to the men and women who served Catherine of Braganza. Two key questions are who they were and where were they from. The answer to the first question sees a clear divide between those individuals, such as

[134] Cited, Davidson, *Catherine of Braganza*, 394–95.

[135] Susannah Lyon-Whaley, 'Queens at the spa: Catherine of Braganza, Mary of Modena and the politics of display at Bath and Tunbridge Wells', *The Court Historian* 27.1 (2022), 24–41.

[136] Pepys, *Diary*, 4, 272.

Mrs Crane or Mr Evans, who were named and those, like the footmen, pages of the backstairs or coachmen, who were referred to by their job title. The type of service these latter sorts of individual provided was what defined them, and it also very precisely located them within the hierarchy of the household. In answer to the second, it may be said that most of the members of the queen's household were English but not all. There was a small cluster of individuals from the Portuguese retinue who accompanied Catherine when she married. Some did not stay long and on 15 December 1663 she paid £6 5s 'To Mr Chiffinch for seuerall necesariess ffor ye Portuguez att Porthmouth'.[137] However, her New Year's gifts in 1668 and most other years included £3 given to her 'Two Portagall Cookes' and £3 to her 'Portagall woman Baker'.[138]

There was also a payment 'To the Lady Wood to the Blackemores Lienning' on 15 August 1663.[139] So far the name of this person has proved elusive, as Susannah Lyon-Whalley has noted, but there were people of African descent in the king's household. Whether the man referred to here was free or enslaved, the king's robes account for 1666–67 included a payment for 'a grey cloth suit lined with tabby trimmed with gold and silver butons and loops for the Tangier moor'. The coat's sleeves were trimmed with 2½ yards of gold and silver lace, while the rest was finished with 10 dozen gold and silver coat buttons and 16 dozen and a half gold and silver breast buttons. There was a second suit, coat and vest for 'the African Moor' with breast buttons, 8 dozen gold and silver buttons for the vest, a rich garniture of scarlet taffeta and figured ribbon and a pair of gloves.[140]

Like the households of other early modern English queens consort and queens regnant before her, Catherine's household offered opportunities for women, both young and older, single and married. Her privy purse accounts contain many references to women in the queen's service and they fell into two main groups. The first included the Maids of Honour, the mother of the Maids, and the ladies of the bedchamber attendant on the queen. They were usually mentioned in a social context, in connection with outings, treats, travel and lodgings. The queen's maids of honour were very visible in London society, for example, when they visited Evelyn's home Sayes court, or when Pepys described their beauty or their clothing.[141] The second group of women referred to in the accounts included those who offered more practical service

137 LAO, 1-Worsley 6, fo.10r.

138 LAO, 1-Worsley 6, fo.41r.

139 LAO, 1-Worsley 6, fo.6r.

140 TNA AO3/915, 22–23, 59. However, in 1682 the secret service accounts listed a payment of £50 to 'Randall McDonnell, for a black his s^d Matie bought of him', Akerman, *Secret Services*, 58.

141 Evelyn, *Diary*, 577, 598, 607 and Pepys, *Diary*, 3, 92 and 7, 347.

to the queen, such as her herb woman and necessary woman. These more humble women cleaned and perfumed the queen's apartments.

Women featured in other ways in the privy purse relation to Catherine's household, most notably in relation to creating and caring for her domestic and personal linens.[142] Of these, the most prominent is Mrs Hemden, who was possibly the seamstress Sarah Hampden, who made frequent purchases for the queen, including linen, gauze, Colbertine, tape and thread. She also received regular payments for mending the queen's linen. All in all, she appeared 110 times between 4 May 1671 and 16 October 1680.[143] On occasion, the queen's seamstresses were paid from the privy purse for making the linen supplied by the Great Wardrobe into sheets and the other domestic linens that Catherine needed. Examples of this include a payment made on 6 July 1663 'ffor transporting of Clouth for shietting', a payment of 16 July 1665 'ffor feching holland from ye Greate Wardrope for y^r^ Ma:^tie^', and two payments of 9 March 1668 and 4 June 1678 for monies 'Laid out by Mrs Hemden at the wardrob'.[144] Payments to Mistress Nun, the queen's laundress and starcher, along with her man, who was possibly delivering things back to the queen, feature in all four account books.[145]

b) Clothes and dressing

Catherine's clothes and appearance were the subject of much discussion at court and beyond.[146] Pepys made this clear when, in July 1663, he observed that he had seen '[the] queen, who looked in this dress (a white laced waistcoat and a crimson short petticoat, and her hair is dressed a la negligence) might pretty'.[147] Most of Catherine's clothing-needs were overseen by the staff of her wardrobe of the robes. However, the occasional purchase did appear in

142 For the seamstresses serving the Stuart kings, see Patricia Wardle, 'Divers necessaries for his Majesty's use and service': Seamstresses to the Stuart Kings', *Costume* 31 (1997), 16–27.

143 Eleven mentions in book7, 66 in book 8 and 33 in book 9.

144 LAO, 1-Worsley 6, fos. 5v, 18v; LAO, 1-Worsley 7, fo. 8v and LAO, 1-Worsley 8, fo. 30v.

145 Eight times in book 6, 6 in book 7, 12 in book 8 and 10 in book 9.

146 Aileen Ribeiro, *Fashion and Fiction: Dress in Art and Literature in Stuart England* (London and New Haven: Yale University Press, 2005), 223, 266, 359; Maria Hayward, 'The best of queens, the most obedient wife': Fashioning a place for Catherine of Braganza as consort to Charles II', in Erin Griffey (ed.), *Sartorial Politics in Early Modern Europe: Fashioning Women* (Amsterdam, Amsterdam University Press, 2020), 227–52; Sarah A. Bendall, 'The queen's dressmakers: women's work and the clothing trades in late seventeenth-century London', *Women's History Review* 32.3, 2023, 389–414.

147 Pepys, *Diary*, 4, 229–30.

her privy purse accounts including a reference to a petticoat bought from Margaret Lorene 'on Lady Garrets recomend' on 30 October 1667 for £30 and 'a french Embrodred Manto as per aquitance' on 7 October 1673, costing £35.[148] There were also more specialist items, including, on 18 October 1666, 'a Box of Morning yt Came outt of france'.[149] This might have been mourning for Catherine's mother, Luisa de Guzman, who died in February 1666.

Catherine also bought materials to be made up into garments by her makers. The implication from the privy purse accounts is that the queen chose these materials, either while out shopping or because they were brought to her to consider, and such purchases included, in December 1675, £21 'for 14 yeards of french stufe as per bill' and £7 'for 14 yeards of silver Ribon by Mrs Cranmer'.[150] She also paid £57 'to Mon:s duplessy for 11 yeards of velvet, for point de vinis & Embrodry as per bill'.[151] While the examples so far were probably for daywear, Catherine also made five payments for wad, a padding material, in 1663. These payments included £5 7s 'ffor wad for 2 gounes', that is, for lining Indian gowns which were worn while relaxing informally.[152] In addition, Catherine purchased some very fine, light-weight fabrics, including £1 'for Gas [gauze], Tap and Threed for Lining' and £5 15s 'ffor striped tifeny & Combs'.[153] To finish garments she added trimmings and lace: for example, on 4 May 1674, she selected 'two peices of satin Ribon & two peices of Colbertin lace by Lady Clenton' costing £5 2s 2d, while on 16 April 1675, she paid £3 'for lace & other things by Mrs Hemden'.[154]

Catherine had her own group of suppliers and some of them featured in her privy purse accounts, including references to the French mercer, the Italian milliner and her shoemakers.[155] Not surprisingly, there were several other French suppliers, including 'a french woman for a tremed pare of Marchalls Gloues' (highly desirable perfumed gloves) and 'Bardou a french woman for seuerall Garniturs of Ruban'.[156] Beyond these individuals, there are some who feature much more frequently in the accounts. One of these was Mrs Marie Cherrett, a fashionable milliner based in Covent Garden, who ran a business with her husband Thomas. Cherrett was mentioned sixteen times in book 8, sometimes in reference to quarterly payments but mostly for bills.[157] Marie

[148] LAO, 1-Worsley 6, fo. 39r, LAO, 1-Worsley 7, fo. 31r.
[149] LAO, 1-Worsley 6, fo. 30v.
[150] LAO, 1-Worsley 8, fo. 10r.
[151] LAO, 1-Worsley 7, fo. 31r.
[152] LAO, 1-Worsley 6, fo. 8v.
[153] LAO, 1-Worsley 6, fo. 27v; LAO, 1-Worsley 7, fo. 16r.
[154] LAO, 1-Worsley 7, fo. 33r; LAO, 1-Worsley 8, fo. 5v.
[155] LAO, 1-Worsley 6, fo. 33v; LAO, 1-Worsley 7, fo. 3v; LAO, 1-Worsley 8, fo. 11v.
[156] LAO, 1-Worsley 6, fos. 17r, 30v.
[157] Gesa Stedman, *Culture Exchange in Seventeenth-Century France and England*

also featured in book 9, when she submitted bills for £13 4s 6d and £23 3s, respectively. A second milliner, mistress Bew, who sold hoods and scarves, appeared far less often, but her entries are interesting because they indicate the scale of her business with the queen, the types of goods she supplied and how they were delivered. Thus, in January 1665 a payment of £2 was made 'To Biews Mayds', in July 1668 £14 5s 6d was paid 'to Mistress Biew as per bill', and in June 1675 £1 16s was given 'to Mrs Biew for a dozen of Gloues'.[158]

While Catherine's tailor, Luis Roche, would have worked closely with the staff of her wardrobe of the robes, he also submitted bills which were paid from the privy purse. Some of these were substantial, such as a bill for £21 in October 1666 'tto La Roche yr Ma:ties Taylor as per bill' and a payment of £167 in April 1669 'to Mons La Roche as per bill'.[159] In addition to these large orders, Roche also provided small items and a payment for £3 2s made in September 1674 indicates how they were delivered, with the accountant noting this had been given 'to Mr Roche [and] Laid out by the pages of the Bakestairs'.[160] Some of the queen's other suppliers followed Roche's example, including the furrier, Monsieur Lenoir, who featured in several entries, including one of 4 August 1668 when a payment was noted 'to yor Maties furier for Mufs per bill' and another on 11 September 1673 'to Mr Lenoir furrier as per bill'.[161] Muffs were clearly highly desirable, as indicated by a payment made on 3 October 1673 'to Mr Lenoir for a Mufe' and on 5 February 1680 'to Mr Le noire for a mufe by Mrs Roper'.[162]

Catherine shared some of her husband's suppliers, including two key individuals: John Eaton and William Watts. John Eaton was the king's laceman and Catherine's accounts include a payment of £42 'To Mr Eaton for a Rich Point as per bill', as well as a reference to Mrs Eaton, who may well have been John's wife.[163] The accounts of the queen's privy purse also refer to Mr Watts, who was probably William Watts, the king's tailor. On 3 October 1673 the accounts record a payment of £26 8s 'to Mr Watts for Maskarad Cloaths as per bill'.[164] Whether this was for a masquerade costume for Catherine herself or for a masquerade that she had commissioned is not clear, but Watts was well known for making costumes of this type for royal and court clientele.

In July 1663, Pepys recorded in his diary an exchange that had been

(London: Routledge, 2013), 88. Jane Ashelford, *The Art of Dress: Clothes and Society, 1500–1914* (London: National Trust, 1996), 115.

158 LAO, 1-Worsley 6, fo. 16r, LAO, 1-Worsley 8, fo. 6r.

159 LAO, 1-Worsley 6, fo. 31r; LAO, 1-Worsley 7, fo. 9v.

160 LAO, 1-Worsley 7, fo.38r.

161 LAO, 1-Worsley 7, fos. 6r, 31r.

162 LAO, 1-Worsley 7, fo. 31r; LAO, 1-Worsley 9, fo. 11v.

163 LAO, 1-Worsley 6, fo. 40r; LAO, 1-Worsley 8, fo. 10r.

164 LAO, 1-Worsley 7, fo. 31r.

overheard at court between Catherine and Castlemaine. Apparently, the latter, 'when she came in and found the Queen under the dresser's hands, and had been so long', expressed surprise: 'I wonder your Majestie', says she, 'can have the patience to sit so long a-dressing'; to which the queen replied, 'I have so much reason to use patience...that I can very well bear with it'.[165] The implication is that Catherine used a prolonged dressing process to avoid Castlemaine. Dressing and undressing were very important parts of Catherine's daily routine, which the countess of Suffolk oversaw, as mistress of the robes, assisted by a team of other women. Catherine was attended by her dressers, and while not identified by their role in the accounts, many featured regularly, including Lady Mary Scrope, Lady Temple, Lady Mary Tuke and Mistress Winifred Wells. The dressing process not only clothed the queen's body, it also trimmed her hair, and the accounts included payments for hair pins and jewelled bodkins, ribbon, combs and 'Curlinge Irons'.[166] Then the queen was made fragrant with sweet powder, sweet water and essence and cosmetics were applied, including patches that were purchased in June and August 1663 for 11s and 6s, respectively.[167] Catherine's purchases combined fashionable luxuries that were suited to her status, while hinting at her personal taste, alongside the less expensive, everyday items that women needed to dress their hair and complete an outfit.

c) Catherine's health: 'the condition of the queen'

The account books offer insights into the queen's health, which was a matter of national interest and consequently a great source of gossip and speculation. People were anxious to hear about Catherine's general state of wellbeing, but they were most interested in her fertility and the prospect of an heir to the throne. Indeed, in May 1662, the very month that she arrived in the country, the politician and diarist Sir John Reresby noted that that queen had 'a constant flux upon her', adding that this 'made her unlikely (if not incapable) to have issue'.[168] Reresby's comments reflected contemporary attitudes to female reproductive health.[169]

Several types of medical treatment feature in the accounts. First was bleeding with bloodletting, from the foot, often recommended for encouraging and regulating menstruation.[170] Catherine was thought to have miscarried in

165 Pepys, *Diary*, 4, 216.

166 LAO, 1-Worsley 6, fo. 2v.

167 LAO, 1-Worsley 6, fos.5r, 6v.

168 Browning, *Memoirs*, 41.

169 Patricia Crawford, 'Attitudes to menstruation in seventeenth-century England', *Past & Present* 91 (1981), 54 [47–73].

170 Laura Gowing, *Common Bodies: Women, Touch and Power in Seventeenth-Century England* (Cambridge: Cambridge University Press, 2003), 24.

May 1668, and again in June 1669, and her privy purse accounts recorded bloodletting on 8 and 12 May 1668 at £11 a time and again on 2 September 1669 'for two seuerall tims' £20 16s 8d.[171] The second recommended treatment was taking the waters, which could include both drinking spa water and bathing in the water of hot spas. The French courtier, Philibert de Grammont (1621–1707), reported that Catherine 'had recourse to all the celebrated secrets against infertility', which included vows, prayers and offerings, while her doctors felt that, as the waters of Tunbridge had not had the desired effect, she should try Bristol (or more probably, Bath).[172] The third treatment that contemporary physicians recommended was drinking and bathing in milk.[173] This might explain why Catherine had her own small dairy (see below), as it would ensure a regular supply of fresh milk. The poet and writer Gervase Markham recommended preparing a milk bath as follows: 'take Rosemary, Featherfew, Orgaine, Pellitory-of-the-wall, Fennell, Mallows, Violet leaves and Nettles, boil all these together, and when it is well sodden, put it to two or three galloons of milk, then let the party stand or sit in it an hour or two, the bath reaching up to the stomach, and when they come out, they must go to bed and sweat, and beware of taking cold'.[174] It was not just queens who used milk medicinally. In January 1682, Evelyn had several fits associated with malaria, otherwise known as the Ague Tertian, and on 7 February, 'bathed my legs to the knees in Milk made as hot as I could endure it, & sitting so in it, in a deepe Churn or vessel, Covered with blanquets & drinking Carduus posset, then going to bed & sweating'.[175]

As the reign progressed and the king's unofficial family grew, poets and the populace alike continued to comment upon the queen's infertility. In 1681, the poet laureate John Dryden (1631–1700) cast Catherine as Michal, the childless wife of David, king of Israel, in his work *Absalom and Achitophel*, observing:

> Michal, of Royal blood, the Crown did wear,
> A Soyl ungratefull to the Tiller's care:
> Not so the rest; for several Mothers bore
> To Godlike David, several sons before.[176]

[171] LAO, 1-Worsley 7, fos. 4r, 11v.

[172] Anthony Hamilton, *Memoirs of the Court de Grammont* (London: George Allen & Unwin Ltd, 1926); Brilliana Harley, *Letters of Lady Brilliana Harley* (Cambridge: Cambridge University Press: 1954), 340.

[173] Joanna Marschner, 'Baths and bathing at the early Georgian court', *Furniture History* 31 (1995), 23–28.

[174] Donald Watts, *Elsevier's Dictionary of Plant Lore* (Burlington, MA: Elsevier, 2007), 85.

[175] Evelyn, *Diary*, 720.

[176] John Dryden, *Absalom and Achitophel* (London: 1681), lines 11–14.

Even so, Charles refused to divorce Catherine on the grounds of infertility, looking to his brother's daughters, Mary (1662–94) and Anne (1665–1714), as his prospective Protestant heirs.

Alongside the ongoing challenges that Catherine faced with her menstrual health, she also experienced several periods of serious illness that were severe enough to raise questions over whether she might live. The first occurred early in her marriage and evidence of it features in the accounts. On 17 October 1663, Arlington informed the duke of Ormond that 'the condition of the queen is much worse, and the physicians give us but little hopes of her recovery; by the next year you will hear she is either in a fair way to it; or dead: to-morrow is a very critical day with her'.[177] Arlington was not the only one to be aware of this. On the same day, Pepys confided to his diary that 'we had some discourse of the queens being very sick, if not dead, the duke and duchess of York being sent for betimes to come to White-hall to her'.[178] By 4 November Pepys was able to record that 'the queen is in a great way to recovery' and six days later he noted with approval that 'the queen I hear is now very well again and that she hath bespoke herself a new gown'.[179] While her renewed health was greeted with pleasure by many on this occasion, when she was taken ill in 1671, some unscrupulous individuals saw this as an opportunity for their own advancement. The diplomat Charles Colbert, marquis de Croissy (1625–96), observed that Louise de Kérouaille 'Having got it into her head that she could become the Queen of England' had taken 'every opportunity of discussing the Queen's indispositions as if they were fatal'.[180] It is pleasant to be able to record that Catherine rallied and thwarted Louise's hopes.

d) Religion

Catherine's Catholicism was central to her life. It shaped the pattern of her day and her year. Key religious feast days featured in the accounts: most notably Maundy Thursday, Good Friday and Easter Saturday, Sunday and Monday. Lent was also mentioned, both directly in relation to Ash Wednesday and indirectly with gifts of suitable 'lean' foods, such as the presents of almond butter given to Catherine by Mr Spencer in February 1665.[181] She was also sent fish, including carp, lampreys, mullet, salmon and trout, some of which had associations with Portugal, and so would have reminded her of home, while also adding to the variety of the dishes served on fish days, which

177 Anthony Hamilton, *Memoirs of the Court de Grammont* (London: George Allen & Unwin Ltd, 1926), 168.

178 Pepys, *Diary*, 4, 337.

179 Pepys, *Diary*, 4, 363, 378.

180 Baird, *Mistress of the House*, 265.

181 LAO, 1-Worsley 6, fo. 17r.

were Wednesday, Friday, Saturday and all of Lent. For Catherine this was a religious observance, while for her English protestant friends it was a matter of national interest as it helped to support the maritime community. In 1563, Cecil had crafted an act promoting fish days 'for the better maintenance and increase of the Navy… and not for any superstition…. (nor) for the saving of the soul of any man'.[182] Its culinary impact was still felt in Restoration England.

While Henry VIII had reduced the number of saints' days observed in England, Catherine's footmen performed a key role in helping her to celebrate the saint's days of the Stuart kingdoms. For St David's day, she was presented with a leek, as was the case on 1 March 1665 – 'To one of yr Ma:tie footemen yt preted a Licke'.[183] In contrast, on 19 March 1666, she gave a rewards 'To one of yr Ma:ties footemen thatt presented a crose one St Patricks Day', and she also received crosses on St George's day and St Andrew's day.[184] The year 1666 also saw a payment to the footmen on 1 August for a making a bonfire.[185] This was probably to celebrate Lammas or Loaf mass, a name derived from the Celtic name, of the fire-festival, Lughnasadh. It marked when the wheat harvest began and was celebrated with bonfires.[186]

Catherine's faith also influenced the composition of her household. This was most obvious in the presence of priests and monks. Several such men, including Father Howard, who was dean of the queen's chapel, and Father Patrick Mackinney, also known as Dom Patricio, who was her Portuguese almoner, appear in the accounts. On occasion, Catherine paid for their travel costs, including 10s 'to a footman sent bake for the fathers' and £1 'to yor Maties Berge to dartford with the fathers' in 1674.[187] She also covered the cost of their lodgings out of her privy purse when necessary. For instance, the accounts record a back payment of £6 11s made on 24 February 1676 'to Mr Slaughter Laid out for the fathers Lodging at winsor in 1674' and a further payment of £51 6s made in September 1678.[188] The queen's religious beliefs also dictated where she spent time and how she accessed the various chapels at her disposal, and this is reflected in the many payments made for barges taking her to and from Somerset House.

182 Eliz. I c.5, *Statutes of the Realm*, 4:1, 422–23; R. C. L. Sgroi, 'Piscatorial politics revisited: the language of economic debate and the evolution of fishing policy in Elizabethan England', *Albion* 35.1 (2003), 2–3.

183 LAO, 1-Worsley 6, fo. 17r. In some years she received a cross rather than a leek, for example, March 1673, LAO, 1-Worsley 7, fo. 29v.

184 LAO, 1-Worsley 6, fo. 24v.

185 LAO, 1-Worsley 6, fo. 28v.

186 Ronald Hutton, *The Rise and Fall of Merry England: The Ritual Year 1400–1700* (Oxford: Oxford University Press, 1994), 44.

187 LAO, 1-Worsley 7, fos. 36v, 40r.

188 LAO, 1-Worsley 8, fos.11r, 33v.

However, Catherine's faith was rarely mentioned explicitly in the accounts and, consequently, there were very few religious purchases. The one notable exception was the payment made on 9 May 1663 'To Mis fountayne Makeing Lining for the Chappell as By Bill'.[189] As Chelsea Reutcke has suggested, this is partly because Catherine obtained, and on occasions sponsored, Catholic books and pamphlets by other means.[190] The same is true for consumables for her chapel. In November 1677, Danby ordered the Customs Commissioners to deliver, customs free, certain items brought from Lisbon to David Rowland, groom of the robes, for the queen. These included four chests of wax candles for her chapel, along with six boxes of sweet meats, a small cask with sweet water, and two quarter casks of bacon.[191]

There were other reminders of Catherine's piety in her engagement with what she would have regarded as acts of mercy.[192] Of the seven merciful acts, some are more visible in the accounts, such as the payments for twelve funerals. Of these, eleven were for members of her household and so could have been seen as an act of good lordship. In addition, on 15 February 1663, £5 was given to 'a Poore woman to Bury her husband by your Maties order'.[193] Two years later on 11 April 1665, she spent 9s 'ffor threde & tape & Making ye poore Childrens aprons'.[194] It is possible that some of the other payments for linens were put to a similar use. In most cases the accounts recorded money give to unnamed poor men and women, including 'a Poore woman sent by Lady Gerrarde'.[195] Other monies were distributed to the poor of specific communities, including 'the poore att oxbri<d>ge' [Oxbridge, Dorset], 'the poore at Audley end', 'the poore of Bery' [Bury St Edmunds] and 'the poore of Ewston' [Euston Hall].[196] In the last account book, it was noted that Mr Cleyton had been repaid £5, which was given on 13 October 1679 'to the poore', and similar payments were made on 31 March and 6 October 1680.[197]

Catherine also sent gifts for six christenings during the 1670s, including on 3 June 1676 the sum of £21 15s 'to Lady fingalls Cristning'.[198] She provided

[189] LAO, 1-Worsley 6, fo. 4r.

[190] Chelsea Reutcke, 'Royal patronage of illicit print: Catherine of Braganza and Catholic books in late seventeenth-century London', in Nina Lamal, Jamie Cumby and Helmer J. Helmers (eds.), *Print and Power in Early Modern Europe, 1500–1800* (Leiden: Brill, 2021), 239–56.

[191] *CTB, 1676–79,* 789.

[192] These are: to feed the hungry, give a drink to the thirsty, clothe the naked, shelter the homeless, minister to the sick, visit the imprisoned and bury the dead.

[193] LAO, 1-Worsley 6, fo. 2v.

[194] LAO, 1-Worsley 6, fo. 17v.

[195] LAO, 1-Worsley 6, fo. 2v.

[196] LAO, 1-Worsley 6, fo. 8r, LAO, 1-Worsley 7, fo.7v, LAO, 1-Worsley 8, fo.16v.

[197] LAO, 1-Worsley 9, fos. 8v, 13r, 20v.

[198] LAO, 1-Worsley 8, fo. 14r.

financial support for the widows of her grooms and footmen, with sums ranging from £5 to £20, including a payment made to 'Mrs Bussy yor Maties grooms wedow' in October 1671.[199] In addition, several individuals who were described as old feature in the accounts. Some received money in return for small gifts, such as the money given to the old groom and footman who gave asparagus, while others appear to have been given money in response to their age. A few were named, including 'old Georg Bar' and 'old Mr Bure', but the most frequent recipient was an unnamed elderly footman of Henrietta Maria.[200] Through such payments, Catherine demonstrated that she was both a good mistress to her household and a pious queen.

e) Politics

Catherine is often presented by historians as a nonpolitical queen consort, yet it was impossible for a queen consort to completely avoid the political world and it is debatable whether she wanted to. This section explores the different ways in which Catherine engaged with politicians and key political institutions, and the less formal ways in which she could be involved in the political sphere. While on the one hand, these accounts deal primarily with Catherine's domestic concerns, on the other, the pages include the names of men and women who were central to the government and court life. Most prominent among these were Henry Bennet, who was referred to in the accounts as Lord Arlington, and his wife, Isabella van Nassau-Beverweert. One reason why they both feature so regularly is that they were members of the queen's household. This reminds us that the household had the potential to be a highly political place: one where individuals with political interests could serve within this 'domestic' context. The Arlingtons' presence was consistent throughout the accounts, with four references in book one (two for him, two for her), twenty-five in book two (two for him, twenty-three for her), thirty-six in book three (four for him, thirty-two for her) and sixteen in book four (seven for him, nine for her). In all, they appeared eighty-one times (fifteen for him, sixty-six for her).

There are several reasons for their consistent presence. Magalotti described Arlington as 'generous to his friends and very affable to deal with', while also noting 'the moderation with which he uses his favour with the King'.[201] Similarly, the Venetian ambassador noted that Arlington was 'always by the king's side'.[202] As a consequence, the king used Arlington's home just outside

199 LAO, 1-Worsley 6, fos. 11r, 14r, 16v. LAO, 1-Worsley 7, fo. 28r.
200 LAO, 1-Worsley 8, fos. 11v, 17v, 29v.
201 Middleton, *Lorenzo Magalotti*, 43.
202 *CSP Venetian, 1666–68*, 14.

St James's park to entertain male friends and the Spanish ambassador.[203] More importantly, Arlington was on the rise in the 1660s, and the fall of Edward Hyde, 1st earl of Clarendon, in 1667 saw him becoming more powerful still with the establishment of the so-called 'Cabal'. Named after the five men who were generally thought to hold power between 1667 and 1674, the Cabal consisted of: Thomas Clifford, 1st baron Clifford of Chudleigh, Henry Bennet, lord Arlington, George Villiers, duke of Buckingham, Antony Ashley-Cooper, later lord Shaftesbury, and John Maitland, duke of Lauderdale. All of these men, apart from Thomas Clifford, featured in Catherine's account books.

After the collapse of the Cabal, Shaftesbury worked alone and he was succeeded by Thomas, viscount Osborne, later the earl of Danby and finally the 1st duke of Leeds. Danby's ardent Protestantism could explain why he did not feature in the account books. However, Arlington survived, and his career took two different routes: firstly, as an ambassador and secondly as a member of the queen's household.[204] Arlington served as Catherine's Lord Chamberlain in 1682 and as Lord Steward of her Revenue between 1682 and 1684 (although both of these offices fell outside the span of the privy purse account books that are being discussed here).[205]

However, it was Arlington's wife Isabella who appeared far more frequently in the accounts. While there has been some doubt over whether Isabella was appointed as a lady of the bedchamber in 1666, she regularly entertained the queen and sent members of her household to deliver many small gifts.[206] She was a woman who took great interest in current fashions. When Evelyn visited the countess on 17 April 1673, he was shown her new dressing room at Goring House 'where was a bed, 2 glasses, silver jarrs & Vasas, Cabinets & other so rich furniture, as I have seldom seene the like; to this ecesse of superfluity wer we now arriv'd, & that not onely at Court, but almost universaly, even to wantonesse, & profusion'.[207] The following year, the privy purse accounts recorded a payment made 'to Lady Arlintons footmen with things from the Custom house for yor Matie'.[208]

Two other men who straddled the divide between the queen's household and wider court and national politics deserve a mention here. The first was Ralph Montagu (1638–1709), who was master of the horse to the queen and a client of Arlington.[209] There are not many references in the account books to Ralph, but

[203] Middleton, *Lorenzo Magalotti*, 77.

[204] Helen Jacobsen, *Luxury and Power: The Material World of the Stuart Diplomat, 1660–1714* (Oxford: Oxford University Press, 2012), 81, 94, 111, 129.

[205] Sainty, Wassmann and Bucholz, *Household officers*, 2.

[206] Sainty, Wassmann and Bucholz, *Household officers*, 2.

[207] Evelyn, *Diary*, 585.

[208] LAO, 1-Worsley 7, fo. 35r.

[209] Jacobsen, *Luxury and Power*, 140.

they allude to his role for the queen and his role as an ambassador to France. The latter is confirmed in other sources, which noted that he bought clothes for the queen in France in 1677 when he imported 'two small boxes with clothes for ye Queene'.[210] The second significant figure was Lord Feversham (1641–1707), who became Master of the Horse to Catherine of Braganza and her Lord Chamberlain in 1680. He featured in the last account book.

Looking beyond the household, the accounts reveal Catherine's engagement with the European ambassadors who came to the Restoration court. While Pepys and Evelyn referred to the formal entrance and reception of foreign ambassadors in their diaries, the privy purse accounts offer a view of the more informal links that the ambassadors had with the queen. At various times the ambassadors from France, the Netherlands, Portugal, Spain and Sweden all sought to engage with Catherine. This could be on a small scale, as was the case with the Dutch, French and Swedish ambassadors, or much more dedicated attendance, as was the case with the Spanish and Portuguese visitors. The latter were particularly noticeable in the 1670s and 1680s, with Francisco del Melo Manoel da Camara and the Maquis of Arronches featuring frequently in the accounts. In all cases, the ambassadors sent various of their household servants to the queen, but this went further with the Spanish and Portuguese ambassadors, who regularly put their chairmen, footmen and on occasion coachmen at her service.[211]

Catherine also engaged with parliament. She could attend in person with her husband, as she did on 21 March 1664, when Pepys recorded that 'This day the House of Parliament met and the King met them, with the Queen with him'.[212] This was a formal and official visit to mark the opening of the parliamentary session. However, Catherine also attended on other occasions, and on 10 December 1666 the accounts recorded a payment of £2 'To ye Doore Keeper of ye parlement when y^{r} Ma:^{tie} went Incognito'.[213] By travelling incognito, Catherine was emulating Henrietta Maria, who had famously gone to plays in disguise. This visit was one of six references to Catherine's engagement with parliament. They record her visiting the house: on 5 August 1664 (when parliament was not in session, as this was the summer recess), 5 January 1665 (part of the session running from 24 November 1664 to 2 March 1665), on 27 September (when MPs were discussing the rebuilding of London bill), on 10 and 14 December 1666 (no debate is recorded on 10th December, while 14th fell in the recess) and finally on 12 April 1678 (part of the session from 15 February 1677 to 13 May 1678).[214] While there is always the possibility that the

[210] Jacobsen, *Luxury and Power*, 99, fn. 24.

[211] For example, LAO, 1-Worsley 8, fos. 5r, 7r, 11r.

[212] Pepys, *Diary*, 5, 93.

[213] LAO, 1-Worsley 6, fo. 32r.

[214] LAO, 1-Worsley 6, fos. 12r, 16r, 30r, 32r, 32v; LAO, 1-Worsley 8, fo., 29v.

dates listed in the accounts reflect the day when payment was made rather than the day when the expense was incurred, the six visits do point to the queen being interested in parliament in the early years of her marriage. There were very few references to women in the diary of John Milward (1599–1670), MP for Derbyshire, or his view of parliamentary business. There were just two mentions of the queen and her mother-in-law.[215] There was also discussion of Lady Isabella Arlington's naturalisation on 4, 6, 12 and 24 October 1666.[216]

We also glimpse less formal methods of lobbying the queen in the accounts, especially during the 1670s, when Barbara made reference to two variants on the idea of petitioning. One, where the word was used as a verb, was a means of asking for money, as was the case in 1670, when £12 was given 'to yor Maties footmen vpon petition'.[217] This may well have been a request for backpay rather than something more political. The other, where the word was used as a noun, may have been when individuals sought the queen's support for a specific petition. For example, in 1677 'a poore man with a petition' received £1, as did 'a poore womane with a petetion' in the following year.[218] In all of these instances, Catherine would have been able to engage with the political sphere in informal ways and the fact that her influence was inconspicuous did not make it any less important.

f) Recreation

In the summer of 1675, Mary of Modena wrote 'we go every night ethiere by watter or by land, or a walking or a fisching, or sometimes to contre gentlemens houses where we dance and play at little plays, and cary our one super and supe in the garden or in the field'.[219] Mary's words provided a good sense of the range of evening entertainments available to women at court, but these are not always easy to track in the accounts. So, this section explores how Catherine spent her spare time in three ways: going to the theatre, gambling, and spending time with her pets (and other animals).

There were close links between the theatre and the Restoration court, ranging from the two companies that were under the patronage of the king and his brother, to the cluster of aristocratic playwrights, such as the dukes of Newcastle and Buckingham, the earls of Bristol and Orrery, as well as Sir George Etherege (1636–92), Sir Robert Howard (1626–98), Sir Charles Sedley

215 Caroline Robbins (ed.), *The Diary of John Milward Esq, Member of Parliament for Derbyshire, September 1666 to May 1668* (Cambridge: Cambridge University Press, 1938), 4, 31.

216 Robbins, *Diary of John Milward*, 14, 16, 21, 30.

217 LAO, 1-Worsley 7, fo. 16v.

218 LAO, 1-Worsley 8, fos. 23r, 34v.

219 Margaret Toynbee, 'A further note on the early correspondence of Queen Mary of Modena', *Notes and Queries* 193 (1948), 293.

(1639–1701) and Sir Samuel Tuke (*c*.1615–74).[220] Not surprisingly, Catherine was often the focus of their work. This could be a positive experience, as in John Dryden's *Tyrannick Love or The Royal Martyr* (1669), which drew on the story of St Catherine of Alexandria and her martyrdom by Maximin.[221] But, on other occasions, she was represented in works that were scurrilous in the extreme, as in the anonymous, *The Farce of Sodom, or The Quintessence of Debauchery* (1672), where Catherine was one of the play's many targets.[222] While *Sodom* was a closet drama, which was intended to be read in private rather than performed on stage, many contemporaries attributed it to John Wilmot, 2nd earl of Rochester, so ensuring its barbed comments were well-known. Even so, Catherine still took a close interest in what was being performed at the London theatres. She regularly received copies of the play bills and made many payments to Mr Hailes, Mr Hill, Mr Murray and Mr Pavy, the theatre box keepers, so much so that they featured in her New Year's gifts lists in the later 1670s.[223]

While Catherine was on display when she went to the theatre, she was still the subject of comment when she hosted or attended events held within the royal palaces. On 17 February 1667 Pepys was shocked to see Catherine playing cards for money on a Sunday.[224] However, her first account book indicates that this was a popular form of entertainment in the early years of her marriage. She played the French card games *Cuba* and *Loo* or *Lanterloo*, as well as *ombre*, a Spanish game, and *Losing Lodam*, an English game, and board games such as the *Game of Goose*. To add a frisson of risk, she regularly placed a wager on the outcome, either receiving cash in advance from the countess of Suffolk or borrowing money from other players whom the countess subsequently repaid.

Catherine engaged in other fashionable sporting pastimes. On 31 July 1663, she paid £16 'ffor a Billyard table' and on 20 September Suffolk paid £1 to 'your Matie att billyards'.[225] A few years later she tried bowls, giving rewards on 16 September 1665 'for ye Ea:rle of pembroucks Boulling Grine Keeper' and 12 June 1666 'To ye Boulling Grine Keeper att Putny'.[226] Catherine also enjoyed archery, having her own bow and arrows, while also making payments

220 Brewer, *The Pleasures of the Imagination*, 359.

221 Johnson, *A Profane Wit*, 158–59.

222 Johnson, *A Profane Wit*, 166–67.

223 LAO, 1-Worsley 8, fos.19r, 28r, 36v.

224 Pepys, *Diary*, 8, 70.

225 LAO, 1-Worsley 6, fos. 5v, 7v.

226 LAO, 1-Worsley 6, fos. 21r, 26v. In 1679, John Locke noted that 'At Marebone and Putney [a stranger] may see several persons of quality bowling two or three times a week all the summer': [Peter] Lord King, *The Life of John Locke*, New Ed. (2 vols) (London: 1830), 1, 248.

to Mr Long, the keeper of the tennis court.[227] Whether she played herself is not clear from the accounts, although she did pay £1 'to the tenise court man for shooess' in June 1669.[228] By the 1670s, Catherine was playing ninepins, first acquiring a set of ninepins on 2 May 1675 and then on 8 July rewarding Lady Arlington's footman who 'keept the ninpins'.[229]

When not indulging in in gentle sporting pursuits, Catherine's pets, and other animals and birds, played an important part in her life. She embraced her husband's love of dogs. In addition to a payment of £1 11s 7d made on 6 January 1681 'to the man that Keeps the Kings dogs', her own dogs featured more frequently.[230] They often appeared in the accounts when they were bought new things, for example, when 3s was recorded to have been paid 'for a dog coler'.[231] These pampered pooches had their own travel arrangements overseen by the queen's footmen and in September 1669 a reward was given 'to one of them that braught the dogs from Hamptoncourt'.[232] They also needed medical care – on one occasion £1 10s was spent on 'a bottle of oyle for the dogs'.[233] And when disaster struck, on 4 May 1669 the accounts paid 'for printed bills & to the Crier when yor Maties dog was Lost'.[234] Other canines had the opportunity to entertain the queen, as was the case on 2 December 1670 when £1 1s 4d was given 'to a man with the dancing doge'.[235]

More exotic pets included the monkey that was presented to Catherine by Lady Arlington's page on 26 October 1671, possibly an early birthday gift.[236] The following year, on 22 April 1672, Mr Hutton supplied 'silver Chains and Colors to yor Maties Munky'.[237] Catherine was not the first Stuart queen to own a monkey. Her mother-in-law was painted by Anthony van Dyck with Jeffrey Hudson and Pug, her pet monkey.[238] Catherine also owned a parrot, which on occasion appears to have been described as 'the bird'. It had its own cage, and the corn-cutter trimmed its beak.[239] Outside her household, Catherine occasionally encountered other unusual animals, as was the case on

227 LAO, 1-Worsley 7, fo. 12r; LAO, 1-Worsley 6, fo. 39r.

228 LAO, 1-Worsley 7, fo. 10v.

229 LAO, 1-Worsley 8, fos. 5v, 6v.

230 LAO, 1-Worsley 9, fo. 24r.

231 LAO, 1-Worsley 8, fo.34r.

232 LAO, 1-Worsley 7, fo. 12v.

233 LAO, 1-Worsley 8, fo.19v.

234 LAO, 1-Worsley 7, fo. 10r.

235 LAO, 1-Worsley 7, fo. 22v.

236 LAO, 1-Worsley 7, fo. 28r.

237 LAO, 1-Worsley 7, fo. 28v.

238 Anthony van Dyck, Queen Henrietta Maria with Sir Jeffrey Hudson, 1633, oil on canvas, National Gallery of Art, Washington, acc. no. 1952.5.39, https://www.nga.gov/collection/art-object-page.41651.html [accessed 24/6/23].

239 LAO, 1-Worsley 9, fos. 11v, 16r.

10 February 1675 when she paid £2 3s 6d 'to the man [who] showed the sea dog', which was probably a sealion or a seal.[240] Most notable was the Indian elephant that arrived in London in August 1675. On 3 August the accounts recorded a payment of 2s 6d 'for a Boat sent for the Elefant'.[241]

Jacob Huysmans' portrait of Catherine of Braganza as a shepherdess (*c*.1662–64) has a large duck in the foreground, which is possibly a Muscovy duck.[242] While native to South America, Muscovy ducks were brought to Europe in the sixteenth century by the Portuguese and Spanish and they featured in the paintings of Dutch still-life painters such as Melchior de Hondecoeter (*c*.1636–95).[243] Charles II was a keen collector of waterfowl, which he kept in St James' Park, and on 18 August 1661 Pepys went there and 'saw [a] great variety of fowle which I never saw before'.[244] The Secret Service accounts of 1684 record a payment of £20 made 'to Capt Wm Legg, in part of 100li to scowre the ditches and watercourses at Hampton Court, to keep the fowle there'.[245] Catherine appears to have shared her husband's interests and this was reflected in a reference made on 10 July 1668 to 'your Majesties Birds' and the gifts of birds that she received.[246] For instance, in April 1674, Lady Arlington's man 'presented Hens from Holand', which might have been Brabanters, a Dutch breed of chicken, or some of the Muscovy ducks mentioned above.[247]

There are also several references in the accounts to domestic animals including horses, asses and a kid, as well as a hog owned by a poor woman that was 'Killed by one of yor Maties Coatches at Chelsy'.[248] Finally, there were Catherine's own cattle, which were cared for by Joan Story, the queen's dairy woman.[249] All of these examples provide evidence of Catherine's use of her leisure time, and her spending on nonessentials such as a collection of fancy waterfowl, yet all were important markers of her status as queen consort.

240 LAO, 1-Worsley 7, fo. 41v.

241 LAO, 1-Worsley 8, fo. 7r.

242 Jacob Huysmans, *Catherine of Braganza*, 1662–64, oil on canvas, Royal Collection, RCIN 405665, https://www.rct.uk/collection/405665/catherine-of-braganza-1638-1705 [accessed 16/4/23].

243 https://www.coe.int/en/web/cdcj/1999-rec-muscovy-and-domestic-ducks [accessed 16/4/23]. For example, Melchior de Hondecoeter, *Ducks*, 1675–80, oil on canvas, Rijksmuseum, SK-A-172.

244 Pepys, *Diary*, 2, 157.

245 Akerman, *Secret Services*, 88.

246 LAO, 1-Worsley 7, fo. 5v.

247 LAO, 1-Worsley 7, fo. 41r.

248 LAO, 1-Worsley 8, fo. 21r.

249 LAO, 1-Worsley 7, fo. 4v.

g) Gardens and flowers

Gardens were an integral part of Stuart palaces and there is a well-established link between the early Stuart queens consort and gardens. When Marcus Gheeraerts the younger (*c*.1561–1636) painted Anna of Denmark (1574–1619) in *c*.1611 to 1614, he placed her in front of gardens with beds arranged on a geometric pattern like those in Robert Smythson's plan for Somerset House.[250] Henrietta Maria brought her love of Italian-style horticulture to England, and she worked with the gardening father and son John Tradescant the elder (*c*.1570–1638) and the younger (1608–62) on the palace gardens.[251] After the Restoration Henrietta Maria's programme of changes at Somerset House included new gravel walks and lawns to provide a space to walk and to display statues, which may have been the work of Roger Looker.[252] Although Looker described himself as the queen's gardener in the 1680s, Sandra Raphael considers this to be a reference to service with the late Henrietta Maria, as queen dowager, rather than Catherine, because Catherine has not been regarded as taking an active interest in garden design.[253] While this might be true, Catherine's privy purse accounts suggest that she very much appreciated flowers and plants.

She was in good company because Charles II continued his mother's interest in gardens, using them as a setting for fancy garden ornaments. The king's Sun Dial was set up in 1669 by the Jesuit, Francis Line (1595–1675), who was sometimes known as Francis Hall. Line described and illustrated the sundial in his *Explication of the Diall*, and it embraced the king's passion for science, along with his love of family, including as it did portraits of himself, his wife, his brother James, his mother and his cousin, Prince Rupert.[254] However, it was not appreciated by all and late on 25 June 1675, while very drunk, Rochester, with the earl of Middlesex and several friends, wandered into the privy garden at Whitehall and smashed it.[255]

In contrast, Catherine's gardens were more decorous places and her later account books recorded numerous barge trips transporting flowerpots up and down the Thames from London to Somerset House.[256] Royal gardeners

250 Simon Thurley, *Somerset House: The Palace of England's Queens, 1551–1692* (London: London Topographical Society, 2009), 96–97, 101.

251 See Prudence Leith-Ross, *The Johns Tradescants: Gardeners to the Rose and Lily Queen* (London and Chester Springs, Peter Edwards, 2006).

252 Thurley, *Somerset House*, 70.

253 Sandra Raphael, 'Looker [Lucre, Lukar], Roger, gardener and nurseryman', *ODNB*, 23 September 2004, https://doi-org.soton.idm.oclc.org/10.1093/ref:odnb/37687 [accessed 11/4/23].

254 Johnson, *A Profane Wit*, 220.

255 Conor Reilly, 'Francis Line, peripatetic', *Osiris* 14 (1962), 238–39.

256 Multiple entries in LAO, 1-Worsley 8 and 9.

also featured in the accounts, including the best known, John Rose, who was keeper of St James' Park.[257] Other rewarded but unnamed gardeners working in the royal palaces included the gardener of St James's palace, the French gardener at St James's park and the gardener at Hampton Court.[258] Catherine also made numerous payments to the gardeners who delivered gifts of plants and fruit to her, including the gardeners of Colonel Richard Talbot (1630–91) and of Richard Winwood (1609–88), who lived at Ditton Park, Buckinghamshire. Women also sent gifts via their gardeners, including Lady Mary Scrope, who was a member of the queen's household. Some of the gardeners were named including Mr Gibbs who worked for Elizabeth Percy (1646–90), lady Northumberland.[259]

Perhaps most interesting of all are the references to the Italian painter, Antonio Verrio (*c*.1636–1707). While Verrio worked for Arlington at Euston Hall, Suffolk, and at Arlington House in London, he is best known for the commissions he undertook for Charles II at Windsor castle, including the ceiling of the queen's audience chamber depicting Catherine in a chariot pulled by swans and surrounded by mythological figures including zephyrs and putti.[260] Verrio's designs also included garlands, vases and swags of flowers, reflecting his interest in plants. He was also a skilled gardener and, on 23 July 1679, Evelyn recorded that 'Signor Verrio shewed us his pretty Garden, choce flowers & curiosities, he himselfe being a skillfull Gardner'.[261] Verrio worked on the royal gardens at Whitehall, and he sent the queen gifts of flowers.

During the spring and summer months, Catherine frequently received gifts of cut flowers in the form of nosegays. The entries make no mention of the flowers they contained but by implication they were made up of colourful, seasonal, fragrant flowers. During the summers of 1677 and 1678, Catherine received delicately perfumed orange blossom from Lord and Lady Bristol, Lady Manchester, Lady Russell, the countess of Oxford and the duchess of Portsmouth.[262] She also acquired several scented plants in the 1670s. On 25 August 1675 a payment was made 'to a Gardner presented Tubroses' and on 6 July 1676 another was made 'to Lady peterbroughs man [who] presented tubros'.[263] On 8 April 1676 Catherine bought 'twenty thre pots of Jongills' costing £1 4s.[264] On 29 August 1676, £1 was given 'to a gardner [who] presented

257 LAO, 1-Worsley 8, fo. 9r.

258 LAO, 1-Worsley 9, fo. 14r; LAO, 1-Worsley 6, fo. 15v; LAO, 1-Worsley 8, fo. 9r.

259 LAO, 1-Worsley 8, fo. 25v.

260 Antonio Verrio, *Catherine of Braganza in a Chariot*, 1675–*c*.1684, Queen's Audience Chamber, Windsor Castle, RCIN 408426.

261 Evelyn, *Diary*, 670.

262 LAO, 1-Worsley 8, fos. 6r, 13v, 14r, 22v, 30v.

263 LAO, 1-Worsley 8, fos. 8r, 15r.

264 LAO, 1-Worsley 8, fo. 12v.

Narsices'.[265] Gardening was an interest that Catherine shared with her husband. For instance, in 1682, John Cottereau was paid £100 in full satisfaction of his bill 'for roots and flowers' delivered to the earl of Clarendon and William Chiffinch for his majesty's use.[266] Some of these plants may have been gifts for Catherine's gardens.

Many of Catherine's friends also liked gardening, including the earl of Arlington and the duke and duchess of Lauderdale, who lived at Ham House, on the Thames near to Richmond. Henry Danckerts painted Ham House in 1675 and the garden view would have been one that Catherine would have seen when she visited.[267] The design reflected the influence of Jan Wyck and John Slezer, who favoured square lawns, bounded by gravel paths, a parterre, an orchard and a wilderness with hornbeam hedges.[268] In contrast, Pepys did not make many references to flowers in his diary, and those that did feature – cowslips, pinks and roses – were traditional English blooms.[269] However, Samuel did note fruit trees, including orange and lemon trees, an interest he shared with Catherine.[270] The fruit and flowers of the orange, along with the trees that produced them, provided the queen with a link to home, a hint of the exotic and a reminder of Portugal's empire.

The queen and seventeenth-century Lincolnshire

There is no evidence from within the privy purse accounts, or elsewhere, to suggest that Catherine ever visited Lincolnshire. If she had, it is interesting to consider what type of reception she might have received, as the county was a bastion of Puritanism.[271] In 1660, the minister of Cawthorpe and Covenham had knocked over one of the bonfires lit to mark the Restoration, exclaiming 'Stay! The rogue is not yet come over'.[272] Even so, there were pockets of Catholicism in the villages of Bottesford, Clixby, Irnham, West Rasen and Wrawby, including some notable families, such as the Thimblebys

265 LAO, 1-Worsley 8, fo. 16r.

266 Akerman, *Secret Services*, 57.

267 Henry Danckerts, *Ham House, the South Front from the Wilderness*, 1675, Victoria and Albert Museum.

268 Jane Brown, *The Art and Architecture of English Gardens: Designs for the Garden from the Collection of the Royal Institute of British Architects 1609 to the Present Day* (London: Weidenfeld and Nicolson, 1989), 21.

269 Pepys, *Diary*, 3, 95; 4, 112; 7, 204.

270 Pepys, *Diary*, 5, 127; 9, 281.

271 Clive Holmes, *Seventeenth-Century Lincolnshire* (Lincoln: History of Lincolnshire Committee, 1980), 220–24.

272 *CSPD Charles II, 1660–61*, 109.

of Irnham.[273] However, except for some points of tension in London during the exclusion crisis, Catherine was generally well received when she travelled outside the capital.

Even if the queen did not visit the county, Catherine was a Lincolnshire landowner. Several entries in Evelyn's diary reveal how her council administered the land holdings that she received from Charles as part of her dower. On 9 May 1676, for example, Evelyn went 'to the Queenes Council at Somerset house about my friend Mrs G: lease of Spalding in Lincolnshire'.[274] The market town of Spalding sits in the Fens on the River Welland and the property was evidently a desirable one because, a month later, on 13 June, Evelyn went again 'To Lond: about Mrs Godolphins Lease at the Queenes Council'.[275] The visit produced the desired result – eventually. It was not until 9 November that Evelyn was able to record 'I sealed & finished the Lease of Spalding for Mrs Godolphin at her Majesties Council at Somerset house'.[276] The beneficiary of Evelyn's efforts was his good friend, Margaret Blagge (1652–78), who had recently married Sidney Godolphin, 1st earl Godolphin (1645–1712). Before her marriage, Margaret was one of Catherine's maids of honour. While she did not appear in the privy purse accounts, Margaret gained access to her mistresses' land holdings in Lincolnshire.

As a landowner, Catherine may have looked at contemporary maps to chart where her dower property was. Her options included John Speed's map of Lincolnshire, which was produced in tandem with Jodocus Hondius, and first published in 1611. The map offers a view of the county, with its long coastline bordering onto the North Sea, a town map of Lincoln and the coat of arms of earls of Lincoln, from their eighth creation in 1572. As such, a county was more than its geography and its towns: it was also seen in seventeenth-century terms as closely tied with the aristocracy, who in turn had ties to the monarchy. Catherine had connections to the Lincolnshire nobility and gentry, several of whom were members of her household. For instance, Elizabeth Gorges (d.1675) was the second wife of Theophilus Clinton, 4th earl of Lincoln (1599–1667), whose family estate was at Sempringham, about 12 miles from Grantham. From 1666 until her death, Lady Clinton served Catherine as one of the queen's dressers and a woman of the queen's bedchamber.[277] Theophilus Clinton's daughter from his first marriage, Catherine, married George Booth,

[273] Charles Brears, *Lincolnshire in the 17th and 18th Centuries* (London: A. Brown and Sons, 1940), 39.

[274] Evelyn, *Diary*, 625.

[275] Evelyn, *Diary*, 626.

[276] Evelyn, *Diary*, 631.

[277] Sainty, Wassmann and Bucholz, *Household officers*, 15.

1st baron Delamer (1622–84), of Cheshire, who presented Catherine with gifts of cheese on several occasions.[278]

The queen consort also had links with members of the Lincolnshire gentry, most notably, with Sir Robert Carr (*c*.1637–82), who was MP for Lincolnshire in four parliaments and chancellor of the duchy of Lancaster.[279] Carr's estate was at Aswarby, near Sleaford.[280] He featured in the diary of John Milward, who noted Carr promoting a range of interests, including a project to drain the Lindsey Levels in November 1667 and February and April 1668.[281] Robert appeared just once in Catherine's privy purse accounts, on 4 August 1672, when she gave £2 3s 'to Sir Robert Cars man [who] presented wild fouls'.[282] The likely reason for this was Robert's close association with Lord Arlington, who was his brother-in-law. Robert's sister, Mary, was the widow of Sir Adrian Scroope, and a member of the queen's household. She held several posts: as a dresser in 1662 to 1663; as second dresser from 1663 to 1677. As these examples demonstrate, while Catherine may not have visited Lincolnshire, she definitely possessed close links to the county and its elite.

Catherine and the Lincolnshire archive

Catherine's privy purse accounts are part of the collection of Worsley manuscripts, which are housed at the Lincolnshire Archives. These documents are associated with, and were collected by, members of the Worsley family of Appuldurcombe, on the Isle of White. An example of the former is *A journal of the travels perform'd by me Robert Worsley began the seventeenth year of my age and finish'd the twentieth*, 1687–90.[283] This was the travel diary of Sir Robert Worsley, 4th baronet Worsley (*c*.1669–1747), who was a direct contemporary of Catherine of Braganza.[284] His brother Henry went to Spain and Portugal on diplomatic missions and then served as the Governor of Barbados.

Catherine's accounts were probably preserved as a result of their falling into the hands of one of the later Worsleys. Dr Nicholas Bennett has very plausibly suggested that the accounts were acquired by the antiquary, Sir Richard

278 LAO, 1-Worsley 7, fos. 14r, 22v, 28v.

279 Pepys, *Diary*, 10, 53.

280 J. S. Crossette, 'Carr, Sir Robert (c.1637–82), of Aswarby, Linc.', https://www.historyofparliamentonline.org/volume/1660-1690/member/carr-sir-robert-1637-82 [accessed 21/2/22].

281 Robbins, *Diary of John Milward*, li-lii.

282 LAO, 1-Worsley 7, fo. 29r.

283 LAO, 1-Worlsey 10.

284 Paula Watson, 'Worsley, Sir Robert, 4th Bt. (?1669–1747), of Appuldurcombe, I.o.W. and Chilton Condover, Hants.', https://www.historyofparliamentonline.org/volume/1715-1754/member/worsley-sir-robert-1669-1747 [accessed 17/6/23].

	li	s	d
Brought from the other side the sume of	123	14	11
26: To your Matie in Gold	005	00	00
To Lady Wood ffor water ffor your Maties gold	002	00	00
To your Matie in Gold	003	00	00
27: To a Poore Man by your Maties order	002	00	00
To the Servants att Maydenhead	001	00	00
28: To the Servants att Nubery	005	00	00
More to Them uppon the way	000	10	00
29: To the Servants att Malbury	005	00	00
30: To Mr Halsey in Gold	002	00	00
More ffor Coathemere	072	00	00
Sep: 4: ffor Browne Clouth	000	12	00
ffor Exchange of 100 pound in gold & Expences	011	00	00
9: To Lord Hally last att imbro in gold	010	00	00
To the Duches of Buckengame in gold	020	00	00
To my selfe in Gold	011	10	00
14: To Lady Wood Last att theare in gold	002	00	00
ffor Blankets	001	06	00
ffor Mending a Silver Box	000	02	06
ffor Making of towells	000	02	00
17: ffor Bristo: Stons	002	00	00
	266	16	05

Figure 2 Page from the privy purse accounts, from I-Worsley/6 – Catherine of Braganza, privy purse accounts 1662–68, fo. 7r. Author's photograph.

Worsley (1751–1805), whom Nigel Aston describes as 'something of a magpie when it comes to collecting antiquities of any kind'.[285] While Sir Richard lived on the Isle of White, on his death, Appuldurcombe and its contents passed to his niece Henrietta Anna Maria Charlotte Simpson. In the following year she married Charles Anderson-Pelham, 1st earl of Yarborough (1781–1846). It seems probable that it was at this point that Catherine's account books, along with many other items, including a set of chairs made by Chippendale for Sir Richard, were transferred to Brocklesby Park, Lincolnshire.[286]

Transcription notes

The layout of the account books is very consistent, within each volume and from volume to volume (**Figure 2**). This edition aims to capture the original layout as closely as possible by arranging the text in three columns of unequal width on each page. The first, narrow column was used to note the year at the top of each page and then the day and month as well as the occasional explanatory comment, most notably the queen's birthday, and the list of the New Year's gifts that she gave. The second, much wider column served to record details of the payment made and the final, narrow column provided details of the payments, beginning and ending each page with the running total. Where the text only partially filled a line, the space was completed with a line filler of dashes.[287] The paper is a sound weight although there is some bleed-though of the ink.

Judging by the quality of the hand and the colour of the ink, which changes at various points, it looks as though the accounts were written up periodically as a fair copy. They were compiled with reference to various bills, warrants and acquittances that are noted in the entries. As a result, the handwriting is generally clear, with very few corrections, crossings out or insertions. There are a few insertions and deletions, such as the crossing out of a payment for harpers on Catherine's birthday in 1665.[288] Some corrections were also made to the figures, both for individual entries and for the running total, which were probable made at the point when the accounts were checked.[289] In addition, on occasion, small errors were noted, as on 28 November 1667, where the comment 'Vndercharged before in this book as per note £8 5s' appeared.[290]

285 Nigel Aston, 'Worsley, Sir Richard, seventh baronet, (1751–1805), antiquary and politician', *ODNB*, 21 May 2009, https://doi-org.soton.idm.oclc.org/10.1093/ref:odnb/29986 [accessed 28/1/23].

286 Lindsay Boynton, 'Sir Richard Worsley and the firm of Chippendale', *The Burlington Magazine*, 110, no. 783 (1968), 352–53, 355.

287 With many thanks to Chris Woolgar for discussing these dashes with me.

288 LAO, 1-Worsley 6, fo. 22r.

289 LAO, 1-Worsley 6, fos. 3v–4r.

290 LAO, 1-Worsley 6, fo. 40r.

Barbara wrote using an italic hand, which was considered most suited to women. Martin Billingsley asserted that 'If any Art be commendable in a women… it is this of Writing' in his manual *The Pens Excellencie or The Secretaries Delight* (1618).[291] The writing was generally very consistent but on occasion it was more cramped. Her spelling was often phonetic, for example, she usually referred to the duck, rather than the duke, of York, and on occasion, it is quite quirky. In most instances, Barbara wrote out the entries in full, as on 13 September 1678, when she made a payment of £2 'to the footmen Runing mony' and £1 5s to unspecified individuals 'for bringing flowrpots from somersethouse'.[292] She did employ some contractions, including 'her Ma^{tis}' and 'y^{r} Maties' in the first account book but her usage of such abbreviated forms of words tailed off in the later volumes. In November 1675 there was a shift to references to the queen's footmen, etc.[293] Barbara also made use of the ampersand (&) for the word 'and'. She generally used u for v and y for i, but not always.

The transcripts have a modest number of short footnotes, which have been used in three ways: to add or explain dates, to clarify some of Barbara's more quirky spellings and to suggest the meaning of some unfamiliar words.

- ***Signatures*** – Catherine usually signed the accounts at the various reckoning points as *Catherina R* (**Figure 3**).
- ***Money and numbers*** – Barbara used Arabic numerals and her accounts were kept in pounds, shillings and pence. She inserted the abbreviations for these units at the top of many but not all pages: lib for *librum* (pounds, £), s for shilling (derived from the Old English word *scilling*), d for *denarius* (for pence). There were 12 pennies to a shilling and twenty shillings to the pound. There are also a few mentions of foreign coins, usually in the context of them being converted into sterling.
- ***Dates*** – The account used old style dates from the Julian calendar, so it notes the change of year on or after 25 March each year. However, in most years Barbara noted the giving of New Year's gifts on 1 January. Barbara also used other ways of marking time, including referring to the quarter days, especially for the payment of allowances and bills: Lady Day (25 March), Midsummer (24 June), Michaelmas (29 September) and Christmas (25 December). In addition, she recorded some saints' days, most notably the days associated with the four national saints of the Stuart kingdoms: 1 March (St David's Day, for Wales), 17 March (St Patrick's Day, for Ireland), 23 April (St George's Day, for England)

[291] Richard Christen, 'Boundaries between liberal and technical learning: Images of seventeenth-century writing masters', *History of Education Quarterly*, 39.1 (1999), 41.

[292] LAO, 1-Worsley 8, fo. 33r.

[293] LAO, 1-Worsley 8, fo. 9v.

and 30 November (St Andrew's Day, for Scotland). She also recorded the king's birthday (29 May) and the queen's (15 November) as these were both occasions of significant expenditure.

- ***Measurements*** – yards, a unit of length (36 inches or 91.44 cm).
- ***Index*** – the transcriptions are supported by a glossary, which aims to provide information on the people, places and objects listed in the account books, followed by an index.

Figure 3 Detail showing Catherine's signature, from I-Worsley/6 – Catherine of Braganza, privy purse accounts 1662–68, fo. 5r. Author's photograph.

TRANSCRIPTS

1-Worsley/6 – Catherine of Braganza, privy purse accounts 1662–68

[recto] 1r

1662:	**Monies Receiued for her Ma^{tis} Privy Purss**	lib s d
	of The Lord Treasurer	500 00 00
Feb^{r}: the 25 1662[1]	of Mr Heruey ~~her~~ y^{r} Ma^{tis} Treasurer	500 00 00
July the 21 1663	of Mr Heruey your Ma^{tis} Treasurer	350 00 00
Augs^{t} 25 1663	of Mr Heruey your Ma^{tis} Treasurer	300 00 00
Sep^{br} 18 1663	of Mr Heruey your Ma^{tis} Treasurer	200 00 00
Nou^{br} the 14 1663[2]	of Mr Heruey your Ma^{tis} Treasurer	360 00 00
June ye 15 1664	of Mr Heruey your Ma^{tis} Treasurer	200 00 00
July ye 26	of Mr Heruey y^{r} Ma^{tis} Treasurer	200 00 00
October ye 13	of Mr Heruey y^{r} Ma^{tis} Treasurer	200 00 00
This was pad[3] out for newse yiers gifts According <to> her Ma^{tis} warantt	of Mr Heruey y^{r} Maties Treasurer	738 00 00
next day Jan 2 & 3 1664[4]	of Mr Heruey y^{r} Maties Treasurer	300 00 00
Apprill ye 12 1665	Of y^{r} Matie	200 00 00
August ye 15 1665	Of y^{r} Matie	400 00 00
Sep^{br} ye 4 1665	of Mr Heruey y^{r} Maties Treasurer	110 00 00
	Ext	**4558 00 00**

1 1663 NS.
2 1664 NS.
3 Paid.
4 1665 NS.

[verso] 1v		lib s d
g: Febuary ye 3 1665[5]	of yr Matie	300 00 00
4:	More of yr Matie	100 00 00
13[6]	More of yr Matie	139 10 10
July ye 1 1666	of Mr Haruy yr Maties Tresurer <by order>	300 00 00
Sepbr[7]	of Mr Haruy yr Maties Tresurer <by order>	300 00 00
Decbr ye 31 1666	of Mr Haruy by yr Maties Tresurer <by order>	300 00 00
Jan: ye: 14: 1666[8]	of Mr Haruy by yr Maties order:	270 00 00
July ye 6: 1667	of Mr Haruy yr Maties Tresurer	500 00 00
		2209 10 00
	Brought from the other side	**4558 00 00**
	Ext	**6767 10 00**
20 Jan: 1667[9]	Of Mr Harvey more	400 00 00[10]

[recto] 2r		
1662:	**Moines Isued forth to, & ffor her Matis use**[11]	lib s d
8th Decembr	Changeinge 450li into Gold	45 00 00
	To her Maiestie Lost att Play	50 00 00
	More Lost to Lord Dunfarlin	52 00 00
	More to Lord Lawtherdale	30 00 00
	More to Lord Chesterfield	20 00 00
	To your Matie By Lady Wood	10 00 00
	To your Matie owne hand	10 00 00

5 1666 NS.
6 Corrected from 19.
7 No day specified.
8 1667 NS.
9 1668 NS.
10 Making the total £7,167 10s 0d.
11 After this reference to 'Her majesty' and another a line or so below, the style of address changes to 'your majesty', in acknowledgement that Catherine will read, or at least sign, her privy purse accounts, and so the text should be addressed to her.

	More to your Ma[tie]	20 00 00
	Musique	10 00 00
	ffoot Men	05 00 00
	Drummers and Trumpeters	15 00 00
	To a Poore Man by your Ma[tie] order	20 00 00
	To the Duches[12] Musique	10 00 00
	Chaire Men and ffootmen	02 00 00
	Transportinge of Trunks from the wardrop: tto Hamton Court as ffees Payed in Receiving 500[li] and Expenses	04 00 00
	More to your Maiestie[13] att Play	53 00 00
	Payed the Necessary woman as By Bill	09 19 00
18	To your Majestie	20 00 00
Decem 19th	More to your Ma[tie]	30 00 00
22	More to your Maiestie	32 00 00
Jan the 16	More to your Maiestie	28 00 00
	Ext	**475 19 00**

[verso] 2v

1662[14]		lib s d
	Braught ffrom The other side	**475 19 00**
Jan the 18	To your Maiestie	20 00 00
	More to your Ma[tie]	08 00 00
the 23	To your Ma[tie]	10 00 00
28	More to you Ma[tie]	10 00 00
30	More to you Ma[tie]	10 00 00
Feb the 3	More to your Ma[tie]	10 00 00
9	More to your Ma[tie]	24 00 00
11	More to your Ma[tie]	20 00 00
13	More to your Ma[tie]	02 00 00

12 Duchess of York.

13 This is one of the occasions where *your Majestie* is not contracted and there are a few more on this page and elsewhere.

14 1663 NS.

15	More to your Matie	10 00 00
	ffor wad	06 02 00
	To ffather Howard by your Maties appoyntment	06 00 00
	To a Poore woman to Bury her husband by your Maties order	05 00 00
	To the Herbe woman	02 00 00
	ffor Suger Trenchers	01 00 00
	Curlinge Irons	00 05 00
	To Queene Mothers ffoottmen	05 00 00
	More tto Queene Mothers Porters	02 00 00
	Gratuitie for the Duches of Albemarles present on Neu yeers Day	05 10 00
	To a Poore woman sent by Lady Gerrarde By your Maties order	06 00 00
	Ext	**638 16 06**

[recto] 3r

1662[15]		lib s d
	Braught ffrom the other side	**638 16 06**
	To Maudlin ffor Brishes[16]	02 00 00
	ffor Tape and Spunges	00 07 00
	Disbursed	**641 03 06**
	Were of Receiued	**500 00 00**
	Soe rests due this 23 ffeb to y^{r} Ma^{tis} Accomptant	**141 03 06**

Catherina R

		lib s d
ffeb^{r} 27	**Resting Deu on ye Last Accompt**	**141 03 06**
March: the 2: 1663	To ye Kings Musique Playing seuerall times tto your Maties	020 00 00

15 1663 NS.

16 Brushes.

	To The Dukes [music] by Lady Wood	005 00 00
	To your Maties hand on Ashwednesday[17]	001 00 00
	To Lady Wood ffor a Glass of water	002 00 00
9	To your Maties owne hand	020 00 00
24	More tto your Maties hand	002 00 00
	To the Countiss of Bathes seruant	006 00 00
	Lady Marshalls	006 00 00
	Countess of Castelmaines	006 00 00
New yeares Guifts[18]	Lady scroopes	005 00 00
	Lady Woods	005 00 00
	Mis: ffraysiers	005 00 00
	Mis: Legards	003 00 00
	Ext	**227 03 06**[19]

[verso] 3v

1662[20]		lib s d
	Braught ffrom the <othr> side	**227 03 06**[21]
	To Mis Killigreus	005 00 00
	Mis Sandersons	003 00 00
	Mis Stewaards	003 00 00
	Mis Prices	003 00 00
	Mis Careys	003 00 00
	Mis Wells	003 00 00
	Mis Boytons	003 00 00
	Mis Narmstones	003 00 00
	To my owne woman	010 00 00
New yiers Gifftes	To your Matie footmen	005 00 00
	To the Drum Major	003 00 00

17 25 February 1663.

18 The entries from the countess of Bath to the sumpter men on the next page are bracketed together under the heading New Year's gifts.

19 227 03 06 corrected from 327 03 06.

20 1663 NS.

21 227 03 06 corrected from 327 03 06.

	To the Litter men	005 00 00
	To 4 Coatchmen	010 00 00
	To 4 postillians	003 00 00
	Groomes	004 00 00
	To the Sumpter Men	002 00 00
	To three Irish foot men on St Patricks Day[22]	001 00 00
26	To Mr David Rauerick as per bill	020 00 00
1663 Aprill 3	To Mis Nun ffor 10 months allowance for needles & thred	010 00 00
15	To The Lord Aubigny for the poore	027 00 00
	Lord Latherdale[23] borrowed by your Matie	006 00 00
20[24]	To your Maties owne hand	020 00 00
	ffor a Boote that Carred your Maties Chaire & Chaire men to Windsor	001 16 00
28	ffor a fane which your Matie Braught	003 10 00
	Ext	**384[25] 09 06**

[recto] 4r

1663		lib s d
Braught ffrom The other Side	**the sume of**	**384[26] 09 06**
Apll[27]	To the Litter Men att Windsor	001 00 00
	To the houskeeper att Windsor	005 00 00
May: the 7:	To Lady Wood ffor a Glase of water	002 00 00
ap:4	To Mich: de Bruijn van Berendrecht as ye bill	020 08 00
	More <to> your Matie may the 4th	020 00 00
9	To your Matie for a poore woman	003 00 00

22 17 March.
23 Lauderdale.
24 19 April.
25 384 corrected from 484.
26 384 corrected from 484.
27 No day given.

	ffor fanns your Matie Baught	006 00 00
	ffor greene Sattin ribben	000 16 00
	To Mis fountayne Makeing Lining for the Chappell as By Bill	011 04 00
11	ffor fanns your Matie Baught	006 00 00
	To Mis Sanford presenting The history of Portengell[28]	010 00 00
	For Buchram for Bands	000 06 00
	Mending ye siluer box in the standish	000 01 00
	For pars[29] Silke & needles	000 07 00
	2 pound & a ½ of wad	002 10 00
	Celler for waters	000 18 00
	Giuen by your Matie tto a Poore wooman	003 10 00
	To an other poore woman	001 00 00
	To a poore woman Mr Carlton Brought	002 00 00
	To an other poore woman	004 00 00
	Ext	**484 09 06**[30]

[verso] 4v

1663		lib s d
Braught from the other side	**the sume off**	**484 09 06**[31]
	To your Matie owne hand	010 00 00
	To Mr Griffith ffor a standing screen for your Matie Clossett	002 00 00
14	To a Poore woman	001 00 00
	To your Matie postelion	001 00 00
17	To your Matie in ~~Gold~~	010 00 00
24	More to your Matie	020 00 00

28 Portugal.

29 Uncertain – possible for Paris silk, see an Irish statute from 1662 which referred to 'Fyllozell or Paris silk', https://www-oed-com.soton.idm.oclc.org/view/Entry/137915?redirectedFrom=paris+silk+#eid31969508 [accessed 28/1/23].

30 484 09 06 corrected from 584 09 06.

31 484 09 06 corrected from 584 09 06.

25	To the poore Kinghts of Windsor	002 00 00
	To your Matie	030 00 00
	ffor Cheryes presented tto your Matie	000 16 00
26	More to your Matie in gold	020 00 00
	More by Mis Legard <tto> Reifell[32] for a Ring	010 00 00
	ffor Lether to put into ~~the Queenes Truncks~~ your Matie Truncks	000 10 10
27	ffor Cheryes	000 10 00
	To the footmen	003 00 00
	To the Litter men	001 00 00
	To the Coatchmen and postelions	003 00 00
30	To your Maties owne hand	005 00 00
	More by Mr Roper tto giue a poore w~~homan~~	002 00 00
	To the Gardenor at St James	001 00 00
	To Lady Wood ffor a glase of water	002 00 00
	To the wind Musique	002 00 00
		610[33] 16 04

[recto] 5r

1663		lib s d
Braught ffrom the other side	**The sume off**	**610[34] 16 04**
	To the Drumes	002 00 00
	ffor Combs	001 00 00
Jun: 2	ffor Dioper Tape and Needles	000 06 01
	ffor Silke for your Maties Rubands	000 05 04
4	To Mr Halsey for your Matie att the Exchange	011 00 00
10	ffor a spong and for gray & white paper	000 03 00
16	ffor Pachies	000 11 00

32 Raffle (?).
33 610 corrected from 710.
34 610 corrected from 710.

25	ffor a pound & a halfe of wad	002 10 00
7[35]	To your Ma[tie]	008 00 00
	To father Howard for your Ma[tie]	012 00 00
	To Morris dauncers att High Parck	001 00 00
	To the water Men	002 00 00
	Totall dispursed	**651 11 09**
	Whereof reciuied	**500 00 00**
	Soe there rests due this 1 of July To this Accomptant	**151 11 09**

Catherina R

[verso] 5v		lib s d
	To my Selfe which I had disbursed	**151 11 09**
July the 6 1663	To a ffootman that Braught a fether	00 02 06
	ffor a Pound and a halfe of wad	02 10 00
	ffor a Box to put your Ma[tis] hankercher in	00 14 00
	ffor Appricokes	02 05 00
	ffor a Seller tto Carry waters	01 05 00
	ffor transporting of Clouth for shietting	00 04 00
	ffor gome[36]	00 00 06
	ffor a treate your Ma[tie] gaue your Ladys	05 07 00
	ffor passing the Coatchehes ouer to Lambet	01 12[37] 06
23	ffor Coatche hiere tto turbrige	08 00 00
	To The Mouther of the Mayds	06 14 00
Senec[38]	To the Morisdansers	01 00 00
	To the Poore	02 00 00
	Att the Ind[39] where your Ma[tie] Eate:	03 00 00

35 The significance of this 7 is unclear.

36 Gum.

37 has been inserted over another number, possibly a 4, crossed out.

38 Sevenoaks.

39 Inn.

	To the Wind Musique	02 00 00
24	Morisdancours	01 00 00
	To Lady Wood ffor watter 4: 10: in gold:	05 05 00
	To your Matie in Gold 10 p:	10 00 00[40]
	For Bringing The billard table hether	00 04 00
	Foe swiete water & perfume for the Chappell and dressing Roume	00 10 00
31	To a Keeper ffor Bringing a Bock	01 00 00
	ffor a Billyard table	16 00 00
	To your Matie in Gold	03 00 00
	Ext	**225 05 09**

[recto] 6r[41]		lib s d
	Braught ffrom the other side	**225 05 09**
Ags^t^ 1	To a Keeper that Braught a Bock[42]	01 00 00
	To Me^tr^ Meadee[43] Coat^c^he hiere and his Expenses ffrom London	08 00 00
8	To your Matie:^ in gold to Play att ombre	20 00 00
10	More to your Matie to play att ombre	10 00 00
12	More to your Matie to play att ombre	10 00 00
13	More to your Majestie att play in Gold	10 00 00
	To a footman that Braught Biesket	01 00 00
15	To two Blind Mayds	05 00 00
	To the water fiellers & those that opned The gates att the wells	19 00 00
	To the Lady Wood ffor the Blackemores Lienning	02 11 00
	To your Matie in gold tto play att ombre	10 00 00
17	To a Garner[44] that braught frute tto your Matie	01 00 00

40 10 00 00 corrected from 11 01 08.
41 The year – 1663 – is not included at the top of this page.
42 For buck.
43 Originally spelt 'Meagee', the g was then changed into a d.
44 For gardener.

	To the Morisdancers	01 00 00
	To the seruants wheare your Matie Lay att tonbridg	05 00 00
18	To the Seruants wheare your Matie Eate	00 05 00
	Ext	**329 01 09**

[verso] 6v[45]		lib s d
	Braught from The <other> side	**329 01 09**
	ffor Coache hiere ffrom tonbrig tto London	31 12 06
	ffor paches	00 06 00
	More tto Mr Miade[46] for his iournys post Beetweene London & The wells & other Expenses	09 15 00
	Changeinge 100li into Gold	10 16 08
	Totall dispursed	**381 11 11**
	Whereof receiued	**350 00 00**
	Soe there Rests Dew this 24 August to this Accomptant *Ext*	**31 11 11**

Catherina R

		lib s d
	Repayd my selfe	**031 11 11**
August 25	To Mr Vanderdos in Gold	006 00 00
	ffor Coatchehiere tto the Bath:	060 00 00
	To Mr Halsey for a fether for your Majestie had	016 00 00
	To Mr Halsey for Coathehiere	010 00 00
	ffor ffileting	000 03 00
	Ex	**123 14 11**

45 The year – 1663 – is not included at the top of this page.

46 For Meade.

[recto] 7r		lib s d
	Braughtt from the other side the sume of	**123 14 11**
26	To your Matie in Gold	005 00 00
	To Lady <Woode> ffor watter for your Matie in Gold	002 00 00
	To your Matie in gold	003 00 00
27	To a Poore man by your Matie order	002 00 00
	To the Seruantts att Maydenhead	001 00 00
28	To the Seruantts att Nubery	005 00 00
	More tto Them uppon the way	000 10 00
29:	To the Seruannts att Malbury[47]	005 00 00
30:	To Mr Halsey in Gold	001 00 00
	More ffor Coathehiere	072 00 00
Sep: 4:	ffor Brouune Clouth:	000 12 00
	ffor Exchange of a 100 li pound in gold & Expences	011 00 00
9	To Lord Hally[48] last att ombro in gold	010 00 00
	To the duches of Buckengame in gold	010 00 00
	To my selfe in Gold	011 10 00
14:	To Lady Wood Last att oheare in gold	001 00 00
	ffor Blanketts	001 06 00
	ffor Mending a Seluer Box	000 02 06
	ffor Making of towells	000 01 00
17:	ffor Bristo: Stons	001 00 00
	Ext	**266 16 05**

[verso] 7v		lib s d
	Braughtt ffrom The <other> side The sume of	**266 16 05**
17:	To your Matie in Gold	020 00 00
18:	To the poore	001 00 00

47 Marlborough.
48 Hawley.

	ffor Bristostones	001 00 00
19:	ffor scoketts ffor your Matie Chappell	000 12 00
20:	To your Matie footmen	012 00 00
	To your Matie att billyards	001 00 00
	To Lord Candish[49] Lost att ombro in gold	010 00 00
21:	To a poore Child in gold	001 00 00
	To a poore woman	001 00 00
	ffor The Mayds of honnors Lodgings ~~att Bath~~	018 00 00
	ffor the Bedchamber wiemens Log<d>ings	010 10 00
	To the Guids att Barth	010 00 00
	Lostt at ombro by your Maiie in Gold	043 00 00
22	To the saruantts att Barth	005 00 00
	To the saruantts att Lord Nubockes	005 00 00
	To Mr Hallsy for Coathehiere from Barth	020 00 00
28:	More tto Mr Hallsy for Coathehiere ffrom Barth:	030 00 00
Octobr 1:	ffor Charges tto Bristo[50] in receuing the Monys	000 05 00
	To the saruantees where yr Matie Lay at weekam:[51]	005 00 00
	Where your Matie Eate at Oxbrige	005 00 00
	Ex	**466 03 05**

[recto] 8r		lib s d
	Braughtt ffrom the other side the sume of	**466 03 05**
	To the poore att oxbri<d>ge	002 00 00
Sep 10:[52]	To the Lady Barthe Lostt att ombro in gold	013 00 00

49 Lord Cavendish.

50 Bristol.

51 For Wickham.

52 Either an error for October 10 or potentially more likely as the end of the accounting period was 6 October, recording an entry omitted from 10 September.

	Exchange of 39 pices & an Angell of Gold	004 05 07
	Totall Disbursed *Ex*	**485 09 00**
	Where of Receued att tto Paymentts	**500 00 00**
	Soe rests oon This 6 october tto your Ma[tie] from this Accomptant	**014 11 00**

Catherina R

		lib s d
Oc:[ber] 8:	To your Ma[tie] att ombro ine gold	03 00 00
	To Queene Mouthers Cooke in gold	01 00 00
	To the Lords maires[53] man in gold	01 00 00
	More tto Queene Mouthers Cooke in gold	01 00 00
	To father Patrick in gold	01 00 00
No:[br] 3	More tto Father Patrick in gold	02 00 00
	To your Ma[tie] att the Lottrey in gold	20 00 00
	To M:[tris] Chiffinchs Child in gold	03 00 00
	To Lady Gillfords man in gold	01 00 00
	To M[tis] Plancett ffor watter in gold	02 00 00
	Ex	**35 00 00**

[verso] 8v		lib s d
	Braughtt from The other Side The sume of	**35 00 00**
	Exchange of sexty pices of glod[54]	06 11 00
More	To M[r] Halsall for Coachehiere ffrom Barth as by bill appiers	165 12 00
	To a Portingall man	00 10 00
	Charges	00 02 06
No:[br] 16[55]	To The foottmen	03 00 00

53 Lord Mayor of London.

54 Gold.

55 The day after Catherine's birthday, which fell on 15 November. Catherine was 25.

Vppon y^{r} Matie Bur:thday giuen	To The Coachemen		02 00 00
	To The Musique		10 00 00
	To The chare men and Litter men		02 00 00
	To The Gromes		01 00 00
	Trompets		06 00 00
	Dromes		03 00 00
18	Wind Musique		03 00 00
	ffor a table		01 00 00
	ffor Mr Car<e>lton ffor his Jornys tto Bath & tonbrige		01 10 00
	To M^{tris} Nons Mayd		03 00 00
	ffor this Booke		00 11 00
	To the sumpter men		01 00 00
20	ffor wad for 2 gounes		05 07 00
	To a poore woman		00 10 00
	ffor checkings[56] presented		00 05 00
	More for checkings presented		00 10 00
		Ex	**251 08 06**[57]

[recto] 9r		lib s d
	Braughtt from The other side ye sume of	**251 08 06**
	ffor Mending your Maties Lining and thred needles and tape	20 00 00
	To Lady Gillfords Man	00 10 00
	To Lady Frayser Laid outt	00 05 00
	To Lady Deuonsheres woman	00 05 00
	To Lady Gillfords Man	00 05 00
25:	More tto Lady Deuonsheres woman	00 10 00
	ffor Perfuming watter and Canuas	04 12 00

56 Chickens.

57 251 08 06 corrected from 250 18 06.

	To a poore Man thatt came from Portungall	01 00 00
	Giuen awaye	00 10 00
	<tto Mr Chiffinch ffor Carreges> ~~for Careing [...]~~ tto ye Barth	00 06 06
26:	To y^{r} Ma:^{tie} in Gold	05 00 00[58]
	To Sr Kellamdigbys[59] Man in Gold	01 00 00
18:[60]	To your Ma:^{tie} in Gold	05 00 00
De:^{br} 3	To ye Kinges Barber in Gold	05 00 00
	To your Ma:^{tie} att ombro in gold	05 00 00
6	To your Ma:^{tie} in Gold	04 00 00
	To Queen Mou^{hs}[61] Cooke in Gold	01 00 00
	To your Ma:^{tie} att oheare in Gold	02 10 00
	Ex	**308 02 00**

[verso] 9v		lib s d
	Braughtt from ye other side ye sume of	**308 02 00**
7	To your Ma:^{tie} tto play att oheare in gold	05 00 00
	More tto your Ma:^{tie} att oheare in Gold	07 00 00
13	To your Ma:^{tie} att Lodom in Gold	01 00 00
14	To one of The Gard ffor Carring your Ma:^{ties} Platte tto ye barth	00 13 00
	To Lady Deuonshiers Man	00 10 00
	To your Ma:^{ties} Page of ye Backsteeres	02 00 00
	To a Man thatt braughtt ponnado	00 05 00
	ffor spunges	00 04 00
	Charges	00 02 00
	To ye Lady Rochesters Seruantt	00 05 00
	To Lady Connwallisces[62] Cooke	01 00 00

58 05 00 00 corrected from 01 00 00.
59 Sir Kenelm Digby.
60 For 28 or an entry omitted from 18 November.
61 For mother.
62 Cornwallace.

	To Lady Linkhornes[63] Cooke	01 00 00
15	To your Ma:tie at ombro in gold	05 00 00
	To Lady Linkhornes Cooke	01 00 00
	To Lady Conwallies Cooke	01 00 00
	To your Ma:tie att oheare in Gold	07 00 00
	More tto your Ma:tie att oheare in Gold	02 00 00
		333 02 00

[recto] 10r		lib s d
	Braughtt from ye other side the sume	**333 02 00**
	To Mr Haruey w:ch he Gaue Lady Woode by your Matie order in Gold	03 00 00
	To Mr Chiffinch for seuerall necesariess ffor ye Portuguez att Porthmouth Mending of waggons and remouing of Goods ffor your Ma:tie	06 05 00
15	To your Matie att Goose in Gold	05 00 00
	To Lady Gillfords Mayd in Gold	02 00 00
	To your Ma:tie att Lodom in Gold	01 00 00
	To your Matie att oheare[64] in Gold	02 00 00
	To your Matie att Lodom in Gold	01 00 00
	To your Matie att oheare in Gold	01 00 00
Jan:ye 7[65]	More tto your Matie att Lodom in gold	01 00 00
l: 11	To your Ma:tie ffor a Riffell in Gold	10 00 00
	To your Ma:tie att Lodom in gold	01 00 00
13	ffor tape	00 05 00
16	To Lady Deuonshiers Mayd	00 10 00
18:	To your Ma:tie att Lodom in Gold	01 00 00
	Ext	**368 02 00**

[verso] 10v		lib s d
	Braughtt ffrom ye other side ye sume	**368 02 00**
20	To your Ma:tie att Cards in gold	01 00 00
	To Lady Linkhorness Man	00 05 00

63 Lincoln.
64 Here.
65 1664 NS.

ffeb. 3	ffor Brad[66] filliting	00 03 00
	Exchange of sexty & one pecess of Gold	06 13 02
	Totall Disbursed *Ex*	**376 03 02**
	Whereof Receud	**360 00 00**
	Dew tto your Matie vppon ye last Accompt	**14 11 00**
	So rests dew This 24 Mar:ch tto This Accomptant[67] *Ex*	**01 12 02**

Catherina R

		lib s d
	Soe there Rests dew This 22 June tto This Accomptantt which I Repay myselfe	**01 12 02**
June ye 17 1664	To the Duchess of yorks Coatchman	01 00 00
	To the Duchess of yorks ffootmen	03 00 00
	To a Bagge pipe Booye in high parck	00 05 00
	Changeinge of 50 pecess of Gold	05 16 08
	To a poore woman yt presented straburys	00 10 00
	Ex	**12 03 10**

[recto] 11r		lib s d
	Braughtt ffrom ye other side ye sume of	**12 03 10**
	ffor Baggs & Charges	00 05 00
	To Lady Wood for water for yr Ma:tie in Gold	04 00 00
	To his Maties Cooke	10 00 00
22	To a man thatt braught watter ffrom Outlands[68] to hampton Court for yr Ma:tie	01 09 00
	To M:s Nun ffor necesarys ffor yr Ma:tie	30 00 00
23	To the ffootmen	15 00 00
New yiers Gifftes	To ye Litter Men	05 00 00
	To ye Coat<c>hmen	10 00 00
	To ye postilliens	03 00 00
	To ye Gromes	04 00 00

66 For broad?

67 There is no mention of Easter in the accounts, which is unusual. Easter Sunday 1664 – 10 April.

68 Oatlands.

	To ye Sumpter Men	02 00 00
	For a Bathelhen[69] tub	03 00 00
27:	To your Ma:tie in Gold	20 00 00
28:	To your Ma:tie Barge Men	38 10 00
July ye 3:	To your Ma:tie Gromes widow	20 00 00
	Ex	**178 07 10**

[verso] 11v		lib s d
	Braughtt ffrom ye other side ye sume of	**178 07 10**
5	To Mr Spencor in Gold	030 00 00
	Exchange of 4 pices of Gold	000 09 04
	Totall Disbursed *Ex*	**208 17 02**
	Where of Receud	**200 00 00**
	Soe there rests due this 7 July to this Accomptant *Ex*	**008 17 02**

Catherina R

	Repayd my selfe	**08 17 02**
	To ye Duchess of Buckengams Chere men	01 00 00
10:	To Lady Linckhornes Man	00 05 00
25:	To Mr Spencors Man	05 00 00
26:	To your Matie at Lodom in Gold	01 00 00
	To ye ffootemen ffor 3 ronning Jornys	06 00 00
27	To yr Ma:tie at ombro in Gold	10 00 00
28	To ye house Keeper & Gardnor att Hampton Court in gold	02 00 00
	Ex	**34 02 02**

[recto] 12r		lib s d
	Braughtt ffrom ye other side ye sume of	**034 02 02**
29:	To your Ma:tie att ombro & Cuba in gold	025 00 00
30	To ye ffoote Men	002 00 00
	Exchange of fefty pecess of Gold	005 16 08

69 Uncertain meaning.

	ffor Baggs & Charges	000 05 00
31	To ye ffoote Men:	002 00 00
	To M:^{r} vanderdouse in Gold	001 00 00
August ye 1	To Lady Wood ffor watter in Gold	002 00 00
	To Lady Wood which she has <layd> outt for your Ma:^{tie} Goieng by watter in Gold	001 00 00
	To a Man y^{t} presented your Ma:^{tie} w:th a fane in Gold	001 00 00
	Exchange of twenty pecess of Gold Gene	001 06 08
	To a poore woman	001 00 00
2	To y^{r} Ma:^{tie} at Cards in Gold	005 00 00
	To Lady Wood wch y^{r} Ma:^{tie} Lostt tto her in Gold	003 10 00
	To y^{r} Ma:^{tie} at Cuba in Gold	001 00 00
	Ex	**086 00 06**

[verso] 12v		lib s d
	Braughtt ffrom ye other side ye sume of	**86 00 06**
3	To his Ma:^{tie} Barge Man	005 00 00
	To Mr Stannop wch he had Laid outt as by Bill ap[piere]	005 09 06
5	To y^{r} Ma:^{tie} Barge Man ffor seuerall seruesses as playnely douth appiere	020 10 00
	To ye Man y:^{t} keepes ye Parlementt house	002 00 00
6	To a pair of oares y^{t} Carred y^{r} Ma:^{tie} Foote Men tto Hammersmith	000 05 00
7	To y^{r} Ma:^{tie} att Cards in Gold	005 00 00
8	To y^{r} Ma:^{tie} att Lodum in Gold	001 00 00
	To ye Lord Beshope of Canterburys seruantts in <Gold>	002 00 00
	To ye Duchess of yorks Coatheman	001 00 00
	To oares y^{t} Carred y^{r} Ma:^{tie} & your follouers tto Lambeth	001 00 00
	ffor ffeleten[70]	000 05 00
9	Exchange of 20 pecess of Gene Gold	001 06 08

70 For filleting (?).

	ffor Mending y^{r} Ma:^{ties} Lenning Deu May Lastt	020 00 00
12	To y^{r} Ma:^{tie} att Cards in Gold	005 00 00
	Ex	**156 01 08**

[recto] 13r		lib s d
	Braughtt ffrom ye other side ye sume of	**156 01 08**
17	To y^{r} Matie ffootemen	002 00 00
	ffor a poin^{t}	025 00 00
18:	To Madame de Gramontts woman in Gold	005 00 00
19:	To ye Carpenter y^{t} made ye steere Casse	000 05 00
23:	To S^{ir} Allgornon May w:^{ch} he had Layd outt ffor y^{r} Ma:^{tie} as douth appiere	005 19 06
24:	To one of y^{r} Ma:^{tie} ffootemen y^{t} is seck	005 00 00
	To Lady Beathe Coatch Man	000 10 00
	Catherina R Total Disbursed	**199 16 04**
	Where <of:> Receud	**200 00 00**
	Soe rests dew This 24 Aug^{stt} tto y^{r} Ma:^{tie} ffrom this Accomptant	**000 03 08**
		lib s d
August ye 29	To y^{r} Ma:^{tie} att Somersett house att play in gold	010 00 00
	To Lady Linckhornes Man	000 05 00
	To y^{r} Ma:^{tie} att Cuba in Gold	002 00 00
	Ex	**012 05 00**

[verso] 13v		lib s d
	Braughtt ffrom ye other side ye sume of	**012 05 00**
Sep^{br} ye 1	To y^{r} Ma:^{tie} Barge Man ffor waitting one y^{r} Ma:^{tie} ouer tto Lambett	002 00 00
6	To Lady Bath Coat<c>h Man	000 10 00
21[71]	To y^{r} Ma:^{tie} att Somersett house in Gold	010 00 00
22	To Queene Mouther Chareett Man & ffottemen	003 00 00

[71] 21 corrected from 24.

	Charges in feching of yr Ma:tie Liening ffrom ye Greate wardrope	000 11 00
	To ye Duke of yorkes gardnor	000 10 00
24	To yr Ma:tie att Cuba in Gold	005 00 00
25	To M:s Wells which yr Ma:tie Lostt in gold	010 00 00
29	To a woman thatt braughtt quincess	001 00 00
	To My selfe and Ms Wells which yr Ma:tie Lostt att ombro att Somersett house in gold	013 10 00
Octobr ye 11	To Lady Wood which yr Ma:tie Lostt in gold	047 08 00
	Exchange of 115 pecess of genny gold	007 13 04
	Ex	**113 07 04**

		lib s d
[recto] 14r	**Braughtt ffrom ye other side ye sume of**	**113 07 04**
	Exchange More for 30 picess of ould gold	003 12 06
	Chargess & Baggs in receuieng ye Newse gifts	001 00 00
15:	To yr Ma:tie ffootemen ffor twise ronning	004 00 00
21	To Mr Meade which he had Laid outt as by <an> bill	004 19 06
22	To yr Matie att ombro in Gold	005 10 00
	ffor ye Buriall of yr Ma:tie postillion	005 00 00
	To yr Ma:tie footemans widdow	005 00 00
26	To yr Matie footemen roning tto wollige[72]	002 00 00
	To yr Matie Barge Man ffor waitting one yr Ma:tie tto wollige with thre barges	004 10 00
Nobr ye 1	To bien[73] ffor sex pare of Gloues & thre houds	001 14 00
2	To yr Ma:tie att Lady Malburys[74] att play in gold	002 00 00
3	To yr Ma:tie att play in Gold	020 00 00[75]

72 Woolwich.
73 For Mistress Bew.
74 Marlborough's.
75 020 00 00 corrected from 022 00 00.

9	To yr Ma:tie att play in Gold	005 00 00
11	To Lady Malbury which yr Ma:tie lost in gold	015 00 00
15 one yr Matie Buth Day giuen[76]	To Quene Mouthers ffootemen	002 00 00
	To yr Ma:tie Mussique	010 00 00
	Ex	**204 13 04**

[verso] 14v		lib s d
	Braughtt ffrom ye other side ye sume of	**204 13 04**
Uppon yr Maties Bu:th Day giuen	To yr Ma:tie footemen	003 00 00
	To his Ma:tie footemen	002 00 00
	To ye Duke of yorkes footemen	002 00 00
	To ye Duchess of Yorkes footemen	002 00 00
	To yr Ma:tie Coatchmen	003 00 00
	To ye Gromes	001 00 00
	To ye Litter Men	002 00 00
	To ye Somptor Men	001 00 00
	To ye Duke of Yorkes trompettors	003 00 00
	Winde Musique	003 00 00
	Harper	001 00 00
	To ye Sargentt trompetor	006 00 00
	To ye Dromes	003 00 00
	To ye Kings Coatchman ffor waitting one yr Ma:tie seuerall times	005 00 00
	Catherina R Totall Disbursed *Ex*	**241 13 04**
	Dew tto yr Matie in ye Last Accompt	**000 03 08**
	Where of Receud	**200 00 00**
	Soe Restts Dew This 20th Noubr tto This Accomptantt *Ex*	**041 09 08**

[recto] 15r		lib s d
	Repayd My selfe	**041 09 08**
Nobr ye 22	To Lady Lincolne her Man	00 05 00

76 Catherine's birthday – she was 26.

De^{br} ye 3	To a Man t^{t} Mended gold bottells	01 15 00
	To Lady Garrd & my self which y^{r} Ma:^{tie} Lostt att ombro in gold	20 00 00
13	To Lady Lincolne her Man	00 05 00
21	To y^{r} Matie att ombro in gold	01 10 00
	To Lady Wood which y^{r} Ma:^{tie} Lostt att ombro <in gold>	04 00 00
23	To Quene Mouther w:^{ch} y^{r} Ma:^{tie} Lostt in gold	05 00 00
	To y^{r} Ma:^{tie} at ombro in gold	02 10 00
Ja^{y} ye 2	Exchange of Eaighty one piecess of genny gold	05 13 04
	Baggs and Chargess	00 10 00
New yiers guifts 1664[77]	To y^{r} Ma:^{tie} Musique	10 00 00
3	To ye Duke of Yorkes Musique	10 00 00
	To ye winde musique	03 00 00
	To ye Harper	01 00 00
	To his Ma:^{ties} Barbers	10 00 00
	To y^{r} Ma:^{tie} footemen	10 00 00
	Ex	**126 18 00**

[verso] 15v		lib s d
	Braughtt ffrom ye other side ye sume of	**126 18 00**
	To y^{r} Ma:^{tie} Coatchmen	10 00 00
	To ye postillions	03 00 00
	To ye Gromes	04 00 00
	To ye Litter Men & Chere Men	05 00 00
	To ye Sumpter Men	02 00 00
	To his Ma:^{ties} Coatchmen	05 00 00
	To y^{r} Ma:^{tie} Cooke	05 00 00
	To his Ma:^{ties} Cooke	05 00 00
	To ye Gallery Keepers	06 00 00
	To two porters att Sumersett House	02 00 00
	To ye Taylors Men	05 00 00

77 1665 NS.

	To ye shouemakers Men	04 00 00
	To Quene Mouthers footmen	03 00 00
4	To yr Ma:ties AppHolster	03 00 00
	To Lady Wood for water in gold	04 00 00
	To a poore woman yt presented orringers	01 00 00
	To ye French Gardiner in Stt James parck	02 00 00
	Ex	**195 18 00**

[recto] 16r		lib s d
	Braughtt ffrom ye other side ye sume of	**195 18 00**
	Dromes[78] and trompets	09 00 00
	To Lady Wood for ye Lord of newcastells Man in gold	02 00 00
	To Lady Wood for Combes	01 05 00
	ffor Basketts presented	01 00 00
	To ye Keeper of ye parlementt house	02 00 00
5	To yr Ma:tie att ombro in gold	20 00 00
7	ffor a Collor & seluer gield buckell for yr Ma:tie Dogge	01 00 00
	To yr Ma:tie att ombro in gold	20 00 00
	To Biews Mayds	02 00 00
	Payd ffor a pare of Andirons shoueuell and tonges	11 00 00
10:	To Lady Wood wch she gaue tto Lord Manchestors Man & to secatary Benetts in gold	02 00 00
twise	To Lady Deuonshieres Man	01 00 00
	Ex	**268 03 00**

[verso] 16v		lib s d
	Braughtt from ye other side ye sume of	**268 03 00**
	To Lady Newports Man	00 10 00
	To Lady Cornwallises Man	01 00 00
21	To M:s Nun for seuerall Nesesarys ffor yr Ma:tie	10 00 00

78 Dromes corrected from Dremes.

23	To Lady Gilfords Man	00 10 00
26	Payd ffor combes	00 16 00
28	To ye Hearbe woman y^t^ present orringers	01 00 00
31	To y^r^ Ma:^tie^ page of ye bakes-teeres y^t^ present a crose[79]	02 00 00
	To one of y^r^ Ma:^tie^ footmen y^t^ present a crose	01 00 00
feb ye 6	To one of y^r^ Ma:^ties^ footmen widdows	05 00 00
	To Lady Lincolnes Man	00 05 00
	Totall Disbursed *Ex*	**290 04 00**
	Where of receud	**300 00 00**
	Catherina R	
	Soe Rests dew This 9: Febu:^y^ tto y^r^ Matie from this Accomptant *Ex*	**009 16 00**

[recto] 17r		lib s d
Feb ye 16	To M:^r^ Spencors footeman y^t^ braught Almond Butter	00 05 00
	To a woman thatt Made Cline y^r^ Ma:^ties^ Closett	00 10 00
19	To Mr Spencors page y^t^ braught almond butter	00 10 00
27	To Lady Wood for watter in gold	02 00 00
March ye 1	To one of y^r^ Ma:^tie^ footemen y^t^ pre^ted^ a Licke[80]	01 00 00
11	To a french woman for a tremed pare of Marchalls Gloues	03 10 00
	ffor tape	00 05 00
17	To Mr Spencors Man y^t^ braught almond butter	00 05 00
24[81]	To M:^s^ Nun for a Glase of watter in Gold	02 00 00
	ffor ye funerall for one of y^r^ Ma:^ties^ footman	10 00 00
	ffor Orringers y^t^ were presented to y^r^ Ma:^tie^	00 05 00

79 Cross.
80 Leek – on St David's Day.
81 Easter Sunday 1665 – 26 March.

Ap^ell^ ye 1	To Lady Montagus Man y^t^ braught venson in gold		02 00 00
11	To y^r^ Ma:^ties^ footmen roning to hampton Courtt		02 00 00
	To y^r^ Ma:^ties^ footemen for seuerall ttimes Rouning as by bill appiers		92 00 00
		Ex	**116 10 00**

[verso] 17v			lib s d
	Braughtt from y^e^ other side		**116 10 00**
	To his Ma:^tie^ Barber for 12 Combes		03 00 00
	To y^r^ Ma:^ties^ Barge Men for two serues one tto Hampton Court & y^e^ other to barne=helmes[82]		10 10 00
	To y^r^ Ma:^ties^ Mussique		30 00 00
	ffor threde & tape & Making y^e^ poore Childrens approns		00 09 00
	To M:^s^ Burton for houds & Carfes[83] and other Nusesarys as by bill appiers		12 10 00
17:	To y^e^ Lord Mountagues Man y^t^ braught venson		02 00 00
20	To y^r^ Ma:^tie^ which you lost att ombro att Sumersett house		05 00 00
	To picot which he Layd out for a pare [of] Andirons		07 00 00
25:	To y^r^ Ma:^ties^ footemen for Roning		02 00 00
	To y^r^ Ma:^ties^ Barge Man goieng ouer tto Lambett		01 10 00
May ye 1	To Lady Deuonshieres Cooke		01 00 00[84]
2	tto my selfe wch y^r^ Ma:^tie^ lost att ombro		01 10 00
8	To a woman y^t^ presented Cheress		01 00 00
		Ex	**193 19 00**

82 Barn Elms.

83 Hoods and cuffs.

84 01 00 00 corrected from 00 00 00.

[recto] 18r		lib s d
	Braughtt from ye other side ye sume of	**193 19 00**
23	To y^{r} Ma:^{ties} footemen Roning tto Lady Chesterfields	02 00 00
24	To y^{r} Ma:^{ties} footemen Roning to hygate	02 00 00
	To y^{r} Maties Barge Man for goieng tto hammer smith	03 00 00
27	To y^{r} Ma:^{ties} footemen Roning a hunting	02 00 00
	To y^{r} Ma:^{ties} Barge Man ouer to fox hall	01 10 00
29	To y^{r} Ma:^{ties} footemen one ye Kings bu<r>thday[85]	03 00 00
	for Cheries in hy parke	01 00 00
30	To y^{r} Ma:^{ties} footemen Roning a hunting	02 00 00
	Totall disbursed *Ex*	**210 09 00**
	Whereof Receued	**200 00 00**
	Dew tto y^{r} Ma:^{tie} my Last Accountt *Ex*	**009 16 00**
	Catherina R	
	Soe rests dew This 31 May tto this Accomptant *Ex*	**000 13 00**

[verso] 18v		lib s d
	Repayd my selfe	00 13 00
June ye 10 1665 g:	To ye Earle of Newcassells Man Thatt braught a horse	10 00 00
g:	To ye Gardnor att Sion house	02 00 00
	To y^{r} Ma:^{ties} footemen Roning tto Sion house	02 00 00
	To y^{r} Ma:^{tie} Barge Man as by Bill Appiers	12 00 00
	To ye M:^{tr} of ye Duke of Yorke barge	05 00 00
July ye 13	To y^{r} Ma:^{ties} footemen	02 00 00
16	To y^{r} Maties footemen Roning tto Hounslay[86]	02 00 00

85 Charles II's birthday – he was 35.
86 Hounslow.

	ffor feching holland from ye Greate Wardrope for y^r Ma:^{tie}	00 10 06
17	To y^r Ma:^{ties} footemen	02 00 00
18	To y^r Ma:^{ties} footemen	02 00 00
	Ex	**40 03 06**

[recto] 19r		lib s d
	Braughtt from ye other side ye sume of	**40 03 06**
	ffor tape	00 05 00
g:	To one y^t sheud y^r Matie ye watter Woorkes att More parke	02 00 00
g:	To a guide thether	01 00 00
	ffor a baskett of Appricokes	01 00 00
g:	To ye parkeepers att Hampton Court	02 00 00
	To ye Duke of yorkes Gardnor	02 00 00
20:[87]	To y^r Ma:^{ties} footemen	02 00 00
	To ye house Keeper and Gardnor att hampton Court	10 00 00
	ffor Chickings thatt were presented	00 10 00
	ffor feching of watter from Epsom ffor y^r Ma:^{tie} as by bill appiers	04 10 00
26:	To y^r Ma:^{tie} footemen	02 00 00
	Ex	**67 08 06**

[verso] 19v		lib s d
	Braughtt from ye other side ye sume of	**67 08 06**
	To ye Cheremen thatt Carred Donoline tto hampton	01 02 06
27	To y^r Ma:^{ties} footemen	02 00 00
	To ye saruants att ye Bishop of Winchisters	05 00 00
28	To y^r Ma:^{ties} footemen	02 00 00
	To ye seruants att Winchister	05 00 00
29:	To y^r Ma:^{ties} footemen	02 00 00

87 20 corrected from 29.

g:	To Sir Henery Tichbornes Man y^{t} Braught a horse	02 00 00
August ye 3	To y^{r} Ma:^{ties} footemen	02 00 00
9	To y^{r} Ma:^{ties} footemen	02 00 00
10 g:	To y^{r} Ma:^{tie} and w^{ht} you Lost att Cuba	05 00 00
	To y^{r} Ma:^{ties} footemen	02 00 00
11	To y^{r} Ma:^{ties} footemen	02 00 00
	Ex	**99 11 00**

[recto] 20r		lib s d
	Braught from ye other side ye sume of	**99 11 00**
14	To Mr Haley[88] for Coacth hiere as by bills appiers	149 15 00
16	To y^{r} Ma:^{ties} footemen	02 00 00
17	To y^{r} Ma:^{ties} footemen	02 00 00
	Your Ma:^{ties} Giuft tto y^{r} footemen	20 00 00
g:	To a guide when y^{r} Ma:^{tie} went tto see ye Duke of Yorkes Children	01 00 00
20	To y^{r} Ma:^{ties} footemen	02 00 00
22	To y^{r} Ma:^{ties} footemen	02 00 00
23	To y^{r} Ma:^{ties} footemen	02 00 00
24 g:	To Lady Lincolnes Man by y^{r} Ma:^{ties} Command	05 00 00
	To y^{r} Ma:^{ties} footemen	02 00 00
25	To y^{r} Ma:^{ties} footemen a hunting	02 00 00
	Ex	**289 06 00**

[verso] 20v		lib s d
	Braughtt from ye other side ye sume of	**289 06 00**
g:	To ye Earle of Pemprocke[89] Keeper	02 00 00
29:	To y^{r} Ma:^{ties} footemen	02 00 00
	Charges in receuieng Monnys	00 02 00
31	To y^{r} Ma:^{ties} footemen	02 00 00

88 Halsey.
89 Pembroke.

	To one of y^{r} Ma:^{ties} pagess wch he had Layd out as by bill	00 09 06
g:	To y^{r} Ma:^{tie} att ombro	05 00 00
Sep^{br} ye 3	To y^{r} Ma:^{ties} footemen	02 00 00
5	To y^{r} Ma:^{ties} footemen	02 00 00
8	To y^{r} Ma:^{ties} footemen	02 00 00
11	To y^{r} Ma:^{ties} footemen	02 00 00
12	To y^{r} Ma:^{ties} footemen	02 00 00
13	To y^{r} Ma:^{ties} footemen	02 00 00
14 g:	To Lord Aschle Coppers Man	01 00 00
	Ex	**313 17 06**

[recto] 21r		lib s d
	Braughtt from ye other side ye sume of	**313 17 06**
14	To y^{r} Ma:^{tie} footemen	02 00 00
g:	To Sr Steeuen foxsess Man thatt Braughtt a horse	05 00 00
	To one of y^{r} Maties footemen y^{t} went of a mesage	01 00 00
16 g:	To y^{r} Matie for ye Ea:rle of pembrowcks Boulling Grine Keeper	05 00 00
17 g:	tto y^{r} Ma:^{tie} att umbro	10 00 00
18	To y^{r} Ma:^{ties} footemen	02 00 00
22	To Mr Haley for Coacthe hiere as by bills appiers	63 12 00
23	To y^{r} Ma:^{ties} footemen	02 00 00
	To ye seruants att Co^{nells} Papp<h>ames[90]	05 00 00
26	To y^{r} Ma:^{ties} footemen	02 00 00
	Ex	**411 09 06**

[verso] 21v		lib s d
	Braughtt from ye other ye sume of	**411 09 06**
Sep:^{br} ye 27:	To y^{r} Ma:^{ties} footemen	02 00 00
Oc^{br} ye 4 g:	Giuen att ye Phesike Garden	01 00 00

90 Possibly Alexander Popham.

16	To y^{r} Ma:^{ties} footemen	02 00 00
18 g:	To ye Earle of Pembrocke Keeper	02 00 00
19	To y^{r} Ma:^{ties} footemen Roning tto Dichly	02 00 00
	For Loding and vnloding y^{r} Ma:^{ties} Goods and Mending of wagons as by bill	06 16 08
No:^{br} ye 15	To ye Mussique	10 00 00
One y^{r} Ma:^{ties} Bu<r>th day[91]	To y^{r} Ma:^{ties} footemen	03 00 00
	To his Ma:^{ties} footemen	02 00 00
	To ye Duke of yorkes footemen	02 00 00
	To ye Duchess of yorke footemen	02 00 00
	To y^{r} Ma:^{ties} Coacthe Men	03 00 00
	To his Ma:^{ties} Coacthe Men	02 00 00
g:	To y^{r} Ma:^{tie} at ombro	10 00 00
	Ex	**461 06 02**

[recto] 22r		lib s d
	Braughtt from ye other side ye sume of	**461 06 02**
	Drumes and trompets	09 00 00
	Wind Mussique	04 00 00[92]
	~~Harper~~	0~~1~~[93] 00 00
	To ye Litter Men	02 00 00
	Sumpter Men	02 00 00
	To ye Gromes	02 00 00
	To ye Ringers att Merten Colidge	00 10 00
	To one of y^{r} Ma:^{ties} footemen thatt presented a Crosse one St Andrues day	01 00 00
De^{br} ye 10 g:	To Lady Lincolnes Mayd	01 00 00
g:	To y^{r} Matie att ombro	10 00 00
13	To a Stone Cotter thatt presented a Marble piece	05 00 00
	Ex	**497 16 02**

[91] Catherine's birthday – she was 27.
[92] 04 00 00 corrected from 03 00 00.
[93] 1 crossed out and made into 0.

[verso] 22v		lib s d
	Braughtt from ye other side ye sume of	**497 16 02**[94]
g: 23 g:	To Mr Cheldons Keeper	02 00 00
New Yieres Guifts	To ye Mussique	10 00 00
Jan: ye 1:[95]	Wind Musique and Harpers	04 00 00
	To ye uniuerssity Mussique	05 00 00
	Dromes and trompets	09 00 00
	Footemen	10 00 00
	Coatchemen	10 00 00
	Postillions	03 00 00
	Litter Men and Cheare Men	05 00 00
	Sumpter Men	02 00 00
	Gromes	04 00 00
	To his Ma:^ties^ Coatchemen	05 00 00
	Ex	**566 16 02**

[recto] 23r		lib s d
	Braughtt from ye other side ye sume of	**566 16 02**
g:	To ye Spanniche Ambasadors Cooke	05 00 00
5 g:	To ye Duke of Cambrige Musique	01 00 00
	To ye showmakers[96] Men	04 00 00
8 g:	To Darbe[97]	02 00 00
	Sume Totall Disbursed is *Ex*	**578 16 02**
	Where of Receuied	**510 00 00**
	Soe Rest dew This 8:^th^ Jan: tto this Accompt *Ex*	**068 16 02**
	Catherina R	
		lib s d
	Repayd My selfe	68 16 02

94 497 16 12 corrected from 473 16 02.

95 1666 NS.

96 Shoemakers.

97 Possibly a reference to Derby Toby who received clothes from the king in 1660–62.

30	To ye Lady Southamtons footman	00 10 00
Fe^{by} ye 5 g:	To ye Spaniche Ambasaders Man	05 00 00
	To a Messenger y^{t} Carred y^{r} Maties <letters> tto London	05 00 00
	Ex	**79 06 02**

[verso] 23v		lib s d
	Braughtt from ye other side	**79 06 02**
	To Lady Croupe wch she had Laid outt	02 02 00
g:	To Lady Lincolnes wooman	05 00 00
5 g:	To M:^{s} Bougie	10 00 00
6	To M:^{s} Cheret for houds and Gloues as by Bill	05 15 00
Dew att Crismus last	To Ann Barker for halfe a yiere	18 00 00
10	To M:^{s} Nun for seuerall nessesarys	10 00 00
12:	To ye Gromes of ye Greate Chamber By y^{r} Ma:^{tie} Command	20 00 00
13 g:	To y^{r} Ma:^{tie}	50 00 00
	To ye house Clenser att Merton Colledge	02 00 00
	To Mr Montague for ye Coatchmen and Gromes and others	50 00 00
	To Mr Halsall for Coatch hiere from Oxford tto London as per bill	96 16 00
	Ex	**348 19 02**

[recto] 24r		lib s d
	Braughtt from ye other side ye sume of	**348 19 02**
	To ye Meusique att Oxford	05 00 00
	To y^{r} Ma:^{tie} footemen Roning from Oxford tto Maydenhead	02 00 00
	To ye Seruants where y^{r} Ma:^{tie} Lay att Maydenhead	05 00 00
	To Mr Montague wch he had laid outt for Coatch hiere	06 00 00

	To y^{r} Ma:^{ties} footemen Roning from Ma<y>denhead tto London	02 00 00
	To Lady Garrets seruant thatt braught a Cheese	02 00 00
	To Mr Jarmans Man for a Peruwegge[98] thatt your Ma:^{tie} had att Salsbury	12 00 00
17	To ye Barge Men for waiting one your Ma:^{tie} from thiessellworth[99] to London with two Bargess	07 10 00
	Ex	**390 09 02**

[verso] 24v		lib s d
	Braught from ye other side	**390 09 02**
March ye 1	To one of y^{r} Ma:^{ties} footemen that Thatt[100] presented a Lieke	01 00 00
8	To ye Spaniche Ambasadors Man thatt Braught Caramell	02 00 00
11	To Lady Lincolnes Man thatt braught venson	01 00 00
12	To your Ma:^{tie} Barge <Man> tto Grinewich	03 00 00
17	To Heames for Houds and Scarfes as per bill	16 05 00
19	For a poin^{t} for y^{r} Ma:^{tie} as per Acquitances	25 00 00
	To one of y^{r} Ma:^{ties} footemen thatt presented a crose one St Patricks Day[101]	01 00 00
21	To Lady Deuonshieres Man thatt braught a presentt of fishe	01 00 00
23:	To Ben for Houds and Scarfes as per bill	06 01 00
	Ex	**447 15 02**

[recto] 25r		lib s d
	Braughtt from ye other side ye sume of	**447 15 02**

98 Periwig.
99 Isleworth.
100 Uncorrected duplication.
101 March.

	To Mr Spencor by y^r Ma:^tie	20 00 00
	ffor two peruweages[102] as per Acquitance	20 00 00
24	Payd ffor Loding and unloding y^r Ma:^ties goods att Oxford and London & Mending of Wagons as per bill	02 11 00[103] 00 00 00
	For fiue fanes as per Acquittance	20 00 00
29, 1666	For a pice of whightt Crape	07 00 00
	To Mr Meade wch he had Disbursed as per bill	02 08 06
Apprill ye 11	To y^r Ma:^tie for ye poore	26 00 00
	To ye Eury Men by y^r Ma:^ties order[104]	02 10 00
	Sume totall disbursed is *Ex*	**548 08 08**
	Catherina R Where of Receued	**540 00 00**
	Soe Rests dew this 12 Apprill tto this Accompt *Ex*	**008 08 08**

[verso] 25v		ll s d
	Repayd My selfe	**08 08 08**
Apprill ye 19 1666	To ye Spanich Ambassadars Man thatt Braughtt Buisquit	02 00 00
30	To y^r Ma:^ties Barge man for thre Seruecies as per bill	10 00 00
	To ye Ma:^ties footemen ye foust[105] time tto High parke	02 00 00
May ye 1	To y^r Ma:^ties footemen Roning tto Parsons Griene	02 00 00
	To ye Duchess of Monmoths Coatch man & footemen	03 00 00
4:	To y^r Ma:^ties footemen Roning to Hemstiede[106]	02 00 00
10	To ye Duchess of Yorkes Coatchmen	01 00 00

102 Periwig.
103 02 11 00 corrected from 02 15 00.
104 Easter Sunday 1666 – 25 April.
105 First.
106 Hampstead.

	To y^{r} Ma:^{ties} footmen Roning tto Kingsington		02 00 00
		Ex	**32 08 08**

[recto] 26r			ll s d
	Braughtt from ye other side		**32 08 08**
12	To Lord Montagues Keeper that braughtt venson		02 00 00
g:	To Lady Deuenshieres Coatchman		05 00 00
14	To y^{r} Ma:^{ties} Barge Men		01 10 00
	To y^{r} Ma:^{ties} footemen		02 00 00
15	ffor seuerall things out of France as per bill		25 00 00
	For a Baskett of Cherrys thatt y^{r} Ma:^{tie} had att High Parke		01 00 00
	To his Ma:^{ties} Coatchman		01 00 00
23	To y^{r} Ma:^{ties} footemen Ro[ning] tto Hampton Courtt		02 00 00
	To a Cabinett Maker as per Acquitts		03 15 00
	ffor Duke Cherrys in High Parke as per Acquits		02 00 00
		Ex	**82 13 08**

[verso] 26v		lib s d
	Braught from ye other side	**82 13 08**
June: 3:	For y^{r} Ma:^{ties} footemen	02 00 00
	To Lady Deuenshieres seruantts that braught Creame	00 10 00
7	To ye Spaninch Ambasadors Cooke	02 00 00
	ffor tape	00 10 00
	To ye Duke of Yorkes Gardnor thatt braught fruete	01 10 00
	ffor Duke Cheryes as per Acquits	01 00 00
	To ye Duchess of Monmouth	10 00 00
11	ffor a Collation att ye Mulbery Gardon as per Acquits	01 12 00

	To M^{s} Bardon ffor a Double vaile and two per[107] of cofes as per Acquits	22 00 00
12	To ye Boulling Grine Keeper att Putny	02 00 00
	Ex	**125 05 08**

[recto] 27r		lib s d
	Braughtt from ye other side	**125 05 08**
	tto one of y^{r} Ma:^{ties} footemen that was sent tto Rohamton of a Mesage	01 00 00
12	To Lady Mordants footemen	00 10 00
	To y^{r} Ma:^{ties} Barge Men tto putny	05 00 00
	To y^{r} Ma:^{ties} footemen Roning to putny	02 00 00
14	To Lady Linclornes footemen that Braught Cheryes	00 10 00
	ffor a Collation at ye Mulbery Gardon as per bill	03 05 00
18	To your Ma:^{tie} att Southampton House	20 00 00
21	To y^{r} Ma:^{tie} at ombro	40 00 00
26	To Lady Mordants Man	01 00 00
	To My selfe wch y^{r} Ma:^{tie} lost att ye Duchess of Munmoths att Lanterlid[108]	10 00 00
28	To Lady Linclornes Man	00 10 00
	Ex	**208 10 08**

[verso] 27v		lib s d
	Braught from ye other side	**208 10 08**
	To a Surgon y^{t} let y^{r} Matie Blood	10 00 00
	To ye Coatchman y^{t} Carred your <Majestie tto> St Jamesses and tto him y^{t} braugh <sume of> your Majestie <Retennu> ~~trayne~~ bake	01 05 00
9	To Lady Haruy Man y^{t} Braught a Nose gaye	01 00 00

[107] Pairs.
[108] Lanterloo.

	Charges goieng tto receuie Monnys	00 10 00
	To Cherrett for hods and Morning as per bill	22 01 06
	ffor a Perwige as per acquits	12 13 00
	ffor striped tifeny & Combs as per Acquis	05 15 00
	To Mr Halsalsy for Coatche hiere tto Turnebrige[109] as per Acquts	33 05 00
	ffor a Bathing tub for y[r] Ma:[tie]	04 00 00
	Sume totall disbursed is *Ex*	**299 05 02**
	Whereof Receuied	**300 00 00**
	Soe Rest Dew tto y[r] Ma:[tie] this 9 July from this Accompt *Ex*	**000 14 10**
	Catherina R	

[recto] 28r		lib s d
July y[e] 10 1666	Expended where y[r] Ma:[tie] Changed Coatchess	00 05 00
	To y[e] Morris Danceours att Seneck[110]	01 00 00
12	To y[e] Contry Musique att Turnebrige	02 00 00
14	To y[r] Ma:[tie] at Lodom	01 00 00
	To y[e] Duchess of Mounmouths Coatchman	00 10 00
17	To Lord Cornetburys Seruant y[t] braught Bt[111]	00 05 00
	To a Man y[t] presented woodcokes	01 00 00
	To one of y[r] Ma:[tie] footemen y[t] presented Busquet	01 00 00
19	To y[e] Duchess of Monmouths CoatchMan	00 10 00
	To y[e] Earle of Lesters[112] Keeper	02 00 00
	To y[e] waites	02 00 00
23	To S[ir] John Pellames[113] Keeper	02 00 00

109 Tunbridge.

110 Sevenoaks.

111 Possibly an abbreviation for Busquet, which is given in full two lines below. Or a person called Busquet.

112 Leicester's.

113 Pelham's.

26	To Lady Muscarys[114] Keeper	02 00 00
	To Lady Sunderlands Man yt braught Nose gayes	00 10 00
27	To a Man yt presented Partrigess	01 00 00
	Ex	**17 00 00**

[verso] 28v		lib s d
	Braught from ye other side	**17 00 00**
August ye 1	To yr Ma:ties footemen ye bone fiere night	02 00 00
	ffor Mending yr Ma:ties Lining dew in May Last	20 00 00
	To Ann Barker halfe a yiere Dew att Miedsomer last	18 00 00
	To Ms Nun for Nesesarys for yr Ma:tie	10 00 00
	To yr Ma:ties Musique for there coatche hiere and horse hiere to Turnebrige	07 00 00
4:	To two Bliend Mayds	02 00 00
	To ye watter fillers and poore women and others at ye wells as per bill	27 10 00
	To ye waites	02 00 00
5	To yr Ma:ties footemen for twinty four times Roning as per bill	48 00 00
	To ye seruants att Bounds[115]	05 00 00
	To ye Men yt keept ye Pauillion	02 00 00
	To Mr Haley for Coatch hiere from Turnebrige as per Acquts	34 07 00
	Ex	**194 17 00**

[recto] 29r		lib s d
	Braught from ye other side ye sume of	**194 17 00**
	To ye Duchess of Yorkes Coatch Men	10 00 00
	ffor bringing a Clock from Turbrige[116]	00 10 00
	To Tege[117] ye Duke of yorkes footeman	01 00 00

114 Muskerry.
115 Uncertain meaning but possibly a reference to the boundary of Tunbridge.
116 Tunbridge.
117 Teague.

12:	To ye Gardnor att Kingsenton	01 00 00
15	To ye Spanich Ambasadors Man y^{t} braught a present	02 00 00
16	To y^{r} Ma:^{ties} footemen	02 00 00
	To ye porter in Sumerset yeard y^{t} Louked tto <y^{e}> Callonch y^{t} was presented	01 00 00
	ffor a Moutton Hankercher	01 00 00
19	To y^{r} Maties footemen Roning tto Hamsted Hearth	02 00 00
	Payd ffor Loding and vnloding y^{r} Ma:^{ties} Goods tto Turbrige and Mending of Wagons as per bill	04 06 10
	Ex	**219 13 10**

[verso] 29v		lib s d
	Braught from ye other side	**219 13 10**
27	To y^{r} Maties footemen for Roning tto Lady Chesterfilds	02 00 00
	To a Man for a littell Challoche	03 12 00
	Summe total disbured is *Ex*	**225 05 10**
	Catherina R	
	Where of Receuied ye Sume of	**300 00 00**
	Soe Rest dew: tto y^{r} Ma:^{tie} from this Accompt *Ex*	**074 14 02**

Sep^{br} ye 4	To two Soldiers thatt Braughtt a Cristall Candellsticke ffrom Sumersett House	01 00 00
	To Lord Arlinton Seruants goieng ~~up~~ tto St Jamesses	05 00 00
	To one of y^{r} Ma:^{ties} Pagess of ye Backe Steares y^{t} Red[118] postt from Turnebrige with <a letter>	01 00 00
	To y^{r} Maties Barge Men[119] y^{t} wayted ye time of ye fiere	03 00 00

118 Rode.

119 men corrected from man.

	To those y^t^ feched in Liters tto lode your Ma:^ties^ goods	01 00 00
	Ex	**11 00 00**

[recto] 30r		lib s d
	Braught from ye other side	**11 00 00**
	ffor Loding & vnloding y^r^ Ma:^ties^ goods ye time of ye fiere as per bill	01 01 00
	To y^r^ Ma:^ties^ footmen Roning tto Lady Malburys	02 00 00
	ffor Bockrome	00 03 00
17	To y^r^ Maties footemen to Roe Hampton	02 00 00
	To y^r^ Matie Barge Men to putney	03 00 00
Paid	To ye duke of yorkes Gardnor	01 00 00
50^lb^ pices	Exchange of gold	03 19 02
	Baggs and Chargess	00 10 00
24:	To y^r^ Ma:^ties^ footmen to Hygate	02 00 00
27:	To y^r^ Ma:^ties^ footemen Roning to Combe[120]	02 00 00
	To y^r^ Ma:^ties^ Barge Men to Lambeth	01 10 00
	To ye Dore Keeper of ye Parlement house	02 00 00
	To Lady Mordants Man y^t^ Braught a Nose gaye	01 00 00
	Ex	**33 08 02**

[verso] 30v		lib s d
1666	**Braught from ye other side**	**33 08 02**
	To one of y^r^ Ma:^ties^ footemen y^t^ was sent of a Mesage	01 00 00
Octob^r^ 6:	To y^r^ Ma:^ties^ footemen Roning to parsons griene	02 00 00
	ffor a table and stands as per Acquit	05 10 00
	To y^r^ Ma:^ties^ Pagess of ye Backe Stares wch they had Disbursed	06 17 06

120 Coombe.

18	To y^{r} Ma:^{ties} footemen tto parsons grine	02 00 00
	To Bardou a french woman for seuerall Garniturs of Ruban as per bill	12 07 00
	Payd ffor ye porte of a Box of Morning y^{t} Came outt of france and ye fecthing itt and other Charge as per bill	03 14 00
	To Cheuillion for Combes and pienes[121] as per bill	03 10 00
	To y^{r} Ma:^{ties} Musique for Coatch Hiere twise tto Lady Mordants	01 10 00
	Ex	**71 16 08**

[recto] 31r		lib s d
	Braught from ye other side ye sume of	**71 16 08**
27	To Lady Lincolnes Man y^{t} braught a present of Amond Butter	00 05 00
28:	To y^{r} Ma:^{ties} footemen	02 00 00
30:	To y^{r} Ma:^{ties} <footemen> Roning tto Lady Mordants	02 00 00
	ffor feching of watter from Epson when y^{r} Ma:^{tie} went to Turnbrige Last as per bill	02 08 00
	tto y^{r} Ma:^{ties} footemen to King<sin>ston	02 00 00
twise	tto ye Duchess of Monmouth Coatchman	01 00 00
	tto her footemen	01 00 00
	tto Lady Falmouths Coatchman	01 00 00
	tto her footemen	01 00 00
	tto a footeman y^{t} Lighted y^{r} Ma:^{tie}	00 05 00
	tto La Roche y^{r} Ma:^{ties} Taylor as per bill	21 00 00
	tto y^{r} Maties Cheremen wch they had Laid out for Lodging y^{r} Ma:^{ties} Chere as per bill	00 12 06
	Ex	**106 07 02**

[121] Pins.

[verso] 31v

	Braught from ye other side	**106 07 02**
	tto ye Spanich Ambasadors Man yt Braught Suger Cakes	02 00 00
On Yr Ma:ties Burth Day[122]	tto ye Swedes Ambasadors trompets	02 00 00
15	tto yr Ma:ties Musiqu	10 00 00
	Wind Musique & Recorders	05 00 00
	tto ye Harper	01 00 00
	tto yr Ma:ties footemen	03 00 00
	tto his Ma:ties footemen	02 00 00
	tto ye Duke of Yorkes footemen	02 00 00
	tto ye Duchess of Yorkes footemen	02 00 00
	tto yr Maties Coatchmen	03 00 00
	tto his Maties Coatchmen	02 00 00
	Dromes & trompets	09 00 00
	Litter Men	02 00 00
	Sumpter Men	01 00 00
	Gromes	02 00 00[123]
	Ex	**154 07 02**

[recto] 32r

		lib s d
	Braughtt from ye other side	**154 07 02**
	tto ye Master of yr Ma:ties Barge	01 00 00
	tto ye Duke of Yorkes trompeters	03 00 00
	Catherina R Sume Disbursed is *Ex*	**158 07 02**
	Due tto yr Matie in ye Last Account *Ex*	**074 14 02**
Debr ye 24: 1666[124]	Soe Rest Dew tto this Accomptant from yr Matie ye sume of *Ex*	**083 13 00**
	Catherina R	

122 Catherine's birthday – she was 28.

123 02 00 00 corrected from 01 00 00.

124 This date is correct – however its placement is interesting as it comes before entries earlier in December.

		lib s d
	Repayd My selfe	**083 13 00**
	ffor seuen yards of skallope as per Acquits	01 13 00
De[br] 10	To y[e] Doore Keeper of y[e] parlement when y[r] Ma:[tie] went Incognito	02 00 00
	ffor tape	00 05 00
	ffor a Crose presented to y[r] Ma:[tie] one St Andrues Day[125]	01 00 00
	Ex	**88 11 00**

[verso] 32v		lib s d
	Braught from y[e] other side y[e] sume of	**88 11 00**
14	ffor a point as per Acquts	35 00 00
	To y[e] Spaniche Ambasadors seruants	01 00 00
	To y[e] Duchess of Mounmouths Coatchman and footemen that waighted one y[r] Ma:[tie] that day y[r] Ma:[tie] went tto y[e] parlement house	02 00 00
	To a footeman that Lighted y[r] Ma:[tie]	00 10 00
15	To y[e] Spaniche Ambasadors seruants	02 00 00
25	To y[e] Yeoman of y[e] Gaurd y[t] waighted alle night att S[t] James	01 00 00
26	To y[e] Keeper of Hampton Court wth wenson[126]	02 00 00
	To y[e] Coatchemen postilliones and footemen that waighted one y[r] Ma:[tie] to Kingsinton	08 00 00
	Baggs & Chargess in Re[d] y[r] moneys	01 00 00
Newe Yiear Jan: y[e] 1[127]	To y[e] two Bands of violines	20 00 00
	To y[e] Wind Musique and recorders	06 00 00
	Ex	**167 01 00**

125 30 November.
126 Venison.
127 1667 NS.

[recto] 33r

	lib s d
Braught from ye side ye sume of	**167 01 00**
To a violin in ordinary	01 00 00
To ye Ducke of Cambriges violine	01 00 00
Harper	01 00 00
To yr Ma:ties Cooke	05 00 00
To his Ma:ties Cooke	05 00 00
To his Ma:ties Cookes Man yt braught Gelly	02 00 00
To yr Ma:ties Coatchmen	10 00 00
Postillions	03 00 00
To his Ma:ties Coatchmen	05 00 00
To yr Ma:ties footemen	10 00 00
Litter Men	05 00 00
Ex	**215 01 00**

[verso] 33v

		lib s d
	Braught from ye other side ye sume of	**215 01 00**
	Sumpter Men	04 00 00
	Grames[128]	05 00 00
	Drumes and trompets	09 00 00
	To ye Ducke of Yorkes trompets	06 00 00
	To ye Barge Men	02 00 00
	To ye shoomakers Men	04 00 00
	ffor pene Ienke[129] & paper	01 00 00
	To ye Gallery Keepers	06 00 00
2	To ye Spanich Ambasadors seruant	01 00 00
	To ye Duchess of Yorkes Coatchman that waighted one yr Ma:tie with ye trenaw[130] in St James Parke	01 00 00
	Ex	**254 01 00**

[128] Grooms.

[129] Ink.

[130] Uncertain meaning, but the term is repeated but spelt differently in the accounts, also in relation to St James Park. Possibly a phonetic spelling of train, which was another term for a duck decoy, and there was a duck decoy in the park.

[recto] 34r		lib s d
	Braught from ye other side ye sume of	**254 01 00**
6	To his Ma:ties Coatchman yt waighted one yr Ma:tie wth ye Done horsess	10 00 00
	To Cherett for whoodes & Carfes[131] as per bill	14 17 06
	To ye Spaniche Ambasadors seruant	01 00 00
	To Bardon for a triming as per Acqt	08 00 00
7	To a surgion yt let yr Ma:tie Blouding	10 00 00
	To Ms Plancys Nephew for swite water out of France as per Acqts	33 00 00
9	To a surgion in gold	10 00 00
	To ye Musique that waighted one yr Ma:tie att Lady Arlingtons	06 00 00
	ffor an Iron Cheest tto Keepe yr Ma:ties preuie purse Monnys in	10 00 00
12	To a surgion	10 00 00
	To ones that Braught orringers	00 05 00
	Ex	**367 03 06**

[verso] 34v		lib s d
	Braught from ye other side ye sume of	**367 03 06**
	To Bew ye Millinor as per bill	07 14 00
14	To a surgion in gold	10 00 00
23	To one yt Braught swite watter in gold	05 00 00
	To ye Spaniche Ambasadors Cooke g:	01 00 00
	To yr Ma:ties Cooke as a Gratuity	05 00 00
Febr ye 3:	To ye Spanich Ambasadors seruants g:	02 00 00
	To Ms Nun Dew at Crismuss	10 00 00
	To Ann Barker for halfe a yeare dew att Crismus last	18 00 00
4	To Lady Cornwalliess Man g:	01 00 00
	Lady Lincornes Man twise	00 10 00
10	To ye Spanich Ambasadours Cooke g:	01 00 00
	Ex	**428 07 06**[132]

131 Cuffs.

132 428 07 06 corrected from 428 17 06.

[recto] 35r		lib s d
	Braught from ye other side ye sume of	**428 07 06**
11	To ye Spanich Ambasadors Man g:	01 00 00
March ye 1	ffor a Lieke presented one St Dauieds day[133]	01 00 00
14	To ye Spanich Ambasadors seruants g:	02 00 00
	For a Crose presented one St Patricks day[134]	01 00 00
29/1667	To Lady Lincornes seruant	00 05 00
	To ye Spanich Ambasadors seruants g:	02 00 00
	ffor a Crine as per Acqts	05 10 06
	To Lord Fizts Hardings seruant y^{t} Braught Cheese	00 05 00
Aprill ye 1	To Lady Cornwallies seruant	00 05 00
	To ye Spanich Ambasadors Cooke g:	01 00 00
	To one that Braught Cheese from ye Duchess g:	01 00 00
	Ex	**443 13 00**

[verso] 35v		lib s d
	Braught from ye other side ye sume of	**443 13 00**
6	To y^{r} Ma:^{ties} Eury Men there Mandy[135]	02 10 00
	To ye Duchessess Coatchmen that waighted one y^{r} Ma:^{tie} Ester Eue[136] at St James	03 00 00
9	To y^{r} <Ma:^{ties}> Musique	10 00 00
	To Mr Spensors Man twise	00 10 00
15	To Lady Mordants seruant with a Nose gaye	00 10 00
17	To ye Sweedes Ambasadors page in gold	10 00 00
	To ye Coatchman & footemen that waighted one y^{r} Ma:^{tie} at St James	01 00 00
19	To Mr Haley for a Belt for y^{r} Ma:^{tie} wth goold Buckells	17 18 00

[133] 1 March.

[134] 17 March.

[135] Maundy Thursday 1667 – 8 April.

[136] Easter Saturday (Easter Eve) 1667 – 9 April. Easter Sunday 1667 – 10 April.

	ffor ye exchange of 70 pecess of gold	07 08 04
	To ye Spanich Ambasadors Cooke g:	01 00 00
	Ex	**497 09 04**

[recto] 36r		lib s d
	Braught from ye other side ye sume of:	**497 09 04**
20	To Lady Chesterfilds seruant that braught ye Legate g:	01 00 00
High parke	To yr Ma:tie footmen	02 00 00
22	To Lord Corneburys Man yt braught Jacolet[137] and tee in gold	03 00 00
23	To ye Musique one St Gorgess day[138]	10 00 00
	To Lady Cornwalliess seruant twise <Coming>	00 10 00
	To ye Beshope of winchister seruant yt Braught Lamprey pyes	00 10 00
27	To Cherett for two points as per Acqts	38 00 00
28	To his Ma:tie Barber for swite pouder and Essence as per bill	19 00 00
	To Lady Deuonshieres seruant wth salmon	00 10 00
19[139]	To ye Duchess of Yorkes Coatchman g:	01 00 00
May ye 1	To Lady Carlyeles seruant that braught a Nose gaye	00 05 00
11	To ye Spanich Ambasadors Cooke	01 00 00
13	ffor Hay and Barley for yr Ma:ties Kine all Last winter as per bill	09 08 09
	Ex	**583 13 01**

[verso] 36v		lib s d
	Braught from ye other side ye sume of	**583 13 01**
	To ye Mayd and ye Man yt Loucked tto yr Ma:ties Kine	06 00 00
	Sume totall Disbursed is *Ex*	**589 13 01**

137 Chocolate.
138 23 April.
139 Error for 29?

	Where of Receuied ye sume of	**570 00 00**
	Soe Rest <dew> this 13th day May 1667: tto this Accompt from yr Matie ye sume of *Ex*	**019 13 01**

Catherina R

		lib s d
	Repayd My selfe	**19 13 01**
May 18	To Lord Montagues Keeper that braught venson	10 00 00
21	To Lady Mordants Page yt Braught a Nose gaye	02 00 00
22	ffor a point as per Acqts	40 00 00
	To Lady Carterts page yt Braught Cherries seuerall <times> to yr Ma:tie g:	02 00 00
24	To yr Ma:ties footman for a Crose one St Georges day[140]	01 00 00
	Ex	**65 13 01**

[recto] 37r		lib s d
	Braught from ye other side ye sume of	**65 13 01**
30	To a poore woman yt presented pi<e>se[141]	01 00 00
	To yr Ma:ties footemen one ye Kings Burthday[142] Last yiere & this	06 00 00
	To ye Musique	10 00 00
31	To ye Spainch Ambasadors Cooke g:	01 00 00
June ye 1 1667	To ye Spainch Ambasadors Cooke g:	01 00 00
4	To yr Ma:ties footemen	02 00 00
6	To Ms Plancys assignes for Essens sent out of France by her g:	24 00 00
	ffor tape	00 05 00
8	To Lord of Oxfords seruants yt Braught a horse	25 00 00

[140] 23 April.
[141] Peas.
[142] Charles II's birthday (29 May) – he was 37.

10	To Lady Newports seruant	00 05 00
15	To yr Ma:ties footemen	02 00 00
16	To Lady Cornwalliss seruant	00 05 00
	Ex	**137 18 01**

[verso] 37v		lib s d
1667[143]	**Braught from ye other side ye sume**	**137 18 01**
June	ffor Mending yr Ma:ties Lening dew in May last	20 00 00
	To yr Ma:ties footemen	02 00 00
	To a Cabinett Maker as per bill	01 18 00[144]
18	To yr Ma:ties footemen	02 00 00
	Watermen to ffoxHall	01 10 00
20	ffor Cheris & aprecoks	01 00 00
25	to my Lady Carlisles man wth a nosgay	00 10 00
July ye 2 1667	to Kingsinton Gardiner wth frute	01 00 00
3	To Lady Carlils seruant wth flowers	00 05 00
4	To yr Ma:tie in gold at newporthouse	05 00 00
5	To Lady Carlils seruant wth flowers	00 05 00
8	to the wattermen in wolige[145]	03 00 00
12	to ye Spanish Embassadors seruant	01 00 00
	to the watermen to Batersie[146]	03 00 00
13	to the watermen to Chelsy	03 00 00
	Ex	**183 06 01**

[recto] 38r		lib s d
1667 July	**Braught from the other side**	**183 06 01**
13	to oares that Caried yr Ma:tie	01 00 00
	to two pair of oars that Caried yr Ma:ties retenue	00 10 00

143 The year appears at the top of the page again.

144 01 18 00 corrected from 01 10 00.

145 Woolwich.

146 Battersea.

	Bags & Charges in receuing money	01 00 00
	to the watermen to Batersy	03 00 00
14	mor to the watermen to Batersy	03 00 00
15	to the watermen to Chelsy	03 00 00
	to Lord Cornberys seruant	02 00 00
16	to the watermen to Chelsy	03 00 00
	to S^ir William Killegrew wch he paid for a treate as per bill	14 12 06
18	To Bew as per bill	22 09 00
	To Ma: Cherett as per bill	17 12 00
	To M^s Nun for necesaries dew at midsumer[147] last	10 00 00
22	To Ann Barker dew at mid sumer	18 00 00
	Ex	**282 09 07**

[verso] 38v		lib s d
1667	**Braught ffrom the other side**	**282 09 07**
July 23	To the Dairy-maid at Mr Mayes	01 00 00
	To other seruants there	01 00 00
25	Gardenor from Kensington wth fruit	01 00 00
30	To y^r Ma:^ties footmen to Rohampton	02 00 00
August 2	Parents of the two Irish Children	05 00 00
	Y^r Maties Bargmen to Lambeth	01 10 00
	One of y^r Maties Coachmens funeralls	10 00 00
	One that brought ffrench gingerbread	01 00 00
6	Y^r Maties Bargemen to Chelsey	03 00 00
	For a mowse trap	00 02 06
7	Y^r Maties Bargmen	03 00 00
	A wherry attending to Chelsey	00 10 00
9	Mr Steuens giuen by y^r Maties direcon	00 05 00
	To ye keepers of Epsome[148] waters	02 00 00
13	To Mr Burden	26 00 00

[147] 24 June.
[148] Epsom.

	Seruant of ye Earl of Warwickes at Chelsey by Mr Roper		02 00 00
13	Keeping yr Maties Calfe as per bill		04 19 00
		Ex	**346 16 01**

[recto] 39r			lib s d
1667	**Brought from the other side**		**346 16 01**
August 13	Lady Arlingtons woaman with Cakes		02 00 00
16	To one who brought Peaches		00 02 00
	To Mr Long at the Teniscourt		05 00 00
	To the Gardenour at Kinsington		01 00 00
	To Mr Sidnies man with ffiggs		02 04 00
	To the Spanish Imbassadors Man		01 02 00
	To Mr Booscher		11 00 00
21	To His Ma:ties Musique		10 00 00
	To the Sentry		01 02 00
22	To the Spanish Imbassadors Man		01 02 00
14 Oct	Sir Barnard Gaskins man		01 02 00
	Lady ffitzHardins man with Puffs		01 02 00
	Rose the Gardenor at St Jamess		05 10 00
	To his man with flowers		01 02 00
17	Spanish Imbassadors man		01 00 00
20	ffootman from Lady Lincolins		00 05 00
30	Margret Lorene for a Petticoat on Lady Garrets recomend		30 00 00
2 Nou	Spainsh Imbassadors Page		01 02 00
12	Spainsh Imbassadors Page		01 02 00
		Ex	**425 13 01**

[verso] 39v		lib s d
1667	**Brought from the other side**	**425 13 01**
15 Nouember being yr Maties Birth day[149]	Jon Pettoes yr footmans Widdow to bury him	15 00 00

[149] Catherine's birthday – she was 29.

	Sir Barnard Jaskyns man	02 04 00
	Charles Euene Harper	01 00 00
	William Mawgridge & other the ffootman	03 00 00
	Robert Bryerly & other the Coachmen	03 00 00
	Wm Mawgridge & other the Drummers	03 00 00
	Richard Deane & other the Trumperters	06 00 00
	John Hosely & other the Litter men	02 00 00
	Robert Osbourn & other the sumptirmen	01 00 00
	Henry Haruey & other the Groomes	02 00 00
	Wm Clark & other his Majesties Coachmen	02 00 00
	ffrank Crake & other His Majesties ffootmen	02 00 00
	Robert ffisher & other the Dukes ffootmen	02 00 00
	Willm Louring & other the Duchesses ffootmen	02 00 00
	John Symson & other the Dukes Trumpeters	03 00 00
	Robert Hill Chieff Bargman	01 00 00
	Michael Ashwell Bottleman of the ffield	00 02 06
	Ex	**475 19 07**

[recto] 40r		lib s d
1667	**Brought from the other side**	**475 19 07**
17 Nouember	To Henry Brockwell & others of the Musicions	10 00 00
	To Isac Stagings & other the Recorders	05 00 00
	To Thomas ffitzt the Musition	01 00 00
23	To my self wch yr Ma:tie lost at play	05 10 00
28	Wm Mawgridge ffootman one St Andrewes day[150]	01 00 00
	To a siruant of the Lady Swanns	01 00 00
	Maddam Shiret for Combes was pd in May 1665	25 00 00

150 30 November.

	Ms Bew for two dozen transparent gloues	07 04 00
	Yr Ma:ties Lyning mending wch was pd 23 June 1665	20 00 00
	Ann Barkir pd then for Clensing yr Roomes	17 00 00
	Madam Sheret for hoodes pd June 1665	37 10 00
	Tho: Greeting & other Musitions pd then also	10 00 00
	John Banester Musitian pd 20 July 1665	10 00 00
	Vndercharged before in this book as per note	08 05 00
	Spanish Embassidars man	01 02 00
4 Decem	To Mr Eaton for a Rich Point as per bill	42 00 00
11 day[151]	To a seruant of the Countess of Deuonsheirs	01 00 00
	Ex	**678 10 07**

[verso] 40v		lib s d
1667	**Brought from the other side**	**678 10 07**
13 Decembr	To Tho: Gourlaw Laid out for the doggs	01 02 10
	Laid out for a new book, paper, ink, penns etc	01 10 00
	Summ totall disbursed	**681 03 05**
	Wherof receiud: July 6th 1667	**500 00 00**
	Soe there rest due from yr Matie this 16th December 1667 To this Accomptant	**181 03 05**
	Catherina R	

30 Decembr	Repaid my selfe resting due as aboue	**181 03 05**
	Henry Brockwell & others ye Musicians of ye two bands to make vp 10li formerly recd 20li Guift on yr Ma:ties birthday	10 00 00

151 Unusual notation for this date.

1 January[152]	To them more by y[e] said Henry Brockwell	20 00 00
	Wind Musique & Recorders by Isaac Stagings	06 00 00
	M[r] Fitz Violen in ordenary	01 00 00
	M[r] Evens the Harper	01 00 00
	M[r] Harcoat y[r] Ma:[ties] Cooke presenting y[r] Ma:[tie]	05 00 00
	His Ma:[ties] Cheife Cook presenting Jelley	05 00 00
	His man that brought it	01 00 00
	Y[r] Ma:[ties] Coachman by M[r] Brierly	10 00 00
	The Postilions by him	03 00 00
	Ex	**243 03 05**

[recto] 41r		lib s d
1667[153]	**Brought from the other side**	**243 03 05**
1 Jan	The Footmen by Thomas Creek	10 00 00
	His Ma:[ties] Coachmen by M[r] Murry	05 00 00
	Y[r] Ma:[ties] Litter and Chayremen by Rich: Gwin	05 00 00
	Sumpter men by Edward Welch	02 00 00
	Groomes by George Askin & xpher[154] Barker	05 00 00
	Drumers by Turtulian Lewis	03 00 00
	Trumpeters by Edward Humerston	06 00 00
	Gallery keepers by M[r] Palles	06 00 00
	Duke of Yorkes Trumpets by Peter Lafauer	06 00 00
	Duke of Cambridges violen Thomas Greeting	01 00 00
	Shomakers men by Thorp Groome	04 00 00
	Two Portagall Cookes	03 00 00

152 1668 NS.
153 1668 NS.
154 Christopher.

	Portagall woman Baker	03 00 00
2nd Jan	To y^{r} Ma:^{tie} at Lord Arlingtons in gold	05 10 00
	Thomas Creek & other footmen for runing fees in September laste	02 00 00
22nd	To Madam Pinzon for Ribben	04 00 00
	To the Musique for waiting at S^{ir} William Killigrewe	05 00 00
	To my Lord Fitchardings man with a Cheese	01 00 00
	Ex	**319 13 05**

[verso] 41v		lib s d
1667[155]	**Brought from the other side**	**319 13 05**
5 February	For Tape by M^{s} Hamden	01 02 10
6	To my Lrd Orserys Coatchman who drew ye slege	01 00 00
	To y^{r} Ma:^{tie} 50 peices in Gold	55 00 00
	To Mr Stevens which he laide out for y^{r} Ma:^{tie}	01 15 00
	Expences in receuing money	00 16 00
	To y^{r} Ma:^{ties} band of violens playing when y^{r} Ma:^{tie} danced	10 00 00
	To Mistresse Bew as per bill	11 00 00
		400 07 00
	Whereof received of Mr Harvey the 20th of January Last	**400 00 00**
	Soe there rests due from y^{r} Matie this 28th of February 1667[156] To this Acomptant *Ex*	**000 07 00**

Catherina R

155 1668 NS.

156 1668 NS.

1-Worsley/7 – Catherine of Braganza, privy purse accounts 1668–75

[recto] 1r

1668	**Moneis Receuid for her Maties Priuey Purss**	lb s d
25 Aprill	Off Mr Heruey yor Maties Treasurer	500 00 00
6 Octob^r 68	Off Mr Heruy	200 00 00
19 Aprill 1669	Off Mr Heruy	500 00 00
2 Sep^tmbr 1669	Off Mr Heruy	400 00 00
8 Aprill 1670	Receuid of Mr Heruey	400 00 00
30 June 1670	Receuid of Mr Heruey	600 00 00
21 Septmbr 1670	Receuid of Mr Heruey	700 00 00
21 Octobr 1670	Receuid of Mr Hervey	400 00 00
25 May 1671	Receuid of Mr Heruey	500 00 00
19 Septmbr 1671	Receuid of Mr Hervey	300 00 00
26 Septmbr 1671	Receuid of Mr Hervey	200 00 00
9 July 1673	Receuid of Mr Hervey for thre Moneths ending at Midsomerlast	300 00 00[1]
		0000 00 00[2]

[verso] 1v

		lb s d
1673	**Brought from the other Syd**	**300 00 00**[3]
12 August	Receuid of Mr Hervey for July last	100 00 00
11 Septembr	Receuid of Mr Hervey for August last	100 00 00
3 Octobr	Receuid of Mr Hervey for Septembr last	100 00 00
6 Novembr	Receuid of Mr Hervey for Octobr last	100 00 00
10 Decembr	Receuid of Mr Heruey for November last	100 00 00
12 January	Receuid of Mr Hervey for December last	100 00 00
7 Febr	Receuid of Mr Hervey for January last	100 00 00
10 March	Receuid of Mr Hervey for Feberuary last	100 00 00

1 A line is drawn above and below this figure, which in light of the summary given on the next page – for money from March 1671 to April 1674 – suggests a notional total of £4,700 up to September 1671, with £300 being taken forward to the next page.

2 Corrected from £5,000, which is correct for the page.

3 See note 1.

9 Aprill 1674	Receuid of Mr Hervey for March last	100 00 00
	Moneis Receuied from the 25 March 1673 to the 9th April: 1674	**1200 00 00**
4 May 1674	Receuid of Mr Hervey for April last	100 00 00
12 June	Receuid of Mr Hervey for May last	100 00 00
30	Receuid of Mr Hervey to pay y^r Maties footmens Areirs	050 00 00
9 July	Receuid of Mr Hervey for June last	100 00 00
3 August	Receuid of Mr Hervey for July last	100 00 00
	Receuid of Mr Hervey to pay the Coatchmens Areirs	050 00 00
4 Septembr	Receuied of Mr Hervey for August last	100 00 00
19	Receuied of Mr Hervey for this Septembr	100 00 00
26	Receuied of Mr Hervey to paye the Grooms Litermen & somptermens Areirs	057 00 00
25 Novembr	Receuied of Mr Hervey for Octobr last	100 00 00
1 Decembr	Receuied of Mr Hervey for Novembr last	100 00 00
		957 00 00

[recto] 2r		lb s d
1674	**Brought from the other Syde**	**957 00 00**
8 Janr	Receuied of Mr Hervey for Decembr last	100 00 00
4 Febr	Receuied of Mr Hervey for Janr last	100 00 00
2 March	Receuied of Mr Hervey for Febr last	100 00 00
3 April 1675	Receuied of Mr Hervey for March last	100 00 00
	Moneis Receuied from the ninth of April: 1674 to the third of April: 1675	**1357 00 00**[4]

[verso] 2v blank

[recto] 3r		
1668	**Moneis disbursed for her Maties vse**	lb s d
6 Aprill	To yor Matie to play for a Jouell	005 10 00

4 Total delivered to the queen in this accounting period – £7,557 00 00.

	To yor Maties footmen who presented a Leeke[5]	001 00 00
7	To a man that Braught watter	000 10 00
	To Lady Devonshirs man	000 10 00
	To Lady Linkehorns[6] footman	000 10 00
15	for a Ratt Trape	000 02 06
26	Bages & Chargess at receueing Money	001 00 00
	to a footman Leighted your Matie	000 10 00
	to Lady Devonshirs footman	000 10 00
28	to the dutchese of Munmouths Coatchman & postilion	002 05 00
	for paper Inke sand wax & pens	001 00 00
	To your Matie at St James on Good Friday[7]	003 06 00
	to the Garde at that time	001 02 00
	to the Spanish Cooke	001 02 00
	to Lady Temple	001 02 00
	to the Spanish Cooke with Pattes	001 02 00
	to the Spanish cooke by Mr Picott	001 02 00
	to the musique for waitting at Easter[8]	010 00 00
	to Mrs Bew as per bill	028 00 00
	Ex	**060 03 06**

[verso] 3v		lib s d
1668	**Braught from the other side**	**060 03 06**
Aprill	To yor Maties footmen the first time to heigh park	002 00 00
	for St Patricks Cross	001 00 00
	to yor Maties footmen who presented St Goerge cross	001 00 00
30	to the french mercer for stufs as per bill	029 15 00

5 Probably on St David's day, which was 1 March.
6 Lincoln.
7 Good Friday 1668: 30 March.
8 Easter Sunday 1668 – 1 April.

	to M:[9] Cherett as per bill	036 19 00
	to Lady Heruys footman	001 02 00
May	for two treats at heighparke as per bill	015 12 06
	to yor Matie which was lost at cards	005 10 00
	paid then which yor Matie Lost at Cards	005 10 00
2	paid then for mending yor Maties Lining due this present May	020 00 00
	to the Spanishe Ambassadors man by Mr Picot	001 02 00
	to Lady Carnwallace footman	000 05 00
6	to Lady Arlingtons Cooke by Mr Picot	001 02 00
	to the Iwry[10] pantry & buttry for waitting on Maundy Thursday[11]	002 10 00
	to Lady Arlingtons footman	000 10 00
	to francisco Corbett	044 00 00
8	to Anne Barker for 3 quartrs allowance due at our lady <day> Last	027 00 00
	Ex	**255 10 00**

[recto] 4r		lib s d
1668	**Braught from the other Side**	**255 10 00**
May 8	to Lady Arlingtons Cooke	001 02 00
	to Mr Bosher for Letting of yor Maties blood	011 00 00
	for a Looking Glass & cace	006 15 00
9	to the Envoies page	001 02 00
	to Lady Devenshirs footman	000 05 00
	to Lady Carnwallace footman	000 05 00
	to your Matie to play[12] for a point	002 04 00
12	to Mr Bosher for letting blood	011 00 00
	for Combs for yor Matie as per bill	003 10 00
	to Lady Arlintons footman	000 05 00

9 For Mistress.

10 Ewery.

11 Maundy Thursday 1668 – 29 March.

12 Uncertain meaning; possible play for a point (in relation to cards) or pay of a point (a piece of lace).

	to yo[r] Ma[tie] to play[13] for Gloues & fans	001 02 00
14	to the Musique for waitting <on> whitson day[14]	010 00 00
16	to Lady Montegues man who presented a bucke	002 04 00
	to Will Jonson for things from the Confectioner to yo[r] Ma[tie]	000 06 00
16	for Ring o Roots canditt	000 05 00
	to Lady Barths Cooke	001 02 00
20	to Lady Arlintons footman	000 10 00
	Ex	**307 18 00**

[verso] 4v		lib s d
1668	**Braught from the other side**	**307 18 00**
May	to a Gardener	000 05 00
29	to Mr Haliard his Ma[ties] Barber which was due per bill y[e] 30th June 1662	008 04 00
	to yo[r] Ma[ties] foottmen on the kings Birth day[15]	003 00 00
	to the Musique then	010 00 00
30	to M[rs] Nun for 3 quartrs of a years allowance due at Lady day last[16]	015 00 00
First June	focleaning yo[r] Ma[ties] Cabinett as per bill	004 00 00
	to yo[r] Ma[ties] darymaid as per bill	007 06 00
3	for 3 Baskitt of Cheris	002 05 00
	to dutchmen put up the Great Candlestick in the drauingroom	001 00 00
8	to Hamon for Baskits of Cheries	003 00 00
	to his Ma[ties] Coatchman for waitting of yo[r] Ma[tie] to My Lord Baiths	001 00 00
	to the Coatchmaker & harnismakers men	005 00 00
	Ex	**367 18 00**

13 Pay.
14 24 May 1668.
15 Charles II’s birthday – he was 38.
16 25 March.

[recto] 5r		lib s d
1668	**Braught from the other Side**	**367 18 00**
June 10	to the womon at Ipsem[17] wells	002 00 00
	to watermen that Loockt for yor Maties bodgine[18]	000 05 00
	to yor Maties bargemen for waitting to Chelsy	003 00 00
11	to yor Maties bargemen to woster[19] house	001 10 00
16	to hamond for Cheris & Aprecoks	002 00 00
	to his Maties Coatchman for waitting of yor Matie to a play	001 00 00
	for a baskitt of Cheris	000 18 00
17	to his Heighness[20] Bargemen for waitting of yor Matie to sumerset house	001 00 00
	to Mrs Lemar for her husbans funerall	005 00 00
19	for a baskitt of Cheris	000 10 00
1 July	to yor Maties footmen to walthem Aby	002 00 00
	to his Maties Coatchman then	002 00 00
	paid att the boullingreen thair	002 04 00
	Pd by yor Maties bottleman by the way	001 02 00
	Ex	**392 07 00**

[verso] 5v		lib s d
1668 2 July	**Braught from the other Side**	**392 07 00**
	to hamond for a baskitt of fruitt	001 10 00
4	to Lady Heruys footman	001 02 00
6	to Mrs Hill for a quaif to yor Matie	000 05 00
7	to yor Maties footmen to Roehampton	002 00 00
8	to hamond for a baskitt of fruitt	001 15 00
10	to Smith for keeping of yor Maties Birds for the space of two yeares	006 13 00

17 Epsom.
18 Bodkin – cf. 2 July 1669.
19 Worcester.
20 His Highness – possibly James, duke of York.

11	to Lady Arlintons Butler	000 10 00
13	to hamond for a baskitt of fruitt	001 10 00
	to Lady Arlintons footman	000 10 00
	to Lady Linkolns Cooke	000 10 00
	to Chaire men waitted of yor Matie to St James Parke	000 05 00
20	to Lady Manchesters footman	000 10 00
21	to Mistress Biew as per bill	014 05 06
	For Remouing yor Maties Trunks	000 02 06
	Ex	**423 15 00**

[recto] 6r		lib s d
1668	**Braught from the other side**	**423 15 00**
23 Due 6 instant	to yor Maties Bargemen to Rohampton	003 00 00
Due 20 instant	to yor Maiesties Bargemen to Chisweeke	003 00 00
25	to a poore man had his Meare[21] killd	010 00 00
26	to the Gardner from Wimilton[22] house with a present of fruitt	001 00 00
27	to Lady Ingroms man braught ffigs	000 02 06
	to Lady Heruys footman with a pye	000 10 00
	to yor Matie which was lost at cards	005 10 00
28	to the Keeper of St James parke who presented a buck to yor Matie	001 02 00
30	to Lord Crafts page with figs	000 05 00
	to Mrs Bointons footman	000 10 00
4 august	to yor Maties furier for Mufs per bill	003 00 00
5	to Lord Crafts page with figs	000 05 00
6	to Lady Arlintons footman	000 05 00
10	to the Tooth Drawer	011 00 00
	to Mr Steuens wch he Laid out	000 06 00
	Ex	**463 10 06**

21 Mare.
22 Wimbledon.

[verso] 6v		lib s d
1668 August	**Braught from the other side**	**463 10 06**
12	to a Gardner from Chisweek wth fruitt	001 00 00
17	to a Gardner with fruite	001 00 00
5 Septr	to a man with Oranges	001 02 00
13	to Lady Portlands footman wth ffigs	000 05 00
14	to the Spanishe Ambassadors Cooke	001 02 00
23	to his Maties Bergmen from foulem[23] to putny	001 00 00
	for Taep[24]	000 05 00
26	for Coatchehire to Audleyend with Sir William Killegre as per bill	006 10 00
	for powder as per bill	001 11 00
	Tottall disbursed *Ex*	**477 05 06**
	Whereof receuid	**500 00 00**
	Catherina R	
	Soe Rests due this first Octobr to yor Matie from this Accompt *Ex*	**022 14 06**

[recto] 7r		
1668		lib s d
6 Octobr	Charges at the Receipt <of> two hundred pounds	000 10 00
	to Mr Halsall for Coatchehire to Audley End	025 16 00
6	to her Heighnes[25] Coatchehire to Hodsdon[26]	022 00 00
	to A man helpt out yor Maties Coatche by the way	001 02 00
	Runeing Money to yor Maties footmen	004 00 00
9	to Mr Bosher for letting yr Matie blood	011 00 00
	for Transporting yor Maties Goods from London to Audley end as per bill	002 01 03

23 Fulham.

24 Tape.

25 Possibly the duchess of York.

26 Hoddesdon.

	to Mr Steuens as per bill	000 16 06
	to the porter was sent for things to London	001 05 00
15	to her Heighnes Coatchemen	001 02 00
	to the Spanish Embassadors Cooke	001 02 00
18	to M[r] Halsall for Coatchehire from Audley End to London as per bill	045 12 00
	Runeing money to yo[r] Ma[ties] footmen	004 00 00
	For Transporting yo[r] Ma[ties] Goods from Audley end to London as per Bill	002 02 00
	Ex	**122 08 09**

[verso] 7v		lib s d
1668	**Braught from the other Side**	**122 08 09**
22 Octobr	to Lady Heruys man with flowers	001 00 00
	to the Page of the Bakstairs cam beffor from Audley end to get Rady the Lodgings	000 10 00
24	to S[ir] Edward Ker as per aquitance	017 00 00
	to M[r] Clerke page of the Bakstairs as per bill	002 10 06
31	to M[rs] Cherrett as per bill	021 12 00
	to M[r] Vahan[27]: lost at Lantrelew[28]	001 02 00
	to Lady Sunderlands footman wth a nosgay	000 10 00
4 Novembr	Paid that yo[r] Ma[tie] lost at ombre	001 02 00
	to M[rs] Bardo as per bill	019 02 06
	to the poore at Audley end	005 00 00
7	to M[r] Steuens to Kinsinton for water	000 05 00
10	to the Countesse of winssellies[29] footman with a doge	001 00 00
	to M[r] Chase as per Bill	013 15 00
	to Lady Gerretts footman with a Cheese	000 10 00

27 Vaughan.
28 For lanterloo, a card game.
29 Winchelsea.

15 on yr Maties Birth day[30]	to the Musique	020 00 00
	to the Harper	001 00 00
	to the wind Musique & Recorders	005 00 00
	to the Violin in ordinarie	001 00 00
	Ex	**234 07 09**

[recto] 8r		lib s d
1668	**Braught from the other Side**	**234 07 09**
15	to yor Maties footmen	003 00 00
	to his Maties footmen	002 00 00
	to the ducke of Yorks footmen	002 00 00
	to the dutchesse footmen	002 00 00
	to yor Maties Coatchemen	003 00 00
	to his Maties Coatchmen	002 00 00
	to the drumes & trompettes	009 00 00
	to the Littermen	002 00 00
	to the sumptermen	001 00 00
	to the Groomes	002 00 00
	to the Duck[31] of Yorks Trompetts	003 00 00
	to yor Maties Bargemen	001 00 00
	to the Bottleman of the feild	000 02 06
	Catherina R Tottall disbursed *Ex*	**266 10 03**
	Wherof Receiued	**200 00 00**
	Due tto yor Matie in the Last Accompt	**022 14 06**
Novembr 16	Rest due from yor Matie to this Accomptant *Ex*	**043 15 09**

[verso] 8v		
1668		lib s d
16 Novembr	Repaid my selfe	**043 15 09**
20	to the Spanish Embassadors Cooke	001 02 00
	to yor Mties footmen presented St Androws Cross[32]	001 00 00

30 Catherine's birthday – she was 30.

31 Duke.

32 30 November.

5 Decembr	for Bringing the Tall woman in a Chaire	000 04 00
9	paid that yor Matie <Lost> at play	008 05 00
	for pen Inke and paper	001 00 00
15	to the Spanish Embassadors Cooke	001 02 00
25	to the Gard att St James	001 02 00
	for Carieing things to St James & bake	000 05 00
2 Jan[33]	to Lady Marshalls pag[34] wth a pye	000 05 00
15	to the Embassadors footman	000 10 00
14 Feb^r^	for Tape	000 05 00
	to lady Falmouth footmen	001 00 00
9 March	to the Spanish Embassaders Cooke	001 01 06
	to lady Devenshirs man wth a sallmon	000 10 00
	paid for bringing the holland for yor Maties sheets from the great Wardrobe	000 10 00
16	to the Spanish Embassaders page	001 01 06
20	to yor Maties footman presented St Patricks Cross	001 00 00
	Ex	**063 18 09**

[recto] 9r		lib s d
1669	**Braught from the other Side**	**063 18 09**
26 March	to the Spanish Embassadors Cooke	001 01 04
19 April	Charges at the Rececpt of 500^li^	000 10 00
New years gifts due from Jan: 1668	to the Trompets	006 00 00
	to the dromers	003 00 00
	to the ducks[35] Trompets	006 00 00
	to the Litermen & Chairemen	005 00 00
	to yor Maties footmen	010 00 00
	to the Portuguese Cook	003 00 00
	to the Portuguese Baker	003 00 00
	to his Maties Coatchmen	005 00 00

33 1669 NS.
34 Page.
35 Duke.

	to yor Mai^{tes} Coatchmen	010 00 00
	to the postilions	003 00 00
	to the two bands of Musique	020 00 00
	to the sumpermen	004 00 00
	to the Groomes	005 00 00
	to the duck of Cambridge violin	001 00 00
	to the shoemakers men	004 00 00
	to yor Maties Bargemaister	002 00 00
	to the Harper	001 00 00
	to the windmusique & Recorders	006 00 00
	to the violine in ordinary	001 00 00
	to the Gallery keepers	006 00 00
	Ex	**169 10 01**

[verso] 9v		lib s d
1669	**Braught from the other Side**	**169 10 01**
19 April	to his Maties Maister Cooke	005 00 00
	to his man	001 00 00
	to yor Maties Maister Cooke	005 00 00
	to his man	001 00 00
27	to the ducke of Yorks Musique that plaid to yor Matie on Twehesday	010 00 00
	to yor Maties Musique that waited in the priuy chamber the 20 Jan:	010 00 00
	to y^{r} Maties Musique that waitted on Eastermunday[36]	010 00 00
	to yor Maties footmen the first day to heigh park	002 00 00
	to the Musique on St Goergday[37]	010 00 00
	to Mon^{s} La Roche as per bill	167 00 00
	to the pantry Iwry & Butry that waitted on Maundy Thursday[38]	002 10 00
	to Lady Sunderlands footman with a nosgay to yor Matie	001 00 00

36 Easter Sunday 1669 – 21 April. Easter Monday 1669 – 22 April.

37 23 April.

38 Maundy Thursday 1669 – 18 April.

27	Mrs Nun for thre quartrs allowance due at Cristmus Last	015 00 00
	to Mrs Nun Laid as per bill	004 01 06
	Ex	**413 01 07**

[recto] 10r		lib s d
1669	**Braught from the other Side**	**413 01 07**
27 Aprill	to Anne Barker for thre quarter allowance due at Cristmus Last	027 00 00
	to Richard Lane yeoman of the wagons by yor Maties order	003 03 08
2 May	for mending yor Maties Lining then due	020 00 00
4	to Mis Bew as per Bill	017 18 00
	for printed bills & to the Crier when yor Maties dog was Lost	001 03 00
8	to Will Jonson for Carieing a picktur to St James	000 03 00
	mor to him for remouing <yor Maties trunks> when the lodgings were whitned	000 04 06
	Paid by yor Maties order to the Coatchman & footmen waitted of yor Matie on Easter eue[39]	005 00 00
12	to yor Maties footman presented St dauids Leek[40]	001 00 00
	to yor Maties footman presented St Goerg Cross[41]	001 00 00
	to the Gentlewoman that waitted of yor Matie with Mrs Eliot	005 03 04
	to Lady Baiths[42] Cooke	001 00 08
	to Lady Cornwallace man	001 00 00
	to Joan Brown for yor Maties Cow as per bill	008 00 08
	Ex	**504 18 05**

39 Easter Eve (Holy Saturday) 1669 – 20 April.
40 For St David's day, 1 March.
41 For St George's day, 23 April.
42 Bath.

[verso] 10v		lib s d
1669	**Braught from the other Side**	**504 18 05**
12 May	*Catherina R* Totall disbursed	**504 18 05**
	Wherof Receuied	**500 00 00**
12 May	Rests due to the Accompt from yor Matie	**004 18 05**
	Repayed my Selfe	**004 18 05**
12	to the Spanish Embassadors man	001 00 06
22	to Lord Montagues man who presented a bucke to yor Matie	002 01 06
	to the porter that braught it	000 02 06
24	to Lady Alintons footman	000 02 06
	to Mr Stevens for Coatchehire	000 03 00
7 June	to a Chaireman	000 10 00
	to Lady Baiths footman	000 10 00
	to yor Maties footmen on the Kings Birthday[43]	003 00 00
16	paid for things to yor Maties dogs	000 04 00
20	to Lady Maldons page	000 10 00
	to the tenise court man for shooess	001 00 00
	Ex	**014 02 05**

[recto] 11r		lib s d
1669	**Braught from the other Side**	**014 02 05**
July 2	to Mr Steuens to goe by water	000 01 00
20	to Mrs Talbots footman w^t^ a pigion pye	000 05 00
	to the Gardiner of Hampton court	001 00 00
	to the dutches of Richmons footman w^t^ Milons	000 05 00
	to a Gardiner from Wimilton[44]	001 00 00
	for Steele Bodgins[45]	001 00 00
	for Tape	000 10 00
August 9	to a poore man at heigh park	000 05 00
	to Lady Sunderlands page with a nosgay	001 01 00

43 Charles II's birthday – he was 39.

44 Wimbledon.

45 Bodkins.

	to Mr Steuens sent by water	000 03 00
	to a man from Wimllton with fruite	001 00 00
	to Lady Arlingtons footman	000 10 00
12	to the Gardner of Hampton court	001 00 00
19	to the Gardner from Wimellton	001 00 00
	to Lady Falmuths footmen	000 10 00
	to a man with millons	001 00 00
	Ex	**024 12 05**

[verso] 11v		lib s d
1669	**Braught from the other Side**	**024 12 05**
2 Septembr	to the Musique due on his Maties Birthday	010 00 00
	to the dutches of Buckingams seruants waited of yor Matie to Lady Arlingtons	005 00 00
	to Mr Halsy for Coatchire to Hamton court as per bill	023 06 00
	to Mrs Nun for halfe a years allowance due at Midsomer last	010 00 00
	to Anne Barker for halfe a years Allowance due at Mid somer last	018 00 00
	to Mr Boscher for leting yor Maties Blood at two seuerall tims	020 16 08
	to Mrs Cherett as per bill	053 12 00
	to the men Braught water for yor Maties Baith as per bill	005 09 00
	paid at the Receit of foure hundred pounds	001 00 00
	for pen Ink and paper	001 00 00
	for Threed	000 10 00
	for Tap	000 10 00
	paid by water to London and bakagaine	000 10 00
	Ex	**174 06 01**

[recto] 12r		lib s d
1669	**Braught from the other Side**	**174 06 01**
9 Septr	to Mr Halsy to Southampton	020 00 00
	to yor Maties footmen for runing money	002 00 00

	for bringing the bows & arous[46] to Hamton court	001 00 00
	to Mr Steuens sent before to Hamptoncourt	000 10 00
	for anglerods hooks & lins to fishe	000 16 00
12	to a man sent to London for Turfe	000 10 00
	for mor anglerods hooks & Lins	000 16 06
	to on of yor Maties footmen for things he paid at fishing	000 05 00
	to the fishermen by yor Maties order	001 01 00
	to on yor Maties footmen Sent to London[47]	001 00 00
	to Lady Arlintons footman	000 10 00
17	to the Houskeeper	008 00 00
	to the Gardner	002 00 00
	to the parke Keepers	002 00 00
	to the page of the Bakstairs sent beffor to London	000 10 00
	Ex	**215 04 07**

[verso] 12v		lib s d
1669	**Braught from the other Side**	**215 04 07**
19 Septmr	to yor Maties Bergemen	008 10 00
	to his Maties Bergemen	005 00 00
	paid by Mr Roche	000 02 00
20	to Mr Halsall for Coachire as per bill	021 00 00
	to yor Maties footmen for Runing money	002 00 00
	to one of them Sent to Stope the Coaches at London	001 00 00
	to one of them that braught the dogs from Hamptoncourt	001 00 00
	to the footman that brought the Bows and arrous	001 00 00

46 Arrows.

47 The writer changed to a new batch of ink at the start of this entry – the ink is much paler than that used previously.

	for Loading & unloading the wagons at London and Hamptoncourt as per bill	002 16 06
	to the yeomon of the wagons as per bill	001 09 06
26	to Mr Steuens the younger as per bill	001 01 11
8[48]	to William Jonson for the Bathe	000 05 06
2 Octobr	for a large prese to keep yor Maties Bows and Arrous as per bill	012 00 00
	to a porter for remouing Trunks	000 03 00
	to Lord Winsellsis[49] man	001 00 00
	Ex	**273 13 00**

[recto] 13r		lib s d
1669 Octobr	**Braught from the other Side**	**273 13 00**
13	paid by Mr Steuens	000 05 00
	to nurse flecher by yor Maties order	010 10 00
21	to yor Maties Darymaid as per bill	005 10 00
	to Lady Baiths man presented a Cheese	001 01 00
	to Mr Oswell Apotecary for a peice of plate for yor Maties vse	004 10 00
	to Lady Gerrets man presented a Cheese	000 10 00
29	for Tape for yor Maties Lining	000 15 00
12 noumbr	to Lord Orseris[50] man presented sweets	002 04 04
13	to Mrs le coq as per bill	017 10 00
	to Mrs Bew as per bill	012 12 06
	to Lord Delamers man	001 01 02
	to Lady Cranburns man	001 01 02
15 yor Maties Birthday[51]	to the Musique	020 00 00
	to the Wind Musique & Recorders	005 00 00
	to the Harper	001 00 00
	to yor Maties footmen	003 00 00
	to his Maties footmen	002 00 00

48 For 28 (?).
49 Winchelsea.
50 Ossory.
51 Catherine's birthday – she was 31.

	to the ducke of Yorks footmen	002 00 00
	to the dutchese footmen	002 00 00
	Ex	**364 03 02**

[verso] 13v		lib s d
1669	**Braught from the other side**	**364 03 02**
15 novembr	to yor Maties Coatchman	003 00 00
	to his Maties Coachman	002 00 00
	to the droms & Trompets	009 00 00
	to his Heighnesse Trompets	003 00 00
	to the violine in ordinary	001 00 00
	to the Littermen	002 00 00
	to the Somptermen	001 00 00
	to the Groomes	002 00 00
	to the Master of yor Maties Berge	001 00 00
	to the Bottleman of the feild	000 02 06
20	to Lord Newports man presented a Cheese	000 10 00
	to Mr Marsh man presented Creams at Hampton court	001 10 03
28	to Lady Newports man	000 10 00
30	to the footman presented St Androws Cross[52]	001 00 00
	Catherina R Totall disbursed *Ex*	**391 06 11**
	Wherof Receiued	**400 00 00**
15 decembr	Rests due to yor Matie from this Acompt *Ex*	**008 13 01**

[recto] 14r		
1669		lib s d
20 decembr	to Lady Baithes man	001 00 00
	to a poore womane by y^r^ Maties order	001 00 00
24	to Lady Devonshirs man	001 00 00
	to the Duck of ormonds man with the Traino in St James parke	002 00 00

52 30 November.

27	to Lady Arlintons man	001 00 00
1 Janr[53]	to a woman presented Pomgranads and pomecitrons	002 00 00
6	for Carieing things to & from St James	000 03 00
	to Lady Manchesters Page wt oranges	001 01 06
2 febr	to Lord delamers man with a Cheese	001 01 04
16	to Burie Charles Eaton yor Maties footman	010 00 00
	for pen Inke and paper	000 10 00
1 March[54]	to the footman presented a Leeke	001 00 00
10	to Burie Edward welch Sompterman	010 00 00
17	to the footman presented St Patricks Crose	001 00 00
	to the dutches of ormonds man	001 00 00
	to the Coatchman & footmen waited of yr Matie to & from St James	005 00 00
	to Lady Abergenis[55] man	001 01 03
	Ex	**039 17 01**

[verso] 14v

1670	**Braught from the other side**	**039 17 01**
3 aprill	for Carieing things to & from St James	000 03 00
	to yor Maties footmen the first day to Heighparke	002 00 00
8	Charges at the Receipt of 400li	001 00 00
	to the Butry pantry & Iwry men that waited on Maundy Thursday[56]	002 10 00
	to Mrs Nun for thre quarters of a yeares Allowance due at our Lady[57] day last	015 00 00
	to Anne Barker for thre quarters of a yeares Allowance due at our Lady day last	027 00 00

53 1670.
54 St David's Day.
55 Bergavenny.
56 Maundy Thursday 1670 – 3 April.
57 25 March.

	to the yeoman of the Gard waited at St James at Easter[58]		001 01 00
	to the footmen Leighted yor Matie		001 00 00
11	to yor Maties Apotecary as per aquitanc		021 10 00
	to an old man presented Sparagrese[59]		001 01 02
	for Tape & other things for yor Maties Lining		001 10 00
	to the Musique on Easter Munday[60]		010 00 00
	to Jane Brown yor Maties dary woman as per bill		021 14 00
	for boats & Berges to Grewich		006 00 00
		Ex	**151 06 03**

[recto] 15r

1670	**Braught from the other side**	**151 06 03**
13 Aprill	to the Musique	020 00 00
New years gifts for the Last yeare	to the wind Musique & Recorders	006 00 00
	to the violine in ordinary	001 00 00
	to the Harper	001 00 00
	to yor Maties Cooke	005 00 00
	to his man	001 00 00
	to his Maties Cooke	005 00 00
	to his man	001 00 00
	to yor Maties Coatchman	010 00 00
	to the postilions	003 00 00
	to yor Maties footmen	010 00 00
	to his Maties Coatchmen	005 00 00
	to yor Maties Litermen & Chairmen	005 00 00
	to yor Maties somptermen	004 00 00
	to your Maties Groomes	005 00 00
	to the dromes	003 00 00
	to the Trompets	006 00 00

58 Easter Sunday 1670 – 6 April.

59 Asparagus.

60 Easter Monday 1670 – 7 April.

	to the Gallrykeepers	006 00 00
	to yo[r] Ma[ties] Bargemen	002 00 00
	to the ducks Trompets	006 00 00
	Ex	**256 06 03**
[verso] 15v		lib s d
1670	**Braught from the other side**	**256 06 03**
15 Aprill	to yo[r] Ma[ties] shoemakers men	004 00 00
	to the duck of Cambridg violin	001 00 00
	to the portugall Cooke	003 00 00
	to the portingell Baker	003 00 00
	to the ducks Musique	010 00 00
15	to the dutchesse of Richmons footmen Leighted yo[r] Ma[tie]	001 00 00
	to Mrs Cheret as per bill	024 00 00
	Mor to Mrs Cheret as per bill	009 17 00
16	Paid by Lady Scrup[61] for Combs and other things as per bill	009 04 02
	to the Coatchmen & footmen waited of yo[r] Ma[tie] to S[t] James	005 00 00
17	to a paire of oares to fox hall	001 00 00
	to Lady Manchesters page w[t] a nosgay	001 01 00
18	to yo[r] Ma[ties] Bergemen to dartford	005 00 00
	to yo[r] Ma[ties] footmen then	001 00 00
23[62]	to the footman presented S[t] Goerge Cross	001 00 00
	to his Ma[ties] Bergemen to dartford	005 00 00
	to yo[r] Ma[ties] footmen then	002 10 00
	for two boats that Caried the Gard	002 00 00
	Ex	**344 18 05**

[recto] 16r		lib s d
1670	**Braught from the other Side**	**344 18 05**
25 Aprill	to the Musique on S[t] Goerge Day	010 00 00

61 Scroop.
62 23 April – St George's day.

	for Gas[63] Tap[64] and Threed for Lining	001 00 00
	to yor Maties Chairemen waited at the Bridge	001 00 00
26	to the dutchesse of Monmuths Coatchman & postilion & footmen waited of yor Matie to Hampton Court	007 00 00
	to the Musique then	010 00 00
	for two Coatches to Hampton court for them	002 16 00
29	to her Heighness Coatchmen & footmen	005 00 00
	to the footmen Leighted yor Matie	001 00 00
4 May	to one of his Maties footmen that had presented yor Maties two yeares agoe	002 02 00
	for Mending yor Maties Lining	020 00 00
18	paid at Sitenburne[65]	010 00 00
	paid at Canterbery & by the way to dover	007 07 00
	to yor Maties footmen for Runing money	006 00 00
23	to the Musique	010 00 00
	to his Heighnes Coatchmen & footmen	005 00 00
24	to Madames Chairemen & footmen	010 10 00
	to Will Jonson for Loading & unloading the wagons	001 04 00
	to his Maties Bergemen	002 00 00
	Ex	**456 16 00**

[verso] 16v		lib s d
1670	**Braught from the other Side**	**456 16 00**
24 May	to the <men> Caried yor Matie a shore	002 00 00
25	to his Maties Bergemen	002 00 00
26	to yor Maties footmen Runing money	002 00 00
28	to yor Maties footmen Runing money	002 00 00
29	to the Musique on his Maties Birthday[66]	010 00 00

63 Gauze.

64 Tape.

65 Sittingbourne.

66 Charles II's birthday – he was 40.

	to yor Maties footmen then	003 00 00
30	to yor Maties footmen vpon petition	012 00 00
31	to yor Maties footmen Runing money	002 00 00
	paid for a Calfe	001 11 00
3 June	paid by the way from Dover to sitenburne	002 02 00
4	paid at sitenburne	010 00 00
	to a Gyd to Greuesend	001 01 00[67]
	for Cheescaks thaire	001 01 00
	Totall disbursed[68]	**507 12 05**
	Wherof Receiued	**400 00 00**
	Rests due to yor Matie from the last Accompt	**008 13 01**
4	Rests due from yor Matie to this Accompant	**098 19 04**

[recto] 17r

1670	**Repayed my selfe due from the Last Accompt**	**098 19 04**
7 June	to yor Maties footmen Runing money	006 00 00
	to yor Maties watermen the first time yor Matie went in the new Berge	005 00 00
10	for two boats when yor Matie went by water	001 10 00
	to the yeoman of yor Maties wagons as per bill	006 12 08
	for a Baskitt of Cheries	001 00 00
12	for thre boats	001 15 00
	for a Baskitt of Cheries	001 00 00
15	to Mr Halsall as per bill	266 00 06
	for boats	001 10 00
16	for Berges Gallys & oares to and from Grauesend as per aquitanc	033 10 00
	to the Trompetts by yor Maties order	010 00 00
	for a Baskitt of Cheris	001 00 00

67 001 01 00 corrected from 001 00 00.

68 No signature by the queen.

17	for boats	001 10 00
	to the pages of the Bakstairs as per bill	002 18 06
	for two Baskits of Cherise & aprecoks	002 00 00
18	for boats	001 15 00
	to Lady Arlintons man with a pye	001 00 00
19	for a Baskitt of Cheris	001 00 00
	for boats	001 10 00
		445 16 00

[verso] 17v		lib s d
1670	**Braught from the other Side**	**445 16 00**
20 June	to Will Jonson for Loading and vnloading the wagons as per bill	001 12 06
	for a Baskitt of fruite	001 00 00
	for pen Inke and paper	000 10 00
21	for boats	001 10 00
24	for Cheris and Aprecoks	001 00 00
	to the footman brought the Calfe by sea	002 04 06
	to yor Maties darymaid as per bill	013 18 00
30	paid in Charges at the Receit of 600^{li}	001 00 00
5 July	to Mrs Bocher for a Baithing tub	004 00 00
	to yor Maties footmen for Runing money from Richmon[69]	002 00 00
	for a baskitt of friute	001 00 00
	for two pigon pyes	000 12 00
	for two baskitt of friute	002 00 00
	to one of yor Maties footmen sent to Richmon	001 00 00
	to yor Maties Berges to Richmon	007 10 00
	to his Heighnes watermen	001 01 00
	paid at Barnellms whan yor Matie dined	005 10 00
	for a Galy[70] with prousions	001 00 00
	for a boat to Call bake the Gally	000 05 00
6	for 3 boats	001 10 00

69 Richmond.
70 For galley.

	for a baskit of fruit	001 00 00
		496 19 00

[recto] 18r		lib s d
1670	**Brought from the other Side**	**496 19 00**
7 July	to Lord Cornberies[71] Gardner	001 00 00
	to yor Maties Berges to Richmon	007 10 00
	to yor Maties footmen Runing money	002 00 00
8	for 3 boats	001 10 00
	for a baskit of fruite	001 00 00
	to Lord Bristolls Gardner	001 01 00
9	for 3 boats	001 10 00
	to Mr Steuens for things for yor Maties fishing	001 04 06
	to the dutchesse of Cleulands man with Cream	000 10 00
	for a baskit of friute	001 00 00
	to the dutchesse of Bukinghams watermen	001 00 00
10	for boats	001 10 00
	for a baskit of friute	001 00 00
11	for boats	001 10 00
12	to yor Maties Berges to Richmon	007 10 00
	to the dutchesse of Cleulands man	000 10 00
	for a baskit of friut	001 00 00
	for Carieing yor Maties dogs by water	000 01 00
	to Lord Cornberies Gardner	001 00 00
		530 06 06

[verso] 18v		lib s d
1670	**Brought from the other Side**	**530 06 06**
16 July	for two baskitts of friut	001 10 00
	to a man presented Mulberies	001 00 00
	to the dutchesse of Cleueland man w^t^ Cheese	000 10 00

71 Cornbury.

	to yor Maties Berges to Richmon	007 10 00
	to the dutchesse Chairemen	002 02 00
	to yor Maties footmen Runing money	002 00 00
	to the French embassador man with Cheese	001 01 00
18	for 3 boats	001 10 00
	to Lord Bristolls man with orange flowers	001 00 00
	to a man with Mulberies	001 00 00
	for a baskit of friut	000 15 00
21	for thre boats	001 10 00
24	for 4 boats	001 15 00
	for a baskit of friut	000 15 00
25	for thre boats	001 10 00
	to Mr Mays man presented a Bird	000 10 00
	to his Maties Bergemen	002 00 00
	to the old footman presented Sparegrase[72]	001 01 02
28	to yor Maties Berges to Richmon	007 10 00
	for thre boats then	001 10 00
	to yor Maties footmen Runing mony	002 00 00
	to Lord Bristols Gardner	001 00 00
		571 05 08

[recto] 19r		lib s d
1670	**Braught from the other Side**	**571 05 08**
28 July	to one of yor Maties footmen sent to Richmon	001 00 00
	to Lord Arondalls Coatchman & footmen	002 00 00
29	for thre boats	001 10 00
	for a baskit of friut	000 15 00
4 August	to Mr Porters man with a pye	001 00 00
	to Lord Bristols Gardner	001 01 02
6	to Lady Geretts man with a Cheese	000 10 00

[72] Asparagus.

	to the dutchesse of Cleulands man w^{t} a Cheese	000 10 00
	to Lord Cornberies Gardner	001 01 02
14	to Lord Bristols man with orangflowres	000 10 00
17	to Sir Barnett Gaskins man w^{t} Cheeses	003 03 06
	paid by Mr Stevens	000 01 00
	The Totall disbursed	**584 07 06**
	Receuied	**600 00 00**
17	Rest due to yor Matie from this Accompt	**015 12 06**

[verso] 19v		lib s d
1670 18 August	Paid to Madame de bord as per bill	**052 10 00**
	for pen Ink and paper	001 00 00
	to the dutchesse of Cleulands man w^{t} Cheese	001 00 00
22	to the page of the Bakstairs went before to Hampton court	000 10 00
	to Lady Arlintons man with wine	001 00 00
	to yor Maties footmen Runing money	002 00 00
	for boats when yor Matie went a fishing	002 05 00
	to the footman Braught the Bows & Arrows	001 00 00
	to Mr Halsall as per bill	021 10 00
23	to a young maid presented a hatt	002 02 08
	for boats	004 00 00
	to a fisherman at Kingston	001 01 04
	to yor Maties footmen Runing mony	002 00 00
24	to the two necesary women for half a years allowance at Midsomer last as per aquitanc	037 00 00
	to Lady Arlingtons man	001 01 04
	to William Jonson for yor ma^{ties} Baithinge at London fiue times as per bill	003 12 06
	to a gyd to windsor	001 01 04
	to yor Maties footmen Runing mony	002 00 00

	for boats at night	002 00 00
25	for boats	004 10 00
26	for boats	005 00 00
27	for boats	004 10 00
28	for boats	001 15 00
		154 09 02

[recto] 20r		lib s d
1670	**Braught from the other side**	**154 09 02**
29 August	paid by one of the pages of the Bakstairs	000 02 00
	for boats	002 15 00
	to one of yor Maties footmen sent for S^ir^ Barnett Gaskin	000 10 00
31	to the Hoyboys Musique	005 00 00
	for boats	002 00 00
	to Lord Mongroos[73] man presented two Cace of Arows	002 02 08
	to yor Maties footmen Runing mony to Rohamton	002 00 00
1 September	for boats	002 15[74] 00
	to a man with a present of Carps	001 01 04
2	for boats	002 15 00
	to Lady Cranburns man with Cheesecak	002 02 08
4	to the footmen by yor Maties order	010 00 00
	to one of his Maties footmen with a dog from windsor	002 02 08
	for yor Maties Bath	000 13 06
5	to Mr Heriot vnder house keeper	008 00 00
	to the Gardner	002 00 00
	to the parke Keepers	002 00 00
	paid at the two farmers houses	012 16 00
	for boats	001 15 00
	for a boat waited w^t^ provisions & from thenc to London	000 10 00

73 Possibly a variation on ‘Montagus’.
74 002 15 00 corrected from 002 05 00.

	to yor Maties footmen Runingmony from Hampton court to London	002 00 00
		219 00 00

[verso] 20v		lib s d
1670	**Braught from the other side**	**219 00 00**
6 septmbr	to the footman Brought the Bows & Arows	001 00 00
	to Mr Halsall as per bill	022 10 00
7	to Mrs Cherett as per bill	028 15 00
	Mor paid by Mr Halsall	000 06 00
	to Sir Thomas Asps[75] man wt sweet water	002 02 08
8	to Lord orserys footman Lighted yor Matie	001 00 00
10	to the yeoman of the wagons as per bill	002 08 06
	to Mrs Bew as per bill	009 00 06
	to Will Jonson for Loading & unloading the wagons to & from Hamptoncourt	002 11 04
15	to yor Maties Berges to putny	003 00 00
	to Lady Devonshirs man with peas	001 01 04
	to yor Maties footmen Runing mony to Hampton court	002 00 00
	for boats waited to Hampton court	003 10 00
	to Lady Arlintons footmen Leighted yor Matie	001 00 00
	paid at Bartlemewfaire[76]	002 02 08
	to Lord Arlintons man wt a bird	002 02 08
18	to the Gardner of Hampton court wt Graps	001 01 08
	paid by the pages of the Bakstairs vpon seuerall occations as per bill	002 14 04
21	to Mr Roch for a diamon watch as per aquitance	400 00 00
	for Coatchire for Sir William Killigre to and from audley end	004 10 00

75 Uncertain who this is.
76 St Bartholomew's feast day falls on 24 August, but the fair lasted for longer.

	paid at the Receit of seuen hundred pounds	001 00 00
		712 16 08

[recto] 21r		lib s d
1670	**Braught from the other Side**	**712 16 08**
23 Septbr	to the dutches of Buckinghams footman	001 00 00
	to the Queen Mothers footman w[t] fruit	001 01 04
	to the Spanish Embassadors man with a present	010 13 04
	to the Gardner of Hampton court	001 01 04
	Sume disbursed	**726 12 08**
	Whereof Receiued	**700 00 00**
	Rests due to yo[r] Ma[tie] from the Lastet acompt	**015 12 06**
26 Septmbr	Rests due from yo[r] Ma[tie] to this Accomptant	**011 00 02**
	Repaid my selfe due from the last accompt	**011 00 02**
27	to yo[r] Ma[ties] footmen Runing mony to Audley end	004 00 00
	to the page of the Bakstairs went before	000 10 00
30	to a man with a leter from Roiston	000 10 00
	paid at the House in Chesterson parke	005 00 00
	to yo[r] Ma[ties] footmen Runing mony	002 00 00
1 October	paid at a fermers house	005 06 08
	to S[ir] Barnet Gaskins man	002 02 08
	to yo[r] Ma[ties] footmen Runing mony	002 00 00
	to the footmen Runing mony effternoon	002 00 00
		034 09 06

[verso] 21v		lib s d
1670	**Braught from the other side**	**034 09 06**
3 Octobr	to Country Musique & hornpype	002 02 08
	paid at a fermers house	005 06 08
	to the footmen Runing mony	002 00 00

	paid at Newport	003 15 00
	paid at Euston to the House	020 00 00
	to Lord Arlingtons two men & page	008 10 08
	to Lady Arlingtons woman	005 06 08
	to the Coatchman & postilion	005 00 00
	to the Groom that danct	002 02 08
	to the foure footmen	003 00 00
	to the Musique	010 00 00
	to the thre Coatches went from Newmarkitt to Euston & bak againe	015 00 00
	to the poore	001 00 00
	to the ducke of ormonds Coatchman	005 00 00
	to a Gyd from Newmarkitt & bak againe	002 02 08
	to the thre Coatches that went from Audley end to Newmarkitt & bak againe	015 00 00
	to the ducke of Buckinghams Coatchman	005 00 00
	to the page of the Bakstairs	001 00 00
	to Will Lee[77] the footman	005 00 00
	to some of y^{r} Maties footmen sent to Cambridg	002 00 00
8	to Mr Halsall for Coatches & horse hire as per bill	080 19 00
	for Letters from Roiston	000 10 00
12	to a woman presented hony	002 02 08
		236 08 02

[recto] 22r		lib s d
1670	**Braught from the other Side**	**236 08 02**
14 octobr	to the vnderhouskeeper	008 00 00
	to the parkekeeper	002 00 00
	to the Gardner	002 00 00
	to the poore	005 00 00
	to yor Maties footmen Runing mony to London	004 00 00
	to the page of the Bakstairs went beffor	000 10 00

77 Leigh.

	to the yeoman of the wagons as per bill	004 05 06
19	to Mr Halsall for Coatches & horse hire as per bill	115 08 00
	to Will Jonson for Loading & unloading the wagons as per bill	002 14 00
21	paid at the Receit of foure hundred pounds	001 00 00
27	Expense for the viz Chamberlan & Mr Mend sent to Audley end as per bill	005 02 03
4 novmbr	paid by the pages of the Bakstairs upon seueral locations as per bill	004 01 00
	to a man [who] presented a Bird	002 02 08
8	to Richard Maley one of yor Maties postilions	005 00 00
	to a man presented a Booke	005 06 08
	disbursed	**403 08 03**
	Receiued	**400 00 00**
12	Remains due from yor Matie to the Accomptant	**003 08 03**

[verso] 22v		lib s d
1670	Repaid my Selfe due from the Last accounte	**003 08 03**
16 novmbr	for pen Inke and paper	001 00 00
	to yor Maties Robs feast[78]	005 00 00
	to Lady Carnwallace man	000 10 00
	to Lord delamers man presented a Cheese	001 00 00
	to the Cryer when a perle was Lost	000 05 00
	to Lady Manchesters page	001 01 04
18	to the Spanish Embassadors Cooke	001 01 04
	for threed and tape for yor Maties Linen	001 00 00
	Lost by yor Matie at Cards	010 13 04
28	to the dutchesse of Buckingams Chairmen and footmen	005 00 00
	to Lady Gerets man presented a Cheese	001 00 00

78 Catherine's birthday – she was 32.

	to the Spanish Embassadors man	001 01 04
30	to the footman presented St Androws cross	001 00 00
	to Lord orseris[79] footmen Lighted yor Matie	001 00 00
2 decmbr	to Lady Carnwallace footman	000 10 00
	to a man with the dancing doge	001 01 04
6	for Carieing things to & from St James	000 05 00
	to Lady Manchesters page presented a Cheese	001 01 04
	to the prince of Orange cooke	005 06 08
	Laid out by the pages of the Bakstairs as per bill	001 16 00
20 Janr[80]	to Mr Hamiltons man with a present	005 06 08
	to the porter to Carye them to St James	000 02 00
	to the prince of orange Trompets	005 06 00
24	to Lady Carnwallace footman	000 10 00
	Lost by yor Matie at Cards	017 01 04
4 Febr	to the Spainsh Embassadors man	001 01 04
1 March	to the footman presented St davids Leeks	001 00 00
	to the Spainsh Embassadors Cooke	001 01 00
10	to the Spainsh Embassadors Cooke	001 00 00
		076 09 11

[recto] 23r		lib s d
1670[81]	**Braught from the other Syde**	**076 09 11**
15 March	to the Spanish Embassadors Cooke	001 00 00
17	to the footman presented St Patriks cross	001 00 00
19	to the Spanish Embassadors Cooke	001 00 00
24	to the Spanish Embassadors Cooke	001 00 00
1 April: 1671	to the Spanish Embassadors Cooke	001 00 00
	to the Late Queens old footman	001 01 03
7	to the Spanish Embassadors Cooke	001 00 00

79 Ossory.
80 1671 NS.
81 1671 NS.

12	to the Spanish Embassadors Cooke	001 00 00
	for thre boats	001 00 00
	Laid out by the pages of the Bakstairs	000 12 06
16	to the Spanish Embassadors Cooke	001 00 00
	to the pantry Butry & Ewry for Mandy[82] thursday	002 10 00
	for four boats	001 05 00
	to the Late Queens old footman	001 01 05
	To yor Maties footmen the first time to Heighpark	002 00 00
22	for thre boats	001 00 00
	for threed & tape for yor Maties Linen	001 00 00
23	to the footman presented St Georg crose[83]	001 00 00
27	to the Spanish Embassadors Cooke	001 00 00
	for thre boats	001 00 00
4 May	paid by the pages of the Bakstairs	000 14 00
	for thre boats	001 00 00
	to Mrs Hemden for Mending yor Maties Linen as per aquitance	030 00 00
7	for thre boats	001 00 00
	for a Baskit of Cheries	001 00 00
8	for two boats	000 15 00
9	for thre boats	001 00 00
10	for thre boats	001 00 00
		135 08 11

[verso] 23v		lib s d
1671	**Brought from the other syde**	**135 08 11**
11 May	for thre boats	001 00 00
12	for thre boats	001 00 00
	to Lady Carnwallace footman	000 10 00
	to Bury the firemaker of yor Maties Gard Chamber	002 00 00
13	for thre boats	001 00 00

82 Maundy Thursday 1671 – 26 March. Easter Sunday 1671 – 29 March.
83 St George's day – 23 April.

	Laid out by the pages of the Bakstairs	000 19 00
	to Lady Sunderlands pag[84] that presented a nosgy	001 01 03
	for a Baskit of Cheris	001 00 00
17	for thre boats	001 00 00
25	Charges at the Receit of fiue hundred pounds	001 00 00
	to Mons ducaila as per bill	013 00 00
	for thre boats	001 00 00
	for a Baskit of Cheris	001 00 00
	to Mr Vernon vpholster as per bill	060 03 06
26	to the pages of the Bakstairs to winsor	000 10 00
	to yor Maties footmen footmen[85] Runing mony	002 00 00
	for a Baskit of Cheris	001 00 00
	to the footman Brought the Bird	001 00 00
	for a boat from the Bakestairs	001 05 00
29	to the violins Musique on his Maties Birthday[86]	010 00 00
	to yor Maties footmen then	003 00 00
	to a man presented a baskit of fruit	001 01 03
1 June	for a Baskit of Cheris	001 00 00
	for Bringing two portingall Mats from London to winsor	001 00 00
	to Sir William Bormans[87] man presented fruite	000 10 00
3	to yor Maties footmen to & from London	004 00 00
	for a Baskit of fruite presented by the way	001 01 02
	for Bringing Cristall Candlestiks & others things from London	001 00 00
		249 10 01

84 Page.
85 Uncorrected duplication of the word footmen.
86 Charles II's birthday – he was 41.
87 Bowerman.

[recto] 24r		lib s d
1671	**Brought from the other syde**	**249 10 01**
3 June	for thre boats	000 15 00
	to the pages of the Bakestairs to & from London	001 00 00
5	to yor Maties footmen Runing mony	002 00 00
6	for thre boats	000 15 00
7	to the footmen Runing mony	002 00 00
	to the yeoman of the wagons as per bill	001 05 00
	for two boats	000 10 00
	to William Jonson as per bill	001 03 06
	for Bringing yor Maties boat to winsor	001 10 00
	to the two boatmen from the 26 May to the 7 of June at 10^s the day as per bill	006 10 00
	to a gyde waited of yor Matie seuerall tims	002 02 04
8	for a Baskit of Cheris	000 15 00
	for thre boats	000 15 00
	paid by the pages of the Bakestairs	000 17 06
	to the footmen Runing mony to & from London	004 00 00
	to the pages of the Bakstairs to & from London	001 00 00
14	for thre boats	000 15 00
15	to the footmen Runing mony	002 00 00
	paid by Mr Stevens for seuerall things	000 10 06
	for two boats	000 10 00
	to Lady Marshalls[88] footman presented Cheesecak	000 10 00
16	for two boats	000 10 00
	to yor Maties Boatmen from the 7 of June to the 17 as per bill	005 00 00
17	for one boate	000 05 00
	for a Baskit of Cheris presented	001 01 02
18	for two boats	000 10 00
		288 00 01

[88] Marischal.

[verso] 24v		lib s d
1671	**Brought from the other syde**	**288 00 01**
18 June	to a man presented a great fishe	001 01 02
19	to the footmen Runingmony	002 00 00
	for two boats	000 10 00
	for a Baskit of Cheris	000 10 00
	to Mr Maginis[89] for a Coatche from franc as per aquitance	046 17 09
	to a man with Buter from yor Maties dary	001 00 00
20	to yor Maties Berges to London	015 00 00
	to the Kings Berges to London	010 00 00
21	to the footmen Runing mony to & ffrom London	004 00 00
	to the pages of the Bakestairs to & from London	001 00 00
	for a Baskit of Cheris	000 10 00
	for two boats	000 10 00
	to yor Maties Bergemen from whitehall to somerset house in May last	000 10 00
	paid by Mr Pirot as per bill	002 19 00
	to Lord Bristols Gardner	001 01 02
22	for Cheris	000 10 00
	for two boats	000 10 00
	paid by Mr Roche	000 13 06
	to the ducks Coatchman & footmen	005 00 00
23	for thre boats	000 15 00
	paid by Mr Roper	001 17 00
	to a man sent to old winsor	000 10 00
24	for two boats	000 10 00
25	to the footmen Runingmony	002 00 00
	for thre boats	000 15 00
		388 09 08

[recto] 25r		lib s d
1671	**Brought from the other syde**	**388 09 08**

89 MacGinnis.

25 June	to Mr Halsall for Coaches as per bill	155 10 00
26	to the two Boatmen from the 17 to the 26 as per bill	004 10 00
	for goeing to & from London with yor Maties boat	002 10 00
	for two boats	000 10 00
	to a man that gatherd worms	001 00 00
27	for two boats	000 10 00
28	for one boat	000 05 00
29	for two boats	000 10 00
	to Lord Bristols Gardner	001 01 02
	to a womane presented fruite & creams	002 02 04
	to the footmen Runing mony	002 00 00
30	for one boate	000 05 00
	to the two boatmen from the 26 of June to the first of July as per bill	002 10 00
1 July	to the footmen Runing mony	002 00 00
2	for two boats	000 10 00
3	for two boats	000 10 00
	to William Jonson for yor Maties Bathe	001 19 00
	to the surgon let yor Maties Blood	010 10 10
8	to Lord Bristols Gardner	001 01 02
	to the Kinsinton gardner	001 01 02
	to the boatmen from the first of July to the eight as per bill	003 10 00
	to a man with a Cheese from London	001 00 00
	to the footmen Runing mony	002 00 00
11	to the fisherman as per aquitanc	006 03 06
		591 18 10

[verso] 25v		lib s d
1671	**Brought from the other Syde**	**591 18 10**
11 July	lost by yor Matie at ohair	005 05 10
	to the footmen Runing mony to stoke	002 00 00
12	to a poore man serued at fishing	000 10 00
	to the footman Runing mony	002 00 00
13	to the Houskeeper	008 00 00

	to the wardrobkeeper	005 00 00
	to the parkekeper	002 00 00
	to the parkegatkeper	001 00 00
	to yor Maties footmen vpon peticion	010 00 00
	to the pages of the Bakstairs to Hamton court	000 10 00
	to the footmen to Hampton court	002 00 00
	to the footman that Brought the Bird	001 15 00
	for bringing y^r^ Maties boat to Hamton court	001 00 00
	to the boatmen from the 9 of July to the twelve as per bill	002 00 00
14	to the Countesse of deuonshirs man with whitears	001 01 02
	to the yeoman of the wagons as per bill	002 10 00
	disbursed	**638 10 10**
	Receiued	**500 00 00**
	Remains due from yor Matie to the Accountant	**138 10 10**

[recto] 26r		lib s d
1671	**Repaid my selfe due from the Last Accounte**	**138 10 10**
14 July	to the boatmen from the 12 to the 17 and to Carie them home as per bill	002 10 00
	to yor Maties footmen to & from London	004 00 00
	to the pages of the Bakstairs to & from London	001 00 00
17	for thre boats	000 15 00
18	for two boats	000 10 00
	to Kinsinton[90] Gardner presented fruite	001 01 00
	for boats over at twitnham[91]	001 06 00
	to the footmen Runing mony to ham house	002 00 00
	to Lady dyserts man presented a pye	001 01 02

90 Kensington.
91 Twickenham.

19	to a womane presented fruite	001 01 02
	to S[ir] Henery Caples Gardner presented fruite	001 01 02
20	to the footmen to Rohamton	002 00 00
	to the ducks Berge & other boat at Richmon	002 07 00
	for seven boats	001 15 00
	to a Messanger with Leters to yo[r] Ma[tie]	002 02 02
21	for eight boats	002 00 00
	to a man presented Mulberis	001 00 00
	to Lord Bristols Gardner presented orang <flowrs>	001 01 01
	paid at Richmon & thistle-worth[92] by water	001 11 01
	for fruite presented by the way from London	001 01 01
	for the footmen to & from London	004 00 00
	to the pages of the Bakstairs to & from London	001 00 00
	for remouing trunks from whitehall to somerset house & bak againe	000 10 00
	Laid out by the pages of the Bakstairs	000 12 00
		175 15 09

[verso] 26v		lib s d
1671	**Brought from the other syde**	**175 15 09**
24 July	to the Howskeeper	008 00 00
	to the parkekeppers	002 00 00
	to the Gardner	002 00 00
	to the fisherman as per aquitance	005 05 05
25	paid by the way to London	001 01 01
	to the footmen Runing mony	002 00 00
	to the footman Brought the Bird	001 10 00
	to the pages of the Bakestairs	000 10 00

92 Isleworth.

	to yor Maties two boatmen from the 17 of July to the 25 as per bill	004 10 00
	for Bringing yor Maties Boat to London	001 00 00
27	to the footmen Runing mony to Twitnham	002 00 00
	to Lord Bristols Gardner presented orang flowrs	001 01 01
	to the yeoman of the wagons as per bill	002 18 00
3 August	to a man presented a sturgon	005 05 05
	for boats to & from somerset house	000 15 00
	to the dutchesse of abemalls womane presented figs	001 01 01
8	for boats to & from somersethouse	000 15 00
19	for boats to & from somersethouse	000 12 06
26	for boats to & from somersethouse	000 10 00
	to the Gardner of Hamton court presented figs	001 01 01
27	for boats to somersethouse	000 12 06
	to the Hoboys from notingam	005 00 00
	for boats to somersethouse [in the] Effternoon	000 12 06
3 septembr	for boats to somersethouse	000 10 00
12	for boats to somersethouse	000 15 00
		227 01 05

[recto] 27r		lib s d
1671	**Brought from the other side**	**227 01 05**
14 septembr	for boats to somersethouse	000 12 06
18	for one boate	000 05 00
	to Mr Green feilds man presented Graps	001 01 02
19	Paid at the Receit of thre hundred pounds	000 10 00
	to Mr Halsall as per bill	153 16 06
20	to Madame debord as per bill	052 00 00
	to yor Maties Berge to somerset house	000 10 00
	to Mr Stevens as per bill	001 17 00
	for two boats	000 12 06

	disbursed	**438 06 01**
	Receiued	**300 00 00**
20	Remains due from yo[r] Ma[tie] to the Accountant	**138 06 01**
22	paid for Careing a table & stands to Hamton court	000 10 00
	Repaid my selfe due from the Last Accounte	138 06 01
26	to yo[r] Ma[ties] footmen Runing mony to Audley end	004 00 00
	to the pages of the Bakstairs	001 00 00
	to the Gyds to pas the waters by the way	001 10 00
	for watching the Coatches all night	000 05 00
		145 11 01
[verso] 27v		lib s d
1671	**Brought from the other side**	**145 11 01**
27 Septembr	to yo[r] Ma[ties] footmen to Ewston[93]	002 00 00
	to the pages of the Bakstairs	000 10 00
	to a Gyde to Ewston	001 00 00
	for watching the Coatches all night	000 05 00
	to the Musique	010 00 00
	to the poore	002 00 00
28	to yo[r] Ma[ties] footmen to Norwiche	002 00 00
	paid by the way	001 01 02
	to the pages of the Bakestairs	000 10 00
29	to the Hoboys	005 00 00
	to a Gyd from S[ir] John Huberds	000 10 00
	to the footmen Runing mony	002 00 00
30	to a Gyd to S[ir] Robert Pastons	000 10 00
	to the footmen Runing mony	002 00 00
	Given to Lord Howards servants	100 00 00
	to the poore thair	030 00 00

93 Euston.

	for watching the Coatches thre nights	000 15 00
1 octobr	to the pages of the Bakestairs to Ewston	000 10 00
	to the footmen Runing mony	002 00 00
	to a Gyde to Ewston	001 01 00
	paid by the way	001 01 02
	Given to the seruants at Ewston	040 00 00
	to Lady Arlintons woman	005 05 10
	for watching the Coatches all night	000 05 00
	to the Musique	005 00 00
	to the poore	002 00 00
		362 15 05

[recto] 28r		lib s d
1671	**Brought from the other syde**	**362 15 05**
2 octobr	to the pages of the Bakstairs to Audley end	000 10 00
	to yor Ma^tes^ footmen Runing mony	002 00 00
	to Gyds by the way	001 07 02
	for watching the Coatches	000 05 00
	Given to the servants at Audley end	010 00 00
	to the poore	002 00 00
	to the vnderHowsekeeper	008 00 00
	to the parkekeeper	002 00 00
	to the Gardner	002 00 00
3	to the pages of the Bakestairs to London	001 00 00
	to yor Maties footmen to London	004 00 00
12	to the yeoman of the wagons as per bill	008 07 00
	to Mrs Bussy yor Maties Grooms wedow	010 00 00
	to Sir John Arondalls footman	000 10 00
	to the Spanish Embassadors Cooke	001 00 00
15	for two boats to somerset house	000 12 06
	to Lady Trevors man presented nosgys	001 01 02
	paid for boats by Mr Roper	000 12 06
	for a boat to Mr Sears	000 02 00
25	to yor Maties Berge seaven times to and from somerset house as per bill	003 10 00

	to the men that keept the swans	000 05 00
26	to Lady Arlintons page presented a Munky	002 02 04
	to the Late Queens old footman	000 10 00
	for pen Inke & paper	000 10 00
		425 00 01

[verso] 28v		lib s d
1671	**Brought from the other side**	**425 00 01**
3 novembr	to the Spanish Embassadors man	001 00 00
15	To yor Maties Robs feast[94]	005 00 00
	for threed & tape for yor Maties Linen	001 00 00
30	to the footmen presented St Andrews Crose[95]	001 00 00
2 febr	to Lord delamers man presented a Cheese	001 00 00
1 March	to the footman presented St David Leeke	001 00 00
	to Sir Francis Goodrichs man presented a samon pye	005 06 08
17	to the footman presented St Patriks Crose[96]	001 00 00
22 Aprill 1672	to Lady trevors man presented nosgys	001 01 04
	to the pantry Butry & Ewry on Mandy thursday[97]	002 10 00
	to yor Maties footmen the first time to Heighparke	002 00 00
	to Mr Huton[98] for silver Chains and Colors to yor Maties Munky as per bill	005 14 00
	to the Late Queens old footman	000 10 00
23	to the footman presented St Georg Crose	001 00 00
30	to y^r^ Maties footmen to Hamersmith	002 00 00
	to the Late Queens old footman	000 10 00

94 Catherine's birthday – she was 33.
95 30 November.
96 17 March.
97 Maundy Thursday 1672 – 14 April. Easter Sunday 1672 – 17 April.
98 Hutton.

2 May	to Mrs Hemden[99] for mending yo[r] Ma[ties] Linen as per aquitance	030 00 00
18	to yo[r] Ma[ties] footmen to & from dalle[100] as per <bill>	008 00 00
	to the page of the Bakstairs to & from dalle as per bill	002 00 00
	paid by Mr Halsall at dalle as per bill	004 00 00
		500 12 01

[recto] 29r		lib s d
1672	**Brought from the other Syde**	**500 12 01**
20 May	to the Late Queens old footman	000 10 00
24	for a boate to & from somersethouse	000 10 00
6 June	to Lord Mairs[101] man presented a sturgon	005 07 06
10	to the Late Queens old footman	000 10 00
	for boats	000 10 00
	to Lady Manchesters page presented orange flowrs	001 01 06
15	to yo[r] Ma[ties] footmen to & from Rochester	006 00 00
	to the footman sent from sea to stope the Coatches	002 00 00
	to the Housekeepers man at somersethouse	000 12 00
18	to the footmen Runing mony to Chelsy	002 00 00
23	to Lord Mairs man presented a sturgon	005 07 06
	to the Late Queens old footman	000 10 00
	for boats over at Richemon	000 15 00
	to the footmen Runing mony to Richemon	002 00 00
4 July	for stra[102] to the Gards at somersethouse	000 15 00

99 For Hamden.

100 Deal (Kent).

101 Mayor's.

102 Meaning uncertain but possibly a variant of straw – compare with a reference in John Lamont's diary of 1657 to 'None should be obleidged to bring any oatts to the English troupe horses any longer, but only stra hireafter', https://www.oed.com/view/Entry/191357?rskey=6FQ0Xo&result=2#eid [accessed 17/3/22].

	for a boat when yo[r] Ma[tie] went incognito	000 10 00
4 August	for a boat to somerset house	000 05 00
	to Sir Robert Cars man presented wild fouls	002 03 00
15	to Tery the waterman presented pears	001 00 00
16	for a boat to & from somersethouse	000 10 00
20	to the Gardner of Hamton court	001 01 06
	to Mr Green fields man presented Graps	001 01 06
	to tery the waterman presented Mulberis	001 00 00
	to a waterman sent to dartford	000 08 00
		536 19 07

[verso] 29v		lib s d
1672	**Brought from the other Syde**	**536 19 07**
24 August	to Lady Arlintons Gardner	002 03 00
6 septembr	to the Gardner of Hamton court	001 01 06
20	to the Gardner of Hamton court	001 01 06
15 novembr	to yo[r] Ma[ties] Robs feast[103]	005 00 00
30	to the footman presented S[t] Androws Crose	001 00 00
10 febr	to Lady Devonshirs man presented flowrs	001 00 00
1 March	to the footman presented S[t] Davids Crose	001 00 00
17	to the footman presented S[t] patricks Crose	001 00 00
24 March	to the pantry Butry & Ewry for Mandy thursday[104]	002 10 00
	disbursed	**552 15 07**
	Receiued	**200 00 00**
	Remains due from yo[r] Ma[tie] to the Accountant	**352 15 07**

[103] Catherine's birthday – she was 34.
[104] Maundy Thursday 1673 – 30 March. Easter Sunday 1673 – 2 April.

25 March 1673	Repaid my selfe due from the Last Accounte	**352 15 07**
23 Aprill	to the footman presented St George Crose	001 00 00
	to yor Maties footmen on the first time to Heighparke	002 00 00
24	to yor Maties footmen to Hamtoncourt	002 00 00
	for two boats at Hamtoncourt	000 15 00
	to one of his Maties Coatchmen from Hamtoncourt when bonard broak his Leg	005 00 00
30	to yor Maties footmen to Hamton court	002 00 00
		365 10 07

[recto] 30r

1673	**Brought from the other Syde**	**365 10 07**
2 May	to Mrs Hemden for mending yor Maties Linen as per aquitance	030 00 00
15 June	to yor Maties footmen to Ham	002 00 00
	for fiue boats waited thair	001 10 00
	to the dutchesse of Lauderdalls Chairemen	001 00 00
9 July	fees & Charges at the Receit of thre hundred pounds	011 00 00
10	paid by Mr Roper for boats	000 15 00
12	for boats to & from somerset house	000 15 00
15	to Mr Hill for Berges as per bill	063 14 00
16	to Francis Charleton for Boats as per bill	027 10 00
	paid by the pages of the Bakestairs as per bill	004 18 06
19	to Mr Lapy of the standing wardrobe as per bill	002 03 00
	to the Master of his Maties Berges as per bill	012 10 00
	to the Herbewoman presented oranges	001 01 06
29	to Lady Peterbroughs Coatchman and footmen	002 00 00
	to yor Maties Berges waited thair	001 10 00
	to a boat waited thair	000 05 00
		528 02 07

[verso] 30v		lib s d
1673	**Brought from the other syde**	**528 02 07**
2 August	to Mrs Alexander as per bill	010 18 03
	for pen Inke and paper	000 10 00
	Laid out by Mrs Hemden as per bill	005 00 00
5	for a boat to & from somerset house	000 10 00
11	for a boat to & from somerset house	000 10 00
12	fees & Charges at the Receite of one hundred pounds for July Last	003 15 00
14	for a boat to & from somerset house	000 10 00
	for a boat in the Effternoon	000 10 00
	to the Late Queens old footman	000 10 00
15	for a boat to & from somerset house	000 10 00
	to tery the waterman presented Mulberis	000 10 00
16	for a boat to & from somerset house	000 10 00
18	for boats to Chelsy	001 00 00
19	to Mr Clark for a Coatche to Hamton court	000 13 00
	to yo[r] Ma[ties] footmen to Hamton court	002 00 00
	to yo[r] Ma[ties] Boat to Hamton court	002 00 00
26	to y[r] Ma[ties] footmen to Hamton court	002 00 00
	to y[r] Ma[ties] Berges to Hamton court	007 10 00
	to y[r] Ma[ties] Boate to Hamtoncourt	002 00 00
	for five other boats thair	001 05 00
11 septembr	fees & Charges at the Receite of one hundred pounds for August Last	003 15 00
		574 08 10

[recto] 31r		lib s d
1673	**Brought from the other syde**	**574 08 10**
11 septembr	to Mr Lenoir furrier as per bill	041 07 06
3 octobr	fees & Charges at the Receipt of one hundred pounds for September last	003 15 00
	to Mr Watts for Maskarad Cloaths as per bill	026 08 00
	to Mr Lenoir for a Mufe as per aquitance	008 00 00
7	for Cages to the Birds by Mr Clarke	000 14 00

	for a french Embrodred Manto as per aquitance	035 00 00
22	to Mon:s duplessy for 11 yeards of velvet for point de vinis[105] & Embrodry as per bill	057 00 00
30	to Lady Arlintons Chairemen and footmen to somerset house	002 00 00
6 novembr	fees & Charges at the Receipt of one hundred pounds for octobr last	003 15 00
15 yor Maties Birthday[106]	to the violin Musique	020 00 00
	to the winde Musique & Recorders	005 00 00
	to the Harper	001 00 00
	to yor Maties footmen	003 00 00
	to the Kings footmen	002 00 00
	to the ducks footmen	002 00 00
	to yor Maties Coatchman	003 00 00
	to the Kings Coatchmen	002 00 00
		790 18 04

[verso] 31v		lib s d
1673	**Brought from the other syde**	**790 18 04**
15 novembr	to the trompets	006 00 00
	to the dromes	003 00 00
	to the ducks trompets	003 00 00
	to the Litermen & Chairemen	002 00 00
	to the somptermen	001 00 00
	to the Grooms	002 00 00
	to the Master of yor Maties Berges	001 00 00
	to the Groom botleman	000 02 06
	to the violine in ordinary	001 00 00
	to the ducks violins Musique	010 00 00
	to yor Maties Robs feaste	005 00 00

105 Point de Venice.
106 Catherine's birthday – she was 35.

30	to the footmen presented St Androws Crose	001 00 00
10 decembr	fees & Charges at the Receipt of one hundred pounds for november last	003 15 00
15	to Madame de bords woman with Cut Lether as per aquitance	027 00 00
	to Mr Hall for things from the Custom house as per bill	007 04 06
20	to yor Maties Berge to somerset house	000 10 00
	Laid out by Mr Stevens	000 14 00
27	to a woman presented wafers	001 01 08
	to Mr Caple Messenger sent to dall[107] as per bill	005 05 00
	to a man presented a nosgye	001 01 08
		872 12 08

[recto] 32r		lib s d
1673[108]	**Brought from the other syde**	**872 12 08**
1 Janr New Years gifts	to the violins Musique	020 00 00
	to the wind Musique & Recorders	006 00 00
	to the violine in ordinary	001 00 00
	to the Harper	001 00 00
	to yor Maties Master Cooke	005 00 00
	to his man	001 00 00
	to the Kings Master Cooke	005 00 00
	to his man	001 00 00
	to yor Maties Coatchmen	010 00 00
	to yor Maties postilions	003 00 00
	to yor Maties footmen	010 00 00
	to the Kings Coatchmen	005 00 00
	to the Litermen & Chairemen	005 00 00
	to the somptermen	004 00 00
	to yor Maties Grooms	005 00 00

107 Deal.
108 1674 NS.

	to the Trompets	006 00 00
	to the droms	003 00 00
	to the Gallery keepers	006 00 00
	to the ducks trompets	006 00 00
	to the violine to the ducks Children	001 00 00
	to the Master of yor Maties[109] Berges	002 00 00
		978 12 08

[verso] 32v		lib s d
1673[110]	**Brought from the other syde**	**978 12 08**
1 Janr	to the shoemakers men	004 00 00
	to the portingall Cooke	003 00 00
	to the portingall Baker	003 00 00
2	to the man that Bring the Gazets	001 01 08
12	fees & Charges at the Receipt of one hundred pounds for decembr last	003 15 00
	to the Herbewoman presented oranges	001 01 08
	to Lady Northumberlands Gardner	001 01 08
28	to yor Maties footmen to Chelsy	002 00 00
7 febr	fees & Charges at the Receipt of one hundred pounds for Janr last	003 15 00
9	to Mr Lightfoot as per bill	012 00 00
	to Major Harwood to paye for Craig the footman being hurte as per bill	010 00 00
12	to Madame de bords woman for Combs as per bill	017 10 00
	to John percivall bonseter as per bill	015 00 00
	for pen Inke and paper	000 10 00
19	to Mrs Browning as per bill	007 12 05
20	to William Jonson as per bill	016 02 08
	Laid out by the pages of the Bakestairs	000 08 00
1 March	to the footman presented St davids Leeke	001 00 00
7	Laid out by Mrs Hemden as per bill	003 05 00

109 Unusually not expressed as Maties.
110 1674 NS.

10	fees & Charges at the Receit of one hundred pounds for febr last	003 15 00
		1088 10 09

[recto] 33r		lib s d
1673[111]	**Brought from the other syde**	**1088 10 09**
17 March	to the footman presented S^t^ patriks Crose	001 00 00
20	for a boat to somerset house	000 05 00
9 April 1674	fees & Charges at the Receipt of one hundred pounds for March last	003 15 00
	Monies disbursed from the twenty fiue of March 1673 to the ninth of Aprill 1674	**1039 10 09**
	Monies Receiued from the twenty fiue of March 1673 to the ninth of Aprill 1674	**1200 00 00**
	Remains due to yor Matie from the Accountant the ninth of Aprill 1674	**0106 09 03**

[verso] 33v		
1674		lib s d
20 April	for a boat to somerset house	000 05 00
23	to the violin Musique St Goerg day[112]	010 00 00
24	to the pantry Butry & Ewry on Mandy thursday[113]	002 10 00
	to Lady Northumberlands Gardner	001 01 08
	to yor Maties footmen the first time to Heighparke	002 00 00
	to the footman present St Georg Crose	001 00 00
	to Mrs Cheret for Ladyday[114] quarter last as per bill	013 08 00
27	Laid out by Mr Stevens	000 14 06
	to Lady Northumberlands Gardner by Mr Stevens	002 03 04
	to the Late Queens old footman presented Sparagras	001 01 08

111 1674 NS.
112 23 April.
113 Maundy Thursday 1674 – 22 March. Easter Sunday 1674 – 25 March.
114 25 March.

	paid at the Cristning Lady Kenouls Child	021 13 04
4 May	fees & Charges at the Receit of one hundred pounds for April: Last	003 15 00
	for two peices of satin Ribon & two peices of Colbertin lace by Lady Clenton	005 02 02
	to Mrs Hemden for Mending yor Maties Linen as per aquitance	030 00 00
14	to William Jonson as per bill	001 06 00
	to Henery Huges Lost his horse in the journy to Norwich as per bill	012 00 00
18	to yor Maties Berges to Greenwich	003 00 00
		111 10 08

[recto] 34r		lib s d
1674	**Brought from the other syde**	**111 10 08**
19 May	to yor Maties footmen to Chelsy	002 00 00
20	to the footmen to windsor	002 00 00
	for a boat from the Bakstairs	001 01 08
21	to the Hoboys	005 00 00
26	to the footmen Runing mony	002 00 00
27	to yor Maties Berges to London	015 00 00
	to the Kings Berge to London	010 00 00
28	to yor Maties Berges to Richmon	007 10 00
	to a Gyde from Richemon to winsor	001 00 00
	to the footmen to & from London	004 00 00
29	to the violin Musique on his Maties Birthday[115]	010 00 00
	to yor Maties footmen then	003 00 00
30	to the footmen Runing mony	002 00 00
31	to the footmen Runing mony	002 00 00
	to another set of Hoboys	005 00 00
	paid by Mr Rogers upon the water	000 02 00
	to yor Maties two Boatmen from the 19th of May to the first of June as per <bill>	007 10 00
1 June	to the footmen Runing mony	002 00 00

115 Charles II's birthday – he was 44.

2	to the footmen Runing mony	002 00 00
3	to the footmen Runing mony	002 00 00
		196 14 04

[verso] 34v		lib s d
1674	**Brought from the other syde**	**196 14 04**
3 June	to Mrs Hemden as per bill	001 19 06
	to a footman sent to Richemon	001 00 00
4	to the footmen Runing mony	002 00 00
5	to the footmen Runing mony	002 00 00
6	to Lord Montagus man presented veneson	002 03 04
7	to the footmen Runing mony	002 00 00
8	to the footmen Runing mony	002 00 00
	to yor Maties Boatmen from the first of June to the 8 as per bill	004 10 00
10	to the footmen Runing mony	002 00 00
12	to the yeoman of the wagons as per bill	001 08 00
	to William Jonson as per bill	001 06 06
	to the footmen Runing mony	002 00 00
	fees & Charges at the Receit of one hundred pounds for May Last	003 15 00
	to Mrs Cheret as per bill	094 07 00
14	to the footmen Runing mony	002 00 00
16	to yor Maties footmen from the eight to the 16 as per bill	004 00 00
	to Lord Bristols Gardner presented orang flowrs	002 03 04
	to the footmen Runing mony	002 00 00
	to Bury Roger hastrik footman as per aqitance	010 00 00
		339 07 00

[recto] 35r		lib s d
1674	**Brought from the other syde**	**339 07 00**
18 June	to one of the Kings trompets vpon the water	005 08 04

	to a woman presented Creams Cheese and other things vpon the water	002 03 04
20	to yo[r] Ma[ties] Berges to & from London	030 00 00
	to the Kings Berge to London as per bill	010 00 00
	to the footmen Runing mony to and from London	004 00 00
	to Lord Bristols Gardner presented orange flowrs	002 03 04
	to Lady Arlintons footmen with things from the Custom house for yo[r] Ma[tie]	002 03 04
23	to yo[r] Ma[ties] Boatemen from the 16 to 23 as per bill	003 10 00
25	to a woman with Leaches	005 08 04
27	to yo[r] Ma[ties] Berges to & from London as per aquitanc	030 00 00
	to the Kings Berge to & from London as per aquitance	020 00 00
	to a woman presented fruite and other things vpon the water	002 03 04
	to a footman sent to Mr Progers	000 10 00
	to Lord Bristols Gardner presented orang flowrs	001 01 08
	to yo[r] Ma[ties] footmen to & from London	004 00 00
		461 18 08

[verso] 35v		lib s d
1674	**Brought from the other syde**	**461 18 08**
29 June	to Mr Clarke Laid out by the pages of the Bakestairs	004 07 00
	to the footmen Runing mony	002 00 00
	to Mrs Cheret for one quarter due at Mid somer last as per bill	011 10 00
30	fees & Charges at the Receit of fifty pounds to pay the footmens ariers	002 00 00
	to yo[r] Ma[ties] footmen as per aquitance	045 00 00
1 July	to the footmen Runing mony	002 00 00
	to Lord tenhams Keeper presented veneson	002 03 04

	to a footman sent from the forest	000 10 00
2	to Mrs Cranmer as per bill	041 15 06
3	to Lord Bristols Gardner	001 01 08
4	to the footmen Runing mony	002 00 00
5	to the footmen Runing mony	002 00 00
6	to the footmen Runing mony	002 00 00
7	to the footmen Runing mony	002 00 00
	to yo[r] Ma[ties] Boatemen from the 24 of June to the eight of July as per bill	008 00 00
8	to the footmen Runing mony	002 00 00
	to a man presented a Melon	001 01 08
9	fees & Charges paid at the Receit for one hundred pounds for May Last	003 15 00
11	to Lord Bristols Gardner presented orang flowrs	001 01 08
		598 04 08

[recto] 36r		lib s d
1674	**Brought from the other syde**	**598 04 08**
12 July	to the footmen Runing mony	002 00 00
13	to the footmen to Hamton court	002 00 00
	paid by Mr Roper at Hamton court	003 05 00
	to a footman sent of earands	000 10 00
	paid by Major Harwood at Hamton court	001 10 00
	to Mr Stevens as per bill	001 06 00
17	to the footmen Runing mony	002 00 00
18	to yo[r] Ma[ties] Boatemen from the ninth to the 18 as per bill	007 00 00
	to Lady Bellings man presented a pigon pye	001 01 07
	to the portingall Embassadors Chairemen	001 00 00
	to Lord Bristols Gardner	001 01 07
	to Lady peterbroughs page presented Cheesecaks	001 01 07
20	to the footmen Runing mony	002 00 00
	to the dutchesse of yorks Chairemen and footmen	005 00 00

23	to the footmen Runing mony	002 00 00
	to yo[r] Ma[ties] boatmen from the nineteen to the 25 as per bill	003 10 00
24	to the footmen Runing mony	002 00 00
	Paid by Major Harwood at Cramburn loge	000 10 00
		637 00 03

[verso] 36v		lib s d
1674	**Brought from the other syde**	**637 00 03**
25 July	to the footmen Runing mony	002 00 00
	to Lord Bristols Gardner presented orange flowrs	001 01 07
26	to the footmen Runing mony	002 00 00
27	to the footmen Runing mony	002 00 00
	for Bringing y[r] Ma[ties] Chair from London	001 01 07
29	to the footmen Runing mony	002 00 00
30	to the footmen Runing mony to London	002 00 00
	paid by Mr Roper at Hamton court	004 06 04
	to a footman sent bake for the fathers	000 10 00
	for a boat with provisions from winsor	001 01 07
3 August	fees & Charges at the Receit of one hundred pounds for July Last	003 15 00
	fees & Charges at the Receit of fifty pounds to pay the Coatchmens Areirs	001 17 06
	to yo[r] Ma[ties] Coatchmen by Mr Muray as per aquitance	048 00 00
	for pen Inke and paper	000 10 00
	to the dutchesse of Monmuths Chairemen	005 00 00
	for a boat to somerset house	000 10 00
4	to yo[r] Ma[ties] footmen Runing mony from London	002 00 00
	to yo[r] Ma[ties] boatmen from the 26 of July to the 10 of August as per bill	010 10 00
5	paid by Mr Roper at fishing	002 18 00
		730 01 10

[recto] 37r		lib s d
1674	**Brought from the other syde**	**730 01 10**
7 August	to two of the Kings Coatchmen waited of yor Maties	002 00 00
	to the footmen Runingmony	002 00 00
9	to the footmen Runingmony	002 00 00
11	to the footmen Runing mony	002 00 00
	paid by Mr Sears at fishing	001 01 07
	to a footman sent for Angles	001 04 00
12	to the footmen Runing mony	002 00 00
13	to the footmen Runing mony	002 00 00
	to the Kings two Coatchmen	002 00 00
	to a man presented a large trout	001 01 07
	to the dutch Embassadors servants	003 10 00
17	to the two boatmen to the tenth to the seventeen as per bill	004 05 00
	to the footmen Runing mony	002 00 00
	for Riben & things for yor Maties Chaire	000 10 00
	to the Hoboys from notingam	005 00 00
	for a Baskit of fruite	001 01 07
	to the portingall Embassadors Chairemen	001 00 00
21	to the footmen Runing mony	002 00 00
22	to the footmen Runing mony	002 00 00
23	to the footmen Runing mony	002 00 00
	to the Kings two Coatchmen	002 00 00
24	to yor Maties Boatmen from the 18 to the 24 as per bill	004 04 00
		776 19 07

[verso] 37v		lib s d
1674	**Brought from the other syde**	**776 19 07**
25 August	to the footmen Runing mony	002 00 00
	for a warant for y^r^ Maties sheets	000 10 00
27	to Mary doule Herbwomane as per bill	003 00 00

	to Lady Suffolks page & footmen at Lord Mainards[116]	002 00 00
29	to the footmen Runing mony	002 00 00
	to Lord Mainards man presented a pigon pye	001 01 07
	paid by Mr Roper & Mr Sears by water	002 15 00
31	to the footmen Runing mony	002 00 00
	for a Baskit of fruite	001 00 00
1 septmbr	to the parke keeper	002 00 00
	to the parke gate keeper	001 00 00
	to the wardrobe keeper	005 00 00
	to Mrs Hemden for journys to & from London & other epense[117] for y^r^ Maties seruice	003 15 00
	to the Hous keeper	008 00 00
	for Lady Eyvis Lodgings by Mr Slaughter	003 00 00
	to vnder Keepers of the greatparke	002 03 04
	to the Guiners[118]	005 08 04
	for a boate for yor Maties Chaire to London	001 01 07
	to yor Maties boatmen from the 25 of august to the first of septembr as per bill	006 09 00
	to the yeoman of the wagons as per bill	001 18 00
	to William Jonson as per bill	002 00 00
		835 01 05

[recto] 38r		lib s d
1674	**Brought from the other syde**	**835 01 05**
1 Septembr	to yor Maties footmen Runing mony to London	002 00 00
4	fees & Charges at the Receit of one hundred pounds for August Last	003 15 00
5	for a boat to & from somerset hous	000 10 00

[116] Maynard's.
[117] Expense.
[118] Gunners.

8	for a boat to & from somerset hous	000 10 00
9	to the footmen Runing mony to Chelsy	002 00 00
17	to the footmen Runing mony to Hamton court	002 00 00
	to Mr Roche Laid out by the pages of the Bakestairs	003 02 00
18	to the footmen Runing mony	002 00 00
19	to the footmen Runing mony	002 00 00
	fees & Charges at the Receit for one hundred pounds for this present Septembr	003 15 00
20	to the footmen Runing mony	002 00 00
22	to the footmen Runing mony	002 00 00
24	to the footmen Runing mony	002 00 00
26	to the footmen Runing mony	002 00 00
27	to the footmen Runing mony	002 00 00
	fees & Charges at the Receit of fifty seven pounds to pay the Litermen Grooms & sompterms Areirs	002 03 00
	Laid out by Mrs Hemden	001 15 00
	to the Litermen as per aquitance	021 00 00
	to the somptermen as per aquitance	015 00 00
		906 11 05

[verso] 38v		lib s d
1674	**Brought from the other syde**	**906 11 05**
27 Septembr	to Mr Price for Keeping of yor Maties Asse as per bill	013 10 00
28	to yor Maties footmen Runing mony	002 00 00
29	to the footmen Runing mony	002 00 00
30	to the Grooms for their Areirs as per aquitance	021 00 00
	for a halfe shirt to yor Matie	001 01 08
2 octobr	to the footmen Runing mony	002 00 00
	to Mrs Cheret for one quarter due at Michalmas[119] last as per bill	028 01 00

119 29 September.

4	to the footmen Runing mony to & from London	004 00 00
6	to the footmen Runing mony to Lord Bellows	002 00 00
7	to the footmen Runing mony	002 00 00
8	to yo[r] Ma[ties] Boatmen from the 17 of Septembr to the 8 of octobr as per bill	012 15 00
	to the footmen Runing mony	002 00 00
	to Mr Winewoods Gardner presented fruite	001 01 08
10	to the footmen Runing mony	002 00 00
11	to the footmen	002 00 00
	to William Jonson as per bill	001 10 06
12	to the footmen Runing mony to Newparke	002 00 00
	to a footman sent to Richemon	001 00 00
	paid by Mr Rogers at Newparke	005 08 06
	to Mr Stevens as per bill	002 08 00
		1016 07 09

[recto] 39r		lib s d
1674	**Brought from the other syde**	**1016 07 09**
15 Octobr	to the footmen Runing mony to Newparke	002 00 00
16	to the footmen Runing mony	002 00 00
17	to the footmen Runing mony	002 00 00
18	to the footmen Runing mony	002 00 00
19	to the footmen Runing mony	002 00 00
20	to the footmen Runing mony	002 00 00
21	to the footmen Runing mony	002 00 00
22	to the Gardner	002 00 00
	to the Housekeeper	008 00 00
	to the wardrobe Keeper	005 00 00
	to the footmen Runing mony to London	002 00 00
	to <the> parkeepers	002 00 00
	to the yeoman of the wagons as per bill	001 03 06

	to yo[r] Ma[ties] Boatemen from the eight to the twenty two as per bill	008 03 00
	for a boat for yo[r] Ma[ties] Chaire	000 10 00
	to the foure Keepers of Both parks Riding fees	006 10 00
	to the womane whair was yo[r] Ma[ties] dary	002 03 04
	to the man keeps the fery boat	001 01 08
28	to Mr Clarke Laid out by the pages of the Bakestairs as per bill	002 17 06
		1071 16 09

[verso] 39v		lib s d
1674	**Brought from the other Syde**	**1071 16 09**
2 Novembr	Laid by Mrs Hemden as per bill	001 17 06
10	Laid out by Mr Mead as per bill	002 09 00
	to Mr Wright for a paire of Butts	005 00 00
	for a boat to carry them to Hamton court	000 10 00
	to the portingall Embassadors Chaire men	001 00 00
15 yo[r] Ma[ties] Birthday[120]	to the violine Musique	020 00 00
	to the wind Musique & Recorders	005 00 00
	to the Harper	001 00 00
	to yo[r] Ma[ties] footmen	003 00 00
	to the Kings Footmen	002 00 00
	to the ducks Footmen	002 00 00
	to the dutchesse footmen	002 00 00
	to yo[r] Ma[ties] Coatchmen	003 00 00
	to the Kings Coatchmen	002 00 00
	to the Trompets	006 00 00
	to the droms	003 00 00
	to the ducks trompts	003 00 00
	to the Litermen & Chairmen	002 00 00
	to the somptermen	001 00 00

120 Catherine's birthday – she was 36.

	to the Grooms	002 00 00
	to the Master of yor Maties Berges	001 00 00
		1140 13 03

[recto] 40r		lib s d
1674	**Brought from the other syde**	**1140 13 03**
15 November	to the violine in ordinary	001 00 00
	to the Groome Bottleman	000 02 06
	to the ducks violin & Musique	010 00 00
	to yor Maties Robs feast	005 00 00
25	fees & Charges at the Receit of one hundred pounds for this octobr Last	003 15 00
	to Lady Lauderdalls man presented an Asse	002 03 04
26	to yor Maties Berge to dartford with the fathers	001 10 00
30	to the footman presented St Androws Crose	001 00 00
1 Decembr	fees & Charges at the Receit of one hundred pounds for Novembr last	003 15 00
2	to Mrs Nun for one years Alowance due at Michalmas[121] last as per aquitance	020 00 00
	to Mrs Crane for Combs	001 10 00
17	to Mr Lightfoot as per bill	010 16 00
	to Mrs Browning as per bill	013 08 04
	Mor to Mrs Browning as per bill	002 03 07
24	to the portingall Embassadors Chairemen	002 00 00
		1219 07 00

[verso] 40v		lib s d
1674[122]	**Brought from the other syde**	**1219 07 00**
1 Janr	to the violine Musique	020 00 00
Newyears gifts	to the winde Musique & Recorders	006 00 00
	to the violine in ordinary	001 00 00

121 29 September.
122 1675 NS.

	to the Harper	001 00 00
	to yo[r] Ma[ties] Master Cooke	005 00 00
	to his man	001 00 00
	to the Kings Master Cooke	005 00 00
	to his man	001 00 00
	to yo[r] Ma[ties] Coatchmen	010 00 00
	to yo[r] Ma[ites] postilions	003 00 00
	to yo[r] Ma[ties] footmen	010 00 00
	to the Kings Coatchmen	005 00 00
	to the Litermen & Chairemen	005 00 00
	to the somptermen	004 00 00
	to the Grooms	005 00 00
	to the Kings trompets	006 00 00
	to the droms	003 00 00
	to the Galery keepers	006 00 00
	to the ducks trompets	006 00 00
	to the violine to the ducks Children	001 00 00
	to the Master of yo[r] Ma[ties] Berge	002 00 00
	to the shoemakers men	004 00 00
		1329 07 00

[recto] 41r

1674[123]	**Brought from the other syde**	**1329 07 00**
1 Janr	to the portingall Baker	0003 00 00
	to the portingall Cooke	0003 00 00
2	to the man that Brings the Gazets	0001 01 08
	to the Herbewomane	0001 01 08
	to Lady Northumberlands Gardner	0001 01 08
8	fees & Charges at the Receit of one hundred pounds for decembr last	0003 15 00
	to Lady Arlintons man presented Hens from Holand	0002 03 04
	to the two men that Brings the play bills	0002 03 04
	to William Jonson as per bill	0001 11 06

[123] 1675 NS.

16	to Mrs pigon as per bill	0012 04 06
21	to a womane gave yor Matie phisique	0010 16 04
	to the portingall Embassadors Chairemen	0002 00 00
	to a man Laid boards at the playe house	0000 02 06
4 febr	fees & Charges at the Receit of one hundred pounds for Janr Last	0003 15 00
5	to Mr Hall for things from the Custom house as per bill	0010 10 00
	to Mr Roper for things from Mr Montegue as per bill	0019 15 00
		1407 08 06

[verso] 41v		lib s d
1674[124]	**Brought from the other syde**	**1407 08 06**
10 febr	to Mrs Cheret for one quarter due at Cristmas last as per bill	0014 01 00
	to the man showed the sea dog	0002 03 06
	Laid out by Mr Stevens	0000 09 00
20	to Criston Lord Tenhams Child	0021 15 00
1 March	to a footman presented S^t^ davids Leeks	0001 00 00
2	fees & Charges at the Receit of one hundred pounds for febr Last	0003 15 00
8	to the portingall Baker for thre years Areirs as per aquitance	0009 00 00
9	to the portingall Cooke for thre years Areirs as per aquitanc	0009 00 00
	Laid out by Mrs Hemden for yor Maties service	0001 01 00
15	to Lady Anglesies man presented Caks	0000 10 00
17	to the footman presented St Patriks Crose	0001 00 00
1 April: 1675	to Lady Northumberland Gardner on Mandy thursday[125]	0002 03 06
3	fees & Charges at the Receit of one hundred pounds for March Last	0003 15 00
		1477 01 06

124 1675 NS.
125 Maundy Thursday 1675 – 11 March. Easter Sunday 1675 – 14 April.

[recto] 42r		lib s d
1675	**Brought from the other syde**	**1477 01 06**
	Moneis disbursed from the ninth of April: 1674 to the third of April: 1675	**1477 01 06**
	Moneis Receiued from the ninth of April: 1674 to the third of April: 1675	**1357 00 00**
	Remained due to yo[r] Ma[tie] from the former Accounte	**0106 09 03**
	Remains due from yo[r] Ma[tie] to the Accountant the third of April: 1675	**0013 12 03**

Catherina R

1-Worsley/8 – Catherine of Braganza, privy purse accounts 1675–79

[recto] 1r

1675	**Moneis Receuid by the Countesse of Suffolke of John Heruey Esqr for her Maties Priuy purse**	**lib s d**
4 May	Receiued of John Heruey Esqr one hundred pounds for the month of April last	100 00 00
2 June	Receiued of John Heruey Esqr one hundred pounds for May last	100 00 00
2 July	Receiued of John Heruey Esqr one hundred pounds for June last	100 00 00
16 July	Receiued of John Heruey Esqr one hundred pounds for this present Month	100 00 00
3 August	Receiued of John Heruey Esqr one hundred pounds for this present Month	100 00 00
17 Septembr	Receiued of John Heruey Esqr one hundred pounds for this present Month	100 00 00
5 Octobr	Receiued of John Heruey Esqr one hundred pounds for this present Month	100 00 00
4 Novembr	Receiued of John Heruey Esqr one hundred pounds for this present Month	100 00 00
3 Decembr	Receiued of John Heruey Esqr one hundred pounds for this present Month	100 00 00
		900 00 00

[verso] 1v

		lib s d
1675[1]	**Brought from the other syd**	**900 00 00**
4 Janr	Receiued of John Heruey Esqr one hundred pounds for this Month	100 00 00
3 Febr	Receiued of John Heruey Esqr one hundred pounds for this Month	100 00 00

[1] 1676 NS.

2 March	Receiued of John Heruey Esq[r] one hundred pounds for this Month	100 00 00
	Moneis Receiued	
	From the fifth of April: 1675 to the fifth of April: 1676	**1200 00 00**
8 April 1676	Receiued of John Heruey Esq[r] one hundred pounds for this present Month	100 00 00
2 May	Receiued of John Heruey Esq[r] one hundred pounds for this Month	100 00 00
6 June	Receiued of John Heruey Esq[r] one hundred pounds for this Month	100 00 00
4 July	Receiued of John Heruey Esq[r] one hundred pounds for this Month	100 00 00
3 August	Receiued of John Heruey Esq[r] one hundred pounds for this Month of August	100 00 00
		500 00 00

[recto] 2r		lib s d
1676	**Brought from the other syd**	**500 00 00**
5 septembr	Receiued of John Heruey Esq[r] one hundred pounds for this Month	100 00 00
11	Receiued of John Heruey Esq[r] one hundred pounds for the Month ofoctober next	100 00 00
31 Octobr	Receiued of John Heruey Esq[r] thre Hundred pounds	300 00 00
2 Novembr	Receiued of John Heruey Esq[r] one hundred pounds for this Month of November	100 00 00
6 Decembr	Receiued of John Heruey Esq[r] one hundred pounds for this Month of December	100 00 00
8 Janr	Receiued of John Heruey Esq[r] one hundred pounds for this present Month	100 00 00
3 Febr	Receiued of John Heruey Esq[r] one hundred pounds for this present Month	100 00 00

5 March	Receiued of John Heruey Esqr one hundred pounds for this present Month	100 00 00
	Moneis Receiued	
	From the eight of April: 1676 to the second of April: 1677	**1500 00 00**

[verso] 2v

1677		lib s d
3 April:	Receiued of John Heruey Esqr one hundred pounds for this present Month	100 00 00
4 May	Receiued of John Heruey Esqr one hundred pounds for this present Month	100 00 00
9 June	Receiued of John Heruey Esqr fiue hundred pounds	500 00 00
26 July	Receiued of John Heruey Esqr	316 10 00
31	Receiued of John Heruey Esqr one hundred pounds for this present month	100 00 00
15 August	Receiued of John Heruey Esqr one hundred pounds for this present Month	100 00 00
5 Septembr	Receiued of John Heruey Esqr one hundred pounds for this present Month	100 00 00
9 Octobr	Receiued of John Heruey Esqr one hundred pounds for this present Month	100 00 00
6 Novembr	Receiued of John Heruey Esqr one hundred pounds for this present Month	100 00 00
4 Decembr	Receiued of John Heruey <Esqr> one hundred pounds for this present Month	100 00 00
3 January	Receiued of John Heruey Esqr one hundred pounds for this present Month	100 00 00
8 Febr	Receiued of John Heruey Esqr one hundred pounds for this present Month	100 00 00
		1816 10 00

[recto] 3r

1667/8	**Brought from the other syd**	**1816 10 00**
5 March	Receiued of John Heruey Esqr one hundred pounds for this present Month	100 00 00

	Moneis Receiued	
	from the second of April: 1677 to the first of April: 1678	**1916 10 00**
		lib s d
4 April 1678	Receiued of John Heruey Esqr one hundred pounds for this present Month	100 00 00
3 May	Receiued of John Heruey Esqr one hundred pounds for this present Month	100 00 00
4 June	Receiued of John Heruey Esqr one hundred pounds for this present Month	100 00 00
4 July	Receiued of John Heruey Esqr one hundred pounds for this present Month	100 00 00
7 August	Receiued of John Heruey Esqr one hundred pounds for this present Month	100 00 00
		500 00 00

[verso] 3v		lib s d
1678	**Brought from the other syde**	**500 00 00**
7 Septembr	Receiued of John Heruey Esqr one hundred pounds for this present Month	100 00 00
8 Octobr	Receiued of John Heruey Esqr one hundred pounds for this present month	100 00 00
21 Novembr	Receiued of John Heruey Esqr one hundred pounds for this present month	100 00 00
	Receiued of John Heruey Esqr five hundred pounds	500 00 00
7 Decembr	Receiued of John Heruey Esqr one hundred pounds for this present Month	100 00 00
9 Janr[2]	Receiued of John Heruey Esqr one hundred pounds for this present Month	100 00 00
4 Febr	Receiued of John Heruey Esqr one hundred pounds for this present Month	100 00 00
8 March	Receiued of John Heruey Esqr one hundred pounds for this present Month	100 00 00
	Moneis Receiued	

2 1679 NS.

	from the first of April: 1678 to the first of April: 1679 seuenteen hundred pounds	**1700 00 00**[3]
[recto] 4r	blank	
[verso] 4v	blank	
[recto] 5r		
1675	**Moneis disbursed by the Countesse of Suffolke for her Ma[ties] vse**	lib s d
5 April:	Remains due from the last Acompt	013 12 03
	to Lady Scrope as per bill	038 14 06
	to the portingall Embassadors Chairmen	002 00 00
	to yo[r] Ma[ties] footmen the first time to Heighparke	002 00 00
	to the yeoman of the Gard at Easter[4]	001 01 09
	Laid out by Mr Roper	002 03 06
6	to the pantry Butry & Ewry on Mandy thursday[5]	002 10 00
	for french Ribon	003 15 00
	for pen Inke & paper	000 10 00
8	to Mrs Cranmer as per bill	034 05 05
9	to Mrs Cheret for one quarter due at our Lady day last[6]	018 02 00
	to Lady Arlintons Chairemen by Mr Stevens	002 03 06
10	to Mrs Nun for halfe a years allowance due at our Lady last	010 00 00
	to Lady Manchesters man presented Caks	000 10 00

3 The total income was £6,316 10s.
4 Easter Sunday 1675 – 14 April.
5 Maundy Thursday 1675 – 11 April.
6 25 March.

	for point for yo[r] Ma[ties] sleeues by Mrs Hemden	002 02 00
	to the duchesse of Lauderdalls man presented a Chaire	002 03 06
		135 13 05

[verso] 5v

1675	**Brought from the other syd**	**135 13 05**
16 April:	to Lady Manchesters man presented flowrs	000 10 00
	for lace & other things by Mrs Hemden	003 00 00
23	to the violin Musique on St Georg day[7]	010 00 00
	Laid out by the pages of the Bakstairs	000 18 00
2 May	to Mrs Hemden for one year Allowance as per Aquitance	030 00 00
	Laid out by Mr Roper	002 03 06
4	to Mrs Guidat for a pointe as per bill	050 00 00
	fees & Charges at the Receit of one hundred pounds for April last	003 15 00
	to the portingall Embassadors Chairmen	002 00 00
	to Mon[s] le noire furrier as per bill	006 02 06
7	for Colbertin by Mrs Hemden	005 06 00
	to a seamans wife presented a statue	005 08 09
	for a set of ninpins by Mr Stevens	000 10 00
12	to Mrs Carleton as per Aquitance	010 00 00
	for Cheries at Heighparke	002 00 00
14	to the portingall Embassadors Chairmen	001 00 00
	to the workemen at somersethouse by Mr Roper	002 06 00
20	to the Herbewomane presented Cheris	001 01 09
	to yo[r] Ma[ties] Boatmen	000 10 00
	to the Late Queens old footman	002 03 06
	for Colbertin by Mrs Hemden	002 15 00

[7] 23 April.

29[8]	to the violine Musique	010 00 00
	to yor Maties footmen	003 00 00
		290 03 05

[recto] 6r

1675	**Brought from the other syd**	**290 03 05**
2 June	to Lord Montegus man presented veneson	002 03 06
	fees & Charges at the Receit of one hundred pounds for May last	003 15 00
	to Mrs Browning as per bill	016 19 04
	for Colberin by Mrs Hemden	004 00 03
	to Lady Northumberlands Gardner for flowrs at [….][9] Easter[10]	001 01 09
	to Lady Northumberlands Gardner	002 03 06
	for things by Mrs Hemden	001 00 00
	to Mrs Biew for a dozen of Gloues	001 16 00
	for this Booke	000 16 00
15	to the portingall Embassadors Chairmen	002 00 00
26	to Mrs Cheret for one quarter due at Midsomerlast[11] as per bill	011 06 00
	paid by Mr Roper at Heighparke	002 03 06
2 July	fees & Charges at the Receit of one hundred pounds for June last	003 15 00
	to Lord Bristols Gardner presented orang flowrs	001 01 09
	to the Keeper of Heighpark with veneson	000 10 00
	to Mr Jonson as per bill	002 12 06
5	Laid out by Mr Stevens	000 09 06
6	to Mr Roper for the Armenian as per bill	022 05 06

8 Charles II's birthday – he was 45.
9 Two words have been deleted here and Easter added.
10 Easter Sunday 1675 – 14 April.
11 24 June.

	for Colbertin by Mrs Hemden	006 00 00
7	to Lord Bristols Gardner presented orang flowrs	001 01 09
8	to yo[r] Ma[ties] Berges to somersethouse	001 10 00
		378 14 03

[verso] 6v

1675	**Brought from the other Syd**	**378 14 03**
8 July	to yo[r] Ma[ties] footmen to winsor	002 00 00
	to Lady Arlintons Chairmen	002 00 00
	to Lady Arlintons footman keept the ninpins	001 00 00
	to the pages of the Bakstairs to winsor	000 10 00
	for bringing yo[r] Ma[ties] to winsor with lights	001 01 09
9	to the footmen Runing mony	002 00 00
10	paid by Mr Halsall at the Greatparke	003 15 00
	to the footmen Runing mony	002 00 00
	to a Gyd	000 10 00
11	to Mr Jonson as per bill	001 05 00
	to the footmen Runing mony	002 00 00
12	to the footmen Runing mony	002 00 00
13	to the footmen Runing mony	002 00 00
14	to the footmen Runing mony	002 00 00
15	to the footmen Runing mony	002 00 00
16	to the footmen Runing mony	002 00 00
	fees & Charges at the Receit of one hundred pounds for this Month	003 15 00
	to Mr Stevens Laid out by the pages	000 15 00
17	to the footmen Runing mony	002 00 00
	to Mrs Hemden to winsor	001 05 00
19	to the footmen Runing mony	002 00 00
21	to the footmen Runing mony	002 00 00
	to Mr Roper Laid out upon seuerall ocations	007 15 00
		426 06 00

[recto] 7r

1675	**Brought from the other syd**	**426 06 00**
21 July	to Mr Sears Laid out upon seuerall ocations	003 05 00
22	to the footmen Runing mony	002 00 00
	to the Hobois by Mr Stevens	002 03 06
23	to the footmen Runing mony	002 00 00
24	for Colbertin by Mrs Hemden	002 10 06
26	to the footmen Runing mony	002 00 00
	to a man with ninepins from Lord orsery	001 01 09
28	to the footmen Runing mony	002 00 00
	to Kinsinton Gardner	001 01 09
29	to the footmen Runing mony	002 00 00
	to yor Maties Bootemen from the eight of July to the thirty one as per bill	017 10 00
30	paid by Mr Sears at Boulls at two seuerall tims	002 03 06
	to the workmen at somerset gardine	001 01 09
31	to the footmen to London	002 00 00
	to the portingall Embassadors footman sent from the Greatparke	001 00 00
3 August	fees & Charges at the Receit of one hundred pounds for this Month	003 15 00
	for a Boat sent for the Elefant	000 02 06
	to Mr Roche Laid out by the Pages	000 14 00
	for Bandstrings by Mrs Hemden	001 00 00
4	to the footmen Runing mony to winsor	002 00 00
		477 15 03

[verso] 7v

1675	**Brought from the other syd**	**477 15 03**
4 August	to the pages of the Bakstairs to and from London	001 00 00
	for a boat to & from whithall	000 10 00
	for friut by the way	000 10 00

	for things by Mrs Hemden	000 12 06
5	to the footmen Runing mony	002 00 00
	to the Hobois from Notingam	003 05 00
8	to the footmen Runing mony	002 00 00
	for a Baskit of friute	001 01 10
9	to the footmen Runing mony	002 00 00
11	to the footmen Runing mony	002 00 00
	to a footman sent from the forest	000 10 00
15	to the footmen Runing mony	002 00 00
16	to the footmen Runing mony	002 00 00
17	to the footmen Runing mony	002 00 00
18	to the footmen Runing mony	002 00 00
19	to the Boatmen from the first of August to the ninteen as per bill	009 16 00
	to the footmen Runing mony	002 00 00
	paid by Mr Rogers	001 08 00
	paid for Making things by Mrs Hemden	000 18 06
20	to the footmen Runing mony	002 00 00
24	to the violine Musique	010 00 00
	to Kinsinton Gardner	001 01 10
		528 08 11

[recto] 8r

1675	**Brought from other syd**	**528 08 11**
25 August	to a Gardner presented Tubroses	002 03 08
	to a man Caried them to London	001 02 00
	to the footmen Runing mony	002 00 00
	to Mr Herbert watch maker sent to London	001 10 00
27	to the footmen Runing mony	002 00 00
	paid by Mr Sands	001 15 00
	to the trompet Marine	002 03 08
29	to the footmen Runing mony	002 00 00
	to Mr winwoods Gardner	001 01 08

31	to the footmen Runing mony	002 00 00
1 Septembr	to the footmen Runing mony	002 00 00
	for a Baskit of friute	001 01 10
2	to the footmen Runing mony	002 00 00
	paid by Lady suffolke at the forest	005 08 09
	paid by Mr Sands	000 05 00
	to the dutchesse of Monmuths man Caried provisions	001 10 00
	to a Keeper in the forest	001 01 10
3	to a woman presented Hony	002 03 06
6	to the Boatmen from the 19 of August to six of Septembr as per bill	009 00 00
7	to the footmen Runing mony	002 00 00
	for friute at the playe	000 12 00
		573 07 10

[verso] 8v

1675	**Brought from the other syd**	**573 07 10**
10 Septembr	to the Housekeeper	008 00 00
	to the parkekeeper	002 00 00
	to the parkgatkeeper	001 00 00
	to the wardrobkeeper	005 00 00
	to the Gards	005 08 09
	to Mr Winwoods Gardner	001 01 09
	for friute by the way to London	000 10 00
	to the footmen Runing mony	002 00 00
	to the pages of the Bakstairs	000 10 00
	to the two keepers of Greate parke	002 03 06
	paid by Mr Hall at Hamton court	002 11 06
11	to the Late Queens old footman	001 01 09
	for shoes had 4 yeares agoe	000 18 00
	Laid out by Mr forbus	000 11 00
	to the yoman of the wagons as per bill	001 13 00
	to Mr Jonson as per bill	001 04 00

	Laid out by Mrs Hemden	000 09 00
15	to Mr Mead as per bill	004 00 00
	Laid out by Mr Roche	000 04 00
	for Bringing yor Maties Chaire	001 01 09
17	to yor Maties Boatmen from the seaven instant to the tenth as per bill	004 12 00
	fees & Charges at the Receit of one hundred pounds for this Month	003 15 00
	for Gaus[12] by Mrs Hemden	000 10 00
		623 12 10

[recto] 9r

1675	**Brought from the other syd**	**623 12 10**
22 Septembr	to Mr Rose the Gardners men	001 01 09
	to Mr Rogers man presented friute	001 01 09
	to Mrs pigon for Ribon	000 10 00
30	To Mrs Nun for halfe a years Allowance due at Michaelmas last	010 00 00
	to the Locksmith	000 10 00
5 Octobr	Laid out by Mrs Hemden	001 00 00
	fees & Charges at the Receit of one hundred pounds for this Month	003 15 00
9	to Mrs Cheret for one quarter due at Michaelmas[13] Last	014 00 00
	to Mrs Chase man presented Caks	001 01 09
	to the Gardner of Hamton court	001 01 09
10	to Mr Rogers man presented fruite	001 01 09
	to Lady Marshalls man presented sweetmeats	000 10 00
	Laid out by Mr Steuens	000 07 06
22	Laid out by Mrs Hemden	001 10 00
	to thre Children at a Birth	005 09 02
30	to Mr Montague as per bill	016 10 00

12 Gauze.

13 29 September.

4 Novembr	fees & Charges at the Receit of one hundred pounds for this Month	003 15 00
		686 18 03

[verso] 9v

1675	**Brought from the other syd**	**686 18 03**
4 Novembr	to Mrs Cranmer as per bill	050 17 09
8	to a womane from winsor presented fishe	001 02 00
15[14]	to the violine Musique	020 00 00
	to the wind Musique & Recorders	005 00 00
	to the Harper	001 00 00
	to the Queens footmen	003 00 00
	to the Kings footmen	002 00 00
	to the ducks footmen	002 00 00
	to the dutches footmen	002 00 00
	to the Queens Coatchmen	003 00 00
	to the Kings Coatchmen	002 00 00
	to the Trompets	006 00 00
	to the droms	003 00 00
	to the Litermen & Chairemen	002 00 00
	to the somptermen	001 00 00
	to the Grooms	002 00 00
	to the Master of the Queens Berge	001 00 00
	to the violine in ordinary	001 00 00
	to the Groom botleman	000 02 06
	to the ducks violine Musique	010 00 00
	to the yeomans of the Gard	002 04 00
	to the Robsfeast	005 00 00
19	to Mons le noire as per bill	016 00 00
		828 04 06

14 Catherine's birthday – she was 37.

[recto] 10r

1675	**Brought from the other Syd**	**828 04 06**
30 Novembr	to the footman presented St Androws Crose	001 00 00
3 decembr	fees & Charges at the Receit of one hundred pounds for this Month	003 15 00
	Laid out by Mrs Hemden	001 00 00
	to Lady Loules[15] womane presented sweet pouders	005 10 00
9	to Mr Lightfoot as per bill	011 04 00
17	for 14 yeards of silver Ribon by Mrs Cranmer	007 00 00
20	for 14 yeards of french stufe as per bill	021 00 00
	to Mrs Eaton as per bill	003 13 06
	for pen Inke and paper	000 10 00
28	to Mrs Cheret for one quarter due at Cristmas last as per bill	014 14 00
	to the yeomans of the Gard	001 02 00
	to a womane from Bramford presented fruite	001 02 00
1 Janr	to the violin Musique	020 00 00
	to the wind Musique & Recorders	006 00 00
	to the violine in ordenary	001 00 00
	to the Harper	001 00 00
	to the Queens Master Cooke	005 00 00
	to his man	001 00 00
		933 15 00

[verso] 10v

1675[16]	**Brought from the other syd**	**933 15 00**
1 Janr	to the Kings Master Cooke	005 00 00
	to his man	001 00 00

15 Lovelace.
16 1676 NS.

	to the Queens Coatchmen	010 00 00
	to the Queens postilions	003 00 00
	to the Queens footmen	010 00 00
	to the Kings Coatchmen	005 00 00
	to the Litermen & Chairemen	005 00 00
	to the somptermen	004 00 00
	to the Grooms	005 00 00
	to the Trompets	006 00 00
	to the droms	003 00 00
	to the Gallery keepers	006 00 00
	to the ducks trompets	006 00 00
	to the violine to the ducks Children	001 00 00
	to the Master of the Queens Berge	002 00 00
	to the shoemakersmen	004 00 00
	to the portingall Baker	003 00 00
	to the portinall Cooke	003 00 00
2	to Lady Northumberlands Gardner	001 02 00
	to the portingall Embassadors Chairmen	002 00 00
	to the Herbewoman	001 02 00
	to the man brings the Gazets	001 02 00
	to the two men brings the play bills	002 04 00
		1023 05 00

[recto] 11r

1675[17]	**Brought from the other syd**	**1023 05 00**
4 Janr	fees & Charges at the Receit of one hundred pounds for this Month	0003 15 00
	to the portingall Embassadors Chairmen	0002 00 00
	to the portingall Embassadors Coatchman	0002 00 00
	to Mrs Alexander for 7 paire gloues	0007 14 00
14	to Mr Jonson as per bill	0001 15 00

17 1676 NS.

	to the portingall Embassadors gentleman by Mr Roper	0003 06 00
3 Febr	fees & Charges at the Receit of one hundred pounds for this Month	0003 15 00
	to Lady Arlintons Chairemen & footmen	0002 00 00
	for a hoode by Mrs Crane	0001 01 10
	to the ducks Trompets due the fifteen of Novembr[18] last as per aquitance	0003 00 00
	to Mrs Chase man presented Caks	0001 01 10
24	to the footmen the first time to Heighparke	0002 00 00
	to Mr Slaughter Laid out for the fathers Lodging at winsor in 1674	0006 11 00
	to the portingall Embassadors Chairemen	0002 00 00
26	to Mrs pigon as per bill	0014 00 00
	to the footmen Runing mony	0002 00 00
		1081 04 08

[verso] 11v

1675[19]	**Brought from the other Syd**	**1081 04 08**
1 March	to the footman presented St Davids Leeke	0001 00 00
2	fees & Charges at the Receit of one hundred pounds for this month	0003 15 00
	for a hood	0001 00 00
	to the footmen Runing mony	0002 00 00
	Laid out by Mr Roper at Chelsey	0002 15 00
	to Lady Arlintons page	0001 01 10
	to Mrs Chase man	0001 01 10
4	to Lady Manchesters man	0001 01 10
	Laid out by Mrs Hemden	0001 01 06

18 A late payment from Catherine's birthday.
19 1676 NS.

	to Lady Arlintons Coatchman and footmen	0002 00 00
6	to the footmen Runing mony	0002 00 00
7	to the footmen Runing mony	0002 00 00
10	to the Italian Miliner for 2 hoods	0003 10 00
15	to Mr Stevens as per bill	0005 11 00
	to Mr Ropers man	0001 00 00
17	to the footman presented St Patriks Crose	0001 00 00
22	to old Georg Bar as per bill	0006 00 00
23	to the yeomans of the Garde Mandy thursday[20]	0001 01 10
	to the pantry Butry & Ewry	0002 10 00
	to Lady Northumberlands Gardner	0002 03 08
	to a woman that Longd to Kisse the Queens hand by Mr Roper	0001 01 10
		1126 00 00

[recto] 12r

1676	**Brought from the other syd**	**1126 00 00**
26 March	to the yeomans of the gard at Easter[21]	0001 01 10
	to Lady Northumberlands Gardner	0001 01 10
27	to the violins Musique on Easter Munday[22]	0010 00 00
	to Mr Chase man	0001 01 10
	to Mrs Nun ten pounds for halfe a Yeares Allowance due at Our Lady day[23] Last as per bill	0010 00 00
28	for Colbertine by Mrs Hemden	0001 12 00
1 April:	to Lady Northumberlands Gardner	0001 01 10
3	to Mrs Cheret as per bill	0010 01 06

20 Maundy Thursday 1676 – 2 April.
21 Easter Sunday 1676 – 5 April.
22 Easter Monday 1676 – 6 April.
23 25 March.

	to the Late Queens old footman	0001 01 09
5	to the poore by the portingall Embassador	0027 03 09
	Laid out by Mr Roper at Mulbery gardine	0003 13 00
	to Mrs Browning as per bill	0012 04 02

Moneis disbursed

from the fifth of April: 1675 to the fifth of April: 1676	**1206 03 06**

Moneis Receiued

from the fifth of April: 1675 to the fifth of April: 1676	**1200 00 00**

Remains due

from yor Matie to the Accomptant	**0006 03 06**

[verso] 12v

1676	**Remains due from the Last Acompt**	**006 03 06**
8 April:	to yor Maties footmen Runing mony to Hakny[24]	002 00 00
	Laid out by Mr Slaughter	002 03 06
	to Lady Manchesters man	001 01 09
	Laid out by Mr Roper as per bill	006 01 06
8[25]	fees & Charges at the Receit of one hundred pounds for this present Month	003 15 00
	for twenty thre pots of Jongills[26]	001 04 00
	to the portingall Embassadors Chairmen	002 00 00
9	to the footmen Runing mony	002 00 00
	for a hood	000 12 00
15	to Lady Northumberlands Gardner	001 01 09

24 Hackney.

25 Date repeated.

26 Jonquils.

16	to the footmen Runing mony	002 00 00
19	to the footmen Runing mony	002 00 00
	to Lady Manchesters man	001 01 09
20	to the footmen Runing mony	002 00 00
21	to yo[r] Ma[ties] Berge to somersethouse	001 00 00
	to the Late Queens old footman	001 01 08
22	to Mr peckering[27] as per bill	013 13 06
23	to Mr Brokall[28] for the violins as per bill	010 00 00
	Laid out by Mrs Hamden	001 05 00
24	to the footmen Runing mony	002 00 00
	to the Berges somersethouse	001 10 00
	Laid out by Mr Rogers	001 15 00
		067 09 11

[recto] 13r

1676	**Brought from the other syd**	**067 09 11**
25 April:	to Mon[s] depuy presented sweetmets	002 03 06
27	to the Berge to somersethouse	001 00 00
	to the portingall Embassadors Coatchman	001 00 00
28	to the Berges to dartford	005 00 00
	to the Late Queenes old footman	001 01 09
	to Lady Manchesters man	001 00 00
2 May	fees & Charges at the Receit of one hundred pounds for this Month	003 15 00
	to Mrs Hemden due this day as per bill[29]	030 00 00
3	to Mr Rogers man presented Cheries	001 01 09
	to Mr Coolins[30] man	000 10 00
	to Mr Jonson as per bill	001 10 04

27 Pickering.
28 Brockwell.
29 This entry has been squashed in between those above and below it.
30 Collin's.

	to the portingall Embassadors Chairmen	002 00 00
	Laid out by Mr Steuens as per bill	001 11 00
	to the dutchesse of Richmons man	001 01 09
4	to Lady Northumberlands Gardner	002 03 06
	to the footmen Runing mony	002 00 00
5	to Mrs Cranmer as per bill	035 15 08
	Laid out by Mr Slaughter	003 05 00
	to the Berges to somersethouse	001 00 00
	Laid out by Mrs Hamden	001 10 06
	Laid out by Mr porter at the southaris[31]	002 03 06
11	to the Berge to somersethouse	001 00 00
	Laid out by father Manwell[32] for virgenells	002 03 06
		171 06 08

[verso] 13v

1676	**Brought from the other Syd**	**171 06 08**
13 May	to the footmen Runing mony to wolege[33]	002 00 00
	to the Berge to wolege	003 00 00
14	to Lady Northumberlands Gardner	002 03 06
	to a footman sent by water	000 05 00
	to Lady Arlintons Gardner presented orangtres	002 03 06
17	to Lord Montegues man presented venesen	002 03 06
	to Lady Northumberlands Gardner	001 01 08
	to Lady Manchesters Gardner presented orangtres	002 03 04
	to the Berge to somersethouse	001 00 00
	to Lord Bristols Gardner presented orange flowrs	001 01 08

31 Possibly Suthrey House in Mortlake.

32 Manuel.

33 Woolwich.

	for thre boats	000 15 00
18	Laid out by Mr porter	001 04 00
	for pen Inke and paper	000 10 00
	to a man sent about the fire	001 01 08
20	to Lady Northumberlands Gardner	001 01 08
22	to Lady Manchesters man presented orang flowrs	001 01 08
24	to Lady Northumberlands Gardner	001 01 08
27	to Lady Northumberlands Gardner	001 01 08
	to Lady Arlintons Butler	001 01 08
29[34]	to the violin Musique as per bill	010 00 00
	to yor Maties footmen	003 00 00
		210 07 10

[recto] 14r

1676	**Brought from the other Syd**	**210 07 10**
2 June	to the footmen Runing mony	002 00 00
	to Lady Northumberlands Gardner	001 01 08
	to the Gardner of somersethouse	001 01 08
	for Colbertin by Mrs Hemden as per bill	006 02 00
	to the Berge to somersethouse	001 00 00
3	to Lady fingalls[35] Cristning	021 15 00
5	to the footmen Runing mony to Hamton court	002 00 00
	Laid out by Mr Roper	003 05 03
	Laid out by Mr Slaughter at Ham	006 13 00
	Laid out by Mr Sands	002 13 06
	to Lord Bristols Gardner presented orange flowrs	001 01 09
6	fees & Charges at the Receit of one hundred pounds for this Month	003 15 00

34 Charles II's birthday – he was 46.

35 Finghall's.

12	to the Countesse of oxfords man presented orang flowrs	001 01 09
	to Lord Bristols Gardner presented orang flowrs	001 01 09
	to Anne Caple for fruite to Barn ellms	004 05 06
	for a boat to Barn ellms	000 10 00
	to Lady Northumberlands Gardner	001 01 09
	to Mrs Davis at Barn ellms	005 08 04
	for an other boat to Barn ellms	000 10 00
	to yo[r] Ma[ties] Berges to Barn ellms	003 00 00
	for a hired Berge with provisions	002 00 00
	to the dutchesse of Richmons man	001 01 08
		282 17 05

[verso] 14v

1676	**Brought from the other Syd**	**282 17 05**
13 June	Laid out by Mr Roche	000 14 00
	for thre boats to somersethouse	000 10 00
15	for thre boats to somersethouse	000 10 00
	to a man sent for yo[r] Ma[ties] Boat	000 02 06
	Laid out by Mr Stevens	000 16 00
16	for thre boats to somersethouse	000 10 00
	to Lady Mardans man	001 01 08
18	to Mr Charleton for boats as per bill	010 02 06
	Laid out by Mrs Hemden	001 05 00
22	to Mr Charleton for boats as per bill	005 08 00
	for a Baskit of cheris	001 01 08
	to Lord Bristols gardner	001 01 08
25	for five boats as per bill	001 10 00
27	to Mr Roe for Birds as per bill	010 00 00
	to Lady Arlintons Butler	001 01 08
28	to Mrs Cheret as per bill	012 08 00
30	for a boat to the tryall	000 02 06
	to a man Caried the blew Cloath	000 05 00

	to Lady Arlintons page	001 01 08
	to yor Maties Berges	001 10 00
3	to Lord Bristols Gardner	001 01 08
4 July	fees & Charges at the Receit of one hundred pounds for this Month	003 15 00
	to Mrs pingon[36] as per bill	044 02 00
5	for a boat to Lady peterbroughs	000 05 00
		383 03 05

[recto] 15r

1676	**Brought from the other Syd**	**383 03 05**
6 July	to Mr Halsall as per bill	019 07 00
	to the dutchesse of ports-mouthsman presented ortolans	001 01 08
	to Lady peterbroughs man presented tubros	001 01 08
7	to Mr Jonson as per bill	002 15 06
10	to Lord Bristols Gardner	001 01 08
	to Sir Robert Howards Gardner	001 01 08
11	for foure boats to somersethouse	001 00 00
	for sleues & Rufles by Lady Tuck[37]	002 10 00
	for a baskit of friute at Heigh parke	001 01 08
	for thre fans by Lady Bellings	004 00 00
12	to Lady Northumberlands Gardner	001 01 08
	for thre boats to somersethouse	000 10 00
13	for thre boats to somersethouse	000 10 00
	to tery the waterman presented Mulberis	000 10 00
19	to the Berges to somersethouse	001 10 00
20	to the Berge to somersethouse	001 00 00
21	to the Berge to somersethouse	001 00 00
	to Mr fowle for a sweetwaterpot as per	007 10 00
22	to the Berge to somersethouse	001 00 00

36 Pinzon.

37 Tuke.

	to Lord Bristols gardner	001 01 08
23	to the Berge to somersethouse	001 00 00
	to Mr Charleton as per bill	005 07 00
	Laid out by Mr Steuens	001 04 00
24	to the Berge to somersethouse	001 00 00
		442 08 07

[verso] 15v

1676	**Brought from the other Syd**	**442 08 07**
25 July	for a Baskit of fruite	001 01 08
	to the Berge to somersethouse	001 00 00
26	to the Berge to somersethouse	001 00 00
27	to the Berge to somersethouse	001 00 00
30	to Lord Bristols gardner	001 01 08
3 August	fees & Charges at the Receit of one hundred pounds for this Month	003 15 00
	to the Berge to somersethouse	001 00 00
6	to the Berge to somersethouse	001 00 00
12	to Lady Northumberlands Gardner	001 01 08
	to the Berges to somersethouse	001 10 00
14	to Mr Noris[38] as per bill	010 00 00
	to Mr Jonson as per bill	001 05 06
	to Mr Caries[39] man presented a staig	002 03 08
15	to Mrs foran as per bill	002 13 06
17	to Mrs dodson by Sir Richard Bellings	010 00 00
	to the Berges to somersethouse	001 10 00
18	to Mrs devet as per bill	021 07 06
	Laid out by Mrs Hemden	001 11 00
21	to Mrs More[40] as per bill	005 00 00
	to the Berges to somersethouse	001 10 00
24	to the Berges to Lambeth	001 10 00

38 Norris.
39 Cary's.
40 Mors.

	for boats to Lambeth	000 05 00
	to the footmen Runing mony to Greenwich	002 00 00
	Laid out by Mr Slaughter	003 05 00
		519 19 09

[recto] 16r

1676	**Brought from the other Syd**	**519 19 09**
29 August	to a Chaireman	000 02 06
	Laid out by Mrs Hemden	000 10 00
	to Lady Scrops man	001 01 08
	to a gardner presented Narsices[41]	001 00 00
5 Septembr	fees & Charges at the Receit of one hundred pounds for the Month	003 15 00
	Laid out by Mr Steuens	000 07 06
	Laid out by Mrs Hemden	000 05 00
9	to Mr Semson as per bill	005 00 00
	to Lady Scrops man	000 10 00
11	fees & Charges at the Receit of one hundred pounds for the Month of october nixt[42]	003 15 00
	to a porter	000 01 00
13	to the footmen Runing mony to Audleyend	004 00 00
	to the page of the Bakstairs sent befor	000 10 00
	paid by the way by Mr Halsall	002 11 06
	for watching the Coatches all night	000 05 00
14	to the Musique at Audleyend	005 00 00
	to the footmen Runing mony to Ewston[43]	002 00 00
	to the page of the Bakestairs	000 10 00
	to Lord Arlingtons groome for a gyd	001 01 10

41 Narcissus.
42 Next.
43 Euston.

15	to Thetford musique	003 00 00
	to the footmen Runing mony	002 00 00
16	to the footmen Runing mony	002 00 00
		559 05 09

[verso] 16v

1676	**Brought from the other Syd**	**559 05 09**
17 Septembr	to the footmen Runing mony	002 00 00
18	to the footmen Runing mony	002 00 00
19	to the footmen Runing mony	002 00 00
20	to the footmen Runing mony	002 00 00
	to Lord Arlintons Keeper	005 09 02
	to Mrs Dickison[44] as per bill	005 00 00
	to the Musique from Epswich[45]	003 00 00
23	to the gardner at Bery[46] presented fruite	002 00 00
	to the footmen Runing mony	002 00 00
24	to the poore of Bery	010 00 00
	to the poore of Thetford	010 00 00
	to the footmen Runing mony	002 00 00
25	to Lord Arlingtons seruants	200 00 00
	to the poore of Ewston	005 00 00
	to the Kings Musique	020 00 00
	to Lord Arlingtons Groome to newmarkit[47]	001 01 09
	to yor Maties footmen to Audleyend	002 00 00
	to the page of the Bakstairs	000 10 00
	to a man with drops[48] from Ewston	000 10 00
26[49]	for watching the Coatches	000 05 00
	to the womane at the Bakstairs	001 01 10

44 Dickenson.
45 Ipswich.
46 Bury St Edmunds.
47 New Market.
48 Uncertain meaning.
49 Saturday.

	to Lady Suffolkes seruants	020 00 00
	to the poore	005 00 00
	to the vnder Houskeeper	008 00 00
		870 03 06

[recto] 17r

1676	**Brought from the other Syd**	**870 03 06**
26 Septembr	Laid out by the pages of the Bakestairs	000 14 00
	Laid out by Mr Slaughter	000 08 00
	to the Musique from Cambridge	003 00 00
	Laid out by Mr Steuens	001 01 10
	to the footmen Runing mony to London	004 00 00
	to the pages of the Bakstairs	000 10 00
	Laid out by Mr Halsall	000 18 06
	to a womane called Kathrine by Mr Sands	001 01 10
13 Octobr	to Mr winwoods garner presented Graps	002 03 08
	to the portingalls Embassadors footman	001 00 00
14	Laid out by Mrs Hemden	001 02 00
16	to Mrs Cheret as per bill	028 04 06
	to the dutchesse of Richemons man	001 01 09
	to Mr smith yeoman of the wagons as per	005 09 00
	to Mr Jonson as per bill	002 08 00
19	to Mrs Nun for halfe a years Allowance due at Michaelmas last	010 00 00
20	to Mon^s le Noire as per bill	013 16 00
	for pen Inke and paper	000 10 00
21	to the portingall Embassadors Chairmen	002 00 00
26	to the portingall Embassadors Chairmen	002 00 00
	to Lady Northumberlands Gardner	001 00 00
31	fees & Charges at the Receit of thre hundred pounds	011 05 00
		963 17 07

[verso] 17v

1676	**Brought from the other syd**	**963 17 07**
2 Novembr	to Sir Richard Bellings man	001 01 09
	fees & Charges at the Receit of one hundred pounds for this Month	003 15 00
	to old Mr Bure as per bill	006 00 00
3	to Mr Bridgwater for a siluer petecot as per bill	024 14 06
4	to Lady peterbrough as per bill	018 00 00
	to Mr Benet as per bill	006 16 06
	to Mon^s le fever as per bill	005 08 00
	to Lady francis Kytlys Cristning	021 15 00
	to Mrs Chase man	001 01 08
15[50]	to Lady Mardans man presented a nosgy	001 01 08
	to Lady Northumberlands Gardner	001 00 00
	to yor Maties Robs feast	005 00 00
	to the violin Musique as per bill	020 00 00
	to the wind Musique & Recorders	005 00 00
	to the Harper	001 00 00
	to yor Maties footmen	003 00 00
	to the Kings footmen	002 00 00
	to the ducks footmen	002 00 00
	to the dutchesse footmen	002 00 00
	to yor Maties Coatchmen	003 00 00
	to the Kings Coatchmen	002 00 00
	to the Kings trompets	006 00 00
		1105 11 08

[recto] 18r

1676	**Brought from the other Syd**	**1105 11 08**
15 Novembr	to the droms	0003 00 00

50 Catherine’s birthday – she was 38.

	to the ducks Trompets	0003 00 00
	to the Litermen & Chairemen	0002 00 00
	to the somptermen	0001 00 00
	to the grooms	0002 00 00
	to the master of yor Maties Berge	0001 00 00
	to the violin in ordinary	0001 00 00
	to the Groome botleman	0000 02 06
	to the ducks violin Musique	0010 00 00
	to the yeomans of the Gard	0002 00 00
22	to Mr Clarke as per bill	0001 00 06
30	to the footman presented St Andreus Crose	0001 00 00
1 decembr	to thre Children at a Birth	0005 08 09
6	fees & Charges at the Receit of one hundred pounds for this Month	0003 15 00
8	to Mr pawlett[51] as per bill	0018 00 00
	to Lady Lovles woman with a present	0005 08 04
	to Lady Arlingtons page	0001 01 08
12	to Mr Lightfoot as per bill	0010 16 06
	to Mrs Hemden for worke done Extraordenary as per bill	0010 00 00
	Laid out by Mr Steuens	0001 03 00
		1188 07 11

[verso] 18v

1676	**Brought from the other Syd**	**1188 07 11**
20 decembr	to Mrs pingon as per bill	0022 14 00
	to Mrs Chaseman	0001 01 00
21	to Mrs Hegeson as per bill	0005 00 00
	to the portingall Embassadors Chairmen	0002 00 00
25	to the yeoman of the Gard at somersethouse	0001 01 08
	to Lady Scrops man	0001 01 08

51 Paulet.

	to Mr Loft that was tryed for his life as per bill	0005 00 00
28	to Mrs ferand as per bill	0007 03 00
	Laid out by Mr Clarke	0000 18 06
1 Janr	to the violin Musique	0020 00 00
	to the wind musique & Recorders	0006 00 00
	to the violin in ordenary	0001 00 00
	to the Harper	0001 00 00
	to the Queenes Master Cooke	0005 00 00
	to his man	0001 00 00
	to the Kings Master Cooke	0005 00 00
	to his man	0001 00 00
	to Queenes Coatchmen	0010 00 00
	to Queenes postilions	0003 00 00
	to the Queenes footmen	0010 00 00
	to the Kings Coatchmen	0005 00 00
	to the Groomes of the stables	0004 00 00
	to the Litermen & Chairemen	0005 00 00
		1311 08 05

[recto] 19r

1676[52]	**Brought from the other Syd**	**1311 08 05**
1 Janr	to the somptermen	0002 00 00
	to the Trompets	0006 00 00
	to the dromes	0003 00 00
	to the Gallery keepers	0006 00 00
	to the ducks Trompets	0006 00 00
	to the violine to the ducks Children	0001 00 00
	to the Master of the Queenes Berge	0002 00 00
	to the shoemakersmen	0004 00 00
	to the portingall Baker	0003 00 00
	to the portingall Cooke	0003 00 00

[52] 1677 NS.

	to Mrs Hemden	0010 00 00
	to John Tough	0020 00 00
	to the men that brings the playe bills	0002 03 04
	to the man that brings the Gazetts	0001 01 08
	to Lady Northumberlands Gardner	0001 00 00
	to the Herbwomane	0001 01 08
	to Mr Muray[53] box keeper as per bill	0002 03 04
	to Mr Hill box keeper at the ducks hous[54]	0002 03 04
8	fees & Charges at the Receit of one hundred pounds for this Month	0003 15 00
	Laid out by the pages of the Bakstairs	0000 06 06
17	to Mrs Cherett for one quarter due at Cristmaslast	0016 14 00
	to the portingalls Embassadors Chairmen	0002 00 00
		1409 17 03

[verso] 19v

1676[55]	**Brought form the other Syd**	**1409 17 03**
18 Janr	to Captan day as per bill	0010 16 08
	to Mon[s] duplessy[56] as per bill	0011 15 00
25	to Mr Jonson as per bill	0002 02 06
1 Febr	to Monsieur Gonzone as per bill	0020 00 00
3	fees & Charges at the Receit of one hundred pounds for this present Month	0003 15 00
	to a womane from Bramford	0001 01 08
7	to Mr Smith as per bill	0007 00 00
	for a bottle of oyle for the dogs	0001 10 00
	to the portingall Embassadors Chairmen	0002 00 00
	Laid out by the pages of the Bakstairs	0000 07 00

53 Murray.
54 The theatre used by the Duke’s Company.
55 1677 NS.
56 du Plessy.

	to the Spanish Envois man	0001 01 07
	Laid out by Mrs Hemden	0001 00 00
15	to Mrs Lenthall	0005 07 06
	to Lady Suffolkes page	0001 01 07
22	to Lord Orseris Coatchman & footmen	0002 00 00
	to the portingalls Embassadors Chairmen	0001 00 00
23	to Teags Cristening as per bill	0010 00 00
1 March	to the footman presented St Dauids Leeke	0001 00 00
	for pen Inke and paper	0000 10 00
5	fees & Charges at the Receit of one hundred pounds for this Month	0003 15 00
7	to Mrs Crane as per	0019 18 10
16	to Mr Steuens as per bill	0002 04 06
		1518 14 01

[recto] 20r

1676[57]	**Brought from the other syd**	**1518 14 01**
19 March	to the footman presented St patriks Crose	0001 00 00
	Laid out by Mrs Hemden	0000 10 06
20	to Mr Roche for balme for the dogs	0001 10 00
24	Laid out by Mr picot at Erif[58]	0002 14 00
29	to Mrs Nuns man	0001 00 00
1677 31	for yellow Calleco	0000 10 00
2 April:	to Mrs ferand for a fan as per bill	0006 09 06[59]

Moneis disbursed

from the eight of April: 1676 to the second of April: 1677 **1532 08 01**

57 1677 NS.

58 Erith.

59 Unusually, the total is not placed immediately below this list of figures.

Moneis Receiued

	from the eight of April: 1676 to the second of April: 1677	**1500 00 00**

Remaines due

	from yo[r] Ma[tie] to the Accomptant this second of April: 1677	**0032 08 01**

[verso] 20v

1677	**Repaid my selfe due from the last Acompt**	**032 08 01**
3 April:	fees & Charges at the Receit of one hundred pounds for this present Month	003 15 00
	Laid out by Mrs Hemden	000 10 00
	Laid out by the pages of the Bakstairs	000 07 06
5	to sentris at somersethouse	001 01 07
	to the wardrobmen at somersethouse	001 01 07
8	to Lady Northumberlands Gardner	001 00 00
	to the portingall Embassadors Chairmen	001 00 00
9	to Mr Steuens as per bill	002 03 00
9[60]	to Mr Groome for his mens Areires as per bill	012 00 00
12	to the yeoman of the gard on Mandy thursdy[61]	001 01 07
	to Lady Northumberlands gardner	001 00 00
	to the panthry Butry & Ewry as per bill	002 10 00
15	to Lady Northumberlands gardner at Easter[62]	002 00 00
17	Laid out by Mrs Hemden	001 00 00
22	to Lady Northumberlands gardner	001 00 00
	Laid out by Mr Roche	000 08 06
23	to the violin Musique as per bill	010 00 00
24	to Mrs Nun as per bill	010 00 00

60 Duplication of the date.
61 Maundy Thursday 1677 – 15 April.
62 Easter Sunday 1677 – 18 April.

	to yor Maties footmen the first day to Heighpark	002 00 00
27	to the footmen Runing mony	002 00 00
1 May	to the footmen Runing mony	002 00 00
2	to Mrs Hemden for Mending yor Maties Linen as per bill	030 00 00
7	fees & Charges at the Receit of one hundred pounds for this present Month	003 15 00
		124 01 10

[recto] 21r

1677	**Brought from the other Syd**	**124 01 10**
7 May	to Lady Northumberlands Gardner	001 00 00
	to the footmen Runing mony	002 00 00
8	to Mr Conyers as per bill	005 00 00
9	to the footmen Runing mony	002 00 00
10	to Mrs Cheret as per bill	019 08 00
	to Mr Noris for a pickture from [....]	000 16 00
	Laid out by Mr Steuens	001 17 00
	to the footmen Runing mony	002 00 00
	to a poore womane had her Hog Killed by one of yor Maties Coatches at Chelsy	001 01 07
11	to the footmen Runing mony	002 00 00
	Laid out by father Manwell[63]	003 05 00
16	to the footmen Runing mony	002 00 00
18	to Mr Burke footman as per bill	005 00 00
20	to the footmen Runing mony	002 00 00
23[64]	to yor Maties Berge to somersethouse	001 00 00
	to Lord Montegus man presented veneson	002 03 02
24	to Lady Northumberlands gardner	002 00 00
	to Mrs Story y^r^ Maties dary[65] woman as per bill	035 01 02

63 Manuel.
64 Sunday.
65 Diary.

29	to the footmen <on his Maties> [….][66] Birthday	003 00 00
	to the violin Musique as per bill	010 00 00
30	to the Berge to somersethouse	000 10 00
	for a box by Mr Steuens	000 08 00
2 June	to Lady Arlingtons gardner	003 05 00
	for thre boats to somersethouse	000 17 06
		231 14 03

[verso] 21v

1677	**Brought from the other Syd**	**231 14 03**
3 June	to Lady Northumberlands Gardner	002 00 00
	Laid out by Mr Steuens	000 09 00
4	to Mr Jonson as per bill	003 00 00
7	to Mrs Ann Mor as per bill	001 00 00
	to Lady Bristols Gardner	001 01 07
9	to Mrs Cranmer as per bill	062 12 09
	for canuas smaks[67] petecots and Colbertin quafs[68] by Mrs Hemden	003 00 00
	to Mr Halsall as per bill	070 00 00
	to Sir Richard Bellings for a warant	006 09 06
	fees & Charges at the Receit of ~~one~~ fiue hundred pounds	018 15 00
	to Mr Maugredge dromer as per bill	006 00 00
	for Colbertin quafe Cornet and hood by Mrs Hemden	007 02 00
	to Mr Fisher for the Trompets as per bill	012 00 00
	to Monsieur Le feubre for the ducks Trompets as per bill	009 00 00
	to Mr Smith page of the presence as per bill	006 00 00
	to Mr Cotter as per bill	006 00 00

66 Illegible deletion. Charles II's birthday – he was 47.

67 Smocks.

68 Coifs.

	to Mr Johns as per bill	006 00 00
	to Mr Hilliar as per bill	006 00 00
		458 04 01

[recto] 22r

1677	**Brought from the other Syd**	**458 04 01**
9 June	to Mr Litlemor of the Ewry as per bill	016 00 00
	to Mr Robinson Groome of the great Chamber as per <bill>	006 00 00
	to Mr Low as per bill	006 00 00
	to Mr Goldsbrough[69] as per bill	006 00 00
	to Mr Colby as per bill	006 00 00
	to Mr Hall as per bill	006 00 00
	to Mr person yeoman Hanger as per bill	012 00 00
	to Father Manwell and father Pall as per bill	040 00 00
	to Mrs Cheret as per bill	016 00 00
	for Colbertin sleues & Rufles by Mr^s^ de bord	001 13 06
	to a womane from Bramford presented friute	001 01 07
11	to the footmen Runing mony to filberds[70]	002 00 00
	to the page of the Bakestairs	000 10 00
	to a porter	000 01 00
12	to the servants at filberds	021 11 08
	to the Musique	005 00 00
	to the footmen to Newbery	002 00 00
	to the page of the Bakstairs	000 10 00
	to the Musique by Mr Roper	002 03 02
13	to the House at Newbery	010 00 00
		618 15 00

69 Goldsborow.

70 Philberts House.

[verso] 22v

1677	**Brought from the other Syd**	**618 15 00**
13 June	to the footmen to Malbrough	002 00 00
	to the page of the Bakstairs	000 10 00
	to the House at Malbrough	010 00 00
14	to the footmen to the Bath	002 00 00
	to the page of the Bakstairs	000 10 00
	paid at Laycok whair yo[r] Ma[tie] dined	002 03 02
	to the Musique by Mr Roper	001 01 07
15	to the two Heigh sherifs Trompets	005 00 00
16	to violin Musique	002 00 00
17	to the footmen Runing mony	002 00 00
	Laid out by Major wherwood as per bill	006 07 06
18	to Hoboys from Bristole	002 00 00
	to a man presented verses	001 01 07
	to the dutchesse of portsmouths man presented orange flowrs	001 01 07
21	to the Musique from Wells	002 00 00
	to Lord Downs man presented veneson	002 03 02
	Laid out by Mr Halsall	001 15 00
22	to a set of Musique	001 00 00
	to the Marquis of wosters man	002 03 02
	Laid out by Mrs Hemden	000 18 00
23	to Lord Downs man presented veneson	002 03 02
	to Lady Hamiltons man by Lady Bellinge	002 03 02
		670 16 01

[recto] 23r

1677	**Brought from the other Syd**	**670 16 01**
24 June	to Mr Smith as per bill	004 03 06
	to Mr Jonson as per bill	002 00 00
	to two sets of Musique	002 00 00
26	Laid out to Mr Roper	003 04 09
	to the footmen Runing mony	002 00 00

	Laid out by Mrs Hemden	001 05 00
27	to thre sets of Musique	002 10 00
	to the footmen Runing mony	002 00 00
	to the Marquis of wosters man	002 03 02
	to a poore man with a petition	001 00 00
28	to a set of trompets by Mr Steuens	002 03 02
30	to Lord downs man with veneson	002 03 02
	to a set of Musique	000 10 00
2 July	to the Marquis of wosters man with foulle	001 01 07
	to the footmen Runing mony	002 00 00
3	to the Marquis of wosters man by Mr Stevens	002 03 02
	Laid out by Mr Roper	000 10 00
	to a set of Musique	001 00 00
	to a Lame solger	001 00 00
	to the footmen Runing mony	002 00 00
4	Laid out by Mr Steuens	001 01 07
		708 15 02

[verso] 23v

1677	**Brought from the other Syd**	**708 15 02**
6 July	to the Marquis of wosters man	002 03 02
	to an other Lame solger	001 00 00
	to a poore womane	001 00 00
7	to Lord downs man with veneson	002 03 02
8	to the footmen Runing mony	002 00 00
	to a Herper	000 10 00
	to a poore old man	001 00 00
	Laid out by Mrs Hemden	000 18 00
10	to the Marquis of wosters <man> by Mr Stevens	002 03 02
12	to the footmen to Bristoll	002 00 00
	Laid out by the pages of the Bakstairs	000 17 06

13	to Bristols Trompets	005 00 00
	Laid out by Mr Rogers	003 04 09
	Expenses to Bristole for Money	001 10 00
	to a Harper by Mr Stevens	002 03 02
	to Lord downs man with veneson	002 03 02
14	to Mr Mead for Lodgings as per bill	069 15 00
	Laid out by Mr Roper	002 03 02
	to Mr Kirkton for the yeomans of the Gard as per bill	024 00 00
	to Mr Colin for a Bathing tub as per bill	003 15 00
	Laid out by Mrs Hemden	001 18 06
		840 02 11

[recto] 24r

1677	**Brought from the other Syd**	**840 02 11**
14 July	to a poore man	002 03 02
	to Mr Masters sergan[71] of the Bath as per bill	020 00 00
	to the Gyds	010 00 00
	to the man keept the puomp	001 00 00
	to doctor peirce for Lodging as per bill	100 00 00
	to the seruants	020 00 00
	to a man presented friute	001 01 07
	Laid out by Mr Roche	000 18 00
	to Mr Shore for the Gard Trompets as per bill	010 00 00
	to a poore old womane	001 00 00
	to the footmen to Badmenton	002 00 00
	Laid out by Major whorwood	002 08 00
	to Mr whitock as per bill	002 00 00
	to Mr Makerty[72] as per bill	003 00 00
	to Mr Tailour as per bill	005 00 00

71 Uncertain meaning, possibly either surgeon or sergeant of the British.
72 MacCarthie.

	Laid out by Mr Porter	001 01 07
	to the Bellman	000 10 00
16	to a woman presented friute	001 01 07
	Laid out by the way to Malbrough[73] by Mr Hallsall	008 12 06
17	to violin Musique at Malbrough	001 00 00
	to a set of Hoboys	001 00 00
	to the Howse	010 00 00
		1043 19 04

[verso] 24v

1677	**Brought from the other Syd**	**1043 19 04**
17 July	to Lord Creuens[74] Gardner	0001 01 07
	Laid out by Mr Hallsall at Newbery whair yor Matie dined	0006 12 00
	Laid out by the way to Redin[75] by Mr Halsall	0002 08 02
18	to the Musique at Redin	0002 00 00
	to the Howse	0010 00 00
	Laid out at Colbrook[76] whair yor Matie dined by Mr Mead	0006 19 06
	to the footmen from the Bath to London as per bill	0008 00 00
	to the pages of the Bakstairs	0001 10 00
	to the footman Loak to Momper[77]	0000 10 00
19	to a womane from Braimford with friute	0001 01 07
	Laid out by Mr Mead as per bill	0001 15 00
	Laid out by Mr Stevens as per bill	0001 19 00
	Laid out by Mr Whorewood	0002 14 00
	to Mr Smith yeoman of the wagons as per bill	0001 18 06

73 Marlborough.
74 Craven.
75 Reading.
76 Colnbrook.
77 Possibly short for Mompesson.

	to Mr Jonson as per bill	0002 02 00
	Laid out by Mrs Hemden	0001 13 00
	Laid out by Mr Porter	0002 03 02
	for pen Inke & paper	0000 10 00
24	to Lady Mardans man	0001 01 07
	for Colbertin Cufs	0001 00 00
		1100 18 05

[recto] 25r

1677	**Brought from the other Syd**	**1100 18 05**
26 July	fees & Charges at the Receit of thre hundred sixteen pounds ten shillings	0017 05 00
	Paid to seuerall people of qualitys Coatchmen Chairemen & footmen that waited of yor Matie in the yeares of 1670: 1671: 1672 as per bill	0056 00 00
27	to Mr Charleton for boats as per bill	0004 02 06
	to Mr Haris as per bill	0002 00 00
31	fees & Charges at the Receit of one hundred pounds for this present Month	0003 15 00
3 August	to Mrs ferand for french Riben	0004 00 00
10	to the footmen Runing mony	0002 00 00
	to yor Maties dary womane	0001 01 08
	to the portinall Embassadors Chairemen	0001 00 00
	for a paire sleeues	0002 10 00
12	to the footmen Runing mony	0002 00 00
14	to Mr Jonson as per bill	0000 18 06
	to a womane presented friute	0001 01 08
	Laid out by Mrs Hemden	0001 06 00
	to the footmen Runing mony	0002 00 00
15	fees & Charges at the Receit of one hundred pounds for this present Month	0003 15 00
	for boats to Chelsy	0001 00 00
18	to Mrs Hemden for worke done Extraordinary as per bill	0010 00 00
		1216 13 09

[verso] 25v

1677	**Brought from the other Syd**	**1216 13 09**
18 August	to the footmen Runing mony	0002 00 00
	to Mr Gibs Lady Northumberlands Gardner as per bill	0004 00 00
	for a fan by Mrs Crane	0002 03 04
19	to the footmen Runing mony	0002 00 00
22	to Mrs pingon as per bill	0051 02 00
	for boats to somersethouse	0000 10 00
	to the portingall Embassadors Chairmen	0002 00 00
	to the man from Barnet presented Graps	0001 01 08
26	to the footmen Runing mony	0002 00 00
27	to Mrs debord as per bill	0024 00 06
	to a sentry	0001 01 08
4 Septembr	for boats to Chelsy	0001 00 00
	to Lady Killigrew as per bill	0015 02 00
5	fees & Charges at the Receit of one hundred pounds for this present Month	0003 15 00
	to Lady Mardans man	0001 01 08
	to the Marquis of wosters man by Mr Roper	0002 03 04
9	Laid out by Mr Roche	0000 16 00
	for a boat to somersethouse	0000 05 00
	to the footmen Runing mony	0002 00 00
12	to Mr woodward as per bill	0001 00 00
	to Mr Caple as per bill	0007 10 00
	to a solger at somersethouse	0001 01 08
21	to the footmen Runing mony	0002 00 00
23	to the footmen Runing mony	0002 00 00
		1348 07 07

[recto] 26r

1677	**Brought from the other Syd**	**1348 07 07**

30 septembr	to Mrs Nore for one quarter & two weeks due this michaelmas[78] as per bill	0001 10 00
1 octobr	to Mrs Nun for halfe a yeares Allowance due at Michaelmas last as per bill	0010 00 00
	Laid out by Mrs Hemden	0001 00 00
	to Mr Rogers man presented friute	0001 01 08
4	to Lady Northumberlands gardner	0002 00 00
5	to Mr winwoods gardner presented graps	0002 03 06
9	fees & Charges at the Receit of one hundred pounds for this Month	0003 15 00
	Laid out by Mr steuens as per bill	0000 19 00
10	giuen at the southaries[79]	0021 15 00
	to the Musique	0001 01 08
	to fiue boats that waited thair	0001 05 00
	to the footmen Runing mony	0002 00 00
	to the Berges to Lambeth	0001 10 00
	to boats to & from Lambeth	0000 10 00
12	to Lady Mardans man	0001 01 08[80]
17	to a solger at somersethouse	0001 01 08
	to Lady Tounsend[81] by Lady Teuk[82]	0005 00 00
	Laid out by Mrs Hemden	0000 05 00
24	to Mr Langrish for a mufe as per bill	0006 00 00
3 novembr	to Mr Maginis[83] to Bury John Gordon yor Maties footman as per bill	0010 00 00
		1422 06 09

[verso] 26v

1677	**Brought from the other Syd**	**1422 06 09**

78 29 September.
79 Possibly Suthrey House in Mortlake.
80 0001 01 08 corrected from 0001 00 08.
81 Townshend.
82 Tuke.
83 MacGinnis.

6 Novembr	fees & Charges at the Receit of one hundred pounds for this Month	0003 15 00
10	to Mrs Cheret for one quarter due at Michaelmas last as per bill	0026 07 00
15[84]	to the violine Musique	0020 00 00
	to the wind Musique & Recorders	0005 00 00
	to the Harper	0001 00 00
	to yor Maties footmen	0003 00 00
	to the Kings footmen	0002 00 00
	to the ducks footmen	0002 00 00
	to the dutchesse footmen	0002 00 00
	to yor Maties Coatchmen	0003 00 00
	to the Kings Coatchmen	0002 00 00
	to the Kings trompets	0006 00 00
	to the dromes	0003 00 00
	to the duckes trompets	0003 00 00
	to the Queenes Litermen & Chairemen	0002 00 00
	to the somptermen	0001 00 00
	to the Groomes of the stables	0002 00 00
	to the Master of yor Maties Berge	0001 00 00
	to the violin in ordinary	0001 00 00
	to the Groome botleman	0000 02 06
	to the dukes violine Musique	0010 00 00
		1521 11 03

[recto] 27r

1677	**Brought from the other Syd**	**1521 11 03**
15 Novembr	to the yeomans of the Gard	0002 00 00
16	to yor Maties Robs feast	0005 00 00
	to Lady Northumberlands gardner	0001 00 00
	to the prince of orange trompets	0005 08 09
	to the Herbewomane	0001 01 09

84 Catherine's birthday – she was 39.

17	to Mrs Blyth as per bill	0004 10 00
	to Mrs Crane as per bill	0030 09 00
	to Lady Loueles[85] womane	0005 08 09
	Laid out by Mrs Hemden	0000 11 06
28	to Mr Lenoire as per bill	0006 17 06
30	to the footman presented St Androws Crose	0001 00 00
4 decembr	fees & Charges at the Receit of one hundred pounds for this Month	0003 15 00
6	to Mrs ferand as per bill	0005 10 00
7	to Mr Thomas as per bill	0012 00 00
	Laid out by Mrs Hemden	0001 00 00
8	to Lady Northumberlands gardner	0002 00 00
12	to Mrs Crane as per bill	0006 00 00
	to a womane w^{t} Eyle pye from Chatham	0002 03 06
13	to Mrs Jonson as per bill	0002 19 00
	to Mr Montegus man w^{t} a present from france	0005 08 09
		1625 14 09

[verso] 27v

1677	**Brought from the other Syd**	**1625 14 09**
14 decembr	Laid out by Mrs Hemden	0000 08 00
	for pen Inke & paper	0000 10 00
26	to Mrs More for one quarter due at Cristmas[86] last as per bill	0001 06 00
	to the yeomans of the Gard	0001 01 08
	to the womane that Lookes to the Lodgings at somersethouse	0005 08 09
27	to the french man that cut yor Maties haire	0005 08 09
first Janr	to the volins Musique as per bill	0020 00 00
	to the windmusique & Recorders	0006 00 00

85 Lovelace's.

86 25 December.

	to the violine in ordinary	0001 00 00
	to the Harper	0001 00 00
	to yor Maties Master Cooke	0005 00 00
	to his man	0001 00 00
	to the Kings Master Cooke	0005 00 00
	to his man	0001 00 00
	to yor Maties Coatchman	0010 00 00
	to yor Maties postilions	0003 00 00
	to yor Maties footmen	0010 00 00
	to the <kings> Coatchmen	0005 00 00
	to the Groomes of the stables	0004 00 00
	to the Litermen & Chairemen	0005 00 00
	to the semptermen	0002 00 00
		1718 17 11

[recto] 28r

1677[87]	**Brought from the other syd**	**1718 17 11**
1 Janr	to the Kings trompets	0006 00 00
	to the dromes	0003 00 00
	to the Gallery keepers	0006 00 00
	to the ducks trompets	0006 00 00
	to the violine to the ducks Children	0001 00 00
	to the Master of yor Maties Berge	0002 00 00
	to the shoemakersmen	0004 00 00
	to the portingall Baker	0003 00 00
	to the portingall Cooke	0003 00 00
	to Mrs Hemden	0010 00 00
	to John Tough	0020 00 00
2	to Lady Northumberlands Gardner	0001 00 00
	to the man that brings the Gazets	0001 01 09
	to a womane from Colbrook presented pudins	0002 03 06

87 1678 NS.

	to Mr Hailes Boxkeeper as per bill	0002 03 06
	to Mr Hill boxkeeper as per bill	0002 03 06
	to the Herbwomane	0001 01 09
	to the men that brings the play bills	0002 03 06
3	fees & Charges at the Receit of one hundred pounds for this Month	0003 15 00
6	Laid out by Mrs Hemden	0000 14 00
8	to Mr Lightfoot as per bill	0011 04 00
		1810 08 05

[verso] 28v

1677[88]	**Brought from the other Syd**	**1810 08 05**
25 Janr	to Mrs Cheret for one quarter due at Cristmas last as per bill	0015 11 00
	to the violins Musique at somer-sethouse as per bill	0010 00 00
	to yor Maties footmen first time to Heighparke	0002 00 00
2 Febr	to Lady Mardans <man> presented a nosgy	0001 01 08
8	fees & Charges at the Receit of one hundred pounds for this Month	0003 15 00
15	to Lady Northumberlands gardner	0000 10 00
	Laid out by Mr Steuens	0000 17 00
1 March	to the footman presented a Leeke	0001 00 00
5	fees & Charges at the Receit of one hundred pounds for this Month	0003 15 00
7	to Mrs Jordan as per bill	0005 00 00
	to Mr Metlans man w^t^ <a> present from the dutchesse of Cleueland from france	0005 08 04
	to Mrs Crane as per bill	0008 00 00
9	to Mr Noris for a pictur fram	0000 15 00
13	to Mr Steuens as per bill	0006 12 00

88 1678 NS.

17	to the footman presented St Patriks Crose	0001 00 00
	to Mrs pingon as per bill	0027 07 00
	to Mrs Nuns man	0001 00 00
		1904 00 05

[recto] 29r

1677[89]	**Brought from the other Syd**	**1904 00 05**
26 March	to Mrs Nore for one quarter due at our Lady Day[90] last	0001 06 00
28	to the yeoman of the Gard on Mandy thursday[91]	0001 01 08
	to Lady Northumberlands Gardner	0001 00 00
	To Mr Earnle[92] for the pantry & Ewry as per bill	0002 10 00
30	to Lady Northumberlands Gardner at Easter[93]	0001 00 00
	to Mr Jonson as per bill	0004 05 00
	to Mrs Nun for halfe a yeare due at our Lady <day> last as per bill	0010 00 00

Moneis disbursed

from the second of April: 1677 to the first of April: 1678 **1925 03 01**

Moneis Receiued

from the second of April: 1677 to the first of April: 1678 **1916 10 00**

Remaines due

from yor Matie to the Accomptant the first of April: 1678 **0008 13 01**

89 1678 NS.

90 25 March.

91 Maundy Thursday 1678 – 7 April.

92 Ernle.

93 Easter Sunday 1678 – 10 April.

[verso] 29v

1678		lib s d
4 April	fees & Charges at the Receit of one hundred pounds for this present Month	003 15 00
	Laid out by Mrs Crane	002 03 04
	Laid out by Mrs Hemden	000 10 00
	to Lady Scrops man	001 01 08
	to yo[r] Ma[ties] Berge to westminster	001 10 00
8	to Lady Northumberlands Gardner	001 00 00
	to Mr Reynolds as per bill	002 03 04
12	to the door keepers of the parliament	002 00 00
	to Mrs Cheseman	001 01 08
	for a paire of stands by Lady wyche	001 10 00
19	to Mr Morgan for the Map of London as per <bill>	010 00 00
	to the Late Queenes old footman	001 01 08
20	to the portingall Embassadors Chairmen	002 00 00
	to a poore womane with Child	001 01 08
23	to Mr Brokhall to the violins Musique as per bill	010 00 00
	to the footmen Runing mony	002 00 00
29	to Mrs deuett as per bill	012 00 00
	to the Late Queenes old footman	001 01 08
	Laid out by Mr Steuens	001 10 00
2 May	to Mrs Hemden as per bill	030 00 00
	Laid out by Mrs Crane as per bill	005 00 00
3	fees & Charges at the Receit of one hundred pounds for this present Month	003 15 00
7	to the footmen Runing mony	002 00 00
		098 05 00

[recto] 30r

1678	**Brought from the other syd**	**098 05 00**
9 May	to Lady Northumberlands gardner	001 00 00
	to Mrs Nunns man	001 00 00
10	for boats to & from somersethouse	001 05 00

	to Mrs Story as per bill	023 03 00
11	for boats to somersethouse	000 12 06
	to Lady Arlintons man	001 00 00
15	to the footmen Runing mony	002 00 00
	to Lady Northumberlands gardner	000 10 00
16	for boats to somersethouse	001 05 00
	Laid out by Mrs Hemden	001 00 00
	Laid out by Mr Steuens	000 13 06
	for pen Ink & paper	000 10 00
	to Mr Noris for two pictur frams	002 00 00
18	to Lady Northumberlands gardner	001 00 00
22	to Mrs Cheret as per bill	018 00 00
	to Mr Makartan[94] as per bill	005 00 00
23	to Mrs Cranmer as per bill	061 16 03
	mor laid out by Mrs Cranmer	000 02 06
	for boats to somersethouse	000 10 00
	to the footmen Runing mony	002 00 00
26	Laid out by Mr Picot	001 05 00
	to Lord Montegus man with veneson	002 03 04
	Laid out by father Mannell for virginells	002 03 04
	to a man sent with a kid to somersethouse	000 02 06
29[95]	to the violine Musique as per bill	010 00 00
	to yor Maties footmen	003 00 00
		241 06 11

[verso] 30v

1678	**Brought from the other Syd**	**241 06 11**
2 June	to Lady Northumberlands gardner	001 00 00
	to Lady Arlintons footmen	001 00 00

94 MacCarthie.

95 Charles II's birthday – he was 48.

4	fees & Charges at the Receit of one hundred pounds for this present Month	003 15 00
	Laid out by Mrs Hemden at the wardrob	000 10 00
	for boats	000 15 00
6	to Lady Northumberlands gardner	001 10 00
9	to the Berges to putny	003 00 00
	to the dutchesse of southamptons man	001 01 08
12	to Mrs Hayfeild[96] as per bill	002 00 00
	Laid out by Mrs Hemden	000 10 00
	for boats	000 15 00
	to Lady Bristols gardner with orangflours	001 01 08
	to the portingall Embassadors Coatchman at putny	001 00 00
13	for boats	000 10 00
18	to Mrs Crane as per bill	006 10 00
19	to Lady Northumberlands gardner	001 00 00
20	for boats	001 10 00
	to Lady Bristols gardner	001 01 08
	Laid out by Mr Steuens	000 14 06
	to the dutchesse of southamptons man	001 01 08
	to Lady Rusells man with orangflowrs	001 01 08
25	to Lady Bristols garner	001 01 08
	Laid out by Mrs Hemden	000 10 00
26	to Mrs Nor dew at Midsomer[97] last	001 06 00
		275 12 05

[recto] 31r

1678	**Brought from the other Syd**	**275 12 05**
1 July	to Lady Bristols gardner	001 01 08
	to Mr Charleton for boats as per bill	003 17 06

96 Hayfield.
97 24 June.

4	fees & Charges at the Receit of one hundred pounds for this present month	003 15 00
	to Mrs Hemden for one quarter for threed and niedles due at Midsomerlast	001 00 00
6	to Lady Bristols gardner	001 01 08
7	to Mr Charleton for boats as per bill	010 07 06
8	to Lady scrops gardner by Mr picot	001 01 08
	to the portingalls Embassadors man by Mr Steuens	001 01 08
12	to Lady Bristols gardner	001 01 08
	to Lady Arlintons gardner	001 01 08
16	to Mrs Cheret as per bill	013 02 00
17	Laid out by Lady Billings as per bill	010 16 08
	to Lady Arlingtons Chairmen & footmen	002 00 00
18	to Lady Bristols gardner	001 01 08
	to Mr Charleton as per bill	014 05 00
	to the thifecatcher by Mr Roche	001 01 08
	to the Late Queenes old footman	001 01 08
24	to Mr Browne as per bill	002 00 00
	for boats	001 00 00
	to Lady Bristols gardner	001 00 00
	to the portingall Embassadors man with birds	001 01 08
	to Mr Johns for thre botles of Essence	000 12 00
		350 04 09

[verso] 31v

1678	**Brought from the other Syd**	**350 04 09**
25 July	to Lady Arlingtons Chairemen & footmen	002 00 00
	for tape for new Lenen by Mrs Hemden	001 00 00
27	to Lady Arlintons Chairemen & footmen	002 00 00
29	to Mr Jonsen as per bill	001 12 06

	for boats by Mr Roper	000 15 00
2 August	to Lady Arlingtons Chairemen & footmen to & from St James	002 00 00
	to father odaly as per bill	005 00 00
7	fees & Charges at the Receit of one hundred pounds for this month	003 15 00
	to the footmen Runing mony	002 00 00
	for pen Inke & paper	000 10 00
	to the Gardner at St James by Mr Heruey	001 01 08
12	to Lady Arlingtons Chairemen & footmen	002 00 00
14	for boats	001 05 00
	to the Kings gardners man	001 01 08
	to Lady Arlintons garner by Mr Picot	002 03 04
	to Mrs ferand for Riben as per bill	003 16 00
15	for boats to somersethouse	000 10 00
16	to the footmen Runing mony to winsor	002 00 00
	to the pages of the bakstairs	000 10 00
	for bringing yor Maties boats & porters	002 08 00
	to Mr Jonson as per bill	002 05 00
	for bringing yor Maties Chaire	001 01 08
		390 19 07

[recto] 32r

1678	**Brought from the other Syde**	**390 19 07**
16 August	for a boat with flowrepots & porters	001 17 06
	for boats by Mr Steuens	002 10 00
17	to the hoboys	002 03 04
	to the footmen Runing mony	002 00 00
	Laid out by Mr Roche	000 18 00
	Laid out by Mr Porter	001 01 08
19	to the footmen Runing mony	002 00 00
	to Mr Porters man presented Cheese	001 00 00
20	to the footmen Runing mony	002 00 00

	to the violins Musique by Mr Brokhall as per bill	010 00 00
	to a groome sent to London	001 00 00
	to Lady Arlintons Butler	001 01 08
25	to the footmen Runing mony	002 00 00
	to a womane presented friute	001 00 00
27	to the footmen Runing mony	002 00 00
	to Lady Arlintons men with flowrpots	001 00 00
	Laid out by Mr Roche	000 14 00
	for a boat by Mr Richards	000 05 00
	to Kinsinton gardner with friute	001 01 08
28	Laid out by Mr Rowland as per bill	004 00 00
	for Anglerods and hooks	001 00 00
	to the footmen Runing mony	002 00 00
		433 12 05

[verso] 32v

1678	**Brought from the other Syd**	**433 12 05**
29 August	for flowrs from garnsy[98]	002 03 04
	to a groome sent to London	001 00 00
	Laid out by Mr Roper	002 08 04
	to Lady Arlintons Butler	001 01 08
	to Lady Arlintons footman sent for water	000 10 00
	Laid out by Mr Steuens as per bill	001 11 08
	Laid out by Mrs Cranmer	002 03 04
	to Lady Arlintons man presented a house Kye by Sir John Arondall	002 03 04
31	Laid out by Lady Arlinton at Cranburn Lodg	003 05 00
	to the footmen Runing mony	002 00 00
	to the gardner by Mr Steuens	001 01 08
	to Lady Arlintons Butler	001 01 08

98 Guernsey.

1 Septembr	to the footmen Runing mony	002 00 00
2	to the footmen Runing mony	002 00 00
	Laid out by Mr Seares at fearnhill[99]	005 08 04
	to Mr Charleton as per bill	008 15 00
	Laid out by Mr Roche	001 01 08
	to Lady Arlintons page	001 01 08
	to the dutchesse of portsmouths man	001 01 08
4	to the footmen Runing mony	002 00 00
	to Mrs Cheseman	001 01 08
5	to the footmen Runing mony	002 00 00
	Laid out by Lady Bellings as per bill	010 00 00
		491 02 05

[recto] 33r

1678	**Brought from the other Syde**	**491 02 05**
6 Septembr	fees & Charges at the Receit of one hundred pounds for this present Month	003 15 00
	Expenses to London for this mony	000 10 00
	to Mr Anger as per bill	002 00 00
8	Laid out by Lady Arlinton at Cleuedon[100]	005 06 04
	to the footmen Runing mony	002 00 00
	Laid out by Mrs Hemden	001 00 00
	to a man sent for water at Cleuden	000 10 00
10	to the footmen Runing mony	002 00 00
	to Mr winwoods gardner with graps	001 01 08
11	to the footmen Runing mony	002 00 00
	Laid out by Mrs Crane	001 01 08
	Laid out by Mr Steuens	000 16 00
	to the parke keeper presented a Kye	001 01 08
12	to Kinsinton gardner by Mr Steuens	001 01 08
13	to the footmen Runing mony	002 00 00

99 Fernhill.
100 Cliveden.

	for bringing flowrpots from somersethouse	001 05 00
15	to the footmen Runing mony	002 00 00
	Laid out by Mr Sands	001 00 00
	Laid out by Lady Bellings in the forest	003 05 00
16	to Mr Charleton as per bill	007 00 00
	to the footmen Runing mony	002 00 00
	to a man presented graps by Mr Roche	001 01 08
18	to the footmen Runing mony	002 00 00
19	to the footmen Runing mony	002 00 00
		538 18 01

[verso] 33v

1678	**Brought from the other Syde**	**538 18 01**
19 Septembr	to a groome sent from filberd to winsor	000 10 00
	for boats to filberds	001 00 00
	to the Kings violins Musique at filberds	010 00 00
	to a groome sent to bray	000 10 00
20	to the fishermen	002 00 00
	to a man presented graps by Mr Steuens	001 01 08
	to Captane Hampot vpon petition	002 00 00
23	to a Groome sent to London	001 00 00
	Laid out by Mr Seares	001 05 00
24	to Mr Randue Houskeeper as per bill	008 00 00
	to Mr Davis wardrobkeeper as per bill	005 00 00
	to sergant Tapham parkekeper	002 00 00
	to the parkgatkeeper	001 00 00
	to Mr Charleton as per bill	012 07 00
	paid for the Maids of honoure and Mrs Ropers Lodgings as per bill	027 00 00
	Laid out by Sir John Arondall	001 01 08
	to the footmen Runing mony to London	002 00 00
	for bringing yor Maties Chaire to London	001 01 08
	for the fathers Lodgings as per bill	051 06 00
	to the pages of the Bakstairs	000 10 00

	to a set of Musique	002 00 00
	to the fishermen	001 00 00
	to the Keepers of the great parke	002 03 04
	Laid out by Mr Steuens	001 07 06
		676 01 11

[recto] 34r

1678	**Brought from the other Syde**	**676 01 11**
24 Septembr	Laid out by Mr Porter	001 01 08
	Laid out by Mr Seares	001 04 00
	for a boat with Clocks & flowrepots	001 00 00
	Laid out by Mrs Hemden as per bill	008 12 06
	Laid out by John Tough as per bill	012 03 00
26	to the yeoman of the wagons	000 17 06
	to Mr Jonson as per bill	001 07 00
30	to Mrs Mor due now as per bill	001 06 00
	to Mr Lambe as per bill	013 00 00
6 Octobr	to Mr winwoods gardner with graps	002 03 04
	to Mrs Hemden for thred & needles due at Michaelmis[101] last	001 00 00
	to Lady orseries man with a Cheese	001 01 08
	Laid out by Mr Clarke	001 02 00
8	fees & Charges at the Receit of one hundred pounds for this Month	003 15 00
	Laid out by Mrs Cranmer	002 03 04
	for a dog coler	000 03 00
10	to Mrs Nun for halfe a years Allowance due at Michaelmis last	010 00 00
	to Mrs Cheret as per bill	022 02 00
11	to Mr Lenoire as per bill	031 10 00
	Laid out by Mr Steuens	001 03 00
	to Mr web that hookes the birds	003 05 00
		796 01 11

[101] 29 September.

[verso] 34v

1678	**Brought from the other Syde**	**796 01 11**
12 Octobr	to Lady Marshalls man	000 10 00
	to a man with a present of Tee from holand	002 03 04
	for a boat	000 01 00
20	for pen Inke & paper	000 10 00
	to Lady Arlintons man by Mr Stevens	001 01 08
	to Mrs Alexander for Riben	002 12 00
	to a poore womane with a petetion	001 00 00
6 Novembr	to Mrs pigon as per bill	039 01 00
	Laid out by Lady Bellings	002 03 04
	Laid out by Mr Roche	000 08 00
15	to Lady Northumberlands gardner	001 00 00
	to the Robs feast by Mr Rutland as per bill	005 00 00
	to Mrs ferands as per bill	002 10 00
	to the violins Musique as per bill	020 00 00
	to the wind Musique & Recorders	005 00 00
	to the Harper	001 00 00
	to yor Maties footmen	003 00 00
	to the Kings footmen	002 00 00
	to the ducks footmen	002 00 00
	to the dutchesse footmen	002 00 00
	to yor Maties Coatchmen	003 00 00
	to the Kings Coatchmen	002 00 00
		894 02 03

[recto] 35r

1678	**Brought from the other syde**	**0894 02 03**
15 Novembr[102]	to the Kings trompets	0006 00 00
	to the droms	0003 00 00

102 Catherine's birthday – she was 40.

	to the ducks trompets	0003 00 00
	to the Litermen & Chairemen	0002 00 00
	to the somptermen	0001 00 00
	to the Groomes of the stables	0002 00 00
	to the Master of yo[r] Ma[ties] Berge	0001 00 00
	to the violine in ordenary	0001 00 00
	to the Gromebotleman	0001 00 00
	to the ducks violins Musique	0010 00 00
	to the yeomans of the gard	0002 00 00
21	fees & Charges at the Receit of one hundred pounds for this present Month	0003 15 00
	to Sir Richard Bellings for a warant	0006 10 00
	fees & Charges at the Receit of fiue hundred pounds	0018 15 00
22	to Mr Suckley as per bill	0015 00 00
	to Mr vancoe as per bill	0015 00 00
	to Mr Smith page of the presence as per bill	0006 00 00
	to Mr Johns as per bill	0006 00 00
	to Mr Coter as per bill	0006 00 00
	to Mr Hilliar as per bill	0006 00 00
	to Mr Lambe for foure yeares New yeares gifts to the officers of yo[r] Ma[ties] Kitchion as per bill	0064 10 00
		1073 12 03

[verso] 35v

1678	**Brought from the other Syde**	**1073 12 03**
22 Novembr	to Mr Jonson bounty as per bill	0020 00 00
	to the Chairemen by Mr tailour bounty as per bill	0020 00 00
	to Mr Clark Areirs of New years gift for the Kings Coatchmen as per bill	0021 00 00
	to Mr Dawson Areires of New years gifts to the porters of whithall as per bill	0030 00 00

	to Mr Sterlin[103] bounty for yor Maties Coatchmen as per bill	0020 00 00
	to Mr old feild bounty for the Groomes of the stables as per bill	0010 00 00
	to Mr Betts for the somptermen bounty as per bill	0010 00 00
	to Mr Eshar[104] for yor Maties footmen bounty as per bill	0020 00 00
	to Mrs Hemden for fiue years Areirs of New yeares gifts as per bill	0050 00 00
	to John Tough for fiue yeares Areirs of New years gifts as per bill	0100 00 00
30	to Mrs sarsfeild as per bill	0010 00 00
	to the footman presented St Androws Cross	0001 00 00
	to Mrs Houlders servant by Mrs Cranmer	0005 08 04
5 decembr	to Captan Berne by Mr Steuens as per bill	0005 00 00
	for 12 pounds of biskit by Mr Steuens	0002 08 00
		1398 08 07

[recto] 36r

1678	**Brought from the other Syde**	**1398 08 07**
6 decembr	Laid out by Mr Steuens	0000 13 00
	to Mr Capell as per bill	0002 00 00
	to Mr woodward as per bill	0001 00 00
7	fees & Charges at the Receit of one hundred pounds for this Month	0003 15 00
17	to Mr Lightfoot as per bill	0011 12 00
25	to the yeomans of the gard at somersethouse	0001 01 08
28	to Mrs Mordneat Cristsmis[105] last as per	0001 06 00

103 Starling.

104 Esharr.

105 25 December.

	to Mrs <Hemden> for thred & nedles due at Cristsmis last	0001 00 00
	to Mons[s] Gloud as per bill	0002 00 00
1 Janr	to the Kings violin Musique as per bill	0020 00 00
	to the wind Musique & Recorders	0006 00 00
	to the violin in ordinary	0001 00 00
	to the Harper	0001 00 00
	to yo[r] Ma[ties] Master Cooke	0005 00 00
	to his man	0001 00 00
	to the Kings Master Cooke	0005 00 00
	to his man	0001 00 00
	to yo[r] Ma[ties] Coatchmen	0010 00 00
	to yo[r] Ma[ties] postilions	0003 00 00
	to yo[r] Ma[ties] footmen	0010 00 00
		1485 16 03

[verso] 36v

1678[106]	**Brought from the other Syde**	**1485 16 03**
1 Janr	to the Kings Coatchmen	0005 00 00
	to the Groomes of the stables	0004 00 00
	to the Litermen & Chairemen	0005 00 00
	to the somptermen	0002 00 00
	to the Kings trompets	0006 00 00
	to the dromes	0003 00 00
	to the Gallery keepers	0006 00 00
	to the duckes trompets	0006 00 00
	to the violin to the duckes Children	0001 00 00
	to the Master of yo[r] Ma[ties] Berge	0002 00 00
	to the shoemakers men	0004 00 00
	to the portingall Baker	0003 00 00
	to the portingall Cooke	0003 00 00
	to Mrs Hemden	0010 00 00

[106] 1679 NS.

	to John Tough	0020 00 00
2	to the men that Brings the playe bills	0002 03 04
	to the man that brings the Gazets	0001 01 09
	to Mr pauy[107] boxkeeper as per bill	0002 03 00
	to Mr Hailes boxkeeper as per bill	0002 03 04
	to the Herbwomane	0001 01 08
	to Lady Northumberlands gardner	0001 00 00
9	to Colonell damsys Cristning by Lady fingall	0016 06 03
		1591 15 07

[recto] 37r

1678[108]	**Brought from the other syde**	**1591 15 07**
9 Janr	fees & Carges[109] at the Receit of one hundred pounds for this Month	0003 15 00
10	to Mr Jonson as per bill	0002 08 06
16	to Mrs Hemden for worke done Extraordinary as per bill	0010 00 00
31	to Mr Langrish for a Mufe as per bill	0004 00 00
4 Febr	fees & Charges at the Receit of one hundred pounds for this Month	0003 15 00
	to Lady Clarindens man presented a samon	0001 00 00
	Laid out by Mr picot for flowrpots sent to winsor last somer	0001 10 00
11	to Mrs Cheret as per bill	0012 11 00
	for pen Inke and paper	0000 10 00
	Laid out by Mrs Hemden	0000 10 00
	to a womane from Colbrooke presented pudins	0001 01 08
	Laid out by Mr Steuens	0000 18 00

107 Pavy.
108 1679 NS.
109 Charges.

20	to Lady Clarindons man presented a samon	0001 00 00
1 March	to the footman presented a Leeke	0001 00 00
5	to Mr Thomas as per bill	0003 03 00
6	to Mrs duett as per bill	0011 17 06
8	fees & Charges at the Receit of one hundred pounds for this present Month	0003 15 00
17	to the footman presented St patriks Crose	0001 00 00
		1655 10 03

[verso] 37v

1678[110]	**Brought from the other Syd**	**1655 10 03**
18 March	to Lady Clarindons man presented a samon	0001 00 00
20	to Mr Coqus as per bill	0015 15 00
28	To Mrs Mor for a quarter due at our Lady day Last	0001 06 00
1679	to Lady Clarindons man presented a samon	0001 00 00
	to Mrs deuett as per bill	0021 03 00
	To Mrs Nun for halfe a yeares Allowance due at our Lady last as per bill	0010 00 00
31	to Lady Clarindons man presented a samon	0001 00 00
	Laid out by Mr Steuens	0001 01 00
	Remains due from yor Matie to the accomptant by the last accompt: mad the first of April: 1678: not set down till now	0008 13 01
	Moneis disbursed	
	from the first of April: 1678: to the first of April: 1679:	**1716 08 04**

110 1679 NS.

Moneis Receiued

from the first of April: 1678: to the first of April: 1679	**1700 00 00**

Remaines due

from yo[r] Ma[tie] to the Accomptant the first of April: 1679	**0016 08 04**

Catherina R

1-Worsley/9 – Catherine of Braganza, privy purse accounts 1679–81

[recto] 1r

1679	**Moneis Receuid by the Countesse of Suffolke of Jn° Heruey Esqr for the Queenes Priuy purse**	lib s d
7 April:	Receiued of Jn°[1] Heruey Esqr one hundred pounds for this present month	100 00 00
2 May	Receiued of Jn° Heruey Esqr one hundred pounds for this present month	100 00 00
5 June	Receiued of Jn° Heruey Esqr one hundred pounds for this present month	100 00 00
1 July	Receiued of Jn° Heruey Esqr one hundred pounds for this present month	100 00 00
7	Receiued of Jn° Heruey Esqr two hundred pounds	200 00 00
11 August	Receiued of Jn° Heruey Esqr one hundred pounds for this present Month	100 00 00
5 Septembr	Receiued of Jn° Heruey Esqr one hundred pounds for this present month	100 00 00
23	Receiued of Jn° Heruey Esqr foure hundred and sixty pounds	460 00 00
20 Octobr	Receiued of Jn° Heruey Esqr one hundred pounds for this present Month	100 00 00
		1360 00 00

[verso] 1v		lib s d
1679	**Brought from the other Syd**	**1360 00 00**
4 Novembr	Receiued of Jn° Heruey Esqr one hundred pounds for this present Month	0100 00 00
5 Decembr	Receiued of Jn° Heruey Esqr one hundred pounds for this present Month	0100 00 00

[1] John.

	Moneis Receiued	
	from the sixth of April: 1679 to the 31: of december 1679 fifteen hundred and sixty pounds	**1560 00 00**
9 Janr	Receiued of Jno Heruey Esqr thre hundred forty eight pounds twelue shillings and eight pence	0348 12 08
8 March	Receiued of the Earle of Clarindon: <yor Maties Treasurer> two hundred poinds	0200 00 00

[recto] 2r

1680		lib s d
3 Septembr	Receiued of the Earle of Clarendon	400 00 00
14	Receiued of the Earle of Clarendon	400 00 00
11 Novembr	Receiued of the Earle of Clarendon	400 00 00
30 decembr	Receiued of the Earle of Clarendon	358 18 08[2]

[verso] 2v blank

[recto] 3r

1679	**Moneis disbursed by the Countesse of Suffolke for her Maties vse**	lib s d
7 April:	Repaid my selfe due from the Last accompt	016 08 04
	for this booke	000 16 00
	Laid out by Lady Cranmer	001 01 08
	to Lady Clarindons man presented samon	001 00 00
	fees & Charges at the Receit of one hundred pounds for this present Month	003 15 00
9	Laid out by Mr Steuens	000 18 00

2 No total given for 9 January to 30 December 1680. It is £2,107 11s 4d. The overall total is £3,667 11s 4d.

	Laid out by Mrs Hemden	001 10 00
15	to Mrs Cheret as per bill	013 04 06
	to Lady Arlingtons man	001 00 00
	to the yeomans of the gard on Mandy thursday[3]	001 01 08
	to Mr Ernly[4] as per bill	002 10 00
	to Mrs Hemden for thred & needles due at our Lady day last[5]	001 00 00
20	to Mrs deuett for stufs as per bill	007 10 00
	Laid out by Mrs Hemden	000 05 00
23	to the violin Musique by Mr Fitts as per bill	010 00 00
	to the portingall Embassadors man	001 01 08
24	to Mrs Story as per bill	022 07 06
		085 09 04

[verso] 3v

1679	**Brought from the other Syd**	**085 09 04**
26 April:	to the Herbwomane	001 01 08
28	to the portingall Embassadors man	001 01 08
	to Lady Clarnidons[6] man presented mulets	001 01 08
30	to the portingall Embassadors man	001 01 08
2 May	fees & Charges at the Receit of one hundred pounds for this present Month	003 15 00
	to the portingall Embassadors man	001 01 08[7]
	Laid out by Mr Clarke	001 02 00
	to Mrs Hemden for mending yo[r] Ma[ties] Linen as per bill	030 00 00
	to Mrs Nuns man	001 00 00

3 Maundy Thursday 1679 – 30 March [Easter Sunday 1679 – 2 April].
4 Ernle.
5 25 March.
6 Clarendons.
7 001 01 08 corrected from 001 00 08.

4	to the portingall Embassadors man	001 01 08
	to yo[r] Ma[ties] footmen the first time to Heigh parke	002 00 00
6	to Lady Arlingtons man	001 01 08
10	to the portingall Embassadors man	001 01 08
	to Lady Northumberlands gardner	001 00 00
14	to Lady Cranmer as per bill	084 10 00
	to the portingall Embassadors man	001 01 08
	to yo[r] Ma[ties] footmen Runing mony	002 00 00
21	to the portingall Embassadors man	001 01 08
28	to Lady Bristols gardner presented orangflowrs	001 01 08
		222 14 08

[recto] 4r

1679	**Brought from the other Syd**	**222 14 08**
29 May[8]	Laid out by Mrs Hemden	000 10 00
	to Lord Montegus man presented veneson	002 03 04
	to the violin Musique by Mr Brokhall as per bill	010 00 00
	to yo[r] Ma[ties] footmen	003 00 00
3 June	to Mrs Burton as per bill	001 06 00
	for pen Ink and paper	000 10 00
	to Mrs deuett as per bill	004 02 00
5	fees & Charges at the Receit of one hundred pounds for this present month	003 15 00
	to Lady Bristols gardner	001 01 08
6	to Mrs Low as per bill	010 00 00
	to the Berge to somersethouse	000 10 00
	to the portingall Embassadors man	001 01 08
7	to Mr Jonson as per bill	001 19 08
	Laid out by Mr Clarke	000 16 00

8 Charles II's birthday – he was 49.

	to the Herbwomane	001 01 08
12	to Lady Bristols gardner	001 01 08
	for Biskit	000 06 00
16	Laid out by Mr Rowland as per bill	025 18 06
	to the gardner of somersethouse	001 01 08
17	to the portingall Embassadors man	001 01 08
19	to yo[r] Ma[ties] footmen Runing mony	002 00 00
		296 01 02

[verso] 4v

1679	**Brought from the other Syd**	**296 01 02**
20 June	to Lady Bristols gardner	001 01 08
	to yo[r] Ma[ties] footmen Runing mony	002 00 00
22	to the portingall Embassadors man	001 01 08
	Laid out by Mrs Hemden	000 15 00
26	to Mrs More due at Midsomerlast[9]	001 06 00
	to Lady Bristols gardner	001 01 08
28	Laid out by Mr Steuens as per bill	004 13 06
	to the footmen Runing mony	002 00 00
	to the Coatchmakersmen	002 00 00
	to the dutchesse of Monmouths man	001 01 08
	to the Countesse of peneluas[10] man	001 01 08
29	to the portingall Embassadors man	001 01 08
	to Mrs Hemden for a quarter due at Midsomerlast	001 00 00
1 July	fees & Charges at the Receit of one hundred pounds for this present month	003 15 00
	to the secretary for a warant	006 00 00
	to the footmen to windsor	002 00 00
	to the pages of the Bakstairs	000 10 00
	to a set of Hoboys	001 00 00
	for bringing of yo[r] Ma[ties] Chaire	001 01 08

9 24 June.
10 Penalva.

2	to a set of Musique	001 00 00
	to the Kings violin Musique as per bill	010 00 00
	to Mr Jonson as per bill	001 10 00
		343 02 04

[recto] 5r

1679	**Brought from the other Syd**	**343 02 04**
3 July	to a set of Hoboys	001 00 00
	Laid out by Mrs Hemden	000 10 00
4	to the footmen Runing mony	002 00 00
	to Mr Verios gardner	001 01 08
5	to the footmen Runing mony	002 00 00
	to Lady Arlingtons footmen	001 00 00
	to Mrs Nuns man	001 00 00
7	fees & Charges at the Receit of two hundred pounds	008 00 00
	to the footmen Runing mony	002 00 00
	Laid out by Mr Steuens as per bill	007 13 00
	to Mr winwoods man	001 01 08
	to the portingall Embassadors man	001 01 08
12	to the footmen Runing mony	002 00 00
13	to the footmen Runing mony	002 00 00
	to a man from somerset-house with flowrs	000 10 00
14	to the footmen Runing mony	002 00 00
15	to the footmen Runing mony	002 00 00
17	to the footmen Runing mony	002 00 00
	to Mrs Nuns man	001 00 00
20	to the portingall Embassadors man	001 01 08
	to Lady Clarindons man with flowrs	001 00 00
	to Mr Verios man	001 01 08
		386 03 08

[verso] 5v

1679	**Brought from the other Syd**	**386 03 08**

22 July	to the footmen Runing mony	002 00 00
	to Collonell Talbots gardner	001 01 08
	for a boats with flowrpots from somersethouse	001 03 00
24	to the footmen Runing mony	002 00 00
	to the Herbwomane	001 01 08
26	to the footmen Runing mony	002 00 00
	to a man from twitnham[11] with Milons	001 01 08
27	to the footmen Runing mony	002 00 00
	to the portingall Embassadors man	001 01 08
30	for a boat with flowrpots from somersethouse	001 03 00
1 August	to the footmen Runing mony	002 00 00
2	to Mr Capell Messenger as per bill	002 00 00
	to Lady Suffolkes footmen	001 01 08
4	to the footmen Runing mony	002 00 00
6	to the footmen Runing mony	002 00 00
	to the portingall Embassadors man	001 01 08
	for a boat from somersethouse	001 02 00
8	to the footmen Runing mony	002 00 00
	to Mrs Nuns man	001 00 08
	Laid out by Mrs Hemden	000 12 06
11	fees & Charges at the Receit of one hundred pounds for this present month	004 05 00
		419 19 10

[recto] 6r

1679	**Brought from the other syd**	**419 19 10**
12 August	to the footmen Runing mony	002 00 00
13	for a boat with flowrpots from somersethouse	001 02 00
	to the footmen Runing mony	002 00 00
14	to Mr Charlton as per bill	010 10 00
	to the portingall Embassadors man	001 01 08

11 Twickenham.

	to a footmen sent from old windsor	000 10 00
16	Laid out by Mr Steuens as per bill	001 11 06
	to Mr winwoods gardner	001 01 08
	to the footmen Runing	002 00 00
20	for a boat with flowrpots to & from somersethouse	002 05 00
	Laid out by Mr Clarke	000 12 06
	to a woman presented osters[12]	001 01 08
	for fishing hooks & Angles	000 10 00
28	for a boat with flowrpots to & from somersethouse	001 02 00
	to the herbwomane	001 01 08
	to the portingall Embassadors man	001 01 08
	Laid out by Mr Steuens	001 04 00
30	to Mr Charleton as per bill	008 00 00
	to Lady orseris man	001 01 08
	for pen Inke & paper	000 10 00
		460 06 10

[verso] 6v

1679	**Brought from the other Syd**	**460 06 10**
1 Septembr	to the footmen Runing mony	002 00 00
	Laid out by Mr Clark as per bill	002 15 00
	to a waterman brought things from London	000 10 00
2	to Lord Clarindons man with Mulets	002 03 04
	to the footmen Runing mony	002 00 00
4	for a boat with flowrpots from somersethouse	001 00 00
	Laid out by Mrs Hemden	000 10 00
5	fees & Charges at the Receit of one hundred pounds for this present month	004 05 00

12 Oysters.

8	for a boat with flowrpots from somersethouse	001 00 00
9	to the footmen Runing mony	002 00 00
	to Mr winwoods gardner	001 01 07
	to Lady orseris man	001 01 07
	to Sir Henery Caples gardner	001 01 07
11	to the footmen Runing mony	002 00 00
13	to Mr Charleton as per bill	007 00 00
15	to Mr verios gardner	001 01 07
	to the fishermen	001 00 00
	to the Corn cuter by Mrs Nun	001 01 07
	for a boat with flowrpots from somersethouse	001 02 00
	to a groome sent to London	001 00 00
		496 00 01

[recto] 7r

1679	**Brought from the other Syd**	**496 00 01**
16 Septembr	for bringing yo[r] Ma[ties] Chaire to London	001 01 07
	for Lodgings as per bill	268 07 00
	to the secretary for a warant for 260[li]	006 00 00
17	to Mr dauis wardrobkeeper as per bill	005 00 00
	to the parkekeeper	002 00 00
	to the parkegatkeeper	001 00 00
	to <Mr> winwoods gardner	001 01 07
	to Mr Rendu as per bill	008 00 00
	to his man	002 00 00
	to Mr Steuens as per bill	002 11 00
	to a set of Musique	001 00 00
	to the garison by Captan pots	005 08 00
	for a horsehire to London	000 05 00
	to the footmen Runing mony to London	002 00 00
	to the pages of the Bakstairs to London	000 10 00

	to the vnder Keepers of the great parke	002 00 00
	to the Kings Coatchman	001 00 00
18	to Mr Charleton as per bill	003 10 00
	to Mr Jonson as per bill	001 10 00
	to Mr Smith as per bill	001 05 00
	to Mr Charleton for a Berge to bring yor Maties goods as per bill	006 00 00
		817 09 03

[verso] 7v

1679	**Brought from the other Syd**	**817 09 03**
19 Septembr	paid to porter for Carieing the goods	000 13 06
22	to the Herbewomane	001 01 07
	to the secretary for a warant for two hundred pounds	006 00 00
	to Sir Henery Caples man	001 01 07
23	fees & Charges at the Receit of foure hundred & sixty pounds	016 02 00
	Laid out by Mrs Hemden	001 04 00
26	to the footmen Runing mony to Newmarkit	004 00 00
	to the seruants at Audley end	005 08 00
	to the pages of the Bakestairs to Newmarkit	001 00 00
	for a horse hire	001 00 00
27	Laid out by Mr Rogers	001 15 00
	to a set of musique	001 00 00
	to Mr Smith as per bill	001 15 06
	to Mr Jonson as per bill	001 10 00
	to the Kings violine Musique by Mr Fitts as per bill	010 00 00
29	to a set of Musique	001 00 00
30	to a set of Musique	001 00 00
	Laid out by Mr Perera[13]	000 13 06
		873 13 11

13 Periera.

[recto] 8r

1679	**Brought from the other Syd**	**0[14]873 13 11**
6 Octobr	Laid out by Mr Steuens as per bill	0019 01 11
7	to the footmen Runing mony	0002 00 00
8	to the footmen Runing mony	0002 00 00
9	for a groome sent to London for the Coatches	0002 00 00
	Laid out by Lady fingall at Euston	0016 02 06
	to the footmen Runing mony	0002 00 00
	to a gyd to Euston	0001 01 07
	to two groomes Lighted the Coatches	0001 00 00
	to seauen Coatchmen as per bill	0035 00 00
10	to two yeomans of the garde Caried yor ma^tie^ in a Chaire	0001 01 07
	to a set of Musique	0001 00 00
	to the footmen Runing mony	0002 00 00
13	for Lodgings as per bill	0048 12 06
	to the wardrobemen	0001 01 07
	to the footmen to London	0004 00 00
	to the pages of the Bakstairs	0001 00 00
	to the Kings Runing horse groomes	0005 08 00
	to the man that Keeps the stand	0002 03 02
	to Mrs frost vnderhouse-keeper as per bill	0008 00 00
		1028 06 09

[verso] 8v

1679	**Brought from the other Syd**	**1028 06 09**
13 Octobr	to Mrs Gregory a Lame womane	0002 03 02
	to the poore by Mr Cleton[15] as per bill	0005 00 00
	to guydes to London	0002 03 02
	to the Coatchmakers men to London	0002 03 02
16	to Mr Johnson as per bill	0001 13 06

[14] This zero and those in the column below were added after the total for the page was calculated as it took the sum over £1,000.

[15] Cleyton.

	to Mr Smith yeomane of the wagons as per bill	0002 06 00
	to Mrs Hemden ffor a quarter threed and Needles due at Michaelmis[16] last	0001 00 00
	for a boat sent to dartford	0000 10 00
	to Mrs More due at Michaelmas last	0001 06 00
20	fees & Charges at the Receit of one hundred pounds for this present monthe	0003 15 00
	to the portingall Embassadors man	0001 01 07
22	to Mrs Nun for halfe a years Allowance due at Michaelmas last as per bill	0010 00 00
24	to Mr Thomas as per bill	0000 12 06
	Laid out by Mr Steuens	0001 01 06
26	to the portingall Embassadors man	0001 01 07
	Laid out by Mrs Hemden for Cloathe and worke done	0002 18 00
4 Novembr	fees & Charges at the Receit of one hundred pounds for this present monthe	0003 15 00
8	to the portingall Embassadors man	0001 01 07
	to Mr Thomas for a Lookinglase	0001 10 00
		1073 08 06

[recto] 9r

1679	**Brought from the other Syd**	**1073 08 06**
13 Novembr	to Mr woodward as per bill	0001 05 00
	Laid out by Mr Clarke	0000 15 06
	for pen Ink & paper	0000 10 00
15	to a womane presented Graps	0002 03 02
	to yor Maties Robs feast by Mr groome[17]	0005 00 00

16 29 September.

17 Catherine's birthday – she was 41.

	to Lady Northumberlands gardner	0001 01 07
	to the violines Musique by Mr Brokwell as per bill	0020 00 00
	to the wind musique & Recorders	0005 00 00
	to the Harper	0001 00 00
	to y[r] Ma[ties] footmen	0003 00 00
	to the Kings footmen	0002 00 00
	to the duckes footmen	0002 00 00
	to the dutchesse footmen	0002 00 00
	to yo[r] Ma[ties] Coatchmen	0003 00 00
	to the Kings Coatchmen	0002 00 00
	to the Kings Trompets	0006 00 00
	to the dromes	0003 00 00
	to the duckes trompets	0003 00 00
	to the Litermen & Chairemen	0002 00 00
	to the somptermen	0001 00 00
	to the groomes of the stables	0002 00 00
		1141 03 09

[verso] 9v

1679	**Brought from the other syd**	**1141 03 09**
15 Novembr	to the Master of yo[r] Ma[ties] Berges	0001 00 00
	to the violine in ordinary	0001 00 00
	to the groome botleman	0001 00 00
	to the duckes violine Musique	0010 00 00
	to the yeomans of the gard	0002 00 00
16	to the portingall Embassadors man	0001 01 07
21	to Mrs Cherett as per bill	0023 03 00
	to Mr Noris as per bill	0005 00 00
22	to the portingall Embassadors man	0001 01 07
	Laid out by Mrs Hemden	0001 10 00
30	to the footman presented St Andrews Crose	0001 00 00
	to the portingall Embassadors man	0001 01 07

1 decembr	to Mr Lambe as per bill	0027 13 00
5	fees & Charges at the Receit of one hundred pounds for this present month	0003 15 00
	Laid out by Mrs Hemden for sleues	0001 12 00
11	to Mr Lightfoot as per bill	0012 16 00
22	to Mrs Langrishe for a Mufe by Mrs Roper	0000 18 00
25	to the yeomane of the gard at somerset house	0001 00 00
26	to Mrs Mor for a quarter due at Cristsmas last	0001 06 00
	to the portengall Embassadors man	0001 01 07
		1240 03 01

[recto] 10r

1679	**Brought from the other Syd**	**1240 03 01**
27 decembr	to Mrs Hemden for a quartr for threed and Needles due at Cristmas Last	0001 00 00
	to the yeomans of the Gard yo[r] Ma[ties] bounty by Mr Persons as per bill	0024 00 00
	to the somptermen y[r] Ma[ties] bounty by Mr Hosey as per bill	0020 00 00
29	to the portingall Embassadors man	0001 01 07
31	to Lady Marshalls man	0001 00 00

Moneis disbursed

from the Six of April: 1679 to the 31 decembr 1679	**1287 04 08**

Moneis receiued

from the Six of April: 1679 to the 31: decembr 1679	**1560 00 00**

Remaines due

to yo[r] Ma[tie] from the Accomptant this 31: decembr 1679	**0272 15 04**

Catherina R

[verso] 10v

1679[18]

1 Janr	to the Kings violine Musique by Mr Twist	020 00 00
	to the wind musique & Recorders	006 00 00
	to the violine in ordinary	001 00 00
	to the Harper	001 00 00
	to yor Maties Master Cooke	005 00 00
	to his man	001 00 00
	to the Kings Master Cooke	005 00 00
	to his man	001 00 00
	to yor Maties Coachemen	010 00 00
	to yor Maties postilions	003 00 00
	to yor Maties footmen	010 00 00
	to the Kings Coachmen	005 00 00
	to the Groomes of the stables	004 00 00
	to the Litermen & Chairemen	005 00 00
	to the somptermen	002 00 00
	to the Kings Trompets	006 00 00
	to the dromes	003 00 00
	to the Gallerykeepers	006 00 00
	to the ducks Trompets	006 00 00
	to the violine to the ducks Children	001 00 00
	to the Master of yor Maties Berges	002 00 00
		103 00 00

[recto] 11r

1679[19]	**Brought from the other Syd**	**103 00 00**
1 Janr	to the shoemakersmen	004 00 00

18 1680 NS.
19 1680 NS.

	to the portingall Baker	003 00 00
	to the portingall Cooke	003 00 00
	to Mrs Hemden	010 00 00
	to John Tough	020 00 00
	to the men that brings the play bills	002 03 02
	to the man that brings Gazets	001 01 07
	to the box keepers of both play houses	004 06 04
	to the Herbewomane	001 01 04
	to the secretarys Clerke	005 00 00
	to the Treasurers Clerke	005 00 00
	to the porters of the Greatgate	002 10 00
	to the womane from Colbrooke with pudins	001 01 07
	to the portingall Embassadors man	001 01 07
	to Lady Northumberlands gardner	001 01 07
2	to the Corncuter	001 01 07
	Laid out by Mrs Hemden	000 10 00
	to the portingall Embassadors man	001 01 07
	to the secretary for a warant for thre hundred forty eight pounds twelue shillings & eight pence	006 00 00
		176 00 07

[verso] 11v

1679[20]	**Brought from the other Syd**	**176 00 07**
9 Janr	fees & Charges at the Receit of thre hundred forty eight pounds twelue shillings & eight pence	013 01 00
14	to the portingall Embassadors men with a present	005 07 05
16	to yor Maties footmen: bounty: by Mr Maugridge as per bill	020 00 00
18	to the portingall Embassadors man	001 01 07
19	to Mr Steuenes as per bill	001 15 00

20 1680 NS.

29	to Mr Thomas for a Cristall cace to a Looking glace as per bill	001 10 00
5 Febr	for a parots cage by Mr Steuens	001 10 00
	Laid out by Mr Clark as per bill	001 03 04
13	to Mr Le noire for a mufe by Mrs Roper as per bill	001 05 00
	to the gardners man of somerset house with flowres	000 10 00
	for pen Inke and paper	000 10 00
	to Lady Clarindons man presented a samon	001 01 07
24	Laid out by Mrs Hemden	000 13 06
		225 09 00

[recto] 12r

1679	**Brought from the other Syd**	**225 09 00**
25 Febr	Laid out by Lady Cranmer for Embrodery	001 00 00
26	Laid out by Mr Johnson as per bill	001 14 10
28	to Lady Clarindons man presented a samon	001 01 07

Moneis disbursed
from the 31: of december: 1679: to the 29: of Febr: 1679[21] **229 05 05**

Moneis receiued
from the 31: of December: 1679: to the 29: of Febr: 1679: and what Remains due to yor Matie from the Last Accompt **621 08 00**

Remains due
to yor Maties from the Accomptant this 29: of Febr: 1679 **392 02 07**

21 1680 NS.

Catherina R

[verso] 12v

1679/80		
1 Marche	to the portingall Embassadors man	001 01 07
	to the footman presented a Leeke	001 00 00
6	to the secretarye for a warant for two hundred pounds	006 00 00
7	to the portingall Embassadors man	001 01 07
8	fees & Charges at the Receit of two hundred pounds	007 10 00
9	to a Joyner by Mr Steuenes	001 00 00
	for Carnelian butons by Lady Killygris[22]	003 00 00
	mor Laid out by Lady Killigrew as per bill	015 08 06
	Laid out by Mrs Hemden	000 07 06
	Laid out by Mr Clarke as per bill	000 07 00
	to Mrs Pinjon as per bill	022 16 00
	Laid out by Mr Steuens as per bill	001 07 09
10	to Mr Johnson for the wagons to Newmarkitt as per bill	003 14 06
	to yor Maties footmen to newmarkitt	004 00 00
	to the page of the Bakstairs	001 00 00
11	to the Kings violine Musique	010 00 00
	to thre sets of Musique	003 00 00
12	to a set of Musique	001 00 00
		084 04 05

[recto] 13r

1679/80	**Brought from the other Syd**	**084 04 05**
13 March	to a set of Musique	001 00 00
15	to two sets of Musique	002 00 00

22 Killigrew.

16	to a set of Musique	001 00 00
17	to the footman presented St patricks Crose	001 00 00
21	to the footmen Runing mony	002 00 00
	to a set of Musique from Epswich[23]	001 00 00
23	to the footmen Runing mony	002 00 00
29	to a set of Musique from Lin[24]	001 00 00
	to the footmen Runing mony	002 00 00
	Laid out by Mrs Crane	005 08 00[25]
31	for Lodgings as per bill	049 10 00
	to the wardrobmen by Mr Rogers	001 10 00
	to a womane for newlaidegers[26]	001 00 00
	to Lady Marshalls man	001 00 00
	to the poore by Mr Cleyton as per bill	005 00 00
	to Mrs Frost vnder houskeeper as per bill	008 00 00
	to the man that keeps the stand	002 03 02
	to yor Maties footmen to London	004 00 00
	to the pages of the bakstairs	001 00 00
	to Lord feuersoms[27] Coatchman	005 00 00
		180 15 07

[verso] 13v

1680	**Brought from the other Syd**	**180 15 07**
2 April:	to Lord orsserys man	001 00 00
	to the Countesse peneluas man	001 01 07
	to Mr Thomas by Lady Killigrew as per bill	001 00 00
	to Lady Arlintons man	001 00 00
	to Mrs More for one quarter due at Our Lady day[28] last as per bill	001 06 00

23 Ipswich.
24 Kings Lynn.
25 005 08 00 corrected from 005 00 00.
26 new ledgers.
27 Feversham's.
28 25 March.

	to Mrs Hemden for one quarter due at Our Lady day last	001 00 00
	to the Coatchmakers man to & from Newmarkitt	002 03 02
	to Mr Johnson for the wagons as per bill	004 03 06
3	to Lord feversoms man sent from New markitt to London for the Coatches as per bill	005 08 00
	to the portingall Embassadors man	001 01 07
	to a footman sent post from Newmarkitt to London	005 08 00
	to Mrs Nun for halfe a yeares Allowance due at our Lady Day last as per bill	010 00 00
4	to the portingall Embassadors man	001 00 00
5	to the Countesse of peneluas man	001 00 00
	to the portingall Embassadors man	001 00 00
		218 07 05

[recto] 14r

1680	**Brought from the other Syd**	**218 07 05**
6 April:	to the portingall Embassadors man	001 00 00
	Laid out by Mr Steuens as per bill	000 11 00
7	to the Countesse of peneluas man	001 00 00
8	to the yeoman of the gard on Mandy thursday[29]	001 01 07
10	to Lady Northumberlands gardner	001 00 00
12	to Lord Orseris man	001 00 00
	to the gardner of St James	001 01 07
	to Lady Clarindons page	001 01 07

Moneis disbursed

29 Maundy Thursday 1680 – 18 April [Easter Sunday 1680 – 21 April].

from the 29: of Febr: 1679[30]: to the 13 of April: 1680	**226 03 02**

Moneis receiued

from the 29: of February: 1679[31]: to the 13 of April: 1680 and what remaines due to yor Matie from the Last Accompt: is	**592 02 07**

Remains due

to yor Matie from the Accomptant this 13: of April: 1680	**365 19 05**

Catherina R

[verso] 14v

1680

15 April:	to yor Maties footmen the first time to Heigh parke	002 00 00
	for a warant for Linnen for sheets	000 10 00
	to Mr Earnle for the pantry Butry & Ewry on Mandy thursday as per bill	002 10 00
	Laid out by Mr Steuens as per bill	000 12 00
19	to the footmen to windsor	002 00 00
	to the page of the Bakstairs	000 10 00
	for a Berge with roods from windsor as per bill	006 17 00
	Laid out by Mr Baptista as per bill	001 13 06
	for Coatches to windsor	000 04 00
20	to two sets of Musique	002 00 00
	Laid out by Mrs Hemden	000 15 00
	to Mr Johnson for wagons as per bill	002 04 00
	For Bringing yor Maties Chaire	001 01 07
	to the parkeeper presented a Kye	001 01 07

30 1680 NS.

31 1680 NS.

21	to a set of Musique	001 00 00
22	to a set of Musique	001 00 00
	for a boat with flowrepots from London	001 03 00
	to the footmen Runing mony as per bill	002 00 00
23	to the Kings violin Musique as per bill	010 00 00
	to a footman sent to old windsor	000 10 00
24	to Lord Clarindons page	001 01 07
		040 13 03

[recto] 15r

1680	**Brought from the other Syd**	**040 13 03**
27 April:	to the footmen Runing mony as per bill	002 00 00
	to Lord Clarindons man	001 01 07
29	to the footmen Runing mony as per bill	002 00 00
1 May	to the portingall Embassadors man	001 00 00
	Laid out by Mr Clark as per bill	000 13 00
	for a boat with flowrpots from London	001 03 00
2	to Mrs Hemden for mending yor Maties Linnen	030 00 00
3	to Mr Charleton for yor Maties two boatmen as per bill	009 00 00
	Laid out by Mr Steuens as per bill	002 04 00
4	to the footmen Runing mony as per bill	002 00 00
	to Mr Ellis door keeper	006 09 06
	to the portingall Embassadors man	001 00 00
7	for a boat with flowrpots to London	001 03 00
	to Lady orseris man	001 01 07
8	to the footmen Runing mony as per bill	002 00 00
	to the portingall Embassadors man	001 00 00
10	to the portingall Embassadors man	001 00 00

	to Lord Clarindons man	001 00 00
	to the footmen Runing mony as per bill	002 00 00
11	to the footmen Runing mony as per bill	002 00 00
12	to the Kings violin Musique for waiting of the maid of Honour at Newmarkit as per bill	020 00 00
		130 08 11

[verso] 15v

1680	**Brought from the other syd**	**130 08 11**
14 May	to Bury Mr Miller one of yor Maties footmen as per bill	010 00 00
	to Mr verios gardner	001 01 07
	to the portingall Embassadors man	001 00 00
	to Lord Montegus man with veneson	002 03 02
17	to Lord Charleton boatman as per bill	007 00 00
19	Laid out by Mr Steuens as per bill	002 00 00
	to Mr Legs man	001 01 07
	to the man that made a Lader	000 10 00
	for pen Inke & paper	000 10 00
20	to yor Maties footmen to London	002 00 00
	to the Kings Coatchman at huntslow[32]	001 01 07
	Laid out by Mrs Hemden	000 07 00
	to Mr Caple messenger as per bill	001 05 00
	to Lord Clarindons man	001 00 00
	to Lord Feuersoms[33] man sent for Coatches	001 01 07
	to Lord Arlingtons gardner	001 01 07
26	to the footmen to London	002 00 00
	to the Kings Coatchman at huntslow	001 01 07

32 Hounslow.

33 Feversham.

	to Lord Feuersoms Coatchman	005 07 11
	to Sir Philip Howards Coatchman	005 07 11
	to Lord Feuersoms man sent for Coatches	001 01 07
		178 11 00

[recto] 16r

1680	**Brought from the other Syd**	**178 11 00**
27 May	to Mr Verios gardner	001 01 07
29[34]	to the Kings violin Musique	010 00 00
	to yor Maties footmen	003 00 00
30	to the Corn cuter cut the paret bill	001 01 07
2 June	to Mr Charleton boatman as per bill	008 00 00
	to Lady Marshals man	001 00 00
10	to the footmen to London	002 00 00
	to the Kings Coatchman to London	002 03 02
	to the portingall Embassadors man	001 00 00
	to Lord Arlingtons Butler	001 01 07
	to Lord feuersoms man	001 01 07
	to Lord Tenhams[35] man presented a buck	002 03 02
	Laid out by Mrs Hemden	001 00 00
	to Mrs Nuns man	001 01 07
12	to Mr Woodward Messenger as per bill	002 19 00
	for a Combe	000 04 00
18	to Mr Charleton as per bill	008 00 00
	to Lady Bristols gardner	001 01 07
	to Lady Marshalls man	001 00 00
	Laid out by Mr Steuens as per bill	001 04 02
	to a waterman with flowrpots & boxes	001 00 00
	Laid out by Mr Clarke as per bill	001 05 00
		230 19 00

34 Charles II's birthday – he was 50.
35 Teynham's.

[verso] 16v

1680	**Brought from the other syd**	**230 19 00**
19 June	to Lord Clarindons man	001 00 00
20	to the footmen Runing mony as per bill	002 00 00
	to Lord orseris man	001 01 07
	to Mr Verios gardner	001 01 07
	to orange nan presented orangflowrs	001 01 07
23	to the man brought flowrpots & boxes	001 00 00
	to the Herbewomane	001 01 07
	to Lady Bristols gardner	001 01 07
26	to Lady Marshalls man	001 00 00
28	to the footmen to London	002 00 00
	to the page of the Bakstairs to London	000 10 00
	to the Kings Coatchman at London	001 01 07
	to Lord feversems man	001 01 07
	Laid out by Mrs Hemden	000 07 00
1 July	to the footmen from London	002 00 00
	to the page of the bakstairs	000 10 00
	to Mr Caple Messenger as per bill	001 05 00
	Laid out by Mr Clarke as per bill	001 05 00
	to Lady Suffolkes maid by Mr baptist	002 03 02
	to Lord orseris Cooke	001 01 07
	to the Kings Coatchmen	002 03 02
3	to the herbewomane	001 01 07
		257 16 07

[recto] 17r

1680	**Brought from the other Syd**	**257 16 07**
4 July	to Mrs Nuns man	001 00 00
	to Mrs Hemden for threed & needles due at Midsomer[36] last	001 00 00

36 24 June.

5	to Lady Marshalls man	001 00 00
	to Mrs More due at Midsomer last	001 06 00
8	to a man brought flowrpots & boxes from somerset house	001 00 00
	to Mr Legs man	001 01 07
	to Mr Charleton as per bill	010 00 00
	to the portingall Embassadors man	001 00 00
	for a Chaseboard[37] by Mr Sayers	003 00 00
9	to Mrs Swans womane	001 01 07
	to Lord Clarindons man	001 00 00
	Laid out by Mrs Hemden	000 12 00
	to the dutchese of portsmouths man	001 01 07
10	to Mr Legs man	001 01 07
12	to the footmen to London	002 00 00
	to the page of the Bakstairs	000 10 00
	to the groomes with Lights	001 00 00
	to Lord feuersoms man sent for Coatches	001 01 07
	Laid out by Mr Sayers	002 03 02
	to Mr Roswan the Chasmary[38] man as per bill	001 10 00
14	for a boat sent to & from windsor	002 00 00
	to Lady Northumberlands gardner	001 01 07
15	to the portingall Embassadors man	001 01 07
		295 08 10

[verso] 17v

1680	**Brought from the other Syd**	**295 08 10**
16 July	to the footmen from London	002 00 00
	to the pages of the Bakstairs	000 10 00
	for Coatchire to & from London	000 07 00

37 Chessboard.

38 Meaning uncertain.

	to Mr Sauingnon[39] in lieu of twelue elles of holland as per bill	006 00 00
17	to Collonell Legs man	001 01 07
	Laid out by Mr Steuens as per bill	004 15 03
	to Lady Marshalls man	001 00 00
20	to the footmen to London	002 00 00
	to the pages of the Bakstairs	000 10 00
	to Lord feuersoms man sent for Coatches	001 00 00
	Laid out by Mrs Hamden	001 08 06
21	to the footmen from London	002 00 00
	to the pages of the Bakstairs	000 10 00
	for Coatchire to & from London	000 07 00
	Laid out by Lady Marshall at London	010 15 10
22	to Mr Verios gardner	002 03 02
26	to a groome sent to London	001 00 00
28	to orange Anne presented friute	001 01 07
	to Mr Charleton as per bill	010 00 00
	to Mr Capelle Messenger as per bill	002 10 00
	to the boatman for bringing flowrpots and boxes from somersethouse	001 00 00
	to Lord Arlingtons groome	002 03 02
	to Mr Johnson as per bill	001 15 06
		351 07 05

[recto] 18r

1680	**Brought from the other Syd**	**351 07 05**
29 July	to the portingall Embassadors groome	001 01 07
	to Mr Verios man by Mr Baptist	001 01 07
	Laid out by Mr Clarke as per bill	001 13 06
1 August	to the footmen to London	002 00 00
	to the page of the Bakstairs	000 10 00

[39] Savingnon.

	to Lord feuersoms man sent for the Coatches	001 01 07
2	to the footmen from London	002 00 00
	to the Kings Coatchman at London	001 01 07
	to the page of the Bakstairs	000 10 00
	for Coatchire to & from London	000 07 00
7	to the portingall Embassadors man	001 01 07
	to Mrs Swans man	001 01 07
	to the herbwoman	001 01 07
	to Mr winwoods gardner	001 01 07
16	to the footman to filberds	002 00 00
	to the groomes Lighted yor Matie	001 00 00
	to Mr Chifins huntsman by Lord feuersom	002 03 02
17	to the portingall Embassadors man	001 01 07
	to Mr Charleton as per bill	010 00 00
18	to the dutchesse of Grafans[40] Coatchmen	002 03 02
	to Mr Carys man presented veneson by Mr Clarke	002 03 02
	to Lord Arlingtons Cooke & Butler	002 03 02
	Laid out by Mr Steuens as per bill	009 01 05
	To the footmen Runing mony as per bill	002 00 00
		400 16 03

[verso] 18v

1680	**Brought from the other syd**	**400 16 03**
19 August	to one of yor Maties footmen by Mrs Crane	002 03 02
	to Mr winwoods gardner	001 01 07
	for pen Inke and paper	000 10 00
	to Lord Clarindons man	001 00 00

[40] Grafton.

25	to the footmen to swalowfeild[41]	002 00 00
	to Lord feuersoms Coatchman as per bill	005 00 00
	to Lord Clarindons groome	001 01 07
	to Lord feuersems man sent for Hauks[42]	001 01 07
	to the Kings Coatchmen	002 03 02
29	to a womane from Lady Clarindons	000 10 00
	to Mr winwoods gardner	001 01 07
	to a sentry by Mr Baptist	001 01 07
	to the Herbwomane	001 01 07
2 Septembr	to the secretary for a warante	006 00 00
3	fees & Charges at the Receit of foure hundred pounds	015 17 00
	to Mr Woodward Messenger as per bill	002 11 00
4	to a waterman with boxes and flowr pots from somersethouse 11 times	001 07 06
	to a womane presented osters[43]	001 01 07
	to Mr Woodward messenger as per bill	005 16 00
6	to the footmen Runing mony as per bill	002 00 00
	Laid out by Mr Rogers at Cleworth[44]	002 08 04
	to a groome	001 01 07
	to a poor womane by Lady Ancrim[45]	001 01 07
		459 16 08

[recto] 19r

1680	**Brought from the other Syd**	**459 16 08**
7 Septembr	to the fishermen	001 05 00
	to the boy that brought the Cow	000 10 00

41 Swallowfield Park, Berkshire.
42 Hawks.
43 Oysters.
44 Possibly for Clewer.
45 Ancram.

	for a Berge and porterige by Mr Charleton as per bill	007 11 00
	to a poore womane had her husband killed over the wall[46]	005 07 11
	to Mr Verios gardner	001 01 07
8	for Lodging yor Maties seruants as per bill	359 14 00
	for John Teughs[47] Lodging	007 00 00
	to Mr Randue Houskeeper as per bill	008 00 00
	to his seruants	002 00 00
	to Mr dauis: wardrobkeeper as per bill	005 00 00
	to Mr Tapham parkeeper & his man per bill	003 00 00
	to the vnderkeepers of the greatparke as per bill	002 00 00
	to a womane for the Meads[48] by Lord feuersom	005 00 00
	for bringing yor Maties Chaire to London	001 01 07
	to the Garison by Captan Potts as per bill	005 07 11
	Mrs Hemdens Expences	012 03 06
	John Toughs Expences	012 03 06
	to the footmen to London	002 00 00
	to the pages of the Bakstairs	000 10 00
	to the Groomes Lighted the Coatches	002 00 00
	Laid out by Mrs Hemden for Coatchire	000 12 06
	to Lord feuersems man sent for Coatches	001 01 07
	for Coatchire to London	000 05 00
		904 11 09

46 Uncertain which wall was referred to here/which incident this was.

47 Tough.

48 The Meads or meadows at Runnymede.

[verso] 19v

1680	**Brought from the other Syd**	**904 11 09**
9 Septembr	to Mr Charleton as per bill	015 10 00
	to Mr Johnson for the wagons as per bill	002 12 00
	to Lord Arlingtons gardner by Lady Ancrime[49]	001 01 07
	Laid out by Mr Sayers	004 06 04
14	Laid out by Mr Clarke as per bill	001 06 00
	to the secretary for a warant	006 00 00
	fees & Charges at the Receit of foure hundred pounds	015 00 00
	to Mrs deuett by Lady Killigry[50] as per bill	002 12 00
15	to Mr Langrish for Riben for girdles as per bill	002 17 00
16	to the footmen to Newmarkitt	004 00 00
	to the page of the Bakstairs	001 00 00
	to a Groome by the way	001 00 00
	to Mr Johnson for the wagons as per bill	003 04 00
	for a horsehire to Newmarkit	001 00 00
	to Lord feuersoms Coatchman as per bill	005 00 00
	Laid out by Mrs Hemden	000 10 00
17	to the Kings violins Musique as per bill	010 00 00
18	to the footmen Runing mony as per bill	002 00 00
	to Lord feuersoms Coatchman	001 00 00
		984 10 08

49 Ancram.
50 Killigrew.

[recto] 20r

1680	**Brought from the other Syd**	**984 10 08**
19 Septembr	to Mr Germins[51] gardner	001 01 07
20	to a set of Musique	001 00 00
21	to a set of Musique	001 00 00
	to Mr Germins gardner by My Steuens	001 01 07
22	to the footmen to Euston	002 00 00
	to the page of the Bakstairs	000 10 00
	to a guyd	001 00 00
	to Lord feuersoms man sent for Coatches	001 01 07
	for a horsehire to & from Euston	001 00 00
23	to a set of Musique	001 00 00
	to the Kings violine Musique	010 00 00
	to the footmen Runing mony as per bill	002 00 00
	to a groome sent to thetford	000 10 00
24	to Euston Musique	002 03 02
	to Lord Arlingtons seruants	053 19 02
	to the footmen to Newmarkitt	002 00 00
	to the page of the Bakstairs	000 10 00
	to Mr Johnson for the wagons as per bill	001 05 00
	to a gyd to Newmarkitt	001 00 00
25	to Lord Clarindons man presented a pickture	003 04 09
	to Lord Arlingtons Coatchman postilion page and footman	005 00 00
		1076 17 06

[verso] 20v

1680	**Brought from the other Syd**	**1076 17 06**
26 Septembr	Laid out by Mr Sayers	0001 15 06

51 Possibly Jermyn.

29	to the footmen Runing mony as per bill	0002 00 00
	to Mr Germans gardner by Mr Steuens	0001 01 07
30	to Lord Arlingtons Coatchman postilion page and footman	0005 00 00
	Laid out by Mr Sayers	0000 12 00
1 Octobr	to the footmen Runing mony as per bill	0002 00 00
	to Lord fuersoms groome	0001 00 00
2	Laid out by Mr Steuens as per bill	0001 10 09
4	to Mrs Nun for halfe a yeares Allowance due at Michaelmis Last per bill	0010 00 00
	to Mr germins gardner by Mr Steuens	0001 01 07
	to Mr Lambs man	0001 01 07
	to Mrs Hemden for one quarters threed and Needles due at Michael in ye last	0001 00 00
5	to two of Lord feuersoms men sent post to London as per bill	0010 15 10
6	for Lodging yor Maties seruants at Newmarkitt as per bill	0048 00 00
	to Mrs Frost vnderhouskeeper	0008 00 00
	to the man that keeps the stand	0002 03 02
	to the wardrobmen by Mr Rogers	0001 10 00
	to the poore by Mr Clyton as per bill	0005 00 00
	to the footmen to London	0004 00 00
		1184 09 06

[recto] 21r

1680	**Brought from the other syd**	**1184 09 06**
6 Octobr	to the page of the Bakstairs	0001 00 00
	to Lord feuersoms man sent for the Coatches	0005 07 11
	Laid out by Mrs Crane by the way	0000 05 00
	Laid out by Mr Fowler by the way	0000 05 00

	to thre groomes sent by order as per bill	0003 00 00
	to seauen Coatchmen & postilions as per bill	0035 00 00
	to Lord feuersoms footman Lighted yor Maties Coatche	0001 00 00
	for a horsehire to London	0001 00 00
	to the Coatchmakers man as per bill	0002 03 02
7	to Mr William sent post to Newmarkitt as per bill	0005 01 06
11	to Lord Clarendons man	0001 00 00
13	to the portingall Embassadors man	0001 01 07
	to Mr Johnson for the wagons as per bill	0004 04 06
	to Lady Marshalls man	0001 00 00
14	to Mr Grill for goeing post thre tymes to and from Newmarkitt as per bill	0016 03 09
	Laid out by Mr Steuens as per bill	0005 16 02
	Laid out by Mr Baptist as per bill	0001 05 06
	to Mr Winwood Messenger as per bill	0006 14 00
15	to Mr Smith by Lady Wych as per bill	0004 00 00
	to Mr Capell Messenger as per bill	0005 06 00
		1285 03 07

[verso] 21v

1680	**Brought from the other Syd**	**1285 03 07**
16 Octobr	to the portingall Embassadors man	0001 01 07
	for glases by Mr Baptist	0002 07 00
	Laid out by Mrs Hemden	0000 18 00
20	to the portingall Embassadors man	0001 01 07
	to Lady Arlingtons man	0001 01 07
29	to the portingall Embassadors man	0001 01 07
	mor to the portingall Embassadors man that day	0001 01 07
30	to the portingall Embassadors man	0001 01 07

	Laid out by Mr Steuens as per bill	0006 15 00
1 Novembr	to the secretary for two warants warants[52] for foure hundred pounds	0007 00 00
	fees & Charges at the Receit of foure hundred pounds	0015 00 00
3	Bounty to yor Maties Coatch men and postilions by Mr Sterline[53] as per bill	0020 00 00
	bounty to yor Maties footmen by Mr Maugrege as per bill	0020 00 00
	bounty to yor Maties Litermen & Chairmen by Mr Salmon as per bill	0020 00 00
	bounty to the somptermen by Mr Betts as per bill	0020 00 00
	bounty to the Groom of the Stables by Mr Lands as per bill	0010 00 00
		1413 13 01

[recto] 22r

1680	**Brought from the other Syd**	**1413 13 01**
3 Novembr	bounty to the yeomans of the Gard by Mr Persons as per bill	0024 00 00
	bounty to the Chasmary[54] man by Mr Rawson as per bill	0003 00 00
4	Laid out by Mr Clarke as per bill	0003 06 06
6	to the portingall Embassadors man	0001 01 07
8	to the portingall Embassadors man	0001 01 07
	Laid out by Mrs Hamden	0001 00 00
10	to Mr Herbert for remouing yor Maties clocks as per bill	0004 09 00
12	to the portingall Embassadors man	0001 01 07
	for pens Inke and paper	0000 10 00

52 Uncorrected duplication.
53 Starling.
54 Uncertain meaning.

15[55]	to the Kings violins Musique as per bill	0020 00 00
	to the wind Musique & Recorders	0005 00 00
	to the Harper	0001 00 00
	to yor Maties footmen	0003 00 00
	to the Kings footmen	0002 00 00
	to the ducks footmen	0002 00 00
	to the dutchesse footmen	0002 00 00
	to yor Maties Coatchmen	0003 00 00
	to the Kings Coatchmen	0002 00 00
	to the Kings Trompets	0006 00 00
		1499 03 04

[verso] 22v

1680	**Brought from the other Syd**	**1499 03 04**
15 Novembr	to the dromes	0003 00 00
	to the ducks Trompets	0003 00 00
	to the Litermen & Chairemen	0002 00 00
	to the somptermen	0001 00 00
	to the Groomes of the stables	0002 00 00
	to the Master of yor Maties Berges	0001 00 00
	to the violine in ordenary	0001 00 00
	to the Groomebotleman	0001 00 00
	to the duckes violine Musique	0010 00 00
	to the yeomans of the Gard	0002 00 00
	to the Robs feast as per bill	0005 00 00
	to Lady Northumberlands gardner	0001 01 07
	to orange Anne presented Graps	0002 03 02
	to the Cornecater[56]	0001 01 07
19	to the portingall Embassadors man	0001 01 07
20	to the secretaris Clarke for his Lodging at windsor as per bill	0010 00 00

55 Catherine's birthday – she was 42.

56 Corn cutter.

23	to Mr Cooqus as per bill	0002 05 10
30	to the footman presented St Androws Crose	0001 00 00
	to the portingall Embassadors man	0001 01 07
	Laid out by Mrs Hamden	0000 11 00
		1550 09 08

[recto] 23r

1680	**Brought from the other Syd**	**1550 09 08**
Decembr 5	to the portingall Embassadors man	0001 01 07
6	to Mr Lightfoot as per bill	0012 16 00
13	for a Comboxe by Lady Killygrew	0001 15 00
16	to the portingall Embassadors man	0001 01 07
25	to two of the portingall Embassadors men	0002 03 02
	to the yeomane of the Gard	0001 01 07
27	to Mrs Mor for a quarter due at Cristmas Last as per bill	0001 06 00
	to Mrs Hamden for a quarters threed and Needles due at Cristmas Last	0001 00 00
29	to Mr Germins gardner by Mr Steuens	0002 03 02
	to the portingall Embassadors man	0001 01 07
30	to the secretary for a warrant	0006 00 00
	fees & Charges at the Receipt of thre hundred fifty eight pounds eighteen shillings and eight pence	0012 16 00
1 Janr	to the Kings violin Musicke as per bill	0020 00 00
	to the wind Musick & Recorders	0006 00 00
	to the violin in ordenary	0001 00 00
	to the Harper	0001 00 00
	to yor Maties Mr Cooke	0005 00 00
	to his man	0001 00 00
	to the Kings Mr Cooke	0005 00 00
	to his man	0001 00 00
		1634 15 04

[verso] 23v

1680[57]	**Brought from the other Syd**	**1634 15 04**
1 Janr	to yor Maties Coatchmen	0010 00 00
	to yor Maties postilions	0003 00 00
	to yor Maties footmen	0010 00 00
	to the Kings Coatchmen	0005 00 00
	to the Groomes of the stables	0004 00 00
	to the Litermen & Chairemen	0005 00 00
	to the somptermen	0002 00 00
	to the Kings Trompets	0006 00 00
	to the dromes	0003 00 00
	to the Gallerykeepers	0006 00 00
	to the duckes Trompets	0006 00 00
	to the violin tto the duckes Children	0001 00 00
	to the Mr of yor Maties Berges	0002 00 00
	to the shoemakersmen	0004 00 00
	to the portingall Baker	0003 00 00
	to the portingall Cooke	0003 00 00
	to Mrs Hamden	0010 00 00
	to John Tough	0020 00 00
	to the men that Brings the play bills	0002 03 02
	to the man that Bring the Gazetts	0001 01 07
	to the Box keepers of both play houses	0004 06 04
	to the Herbwomane	0001 01 07
	to the secretarys Clerke	0005 00 00
		1751 08 00

[recto] 24r

1680[58]	**Brought from the other Syd**	**1751 08 00**
1 Janr	to the Treasurers Clerke	0005 00 00
	to the porters of whitehall gatt	0002 00 00

57 1681 NS.
58 1681 NS.

	to their men	0000 10 00
	to yor Maties wachmakers	0010 00 00
2	to a womane from Colbrook presented pudins	0001 01 07
	to Lady Northumberlands gardner	0001 01 07
	to the Cornecuter	0001 01 07
6	to the smith presented a Kye	0001 01 07
	to the man that Keeps the Kings dogs	0001 11 07
13	to the portingall Embassadors man	0001 01 07
	to Lady Arlingtons Housekeeper	0002 03 02
20	Laid out by Mrs Hamden	0000 06 00
24	Laid out by Mr Steuens as per bill	0003 03 00

Moneis disbursed

from the 13 of April: 1680: to the 25 of January 1680[59] **1781 09 08**

Moneis Receiued

from the 13 of April: 1680: to the 25 of January 1680:[60] and what remaines due to yor Matie from the Last Accompt **1924 18 01**

Remaines due

to yor Matie from the Accomptant this 25: of January 1680[61] **0143 08 05**

[verso] 24v

1680[62]

5 Febr	Laid out by Mr Clarke as per bill	0001 16 06
12	for a Lookinglas by Mr Rowland	0001 05 00
	to Lady Marshalls womane & page	0012 19 00

59 1681 NS.
60 1681 NS.
61 1681 NS.
62 1681 NS.

17	to Lady Arlingtons Coatchmane Chairemen and footmen	0003 00 00
18	to two Girles that cam to spine[63]	0002 03 02
	to the portingall Embassadors man	0001 01 07
	to Lady Clarindons man presented a salmon	0001 01 07
21	to the portingall Embassadors man	0001 01 07
24	to the portingall Embassadors man	0001 01 07
26	to the portingall Embassadors man	0001 01 07
27	to yor Maties footmen first time to Heigh parke	0002 00 00
	to Lord feuersoms man	0001 01 07
1 March	to the footman presented a Leeke	0001 00 00
2	to Mrs deuett by Lady Killigrew as per bill	0015 01 00
	Laid out by Mr Johnson as per bill	0001 05 06
7	Laid out by Mr Steuens as per bill	0001 11 10
8	Laid out by Mr Clarke as per bill	0000 13 06
	for pen Inke and paper	0000 10 00
		0049 15 00

[recto] 25r

		lib s d
1680/81	**Brought from the other Syd**	**0049 15 00**
	Moneis disbursed	
	from the 25: of January 1680: to the 9th: of March 1680[64]	**0049 15 00**
	Moneis Receiued	

63 Spin.
64 1681 NS.

from the 25 of January 1680: to the 9th: of March: 1680[65] and what remaines due to yor Matie from the Last Accompt	**0143 08 05**

Remaines due

To yor Matie from the Accomptant this 9th: of March 1680[66]	**0093 13 05**

Catherina R

[65] 1681 NS.
[66] 1681 NS.

Catherine of Braganza's itinerary

Early modern queens rarely travelled light.[1] Long journeys required substantial quantities of people, baggage, horses and carts, or boats and barges, while even short outings needed female attendants in charge of everyday accessories, as well as footmen, chairmen, coachmen and bargemen, depending on the mode of transport. Travel called for trunks, coffers and cases that were designed to protect and keep secure the queen's personal possessions as she journeyed while also proclaiming her ownership of them. Several surviving examples of royal luggage with connections to Catherine of Braganza offer a hint of the quality of these specialist items. The queen's cypher, KR for *Katherine Regina*, worked in gilt dome-headed nails adorn a leather covered trunk or coffer at Holyroodhouse in Edinburgh.[2] This trunk now sits on a decorative wooden stand, revealing how luggage could easily transform into a decorative piece of furniture. A second example, this time of a leather-covered trunk with two integral drawers, with a marvellous quilted salmon pink silk lining, was possibly left behind after the queen's visit in 1671 to Oxnead Hall.[3] Oxnead was the home of Sir Robert Paston and the queen's visit featured in her privy purse accounts on 30 September as part of a longer tour of Norfolk, which explains why the trunk now belongs to collection at Strangers' Hall, Norwich.[4]

The queen's short stay with Sir Robert is one of many places listed in the accounts and the itinerary given below records the references to where Catherine went and who she visited. The details aligned to the left note where Catherine, and members of her household, were on a given date followed by the document reference. These are supplemented by brief notes recording where the king was, so placing Catherine's movements in context and showing when and where their travel plans overlapped or diverged. Charles II's details are in italic and aligned to the right. In addition, some brief details for the

1 For example, see Mary Hill Cole, *The Portable Queen: Elizabeth I and the Politics of Ceremony* (Amherst, MA: University of Massachusetts Press, reprint 2011).

2 Coffer on a stand, 1650–1700, leather, iron and walnut, Great Gallery, Palace of Holyroodhouse, RCIN 31154. https://www.rct.uk/collection/search#/1/collection/31154/coffer-on-stand [accessed 31/10/22].

3 Trunk with two drawers, 1660–70, leather, iron and wood, Strangers Hall, Norfolk, NWHCM 1992:110.9. https://shinealightproject.wordpress.com/2015/01/13/unlocking-hidden-gems-a-trunk-fit-for-a-queen [accessed 31/10/22]. Also see Olivia Fryman, 'Coffer-makers to the late Stuart court, 1660–1714', *Furniture History* 52 (2016), 8, 10.

4 LAO, 1-Worsley 7, fo. 27v. See R. W. Ketton-Cremer, 'The visit of King Charles II to Norfolk', in *Norfolk Portraits* (London: Faber and Faber, 1944), 9–21.

periods not covered by the accounts have been included: so, from Catherine's arrival in Portsmouth on 13 May 1662 and the first reference to her whereabouts in the accounts six months later, on 8 December, and from the last reference in the accounts on 27 February 1681 and the period running up to the king's death in February 1685.

Catherine's itinerary records over 126 destinations, including the homes of courtiers such as Moor Park, Hertfordshire, Euston Hall, West Suffolk, and Worcester House, on the Strand, as well as parks and pleasure gardens such as Hyde Park, St James' Park and Mulberry gardens. As **Map 1** shows, Catherine's travel was concentrated in the south of England, with a particular focus on the Thames Valley. In that respect, her itinerary has many things in common with those of the Tudor kings in terms of its scope and the underlying reasons for travel. As Fiona Kisby has demonstrated, Henry VII's travels can be described in three main ways: as domestic, with regards to his usually remaining within a 30 mile radius on London and making use of royal properties; as centred on the progress and royal ceremony; and as a festive itinerary governed by the liturgical or festive calendar.[5] Building on this, Simon Thurley observed that during Henry VIII's reign the hunt dictated the placement of many royal properties in and around the Thames Valley.[6] Catherine's travel was influenced by her husband's interests, including hunting and horse racing – as well as her own health drawing her to Tunbridge Wells and Bath and by friendship or politics taking her to the homes of the leading courtiers and politicians.

Considered another way, the itinerary also reveals that her patterns of travel consisted of long journeys, including summer progresses, short trips in and around Westminster, St James's and the city of London and removals between the various royal palaces where the queen had apartments. In most years, at the simplest level of analysis, Catherine spent the winter months in and around London. She started to travel further afield in the spring (March/April) and stopped in the autumn (by the end of September), with her most ambitious travel occurring in late summer (July and August). In the summer of 1663, Catherine went to Windsor and then on progress, while in 1664 there was no major summer travel. In 1665, royal travel was described as a progress but was driven by a wish to avoid the plague in and around the capital, while in 1666 there was some travel early in the summer but the Great Fire in early September ensured that the king and queen remained in and around London. While Catherine's travels in 1665 were prompted by a wish to preserve her

5 Fiona Kisby, 'Kingship and the royal itinerary: a study of the peripatetic household of the early Tudor kings, 1485–1547', *The Court Historian* 4.1 (1999), 29.

6 Simon Thurley, *The Royal Palaces of Tudor England: Architecture and Court Life, 1460–1547* (New Haven and London: Yale University Press, 1993), 68–69.

Map 1 Places visited in England by the queen.

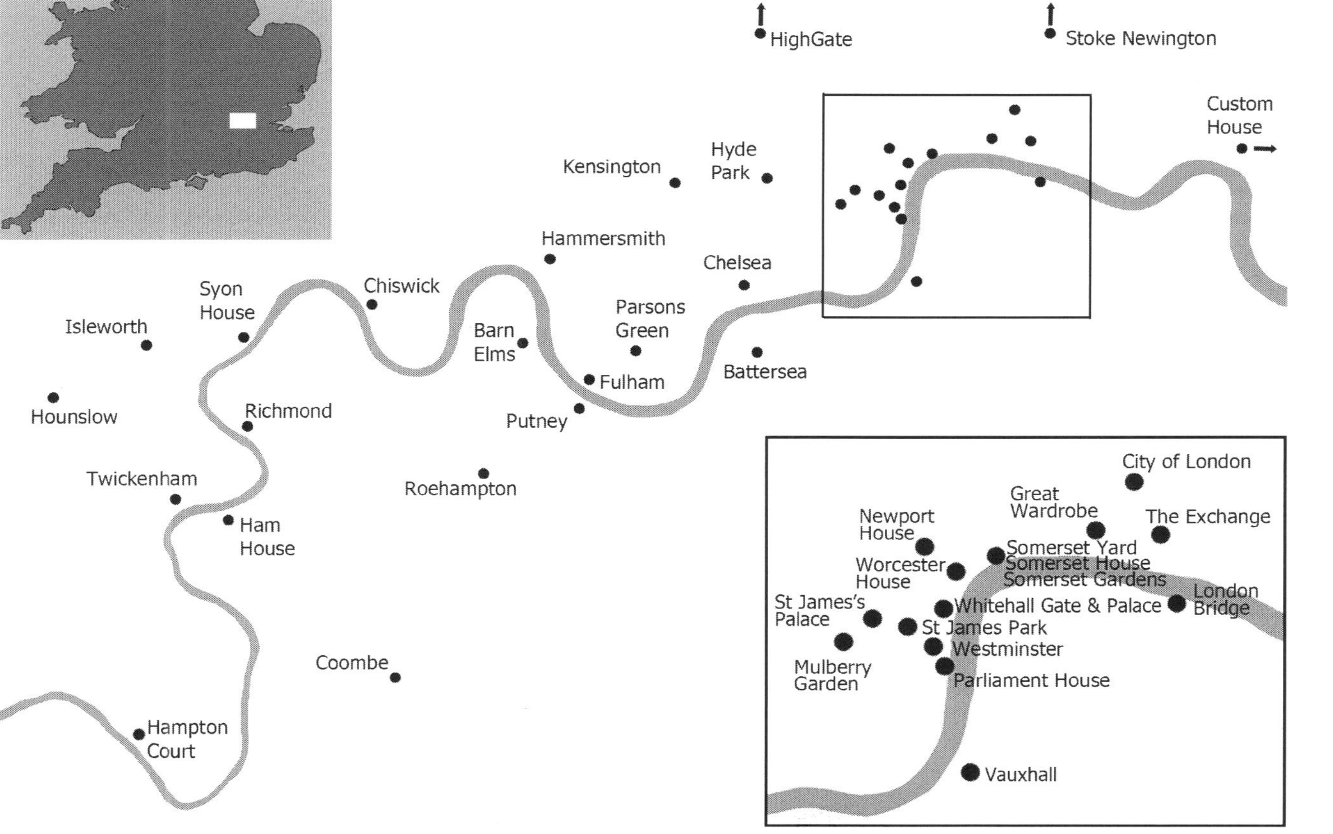

Map 2 Places visited by the queen in and around the Thames Valley.

health, in other years she went to bathe at spa towns including Bath, Tunbridge Wells and Epsom to promote her health and hopefully improve her fertility.[7]

The queen's shorter trips focused in and around the city of London and the suburbs of Westminster as well as slightly further afield along the Thames Valley (**Map 2**). From 1662 she was mainly resident at Whitehall, although this is implicit rather than explicit in the privy purse accounts. Fortunately, the accounts of the King's Works offer more detail of the work that was undertaken from April 1662 to prepare and extend the queen's apartments. These included a substantial new privy chamber, while the wooden carvings supplied for her bedchamber and bed alcove included swags of tulips and other flowers.[8] Payments were also made for her chapel in 1662, including altering silvered altar rails and providing a wooden altar.[9] Her apartments were developed further in 1664 with the addition of a new closet, while in 1668 more rooms were added near the privy stairs and a bathing room in 1670.[10]

In contrast, there were specific references to her visiting the city of London, including a cluster noting her attendance at Parliament. When Catherine arrived in England, Somerset House was the home of the queen dowager, Henrietta Maria, and Catherine visited her mother-in-law there.[11] Samuel Pepys noted that in October 1664 he 'saw the Queen's new rooms, which are most stately and nobly furnished'.[12] However, after Henrietta Maria's death on 10 September 1669, the palace passed to Catherine of Braganza, and the royal arms of France were taken down from the bedchamber and replaced with those of Portugal.[13] While she did not live there, from this point on, Somerset House was her most visited palace during the 1670s because she used the chapel, which was larger than the chapel at St James'.[14] She also celebrated Maundy Thursday in the Guard chamber.[15] The significance of Somerset House was reflected by the numerous short journeys there by boat, both when the house was the London home of the queen dowager, her mother-in-law Henrietta Maria, and during the 1670s. The palace gained a degree of

7 Susannah Lyon-Whaley, 'Queens at the spa: Catherine of Braganza, Mary of Modena and the politics of display at Bath and Tunbridge Wells', *The Court Historian* 27.1 (2022), 24–41.

8 Howard M. Colvin, J. Mordaunt Crook, K. Downes, J. Newman (eds.), *The History of the King's Works: Volume 5 1660–1782* (London: HMSO, 1976), 5, 267.

9 Colvin, *History of the King's Works*, 5, 267.

10 Colvin, *History of the King's Works*, 5, 269.

11 Colvin, *History of the King's Works*, 5, 256–57.

12 Pepys, *Diary*, 5, 300.

13 Colvin, *History of the King's Works*, 5, 257.

14 Simon Thurley, *Somerset House: The Palace of England's Queens, 1551–1692* (London: London Topographical Society, 2009), 70–71.

15 Thurley, *Somerset House*, 71.

notoriety during the Popish Plot when Catherine was accused of conniving at the murder of Sir Edmund Godfrey by her servants at the palace.[16]

The itinerary also highlights fashionable outings made by the queen, such as her visits to Hyde Park, with the first trip each year by carriage noted in the accounts. As Lorenzo Magalotti described, this was a key point of the society year. Consequently, 'the carriage promenade, which begins only the Sunday after Easter and first of May, is very crowded: it takes place in the great meadow of Hyde Park, going round in several concentric circles that sometimes turn out to be as many as four in number'.[17] Pepys provided a more personal view of these trips to the park. For instance on 4 April 1663 he recalled how 'After dinner to Hide Park; my aunt, Mrs Wright, and I in one Coach, and all the rest of the women in Mrs Turners….At the parke was the King, and in another coach my Lady Castlemayne, they greeting one another at every Tour'.[18] Catherine's accounts offer a further nuance on this. Pepys noted his first visit on 19 March 1665 while the queen's first reference was attending on the king's birthday.[19] In 1668, Pepys went first on 30 March, unlike Catherine who did not attend until 1 May.[20]

Catherine's travel, especially when she left London, generally followed the pattern set by the king for his summer travels, although she did not always accompany him to Newmarket. For instance, she did in 1671 but not in 1669 or 1670. There are different ways of thinking about the king's movements, both of which are helpful in this context. The first, which is incorporated into the itinerary below, draws on the work of Andrew Ashbee, who has painstakingly explored household records for evidence relating to music, musical instruments and musicians in Charles II's court and household.[21] Ashbee's work reveals that the king took his musicians with him whenever he travelled for any length of time, so the location of the court musicians is indicative of where the king was. The second draws on the work of Brian Weiser, who analysed the number of days that Charles II resided in his various palaces. Between 1661 and 1679 the king spent between 258 and 365 days a year at Whitehall, except in 1665 when the figure dipped to 180 days, and then from 1680 to 1684 the number dropped further to between 173 and 191 days.[22] Put more simply, Weiser observed that from 1673 Charles spent less and less time

16 Thurley, *Somerset House*, 71.

17 Middleton, *Lorenzo Magalotti*, 129.

18 Pepys, *Diary*, 4, 95.

19 Pepys, *Diary*, 6, 60.

20 Pepys, *Diary*, 9, 141–42.

21 Andrew Ashbee ed, *Records of English Court Music volume 1 (1660–1685)* (Snodland: T. J. Press (Padstow), Ltd, 1986).

22 Brian Weiser, *Charles II and the Politics of Access* (Woodbridge: The Boydell Press, 2003), 39, figure 6.

in London and at Whitehall. When not at Whitehall, the king and queen made use of other royal palaces.

At the start of their marriage Hampton Court was used for the reception of the queen and her honeymoon in 1662 and the preparation of the palace included creation of a chapel royal.[23] In addition, Charles spent important but variable amounts of time at Hampton Court during the 1660s: in 1661–62, 1665–66 and 1668–69.[24] The duke and duchess of York also had apartments there, which provided another reason for Catherine to visit.[25] During the 1660s she also visited Richmond and made a few visits to Greenwich where she stayed in the Queen's House.[26]

As the reign progressed, Newmarket became a royal favourite. From 1668, the king visited the town regularly (1668–72 and then 1674–84), usually in the spring and autumn. Sir John Reresby recorded that Charles was able to relax while at Newmarket:

> The king was so much pleased in the country, and so great a lover of the diversions which that place did afford... he mixed himself amongst the crowd, allowed every man to speak to him that pleased, went a hawking in mornings, to cock matches in the afternoons (if there were no horse races) and to plays in the evening, acted in a barn, and by very ordinary Bartholomew fair comedians.[27]

Consequently, Charles kept a house at Newmarket with apartments for himself and his queen, as well as the duchess of York and the duke of Monmouth.[28] In addition he acquired Audley End for Catherine to use in 1669 and the privy purse accounts indicate that she stayed there regularly in 1668, 1670, 1671 and 1679.[29] Her presence resulted in some repairs and alterations, including the addition of a chapel.[30]

Catherine, like her husband, also spent increasing amounts of time at Windsor (1670–71, 1674–75 and 1677–84).[31] Their presence prompted building work in 1674–75 and 1676–77 on the king and queen's apartments. The Italian

23 Simon Thurley, 'The Stuart kings, Oliver Cromwell, and the Chapel Royal, 1618–1685', *Architectural History* 45 (2002), 256.

24 Weiser, *Politics of Access*, 39, figure 7.

25 Colvin, *History of the King's Works*, 5, 153.

26 Simon Thurley, 'A country seat fit for a king: Charles II, Greenwich and Winchester', in Eveline Cruickshanks (ed.), *The Stuart Court* (Stroud: Sutton, 2000), 222–23.

27 Browning, *Reresby*, 259.

28 Colvin, *History of the King's Works*, 5, 214.

29 See the itinerary below.

30 Colvin, *History of the King's Works*, 5, 132.

31 Weiser, *Politics of Access*, 39, figure 7.

painter Antonio Verrio placed Catherine in a chariot as the centrepiece of his design for the painted ceiling for the Queen's Audience Chamber, while she was depicted vanquishing Sedition and Envy on the ceiling of the Queen's Presence Chamber.[32] By the end of the reign, Charles began a new palace at Winchester (1683–84), which included lodgings for his queen.[33]

Royal travel was expensive and by the mid-1670s Catherine was allowed £1,000 a year for her 'removes and progresses'.[34] However, this money was not always paid promptly. For instance, on 5 July 1675 a warrant was ordered for £1,000 'for the Queen' but it was not until the following February when a warrant for this sum was issued 'to the Honble. John Hervey, Treasurer to the Queen, for the charge of the removing or progress of the Queen this last summer, 1675'.[35] On 28 June 1677 Hervey received £2,000 'for defraying the charge of the removing or progress of her Majesty both for the last and this summer'.[36] The privy purse was used to pay for some of these expenses in the short-term and the cost of the various journeys has been included below to show how expensive the different travel options were. The accounts also reveal how and when footmen, postilions, coachmen, sumptermen and wagons with the baggage attended the queen. When necessary, the queen travelled at night, with men being paid to light the way on various occasions and, when she journeyed further afield, local guides were employed to help find the way. Another key feature of the queen's travel is that Catherine regularly relied on the coaches, barges and sedan chairs of friends and other members of the royal family. On 26 July 1677, a payment of £56 was 'Paid to seuerall people of qualitys Coatchmen Chairemen & footmen that waited of yor Matie in the yeares of 1670: 1671: 1672 as per bill'.[37]

Despite the richness of the material recorded here, there are four challenges in using the privy purse accounts to piece together Catherine's itinerary. The first relates to dating, which occasionally reveals a difference between the date of payment and the date of travel, resulting in some slight discrepancies in the timings. Second, there were multiple short journeys where the destination was not recorded and some days with several payments for the same location, so making a place look more popular than it was. Third, the accounts consist of a combination of direct references to how and when Catherine travelled alongside indirect references to gifts being given to the servants of people that she visited as well as presents sent to her from people who were identified by their location. For instance, on 25 August 1665, a payment of

32 RCIN 408426 and RCIN 408427.

33 Thurley, 'A country seat', 228–29.

34 *CTB, 1672–75*, 318.

35 *CTB, 1672–75*, 318, *CTB, 1676–79*, 129.

36 *CTB, 1676–79*, 671.

37 LAO, 1-Worsley 8, fo. 25r.

£2 was made to 'ye Earle of Pemprocke[38] Keeper'.[39] This was Philip Herbert, 5th earl of Pembroke and 2nd earl of Montgomery (1621–69), and the country home of the earls of Pembroke was Wilton House at Wilton, near Salisbury in Wiltshire. Fourth, there were some references to journeys made by others, either on the queen's business or on the queen's behalf, such as on 15 December 1663 when Mr Chiffinch purchased 'seuerall necesariess for ye Portuguez att Porthmouth'.[40] Books 1 and book 2 include references to travel by 'Mr Halsey'. This was Edward Hallsall, who was equerry to the queen from 1662 to 1678. Some of his travel was linked to the movement of the queen's household but not all, as on 9 September 1669 when he received £20 for travelling 'to Southampton'.[41] Richard Stevens, a page of the presence chamber and later a page of the backstairs, also travelled with the queen or went ahead to ensure her accommodation was ready for her arrival.[42] Even so, these caveats aside, the accounts still provide a very good indication of who and where Catherine visited most and how this changed over time.

By the same token, the accounts also indicate places that Catherine did not visit, such as Basingstoke and Old Basing. This apparent lack of a visit is interesting in the context of the Basing House raised work embroidery, which is dated to the 1660s. It depicts a regal figure, often interpreted as being Charles II, standing before a chair of state and under a canopy with a queenly individual approaching him from the left, who by implication is Catherine. In the background is a substantial Tudor house and the motto of the Paulet family, *Aymez Loyalty* (Love Loyalty). This has led to the suggestion that the unidentified man next to the royal canopy is John Paulet, 5th marquis of Winchester (1598–1675), who owned Basing House.[43] The difficulty is that Catherine and Charles could never have visited the Tudor house because it was destroyed on Oliver Cromwell's orders after the siege was ended on 13 October 1645. As such, the embroidery is more a celebration of the Restoration, represented by the oak tree associated with the king's escape from parliamentary troops at Boscobel House, Shropshire. It was also a reminder of Hampshire's loyalty to the monarch, expressed by the presence of the Hampshire Hog, and the high price of that loyalty. Basing House was lost, as were many royalist lives

38 Pembroke. The country home of the earls of Pembroke was Wilton House at Wilton, near Salisbury in Wiltshire. Built on the site of Wilton Abbey.

39 LAO, 1-Worsley 6, fo. 20v.

40 LAO, 1-Worsley 6, fo. 10r.

41 LAO, 1-Worsley 7, fo. 12r.

42 For example, on 9 September 1669, Mr Stevens was 'sent before to Hamptoncourt': LAO, 1-Worsley 7, fo. 12r.

43 Embroidery, polychrome silk and metal thread on a cream satin ground, c. 1660–65, HMCMS: C1991:20 https://collections.hampshireculture.org.uk/object/basing-house-raised-work-embroidery [accessed 28/9/22].

at the ending of the siege, and Paulet went to live at Englefield, Berkshire. Yet despite the various difficulties, what the embroidery does highlight is the value that was placed on a royal visit, real or imagined, by the friends and supporters of the Charles II and his queen.

1-Worsley/6 – Catherine of Braganza, privy purse accounts 1662–68

13 May – Catherine landed at ***Portsmouth*** *– 13 May.*[44]
[Lord Sandwich] hath left the King and Queene at ***Portsmouth****' – 23 May*[45]
'the Queene this day comes to ***Hampton Court****' – 29 May.*[46]
Musicians attending on the king at ***Hampton court*** *29 May to 23 August.*[47]
the King and Queene entends to come to ***White-hall*** *from* ***Hampton Court*** *next week – for all winter' – 26 July.*[48]
it be []ing the day of the Queenes coming to ***town*** *from* ***Hampton Court****' – 23 August.*[49]
8 December – Transportinge of Trunks from the wardrop to **Hamton Court** – £4 [fo. 2r]

1663

20 April – a Boote that Carred your Maties Chaire & Chaire men to **Windsor** – £1 16s [fo. 3v]
a list of the household at ***Windsor*** *for St George's feast, 23 April.*[50]
[...] April – the Litter Men at **Windsor** – £1 [fo. 4r]
[...] April – the houskeeper att **Windsor –** £5 [fo. 4r]
25 May – the poore Knights of **Windsor** – £2 [fo. 4v]
Gervase Price, sergeant trumpeter, for four trumpeters in ordinary, at ***Tunbridge*** *from 10 June to 7 July.*[51]
25 June – Morris dauncers att **High Parck**[52] – £2 [fo. 5r]
6 July – passing the Coatchehes ouer to **Lambet** – £2 12s 6d [fo. 5v]
John Bannister and six musicians for attending his majesty to ***Tunbridge*** *and* ***Bath*** *from 23 July to 1 October.*[53]
23 July – Coatche hiere tto **turbrige**[54] – £8 [fo. 5v]
1 August – Mr Meadee Coache hiere and his Expenses ffrom **London** – £8 [fo. 6r]

44 Ashbee, *Records*, 31.
45 Pepys, *Diary*, 3, 89.
46 Pepys, *Diary*, 3, 95.
47 TNA LC5/137, pp. 131, 221; Ashbee, *Records*, 35.
48 Pepys, *Diary*, 3, 146.
49 Pepys, *Diary*, 3, 174–75.
50 TNA LC5/137, p. 296; Ashbee, *Records*, 44, 46, 47.
51 TNA LC5/138, p. 91; Ashbee, *Records*, 49.
52 Hyde Park.
53 TNA LC5/138, p. 90; Ashbee, *Records*, 48, 61.
54 Tunbridge.

15 August – the water fiellers & those that opned The gates att **the wells** – £19 [fo. 6r]
17 August – the seruants wheare your Matie Lay att **tonbridg** – £5 [fo. 6r]
18 August – Coache hiere ffrom **tonbrig** tto **London** – £31 12s 6d [fo. 6v]
25 August – Coachehiere tto the **Bath** – £60 [fo. 6v]
27 August – the Seruantts att **Maydenhead**[55] – £1 [fo. 7r]
28 August – the Seruantts att **Nubery**[56] – £5 [fo. 7r]
29 August – the Seruannts att **Malbury**[57] – £5 [fo. 7r]
21 September – the Guids att **Barth** – £10 [fo. 7v]
22 September – the saruantts att **Barth** – £5 [fo. 7v]
22 September – the saruantts att **Lord Nubockes**[58] – £5 [fo. 7v]
22 September – Mr Hallsy for Coathehiere from **Barth** – £20 [fo. 7v]
28 September – Mr Hallsy for Coathehiere from **Barth** – £30 [fo. 7v]
1 October – Charges tto **Bristo**[59] in receuing the Monys – 15s [fo. 7v]
1 October – the saruantees where yr Matie Lay at **weekam**[60] – £5 [fo. 7v]
1 October – Where your Matie Eate at **Oxbrige** – £5 [fo. 7v]
1 October – the poore att **Oxbridge** – £2 [fo. 8r]
3 November – Mr Halsall for Coachehiere ffrom **Barth –** £165 12s [fo. 8v]
18 November – Mr Carelton ffor his Jornys tto **Bath** & **tonbrige –** £1 10s [fo. 8v]
25 November – Mr Chiffinch ffor Carreges> ~~for carring [...]~~ tto ye **Barth –** 6s 6d [fo. 9r]
14 December – one of The Gard ffor Carring your Maties platte tto ye **barth** – 13s [fo. 9v]
15 December – Mr Chiffinch for seuerall necesariess for ye Portuguez att **Porthmouth**
Mending of waggons and remouing of Goods ffor your Matie – £6 5s [fo. 10r]

1664

17 June[61] – a Bagge pipe Booye in **high parck** – 5s [fo. 10v]
22 June – a man thatt braughtt watter from **Outlands**[62] to **hampton Court** for yr Matie – £1 9s [fo. 11r]
28 July – ye house Keeper & Gardnor att **Hampton Court** – £2 [fo. 11v]
5 August – ye Man yt keepes ye **Parlementt house** – £2 [fo. 12r]
6 August – a pair of oares yt Carred yr Matie Foote Men tto **Hammersmith** – 5s [fo. 12r]

55 Maidenhead.
56 Newbury.
57 Melbury House, Melbury Park, Dorset.
58 His constituency was Cirencester, Gloucestershire.
59 Bristol.
60 Wickham.
61 There is a gap in the account with no entries between 3 February and 17 June.
62 Oatlands.

7 August – oares y^t Carred y^r Matie & your follouers tto **Lambeth** – £1 [fo. 12r]
29 August – y^r Matie att **Somersett house** att play – £10 [fo. 13r]
1 September – y^r Matie Barge Man ffor waitting one y^r Matie ouer tto **Lambett** – £2 [fo. 13v]
21 September – y^r Matie att **Somersett house** – £10 [fo. 13v]
29 September – My selfe and M^s Wells which y^r Matie Lostt att ombro att **Somersett house** – £13 10s [fo. 13v]
26 October – y^r Matie footemen running tto **wollige**[63] – £4 10s [fo. 14r]
26 October – y^r Matie Barge Man for waiting one y^r Matie tto **wollige** with thre barges – £2 [fo. 14r]
2 November – To y^r Matie **att Lady Malburys**[64] – £2 [fo. 14r]

1665

4 January – ye Keeper of **ye parlementt house** – £2 [fo. 16r]
11 April – y^r Maties footmen roning to **hampton Courtt** – £2 [fo. 17r]
11 April – y^r Maties footemen for seuerall ttimes Rouning – £92 [fo. 17r]
11 April – y^r Maties Barge Men for two jernes one to **Hampton Court** & ye other to **barnehelmes**[65] – £10 10s [fo. 17v]
20 April – y^r Matie which you lost att ombro att **Sumersett house** – £5 [fo. 17v]
25 April – y^r Maties footemen for Roning – £2 [fo. 17v]
25 April – y^r Maties Barge Man goieng ouer tto **Lambett** – £1 10s [fo. 17v]
23 May – y^r Maties footemen Roning tto **Lady Chesterfields**[66] – £2 [fo. 18r]
24 May – y^r Maties footemen Roning to **hygate** – £2 [fo. 18r]
24 May – y^r Maties Barge Man for goieng tto **hammer smith** – £3 [fo. 18r]
27 May – y^r Maties Barge Man ouer to **foxhall** – £1 [fo. 18r]
29 May – Cheries in **hy park** – £1 [fo. 18r]
30 May – y^r Maties footemen Roning a hunting £2 [fo. 18r]
*Sergeant trumpeter and six trumpeters to accompany the king to **Salisbury** [undated, June 1665].*[67]
10 June – To ye Gardnor att **Sion house** – £2 [fo. 18v]
10 June – To y^r Maties footemen Roning tto **Sion house** – £2 [fo. 18v]
***Syon House, Isleworth** – 29 June*
***Hampton Court** – 9 July*
13 July – y^r Maties footemen – £2 [fo. 18v]
13 July – y^r Maties footemen Roning tto **Hounslay**[68] – £2 [fo. 18v]
17 July – y^r Maties footemen – £2 [fo. 18v]

63 Woolwich.

64 Uncertain but possibly Melbury.

65 Barn Elms.

66 Her husband, Lord Chesterfield, was recorded as dying at his house in Middlesex, which is probably where the queen visited Lady Chesterfield.

67 TNA LC5/138, p. 374; Ashbee, *Records*, 64–65, 70.

68 Hounslow.

18 July – y^{r} Maties footemen – £2 [fo. 18v]
18 July – one y^{t} sheud y^{r} Matie ye watter Woorkes att **More parke** – £2 [fo. 19r]
18 July – ye parkeepers att **Hampton Court** – £2 [fo. 19r]
20 July – ye house Keeper and Gardnor att **hampton Court** – £10 [fo. 19r]
20 July – ffor feching of watter from **Epsom** ffor y^{r} Matie – £4 10s [fo. 19r]
20 July – y^{r} Maties footemen – £2 [fo. 19r]
26 July – y^{r} Maties footemen – £2 [fo. 19r]
26 July – ye Cheremen thatt Carred Donoline tto **Hampton** – £1 2s 6d [fo. 19r]
27 July – ye saruants att y^{e} **Bishop of Winchisters**[69] – £3 [fo. 19v]
27 July – y^{r} Maties footemen – £2 [fo. 19v]
28 July – ye seruants att **Winchister** – £5 [fo. 19v]
28 July – y^{r} Maties footemen – £2 [fo. 19v]

***Salisbury** – 1 August*

3 August – y^{r} Maties footemen – £2 [fo. 19v]
9 August – y^{r} Maties footemen – £2 [fo. 19v]
10 August – y^{r} Maties footemen – £2 [fo. 19v]
11 August – y^{r} Maties footemen – £2 [fo. 19v]
16 August – y^{r} Maties footemen – £2 [fo. 20r]
17 August – y^{r} Maties footemen – £2 [fo. 20r]
17 August – a guide when y^{r} Matie went tto see y^{e} **Duke of Yorkes Children** – £1 [fo. 20r]
20 August – y^{r} Maties footemen – £2 [fo. 20r]
22 August – y^{r} Maties footemen – £2 [fo. 20r]
23 August – y^{r} Maties footemen – £2 [fo. 20r]
24 August – y^{r} Maties footemen – £2 [fo. 20r]
25 August – y^{r} Maties footemen a hunting – £2 [fo. 20v]
25 August – To y^{e} **Earle of Pemprocke**[70] **Keeper** – £2 [fo. 20v]
29 August – y^{r} Maties footemen – £2 [fo. 20v]
31 August – y^{r} Maties footemen – £2 [fo. 20v]
3 September – y^{r} Maties footemen – £2 [fo. 20v]
5 September – y^{r} Maties footemen – £2 [fo. 20v]
8 September – y^{r} Maties footemen – £2 [fo. 20v]
11 September – y^{r} Maties footemen – £2 [fo. 20v]
12 September – y^{r} Maties footemen – £2 [fo. 20v]
13 September – y^{r} Maties footemen – £2 [fo. 20v]

[69] His official residences outside London were Bishop's Waltham palace, Hampshire, Farnham castle, Surrey, Wolvesey palace, Winchester and Winchester palace, Southwark, Surrey. Prior to the Civil War, the bishop's London home was Winchester House in Southwark. In 1642, it was converted into a prison and sold in 1649. After the Restoration the bishop recovered the property but chose to live at Chelsea. https://medievalarchaeology.co.uk/projects/a-lost-palace-of-the-bishops-of-winchester [accessed 27/1/23].

[70] Pembroke. The country home of the earls of Pembroke was Wilton House at Wilton, near Salisbury in Wiltshire. Built on the site of Wilton Abbey.

1? September – y^{r} Matie for y^{e} **Earle of pembroucks** Boulling Grine keeper – £5 [fo. 21r]
18 September – y^{r} Maties footemen – £2 [fo. 21r]
23 September – y^{r} Maties footemen – £2 [fo. 21r]
23 September – To y^{e} seruants att **Co**^{nells} **Papphames**[71] – £5 [fo. 21r]

__Oxford__ – 23 September

26 September – y^{r} Maties footemen – £2 [fo. 21r]
27 September – y^{r} Maties footemen – £2 [fo. 21v]
4 October – Giuen att y^{e} **Phesike Garden**[72] – £1 [fo. 21v]
16 October – y^{r} Maties footemen – £2 [fo. 21v]
18 October – To y^{e} **Earle of Pembrocke** Keeper – £1 [fo. 21v]
19 October – To y^{r} Maties footemen Roning tto **Dichly –** £2 [fo. 21v]
15 November – To y^{e} Ringers at **Merten Colidge** – 10s [fo. 21v]

1666

the king left Oxford for __Hampton Court__, 23 January
the king at __Whitehall__, 1 February[73]

5 February – a Messenger y^{t} Carred y^{r} Maties <letters> tto **London** – £5 [fo. 23r]
13 February – y^{e} house Clenser att **Merton Colledge** – £2 [fo. 23v]
13 February – Mr Halsall for Coatch hiere from **Oxford** tto **London** – £96 16s [fo. 23v]
13 February – y^{e} Meusique att **Oxford** – £5 [fo. 24r]
13 February – y^{r} Matie footemen Roning from **Oxford** tto **Maydenhead** – £2 [fo. 24r]
13 February – ye Seruants where y^{r} Matie Lay att **Maydenhead** – £5 [fo. 24r]
13 February – y^{r} Maties footemen Roning from **Maydenhead** tto **London** – £2 [fo. 24r]
13 February – a Peruwegge[74] thatt y^{r} Matie had att **Salsbury** – £12 [fo. 24r]
17 February – ye Barge Men for waiting one your Matie from **thiessellworth**[75] to **London** with two Bargess – £7 10s [fo. 24r]
12 March – To your Matie Barge <Man> tto **Grinewich** – £3 [fo. 24v]
24 March – Payd ffor Loding and unloding y^{r} Maties goods att **Oxford** and **London** & Mending of Wagons – £2 11s [fo. 25r]
30 April – y^{r} Maties Barge man for thre Seruecíess – £10 [fo. 25v]
30 April – ye Maties footemen ye foust[76] time tto **High parke** – £2 [fo. 25v]
1 May – y^{r} Maties footemen Roning tto **Parsons Griene** [fo. 25v]

[71] Probably Alexander Popham, whose family home was Littlecote House, Wiltshire.

[72] This was the Oxford physic garden.

[73] Ashbee, *Records*, 65, 69, 73.

[74] Periwigs?

[75] Isleworth.

[76] First.

4 May – y^{r} Maties footemen Roning to **Hemstiede**[77] – £2 [fo. 25v]
10 May – y^{r} Maties footmen Roning tto **Kingsington** – £2 [fo. 25v]
14 May – y^{r} Maties Barge Men – £1 10s [fo. 26r]
14 May – y^{r} Maties footemen £2 [fo. 26r]
15 May – a Baskett of Cherrys thatt y^{r} Matie had att **High Parke** – £1 [fo. 26r]
23 May – y^{r} Maties footemen Roning tto **Hampton Courtt** – £2 [fo. 26r]
23 May – Duke Cherrys in **High Parke** – £2 [fo. 26r]
3 June – y^{r} Maties footemen – £2 [fo. 26v]
11 June – a Collation att y^{e} **Mulbery Gardon** – £1 12s [fo. 26v]
12 June – ye Bouling Grine Keeper att **Putny** – £2 [fo. 26v]
12 June – one of y^{r} Maties footemen that was sent tto **Rohamton** – £1 [fo. 27r]
12 June – y^{r} Maties Barge Men tto **Putny** – £5 [fo. 27r]
12 June – y^{r} Maties footemen Roning to **Putny** – £2 [fo. 27r]
14 June – a Collation at y^{e} **Mulbery Gardon** – £3 5s [fo. 27r]
18 June – your Matie att **Southampton House** – £20 [fo. 27r]
28 June – ye Coatchman y^{t} Carred your <Majestie tto> St **Jamesses** and tto him y^{t} braugh <sume of> your Majestie <Retennu> ~~trayne~~ bake – £1 5s [fo. 27v]

John Bannister and six musicians in ordinary with violins accompanied the queen to ***Tunbridge Wells*** *from 9 July to 5 August.*[78]

9 July – Mr Halsalsy for Coatche hiere tto **Turnebrige**[79] – £33 5s [fo. 27v]
10 July – ye Morris Danceours att **Seneck**[80] – £1 [fo. 28r]
12 July – ye Contry Musique att **Turnebrige** – £2 [fo. 28r]
1 August – y^{r} Maties Musique for there coatche hiere and horse hiere to **Turnebrige** – £7 [fo. 28v]
4 August – ye watter fillers and poore women and others at **ye wells** – £27 10s [fo. 28v]
5 August – Mr Haley for Coatch hiere from **Turnebrige** – £34 7s [fo. 28v]
5 August – ffor bringing a Clock from **Turbrige**[81] – 10s [fo. 29r]
12 August – ye Gardnor at **Kingsenton** – £1 [fo. 29r]
16 August – y^{r} Maties footemen – £2 [fo. 29r]
16 August – ye porter in **Sumerset yeard** y^{t} Louked tto <y^{e}> Callonch – £1 [fo. 29r]
19 August – y^{r} Maties footemen Roning tto **Hamsted Hearth** – £2 [fo. 29r]
19 August – ffor Loding and vnloding y^{r} Maties Goods tto **Turbrige** – £4 6s 10d [fo. 29r]
27 August – y^{r} Maties footemen for Roning tto **Lady Chesterfilds** – £2 [fo. 29v]
4 September – the Soldiers thatt Braughtt a Cristall Candellsticke ffrom **Sumersett House** – £1 [fo. 29v]
4 September – Lord Arlinton Seruants goieng tto St **Jamesses** – £5 [fo. 29v]

77 Hampstead.
78 TNA LC5/138, 363; Ashbee, *Records*, 72.
79 Tunbridge.
80 Sevenoaks.
81 Tunbridge.

4 September – yr Maties Barge Man yt wayted ye time of ye fiere – £3 [fo. 29v]
4 September – yr Maties footmen Roning tto **Lady Malburys** – £2 [fo. 30r]
17 September – yr Maties footemen to **Roe Hampton** – £2 [fo. 30r]
17 September – yr Matie Barge Men to **Putney** – £3 [fo. 30r]
24 September – yr Maties footmen to **Hygate** – £2 [fo. 30r]
27 September – yr Maties footemen Roning to **Combe**[82] – £1 10s [fo. 30r]
27 September – yr Maties Barge Men to **Lambeth** – £1 10s [fo. 30r]
27 September – ye Dore Keeper of **ye Parlement house** – £2 [fo. 30r]
8 October – yr Maties footemen Roning to **parsons griene** – £2 [fo. 30v]
18 October – yr Maties footemen tto **parsons grine** – £2 [fo. 30v]
18 October – yr Maties Musique for Coatch Hiere twise tto **Lady Mordants**[83] – £1 10s [fo. 30v]
28 October – yr Maties footemen – £2 [fo. 31r]
30 October – yr Maties <footemen> Roning tto **Lady Mordants** – £2 [fo. 31r]
30 October – feching of watter from **Epson** when yr Matie went to **Turnbrige** Last – £2 8s [fo. 31r]
30 October – yr Maties footemen to **King<sin>ston** – £2 [fo. 31r]
10 December – ye Doore Keeper of **ye parlement** when yr Matie went Incognito – £2 [fo. 32r]
14 December – ye Duchess of Mounmouths Coatchman and footemen that weighted one yr Matie that day yr Matie went tto **ye parlement house** – £2 [fo. 32v]
25 December – ye Yeoman of ye Guard yt weighted all night att **St James** – £1 [fo. 32v]
26 December – ye Coatchemen postilliones and footemen that weighted one yr Matie to **Kingsinton** – £8 [fo. 32v]

1667

2 January – ye Duchess of Yorkes Coatchmen that waighted one yr Matie with ye trenan in **St James Parke** – £10 [fo. 33v]
9 January – ye Musique that weighted one yr Matie att **Lady Arlingtons**[84] – £6 [fo. 34r]
6 April – ye Duchessess Coatchmen that waighted one yr Matie Ester Eue at **St James** – £3 [fo. 35v]

82 Coombe.

83 Lady Mordaunt was a widow at this point – Sir Charles Mordaunt died in 1663 and she did not marry her second husband, Francis Godolphin, until 1669. It is uncertain where she was living.

84 The time of year suggests this would be the Arlington's London home. Lord Arlington bought Goring house in 1665 and after a fire in 1674 much was rebuilt and renamed Arlington House. It had been the home of George Goring, 1st earl of Norwich.

17 April – ye Coatchman & footemen that waighted one y^{r} Matie at **St James** – £1 [fo. 35v]
4 June – y^{r} Maties footemen – £2 [fo. 37r]
15 June – y^{r} Maties footmen – £2 [fo. 37r]
16 June – y^{r} Maties footemen – £2 [fo. 37v]
18 June – y^{r} Maties footemen – £2 [fo. 37v]
18 June – Watermen to **ffoxHall** – £1 10s [fo. 37v]
4 July – y^{r} Matie in gold at **newporthouse**[85] – £5 [fo. 37v]
8 July – the wattermen in **wolige**[86] – £3 [fo. 37v]
12 July – the watermen to **Batersie**[87] – £3 [fo. 37v]
13 July – the watermen to **Chelsy** – £3 [fo. 37v]
13 July – oares that Caried y^{r} Matie – £1 [fo. 38r]
13 July – two pair of oars that Caried y^{r} Maties retenue – £1 10s [fo. 38r]
13 July – the watermen to **Batersy** – £3 [fo. 38r]
14 July – mor to the watermen to **Batersy** – £3 [fo. 38r]
15 July – the watermen to **Chelsy** – £3 [fo. 38r]
16 July – the watermen to **Chelsy** – £3 [fo. 38r]
23 July – the Dairy-maid **at Mr Mayes** – £1 [fo. 38v]
30 July – y^{r} Maties footmen to **Rohampton** – £2 [fo. 38v]
2 August – Y^{r} Maties Bargmen to **Lambeth** – £1 10s [fo. 38r]
6 August – Y^{r} Maties Bargemen to **Chelsey** – £3 [fo. 38r]
7 August – A wherry attending to **Chelsey** – 10s [fo. 38r]
9 August – To ye keepers of **Exsome**[88] **waters** – £2 [fo. 38r]
16 August – To be Mr Long at the **Teniscourt** – £5 [fo. 39r]
16 August – To the Gardenour at **Kinsington** – [fo. 39r]
14 October – Rose the Gardenor at **St Jamess** – £5 10s [fo. 39r]

1668

22 January – the Musique for waiting at **S^{ir} William Killigrewe**[89] – £5 [fo. 41r]

85 Newport House, London, in the area around St Martin's Field.

86 Woolwich.

87 Battersea.

88 Epsom.

89 Sir William Killigrew had property in Lincolnshire which he lost in 1650 after the Civil War. He also lost property in Lincoln's Inn Field and Kempton Park, Middlesex, see Paul Hunneyball, 'Killigrew, Sir William II (1606–1695) of Pendennis Castle, Cornw.; later of Lincoln's Inn Fields, London and Kempton Park, Mdx.', http://www.historyofparliamentonline.org/volume/1604-1629/member/killigrew-sir-william-ii-1606-1695 [accessed 22/10/22]. While he was the queen's vice-chamberlain he had apartments at Whitehall and on his retirement, he had rooms at Hampton Court and then spent time in Twickenham, http://www.twickenham-museum.org.uk/detail.php?aid=301&ctid=1&cid=9 [accessed 22/10/22].

1-Worsley/7 – Catherine of Braganza, privy purse accounts 1668–75

1668 [continued]

28 April – yor Matie at **St James** on Good Friday – £3 6s [fo. 3r]
28 April – to the musique for waitting at Easter – £10 [fo. 3r]
28 April – yor Maties footmen the first time to **Heigh Park** – £2 [fo. 3v]
1 May – two treats at **Heigh Parke** – £15 12s 6d [fo. 3v]
Thomas Fitz musician ordinary attending the king at ***Newmarket*** *in May, 21 days at* ***Bagshot*** *and* ***Portsmouth*** *in June, 11 days at* ***Newmarket****, 33 days at* ***Audley End*** *– 65 days.*[90]
29 May – to yor Maties footmen on the kings Birth day – £3 [fo. 4v]
8 June – to his Maties Coatchman for waitting on yor Matie to **My Lord Baiths**[91] – £1 [fo. 4v]
10 June – the womon at **Ipsem**[92] **wells** – £2 [fo. 5r]
10 June – yor Maties bargemen for waitting to **Chelsy** – £3 [fo. 5r]
11 June – yor Maties bargemen to **woster**[93] **house** – £3 10s [fo. 5r]
16 June – his Maties Coatchman for waitting of yor Matie **to a play** – £1 [fo. 5r]
17 June – his Heighness Bargemen for waitting of yor Matie to **sumerset house** – £1 [fo. 5r]
1 July – yor Maties footmen to **walthem Aby** – £2 [fo. 5r]
1 July – Paid att **the boullingreen their** – £2 4s [fo. 5r]
7 July – yor Maties footmen to **Roehampton** – 5s [fo. 5v]
11 July – **Lady Arlintons Butler** – 10s [fo. 5v]
13 July – Chaire men waitted on yor Matie to **St James Parke** – 5s [fo. 5v]
23 July [due 6 July] – yor Maties Bargemen to **Rohampton** – £3 [fo. 6r]
23 July [due 20 July] – yor Maties Bargmen to **Chisweeke** – £3 [fo. 6r]
28 July – to the Keeper of **St James parke** who presented a buck to y^r^ Matie [fo. 6r]
23 September – his Maties Bergmen from **foulem**[94] to **putny** – £1 [fo. 6v]
26 September – for Coatchehir to **Audleyend** with S^ir^ William Killegre – £6 10s [fo. 6v]
6 October – Mr Halsall for Coatchehire to **Audley End** – £25 16s [fo. 7r]

90 TNA LC5/12, p. 21; Ashbee, *Records*, 94.

91 Worcester House on the Strand, which reverted to Henry, marquis of Worcester in 1667.

92 Epsom.

93 Worcester.

94 Fulham.

6 October – her Heighnes Coatchehire to **Hodsdon**[95] – £22 [fo. 7r]
9 October – Transporting yor Maties Goods from **London** to **Audley End** – £2 1s 3d [fo. 7r]
9 October – the porter was sent for things to **London** – £1 5s [fo. 7r]
18 October – Mr Halsall for Coatchehire from **Audley End** to **London** – £45 12s [fo. 7r]
18 October – Runeing money to yor Maties footmen – £4 [fo. 7r]
18 October – Transporting yor Maties Goods from **Audley End** to **London** [fo. 7r]
22 October – the Page of the Bakstairs cam beffor from **Audley End** to get Rady the Lodgings – 10s [fo. 7v]
4 November – the poore at **Audley End** – £4 [fo. 7v]
7 December – Mr Steuens to **Kinsinton** for water – 5s [fo. 7v]
25 December – the Gard att **St James** – 5s [fo. 8v]
25 December – Carieing things to **St James & bake** – 5s [fo. 8v]

1669

Thomas Fittz musician ordinary attending the king at ***Newmarket*** *in March for 15 days and in April for 6 days – 21 days.*[96]
27 April – yor Maties footmen the first day to **heigh park** – £2 [fo. 9v]
8 May – Will Jonson for Carieing a picktur to **St James** – 3s [fo. 10r]
8 May – Mor to him for remouing <yor Maties trunks> when the lodgings were whitned – 4s 6d [fo. 10r]
24 May – Mr Stevens for Coatchehire – 3s [fo. 10v]
7 June – a Chaireman – 10s [fo. 10v]
7 June – yor Maties footmen on the Kings Birthday – £3 [fo. 10v]
2 July – Mr Steuens to goe by water – 1s [fo. 11r]
9 August – a poore man at **Heigh park** – 5s [fo. 11r]
12 August – Mr Steuens sent by water [fo. 11r]
2 September – the dutches of Buckingams seruants waited of yor Matie **to Lady Arlingtons**[97] – £5 [fo. 11v]
2 September – Mr Halsy for Coatchire to **Hamton court** – £23 6s [fo. 11v]
2 September – paid by water to **London** and **bakagaine** – 10s [fo. 11v]
9 September – yor Maties footmen for runing money – £2 [fo. 12r]
9 September – bringing the bows & arous to **Hamton court** – £1 [fo. 12r]
9 September – Mr Steuens sent before to **Hamptoncourt** – 10s [fo. 12r]
12 September – yor Maties footmen Sent to **London** – £1 [fo. 12r]
17 September – the page of the Bakstairs sent beffor to **London** – 10s [fo. 12r]

95 Hoddesdon.
96 TNA LC5/12, p. 21; Ashbee, *Records*, 94.
97 Probably another reference to Goring House, as opposed to her county home Euston Hall, Suffolk.

19 September – yor Maties Bergemen – £8 10s [fo. 12v]
20 September – Mr Halsall for Coatchire as per bill – £21 [fo. 12v]
20 September – yor Maties footmen for Runing money – £2 [fo. 12v]
20 September – one of them Sent to Stope the Coatches at **London** – £1 [fo. 12v]
20 September – one of them that braught the dogs from **Hamptoncourt** – £1 [fo. 12v]
20 September – Loading & unloading the wagons at **London** and **Hamptoncourt** – £2 16s 6d [fo. 12v]
20 November – Mr Marsh man presented Creams at **Hampton court** – £1 10s 3d [fo. 13v]
24 December – the duck of Ormonds man with the Traine in **St James parke** – £2 [fo. 14r]

1670

6 January – Carieing things to & from **St James** – 3s [fo. 14r]
17 March – the Coatchman & footmen waited of yor Matie to & from **St James** – £5 [fo. 14r]
3 April – Carieing things to & from **St James** – 3s [fo. 14v]
3 April – yor Maties footmen the first day to **Heigh parke** – £2 [fo. 14v]
8 April – the yeoman of the Gard waited at **St James** at Easter – £1 1s [fo. 14v]
11 April – boats & Berges to **Grewich** – £6 [fo. 14v]
15 April – the dutchesse of Richmons footmen Leighted yor Matie – £1 [fo. 15v]
16 April – the Coatchmen & footmen waited of yor Matie to **St James** – £5 [fo. 15v]
17 April – a pair of oares to **fox hall** – £1 [fo. 15v]
18 April – yor Maties Bergemen to **Dartford** – £5 [fo. 15v]
18 April – yor Maties footmen then – £1 [fo. 15v]
23 April – his Maties Bergemen to **Dartford** – £5 [fo. 15v]
23 April – yor Maties footmen then – £2 10s [fo. 15v]
23 April – for two boats that caried the Gard – £2 [fo. 15v]
25 April – yor Maties Chairemen waited at **the Bridge** – £1 [fo. 16r]
26 April – the dutchesse of Monmuths Coatchman & postilion & footmen waited of yor Matie to **Hampton Court** – £7 [fo. 16r]
29 April – her Heighness Coatchmen & footmen – £5 [fo. 16r]
29 April – the footmen Leighted yor Matie – £1 [fo. 16r]
Lewis Grabu, master of His Majesty's music, attending his Majesty to ***Dover*** *for 20 days, 16 May to 4 June.*[98]
18 May – paid at **Sitenburne**[99] – £10 [fo. 16r]
18 May – paid at **Canterbery** & by the way to **dover** – £7 7s [fo. 16r]

98 TNA LC5/140, p. 8; Ashbee, *Records*, 113.
99 Sittingbourne.

18 May – yor Maties footmen for Runing money – £6 [fo. 16r]
23 May – the <men> Caried yor Matie ashore – £2 – [fo. 16v]
26 May – yor Maties footmen Runing money – £2 [fo. 16v]
28 May – yor Maties footmen Runing money – £2 [fo. 16v]
29 May – yor Maties footmen then – £3 [fo. 16v]
31 May – yor Maties footmen Runing money – £2 [fo. 16v]
3 June – paid by the way from **Dover** to **Sitenburne** – £2 2s [fo. 16v]
4 June – paid at **Sitenburne** – £10 [fo. 16v]
4 June – a Gyd to **Greuesend** – £1 1s [fo. 16v]
7 June – yor Maties footmen Runing money – £6 [fo. 17r]
7 June – yor Maties watermen the first time yor Matie went in the new Berge – £5 [fo. 17r]
10 June – for two boats when yor Matie went by water – £1 10s [fo. 17r]
12 June – for thre boats – £1 15s [fo. 17r]
15 June – for boats – £1 15s [fo. 17r]
16 June – for Berges Gallys & oares to and from **Grauesend** as per aquitance – £33 10s [fo. 17r]
18 June – for boats – £1 15s [fo. 17r]
19 June – for boats – £1 10s [fo. 17r]
21 June – for boats – £1 10s [fo. 17v]
5 July – yor Maties footmen for Runing money from **Richmon**[100] – £2 [fo. 17v]
5 July – one of yor Maties footmen sent to **Richmon** – £1 [fo. 17v]
5 July – yor Maties Berges to **Richmon** – £7 [fo. 17v]
5 July – paid at **Barnellms** whan y^{r} Matie dined – £5 10s [fo. 17v]
6 July – for 3 boats – £1 10s [fo. 17v]
7 July – yor Maties Berges to **Richmon** – £7 10s [fo. 18r]
8 July – for 3 boats – £1 10s [fo. 18r]
9 July – for 3 boats – £1 10s [fo. 18r]
10 July – for 3 boats – £1 10s [fo. 18r]
12 July – yor Maties Berges to **Richmon** – £7 10s [fo. 18r]
16 July – yor Maties Berges to **Richmon** – £7 10s [fo. 18v]
18 July – for 3 boats – £1 10s [fo. 18v]
21 July – for thre boats – £1 10s [fo. 18v]
21 July – for 4 boats – £1 15s [fo. 18v]
25 July – for thre boats – £1 10s [fo. 18v]
28 July – yor Maties Berges to **Richmon** – £7 10s [fo. 18v]
28 July – one of yor Maties footmen sent to **Richmon** – £1 [fo. 19r]
22 August – the page of the Bakstairs went before to **Hampton court** – 10s [fo. 19v]
23 August – for boats – £4 [fo. 19v]
23 August – a fisherman at **Kingston** – £1 1s 4d [fo. 19v]
24 August – a gyd to **Windsor** – £1 1s 4d [fo. 19v]

100 Richmond.

31 August – yor Maties footmen Runing mony to **Rohamton** £2 [fo. 20r]
1 September – for boats – £2 15s [fo. 20r]
2 September – for boats – £2 15s [fo. 20r]
4 September – one of his Maties footmen with a dog from **Windsor** – £2 2s 8d [fo. 20r]
5 September – for a boat waited w^t^ provisions & from thenc to **London** – 10s [fo. 20r]
5 September – yor Maties footmen Runing mony from **Hampton court** to **London** – £2 [fo. 20r]
10 September – for Loading & unloading the wagons **to & from Hamptoncourt** – £2 11s 4d [fo. 20v]
15 September – yor Maties Berges to **putny** – £3 [fo. 20v]
15 September – yor Maties footmen Runing mony to **Hamptoncourt** – £2 [fo. 20v]
15 September – for boats waited to **Hamptoncourt –** £3 10s [fo. 20v]
15 September – paid at **Bartlemewfaire**[101] – £2 2s 8d [fo. 20v]
21 September – for coatchire for S^ir^ William Killigre to and from **audley end** – £4 10s [fo. 20v]

*John Singleton and others for their attendance on the queen at **Audley End** for 20 days from 26 September to 15 October.*[102]

27 September – yor Maties footmen Runing mony to **Audley end** – £4 [fo. 21r]
30 September – a man with a leter from **Roiston** – 10s [fo. 21r]
30 September – paid at the House in **Chesterson parke**[103] – £5 [fo. 21r]
3 October – paid at **Newport**[104] – £3 15s [fo. 21v]
3 October – paid at **Euston**[105] to the House – £2 [fo. 21v]
3 October – a Gyd from **Newmarkitt & bak againe** – £2 2s 8d [fo. 21v]
3 October – the thre Coatches went from **Newmarkitt** to **Euston & bak againe** – £15 [fo. 21v]
3 October – some of yor Maties footmen sent to **Cambridg** – £2 [fo. 21v]
8 October – for letters from **Roiston** – 10s [fo. 21v]
14 October – yor Maties footmen Runing mony to **London** – £4 [fo. 22r]
27 October – Expense for the viz Chamberlan & Mr Mend sent to **Audley end** – £5 2s 3d
6 December – for Carieing things to & from **St James** – 5s [fo. 22v]

[101] St Bartholomew's feast day falls on 24 August, but the fair lasted for longer and was held at Smithfield.

[102] TNA LC5/13, p. 51; Ashbee, *Records*, 102.

[103] Possibly Chesterton Hall, Chesterton, Cambridge.

[104] Newport, Essex.

[105] Euston Hall, West Sussex.

1671

20 January – to the porter to Carye them to **St James** – 5s – [fo. 22v]
12 April – for thre boats – £1 [fo. 23r]
16 April – for four boats – £1 5s [fo. 23r]
16 April – yor Maties footmen the first time to **Heigh park** – £2 [fo. 23r]
22 April – for thre boats – £1 [fo. 23r]
27 April – for thre boats – £1 [fo. 23r]
7 May – for thre boats – £1 [fo. 23r]
8 May – for two boats – 15s [fo. 23r]
9 May – for thre boats – £1 [fo. 23r]
10 May – for thre boats – £1 [fo. 23r]
11 May – for thre boats – £1 [fo. 23v]
12 May – for thre boats – £1 [fo. 23v]
13 May – for thre boats – £1 [fo. 23v]
17 May – for thre boats – £1 [fo. 23v]
25 May – for thre boats – £1 [fo. 23v]
26 May – the pages of the Bakstairs to **winsor** – 10s [fo. 23v]
*servants appointed to attend His Matie at **St George's Feast** the 29 May 1671.*[106]
*Captain Henry Cook for the gentlemen of the chapel, an organist and two base viols for their attendance on his Majestie in **Windsor**, 30 May to 15 July.*[107]
1 June – Bringing two portingall mats from **London** to **winsor** – £1 [fo. 23v]
3 June – yor Maties footmen to & from **London** – £4 [fo. 23v]
3 June – Bringing Crystall Candlestiks & other things from **London** – £1 [fo. 23v]
3 June – for thre boats – 15s [fo. 24r]
3 June – the pages of the Bakestairs to & from **London** – £1 [fo. 24r]
6 June – for thre boats – 15s [fo. 24r]
7 June – for two boats – 10s [fo. 24r]
7 June – bringing yor Maties boat to **winsor** – £1 10s [fo. 24r]
8 June – for thre boats – 15s [fo. 24r]
8 June – the footmen Runing mony to & from **London** – £4 [fo. 24r]
14 June – for thre boats – 15s [fo. 24r]
15 June – for two boats – 10s [fo. 24r]
16 June – for two boats – 10s [fo. 24r]
17 June – for one boate – 5s [fo. 24r]
18 June – for two boats – 10s [fo. 24r]
19 June – for two boats – 10s [fo. 24v]
20 June – y^r Maties Berges to **London** – £15 [fo. 24v]

106 TNA LC5/193, p. 17; Ashbee, *Records*, 105–06.
107 TNA LC5/14, p. 63; Ashbee, *Records*, 108–09.

20 June – the Kinges Berges to **London –** £10 [fo. 24v]
21 June – the footmen Runing mony to & from **London** – £1 [fo. 24v]
21 June – for two boats – 10s [fo. 24v]
21 June – yo[r] Ma[ties] Bergemen from **whitehall** to **somerset house** in May last – 10s [fo. 24v]
22 June – for two boats – 10s [fo. 24v]
23 June – for thre boats – 15s [fo. 24v]
24 June – for two boats – 10s [fo. 24v]
25 June – for thre boats – 15s [fo. 24v]
26 June – for goeing to & from **London** with yo[r] Ma[ties] boat – £2 10s [fo. 25r]
26 June – for two boats – 10s [fo. 25r]
27 June – for two boats – 10s [fo. 25r]
28 June – for one boat – 5s [fo. 25r]
29 June – for two boats – 10s [fo. 25r]
29 June – to the footmen Runing mony – £2 [fo. 25r]
30 June – for one boate – 5s [fo. 25r]
30 June – to the two boatmen from the 26 of June to the first of July as per bill – £2 10s [fo. 25r]
1 July – to the footmen Runing mony – £2 [fo. 25r]
2 July – for two boats – 10s [fo. 25r]
3 July – for two boats – 10s [fo. 25r]
8 July – to the boatmen from the first of July to the eight as per bill – £3 10s [fo. 25r]
8 July – to the footmen Runing mony – £2 [fo. 25r]
11 July – the footmen Runing mony to **stoke**[108] – £2 [fo. 25v]
13 July – the pages of the Bakstairs to **Hamton court** – 10s [fo. 25v]
13 July – the footmen to **Hampton court** – £2 [fo. 25v]
13 July – bringing yo[r] Ma[ties] boat to **Hamton court** – £1 [fo. 25v]
14 July – yo[r] Ma[ties] footmen to & from **London** – £4 [fo. 26r]
14 July – the pages of the Bakstairs to & from **London –** £1 [fo. 26r]
17 July – for thre boats – 15s [fo. 26r]
18 July – for two boats – 10s [fo. 26r]
18 July – for boats over **twitnham**[109] – £1 6s [fo. 26r]
18 July – to the footmen Runing mony from **ham house** – £2 [fo. 26r]
20 July – to the footmen to **Rohamton** – £2 [fo. 26r]
20 July – to the ducks Berge & other boat at **Richmon** – £2 7s [fo. 26r]
20 July – for seven boats – £1 15s [fo. 26r]
21 July – for eight boats – £2 [fo. 26r]
21 July – paid at **Richmon** & **thistleworth**[110] by water – £1 11s 1d [fo. 26r]
21 July – fruite presented by the way from **London –** £1 1s 1d [fo. 26r]

108 Stoke Newington, Middlesex.
109 Twickenham.
110 Isleworth.

21 July – for the footmen **to & from London** – £4 [fo. 26r]
21 July – remouing trunks from **whitehall** to **somerset house** & **bak againe** – £1 1s [fo. 26r]
25 July – Bringing yor Maties Boat to **London** – £1 [fo. 26v]
27 July – the footmen Runing mony to **Twitnham** – £2 [fo. 26v]
3 August – for boats to & from **somerset house** – 15s [fo. 26v]
8 August – for boats to & from **somersethouse** – 15s [fo. 26v]
19 August – for boats to & from **somersethouse** – 15s [fo. 26v]
26 August – for boats to & from **somersethouse** – 12s 6d [fo. 26v]
27 August – for boats to **somersethouse** – 12s [fo. 26v]
27 August – for boats to **somersethouse** [in the] Effternoon – 12s [fo. 26v]
3 September – for boats to **somersethouse** – 10s [fo. 26v]
12 September – for boats to s**omersethouse** – 15s [fo. 26v]
14 September – for boats to **somerset house** – 12s [fo. 26v]
18 September – for one boate – 5s [fo. 26v]
20 September – yor Maties Berge to **somerset house** – 10s [fo. 27r]
20 September – for two boats – 12s 6d – [fo. 27r]
22 September – Careing a table & stands to **Hamton court** – 10s [fo. 27r]
Gervase Price and four trumpeters attending on his Majesty to ***Norwich, Yarmouth, Newmarket, Cambridge*** *and elsewhere, 25 September to 21 October.*[111]
26 September – yor Maties footmen Runing mony to **Audley end** – £4 [fo. 27r]
27 September – yor Maties footmen to **Ewston**[112] £2 – [fo. 27v]
28 September – yor Maties footmen to **Norwiche** – £2 [fo. 27v]
29 September – a Gyd from **S^ir John Huberds**[113] – 10s [fo. 27v]
30 September – a Gyd to **S^ir Robert Pastons**[114] – 10s [fo. 27v]
30 September – given to **Lord Howards servants**[115] – £100 [fo. 27v]
1 October – the pages of the Bakestairs to **Ewston** – 10s [fo. 27v]
1 October – the seruants at **Ewston** – £40 2d [fo. 27v]
2 October – the pages of the Bakstairs to **Audley end** – 10s [fo. 28r]
3 October – the pages of the Bakstairs to **London** – £1 – [fo. 28r]
15 October – two boats to **somerset house** – 12s 6d [fo. 28r]
15 October – a boat to Mr Sears – 2s [fo. 28r]
25 October – yor Maties Berge seaven times to and from **somerset house** – £3 10s [fo. 28r]

111 TNA LC5/14, p. 92; Ashbee, *Records*, 110.
112 Euston Hall, West Suffolk.
113 Blickling Hall, Norfolk.
114 Oxnead, Norfolk.
115 Probably a reference to Barbara's husband, James Howard, 3rd duke of Suffolk, who lived at Audley End.

1672

22 April – your Majesties footmen the first time to **Heigh parke** – £2 [fo. 28v]
30 April – yor Maties footmen to **Hamersmith** – £2 [fo. 28v]
18 May – yor Maties footmen to & from **dalle**[116] – £8 [fo. 28v]
18 May – the pages of the Bakstairs to & from **dalle** – £2 [fo. 28v]
24 May – for a boate to & from **somersethouse** – 10s [fo. 29r]
10 June – for boats – 10s [fo. 29r]
15 June – yor Maties footmen **to & from Rochester** – £6 [fo. 29r]
15 June – the footman sent from sea to stope the Coatches – £2 [fo. 29r]
15 June – the Housekeepers man at **somersethouse** – 12s [fo. 29r]
18 June – the footmen Runing mony to **Chelsy** – £2 [fo. 29r]
23 June – for boats over at **Richemon** – 12s [fo. 29r]
23 June – to the footmen Runing mony to **Richemon** – £2 [fo. 29r]
4 July – for stra to the Gards at **somersethouse** – 15s [fo. 29r]
4 August – for a boat to **somerset house** – 5s [fo. 29r]
16 August – for a boat to & from **somersethouse** – 10s [fo. 29r]
20 August – a waterman sent to **Dartford –** 8s [fo. 29r]
Henry Brockwell and six musicians in attendance on the king at ***Newmarket****, 1 to 21 October.*[117]

1673

23 April – yor Maties footmen on the first time to **Heigh parke** – £2 [fo. 29v]
24 April – yor Maties footmen to **Hamton court** – £2 [fo. 29v]
24 April – for two boats at **Hamton court** – 10s [fo. 29v]
30 April – yor Maties footmen to **Hamton court** – £2 [fo. 29v]
15 June – yor Maties footmen to **Ham** – £2 [fo. 30r]
15 June – for fiue boats waited their – £1 10s [fo. 30r]
10 July – paid by Mr Roper for boats – 15s [fo. 30r]
12 July – for boats to & from **somerset house** – 15s [fo. 30r]
15 July – to Mr Hill for Berges – £63 14s [fo. 30r]
16 July – to Francis Charleton for Boats – £27 10s [fo. 30r]
29 July – to yor Maties Berges waited their[118] – £1 10s [fo. 30r]
29 July – to a boat waited their – 5s [fo. 30r]
5 August – for a boat to & from **somerset house** – 10s [fo. 30v]
11 August – for a boat to & from **somerset house** – 10s [fo. 30v]
14 August – for a boat to & from **somerset house** – 10s [fo. 30v]
14 August – for a boat in the Effternoon – 10s [fo. 30v]
15 August – for a boat to & from **somerset house** – 10s [fo. 30v]

116 Deal, Kent.
117 TNA LC5/140, p. 263; Ashbee, *Records*, 126.
118 At Lady Peterborough's home (?).

16 August – for a boat to & from **somerset house** – 10s [fo. 30v]
18 August – for boats to **Chelsy** – £1 [fo. 30v]
19 August – to Mr Clark for a Coatche to **Hamton court** – 13s [fo. 30v]
19 August – to yor Maties Boat to **Hamton court** – £2 [fo. 30v]
26 August – to yor Maties Berges to **Hamton court** – £7 10s [fo. 30v]
26 August – to yor Maties Boat to **Hamton court** – £2 [fo. 30v]
26 August – for five other boats their – £1 5s [fo. 30v]
30 October – to Lady Arlintons Chairemen and footmen to **somerset house** – £2 [fo. 31r]
20 December – to yor Maties Berge to **somerset house** – 10s [fo. 31v]
27 December – to Mr Caple Messenger sent to **dall**[119] – £5 5s [fo. 31v]

1674

28 January – yor Maties footmen to **Chelsy** – £2 [fo. 32v]
20 March – a boat to **somerset house** – 5s [fo. 33r]
20 April – a boat to **somerset house** – 5s [fo. 33v]
24 April – yor Maties footmen the first time to **Heighparke** – £2 [fo. 33v]
14 May – Henry Huges Lost his horse in the journey to **Norwich** – £12 [fo. 33v]
18 May – yor Maties Berges to **Greenwich** – £3 [fo. 33v]
John Blow, master of the children of the Chapel Royal and eight children, 109 days in ***Windsor****, 18 May to 3 September.*[120]
19 May – yor Maties footmen to **Chelsy** – £2 [fo. 34r]
20 May – the footmen to **winsor** – £2 [fo. 34r]
20 May – a boat from the Bakstairs – £1 1s 8d [fo. 34r]
27 May – yor Maties Berges to **London** – £15 [fo. 34r]
27 May – the Kings Berge to **London** – £10 [fo. 34r]
28 May – yor Maties Berges to **Richmon** £7 10s [fo. 34r]
28 May – a Gyde from **Richmon** to **winsor** – £1 [fo. 34r]
28 May – the footmen to & from **London** – £4 [fo. 34r]
31 May – yor Maties two Boatmen from the 19th of May to the first of June – £7 10s [fo. 34r]
3 June – a footman sent to **Richemon** – £1 [fo. 34v]
4 June – the footmen Runing mony – £2 [fo. 34v]
5 June – the footmen Runing mony – £2 [fo. 34v]
7 June – the footmen Runing mony – £2 [fo. 34v]
8 June – the footmen Runing mony – £2 [fo. 34v]
8 June – yor Maties Boatmen from the first of June to the 8 – £4 10s [fo. 34v]
10 June – the footmen Runing mony – £2 [fo. 34v]
12 June – the footmen Runing mony – £2 [fo. 34v]

119 Deal, Kent.
120 TNA LC5/141, p. 54; Ashbee, *Records*, 144, 147.

14 June – the footmen Runing mony – £2 [fo. 34v]
16 June – yor Maties footmen from the eight to the 16 – £4 [fo. 34v]
16 June – the footmen Runing mony – £2 [fo. 34v]
20 June – yor Maties Berges to & from **London** – £30 [fo. 35r]
20 June – the Kings Berge to **London** – £10 [fo. 35r]
20 June – the footmen Runing mony to and from **London –** £4 [fo. 35r]
23 June – yor Maties Boatemen from the 16 to 23 – £3 10s [fo. 35r]
27 June – yor Maties Berges to & from **London** – £30 [fo. 35r]
27 June – the Kings Berge to & from **London** – £20 [fo. 35r]
27 June – yor Maties footmen to & from **London** – £4 [fo. 35r]
29 June – the footmen Runing mony – £2 [fo. 35v]
30 June – yor Maties footmen – £45 [fo. 35v]
1 July – the footmen Runing mony – £2 [fo. 35v]
1 July – a footman sent from **the forest**[121] – 10s [fo. 35v]
4 July – the footmen Runing mony – £2 [fo. 35v]
5 July – the footmen Runing mony – £2 [fo. 35v]
6 July – the footmen Runing mony – £2 [fo. 35v]
7 July – the footmen Runing mony – £2 [fo. 35v]

*Violins at **Windsor**, 11 July to 1 September.*[122]

*Nicholas Staggins, accompanying the king to **Windsor**, 15 August to 1 September.*[123]

12 July – the footmen Runing mony – £2 [fo. 36r]
13 July – the footmen to **Hamton court** – £2 [fo. 36r]
17 July – the footmen Runing mony – £2 [fo. 36r]
18 July – yor Maties Boatemen from the ninth to the 18 – £7 [fo. 36r]
20 July – the footmen Runing mony – £2 [fo. 36r]
23 July – the footmen Runing mony – £2 [fo. 36r]
23 July – yor Maties boatemen from the nineteen to the 25 – £3 10s [fo. 36r]
24 July – the footmen Runing mony – £2 [fo. 36r]
24 July – Paid by Major Harwood at **Cramburn loge**[124] – 10s [fo. 36r]
25 July – the footmen Runing mony – £2 [fo. 36v]
26 July – the footmen Runing mony – £2 [fo. 36v]
27 July – the footmen Runing mony – £2 [fo. 36v]
27 July – Bringing yor Maties Chair from **London** – £1 1s 7d [fo. 36v]
27 July – the footmen Runing mony – £2 [fo. 36v]
30 July – the footmen Runing mony to **London** – £2 [fo. 36v]
30 July – paid by Mr Roper at **Hamton court –** £4 6s 4d [fo. 36v]
30 July – a boat with provisions from **winsor** – £1 1s 7d [fo. 36v]

121 Possibly 1) Epping Forest, Essex or 2) part of Waltham Forest.

122 TNA LC5/141, p. 44; Ashbee, *Records*, 143.

123 TNA LC5/141, p. 248; Ashbee, *Records*, 142.

124 Cranbourne Lodge, Berkshire, which was the lodge for Cranbourne Chase, next to Windsor Great Park.

3 August – a boat to somerset house – 10s [fo. 36v]
4 August – yor Maties footmen Runing mony from **London** – £2 [fo. 36v]
4 August – yor Maties boatmen from the 26 of July to the 10 of August – £10 10s [fo. 36v]
7 August – the footmen Runing mony – £2 [fo. 37r]
9 August – the footmen Runing mony – £2 [fo. 37r]
11 August – the footmen Runing mony – £2 [fo. 37r]
12 August – the footmen Runing mony – £2 [fo. 37r]
13 August – the footmen Runing mony – £2 [fo. 37r]
17 August – to the two boatmen to the tenth to the seventeen – £4 5s [fo. 37r]
21 August – the footmen Runing mony – £2 [fo. 37r]
22 August – the footmen Runing mony – £2 [fo. 37r]
23 August – the footmen Runing mony – £2 [fo. 37r]
24 August – yor Maties Boatmen from the 18 to the 24 – £4 4s [fo. 37r]
25 August – the footmen Runing mony – £2 [fo. 37v]
29 August – the footmen Runing mony – £2 [fo. 37v]
31 August – the footmen Runing mony – £2 [fo. 37v]
1 September – Mrs Hemden for journeys to & from **London** & other epense[125] – £3 15s [fo. 37v]
1 September – to vnder keepers of **the greatparke**[126] – £2 3s 4d [fo. 37v]
1 September – a boat for yor Maties Chaire to **London –** £1 1s 7d [fo. 37v]
1 September – yor Maties boatmen from the 25 of august to the first of September – £6 9s [fo. 37v]
1 September – yor Maties footmen Runing mony to **London** – £2 [fo. 38r]
5 September – for a boat to & from somerset hous – 10s [fo. 38r]
8 September – for a boat to & from somerset hous – 10s [fo. 38r]
9 September – to the footmen Runing mony to **Chelsy** – £2 [fo. 38r]
17 September – to the footmen Runing mony to **Hamton court** – £2 [fo. 38r]
*Six violins in ordinary for their attendance on the queen at **Hampton Court** for 36 days from 17 September to 24 October.*[127]
18 September – the footmen Runing mony – £2 [fo. 38r]
19 September – the footmen Runing mony – £2 [fo. 38r]
20 September – the footmen Runing mony – £2 [fo. 38r]
22 September – the footmen Runing mony – £2 [fo. 38r]
*Nicholas Staggins, master of his Majesty's violins, for himself and six violins, for attendance on His Majesty at **Newmarket**, 22 September to 12 October.*[128]
24 September – the footmen Runing mony – £2 [fo. 38r]
26 September – the footmen Runing mony – £2 [fo. 38r]
27 September – the footmen Runing mony – £2 [fo. 38r]

125 Expense.
126 The Great Park, Windsor. So, this and other payments mark her departure.
127 TNA LC5/141, p. 23; Ashbee, *Records*, 143.
128 TNA LC5/141, p. 63; Ashbee, *Records*, 144.

28 September – yor Maties footmen Runing mony – £2 [fo. 38v]
29 September – the footmen Runing mony – £2 [fo. 38v]
2 October – the footmen Runing mony – £2 [fo. 38v]
4 October – the footmen Runing mony to & from **London** – £4 [fo. 38v]
6 October – the footmen Runing mony **to Lord Bellows**[129] – £2 [fo. 38v]
7 October – the footmen Runing mony – £2 [fo. 38v]
8 October – yor Maties Boatmen from the 17 of September to the 8 of October – £12 15s [fo. 38v]
10 October – the footmen Runing mony – £2 [fo. 38v]
11 October – the footmen – £2 [fo. 38v]
12 October – the footmen Runing mony to **Newparke** – £2 [fo. 38v]
12 October – a footman sent to **Richemon** – £1 [fo. 38v]
12 October – paid by Mr Rogers at **Newparke** – £2 8s [fo. 38v]
15 October – to the footmen Runing mony to **Newparke** – £2 [fo. 39r]
16 October – to the footmen Runing mony – £2 [fo. 39r]
17 October – to the footmen Runing mony – £2 [fo. 39r]
18 October – to the footmen Runing mony – £2 [fo. 39r]
19 October – to the footmen Runing mony – £2 [fo. 39r]
20 October – to the footmen Runing mony – £2 [fo. 39r]
21 October – to the footmen Runing mony – £2 [fo. 39r]
22 October – to yor Maties Boatemen from the eight to the twenty two as per bill – £8 3s [fo. 39r]
22 October – for a boat for yor Maties Chaire – 10s [fo. 39r]
22 October – to the man keeps the fery boat – £1 1s 8d [fo. 39r]
26 November – to yor Maties Berge to **Dartford** with the fathers – £1 10s [fo. 40r]

[129] Uncertain location.

1-Worsley/8 – Catherine of Braganza, privy purse accounts 1675–79

1675

*Musicians attending on the king at **Newmarket** 9 to 27 March.*[130]

5 April – yor Maties footmen the first time to **Heighparke** – £2 [fo. 5r]
12 May – Cheries at **Heighparke** – £2 [fo. 5v]
20 May – yor Maties Boatmen – 10s [fo. 5v]
29 May – yor Maties footmen – £3 [fo. 5v]
*Nicholas Staggins for riding charges in attendance on the king at **Windsor**, 7 July to 11 September.*[131]
8 July – yor Maties Berges to **somersethouse** – £1 10s [fo. 6r]
8 July – yor Maties footmen to **winsor** – £2 [fo. 6v]
9 July – the footmen Runing mony – £2 [fo. 6v]
10 July – paid by Mr Halsall at the **Greatparke** – £3 15s [fo. 6v]
10 July – the footmen Runing mony – £2 [fo. 6v]
11 July – the footmen Runing mony – £2 [fo. 6v]
12 July – the footmen Runing mony – £2 [fo. 6v]
13 July – the footmen Runing mony – £2 [fo. 6v]
14 July – the footmen Runing mony – £2 [fo. 6v]
15 July – the footmen Runing mony – £2 [fo. 6v]
16 July – the footmen Runing mony – £2 [fo. 6v]
17 July – to the footmen Runing mony – £2 [fo. 6v]
19 July – the footmen Runing mony – £2 [fo. 6v]
21 July – the footmen Runing mony – £2 [fo. 6v]
22 July – the footmen Runing mony – £2 [fo. 7r]
23 July – the footmen Runing mony – £2 [fo. 7r]
26 July – the footmen Runing mony – £2 [fo. 7r]
28 July – the footmen Runing mony – £2 [fo. 7r]
29 July – the footmen Runing mony – £2 [fo. 7r]
29 July – yor Maties Bootemen from the eight of July to the thirty one – £17 [fo. 7r]
31 July – the footmen to **London** – £2 [fo. 7r]
4 August – the footmen Runing mony to **winsor** – £2 [fo. 7r]
4 August – the pages of the Bakstairs to and from **London** – £1 [fo. 7v]
4 August – a boat to & from **whithall** – 10s [fo. 7v]
5 August – the footmen Runing mony – £2 [fo. 7v]

130 TNA LC5/141, p. 177; Ashbee, *Records*, 149.
131 TNA LC5/141, p. 248; Ashbee, *Records*, 152, 164.

9 August – the footmen Runing mony – £2 [fo. 7v]
11 August – the footmen Runing mony – £2 [fo. 7v]
11 August – a footman sent from **the forest** – £2 [fo. 7v]
15 August – the footmen Runing mony – £2 [fo. 7v]
16 August – the footmen Runing mony – £2 [fo. 7v]
17 August – the footmen Runing mony – £2 [fo. 7v]
18 August – the footmen Runing mony – £2 [fo. 7v]
19 August – the footmen Runing mony – £2 [fo. 7v]
20 August – the footmen Runing mony – £2 [fo. 7v]
25 August – the footmen Runing mony – £2 [fo. 8r]
27 August – the footmen Runing mony – £2 [fo. 8r]
29 August – the footmen Runing mony – £2 [fo. 8r]
31 August – the footmen Runing mony – £2 [fo. 8r]
1 September – the footmen Runing mony – £2 [fo. 8r]
2 September – the footmen Runing mony – £2 [fo. 8r]
7 September – the footmen Runing mony – £2 [fo. 8r]
10 September – friute by the way to **London** – 10s [fo. 8v]
10 September – paid by Mr Hall at **Hamton court** – £2 11s 6d [fo. 8v]
17 September – yor Maties Boatmen from the seaven instant to the tenth – £4 12s [fo. 8v]

1676

24 February – the footmen the first time to **Heigh parke** – £2 [fo. 11r]
2 March – the Footmen Runing mony – £2 [fo. 11v]
2 March – Laid out by Mr Roper at **Chelsey** – £2 15s [fo. 11v]
6 March – the Footmen Runing mony – £2 [fo. 11v]
7 March – the Footmen Runing mony – £2 [fo. 11v]
Musicians in ordinary for their attendance at ***Newmarket****, 27 March to 17 April.*[132]
5 April – Laid out by Mr Roper at **Mulbery gardine** – £3 13s [fo. 12r]
8 April – yor Maties footmen Runing mony to **Hakny**[133] – £2 [fo. 12v]
9 April – the footmen Runing mony – £2 [fo. 12v]
16 April – the footmen Runing mony – £2 [fo. 12v]
19 April – the footmen Runing mony – £2 [fo. 12v]
20 April – the footmen Runing mony – £2 [fo. 12v]
21 April – yor Maties Berge to **somersethouse** – £1 [fo. 12v]
24 April – the footmen Runing mony – £2 [fo. 12v]
24 April – the Berges **somersethouse** – £1 10s [fo. 12v]
27 April – the Berge to **somersethouse** – £1 [fo. 13r]
28 April – the Berges to **Dartford** – £5 [fo. 13r]

132 TNA LC5/141, p. 401; Ashbee, *Records*, 160.
133 Hackney.

4 May – the footmen Runing mony – £2 [fo. 13r]
5 May – the Berges to **somersethouse** – £1 [fo. 13r]
5 May – Laid out by Mr porter at **the southaris**[134] – £2 3s 6d [fo. 13r]
11 May – the Berge to **somersethouse** – £1 [fo. 13r]
13 May – the footmen Runing mony to **wolege**[135] – £2 [fo. 13v]
17 May – the Berge to **somersethouse** – £1 [fo. 13v]
17 May – for thre boats – 15s [fo. 13v]
2 June – the footmen Runing mony – £2 [fo. 14r]
2 June – the Berge to **somersethouse** – £1 [fo. 14r]
5 June – the footmen Runing mony to **Hamton court** – £2 [fo. 14r]
5 June – Laid out by Mr Slaughter at **Ham** – £6 13s [fo. 14r]
12 June – for a boat to **Barn ellms**[136] – 10s [fo. 14r]
13 June – for thre boats to **somersethouse** – 10s [fo. 14v]
15 June – for thre boats to **somersethouse** – 10s [fo. 14v]
16 June – for thre boats to **somersethouse** – 10s [fo. 14v]
18 June – Mr Charleton for boats – £10 2s 6d [fo. 14v]
22 June – Mr Charleton for boats – £5 8s [fo. 14v]
25 June – for five boats – £1 10s [fo. 14v]
30 June – for a boat to **the tryall** – 2s 6d [fo. 14v]
5 July – For a boat to **Lady peterbroughs** – 5s [fo. 14v]
11 July – for foure boats to **somersethouse** – £1 [fo. 15r]
11 July – for a baskit of friute at **Heigh parke** – £1 1s 8d [fo. 15r]
12 July – for thre boats to **somersethouse** – 10s [fo. 15r]
13 July – for thre boats to **somersethouse** – 10s [fo. 15r]
19 July – the Berges to **somersethouse** – £1 10s [fo. 15r]
20 July – the Berge to **somersethouse** – £1 [fo. 15r]
21 July – the Berge to **somersethouse** – £1 [fo. 15r]
22 July – the Berge to **somersethouse** – £1 [fo. 15r]
23 July – the Berge to **somersethouse** – £1 [fo. 15r]
24 July – the Berge to **somersethouse** – £1 [fo. 15r]
25 July – the Berge to **somersethouse** – £1 [fo. 15v]
26 July – the Berge to **somersethouse** – £1 [fo. 15v]
27 July – the Berge to **somersethouse** – £1 [fo. 15v]
3 August – the Berge to **somersethouse** – £1 [fo. 15v]
6 August – the Berge to **somersethouse** – £1 [fo. 15v]
12 August – the Berge to **somersethouse** – £1 [fo. 15v]
17 August – the Berges to **somersethouse** – £1 10s [fo. 15v]
21 August – the Berges to **somersethouse** – £1 10s [fo. 15v]
24 August – the Berge to **Lambeth** – £1 10s [fo. 15v]

134 Uncertain meaning but possibly Suthrey House in Mortlake; a designation for Catherine's house in Hammersmith, or less likely, a reference to South Hayes, close to Hammersmith.

135 Woolwich.

136 Several other boats and the queen's barge.

24 August – the footmen Runing mony to **Greenwich** – £2 [fo. 15v]
13 September – the footmen Runing mony to **Audleyend** – £4 [fo. 16r]
14 September – the Musique at **Audleyend** – £5 [fo. 16r]
14 September – the footmen Runing mony to **Ewston** – £2 [fo. 16r]
15 September – the footmen Runing mony – £2 [fo. 16r]
16 September – the footmen Runing mony – £2 [fo. 16r]
17 September – the footmen Runing mony – £2 [fo. 16v]
18 September – the footmen Runing mony – £2 [fo. 16v]
19 September – the footmen Runing mony – £2 [fo. 16v]
20 September – the footmen Runing mony – £2 [fo. 16v]
23 September – the footmen Runing mony – £2 [fo. 16v]
24 September – the poore of **Bery**[137] – £10 [fo. 16v]
24 September – the poore of **Thetford** – £10 [fo. 16v]
24 September – the footmen Runing mony – £2 [fo. 16v]
25 September – the poore of **Ewston** – £5 [fo. 16v]
25 September – yor Maties footmen to **Audleyend** – £2 [fo. 16v]
26 September – the footmen Runing mony to **London** – £4 [fo. 17r]
Musicians, riding charges to ***Newmarket****, 2 to 21 October.*[138]

1677

24 March – Laid out by Mr picot at **Erif**[139] – £2 14s [fo. 20r]
5 April – sentris at **somersethouse** – £1 1s 7d [fo. 20r]
Musicians, in attendance on the king at ***Newmarket****, 16 to 30 April.*[140]
24 April – yor Maties footmen the first day to **Heighpark** – £2 [fo. 20v]
27 April – the footmen Runing mony – £2 [fo. 20v]
1 May – the footmen Runing mony – £2 [fo. 20v]
7 May – the footmen Runing mony – £2 [fo. 21r]
9 May – the footmen Runing mony – £2 [fo. 21r]
10 May – the footmen Runing mony – £2 [fo. 21r]
10 May – one of yor Maties Coatches at **Chelsy** – £1 1s 7d [fo. 21r]
11 May – the footmen Runing mony – £2 [fo. 21r]
16 May – the footmen Runing mony – £2 [fo. 21r]
20 May – the footmen Runing mony – £2 [fo. 21r]
23 May – yor Maties Berge to **somersethouse** – £1 [fo. 21r]
30 May – the Berge to **somersethouse** – 10s [fo. 21r]
2 June – thre boats to **somersethouse** – 17s 6d [fo. 21r]
11 June – the footmen Runing mony to **filberds**[141] – £2 [fo. 22r]
12 June – the servants at **filberds** – £21 11s 8d [fo. 22r]

137 Bury St Edmunds.
138 TNA LC5/141, p. 479; Ashbee, *Records*, 166.
139 Erith.
140 TNA LC5/142, p. 153; Ashbee, *Records*, 175.
141 Philberts House, Buckinghamshire.

12 June – the footmen to **Newbery** – £2 [fo. 22r]
13 June – the House at **Newbery** – £10 [fo. 22r]
13 June – the footmen to **Malbrough**[142] – £2 [fo. 22v]
14 June – the footmen to the **Bath** – £2 [fo. 22v]
14 June – paid at **Laycok**[143] whair yor Matie dined – £2 3s 2d [fo. 22v]
17 June – the footmen Runing mony – £2 [fo. 22v]
26 June – the footmen Runing mony – £2 [fo. 23r]
27 June – the footmen Runing mony – £2 [fo. 23r]
2 July – the footmen Runing mony – £2 [fo. 23r]
3 July – the footmen Runing mony – £2 [fo. 23r]
8 July – the footmen Runing mony – £2 [fo. 23v]
12 July – the footmen to **Bristoll** – £2 [fo. 23v]
13 July – Expenses to **Bristole** for Money – £1 10s [fo. 23v]
14 July – the footmen to **Badmenton** – £2 [fo. 23v]
16 July – Laid out by the way to **Malbrough** – £8 12 6d [fo. 23v]
17 July – to violin Musique at **Malbrough** – £1 [fo. 23v]
17 July – Laid out by Mr Hallsall at **Newbery** whair yor Matie dined – £6 12s [fo. 24r]
17 July – Laid out by the way to **Redin**[144] – £2 8s 2d [fo. 24r]
18 July – to the Musique at **Redin** – £2 [fo. 24r]
18 July – Laid out at **Colbrook**[145] whair yor Matie dined – £6 18s 6d [fo. 24r]
18 July – the footmen from the **Bath** to **London** – £8 [fo. 24r]
27 July – Mr Charleton for boats – £4 2s 6d [fo. 25r]
10 August – to footmen Runing mony – £2 [fo. 25r]
12 August – to footmen Runing mony – £2 [fo. 25r]
14 August – to footmen Runing mony – £2 [fo. 25r]
15 August – for boats to **Chelsy** – £1 [fo. 25r]
18 August – to footmen Runing mony – £2 [fo. 25v]
19 August – to footmen Runing mony – £2 [fo. 25v]
22 August – for boats to **somersethouse** – 10s [fo. 25v]
26 August – to footmen Runing mony – £2 [fo. 25v]
4 September – boats to **Chelsy** – £1 [fo. 25v]
9 September – a boat to **somersethouse** – 5s [fo. 25v]
9 September – to footmen Runing mony – £2 [fo. 25v]
12 September – a solger at **somersethouse** – £1 1s 8d [fo. 25v]
21 September – to footmen Runing mony – £2 [fo. 25v]
23 September – to footmen Runing mony – £2 [fo. 25v]

Musicians, riding charges in attendance on the king at ***Newmarket****, 24 September to 13 October.*[146]

142 Marlborough.
143 Lacock.
144 Reading.
145 Colnbrook.
146 TNA LC5/142, p. 153; Ashbee, *Records*, 175–76.

10 October – giuen at **the southaries** – £21 15s [fo. 25v]
10 October – the Berges to **Lambeth** – 10s [fo. 25v]
17 October – a solger at **somersethouse** – £1 1s 8d [fo. 25v]

1678

25 January – yor Maties footmen first time to **Heighparke** – £2 [fo. 28v]
4 April – yor Maties Berge to **Westminster** – £1 10s [fo. 29v]
12 April – the door keeper of the **parliament** – £2 [fo. 29v]
29 April – the footmen Runing mony – £2 [fo. 29v]
7 May – the footmen Runing mony – £2 [fo. 29v]
10 May – boats to & from **somersethouse** – £1 5s [fo. 30r]
11 May – boats to & from **somersethouse** – 12s 6d [fo. 30r]
15 May – the footmen Runing mony – £2 [fo. 30r]
16 May – for boats to **somersethouse** – £1 5s [fo. 30r]
23 May – for boats to **somersethouse** – 10s [fo. 30r]
23 May – the footmen Runing mony – £2 [fo. 30r]
29 May – yor Maties footmen – £3 [fo. 30r]
4 June – for boats – 15s [fo. 30v]
9 June – the Berges to **putny** – £3 [fo. 30v]
12 June – for boats – 15s [fo. 30v]
13 June – for boats – 10s [fo. 30v]
20 June – for boats – £1 10s [fo. 30v]
1 July – Mr Charleton for boats – £3 17s 6d [fo. 31r]
7 July – Mr Charleton for boats – £10 7s 6d [fo. 31r]
24 July – for boats – £1 [fo. 31r]
29 July – for boats by Mr Roper – 15s [fo. 31r]
2 August – Lady Arlingtons Chairemen & footmen to & from **St James** – £2 [fo. 31r]
7 August – the footmen Runing mony – £2 [fo. 31r]
14 August – for boats – £1 15s [fo. 31r]
Notification to the Dean of His Majesty's chapel that the court will be at ***Windsor Castle*** *from 14 August for one month.*[147]
Payment to the Chapel Royal in attendance on the king at ***Windsor*** *14 August to 26 September 1678.*[148]
15 August – for boats to **somersethouse** – 10s [fo. 31r]
16 August – the footmen Runing mony to **winsor** – £2 [fo. 31r]
17 August – the footmen Runing mony – £2 [fo. 31v]
19 August – the footmen Runing mony – £2 [fo. 31v]
20 August – the footmen Runing mony – £2 [fo. 31v]

[147] TNA LC5/143, p. 141; Ashbee, *Records*, 180.
[148] TNA LC5/143, pp. 302–03; Ashbee, *Records*, 183.

20 August – to a groome sent to **London** – £1 [fo. 31v]
25 August – the footmen Runing mony – £2 [fo. 31v]
27 August – the footmen Runing mony – £2 [fo. 31v]
27 August – for a boat by Mr Richards – 5s [fo. 31v]
29 August – to a groome sent to **London** – £1 [fo. 32r]
31 August – Laid out by Lady Arlinton at **Cranburn Lodg** – £3 5s [fo. 32v]
31 August – the footmen Runing mony – £2 [fo. 31v]
1 September – the footmen Runing mony – £2 [fo. 32v]
2 September – the footmen Runing mony – £2 [fo. 32v]
2 September – Laid out by Mr Seares at **fearnhill**[149] – £5 8s 4d [fo. 32v]
4 September – the footmen Runing mony – £2 [fo. 32v]
5 September – the footmen Runing mony – £2 [fo. 32v]
8 September – Laid out by Lady Arlinton at **Cleuedon**[150] – £5 6s 4d [fo. 33r]
8 September – the footmen Runing mony – £2 [fo. 33r]
8 September – a man sent for water at **Cleuden** – 10s [fo. 33r]
10 September – the footmen Runing mony – £2 [fo. 33r]
11 September – the footmen Runing mony – £2 [fo. 33r]
13 September – the footmen Runing mony – £2 [fo. 33r]
13 September – for bringing flowrpots from **somersethouse** – 15s [fo. 33r]
15 September – the footmen Runing mony – £2 [fo. 33r]
15 September – Laid out by Lady Bellings in **the forest** – £3 5s [fo. 33r]
16 September – the footmen Runing mony – £2 [fo. 33r]
18 September – the footmen Runing mony – £2 [fo. 33r]
19 September – the footmen Runing mony – £2 [fo. 33r]
19 September – to a groome sent from **filberd** to **winsor** – 10s [fo. 33v]
19 September – for boats to **filberds** – £1 [fo. 33v]
19 September – to a groome sent to **bray** – 10s [fo. 33v]
23 September – to a Groome sent to **London** – £1 [fo. 33v]
24 September – to the footmen Runing mony to **London** – £2 [fo. 33v]
24 September – for bringing y^r^ Maties Chaire to **London** – £1 1s 8d [fo. 33v]
24 September – for a boat with Clocks & flowrepots – £1 [fo. 33v]
12 October – for a boat – 1s [fo. 34v]
25 December – to the yeomans of the gard at **somersethouse** – £1 1s 8d [fo. 36r]

1679

4 February – Laid out by Mr picot for flowrpots sent to **winsor** last somer – £1 10s [fo. 37r]

149 Fernhill.
150 Cliveden.

1-Worsley/9 – Catherine of Braganza, privy purse accounts 1679–81

1679 [continued]

4 May – yor Maties footmen the first time to **Heigh parke** – £2 [fo. 3v]
14 May – yor Maties footmen Runing mony – £2 [fo. 3v]
29 May – yor Maties footmen – £3 [fo. 4r]
6 June – the Berge to **somersethouse** – 10s [fo. 4r]
19 June – yor Maties footmen Runing mony – £2 [fo. 4r]
20 June – yor Maties footmen Runing mony – £2 [fo. 4v]
28 June – the footmen Runing mony – £2 [fo. 4v]
Musicians in attendance on his majesty at ***Windsor*** *from 30 June to 17 September 1679.*[1]
1 July – the footmen to **Windsor** – £2 [fo. 4v]
5 July – the footmen Runing mony – £2 [fo. 5r]
7 July – the footmen Runing mony – £2 [fo. 5r]
12 July – the footmen Runing mony – £2 [fo. 5r]
13 July – the footmen Runing mony – £2 [fo. 5r]
14 July – the footmen Runing mony – £2 [fo. 5r]
15 July – the footmen Runing mony – £2 [fo. 5r]
17 July – the footmen Runing mony – £2 [fo. 5r]
22 July – the footmen Runing mony – £2 [fo. 5v]
22 July – boats with flowrpots from **somersethouse** – £1 3s [fo. 5v]
24 July – the footmen Runing mony – £2 [fo. 5v]
26 July – the footmen Runing mony – £2 [fo. 5v]
27 July – the footmen Runing mony – £2 [fo. 5v]
30 July – boats with flowrpots from **somersethouse** – £1 3s [fo. 5v]
1 August – the footmen Runing mony – £2 [fo. 5v]
4 August – the footmen Runing mony – £2 [fo. 5v]
6 August – the footmen Runing mony – £2 [fo. 5v]
6 August – for a boat from **somersethouse** – £1 2s [fo. 5v]
8 August – the footmen Runing mony – £2 [fo. 5v]
12 August – the footmen Runing mony – £2 [fo. 6r]
13 August – a boat from **somersethouse** – £1 2s [fo. 6r]
13 August – the footmen Runing mony – £2 [fo. 6r]
14 August – a footmen sent from **old Windsor** – 10s [fo. 6r]
16 August – the footmen Runing mony – £2 [fo. 6r]

1 TNA LC5/144, pp. 218–19; Ashbee, *Records*, 186.

20 August – a boat with flowrpots to & from **somersethouse** – £2 5s [fo. 6r]
28 August – a boat with flowrpots to & from **somersethouse** – £1 2s [fo. 6r]
1 September – the footmen Runing mony – £2 [fo. 6v]
1 September – a waterman brought things from **London** – 10s [fo. 6v]
2 September – the footmen Runing mony – £2 [fo. 6v]
4 September – a boat with flowrpots from **somersethouse** – £1 [fo. 6v]
8 September – a boat with flowrpots from **somersethouse** – £1 [fo. 6v]
9 September – the footmen Runing mony – £2 [fo. 6v]
11 September – the footmen Runing mony – £2 [fo. 6v]
15 September – a boat with flowrpots from **somersethouse** – £1 2s [fo. 6v]
15 September – a groome sent to **London** – £1 [fo. 6v]
17 September – a horsehire to **London** – 5s [fo. 6v]
17 September – the footmen Runing mony to **London** – £2 [fo. 6v]
26 September – the footmen Runing mony to **Newmarkit** – £4 [fo. 7v]
26 September – the seruants at **Audley end** – £5 8s [fo. 7v]
26 September – the pages of the Bake stairs to **Newmarkit** – £1 [fo. 7v]
*Musicians for riding charges for being in attendance on the king at **Newmarket**, 1 to 17 October 1679.*[2]
7 October – the footmen Runing mony – £2 [fo. 8r]
8 October – the footmen Runing mony – £2 [fo. 8r]
9 October – a groome sent to **London** for the Coatches – £2 [fo. 8r]
9 October – the footmen Runing mony – £2 [fo. 8r]
9 October – a gyd to **Euston** – £1 1s 7d [fo. 8r]
10 October – two yeomans of the garde Caried yor ma^{tie} in a Chaire – £1 1s 7d [fo. 8r]
10 October – the footmen Runing mony – £2 [fo. 8r]
13 October – the footmen to **London** – £4 [fo. 8r]
13 October – guydes to **London** – £2 3s 2d [fo. 8v]
16 October – a boat sent to **Dartford –** 10s [fo. 8v]
25 December – the yeoman of the gard at **somerset house** – £1 [fo. 9v]

1680

10 March – yor Maties footmen to **newmarkitt** – £4 [fo. 12v]
21 March – the footmen Runing mony – £2 [fo. 13r]
23 March – the footmen Runing mony – £2 [fo. 13r]
29 March – the footmen Runing mony – £2 [fo. 13r]
31 March – yor Maties footmen to **London** – £4 [fo. 13r]
2 April – the Coatchmakers man to & from **Newmarkitt** – £2 3s 2d [fo. 13v]

2 TNA LC5/143, p. 322; Ashbee, *Records*, 184.

3 April – Lord feversoms man sent from **Newmarkitt** to **London** for the Coatches – £5 8s [fo. 13v]
3 April – a footman sent post from **Newmarkitt** to **London** – £5 8s [fo. 13v]
15 April – yor Maties footmen the first time to **Heigh parke** – £2 [fo. 14v]

*Musicians attending the king at **Windsor** from 19 April to 9 September.*[3]

19 April – the footmen to **Windsor** – 12s [fo. 14v]
19 April – a Berge with roods from **windsor** – £6 [fo. 14v]
19 April – Coatches to **Windsor** – 14s [fo. 14v]
22 April – a boat with flowrepots from **London** – £1 3s [fo. 14v]
22 April – the footmen Runing mony – £2 [fo. 14v]
23 April – a footman sent to old **Windsor** – 10s [fo. 14v]
27 April – the footmen Runing mony – £2 [fo. 15r]
29 April – the footmen Runing mony – £2 [fo. 15r]
1 May – a boat with flowerpots from **London** – £1 3s [fo. 15r]
3 May – Mr Charleton for yor Maties two boatmen – £9 [fo. 15r]
4 May – the footmen Runing mony – £2 [fo. 15r]
7 May – a boat with flowrpots to **London** – £1 3s [fo. 15r]
8 May – the footmen Runing mony – £2 [fo. 15r]
8 May – the footmen Runing mony – £2 [fo. 15r]
11 May – the footmen Runing mony – £2 [fo. 15r]
12 May – the Kings violin Musique for waiting of the maid of Honour at **Newmarkit** – £20 [fo. 15r]
20 May – yor Maties footmen to **London** – £2 [fo. 15v]
20 May – the Kings Coatchman at **huntslow**[4] – £1 1s 7d [fo. 15v]
26 May – the Kings Coatchman to **huntslow** – £1 1s 7d [fo. 15v]
10 June – the footmen to **London** – £2 [fo. 16r]
10 June – the Kings Coatchmen to **London** – £2 3s 2d [fo. 16r]
18 June – a waterman with flowrpots & boxes – £1 [fo. 16r]
20 June – the footmen Runing mony – £2 [fo. 16r]
23 June – the man brought flowrpots & boxes – £1 [fo. 16r]
28 June – the footmen to **London**[5] – £2 [fo. 16r]
1 July – the footmen from **London** – £2 [fo. 16v]
8 July – a man brought flowrpots & boxes from **somerset house** – £1 [fo. 17r]
12 July – the footmen to **London**[6] – £2 [fo. 17r]
14 July – a boat sent to & from **Windsor** – £2 [fo. 17r]
16 July – the footmen from **London**[7] – £2 [fo. 17v]

3 TNA LC5/145, p. 116; Ashbee, *Records*, 191, 192, 193.
4 Hounslow.
5 And two more entries for London.
6 And two more entries for London.
7 And two more entries for London.

20 July – the footmen to **London**[8] – £2 [fo. 17v]
21 July – the footmen from **London**[9] – £2 [fo. 17v]
26 July – a groome sent to **London** – £1 [fo. 17v]
28 July – the boatman for bringing flowrpots and boxes from **somersethouse** – £1 [fo. 17v]
29 July – the footmen from **London** – £2 [fo. 17v]
2 August – the footmen from **London**[10] – £2 [fo. 18r]
16 August – the footman to **filberds** – £2 [fo. 18r]
18 August – the footmen Runing mony – £2 [fo. 18r]
25 August – the footmen to **swalowfeild**[11] – £2 [fo. 18v]
4 September – a waterman with boxes and flowr pots from **somersethouse** 11 times – £1 7s 6d [fo. 18v]
6 September – the footmen Runing mony – £2 [fo. 18v]
6 September – Laid out by Mr Rogers at **Cleworth**[12] – £2 8s 4d [fo. 18v]
8 September – a womane for the **Meads**[13] by Lord feuersom – £5 [fo. 19r]
8 September – the footmen to **London** – £2 [fo. 19r]

*John Fashion, musician at **Newmarket** from 16 September to 9 October.*[14]

16 September – the footmen to **Newmarkitt**[15] – £4 [fo. 19v]
22 September – the footmen to **Euston** – £2 [fo. 20r]
22 September – a horsehire to & from **Euston** – £1 [fo. 20r]
23 September – the footmen Runing mony – £2 [fo. 20r]
23 September – a groome sent to **Thetford** – 10s [fo. 20r]
24 September – the footmen to **Newmarkitt** – £2 [fo. 20r]
24 September – a gyd to **Newmarkitt** – £1 [fo. 20r]
29 September – the footmen Runing mony – £2 [fo. 20v]
1 October – to the footmen Runing mony – £2 [fo. 20v]
6 October – for Lodging of your Majesties seruants at **Newmarkitt** – £48 [fo. 20v]
6 October – the footmen to **London** – £4 [fo. 20v]
6 October – for a horsehire to **London** – £1 [fo. 20v]
7 October – Mr William sent post to **Newmarkitt** – £5 1s 6d [fo. 20v]
14 October – Mr Grill for goeing post thre tymes to and from **Newmarkitt** – £16 3s 9d [fo. 20v]

8 And one more payment.
9 And three more payments.
10 And two more entries for London.
11 Swallowfield Park, Berkshire.
12 Possibly for Clewer.
13 The Meads or meadows at Runnymede.
14 TNA LC5/144, p. 629; Ashbee, *Records*, 192.
15 And one more entry.

1681

27 February – yor Maties footmen first time to **Heigh parke** – £2 [fo. 24v]
Musician attending his majesty at ***Windsor*** *for 122 days from 28 April to 27 August.*[16]
Joseph Fashion, musician at ***Newmarket*** *8 September to 12 October.*[17]

1682

the court at ***Newmarket****, 4 March to 7 April.*[18]
William Clayton, musician at ***Windsor****, 22 April to 23 June.*[19]
Their majesties and royal highnesses continue in good health at ***Windsor*** *whence his Royal Highness comes tonight and lodges at* ***St James****, May.*[20]
'to come from ***Winsore*** *where the Court now was', 19 May.*[21]
William Clayton, musician at ***Windsor****, 8 July to 10 September.*[22]
John Abel at ***Newmarket****, 2 to 21 October.*[23]
their majesties and his royal highness with the whole court returned today from ***Newmarket****, 21 October.*[24]

1683

Nicholas Staggins, attending the king at ***Newmarket****, 3 to 26 March.*[25]
Nicholas Staggins, attending the king at ***Windsor****, 14 April to 25 June.*[26]
Nicholas Staggins, attending the king at ***Windsor****, 31 July to 29 August.*[27]
Nicholas Staggins, attending the king at Winchester, 29 August to 25 September.[28]
5 Oct 1683 – ***the Newmarket journey*** *which is to be on Monday. I do not yet know if her majesty goes.*[29]

16 TNA LC5/145, p. 116; Ashbee, *Records*, 196.
17 TNA LC5/144, p. 629; Ashbee, *Records*, 198.
18 Ashbee, *Records*, 199.
19 TNA LC5/144, p. 318; Ashbee, *Records*, 201.
20 *CSPD 1681–82*, 194.
21 Evelyn, *Diary*, 725.
22 TNA LC5/144, p. 318; Ashbee, *Records*, 201.
23 TNA LC5/144, p. 306; Ashbee, *Records*, 202.
24 *CSPD 1681–82*, 489.
25 TNA LC5/144, p. 707; Ashbee, *Records*, 207.
26 TNA LC5/144, p. 707; Ashbee, *Records*, 207.
27 TNA LC5/144, p. 707; Ashbee, *Records*, 207.
28 TNA LC5/144, p. 707; Ashbee, *Records*, 207.
29 *CSPD 1683–84*, 13.

Nicholas Staggins, attending the king at Newmarket, 8 to 20 October.[30]
9 Oct 1683 – as for news here his majesty went yesterday for ***Newmarket****, ... the queen does not go.*[31]

1684

May 1684 – their majesties having been to visit lady Anne returned for ***Windsor*** *on Tuesday and the duke yesterday morning.*[32]
3 June 1684 – one day this week his majesty goes for ***Winchester*** *and will stay there three or four days during which her majesty comes here. Her majesty has been very much indisposed but is now something better and in a few days will prepare for* ***Tunbridge****.*[33]
14 Oct 1684 – His Majesty having advice of the queen's being indisposed sent a messenger on purpose to ***Whitehall*** *to see how she did, who found her somewhat better and in a fair way to recovery.*[34]

1685

6 February – death of Charles II at the palace of ***Whitehall***

30 TNA LC5/144, p. 707; Ashbee, *Records*, 208.
31 *CSPD 1683–84*, 22.
32 *CSPD 1684–85*, 24.
33 *CSPD 1684–85*, 43.
34 *CSPD 1684–85*, 173.

Glossary

This glossary, and the index that follows it, have two functions. The first is to record the page references for the people, places and things listed in the accounts. The second is to provide some brief notes about those people, places and things and where appropriate to make reference to contemporary sources, in particular the diaries of Samuel Pepys and John Evelyn, to provide a sense of what is interesting about Catherine's privy purse accounts.

In terms of navigating the glossary and index, people are listed by their title because this is how they were identified in the accounts and so this makes it simplest to find them. There are also various passing references to unnamed servants and to various household officials. For a discussion of the various posts, see under the heading for the queen's household. Entries for everything else are clustered under headings – these are: accessories, accounts, ambassadors, animals, beverages, birds, books, calendar, christenings, clothing, craftsmen and women, fastenings, fish, fishing, flowers, food, fruit, funerals, furniture, games and pastimes, gardeners, gifts, guides, hairdressing, household items, jewellery, lace, letters, linens, lodgings, maps, meals, meat, medical attendants, medicine/medical attendants, messengers, money, music/musicians, musical instruments, passementerie, perfume and cosmetics, pets, pictures, places, plate, poor, suppliers, textiles, theatres, transport, vegetables, widows and women. Places are given their seventeenth-century location; for example, Richmond is listed as being in Surrey, which was the case until 1965 when it became a London Borough.

In most instances it has been possible to identify the people, places and things mentioned in the accounts. However, occasionally it has not. Where this has occurred, suggestions are made about who the accounts might refer to or there is a brief note indicating why they were mentioned in the accounts. Frequently this was for submitting a bill for unspecified goods or services. The index uses modern spelling and where this differs to the spelling given in the transcript, the alternative is given immediately afterwards in square brackets.

Abergavenny [Abergenis], **Lady** – *see Bergavenny, Lady*

accessories – *also see clothing, fastenings, linens*

belts – a flat, narrow strip of leather or textile, often worn round the waist or hips, or over one shoulder.

fans – fans, including feather fans and folding fans, with fancy handles were popular accessories in the seventeenth century.[1] In 1664, Evelyn

[1] C. Willett Cunnington and Phillis Cunnington, *Handbook of English Costume in the Seventeenth Century* (London: Faber & Faber, 1972), 128, 192.

saw a range of Japanese and Chinese goods brought to London by the East India Company including 'Fanns like those our Ladys use, but much larger, & with long handles curiously carved, & filled with Chineze Characters'.[2] In June 1663, Samuel Pepys observed that his wife Elizabeth bought 'a fan that she did not a mind that I should know of'.[3]

feathers [fether] – these were probably feathers from the African ostrich (*Struthio camelus*) in their natural black or white, although feathers dyed in a wide range of shades were also available. On 13 July 1663, Pepys described the court women at Whitehall who 'walked, talking and fidling with their hats and feathers' considering that it was 'the finest sight to me'. He admired 'Mrs Steward…with her hat cocked and a red plume' while Lady Castlemaine 'had a Yellow plume in her hat (which all took notice of)'.[4]

girdles – a type of belt worn round the waist. They could be decorative, with fancy buckles and fittings, and used to carry items or to keep clothes closed.

gloves – gloves were an essential accessory for men and women[5] and on 25 January 1669 William Batelier showed 'a great many gloves perfumed, of several sorts' to Elizabeth Pepys, many of which were too big for her hands.[6]

Martial *[Mareschal]* – Martial was a famous French perfume maker, who Mary Evelyn described as 'emulating the Frangipani of Rome', so this was a specific and highly desirable type of perfumed gloves.[7]

transparent – possibly chicken skin gloves, which Mary Evelyn described in the following terms in *Mundus Muliebris*:

Some of chicken skin for night
To keep her Hands plump, soft and white.[8]

hats – Women wore a variety of hats and head coverings, but they could also go bare-headed when outside.[9] On 11 August 1667, Pepys noted

2 Evelyn, *Diary*, 461.

3 Pepys, *Diary*, 4, 172.

4 Pepys, *Diary*, 4, 230.

5 Willett Cunnington and Cunnington, *Handbook*, 74–76, 189–91.

6 Pepys, *Diary*, 9, 427.

7 Mary Evelyn, *Mundus Muliebris: or, The ladies dressing-room unlock'd, and her toilette spread In burlesque. Together with the fop-dictionary, compiled for the use of the fair sex* (London: printed for R. Bentley, in Russel-Street in Covent-Garden, 1690), 18; https://quod.lib.umich.edu/e/eebo/A38815.0001.001/1:5?rgn=div1;submit=Go;subview=detail;type=simple;view=fulltext;q1=Frangipani [accessed 1/5/22].

8 Evelyn, *Mundus Muliebris*, 6. https://quod.lib.umich.edu/e/eebo/A38815.0001.001/1:3?rgn=div1;submit=Go;subview=detail;type=simple;view=fulltext;q1=plump [accessed 1/5/22]; Willett Cunnington and Cunnington, *Handbook*, 191.

9 Willett Cunnington and Cunnington, *Handbook*, 179–81.

that 'the women had pleasure in putting on some straw hats … and did become them mightily, but especially my wife'.[10]

hoods – a close fitting head covering for women. Pepys mentioned women's hoods made in a variety of colours and fabrics (bird's eye, black, French, white, and yellow) in his diary.[11] Evelyn stressed the same point in *Mundus Muliebris*:

Hoods by the whole dozens, White and Black
And store of Coiffs she must not lack.[12]

muffs – a covering to keep the hands warm, often made of fur and cylindrical in shape.[13] Muffs were fashionable for men and women, as Pepys' comment on 30 November 1662 demonstrates: 'this day I did wear a muffe, being my wife's last year's muff; and now I have bought her a new one'.[14] A sense of the variety was hinted at in Dr James Smith's *The Burse of Reformation*:

Here is an English conny furr
Rushia hath no such stuffe
Which for to keep your fingers warme
Excells your sable muffe.[15]

scarves – a strip of fabric, of varying widths and weights worn round the neck or over the shoulder.[16] On 28 September, Elizabeth Pepys received 'a new scarfe, laced, as a token' from a relative.[17] On 6 January 1663, Pepys was 'somewhat vexed at my wife's neglect in leaving of her scarf, waistcoat and night-dressings in the coach today'.[18]

shoes – the popular style for women from *c*. 1660 to *c*. 1680 had a long, squared-off toe, a long tongue, latchets, which would have fastened over the tongue with a ribbon or a buckle, and a modest heel.[19] Surviving examples include a dyed kid shoe, decorated with crimson silk ribbon.[20] Women also wore mules or slippers indoors, with a square toe and moderate to high heels, and decorative uppers, as in

10 Pepys, *Diary*, 8, 382.

11 Pepys, *Diary*, 1, 42; 6, 102; 8, 124; 9, 453.

12 Evelyn, *Mundus Muliebris*, 10 https://quod.lib.umich.edu/e/eebo/A38815.0001.001/1:3?rgn=div1;submit=Go;subview=detail;type=simple;view=fulltext;q1=black [accessed 1/5/22].

13 Willett Cunnington and Cunnington, *Handbook*, 191–92.

14 Pepys, *Diary*, 3, 271.

15 Dr James Smith's *The Burse of Reformation* (London: 1658), cited in Willett Cunnington and Cunnington, *Handbook*, 191.

16 Willett Cunnington and Cunnington, *Handbook*, 178–79.

17 Pepys, *Diary*, 5, 274.

18 Pepys, *Diary*, 4, 6.

19 Lucy Pratt and Linda Woolley, *Shoes* (London: V&A Publications, 2005), 31.

20 V&A T.107A-1917, illustrated in Pratt and Woolley, *Shoes*, 31, plate 10.

the case of a crimson velvet mule with metal thread embroidery *c.* 1650s – *c.* 1660s.[21]

tennis shoes – specific shoes for playing royal tennis, which often had cork soles.

accounts – keeping household accounts was an important task. On the morning of Sunday 7 April 1661, Pepys noted that he had just made up his accounts, adding 'God forgive me' for undertaking this task on the Lord's day.[22] Evelyn, like Pepys, reviewed his accounts at the end of the calendar year, noting on 31 December 1669 'I made up my accompts'.[23]

account books –

arrears – outstanding payments; being behind in the payment of debts and liabilities.

bounty – an act of generosity, a gift or gratuity.[24]

Albemarle [albemalls]**, duchess of** – either 1) Anne Radford (1619–70), daughter of John Clarges and Anne Leaver, married George Monck, 1st duke of Albemarle (1608–70).[25] Previously she had been married to Thomas Radford, a farrier. Pepys described her as 'a plain, homely dowdy'.[26] Or 2) Elizabeth (1654–1734), eldest daughter of Henry Cavendish, 2nd duke of Newcastle and Frances Pierrepoint. She married Christopher Monck (1653–88), 2nd duke of Albemarle in 1669 and by 1682 she was suffering from periodic insanity. After Monck's death she married Ralph Montagu, 1st duke of Montagu in 1692.[27] The dating of the entry indicates it is the latter.

woman –

Alexander, Mrs – for gloves. This was possibly the wife of Francis Alexander, gentleman usher, quarter waiter from September 1671 to Michaelmas 1677.[28]

21 V&A T.631-1972, illustrated in Pratt and Woolley, *Shoes*, 27, plate 8. A similar mule, associated with Henrietta Maria and dated 1660–65, belongs to the collection of Northampton Museum.

22 Pepys, *Diary*, 2, 67.

23 Evelyn, *Diary*, 536.

24 https://www.oed.com/view/Entry/22084?redirectedFrom=bounty+#eid [accessed 19/4/22].

25 Anne does not have her own *ODNB* entry, but she does feature in Ronald Hutton, 'Monck [Monk], George, first duke of Albemarle, (1608–70), army officer and navy officer', *ODNB*, 4 October 2021, https://doi-org.soton.idm.oclc.org/10.1093/ref:odnb/18939 [accessed 20/4/22].

26 Pepys, *Diary*, 2, 51.

27 Robin Clifton, 'Monck, Christopher, second duke of Albemarle (1653–88), army officer and colonial governor', *ODNB*, 3 January 2008, https://doi-org.soton.idm.oclc.org/10.1093/ref:odnb/18938 [accessed 18/8/22].

28 Sainty, Wassmann and Bucholz, *Household officers*, 1.

ambassadors – an emissary usually of high social rank and political standing sent on diplomatic missions.

Dutch, *also see Holland* – John Evelyn observed on 11 December 1667 that 'I had discourse with the Dutch Ambassador concerning the present state of Flanders'.[29]

Hieronymus van Beverningh (1614–90) – a diplomat, with a keen interest on botany. He was sent as ambassador to Oliver Cromwell's Commonwealth in 1653–54, the elector of Brandenburg in 1665, and returned to England in 1667 to negotiate the Treaty of Breda, which ended the Second Anglo-Dutch War. Hieronymus revisited this role in 1674 when he came to discuss the Treaty of Westminster, which ended the Third Anglo Dutch War.[30]

servant –

French – *also see France.* In August 1668 Pepys was disparaging of the French ambassador's unfashionable clothes, commenting that he was dressed in 'a black suit and a cloak of silk; which is a strange fashion now; it hath been so long put off'.[31]

Charles Colbert, marquis de Croissy (1625–96), was ambassador to England 1668 to 1674 and on 8 August 1668 Pepys noted that 'I hear that Colbert the French Imbassador is come, and hath been at Court incognito'.[32] He was the brother of Jean-Baptiste Colbert, and he played an important role in the Secret Treaty of Dover in 1670.

man –

Portuguese – *also see Portugal.* The Portuguese ambassador was present for the marriage of Catherine to Charles in 1662. Lady Fanshawe, whose husband had been the English ambassador to Portugal noted that 'there was a rail across the upper part of the room, in which entered only the King and Queen, the Bishop of London, the Marquis de Sande, the Portuguese Ambassador, and my husband'.[33]

Francisco del Melo Manoel da Camara (7 December 1671 to 9 August 1678) was sent by Peter, prince Regent. In 1675, he was made Catherine's lord chamberlain. On 9 May 1667 Evelyn 'dined with L. Cornbury with Don Francisco de Melos Portugal Ambassador & kindred to the Queene, here also dined Mr Henry Jarmine, Sir

29 Evelyn, *Diary*, 519.

30 Albert Valente, *Chronicles of the Dutch Republic, 1566–1702* (Lisbon: Albert Valente, 2022), 88.

31 Pepys, *Diary*, 9, 284.

32 Pepys, *Diary*, 9, 275.

33 Herbert Charles Fanshawe (ed.), *Memoirs of Ann, Lady Fanshawe, wife of Sir Richard Fanshawe, bart. 1600–1672* (London: J. Lane, 1907), 99.

Hen Capell & severell persons of qualitie'.[34] He lost his post in the queen's household after authorising the printing of a Catholic book.[35]

chairmen –
coachman –
footmen –
gentleman –
man –

Maquis of Arronches – D. Henrique de Sousa Tavares (1626–1706), 3° conde de Miranda do Corvo e 28° senhor da Casa de Sousa, in his role as Portuguese ambassador, called on Lord Chief Justice William Scroggs after the acquittal of Sir George Wakeman, the queen's physician, in 1679.[36] On 7 June 1679, Evelyn witnessed his spectacular formal entry and on 4 December he dined with the marquis who had moved to Cleveland House 'a noble Palace, too good for that infamous----'.[37]

chairman –
groom –
man –

Spanish – There was intense competition between the Spanish and French ambassadors and in September 1661 Pepys 'heard of a fray between the two Embassadors of Spaine and France; and that this day being the day of the entrance of an Embassador from Sweden, they were entended to fight for the precedence'.[38] Charles de Watteville de Joux, baron de Batteville (1605–70) was Spanish ambassador at the start of Charles II's reign (from 1660 to 1663). He opposed the marriage to Catherine of Braganza. After Charles signed the marriage treaty, he tried to drum up opposition to Catherine but failed and was expelled from the country.[39] He was followed by Patricio Moledi, who was ambassador from 1663 to 1665.[40]

34 Evelyn, *Diary*, 509.

35 For Catherine's involvement with Catholic printing, see Chelsea Reutcke, 'Royal patronage of illicit print: Catherine of Braganza and Catholic books in late seventeenth century London', in Nina Lamal, Jamie Cumby and Helmer J. Helmers (eds.), *Print and Power in Early modern Europe, 1500–1800* (Leiden: Brill, 2021), 239–56.

36 John Philipps Kenyon, 'The acquittal of Sir George Wakeman: 18 July 1679', *The Historical Journal* 14.4 (1971), 693–708.

37 Evelyn, *Diary*, 666, 677.

38 Pepys, *Diary*, 2, 187–91.

39 Claire Jackson, *Devil-Land: England Under Siege, 1588–1688* (London: Penguin, 2022), 39.

40 For Moledi's earlier career, see Gerald Belcher, 'Spain and the Anglo-Portuguese

Molina, el Conde de, Antonio Francesca Mesia was the Spanish ambassador 1665–69 and 1671–72. On 23 June 1665 Evelyn 'saw the pompous reception & audience of el *Conde de Molino* the Spanish Ambassador in the Banqueting House: both their Majesties siting together under the state'.[41]

cook –

man –

servants –

Swedish – Sweden engaged in the peace discussion between England and the Dutch and Pepys noted the presence of the 'Swedes Embassadresse' in the list of attendees at Catherine's birthday ball in 1666.[42] She has been identified as baroness Leijonbergh.

Gőran Claesson Fleming, baron (1628–67), leader of the Swedish delegation to England, and ***Peter Julius Coyet*** (1618–67) were sent by the Regency council to secure English support for an agreement with the Netherlands. They arrived in London in spring 1666, stayed just over a year, and arrived in Hellevoesluis on the *Haringvliet* on 20 May 1667.[43]

page –

trumpets –

Ancram [Ancrim]**, Frances** – countess of, lady of the Bedchamber, 1677–82.[44] She was married to Charles Ker, 2nd earl of Ancram (1624–90). She was named in *The Ladies March* (1681) and described as too old to engage in the sexual exploits of the other women described in the poem:

Behold a dame too old to chancre 'em,
Vulgarly called my Lady Ancram,
Lodged in a garret at Whitehall,
Hard by the Countess of Fingal.[45]

Anger, Mr – as per bill.

animals – also see *birds*, *pets*

ass – another name for a donkey, a domesticated equid, used as a pack animal.[46] Zebras were known as the 'striped ass', which explains why

alliance of 1661: a reassessment of Charles II's foreign policy at the Restoration', *Journal of British Studies* 15.1 (1975), 86–87.

41 Evelyn, *Diary*, 477.

42 Pepys, *Diary*, 7, 372.

43 Frans Gooskens, 'Sweden and the Treaty of Breda in 1667: Swedish diplomats help to end naval warfare between the Dutch Republic and England', *Forum Navale: Swedish Society for Naval History* 74 (2018), 54–80.

44 Sainty, Wassmann and Bucholz, *Household officers*, 2.

45 John Harold Wilson, *Court Satires of the Restoration* (Columbus, OH: Ohio State University Press, 1976), 57, 59.

46 https://www.oed.com/view/Entry/11702?rskey=6d7PAB&result=1#eid [accessed 19/4/22].

Queen Charlotte's zebra, which was given to her as a wedding gift in 1762, was referred to as the 'Queen's Ass'.[47]

calves – young cows, up to a year old, after which they are yearlings.[48]

cows – usually a female domesticated cow (*Bos Taurus*) but the terms can be applied to female animals of all bovine species.[49] Their milk was drunk but it was also used medicinally, as when Evelyn noted that he had been 'bathing my leggs to the knees in Milk made as hot as I could endure it'.[50]

elephant – in August 1675 an Indian elephant calf (*Elephas maximus indicus*) arrived in London, probably on a ship belonging to the East India Company.[51] The elephant was sold by Lord Berkeley and then displayed at Garraway's Coffee House in the city of London.[52] Earlier in the year, Evelyn met Mr Sheeres, who told him 'that all the Teeth of Elephants grew downewards & not as commonly painted'.[53] It was one of a number of exotic animals on view in London. In 1684, Evelyn went with Sir William Godolphin to see a rhinoceros and 'a living Crocodile brought from some of the W: Indian Islands'.[54]

hogs – domesticated pigs (*Sus domesticus*) kept for meat which were often castrated males. However, some lived happier lives. In 1644, Evelyn enjoyed 'A dish of Truffles, which is a certaine earth-nut, found out by an hogg, train'd up to it'.[55]

horses – (*equus feus caballus*) for riding for pleasure, hunting, racing or travel, pulling carts and coaches.

Done horses – probably 1) done as in tired, or less likely 2) a reference to a horse with a dun coat, a colour that is the result of a dilution gene, which affects red and black coats, along with a dark strip along the spine, and a dark tail and mane.[56]

47 Christopher Plumb, 'Exotic animals in eighteenth century Britain' (unpublished PhD thesis, University of Manchester, 2010), 168–71.

48 https://www.oed.com/view/Entry/26330?rskey=lSYsAX&result=1#eid [accessed 19/4/22].

49 https://www.oed.com/view/Entry/43415?rskey=J3dgM4&result=1#eid [accessed 19/4/22].

50 Evelyn, *Diary*, 720.

51 Anon., *A full and true relation of the elephant that is brought over into England from the Indies, and landed at London, August 3d. 1675* (London: Printed for William Sutten, 1675).

52 Caroline Grigson, *Menagerie: The History of Exotic Animals in England* (Oxford: Oxford University Press, 2015), 33, 37, 40–42; Plumb, 'Exotic Animals', 197–204.

53 Evelyn, *Diary*, 608.

54 Evelyn, *Diary*, 778–79.

55 Evelyn, *Diary*, 90.

56 https://www.animalgenetics.eu/Equine/Coat_Colour/Dun.asp [accessed 2/5/22].

horse hire – horses could be hired from the various staging points along the royal post routes.[57]

mare, killed – a female horse, or equine, that is mature and of breeding age.

kid – a term for male and female juvenile goats, less than a year old.

kine – an archaic plural for cows.[58]

mules – strong and so often used to pull carts and as pack animals, mules (*equus mulus*) are the result of breeding a jack (male donkey) with a mare (female horse). In August 1668 Pepys saw the French ambassador's mules '(the first I ever saw) with their sumpter cloths mighty rich'.[59]

sea dog – a term for a seal, specifically, the common or harbour seal, *Calocephalus vitulinus*, or a dogfish or small shark.[60]

animal feed – domesticated animals like the queen's cattle or wild animals such as the deer in the royal parks were fed hard feed, as well as being provided with grazing. In January 1681, Edward Sawyer received £20 for hay for the deer as keeper of Cranbourne Lodge, Windsor, while in December of that year Anthony Meek provided £25 worth of hay for deer in Greenwich Park.[61]

barley – a grass (*Hordeum vulgare*) producing grain, which was used as animal feed, as well as in brewing and to make flour for bread.

hay – grasses and other herbaceous plants, such as legumes, which are cut and dried as animal feed. The quantity of leaves and seeds determines the quality.

Arlington, lady – Isabella van Nassau-Beverweert (28 December 1633–18 January 1718) was the daughter of Lodewyck van Nassau, Heer van Beverweerd, and Elizabeth, countess van Hornes, and was born at The Hague. She married Henry Bennet, baron Arlington, in March 1665 and their daughter Isabelle was born in *c.* 1668. Isabella was appointed as first lady of the Bedchamber 1682–85.[62] Her sister married the earl of Ossory, son of the duke of Ormond. After the death of countess of

[57] For the origins of this system, see Mark Brayshay, 'Royal post-horse routes in England and Wales: the evolution of the network in the late-sixteenth and early-seventeenth century', *Journal of Historical Geography* 17.4 (1991), 373–89.

[58] https://www.oed.com/view/Entry/103476?rskey=IQZZlJ&result=1#eid [accessed 19/4/22].

[59] Pepys, *Diary*, 9, 281.

[60] https://www.oed.com/view/Entry/174136?redirectedFrom=sea+dog#eid [accessed 19/4/22].

[61] Akerman, *Secret Services*, 23, 41.

[62] No *ODNB* entry but listed in Alan Marshall, 'Bennet, Henry, first earl of Arlington, (1618–85), politician', *ODNB*, 3 January 2008, https://doi.org/10.1093/ref:odnb/2104 [accessed 15/4/22].

Suffolk, she was Catherine's groom of the stool and mistress of the robes from 1681 to 1692.[63]

butler –
chairmen –
cook –
footman –
man –
page –
woman –

Arlington, lord – Henry Bennet, 1st earl of Portland (1618–85), was the second son of Sir John Bennet of Dawley, Middlesex and Dorothy, daughter of Sir John Crofts. He became keeper of the king's privy purse in 1661. He was made baron Arlington in 1665, earl in 1672, and he was secretary of state from 1662 to 1674.[64] During this time Pepys noted that Arlington allied with Lady Castlemaine and Frances Stuart, and that he was rumoured to be crypto-Catholic.[65] According to Evelyn 'there is no man more hospitably easy to be withall than my L: Arlington'.[66] His London home was Goring House, which was renamed Arlington House when it was rebuilt after a fire in 1674. It was located near St James's Park, while his country home was Euston Hall, Suffolk, which he bought in 1666. He converted to Catholicism on his deathbed.

butler –
men –
page –

Armenian, the – possibly an individual engaged in trade between Armenia and the English East India Company.[67]

Arundel [Arondall]**, Lord** – the honourable John, called Sir from 1668. He was master of the queen's horse from 1678 to 1679 and from 1686 to 1702.[68]

coachmen and footmen –
footman –

63 Sainty, Wassmann and Bucholz, *Household officers*, 2; MacLeod, *Painted Ladies*, 244.

64 Alan Marshall, 'Bennet, Henry, first earl of Arlington, (1618–1685), politician', *ODNB*, 3 January 2008, https://doi.org/10.1093/ref:odnb/2104 [accessed 12/1/22]; Sainty, Wassmann and Bucholz, *Household officers*, 2.

65 Pepys, *Diary*, 3, 289; 4, 366 and 4, 48.

66 Evelyn, *Diary*, 560.

67 See Vahé Baladouni and Margaret Makepeace, 'Armenian merchants of the seventeenth and early eighteenth centuries: English East India Company sources', *Transactions of the American Philosophical Society* New Series 88.5 (1998), i–xxxvii, 1–294. For Armenia more generally, see Henry Shapiro, 'The great Armenian flight: migration and cultural change in the seventeenth-century Ottoman empire', *Journal of Early Modern History* 23.1 (2019), 67–89.

68 Sainty, Wassmann and Bucholz, *Household officers*, 2.

Ashwell, Michael – a bottleman of the field. Possibly Michael Ashley, groom of the queen's bottle horse from 1669 to 1674.[69]

Askin, George – the queen's groom.

Asp, Sir Thomas – for perfume delivered by his man.

man –

Aubigny, lord – Ludovic Stuart (1619–65), 10th Seigneur d'Aubigny, was the son of Esmé Stuart, 3rd duke of Lennox and Katherine Clifton, baroness of Clifton of Leighton Bromswold, and almoner to Henrietta Maria, the queen dowager.[70]

Bannister, John – musician.

Baptist, Mr – for glasses.

Baptista, Mr – possibly Giovanni Battista Draghi, musician, who was the queen's principal organist from 1677 to 1691.[71]

Bar, George, old – for his bill.

Bardo/Bardon/Bardou, Mrs – possibly Mrs Beatrice Baradas, a Portuguese woman listed as a member of the queen's household in 1665.[72]

Barker [Barkir], **Ann** – necessary woman or looker to the privy lodgings, 1665–79.[73]

Barker, Christopher – the queen's groom.

Bath [Beath], **countess of** – Jane Wyche (d.1692), daughter of Sir Peter Wyche, a London merchant who had served in the royal household and who was the English ambassador to the Ottoman Empire. She was the wife of Sir John Grenville from 1652, 1st earl of Bath, mother of five children and a lady of the bedchamber to Catherine of Braganza.[74]

coachman –

cook –

footman –

man –

servant –

Bath, lord – Sir John Grenville, 1st earl of Bath (1628–1701), was the son of Sir Bevil Grenville and Grace, daughter of Sir George Smythe. He married Jane Wyche in 1652 and was active during the Restoration. He

69 Sainty, Wassmann and Bucholz, *Household officers*, 3.

70 No *ODNB* entry; see Gaby Mahlberg, *The English Republican Exiles in Europe during the Restoration* (Cambridge: Cambridge University Press, 2020), 78–79.

71 Sainty, Wassmann and Bucholz, *Household officers*, 23.

72 Sainty, Wassmann and Bucholz, *Household officers*, 4.

73 Sainty, Wassmann and Bucholz, *Household officers*, 4.

74 She received a brief mention in the *ODNB* entry of her husband, see Victor Stater, 'Grenville, John, first earl of Bath, (1628–1701), nobleman', *ODNB*, 3 January 2008, https://doi.org/10.1093/ref:odnb/11492 [accessed 1/2/22]; Sainty, Wassmann and Bucholz, *Household officers*, 5.

was made an earl in 1660, a privy councillor in 1663, and was appointed as Lord Lieutenant of Ireland in 1665.[75]

coachman –

bathing – Queen Leonor of Portugal made the spa town of Caldas de Rainha with its warm, sulphurous springs popular in the fifteenth century for bathing for health benefits. So, it is not surprising that Catherine visited English spas. She also had the opportunity to bath at the English royal palaces. In May 1664, Pepys visited the very well-appointed home of his friend Mr Povey in Lincoln's Inn Field which boasted 'a bath at the top of his house'.[76]

bathtubs – bathtubs were made from a variety of materials including wood, cast iron and copper. They were used for emersion and to sweat. In May 1667, Pepys noted that Mr Lowther 'is come to use the Tubb; that is to bathe and sweat himself'.[77]

pumps **–** to pump the water out at spas to fill jugs, bottles and glasses for people to drink.

Belling [Bellings, Billings], **lady** – Lady Frances, chief chamberer or woman of the bedchamber from 1675 until the death of the queen. She was also keeper of the sweet coffers from 1687.[78]

Belling, Sir Richard – the eldest son of Richard Belling (1603–77) and Margaret Butler.[79] He was Catherine of Braganza's principal secretary and master of requests from 1663 until her death. He was knighted in 1666.[80]

man –

Bellows, lord – possibly 1) John Bellew of Williston (1605/6–1679), son of Patrick Bellew of Lisraney. He spent some time in London between 1661 and 1668, and so may have visited England in the 1670s. However, he did not have a title, so referring to him as lord Bellews is unusual[81] Or 2) Sir John Bellew (d.1693), son of Sir Christopher Bellew of Bellewstown and Frances Plunkett, Lord Louth.[82]

75 Victor Stater, 'Grenville, John, first earl of Bath (1628–1701), nobleman', *ODNB*, 3 January 2008, https://doi.org/10.1093/ref:odnb/11492 [accessed 1/2/22].

76 Pepys, *Diary*, 5, 161.

77 Pepys, *Diary*, 8, 217.

78 No *ODNB* entry; Sainty, Wassmann and Bucholz, *Household officers*, 6.

79 Mentioned in Tadhg Ó hAnnracháin, 'Bellings, Richard, (c.1603–1677), politician and historian', *ODNB*, 23 September 2004, https://doi-org.soton.idm.oclc.org/10.1093/ref:odnb/2059 [accessed 27/4/22].

80 Sainty, Wassmann and Bucholz, *Household officers*, 6.

81 Robert Armstrong, 'Bellew, John', *Dictionary of Irish Biography*, https://www.dib.ie/biography/bellew-john-a0559 [accessed 26/10/22].

82 Richard Hawkins, 'Bellew, Sir John', *Dictionary of Irish Biography*, https://www.dib.ie/biography/bellew-sir-john-a0560 [accessed 21/3/22].

bell man [Bellman] – town crier.

Bennet, secretary – Henry Bennet – see *Arlington, lord*

Bennett, Mr – possibly Philip Bennett, groom of the Great Chamber, extraordinary.[83]

Bergavenny Lady – Mary Gifford (d.1699), daughter of Thomas Gifford and Anne Brooksby, wife of George Neville, 9th baron of Bergavenny (1615–66).[84] Mary brought up their son after she was widowed, and in 1681 she remarried Sir Charles Shelley.

man –

Berne, captain – by his bill.

Betts, Mr – probably Henry Betts, groom sumpterman, who was listed in the establishment books of 1674 and 1682.[85]

beverages – these included popular nonalcoholic hot drinks such as coffee, tea and hot chocolate, as well as milk, which was drunk hot or cold, and alcoholic drinks including wine, beer and spirits.

tea [tee] – green and black tea from China, which was made from the leaves of the tea plant (*Camellia sinensis*).[86] On 25 September 1660, Pepys 'did send for a Cupp of Tee (a China drink) of which I never had drank before'.[87] However, tea did not appear in the accounts at Woburn until 1685, when the tea cost over £10 and Lady Margaret Russell was bought a set of tea dishes, which cost £1 14s 0d.[88]

water – In September 1659 Evelyn met Sir Henry Blount 'the famous Travellor, & water drinker'.[89] Pepys described Jemima, countess of Sandwich, as 'not very well' adding that 'it seems her drinking of the water at Tunbridge did almost kill her before she could with the most violent physic get it out of her body again' in July 1665.[90] Celia Fiennes said of the waters at Tunbridge that 'the waters I have dranke many years wch great advantage… it being a spiriteous water that is ready to Evaporate if Carry'd any way'.[91] London water was evidently not as sweet as water in Lisbon, because the women of Catherine's

83 Sainty, Wassmann and Bucholz, *Household officers*, 6.

84 No *ODNB* entry. http://www.thepeerage.com/p1443.htm http://www.thepeerage.com/p1442.htm#i14420 [accessed 2/9/22].

85 Sainty, Wassmann and Bucholz, *Household officers*, 7.

86 Erika Rappaport, *A Thirst for Empire: How Tea Shaped the Modern World* (New Jersey: Princeton University Press, 2019), 23–24.

87 Pepys, *Diary*, 1, 253.

88 Gladys Scott Thomson, *Life in a Noble Household, 1641–1700* (London: Jonathan Cape, 1937), 169–70.

89 Evelyn, *Diary*, 399.

90 Pepys, *Diary*, 6, 152.

91 Celia Fiennes, *Through England on a Side Saddle in the Time of William and Mary* (Cambridge: Cambridge University Press, 2010), 109.

household who arrived before she did in 1662 'complain much for lack of good water to drink'.[92]

glasses of –

wine – the fermented juice of grapes (*vitis*) used to make a variety of alcoholic drinks including Champagne, Port, Claret, Burgundy, Bordeaux and Rhenish, all of which were purchased by the earl of Bedford.[93]

Bew [Biews], **mistress** – the milliner, her bills, selling hoods and scarves.

her maids –

birds – birds were kept as pets, for example, canaries,[94] in collections, for instance the royal waterfowl in St James's park,[95] or for food.

a bird – unspecified type of bird given to the queen.

the bird – probably a reference to the queen's parrot, see below.

your Majesties Birds – possibly the queen's collection of birds, which included the gifts of live chickens and other birds that she was given.

chickens – a domesticated bird (*Gallus gallus domesticus*) kept for meat and eggs. Gervase Markham commented that 'the sauce for chickens is divers, according to men's tastes: for some will only have butter, verjuice, and a little parsley rolled in their bellies mixed together: others will have butter, verjuice, and sugar boiled togethers with toasts of bread: and others will have thick sippets with the juice of sorrel and sugar mixed together'.[96]

fowl – a generic term for birds of the family *Galliformes,* which were bred and kept for their meat, feathers and eggs. Pepys made numerous references to fowl in his diary.[97]

hawks – a group of birds of prey from the *Accipitridae* family; native species include sparrowhawks and goshawks. However, in this context, this term might be used as a generic term to encompass other birds used for hunting, including merlins, kestrels, hobbies and peregrines. In November 1662, Pepys saw the Russian envoy and his attendants 'most of them with Hawkes upon their fists to present to the King'.[98]

hens from Holland – these might have been Brabanters (*gallus gallus domesticus*), a breed of chicken from the duchy of Brabant, which was part of the southern Netherlands, 1648–1794. A Brabanter hen

92 Pepys, *Diary*, 3, 2.
93 Scott Thomson, *Life in a Noble Household*, 183–97.
94 Pepys, *Diary*, 2, 23.
95 Pepys, *Diary*, 2, 157; 3, 47.
96 Gervase Markham, *The Well-Kept Kitchen* (London: Penguin, 2011), 41–42.
97 Pepys, *Diary*, 2, 157; 3, 47; 8, 68.
98 Pepys, *Diary*, 3, 268.

and cockerel featured in Melchior d'Hondecoeter's painting, 'Hens and ducks', dated 1676.[99]

Ortolan – the ortolan bunting (*Emberiza hortulana*) was a small bird weighing approximately 20g. They were caught on their autumn migration from Europe to Africa, then roasted and eaten whole. On 10 July 1666 Pepys saw 'in Cages some Birds brought from about Bordeaux, that are all fat', which may have been ortolans.[100] In 1622, Giovanni Pietro Olina noted in his *Uccelliera* (*The Aviary*) that 'the goodness and flavour of the Meat of this bird have caused observation of its song to be forgotten' adding that 'with care… it fattens so well that some come to weigh three to four ounces, whence being exquisitely delicious they are sent preserved in their skins, and rolled in flour, to be served up in Rome and elsewhere to noblemen'.[101]

parrot – this is a problematic term, which might refer to a true parrot (*Psittacoidea*) or a cockatoo (*Cacatuoidea*). However, the characteristic curved beak, upright body, strong legs and feet with two toes forward and two toes back were common to both. On 22 August 1662, Pepys spoke to Mr Creede 'to have begged a parrett for my wife' but Creede suggested he asked St John Steventon, the clerk of the Cheque, at Portsmouth.[102] Samuel's interest might well have been caused by seeing the parrot the earl of Sandwich brought back with him 'which speaks very well'.[103] Lady Anne Russell was painted as a little girl with a cockatoo, identified as a greater sulphur crested cockatoo.[104] This can be compared with the African grey parrot depicted in *The Paston Treasure*.[105]

parrot's cage –

partridges [partrigess] – probably the grey partridge (*Perdix perdix*), which arrived in Britain after the last ice age. It is a medium sized bird with an orange face. Pepys recorded eating them on several occasions, including 12 August 1668, when 'Pelling dines with us and brings some patriges with him, very good meat'.[106]

pigeon [pigon] – pigeons (*Columba livia domestica*) were bred for meat, with four-week-old chicks known as squabs being a delicacy. In

99 Melchior d'Hondecoeter, *Hens and ducks*, 1676, oil on canvas, Mauritshuis, no. 62.

100 Pepys, *Diary*, 7, 200.

101 Sarah Kane (ed.), *Pasta for Nightingales: A 17th Century Handbook of Bird-care and Folklore* (London: Royal Collection Trust, 2018), 49–51.

102 Pepys, *Diary*, 3, 174.

103 Pepys, *Diary*, 3, 105.

104 Scott Thomson, *Life in a Noble Household*, 291.

105 Unknown artist, Dutch school, *The Paston Treasure*, c.1663, oil on canvas, Norwich Castle Museum. See also Francesca Vanke, *The Paston Treasure: Riches and Rarities of the Known World* (Norwich: Norfolk Museums Service, 2018), 18–19.

106 Pepys, *Diary*, 9, 278. Also 6, 199; 7, 79.

May 1667 Pepys 'dined upon nothing but pigeon pyes … that I was ashamed of it'.[107] Evelyn commented on 12 April 1682 that 'nothing exceeded the pigeons, which tasted just as if baked in a pie, all these being stewed in their own juice, without any addition of water save what swam about the digester'.[108]

swans – probably mute swans (*Cygnus olor*). On 10 January 1664 Pepys went to his uncle 'and there eat some of their swan pie' and then 'invited them to my house to eat a roasted swan on Tuesday next'.[109] In 1695, Robert Laxton received 12s for delivering a gift of 'a brace of fat swans' from Mr Peirson to his Grace at Woburn.[110]

wheatears [whitears] – a small passerine (*Oenanthe oananthe*). They are migratory birds, arriving in Britain in spring and leaving for Africa in September or October and they were considered a delicacy.

wild fowl – a broad term covering aquatic game birds including ducks, geese and swans. In February 1665, Evelyn noted that 'the Parke was at this time stored with infinite flocks of several sorts of ordinary & extraordinary Wild Foule, breeding about the Decoy'.[111] When Gervase Markham discussed how to 'to boil any wild fowl' he described them 'as mallard, teal, widgeon, or such like'.[112]

woodcock [woodcokes] – a large wading bird with a long beak (*Scolopax rusticola*). While Pepys made no mention of eating them, they were highly prized. *The Whole Duty of a Woman Or A Guide to the Female Sex* (1696) advised the cook to 'truss them, parboil them, and so season them with pepper, salt and ginger, and if you please, lard them, then put them in a coffin, covered with butter, mixed with a few sweet herbs, all shred and beaten in a mortar, and being baked enough, draw them and pour in other butter, beaten with the yolk or two of an egg'.[113]

blackamoor – a black servant or enslaved person of Moorish or African descent. It is uncertain who was referred to here and if they were a member of the queen's household.[114] There were people of colour living and working in Restoration London, as is clear from Pepys's comment

107 Pepys, *Diary*, 8, 234.

108 Evelyn, *Diary*, 724.

109 Pepys, *Diary*, 5, 10.

110 Scott Thomson, *Life in a Noble Household*, 159.

111 Evelyn, *Diary*, 472.

112 Markham, *Well-Kept Kitchen*, 26.

113 Anon., *The Whole Duty of a Woman Or A Guide to the Female Sex* (London: printed for J. Gwillim against the Great James Tavern in Bishopsgate street, 1696), 128. https://quod.lib.umich.edu/e/eebo2/A65957.0001.001/1:4.6?rgn=div2;view=fulltext [accessed 18/8/22].

114 https://manyheadedmonster.com/2023/05/18/black-lives-in-the-restoration-household-the-queens-account [accessed 14/6/23].

on 2 March 1669, when he described the dancing after a dinner he had attended in London. Amongst the couples were 'W. Batelier's blackmore and blackmore maid'.[115]

Blyth, Mrs – as per bill.

books – from the sixteenth century, St Paul's churchyard was the centre of the book trade in London and for the country.[116]

History of Portugal – *The Portugal History: Or, A relation of the troubles that happened in the court of Portugal in the years 1667 and 1668* (London: printed for Richard Tonson, 1677). Covering the reign of Alfonso VI and the Treaty of Lisbon of 1668, when Spain recognised Portugal's independence. It was written by Fernando Correa de Lacerda and a French translation was produced by Michel Blouin de la Piquetierre.[117]

Bonard – when he broke his leg.

Bord, de, Mistress – for her bill. This was possibly the 'Madame de boord' mentioned by Evelyn in 1671, who he described as 'a French peddling woman … that used to bring petticoats & fans & baubles out of France to Ladys'.[118]

Bougie, Mistress – possibly a relative of Zachariah Bourgeais, groom of the privy chamber, 1680–1706.[119]

Bowerman [Borman, Boreman]**, Sir William** – clerk comptroller of the king's household in 1661.[120] He was junior clerk of the Green Cloth in 1680 and a resident of Greenwich.

man –

Boynton [Bointon, Boytons]**, Mistress** – Catherine, maid of honour, from 1662–63 to 1669. On 26 October 1664, while attending the launch of the *Royal Catherine*, Pepys noted that 'Mrs Boynton and the Duchesse of Buckeingham, had been very sick coming by water in the barge (the

115 Pepys, *Diary*, 9, 464.

116 See Margaret Willes, *In the Shadow of St Paul's Cathedral: The Churchyard that Shaped London* (New Haven and London: Yale University Press, 2022).

117 https://quod.lib.umich.edu/e/eebo/A54299.0001.001/1:4?rgn=div1;view=fulltext [accessed 14/1/23].

118 Evelyn, *Diary*, 551.

119 Sainty, Wassmann and Bucholz, *Household officers*, 8.

120 There is no *ODNB* entry for Sir William, but see the History of Parliament entry for George Bowerman, for context on the family, John P. Ferris, 'Bowerman (Boreman), George (c.1646–83), of East Greenwich, Kent', http://www.historyofparliamentonline.org/volume/1660-1690/member/bowerman-(boreman)-george-1646-83 [accessed 2/5/22]. For Sir William's will see https://greenwichpeninsulahistory.wordpress.com/2013/08/01/william-boreman-will-and-land-holdings [accessed 2/5/22].

water being very rough)'.[121] She surrendered her post after her marriage to Richard Talbot.[122]

footman –

Bridgewater, Mr – for a petticoat.

Bristol, lady – Lady Anne Russell (d.1697) was the second daughter of Francis, 4th earl of Bedford. She had two sons and two daughters with her husband, George Digby (1612–77), 2nd earl of Bristol. She survived him and oversaw his burial at Chenies, Buckinghamshire, in the Russell family chapel in 1677.[123]

gardener –

Bristol, lord – George Digby (1612–77), 2nd earl of Bristol, son of John Digby, 1st earl of Bristol, and Beatrice or Beatrix Wharton.[124] In 1635 or 1636, he married Lady Anne Russell (d.1697), he fought for the king in 1642 and went into exile in 1646. In 1659, George converted to Catholicism and in 1661 he supported an Italian marriage for Charles II to one of the princesses of Parma. He got into difficulty in 1663 and went into hiding until 1667. He did not recover the king's support.

gardener –

man –

Bristol [bristo] **stones** – Bristol stones or Bristol diamonds are quartz crystals or geodes.[125] In 1654, Evelyn visited Bristol and 'went searching for Bristol diamonds and to the Hotwells at its foot'[126] Celia Fiennes noted that 'Bristol Diamonds wch Look very bright and sparkling and in their native Rudeness have a great lustre and are pointed and Like ye Diamond cutting'.[127]

Brockwell [Brokall, Brokhall], **Henry** – a musician. He was described as a master musician attending the queen's dancing on 14 November 1674.[128] He was a violinist and keeper of the stringed instruments.[129]

121 Pepys, *Diary*, 5, 306.

122 Sainty, Wassmann and Bucholz, *Household officers*, 8.

123 She does not have an *ODNB* entry; see Ronald Hutton, 'Digby, George, second earl of Bristol (1612–77), politician', *ODNB*, 21 May 2009 https://doi.org/10.1093/ref:odnb/7627 [accessed 11/2/22].

124 Ronald Hutton, 'Digby, George, second earl of Bristol (1612–1677), politician', *ODNB*, 21 May 2009 https://doi.org/10.1093/ref:odnb/7627 [accessed 4/1/22].

125 Maurice Tucker, 'Quartz replaced anhydrite nodules ('Bristol diamonds') from the Triassic of the Bristol district', *Geological Magazine* 113.6 (1976), 569–74.

126 Evelyn, *Diary*, 338.

127 Fiennes, *Through England on a Side Saddle*, 201.

128 Sainty, Wassmann and Bucholz, *Household officers*, 9.

129 Ashbee, *Records*, 143.

Brown, Joan, Mrs – keeper of the queen's cow.

Browne, Mr – for his bill.

Browning, Mrs – for her bill.

Bruijn van Berendrecht, Michael de – for his bill.

Bryerly, Robert Mr – the queen's coachman, 1669–74.[130]

Buckingham [Buckengame]**, duchess of** – Mary Fairfax (1638–1705), daughter of Thomas Fairfax, 3rd lord Fairfax of Cameron and Anne, daughter of Horace Vere, baron Vere of Tilbury. In 1657, she became the wife of George Villiers, 2nd duke of Buckingham.[131] She was a lady of the bedchamber, 1662–63 to 1706.[132]

__chairmen__ –

__footmen__ –

__watermen__ –

Buckingham, duke of – George Villiers (1628–87), 2nd duke of Villiers, was the third child of George Villiers, 1st duke of Buckingham and Lady Katherine Manners.[133] In 1649, he joined Charles II in exile and in 1661 he was made a gentleman of the king's bedchamber.

__coachman__ –

Burden, Mr – payment of £26.

Bure, Mr, old – possibly Symon Burr, musician.[134]

Burke, Mr – described as footman but possibly John Burt, groom of the great chamber.[135]

Burton, mistress – by her bill.

busquet – uncertain meaning. Possibly 1) a person called Busquet, 2) for biscuits (for other entries for biscuits, see below under food), 3) for busket, a small bush or scrub or 4) a bouquet, a bunch of flowers or a nosegay (see below).[136]

Bussy, Mrs – widow of one of the queen's grooms.

130 Sainty, Wassmann and Bucholz, *Household officers*, 10.

131 No *ODNB* entry but she does appear briefly in Jacqueline Eales, 'Fairfax [née Vere], Anne, Lady Fairfax, (1617/18–1665), noblewoman', *ODNB*, 23 September 2004 https://doi-org.soton.idm.oclc.org/10.1093/ref:odnb/66848 and in Bruce Yardley, 'Villiers, George, second duke of Buckingham, (1628–1687), politician and wit', *ODNB*, 21 May 2009, https://doi.org/10.1093/ref:odnb/28294 [accessed 21/3/22].

132 Sainty, Wassmann and Bucholz, *Household officers*, 10.

133 Bruce Yardley, 'Villiers, George, second duke of Buckingham, (1628–1687), politician and wit', ODNB, 21 May 2009, https://doi.org/10.1093/ref:odnb/28294 [accessed 21/3/22].

134 Ashbee, *Records*, 104.

135 Sainty, Wassmann and Bucholz, *Household officers*, 10.

136 https://www.oed.com/view/Entry/25244#eid11514535 [accessed 17/3/22]. https://www.oed.com/view/Entry/22086?redirectedFrom=bouquet& [accessed 17/3/22].

cages – for birds.

calendar – the calendar celebrated the Stuart ceremonial year by marking royal birthdays, the legal year and most importantly the liturgical year. As Lancelot Andrews, bishop of Winchester, observed in 1619, 'it never be out of season to speak of Christ, yet even Christ hath his season'.[137] Pepys marked the liturgical year in his diary while also observing his personal milestones, as on 23 February 1660 when he noted 'My birthday: now 27 years', while in 1667 'this day I am by the blessing of God 34 years old – in very good health and mind's content'.[138]

Ash Wednesday (a moveable feast) – the day after Shrove Tuesday, and the first day of Lent. As such, it marks the start of six weeks of abstinence and penitence before Easter with the foreheads of those attending church on that day being marked with the ashes of the burnt palms kept from the previous Palm Sunday. Food purchases made at Woburn Abbey during March 1661 included fresh cod, flounders, oysters, salmon, smelts and sole as well as salted fish, all of which could be termed 'thin dishes' and so suitable for Lent.[139] Pepys noted that music was not performed in the king's chapel at Whitehall during Lent.[140]

Bartholomew fair – a fair held at Smithfield on 24 August, St Bartholomew's day, as well as the days before and after. There were opening ceremonies, as well as performing monkeys, rope dancing and sideshows. Pepys visited several times and observed on 28 August 1667 that he 'was glad to see again, after two years missing it by the plague'.[141] *Bartholomew Fair* was also the name of a play by Ben Jonson, otherwise known as *The Modern History of Hero and Leander*, which included a puppet show and on 7 September 1661 Pepys noted that it was 'acted today, which had not been these forty years (it being so satyricall against puritanisme, they durst not till now)'.[142]

bonfire night [bone fiere night] – while associated with 5 November, the anniversary of the Gunpowder plot, bonfires were used to mark various occasions, including the arrival of Catherine of Braganza and the king's birthday.[143] In this instance, the fire was paid for on 1 August, which was also known as Lammas or Loaf mass and marked when

137 Cressy, *Bonfires & Bells*, 36.

138 Pepys, *Diary*, 1, 65; 8, 77.

139 Scott Thomson, *Life in a Noble Household*, 141.

140 Pepys, *Diary*, 4, 69.

141 Pepys, *Diary*, 8, 405; also see 2, 166; 5, 260.

142 Pepys, *Diary*, 2, 174.

143 David Cressy, *Bonfires and Bells* (Stroud: Sutton Publishing Ltd, 2004), 56–87. Also see Pepys, *Diary*, 1, 89; 3, 83; 3, 95.

the wheat harvest began. It was celebrated with bonfires as this was on the same day as the fire-festival or Lughnasadh (Commemoration of Lugh), an important date in the Celtic calendar.

Christmas (25 December) – One of the four quarter days and the celebration of Christ's birth or nativity. On 24 December 1667, Pepys went to St James's, 'my design being to see the Ceremonys, this night being the Eve of Christmas, at the Queen's Chapel'.[144]

Easter (a moveable feast) – while not specified, it is likely to be a reference to Easter Sunday, the most important point in the liturgical year, marking as it does Christ's resurrection from the dead. It was the day when Mary, Mary Magdalene and John the evangelist visited Christ's tomb, found it empty and learnt that he had risen from the dead. However, Pepys felt it was important in sartorial terms as well and in 1667 he noted that it was 'in vain to make new clothes till Easter, that they might see the fashions as they are like to be this summer'.[145]

Easter eve (a moveable feast) – also known as Holy Saturday and Black Saturday, Easter eve was the last day of Lent, and the one full day when Christ was dead, prior to his resurrection on Easter Sunday.

Easter Monday (a moveable feast) – the day after Easter Sunday.

Good Friday (a moveable feast) – the Friday before Easter Sunday, it was the day of the Crucifixion, and it can fall between 20 March and 23 April.

King's birthday (29 May) – Charles II's birthday. It was chosen as the day when the king made his ceremonial entrance into London in 1660.[146] During Charles's reign, increased emphasis was placed on his birthday as a day of national celebration. Not surprisingly, this was the day selected for the celebration of Royal Oak Day, which remained a public holiday until its abolition in 1859.

Lady Day (25 March) – one of the four quarter days and the Feast of the Annunciation or the Annunciation of the Blessed Virgin Mary. It was the day when the angel Gabriel told Mary that she was with child. It was also the first day of the fiscal and legal year in the Julian calendar.

Maundy Thursday (a moveable feast) – the Thursday before Good Friday, part of Holy Week, and it commemorates the Last Supper. It was marked by the royal Maundy ceremonies.

Michaelmas (29 September) – One of the four quarter days and the feast of St Michael and All Angels. It falls very close to the autumn equinox, which takes place on 22 or 23 September in the northern hemisphere.

144 Pepys, *Diary*, 8, 588.

145 Pepys, *Diary*, 8, 63.

146 Exwood and Lehmann, *Journal of William Schellinks*, 89.

Midsummer (24 June) – one of the four quarter days, the summer solstice, and the feast of the nativity of St John the Baptist, which was often celebrated with bonfires, processions and pageants.

New Year's day (1 January) – also the feast of the circumcision of Christ, taking place eight days after his birth. During this period there were two calendars in use: the Gregorian or New Style calendar established in 1582 by Pope Gregory XIII with 365 days a year apart from in leap years and which began on 1 January and the Julian or Old Style calendar, which was ten days behind the Gregorian calendar and the new financial year, started on 25 March. The Gregorian calendar was not officially adopted in Britain until 1752.[147]

Queen's birthday (15 November) – on this day in 1674, Evelyn recorded in his diary that 'This night being her Majesties Birth-day: the Court was exceeding splendid, in Clothes & Jewells to the height of excesse'.[148]

Robes feast (15 November) – the phrasing and timing suggests it was a feast held to mark the queen's birthday. In a similar way, Pepys sent his father some wine on 8 January 1663 'for to make his feast' because it was his birthday on 14 January.[149]

St Andrew's day (30 November) – St Andrew is patron saint of Scotland and of the Royal Society. Evelyn noted that 30 November 1664 'Was the first Anniversary our Society for the Choice of new Officers … it being St Andrews day, who was our Patron, each fellow wearing a Saint Andrews Crosse of ribbon on the crowne of his hatt'.[150] The previous year Pepys recorded that 'it being St Andrew's and a Collar-day, he [the duke of York] went to Chappell'.[151]

St David's day (1 March) – St David is the patron saint of Wales. On 1 March 1667 Pepys recorded that 'in the street in Mark-lane do observe (it being St David's day) the picture of a man dressed like a Welchman, hanging by the neck upon one of the poles that stand at the top of one of the merchants' houses'.[152]

St George's day (23 April) – St George is the patron saint of England and of the Order of the Garter. On 23 April 1667 Pepys noted that 'the feast being kept at White-hall, out of design, as it is thought, to make

147 Christopher R. Cheyney, *A Handbook of Dates, for Students of British History* (Cambridge: Cambridge University Press, 2004), 1, 17–19.

148 Evelyn, *Diary*, 605.

149 Pepys, *Diary*, 4, 7.

150 Evelyn, *Diary*, 457.

151 Pepys, *Diary*, 4, 401.

152 Pepys, *Diary*, 8, 89.

the best countenance we can to the Swedes Imbassadors, before their leaving us'.[153]

St Patrick's day (17 March) – St Patrick is the patron saint of Ireland.

Irish footmen –

Whitsun (moveable feast) – the festival of Pentecost, which falls on the seventh Sunday after Easter, and as recorded in Acts 2, this was when the Holy Spirits descended upon Jesus's disciples. On Whitsunday 1661 Pepys when to church, after visiting his barber and 'there heard a good sermon of Mr Mills, fit for the day' while on Whit Monday 1662 'the shops being but some shut and some open'.[154]

Cambridge, duke of – James Stuart (1663–67), earl of Cambridge, baron of Dauntsey, son of James, duke of York and Anne Hyde.[155]

music –

violins –

Canterbury, archbishop of – Gilbert Sheldon (1598–1677), son of Roger Sheldon. In 1660, he was elected bishop of London as well as dean of the Chapel Royal and three years later he was made archbishop of Canterbury, an office he held until his death in 1677.[156]

servants –

Capel, Anne – for fruit.

Capel, Sir Henry – Sir Henry Capel (d.1696), second son of Arthur Capel, first Baron Capel of Hadham and Lucy, daughter of Sir Charles Morrison. He was MP for Tewksbury, Gloucestershire.[157] In February 1659 he married Dorothy Bennet. In August 1678 Evelyn went to stay at 'my worthy friends Sir Hen: Capels (bro: to the Earle of Essex) it is an old timber house but his Garden has certainely the Choicest fruite of any plantations in England, as he is the most industrious & understanding in it'.[158] He was created baron Capel in 1692.

gardener –

man –

153 Pepys, *Diary*, 8, 177. The St George's day celebrations were usually held at Windsor in St George's chapel.

154 Pepys, *Diary*, 2, 112; 3, 85.

155 No *ODNB* entry of his own, but he was mentioned briefly in John Miller, 'Anne [née Hyde], duchess of York (1637–1671), first wife of James II', *ODNB*, 3 January 2008, https://doi.org/10.1093/ref:odnb/14325 [accessed 19/4/22].

156 John Spurr, 'Sheldon, Gilbert (1598–1677), archbishop of Canterbury', *ODNB*, 24 May 2008, https://doi.org/10.1093/ref:odnb/25304 [accessed 19/4/22].

157 Paula Watson and Andrew A Hanham, 'Capel, Sir Henry (1638–96), of Kew, Surr.', https://www.historyofparliamentonline.org/volume/1690-1715/member/capel-hon-sir-henry-1638-96 [accessed 10/4/22]. Also see Thomas Doyle, 'Capel, Henry, Baron Capel of Tewkesbury, (bap.1638–96), politician and government official', *ODNB*, 3 January 2008, https://doi-org.soton.idm.oclc.org/10.1093/ref:odnb/4585 [accessed 10/4/22].

158 Evelyn, *Diary*, 653.

Capell, Mr – messenger, as per bill.

Carlisle, lady – Anne Howard (d.1698), daughter Edward Howard, 1st baron Howard of Escrick. She married Charles Howard (1628–85), 1st earl of Carlisle, son of Sir William Howard and Mary, daughter of William, lord Eure.[159]

man –

servant –

Carr, Sir Edward – see *Kerr, Sir Edward.*

Carr [Car], **Sir Robert** – Robert (*c*.1637–82) was the son of Sir Robert Carr and Mary Gargrave and the family estate was at Aswarby, near Sleaford, Lincolnshire.[160] He married twice: first to Isabel Falkingham in 1662 and then to Elizabeth Bennet at some point after March 1664. Knighted in 1664, he succeeded to his father's title in 1667 and was Captain of Lord Gerard's horse 1666–67. Sir Robert was a gentleman of the king's privy chamber 1671–78 and the MP for Lincolnshire in 1665, 1679 and 1681.

man –

Cary [Carey], **Mistress** – possibly Mary Cary, maid of honour to the queen, 1662–69.[161]

Cary [Caries], **Mr** – as per bill. Possibly John Cary, master of the King's Buckhounds 1660–85.

Castlemaine, countess of – Barbara Villiers (1640–1709), daughter of William Villiers, 2nd viscount Grandison and Mary Bayning. She married Roger Palmer, later 1st earl of Castlemaine in 1659. The following year she became the king's mistress and in 1662 she was appointed as a lady of the bedchamber to Catherine of Braganza, a post she held until 1673. In 1670, she was made the duchess of Cleveland. The king acknowledged five of their children but her last child, was probably John Churchill's. From 1676 to 1682, she lived in France and in 1705 she married Major-General Robert Feilding.[162] However, Feilding was already married, and their bigamous marriage was annulled two years later.

man –

servant –

Cavendish [Candish], **lord** – William Cavendish, lord Cavendish (1641–1707), first son of William Cavendish, 3rd earl of Devonshire and Lady Elizabeth

159 She does not have an *ODNB* entry of her own but she is mentioned briefly in Gordon Goodwin, revised by Sean Kelsey, 'Howard, Charles, first earl of Carlisle, (1628–1685), army officer and politician', *ODNB*, 8 October 2009, https://doi-org.soton.idm.oclc.org/10.1093/ref:odnb/13886 [accessed 4/1/22].

160 https://www.historyofparliamentonline.org/volume/1660-1690/member/carr-sir-robert-1637-82 [accessed 21/2/22].

161 Sainty, Wassmann and Bucholz, *Household officers*, 12.

162 Sonia Wynne, Palmer [*née* Villiers], 'Barbara, countess of Castlemaine, and *suo jure* duchess of Cleveland, (bap.1640–1709), royal mistress', *ODNB*, 24 October 2019. https://doi-org.soton.idm.oclc.org/10.1093/ref:odnb/28285 [accessed 14/4/22]; MacLeod, *Painted Ladies*, 245.

Cecil. He was an MP for Derbyshire in 1661, 1679 and 1681 and by 1676 he was considered one of the leaders of the opposition.[163]

Charleton, lord – Sir Edward (of Heslyside), Bt. He was a gentleman usher of the queen's privy chamber, 1672–74.[164]

boatman –

Charleton, Mr Francis – Francis (John) Charleton/Chalton, was the queen's barge keeper/waterman from 1666 to 1706.[165]

Chase, Mr – for his bill. Possibly John Chase, the royal apothecary from 1660. In 1664–65, John was Master of the Society of Apothecaries.[166]

Chase, Mrs – possibly the wife of John Chase, royal apothecary.

Chaseman, Mrs – payments made to her.

Cheldon, Mr – payments to his keeper.

Cherrett [Madame Sheret/Shiret], **Mistress** – for hoods, ribbon. She was a milliner with premises at 'The French House' in Covent Garden.[167]

Cheseman, Mrs – for unspecified goods or services.

Chesterfield, 2nd earl of – Philip Stanhope, lord Stanhope, 2nd earl of Chesterfield (1634–1714), was the son of Henry and Katherine Stanhope. He became lord chamberlain to the queen on 24 February 1662, a post he held until 1665. He married three times: to Lady Anne Percy (1652–54), Elizabeth Butler (1660–65), and Lady Elizabeth Dormer (1658–77).[168]

Chesterfield, lady – Elizabeth Butler (1640–65), countess of Chesterfield. Born in Ireland, Elizabeth was the daughter of James, 1st duke of Ormond and Lady Elizabeth Preston and the second wife of Philip Stanhope, 1st earl of Chesterfield. She was a court beauty painted by Sir Peter Lely and gossip linked her with James, duke of York, and James Hamilton.[169] She was a lady of the queen's bedchamber from 1662–63 to 1665.[170]

Cheuillion – for combs and pins.

Chiffinch, mistress – There are four possible candidates. 1) Dorothy Thanet

[163] E. R. Edwards, 'Cavendish, William, Lord Cavendish (1641–1707), of Chatsworth, Derbys.', https://www.historyofparliamentonline.org/volume/1660-1690/member/cavendish-william-1641-1707 [accessed 2/2/22].

[164] Sainty, Wassmann and Bucholz, *Household officers*, 13.

[165] Sainty, Wassmann and Bucholz, *Household officers*, 13.

[166] Pepys, *Diary*, 10, 59.

[167] Pepys, *Diary*, 10, 60.

[168] Stuart Handley, 'Stanhope, Philip, second earl of Chesterfield (1633–1714), courtier and politician', *ODNB*, 23 September 2004, https://doi.org/10.1093/ref:odnb/26253 [accessed 15/4/22].

[169] She does not have an *ODNB* entry of her own but she does feature in the entry for her husband – see Stuart Handley, 'Stanhope, Philip, second earl of Chesterfield, (1633–1714), courtier and politician', *ODNB*, 23 September 2004, https://doi.org/10.1093/ref:odnb/26253 [accessed 15/4/22], MacLeod, *Painted Ladies*, 241.

[170] Sainty, Wassmann and Bucholz, *Household officers*, 13.

of Merioneth, wife of William Chiffinch.[171] At the Restoration she was appointed as the king's laundress and seamstress. 2) Barbara Nunn, wife of Thomas Chiffinch.[172] 3) Mary Chiffinch, laundress of the body, 1662–63 to 1665.[173] 4) Elizabeth Chiffinch, who was listed as a laundress in 1669.[174]

child –

Chiffinch [Chifins], **Thomas** – possibly of the Chiffinches of Staplehurst, Thomas (1600–66) was a page of the king's bedchamber and keeper of the king's privy closet.[175] Unlike his brother, he was very trustworthy and given charge of the king's private finances. He was also a groom of the privy chamber in the queen's household.[176] He was married to Dorothy Thanet (d.1680) and they had a son, Thomas. On his death, Thomas senior was buried in Westminster Abbey.[177]

Chiffinch, Mr – William (1602–91), younger brother of Thomas Chiffinch. In 1662, he was appointed as a page of the backstairs to the queen and around this time he married Barbara Nunn, who was a Catholic.[178] He was a page of the king's bedchamber and keeper of the king's privy closet from 1666 to 1685.[179] He controlled access to the king via the backstairs as noted in a contemporary satire:

It happen'd in the twilight of the day
As England's monarch in his closet lay,
And Chiffinch stepp'd to fetch the female pray.[180]

huntsman –

171 Ewan Fernie, 'Chiffinch, William, (1602–91), courtier and royal official', *ODNB*, 23 September 2004, https://doi.org/10.1093/ref:odnb/5281 [accessed 18/1/22].

172 Ewan Fernie, 'Chiffinch [Cheffin], Thomas, (1600–1666), courtier and royal official', *ODNB*, 23 September 2004, https://doi.org/10.1093/ref:odnb/5281 [accessed 18/1/22].

173 Sainty, Wassmann and Bucholz, *Household officers*, 13.

174 Sainty, Wassmann and Bucholz, *Household officers*, 13.

175 Ewan Fernie, 'Chiffinch [Cheffin], Thomas, (1600–1666), courtier and royal official', *ODNB*, 23 September 2004, https://doi.org/10.1093/ref:odnb/5281 [accessed 18/1/22].

176 Sainty, Wassmann and Bucholz, *Household officers*, 13.

177 https://www.westminster-abbey.org/abbey-commemorations/commemorations/thomas-chiffinch [15/1/23].

178 Leonard Naylor and Geoffrey Jagger, 'Chiffinch, William, (d.1691), of Whitehall and Philberts, Bray, Berks.', https://www.historyofparliamentonline.org/volume/1660-1690/member/chiffinch-william-1691 [accessed 15/1/23].

179 Ewan Fernie, 'Chiffinch, William, (1602–1691), courtier and royal official', *ODNB*, 23 September 2004, https://doi.org/10.1093/ref:odnb/5281 [accessed 18/1/22].

180 Ewan Fernie, 'Chiffinch, William, (1602–1691), courtier and royal official', *ODNB*, 23 September 2004, https://doi.org/10.1093/ref:odnb/5281 [accessed 18/1/22].

children – also see *christenings*. While Catherine did not have any children of her own, she took an interest in those of her friends, and household.

duke of York's –

Irish children –

poor children –

three children at a birth –

christenings – These were often held privately in the home rather than at church, as on 10 July 1663, when Samuel and Elizabeth went to 'Kate Joyces christening – where much company – good service of sweetmeats'.[181] When Pepys was asked to be a god-parent at a catholic christening he observed that 'being a Protestant, a man stood by and was my proxy to answer for me … The ceremonies many and some foolish. The priest in gentleman's dress, more then my own; but is a Capuchin, one of the Queen-mother's priests'.[182]

M:tris Chiffinchs Child in gold [1663] –

colonel damsys Cristning by Lady Fingall [1678] – it is uncertain who Colonel Damsys was.

Lady Fingals christening [1676]– probably a child of Margaret, countess of Finghall. She had six children, three sons and three daughters. The first two sons died young and their names were not recorded, and their third son, Peter was born in 1678.[183]

Lady Frances Kytlys Cristning [1676] – uncertain who Lady Frances was.

Lady Kenouls child [1674] – Lady Catherine, wife of William Hay, 4th earl of Kinnoull (d.1677) had two children, George (d.1687) and William (d.1709).[184]

Lord Tenham's child [1675] – Lord Teynham's first child was Anne Roper (d.1744).[185]

Teags Cristening [1677] – possibly the child of the same Teague listed as a footman of the duke of York in August 1666.

Clarendon, lady – Frances Aylesbury (d.1667), daughter of Sir Thomas Aylesbury, master of the royal mint and a master of requests. She became the second wife of Edward Hyde in 1634 and they had six children, including Anne (1638–71) who married James, duke of York.[186]

Also, David Allen, 'The political function of Charles II's Chiffinch', *Huntington Library Quarterly*, 39 (1976), pp. 277–90.

181 Pepys, *Diary*, 10, 62; Pepys, *Diary*, 5, 200.

182 Pepys, *Diary*, 7, 329.

183 Anne Creighton, 'Plunket, Luke', *Dictionary of Irish Biography*, https://www.dib.ie/biography/plunket-luke-a7370 [accessed 27/4/22].

184 James Balfour Paul, *The Scots Peerage* (1908), 228.

185 http://www.thepeerage.com/p531.htm#i5302 [accessed 2/4/22].

186 Paul Seaward, 'Hyde, Edward, first earl of Clarendon (1609–1674), politician and

Clarendon, lady – Flower Backhouse (d.1700), daughter of William Backhouse and Anne Richards.[187] She was the second wife of Henry Hyde, 2nd earl of Clarendon and he was her third husband, her second having been her cousin Sir William Backhouse. She was a Lady of the bedchamber 1680–1700. She was first lady of the bedchamber to Queen Anne.

man –

page –

Clarendon, lord – Edward Hyde (1609–74), 1st earl of Clarendon, was the son of Henry and Mary Hyde.[188] A lawyer by training, he took part in the Short and Long and Parliaments, fought for the king in the Civil war and went into exile, first in Jersey, and then in the Hague and Paris. He played an important role in the Restoration and promoted the Portuguese marriage. Hyde fell from power in 1667 and went into exile in France where he worked on his *Life* and *History*. He died at Rouen in 1674. He was buried in Westminster Abbey.[189]

Clarendon, lord – Henry Hyde (1638–1709), 2nd earl of Clarendon, eldest son of Edward Hyde, 1st earl of Clarendon and Frances Aylesbury, and brother of Anne Hyde, duchess of York. He married twice: first to Theodosia Capell (d.1661), daughter of Arthur Capell, 1st baron Capell of Hadham and Elizabeth Morrison in 1660, and he married again in 1670 to Flower Backhouse (d.1700), daughter of William Backhouse and Anne Richards.[190] From 1661 to 1674 he used the title lord Cornbury. In 1662, he became Catherine of Braganza's private secretary and then in 1665 became her lord Chamberlain. In 1680, he was made keeper of Denmark House and treasurer and receiver-general of the queen's revenue. In 1688, he was in dispute with Catherine over money from when he had been part of her household resulting in a lengthy legal case. He became involved with the Jacobite cause.[191]

---

historian', *ODNB*, 4 October 2008, https://doi.org/10.1093/ref:odnb/14328 [accessed 19/4/22].

187 She does not have an ODNB entry; see W. A. Speck, 'Hyde, Henry, second earl of Clarendon, (1638–1709), politician', *ODNB*, 5 January 2012, https://doi.org/10.1093/ref:odnb/14329 [accessed 19/4/22].

188 Paul Seaward, 'Hyde, Edward, first earl of Clarendon, (1609–1674), politician and historian', *ODNB*, 4 October 2008, https://doi.org/10.1093/ref:odnb/14328 [accessed 19/4/22].

189 https://www.westminster-abbey.org/abbey-commemorations/commemorations/edward-hyde-family [accessed 15/1/23].

190 She does not have an ODNB entry; see W. A. Speck, 'Hyde, Henry, second earl of Clarendon, (1638–1709), politician', *ODNB*, 5 January 2012, https://doi.org/10.1093/ref:odnb/14329 [accessed 19/4/22].

191 W. A. Speck, 'Hyde, Henry, second earl of Clarendon, (1638–1709), politician', *ODNB*, 5 January 2012, https://doi.org/10.1093/ref:odnb/14329 [accessed 19/4/22].

groom –

man –

page –

Clark, Mr – Matthew Clark, the queen's coachman in 1666, and chief coachman 1682–84.[192]

Clark, William – the king's coachman.

Clarke [Clerke] **Mr** – possibly James Clarke, page of the backstairs, 1682.[193] Although this Mr Clarke was listed as page in the queen's accounts in 1668.

Cleyton [Cleton], **Mr** – giving money to the poor.

Cleveland, duchess, *see Castlemaine*

Clinton [Clenton], **Lady** – Lady Elizabeth Clinton, was the second wife of Theophilus Clinton, 4th earl of Lincoln (1599–1667). She was one of the queen's dressers and a woman of queen's bedchamber from 1666 to 1678.[194] She appears to have retained the title of Lady Lincoln until Edward Clinton, 5th earl of Lincoln (1645–92), who was the son of Edward Clinton, Lord Clinton, and Lady Anne Holles, married Jeanne de Guliere in 1674. At that point she was referred to as Lady Clinton.

clocks – a mechanical instrument to measure the time. The faces and cases could be very decorative. For instance, in spring 1683 William Chiffinch paid Samuel Watson £215 for a clock bought by the king 'wch showes the rising and setting of the sun and moon, and many other motions'.[195] Other clocks had more specific functions. Catherine kept a clock in her bedchamber designed to help her observe the various time for prayer during the night: 'And her holy water at her head as she sleeps with a clock by her bed-side wherein a lamp burns that tells her the time of night at any time'.[196]

clothing, *also see accessories, fastenings* – Pepys was a keen observer of women's clothing and in October 1666 he noted that 'the ladies are to go into a new fashion shortly; and that is to wear short coats above their ankles'.[197] While most of Catherine's clothing was paid for by the wardrobe of the robes, a few items do feature in her privy purse accounts.[198]

192 Sainty, Wassmann and Bucholz, *Household officers*, 14.

193 Sainty, Wassmann and Bucholz, *Household officers*, 14.

194 Sainty, Wassmann and Bucholz, *Household officers*, 15.

195 Akerman, *Secret Services*, 66.

196 Pepys, *Diary*, 5, 188.

197 Pepys, *Diary*, 7, 325.

198 Sarah A Bendall, 'The queen's dressmakers: women's work and the clothing trades in late seventeenth century London', *Women's History Review*, 32.3, 2023, 389–414.

French embroidered mantua [manto] – According to Randle Holme the mantua was 'a kind of loose Garment without and stiffe Bodies under them, and was a great fashion for Women about the year 1676. Some call them Mantua's, they have very short Sleeves, nay some of the Gallants of the times have the Sleeves gathered up to the top of the Shoulders and there stayed or fastened with a Button and Loope, or set with a rich Jewel'.[199] The mantua was a loose, informal garment, tied at the waist, with pleating at the back and the fronts pulled back to reveal the wearer's petticoat.[200]

gown [goun] – a loose, flat-cut gown or Indian gown, also known as a Japanese gown, similar in shape to a kimono, made with silk padding often referred to as wad.[201] These informal gowns may be what Pepys was describing on 17 August 1667 when he happened 'to see her [Elizabeth Knepp, an actress] come out in her nighte-gowne with no lockes on, but her bare face and hair only tied up in a knot behind'.[202]

incognito – dressing down to avoid being recognised, which Catherine tried with varying degrees of success. For instance, in 1670 when queen, the duchess of Richmond and the duchess of Buckingham were at Audley End, they decided that 'it was a frolick to disguise themselves like country lasses, in red petticoats, wastcoats etc and so goe to see the faire' but 'they had all so overdone it in their disguise, and look'd so much like Antiques than country folk'.[203]

masquerade clothes [Maskarad Cloaths] – costumes made for court masquerades. The most sumptuous were made for the performance of *The Masque of Callisto* by John Crowne in 1675, so two years after these were supplied. Charles and Catherine's nieces, the princesses Mary and Anne, took part in the performance.[204]

mourning – mourning dress in the late seventeenth-century encompassed specific clothing and accessories worn as an expression of sorrow

199 Randle Holme, *An Accademie of Armorie; Or A Store House of Armory and Blazon*, vol. 2 (Chester: 1688), 19.

200 Willett Cunnington and Cunnington, *Handbook*, 176; Aileen Ribeiro, *Fashion and Fiction: Dress in Art and Literature in Stuart England* (London and New Haven: Yale University Press, 2005), 246–48.

201 Wardle, *For Our Royal Person*, 63.

202 Pepys, *Diary*, 8, 388–89.

203 John Heneage Jesse, *Memoirs of the Court of England During the Reigns of the Stuarts including the Protectorate of Oliver Cromwell*, vol. 3 (Boston, MA: L. C. Page, 1901), 341.

204 Andrew Walkling, 'Masque and politics at the Restoration Court: John Crowne's "Callisto"', *Early Music* 24.1 (1996), 27–62.

for a deceased family member, friend or member of royalty.[205] On 8 December, Pepys saw the duchess of York 'in a fine dress of second mourning for her mother, being black, edged with Ermin'.[206] After the first phase of black mourning, people adopted grey clothing and then mauve for the second and third periods of mourning. On 12 May 1667, Pepys agreed to give Elizabeth the money 'to lace her gown for second mourning' for his mother.[207]

petticoat – slightly shorter than the skirt of the gown, the petticoat was often highly decorative and could have a short train.[208] This sense of variety is evident in the *Mundus Muliebris* (1690) which recommended:

Short under Petticoats pure fine
Some of Japan Stuff, some of Chine,
With knee-high Galoon bottomed,
Another quilted white and red;
With a broad Flanders lace below.[209]

On 13 July 1663, when Pepys saw Catherine with the king, she wore 'a white laced waistcoat and a crimson short petty-coate and her hair dressed a la negligence, mighty pretty'.[210]

sleeves – sleeves on gowns were elbow length or longer, often with a turned back cuff up to *c*. 1680 and then short and straight, while those on the smock or chemise were often frilled and ruffled.[211] With evident pleasure, Pepys saw Nell Gwyn on 1 May 1667 'in her smock-sleeves and bodice'.[212]

Clyton, Mr – gave money to the poor.

Colby, Mr – possibly Hobart Colby, groom of the queen's great chamber, 1668–78.[213]

Collins [Colin, Coolins], **Mr** – possibly Henry Collins, groom of the queen's great chamber, 1672–77.[214]

man –

205 Lou Taylor, *Mourning: A Costume and Social History* (Abingdon: Routledge, reprint, 2010), 92–105.

206 Pepys, *Diary*, 8, 570.

207 Pepys, *Diary*, 8, 210.

208 Willett Cunnington and Cunnington, *Handbook*, 175.

209 Evelyn, *Mundus Muliebris*, 2–3; https://quod.lib.umich.edu/e/eebo/A38815.0001.001/1:3?rgn=div1;submit=Go;subview=detail;type=simple;view=fulltext;q1=petticoats [accessed 1/5/22].

210 Pepys, *Diary*, 4, 229–30.

211 Willett Cunnington and Cunnington, *Handbook*, 172, 175.

212 Pepys, *Diary*, 8, 193.

213 Sainty, Wassmann and Bucholz, *Household officers*, 15.

214 Sainty, Wassmann and Bucholz, *Household officers*, 16.

Conyers, Mr – for a bill.

Cooper, lord – Anthony Ashley (1621–83), son of Sir John Cooper and Anne Ashley. Of Puritan beliefs, he married Lord Coventry's daughter in 1639. Initially Anthony fought for the king but in 1644 he changed sides. During the 1650s he was a member of Cromwell's council of state and rejected two appeals from Charles II, but he was part of the parliamentary group that invited the king to return in 1660. On the fall of Clarendon, Ashley became a member of the Cabal and in 1672 he was created 1st earl of Shaftesbury. He was also Chancellor of the Exchequer and Treasurer of the Commission for Prizes and Treasury Commissioner.[215] He was a leading member of the opposition to James, duke of York.

Coq, mistress le – her bill.

Coqus [Cooqus], **Mr** – for his bill. Probably Jean-Gérard Cockus, alias John Cooqus who was entered by the Lord Chamberlain in 1661 as 'Silversmith in Ordinary to His Matie for chastwork within His Maties Closett and Bedchamber, and also the Closett and Bedchamber of the Queen' in van Vianen's place.[216] He is perhaps best known for the bill he submitted for the silverwork on a bed made for Nell Gwyn in 1674.[217]

Corbetta [Corbett], **Francisco** – groom of the queen's privy chamber. He was appointed in 1662/63 and relinquished the office in 1665, appearing again in the listing in 1668 and listed as supernumerary in 1674.[218] He was an Italian guitarist and composer.[219]

corn cutter [Cornecater] – paid by Mrs Nun. An estimate of the annual expenses of the Great Wardrobe included £20 for the livery of two corn cutters' coats embroidered with bullion, along with 'the rat killer a coat of the same about £9'.[220]

cutting the parrot's bill –

Cornbury, lord – see *lord Clarendon, Henry Hyde.*

Cornwallis, lady – Margaret Playsted (d.1668), daughter of Sir Thomas Playsted of Arlington, East Sussex. She married Charles Cornwallis,

215 Tim Harris, 'Cooper, Anthony Ashley, first earl of Shaftesbury (1621–1683), politician', *ODNB*, 3 January 2008, https://doi.org/10.1093/ref:odnb/6208 [accessed 14/2/22].

216 Charles Oman, *Caroline Silver 1625–1688* (London: Faber & Faber, 1970), 26–27.

217 Oman, *Caroline Silver*, 32. For the transcript of the bill, see Peter Cunningham, *The Story of Nell Gwyn and the Sayings of Charles II* (London: Hutchinson & Co, Paternoster Row, 1892), 226–28.

218 Sainty, Wassmann and Bucholz, *Household officers*, 17.

219 Ashbee, *Records*, 146.

220 Folger MS X.d.76.

2nd baron Cornwallis of Eye (1632–73), son of Sir Frederick Cornwallis, 1st baron Cornwallis and Elizabeth Ashburnham in 1651. He was elected as an MP in 1660 and 1661, and he was created a knight of the Bath in the same year.[221] Margaret was listed as a lady of the queen's privy chamber in extraordinary in 1669.[222]

cook –

footman –

man –

servant –

Cotter, Mr – James Cotter, gentleman usher, daily waiter to the queen from 1674 to 1677.[223]

craftsmen/craftswomen, the queen's – Catherine had her own set of makers or artificers and suppliers. As such it was a parallel set to those of the king but with some overlap of personnel.

cabinet maker – someone who made cabinets, whose work was comparable to a joiners, with a high level of decorative work.

carpenter – a worker in wood who undertook more robust work such as structural woodwork in houses.

coach maker – maker of open and closed carriages, often with highly decorative interiors and exteriors.

furrier – someone who traded in and/or dressed furs and skins. An alternative term for a skinner and the associated Skinners' livery company.

joiner – a wood-worker who joined and pieced wood. Their work was often more skilled and decorative than that of carpenters.

locksmith – a person who made, repaired or fitted locks.

milliner, Italian – in the seventeenth century milliners made and supplied hats and other headwear but they also sold a range of trimmings and fancy goods. Italian, French and English milliners were working in London at this time and goods were also imported.

shoemaker – shoemakers made bespoke footwear for the queen. By 1665, Thomas Jervas was the queen' shoemaker and from 10 December 1666 the post was held by Thorpe Groome.[224] By 1671, the shoemaker received £26 10s a year or a daily fee of 2s. He also received a New Year's gift of £10 a year.

smith – a blacksmith who would supply a range of metal work for use in the queen's apartments.

221 M. W. Helms, 'Cornwallis, Charles (1632–73), of Brome Hall, Suffolk', https://www.historyofparliamentonline.org/volume/1660-1690/member/cornwallis-charles-ii-1632-73 [accessed 1/5/22].

222 Sainty, Wassmann and Bucholz, *Household officers*, 17.

223 Sainty, Wassmann and Bucholz, *Household officers*, 17.

224 Sainty, Wassmann and Bucholz, *Household officers*, 42, 33.

tailor – male tailors made gowns and petticoats for female clients. For instance, on 8 August 1667, Pepys accompanied 'my wife to the Temple, where I light and sent her to her tailor's'.[225]

tailor, La Roche – the queen's tailor.[226]

upholsterer [AppHolster] – a person who made or repaired furnishings covered with or including textiles and padding. While outside the scope of these accounts, P. Olivan was listed as the queen's upholster by 1692.[227]

watchmakers – made, sold and repaired watches, which were popular accessories for men and women.

Crake, Frank – the king's footman.

Crake [Creek], **Thomas** – the queen's footman, and yeoman footman, 1667–87.[228]

Cranborne [Cranburn]**, lady** – Lady Margaret Manners (*c.*1645–82), daughter of John Manners, 8th earl of Rutland, and Frances Montague. In 1665, she married James Cecil, Viscount Cranborne and later 3rd earl of Salisbury (d.1683). She looked after the family home of Hatfield and had ten children.[229]

man –

Crane, Mrs – Mary was a woman of the queen's bedchamber and a dresser, from February 1674 to 1692.[230]

Cranmer, mistress – Lelis Wood Cranmer was a woman of the queen's bedchamber and a dresser. She was appointed in 1671, and last received a salary in 1706, the year after Catherine's death in 1705.[231]

for embroidery –

Craven [Creuens], **lord** – William Craven, 1st earl of Craven (1608–97), son of William Craven and Elizabeth Whitmore, was a soldier. He loved Elizabeth of Bohemia (Charles II's aunt) and he never married. At the Restoration, Charles II made him earl of Craven; he was a member of the privy council and he was given a share in North Carolina.[232] When

225 Pepys, *Diary*, 8, 377.

226 Bucholz, Sainty and Wassmann, *Household of Queen*, 31.

227 Bucholz, Sainty and Wassmann, *Household of Queen*, 31.

228 Sainty, Wassmann and Bucholz, *Household officers*, 18.

229 She does not have an ODNB entry but is mentioned briefly in Victor Stater, 'Cecil, James, third earl of Salisbury, (d.1683), politician', *ODNB*, 23 September 2004, https://doi-org/10.1093/ref:odnb/4976 [accessed 17/12/21].

230 Sainty, Wassmann and Bucholz, *Household officers*, 18.

231 Sainty, Wassmann and Bucholz, *Household officers*, 18.

232 Malcolm Smuts, 'Craven, William, earl of Craven (bap.1608–d.1697), army officer and royal servant', *ODNB*, 24 May 2007, https://doi.org/10.1093/ref:odnb/6636 [accessed 17/12/21].

Pepys went to see *The Witts* on 17 August 1661, he noted 'the Queen of Bohemia was here, brought by my Lord Craven'.[233]

gardener –

crier – an urban official, who shouted out news.

crosses – given to Catherine on various saints' days including St Patrick's Day and St Andrew's Day. They may have been similar to the crosses made to mark St Brigid's Day on 1 February, which coincides with Candlemas.

Croft [Craft], **lord**, Sir Herbert Croft (*c*.1651–1720), son of Herbert Croft, bishop of Hereford and Anne Browne. He was made a baronet in 1671 and he was elected MP for Herefordshire in 1679, 1690 and 1695.[234]

page –

Croupe, lady – possibly Elizabeth Crump, a lady of the privy chamber extraordinary in 1668.[235]

Damsys, Colonel – for the christening of his child.

dancing – dancing was a popular social skill and entertainment. Pepys recorded dancing for the first time in his diary on 27 March 1661 adding 'which I did wonder to see myself do'.[236] On 31 December 1662, Pepys attended a ball at Whitehall noting that 'the manner, was when the King dances, all the ladies in the room, and the Queen herself, stands up'.[237] The king's French dancing master, Antoni Robert, taught 'the King, and all the King's children, and the Queen-Mother herself'.[238]

morris dancing –

a groom that danced –

dancing dog –

Darbe – a payment of £2. Uncertain meaning. Possibly 1) a reference to Derby Toby who was supplied with a cloth suit, cloak and justacort that was paid for by the king's wardrobe of the Robes, 1660–62.[239] Or less likely, 2) an incomplete reference to Charles Stanley, 8th earl of Derby (1628–72), who was the son of James Stanley, 7th earl of Derby and Charlotte de La Trémouille.[240]

233 Pepys, *Diary*, 2, 156.

234 He does not have an *ODNB* entry but is mentioned briefly in William Marshall, 'Croft, Herbert (1603–1691), bishop of Hereford', *ODNB*, 3 January 2008, https://doi-org/10.1093/ref:odnb/6717 [accessed 7/1/22].

235 Sainty, Wassmann and Bucholz, *Household officers*, 19.

236 Pepys, *Diary*, 2, 61.

237 Pepys, *Diary*, 3, 301.

238 Pepys, *Diary*, 9, 507.

239 TNA AO3/910/6, p. 54.

240 Barry Coward, Stanley, 'James, seventh earl of Derby (1607–1651), royalist army officer', *ODNB*, 3 January 2008, https://doi-org/10.1093/ref:odnb/26274 [accessed 26/4/22].

Davis [dauis], **Mr** – wardrobe keeper.

Davis, Mrs – at Barn Elms. Possibly Mary (Moll) Davis (*c*.1651–1708), who may have been the illegitimate daughter of Thomas Howard, 4th earl of Berkshire. She was an actress in the Duke's Company from 1660. She retired from the stage in 1668, the year that she became the king's mistress. However, she performed in the court productions of *Calisto* (1673) and *Venus and Adonis* (1681/2). She had one daughter with the king, Lady Mary Tudor. In 1686, she married James Paisible, a court musician. They lived in France during the Glorious Revolution but returned to England in 1698.[241]

Dawson, Mr – gifts to the porters at Whitehall.

Day, captain – for his bill.

Deane, Richard – a trumpeter.[242]

Delamer, lord – George Booth, 1st baron Delamer (1622–84), second son of William Booth and Vere, daughter of Sit Thomas Egerton. He married twice: first to Lady Catherine Clinton, daughter of Theophilus Clinton, 4th earl of Lincoln, and second, to Lady Elizabeth Grey, daughter of Henry Grey, 1st earl of Stamford.[243]

man –

Depuy, Monsieur – for sweetmeats.

Devet, Mrs – as per bill.

Devonshire [Deuonsheres]**, lady** – Lady Elizabeth Cecil (1620–89), second daughter of William Cecil, second earl of Salisbury and wife of William Cavendish, 3rd earl of Devonshire (1617–84). They were married in 1639.[244]

cook –

footmen –

maid –

man –

Dickenson [Dickison], **Mrs** – for a bill.

Digby, Sir Kenelm – Sir Kenelm (1603–65) was the son of Sir Everard Digby and Mary Mulsho. He married Venetia Stanley in 1625 who died in 1633.

241 Wilson, *Court Satire*, p. 241. Olive Baldwin and Thelma Wilson, 'Davis [Davies; *married name* Paisible], Mary [Moll] (c.1651–1708), actress and royal mistress', *ODNB*, 3 January 2008, https://doi.org/10.1093/ref:odnb/7291 [accessed 19/4/22].

242 Ashbee, *Records*, 22, 44, 45, 53, 95, 216, 223, 230, 233.

243 Sean Kelsey, 'Booth, George, first Baron Delamer [Delamere] (1622–1684), politician', *ODNB*, 5 January 2006, https://doi.org/10.1093/ref:odnb/2877 [accessed 19/4/22].

244 She does not have an *ODNB* entry but is mentioned briefly in Victor Stater, 'Cavendish, William, third earl of Devonshire (1617–1684)', *ODNB*, 25 May 2006, https://doi-org/10.1093/ref:odnb/4947 [accessed 15/2/22].

In 1644, he went into exile and became Henrietta Maria's chancellor.[245] After the Restoration he returned home and was an early member of the Royal Society.

Dodson, Mrs – given money by Sir Richard Belling.

Donoline – carried to Hampton Court. Possibly a reference to James Donnellan, gentleman usher daily waiter in extraordinary who was listed in the queen's accounts in 1666.[246]

Doule, Mary – herbwoman.

Down, lord – for a gift.

man –

drops – uncertain meaning in this context. Possibly an earring or ear-drop, a pendant of metal or precious stone or a lozenge or sugar-plum that is spherical in shape.[247]

Ducaila, Monsieur – for his bill.

Duett, Deuett, Mrs – for her bill.

Dunfermline [Dunfarlin], **lord** – Charles Seton (1615–72), 2nd earl of Dunfermline, son of Alexander Seton, 1st earl of Dunfermline and Margaret Hay. He married Mary Douglas, daughter of William Douglas, 7th earl of Morton and Anne Keith. He went into exile in 1649, returning at the Restoration and then was keeper of the privy seal of Scotland from 1661 to 1672.[248]

Dutchmen – a reference to people from the Netherlands, and there was a Dutch community in Restoration London with their own church. On 26 November 1663 Pepys met Mr Cutler, a merchant, at his home 'by the Dutch church' which was close to Austin Friars passage.[249]

Dysart, lady – see *Lauderdale, duchess of* – the title, earl of Dysart, was created for William Murray (?1600–55) in 1643. On his death, the title passed to his daughter, Elizabeth, who was known as the 2nd countess of Dysart.[250]

man –

245 Michael Foster, 'Digby, Sir Kenelm (1603–1665), natural philosopher and courtier', *ODNB*, 8 January 2009, https://doi-org/10.1093/ref:odnb/7629 [accessed 1/5/22].

246 Sainty, Wassmann and Bucholz, *Household officers*.

247 https://www.oed.com/view/Entry/57881?rskey=YNLxXK&result=1#eid [accessed 22/3/22].

248 T. F. Henderson, revised Edward M. Furgol, 'Seton, Charles, second earl of Dunfermline (1615–1672), politician and army officer', *ODNB*, 23 September 2004, https://doi.org/10.1093/ref:odnb/25117 [accessed 19/4/22].

249 Pepys, *Diary*, 4, 398.

250 Rosalind Marshall, 'Murray [*married names* Tollemache, Maitland], Elizabeth, duchess of Lauderdale, and *suo jure* countess of Dysart (bap.1626–1698), noblewoman', *ODNB*, 23 September 2004, https://doi.org/10.1093/ref:odnb/19601 [accessed 16/1/22].

Eaton, Charles – the queen's yeoman footman, 1667–74.[251]
Eaton, Mr – for rich point. John Eaton, lace seller and Charles II's laceman.[252]
Eaton, Mrs – probably the wife of John Eaton.
Ellis, Mr – door keeper.
Elliott [Eliot], **mistress** – Elizabeth Elliott, seamstress to the queen, from 1662–63 to 1678.[253]
envoy – a representative of a country sent on a diplomatic mission or embassy. On 27 August 1667, the Russian envoy was received in the queen's presence chamber, gave an effusive speech 'with much compliment & froth of Language, then they kissed their Majesties hands & went as they came'.[254]
page –
Spanish envoy, his man [1677] –
errands [earands] – a short journey to deliver a message, written or verbal.
Ernle [Earnle], **Mr** – William, yeoman of the queen's wine cellar, 1671–78, yeoman of the buttery and cellar, 1685–90 and gentleman of the buttery and cellar, 1687.[255]
Esharr [Eshar], **Mr** – John Esharr, yeoman footman of the queen, from 1674 to 1682.[256]
Evans, Charles Mr – listed as harper in ordinary to the king in January 1661.[257]
Eyvis, lady – for lodgings.

Falmouth, lady – Mary Bagot (1645–79), daughter of Colonel Hervey Bagot. She married Charles Berkeley (1630–65), 1st earl of Falmouth, son of Charles Berkeley and Penelope Godolphin, in 1664. He was in exile with the Stuarts and in 1652 joined the service of the duke of York. In 1662, he became keeper of the king's privy purse and was a favourite of Charles II. He was killed at the battle of Lowestoft in 1665, part of the Second Anglo-Dutch war.[258] After his death, Elizabeth went on to become one of Charles II's mistresses and she was painted by Lely

251 Sainty, Wassmann and Bucholz, *Household officers*, 24.
252 Patricia Wardle, *For Our Royal Person: Master of the Robes Bills of King-Stadholder William III* (Apeldoorn: Paleis Het Loo National Museum, 2002), 65.
253 Sainty, Wassmann and Bucholz, *Household officers*, 24.
254 Evelyn, *Diary*, 515.
255 Sainty, Wassmann and Bucholz, *Household officers*, 25.
256 Sainty, Wassmann and Bucholz, *Household officers*, 25.
257 TNA LC5/137, p. 64. Ashbee, *Records*, 10.
258 Ronald Hutton, 'Berkeley, Charles, earl of Falmouth (bap.1630–d.1665), courtier', *ODNB*, 3 January 2008, https://doi-org/10.1093/ref:odnb/37185 [accessed 27/4/22].

as one of the Windsor Beauties. In 1674, she married a second time to Charles Sackville, 6th earl of Dorset (1643–1706).[259]

footmen –

farmer, a – that Catherine stopped with while travelling.

fastenings – *also see clothing*

buttons, cornelian [carnelian] – cornelian, a form of chalcedony, is a semi-precious, red to orange translucent stone, associated with fertility and conception, and thought to calm the blood. Carnelian was very popular in England, Portugal and the Netherlands for making beads.[260]

Fathers, the – the queen's priests

to a footman sent bake for the fathers –

to yor Maties Berge to dartford with the fathers –

Ferand, Mrs – by her bill.

Feubre, Monsieur le – for the duke's trumpets.

Fever, Monsieur le – as per bill.

Feversham [Feuersham]**, lord** – Louis de Duras (1641–1707), 2nd earl of Feversham, son of Guy Aldonce, marquis of Duras and Count of Rozan, and Elizabeth de la Tour d'Auvergne. He was a Huguenot who came to England in the early 1660s in the service of the duke of York. In 1679, he became Master of the Horse to Catherine of Braganza and her Lord Chamberlain in 1680. He remained in her service until her death. He was present at Charles II's death and became a member of James II's privy council. In 1698, with Catherine's intervention, he was appointed master of the Royal Hospital of St Katherine.[261]

coachman –

groom –

man –

filleting [filliting] – *see under hair*

Finghall [Fingal], **lady** – Margaret, countess of Fingall, was the daughter of Donough MacCarthy, 1st earl of Clancarty and Eleanor Butler. She married Luke Plunket (1639–84), 3rd earl of Fingall and 12th baron Killeen, shortly before 1666. In 1661, he had signed the Catholic Remonstrance, which he presented to James Butler, 1st duke of Ormond, who gave it

[259] Harold Love, 'Sackville, Charles, sixth earl of Dorset and first earl of Middlesex (1643–1706), poet and politician', ODNB, 3 January 2008, [accessed 12/4/22].

[260] Hazel Forsyth, *The Cheapside Hoard: London's Lost Jewels* (London: Museum of London, 2013), 130.

[261] Stuart Handley, 'Duras, Louis, second earl of Feversham (1641–1709), soldier and diplomat', *ODNB*, 26 May 2016, https://doi.org/10.1093/ref:odnb/8309 [accessed 12/4/22].

to Charles II.[262] She was a lady of the queen's bedchamber 1673 to 1676 and she was listed as a pensioner 1687–1704.[263]

Fire [fiere] – the Great Fire of London began on 2 September 1666 in a bakery on Pudding Lane and continued to burn until 5 September. While the biggest fire in London, it was not the only fire of Charles II's reign. On March 1682 Thomas Silver, gunner, received £20 as a reward 'for himself and other gunners in blowing up several buildings and suppressing the late fire at St James's'.[264]

fish – fish was popular on fish days and more generally. A wide range of fish and shellfish featured in Pepys' *Diary* when he went out for dinner, including anchovies, cod, crab, crayfish, ells, herrings, mackerel, prawns, scallops and tench. Pepys also bought fish and sent it to a tavern to be cooked.[265] For the earl of Bedford, most of the fish he served were perch and pike from the ponds at Woburn.[266]

carp – the Common carp (*Cyprinus carpio*), a large freshwater fish with a round body was introduced into England in the Middle Ages. On 4 April 1663, Pepys had 'three carps in a dish' as part of his dinner.[267] When Evelyn visited Bagshot in October 1685, he 'had Carps & Pike &c of size fit for the table of a Prince … and what added to the delight, the seeing hundreds taken in the drag, out of which the Cooke standing by, we pointed what we had most mind to'.[268] Gervase Markham recommended that 'after you have drawn, washed and scalded a fair large carp, season it with pepper, salt and nutmeg, and then put it in a coffin [pastry case] with a good store of sweet butter and then cast on raisins…, the juice of lemons and some slices of orange peals'.[269]

eel – there are about 800 species of fresh- and salt-water eels (*Anguilliformes*). They are ray-fined fish with long, thin bodies with a single fin and skin without scales, which begin as larvae, maturing into grass ells, elvers, yellow and then silver eels. In 1689, the earl of Bedford paid 17s for 'a stand of all sort of pickle and collared eels'.[270]

great fish, a – This was probably a sturgeon, see below.

262 Anne Creighton, 'Plunket, Luke', *Dictionary of Irish Biography*, https://www.dib.ie/biography/plunket-luke-a7370 [accessed 23/3/22].

263 Sainty, Wassmann and Bucholz, *Household officers*, 27.

264 Akerman, *Secret Services*, 50.

265 Pepys, *Diary*, 6, 240; 9, 496.

266 Scott Thomson, *Life in a Noble Household*, 141.

267 Pepys, *Diary*, 4, 95.

268 Evelyn, *Diary*, 830.

269 Markham, *Well-Kept Kitchen*, 46–47.

270 Scott Thomson, *Life in a Noble Household*, 218.

lamprey pies – the lamprey (*Petromyzontiformes*) is a long thin fish that has a sucking mouth with teeth rather than jaws. Lampreys were eaten during Lent, and they were a delicacy in Portugal. Indeed, Romoli noted in his cookbook that the Portuguese often roasted lampreys on a spit.[271] However, on 4 April 1663 Pepys had a lamprey pie which he described as 'a most rare pie'.[272]

mullet [mulets] – these are likely to have been grey mullet (*muglidae*) although three species are found in British waters: the thick lipped, thin lipped and golden grey mullet.[273] Grey mullet also live along the Atlantic coasts of France, Portugal and Spain, so these fish might have reminded Catherine of home. On 23 July 1663, Pepys dined with Sir William Batten on a 'soused mullett', which he described as 'very good meat'.[274]

oysters [osters] – true oysters (*Ostreidae*) or edible oysters are a bivalve mollusc with well-known British examples coming from Whitstable and Colchester. Even so, oysters were quite rare – the earl of Bedford bought barrels occasionally when at home and, in October 1689, while staying in Cambridge, he ate 'a dish of stewed oysters' costing 6s and 'a stand of pickles with oysters, anchovies, and tongue' for 4s.[275]

salmon [sallmon] – salmon or Atlantic salmon (*Salmo salar*), a large fish that is spawned in freshwater, lives in the sea as an adult and returns to freshwater to spawn. On 20 April 1667, Pepys recorded 'having brought home...a hundred of sparrowgrass, cost 18d, we had them and a little bit of salmon which my wife had a mind to, cost 3s'.[276]

sturgeon [sturgon] – the European sea sturgeon or Common sturgeon (*Acipenser sturio*) is a very large fish, valued for its flesh and its caviar. They were found in large rivers and coastal waters. When Pepys saw a sturgeon that had been caught in the Thames in May 1667, he noted it 'was but a little one'.[277] On 15 October 1689, the earl of Bedford dined at the Red Lion in Cambridge and one of the dishes presented was 'a large jowl of sturgeon with a rand about it' costing £1 15s.[278] Gervase Markham suggested roasting a piece of sturgeon stuck

[271] Romoli, *La singolare dottrina*, ff. 162v, cited in Ken Albala, *The Banquet: Dining in the Great Courts of Late Renaissance Europe* (Urbana and Chicago, IL: University of Illinois Press, 2007), 134.

[272] Pepys, *Diary*, 4, 95.

[273] https://britishseafishing.co.uk/mullet-species [accessed 23/12/21].

[274] Pepys, *Diary*, 4, 242.

[275] Scott Thomson, *Life in a Noble Household*, 219–20.

[276] Pepys, *Diary*, 8, 173.

[277] Pepys, *Diary*, 8, 232–33.

[278] Scott Thomson, *Life in a Noble Household*, 218.

with cloves and then serving it with a venison sauce.[279] Domenico Romoli of Florence offered a Portuguese recipe for sturgeon: after frying the fish in butter, it was to be eaten with a sauce made with wine, fried onions, herbs and spices and coloured with saffron.[280]

trout – the brown trout (*Salmo trutta*) is the only native British trout species.[281] When Evelyn visited Cassiobury Park in 1680 he noted 'a very swift & cleare stream … it being excessive Cold, yet producing faire Troutes'.[282] This fits with Izaak Walton's observation that 'The Trout is a fish highly valued, both in this and foreign nations … he is a fish that feeds clean and purely, in the swiftest streams, and on the hardest gravel; and that he may justly contend with all fresh water fish, as the Mullet may with all sea fish, for precedency and daintiness of taste'.[283] Brown trout were also available and popular in Portugal. Gervase Markham recommended cooking trout stuffed with mace, parsley, savoury, thyme, butter and wine, and after cooking to serve the fish sprinkled with diced hard-boiled egg, herbs and grated sugar.[284]

Fisher, Mr – for the trumpeters.

Fisher, Robert – the duke of York's footman.

fishing – fishing was a popular seventeenth century activity and the subject of several books, including John Dennys, *The Secrets of Angling* (1613), Izaak Walton, *The Complete Angler* (1653) and Robert Venables, *The Complete Angler* (1683).[285] Pepys described winter fishing through the ice in December 1663.[286] Charles very keen on fishing and in 1680 Sir John Reresby visited the king at Windsor where 'he passed his day in fishing or walking in the parke'.[287] Lord Rochester more rudely noted:

Fine representative indeed of God,
Whose sceptres' dwindled to a fishing-rod!
….

[279] Markham, *Well-Kept Kitchen*, 38–39.

[280] Romoli, *La singolare dottrina*, ff. 163r–v, cited in Albala, *The Banquet*, 134.

[281] https://www.wildtrout.org/content/brown-trout [accessed 21/1/23].

[282] Evelyn, *Diary*, 682.

[283] Izaak Walton, *The Complete Angler* (London: printed by T. Maxey for Richard Marriot, 1653), chapter 4.

[284] Markham, *Well-Kept Kitchen*, 47.

[285] Francis Manley, 'An early seventeenth-century manuscript art of angling', *The Yale University Library Gazette* 35.1 (1960), 1–10; Ralph Lytton Bower, 'An early seventeenth century angler', *The Sewanee Review* 10.2 (1902), 199–206.

[286] Pepys, *Diary*, 4, 412.

[287] Andrew Browning (ed.), *Memoires of Sir John Reresby* (London: Royal Historical Society, 1991), 194.

But see, he now from Datchet up does come,
Laden with spoils of slaughter'd gudgeons, home.[288]

angles – a fishing hook, hence fishing being known as angling, as seen in Charles Cotton's Being Instructions How to Angle For a Trout or Grayling in a Clear Stream, which was included in the fifth edition of Izaak Walton's *The Complete Angler* (1676).[289]

fisherman/fishermen – while Catherine and Charles regularly went fishing, they were accompanied by men who earnt their living by fishing.

rods, hooks, and lines – rods could be short or long, with long, jointed rods of up to 16 feet were not uncommon.[290] Examples of sixteenth century u-shaped iron hooks with a tin (?) coating have been found in London.[291] Pepys used gut for lines.[292]

worms – As John Dennys noted in *The Secret of Angling*, seventeenth-century anglers chose their bait dependent on the type of fish that they wished to catch:

The Roache, the Bream, the Carpe, the Chub and Bleik,
With paste or Corne, their greedy hunger tame,
The Dace, the Ruffe, the Goodgion and the rest,
The smaller sort of crawling wormes loue best.
The Chaueunder and Chub doe more delight,
To feede on tender Cheese or Cherries red,
Blacke snayles, their bellies slit to show their white,
Or Grasshoppers that skip in euery Meade,
The Perche, the Tench, the Eele, doth rather bite
At great red worms, in Field or Garden bred.[293]

Fitz [ffitzt], **Thomas** – violin in ordinary, 1666–71.[294]

Fitz [Fitts], **Mr** – possibly Thomas, noted above, or Theophilus Fitz, who played the violin and flute.[295]

Fitzharding, lady – Mary Bagot (1645–79), was the daughter of Colonel Henry Bagot and Dorothea Arden. She married Sir Charles Berkeley

[288] Heneage Jesse, *Memoirs of the Court of England*, 335.

[289] https://pitt.libguides.com/compleatangler/17thcenturyeditions [accessed 15/1/23].

[290] http://www.fishingmuseum.org.uk/rods_overview.html [accessed 15/1/23].

[291] Geoff Egan, *Material Culture in London in an Age of Transition: Tudor and Stuart Period Finds c.1450–c.1700 from Excavations at Riverside Sites in Southwark* (London: Museum of London Archaeology Service, 2005), 157.

[292] Pepys, *Diary*, 8, 119.

[293] John Dennys, *The Secrets of Angling, 1613* (London: W. Satchell & Co, 1883), 48.

[294] Sainty, Wassmann and Bucholz, *Household officers*, 28; Multiple references in Ashbee, *Records*, including 59, 76, 80, 168, 229.

[295] Multiple references in Ashbee, *Records*, including 11, 15, 171, 287.

in 1663, who died in 1665. Mary was one of the women painted as part of the Windsor Beauties by Sir Peter Lely and for a short period she was a mistress of the king. In 1674, she married Charles Sackville, 6th earl of Dorset.[296]

man –

Fitzharding, lord – Sir Charles Berkeley (1630–65), son of Sir Charles Berkeley and Penelope Godolphin. He served as a soldier under James, duke of York, and Charles II and he was knighted in May 1660. In 1662, he was appointed keeper of the privy purse and in 1663 he was created viscount Fitzhardinge. In the following year he became earl of Falmouth. He married Mary Bagot, a lady of the queen's bedchamber in 1663 and he was killed at the battle of Southwold Bay on 2 June 1665, one of the engagements in the Second Anglo-Dutch war.[297]

Fletcher [Flecher] – possibly Robert Fletcher, physician in extraordinary, who was listed in the queen's household in 1673.[298]

flowerpots – the late seventeenth century saw increased use of potted plants in gardens to change the planting rapidly and to allow delicate plants to be moved inside in the winter. Lists of plants in pots were recorded at Ham House in 1682.[299] A plant list for Beaufort House Gardens, Chelsea, dating from 1691, recorded that there were many plants in pots including one of Persian jasmine, twelve of 'double Stock-gillyflowers' and three of double sweet williams in the West Walk next to the Kitchen Garden.[300]

flowers – the queen received many gifts of flowers, as well as making some purchases.

jonquils [jongills] – a rush daffodil (*Narcissus jonquilla*), native to Portugal and Spain, with rush-like leaves and white or yellow, scented flowers.

narcissus [narsices] – the sixteenth and seventeenth centuries saw new types of narcissi developed in Spain, Portugal and Turkey. They were very popular, featuring in the paintings of Jan Brueghel, while John Parkinson recorded 78 narcissi varieties.[301]

296 Ronald Hutton, 'Berkeley, Charles, earl of Falmouth (bap.1630–d.1665), courtier', *ODNB*, 3 January 2008, https://doi-org/10.1093/ref:odnb/37185 [accessed 27/4/22].

297 Ronald Hutton, 'Berkeley, Charles, earl of Falmouth (bap.1630–d.1665), courtier', *ODNB*, 3 January 2008, https://doi-org/10.1093/ref:odnb/37185 [accessed 27/4/22].

298 Sainty, Wassmann and Bucholz, *Household officers*, 28.

299 Ruth Duthie, 'The planting plans of some seventeenth-century flower gardens', *Garden History* 18.2 (1990), 98.

300 Duthie, 'Planting plans', 90–91.

301 Celia Fisher, *The Golden Age of Flowers: Botanical Illustration in the Age of Discovery 1600–1800* (London: The British Library, 2011), 105.

nosegays – a bunch of sweet-smelling flowers, as the character Willmore in Aphra Behn's *The Rover* (1677), described: ''Tis a delicate shining wench. By this hand, she's perfumed and smells like a nosegay'.[302] John Parkinson went further, noting that Indian cress or yellow Larks heals, along with carnations or gillyflowers 'make a delicate Tussimussie, as they call it, or Nosegay, for both sight and sent'.[303] He commented that 'the sweete marieromes are not only much used to please the outward senses in nosegays, and in the windows of houses … but are also in much use in Physicke, both to comfort the outward members, or parts of the body, and in the inward also'.[304]

orange flowers – the flowers of the bitter orange (*Citrus aurantifolium var. myrtifolia*) have been used since the fourteenth century to make perfumed waters by distillation and they have been grown in the south of France from the sixteenth century. On 27 August 1663, Pepys received a case of orange flower water from Captain Robert Cocke, the navy victualling agent in Lisbon as a gift for his help.[305]

orange trees – there are two types of orange – sweet oranges (*Citrus x sinensis*) and bitter oranges (*Citrus x aurantium*). Portuguese and Italian merchants introduced the sweet orange to Europe in the late fifteenth/early sixteenth century and by the mid-seventeenth century it was a well-known luxury. On 27 September 1658, Evelyn visited Beddington 'famous for the first Orange garden of England', which had 'now over-growne trees & planted in the ground, & secured in winter with a wooden tabernacle & stoves'.[306] By the 1690s, the Beddington orangery produced around 10,000 oranges annually.[307] Pepys also encountered orange trees in the physic garden in St James's park, which he described as having seen for the first time on 19 April 1665.[308] Royal Portuguese gardens, including those at the Palace of Sintra, the Villa of Belém and Queluz, all had orange groves.

tuberoses [Tubroses] – a perennial plant native to Mexico (*Agave amica*),

302 James Fitzmaurice et al., *Major Women Writers of Seventeenth Century England* (Ann Arbor, MI: University of Michigan Press, 1997), 257.

303 John Parkinson, *Paradisi in Sole Paridisus Terrestris, Or, A Garden of All Sorts of Pleasant Flowers* (London: printed by Humphrey Lownes and Robert Young at the Sign of the Starre on Bread-Street Hill, 1629), 281.

304 Parkinson, *Paradisi in Sole*, 453.

305 Pepys, *Diary*, 4, 290.

306 Evelyn, *Diary*, 393.

307 David Stuart, *The Kitchen Garden: An Historical Guide to Traditional Crops* (Gloucester: Alan Sutton, 1984), 174.

308 Pepys, *Diary*, 5, 127.

brought to Europe in the seventeenth century and used to make perfume.

food, also see *fish, fruit*, *meat*, *vegetables*

almond butter – almonds (*Prunus dulcis*) are native to Asia, and they were brought to Britain by the Romans where they grew well. The ground nuts were used for marzipan and to make nut butter as Castelvetro noted.[309] Almond butter was also a creamy pudding as described in Andrew Borde's *Compend. Regyment Helth* (1542) 'Almon butter made with fyne suger and good rose water, and eaten with the flowers of many vyolettes, is a commendable dysshe'.[310] Almond milk and butter were used on 'lean' days including Lent.[311]

biscuits [Biskit] – they were often served at funerals, as was the case with Pepys's brother on 18 March 1664, when mourners received 'six biscuits a-piece and what they pleased of burnt claret'. Biscuits were popular for a snack. In 1665, Pepys stopped at the Bear at the Bridge-foot where he ordered 'a biscuit and a piece of cheese and a gill of sack'.[312]

butter [buter] – a pale yellow fat made by churning cream or milk.[313] Eating bread and butter was popular, as Pepys recorded on 30 January 1663 which was 'A solemne Fast for the King's murther' and when he came home for dinner he decided 'to eat something, such as we have, bread, butter and milk'.[314]

cakes – Pepys's diary indicates that cake was often associated with celebrations such as Twelfth Night, Whitsun, christenings and weddings, and at solemn occasions such as funerals.[315] Gervase Markham offered his readers recipes for spice cakes and Banbury cakes.

caramel – made by heating sugar, the name caramel came from the French word and possibly from *caramelo* (Portuguese).[316] By *c*. 1600 Portugal

309 Giacomo Castelvetro, *The Fruit, Herbs & Vegetables of Italy: An Offering to Lucy, Countess of Bedford*, translated by Gilliam Riley (London: British Museum/ Viking, 1989), Stuart, *Kitchen Garden*, 59–60.

310 Andrew Borde, *The* Compendious Regiment, or, Dyetary of Health (London: 1542), xiii. sig.H.i. https://www.oed.com/view/Entry/5593?redirectedFrom=almond+butter#eid [accessed 10/1/22].

311 Castelvetro, *Fruit, Herbs & Vegetables*, 156.

312 Pepys, *Diary*, 5, 90; 6, 224.

313 Pepys, *Diary*, 1, 222.

314 Pepys, *Diary*, 4, 29.

315 Pepys, *Diary*, 2, 7; 2, 112; 5, 211; 7, 250; 8, 19.

316 https://www.oed.com/view/Entry/27703?rskey=4Lxkw4&result=1&isAdvanced=false#eid [accessed 27/4/22].

was very important in the production and trade of white sugar and the Portuguese were also very skilled in using sugar to make sweets and confectionary. Portuguese caramel recipes featured in the Japanese seventeenth century manuscript *Nanban ryōrisho* (the *Southern Barbarians' Cookbook*).[317]

cheese – Pepys described several types of cheese in his diary including home-produced cheese from Cheshire and Suffolk, as well as imported Dutch cheeses and Parmesan.[318] He also noted that Baldock Fair was famous for its cheese.[319] Gervase Markham provided a recipe to make 'an excellent fresh cheese' combining fresh milk with cream and rennet leave to stand, meanwhile mix egg yolks, rose water, a little salt, sugar and nutmeg and add them to the curds and then place in a cheese vat.[320]

cheesecake [Cheesecak] – on 25 April 1669, Samuel Pepys recorded that he 'carried my wife to the Lodge, the first time this year, and there in our coach eat a cheesecake and drank a tankard of milk'. The recipe for cheesecake given in Elizabeth Cromwell's cookery book (1654) included curd cheese, thick cream, butter and eggs, and flavoured with cloves, nutmeg, mace and currants, all in a pastry case.[321] Elizabeth's book also included a recipe for cheesecake which began 'take two gallons of new milk and put into it 2 spoonfuls and a half of runnet, heat the milk a little less than blood warm, cover it close' and the resulting curd cheese was mixed with thick cream, butter, eggs, currants, cloves, nutmeg, mace, sugar and rose water and then placed in a pastry case and baked.[322]

chocolate [jacolet] – chocolate was available in England by *c.* 1652. At the banquet to entertain the Moroccan ambassador in January 1682, Evelyn reported that 'they drank of a sorbett & Jacolatte'.[323] On Christmas day 1715 Lady Grisell Baillie served [jacolet].[324] Chocolate

317 Erik Rath, *Food and Fantasy in Early Modern Japan* (Berkeley, CA: University of California Press, 2010), 92–93.

318 Pepys, *Diary*, 1, 6; 2, 191; 4, 64; 7, 274.

319 Pepys, *Diary*, 4, 314.

320 Markham, *Well-Kept Kitchen*, 71–72.

321 Christopher Driver and Michelle Berriedale-Johnson, *Pepys at Table: Seventeenth Century Recipes for the Modern Cook* (London: Bell & Hyman, 1984), 96.

322 This was a satirical pamphlet attributed to Elizabeth Cromwell, see Mary Liquorice (ed.), *Mrs Cromwell's Cookery Book: The Court and Kitchen of Elizabeth Wife of Oliver Cromwell* (Peterborough: Cambridgeshire Libraries, 1983), 78.

323 Evelyn, *Diary*, 718.

324 Robert Scott-Moncrieff (ed.), *The Household Book of Lady Grisell Baillie, 1692–1733* (Edinburgh: W. S. 1911), 282.

could also be taken medicinally as on 24 April 1661 when Pepys took a hangover cure of 'Chocolate to settle my stomach'.[325]

cream/creams – churned cream was popular as a dessert as is evident from Pepys' diary. On 1 July 1667, Samuel had 'a dish of very good cream'. John Nott included a recipe in *The Cook's Dictionary* (1723) for churned cream made from two quarts of cream that was flavoured with rose water, sweetened with sugar and churned until it was frothy.[326] Cream was also used to make cream cheese[327] and Evelyn noted that the best cream cheese was made when the cows grazed on the autumn grass, in other words, the second crop or rowen.[328] Also, see the entry above for cheesecake.

fool/foole [foulle] – popular in the seventeenth century, a fool is a dessert made from custard and stewed fruit. *The Complete Cook* (1658) included the following recipe:

> Take your gooseberries and put them in a silver or earthen pot, and set it in a skillet of boiling water, and when they are coddled enough, strain them; when they are scalding hot beat them well with a good piece of butter, rose-water and sugar, and put in the yolk of two or three eggs, you may put rose-water into them, and so stir it altogether and serve it to the table when it is cold.[329]

gingerbread, French – a sweet, baked cake flavoured with ginger and other spices. On 28 February 1669 Pepys had 'some ginger-bread made in cakes like chocolate, very good'.[330] The recipe given in *The Receipt Book of Mrs Ann Blencowe* (1694) consisted of sugar, ginger, cinnamon, flour, treacle and melted butter.[331]

honey – a sweet liquid made by bees gathering nectar that was used to sweeten drinks including tea, and in cooking. Pepys mentioned Baltic honey in this context.[332] He also referred to eating or drinking honey

325 Pepys, *Diary*, 2, 88.

326 Driver and Berriedale-Johnson, *Pepys at Table*, 94.

327 A very soft cheese sometimes described as 'rewain' or 'ruayn', see Darra Goldstein (ed.), *The Oxford Companion to Sugar and Sweets* (Oxford: Oxford University Press, 2015), 125.

328 Goldstein, *Oxford Companion*, 125; https://www.oed.com/view/Entry/168191?redirectedFrom=ruayn#eid [accessed 28/4/22].

329 Anon., *The Complete Cook* (London: printed for E. B. for Nath. Brooke, at the Angel in Cornhill, 1658); https://thehistoricfoodie.wordpress.com/2011/06/24/200 [accessed 3/2/22].

330 Pepys, *Diary*, 9, 460.

331 Driver and Berriedale-Johnson, *Pepys at Table*, 102.

332 Pepys, *Diary*, 4, 413.

for a cold and for the colic (an intense pain associated with the urinary tract or the intestines).[333]

jelly [Gelly, jelley] – a dessert that could be coloured and flavoured, as indicated by Randle Holme's comment that 'a Jelly of five or six colours' was a suitable pudding in a home of the middling sort.[334] Gervase Markham included recipes for jelly made from boiled calves' feet, the resulting jelly flavoured with sack, cinnamon, ginger, sugar and rose water. After adding an egg white, the jelly was boiled again and run through a jelly bag with some rosemary in the bottom.[335]

panada *[ponnado]* – bread boiled in milk or water to make soup and then flavoured with sugar and nutmeg or with garlic, coriander and shellfish. Domingo Rodrigues's *Arte de Cozinha* (The Art of Cooking) (1680) included three recipes for sweet panada.[336]

pates [pattes] – provided for Catherine by her Spanish cook at Easter, this was probably a reference to paté, a dish of potted diced or minced meat or fish, encased in pastry (a paté) or cooked in a dish (a terrine).

pies [pye] – a sweet or savoury baked dish, either encased or covered with pastry. They were very popular in the seventeenth century and were sometimes sent as gifts, as on 10 May 1639, when Lady Brilliana Harley wrote to her son Ned commenting 'I haue made a pye to send you; it is a kide pye'.[337]

eel – *see under fish*; On 10 May 1666, Pepys noted that he had 'an eele-pie, of which my wife eat part, and brought home the rest'.[338] A recipe for eel pie with oysters was included in Elizabeth Cromwell's cookbook.[339]

lamprey – *see under fish*. They were popular in pies, so much so that the city of Gloucester has sent the monarch a lamprey pie at Christmas from 1200 until 1836 and to mark their coronation and jubilees.[340]

pigeon – *see under birds*. Robert May included recipes 'to bake pigeons wild or tame' noting that if the pie was to be eaten hot the cook

333 Pepys, *Diary*, 2, 36; 4, 385.

334 Nancy Cox, *Retailing and the Language of Goods, 1550–1820* (London and New York: Routledge, 2016), 155.

335 Markham, *Well-Kept Kitchen*, 68–69.

336 https://www.virgiliogomes.com/index.php/chronicles/109-acorda-sord-the-portuguese-bread-panada [accessed 1/2/22].

337 Brilliana Harley, *Letters of Lady Brilliana Harley* (Cambridge: Cambridge University Press, 1954), 53.

338 Pepys, *Diary*, 7, 121.

339 Liquorice, *Mrs Cromwell's Cookery Book*, 70.

340 Alan Davidson, *The Oxford Companion to Food* (Oxford: Oxford University Press, 2014), 622.

should add 'yolks of hard eggs, sweet-breads' lambs stones [testicles], sparagus or bottoms of artichocks, chesnuts, grapes or gooseberries'.[341]

salmon – *see under fish.* Robert May's recipe for salmon pie in *The Accomplisht Cook* (1660) included asparagus, grapes, and oysters.[342]

provisions, provisioning – the act of supplying a household or journey with food and so by implication the food supplied.[343]

puddings – sweet and savoury puddings were a key part of seventeenth century menus. On Sunday 27 January 1661, Pepys dined on 'a fine pudding (made me by Slater the Cooke last Thursday)'.[344]

puffs – there are several possible meanings of this term: 1) a dessert made from puff pastry, such as the recipe recorded by Hannah Baker in 1692; 2) meringues, a suggestion made by Marissa Nicosia;[345] or 3) a sweet fritter, such as the 'Apple puffes' that John Murrell offered recipes for which were made from minced or grated apple, mixed with sugar and eggs, flavoured with ginger, raisins, rose water and nutmeg, then fried and sprinkled with lemon or orange juice.[346]

Ring o Roots canditt – the meaning is uncertain, but it is possibly a reference to candied fruit. In January 1674 Etienne Emery sold '2 pounds and halve oranges and lemons and zingo roots' for 10s to the earl of Bedford.[347]

sugar cakes – sugar was included in many recipes in the sixteenth and seventeenth centuries. In August 1663, Pepys received 'a feacho' or small case of 'fine Sugar' from Lisbon.[348] Sarah Long included a recipe for sugar cakes in her receipt book, *c.* 1610: 'Take a pound of butter, and wash it in rose-water, and halfe a pound of sugar, and halfe a douzen sponefulls of thicke Creame, and the yelkes of 4 Eggs, and a little mace finely beaten, and as much fine flower as it will wett, and work it well together; then roll them out very thin, and cut them

341 Robert May, *The Accomplisht Cook, Or The whole art and mystery of cookery, fitted for all degrees and qualities* (London: printed by R. W. for Nath. Brooke at the sign of the Angel in Cornhill, 1660), 214–15.

342 See Shakespeare & Beyond https://shakespeareandbeyond.folger.edu/2017/08/08/recipe-salmon-pastry-shakespeare-kitchen-francine-segan [accessed 3/8/22].

343 https://www.oed.com/view/Entry/153483?rskey=WVq3Q5&result=1#eid [accessed 22/3/22].

344 Pepys, *Diary*, 2, 24.

345 For meringues, see Marissa Nicosia, https://rarecooking.com/2020/03/02/meringues-to-make-lemmon-or-chocolett-puffs [accessed 2/3/22].

346 Albala, *The Banquet*, 88.

347 Scott Thomson, *Life in a Noble Household*, 173.

348 Pepys, *Diary*, 4, 290.

with a glasse, and pricke them very thicke with a great pin, and lay them on plates, and so bake them gently'.[349]

sweets – short for sweetmeats, which included sugared confectionary or cakes, sugared fruit and nuts, and lozenges of sugar flavoured or filled with fruit. Evelyn attended a dinner in Ipswich in September 1677 'where they presented us a noble Collation of dried Sweetmeates & Wine' and in January 1682 he was at 'a greate banquet of Sweetemeates & Musique' held 'at the Dut. of Portsmouths glorious Appartment at W.hall'.[350] The earl of Bedford bought confectionary from Etienne Emery, referred to as Monsieur, including 5 lb 6 oz of 'all sorts of sweetmeats' costing £1 7s in December 1673 and in the following January '2 pounds of sweetmeats' for 10s.[351] For a display of Portuguese sweets, see the paintings of Josefa d'Óbidos.[352]

wafers – very thin cakes or biscuits cooked using wafer irons. Gervase Markham included a recipe for wafers in *The English Housewife*: 'To make the best Wafers, take the finest wheat-flowers you can get, and mix it with Cream, the yelks of Eggs, Rose-water, Sugar, and Cinamon, till it be a little thicker than Pancake-batter, and then warming your Wafter Irons on a charcoal-fire, anoint them first with sweet Butter, and then lay on your batter, and press it, and bake it white or brown at your pleasure'.[353] Wafers were often served at Christenings as on 5 May 1667 when Pepys went to his niece's baptism 'so we had gloves and wine and wafers'.[354]

Foran, Mrs – for her bill.

Forbes [Forbus], **Mr** – John Forbes, page of the queen's backstairs, from 1662–63 to 1678.[355]

Fountain [Fountayne], **mistress** – making linen for the chapel. Possibly a seamstress.

Fowl [fowle], **Mr** – for a sweet water pot. Possibly a goldsmith.

Fowler, Mr – possibly Richard Fowler, equerry, from 1682 to 1689.[356]

Fox, Sir Stephen – Stephen (1627–1716) was the son of William Fox and

349 May Anne Caton (ed.), *Fooles and Fricassees: Food in Shakespeare's England* (Washington: Folger Shakespeare Library, 1999), 105.

350 Evelyn, *Diary*, 638, 718.

351 Scott Thomson, *Life in a Noble Household*, 173.

352 For example, Josefa d'Óbidos, *Still Life with Flowers, Sweets and Cherries* (1676), oil on canvas, Museu Municipal de Santarem, Portugal, RM RKN734.

353 Gervase Markham, *The English Housewife* (Montreal, QC: McGill-Queens Press, 1994), 117.

354 Pepys, *Diary*, 8, 202.

355 Sainty, Wassmann and Bucholz, *Household officers*, 28.

356 Sainty, Wassmann and Bucholz, *Household officers*, 28.

Margaret Pavy. He went into exile with the future Charles II where he was appointed by Edward Hyde to the royal household. At the Restoration he was made the clerk comptroller of the king's household and the following year he became paymaster general of the army.[357] He was Catherine's Treasurer and receiver general, 1696–97.[358]

man –

France/French – the fashionable court of Louis XIV, Charles II's cousin and king of France, exerted considerable influence at the English court. In May 1671 Evelyn noted that 'a vast number of [French] Gentlemen & Cadets in fantastical habites, came flocking over to see our Court & complement his Majestie. I was present when they first were conducted into the Queenes with-drawing roome where saluted their Majesties'.[359]

French man that cut the queen's hair –

present from France –

Frazier [Frayser], **mistress** – the date of these entries indicates this was Lady Mary Frazier, who was dresser to the queen, from 1662–63 to 1697, and wife of Sir Alexander Frazier, who had been the king's physician while in exile. He was popular with ladies at court, according to Pepys, because he helped them 'to slip their calfes when there is occasion, and with the great men in curing of their claps, that he can do what he pleases with the King'.[360] Her beautiful daughter, Cary Fraser, was a maid of honour, from 1674 to 1681.[361] On 2 November 1676, Lady Chaworth described the women at court as 'Mighty bravery in clothes preparing for the Queen's birthday' noting 'Mrs Phraser, whose gown is ermine upon velvet imbroiderd with gold and lined with cloth of gold'.[362] In 1681, Lady Mary married Charles, viscount Mordaunt.

Frost, Mrs – under-housekeeper.

fruit – many households grew their own fruit and in 1658 Evelyn lamented that bad weather had destroyed much of the winter fruit at Sayes Court.[363] Households could also supplement home-grown fruit with purchases, as was the case at Bedford House in June and July 1663 where they

357 Michael J. Braddick, 'Fox, Sir Stephen (1627–1716), financier and government official', *ODNB*, 23 September 2004, https://doi.org/10.1093/ref:odnb/10043 [accessed 30/1/22].

358 Sainty, Wassmann and Bucholz, *Household officers*, 28.

359 Evelyn, *Diary*, 553.

360 Wilson, *Court Satires*, 239; Pepys, *Diary*, 5, 275.

361 Sainty, Wassmann and Bucholz, *Household officers*, 29.

362 Wilson, *Court Satires*, 239.

363 Evelyn, *Diary*, 393.

bought codlins, currants, gooseberries, lemons, pears, pippins, plums and raspberries.[364] Fruit was a popular gift to the queen.

apricots [Appricokes] – originating in China, apricots (*Prunus armeniaca*) were well known in seventeenth century England with the Tradescants having five varieties in their garden in 1634.[365]

cherries [cheryes] – these were likely to be the sweet cherry (*Prunus avium*), which is native to England, and they were very popular in the seventeenth century, so much so that fifteen varieties were listed in the 1634 Tradescant catalogue, while in 1688 John Rae offered twenty-four types.[366] Purchases for Bedford House in mid-June 1663 included 'a pound of Duke cherries and a pound and a half heart cherries' for 5s, while in the following July, four pounds of carnation cherries costing 8s and a pound of dried cherries stuffed with raspberries costing 6s along with candied cherries and white cherries were purchased.[367] When Evelyn visited Carshalton in 1658 he found it 'full planted with Walnuts & Chery trees, which afford a considerable rent'.[368]

figs – according to Castelvetro, figs (*ficus carica*) fruited twice: 'these early, or first-crop, figs are so called because this noble tress produces, instead of flowers, a fruit even bigger than the real fruit which is bears early in September'.[369] On 21 July 1662, Pepys visited the garden of Mr Sheldon, where they were 'eating more fruit and drinking and eating figs, which were very good'.[370]

grapes [Graps] – technically a berry, grapes are the fruit of deciduous vines (*Vitis*). They are eaten as fresh fruit, dried to make raisins, or used to make wine. Castelvetro listed three main types of grapes: luglienga grapes ready in early July but 'not the best in the world', muscat grapes 'which are much better' and tremarina grapes which were 'without doubt the same dried grapes which are imported into England'.[371]

melons [milons, millons] – technically, the melon is a berry with sweet flesh. John Parkinson recorded melons (*Cucumis melo*) being grown

364 Scott Thomson, *Life in a Noble Household*, 145–46.

365 Mea Allan, *The Tradescants: Their Plants, Gardens and Museum* (London: Michael Joseph, 1964); David Stuart, *The Kitchen Garden: An Historical Guide to Traditional Crops* (Gloucester: Alan Sutton, 1984), 64–65.

366 Stuart, *Kitchen Garden*, 103.

367 Scott Thomson, *Life in a Noble Household*, 145–46.

368 Evelyn, *Diary*, 393.

369 Castelvetro, *Fruit, Herbs & Vegetables*, 82.

370 Pepys, *Diary*, 3, 142.

371 Castelvetro, *Fruit, Herbs & Vegetables*, 84.

in England in 1629 under glass with hot beds (the heat provided by rotting horse manure).[372] On 9 August 1654 Evelyn visited Leicester where he was 'Entertain'd at a very fine Collation of Fruite, such as I did not expect to meete with so far north, (especially very good Melons)'.[373] Melons were also imported as Pepys recounted on 27 September 1661: 'we find Captain Country … come with some Grapes and Millons from my Lord at Lisbone – the first that ever I saw any'.[374]

mulberries – the black mulberry (*Morus nigra*) produces very tasty fruit.[375] It is native to Asia Minor but was growing at Syon in 1548. When Pepys visited Captain Cockes in Greenwich in August 1662 he ate 'much mulberrys, a thing I have not eat of these many years'.[376]

oranges [orringers] – bitter or Seville oranges were known in Europe in the Middle Ages with sweet oranges brought to Europe from China in the fifteenth century. Two centuries later, Josefa d'Óbidos' painting *Still Life with fruit, vegetables and flowers* (1666–70) depicted three popular types of Portuguese citrus fruits: citrons, oranges and a citrus medica.[377] While a popular refreshment at the theatre, oranges were also be put to other uses. During a dispute between Lady Harvey and the duchess of Castlemaine, Pepys noted that 'Lady Harvy provided people to hiss her [Doll Common] and fling oranges at her'.[378]

pears – a sweet fruit with a delicate flavour. Gerard recorded many British pear (*pyrus communis*) varieties in his *Herbal*, while Parkinson noted that there were 64 types available in England. Pears were eaten as fresh fruit, cooked and made into perry.[379]

peaches [Pachies] – while originating in China, peaches (*Prunus persica*) were hardy in England and were probably brought to the country by the Romans. From the sixteenth century, peaches were regularly grown for their sweet juicy fruit.[380]

pomecitrons – the pomecitron is a cultivar of the lemon (*Citrus limon*), a yellow citrus fruit thought to originate in India. Barnaby Googe in his *Foure Books of husbandrie* (1578) made the following observation

372 Parkinson, *Paradisi in Sole*, 15.

373 Evelyn, *Diary*, 393.

374 Pepys, *Diary*, 2, 185–86.

375 Stuart, *Kitchen Garden*, 166.

376 Pepys, *Diary*, 3, 152.

377 Josefa d'Óbidos, *Still Life with fruit, vegetables and flowers* (1666–70), oil on canvas, National Museum of Ancient Art, Lisbon.

378 Pepys, *Diary*, 9, 415.

379 Stuart, *Kitchen Garden*, 188–89.

380 Stuart, *Kitchen Garden*, 187.

about citrus fruit: 'if they be yellow, are called Citrons, if they be green, Lemons: if they be very great and round like Pompeons, they call them Pomecitrons'.[381]. In December 1665, Pepys bought lemons costing 6d each with oranges costing 3d.[382] Evelyn noted in his *Acetaria: A discourse on Sallets* (1699) that pickled lemon peel made a good addition to salads.[383]

pomegranates – juicy round red fruit (*Punica granatum*) with lots of edible seeds. Castelvetro observed that 'They are a very good fruit on their own, and make an excellent seasoning for cooked dishes'.[384] The trees grow in England but only produce good fruit under glass. Evelyn noted proudly in 1658 that 'the pomegranads beare here' at Beddington.[385]

quinces [quincess] – a small tree (*Cydonia oblonga*) producing pear-shaped, highly scented fruit. The Tradescants imported new varieties including 'Portugal'. *Marmelo* is the Portuguese word for quince and it was also used to describe quince preserve or marmalade.[386] Gervase Markham included recipes for 'marmalade or quinces red' and 'marmalade white'.[387]

strawberries [straburys] – smaller fruited strawberries of the 'Alpine' variety (*Fragaria vesca*) were supplemented by imported larger-fruited strawberries from America (*Fragaria x ananassas*) in the seventeenth century. Grown by Parkinson they ripen by the first week of May.[388] According to Evelyn 'what was pretiest' in Lady Brooks' gardens at Hackney in 1654 was 'the Vine-yard planted in Strawberry-borders, staked at 10 foote distance'.[389]

funerals – as a good mistress, Catherine paid for the funerals of members of her household. She was not alone. The earl of Bedford paid the care of his gardener, John Field, during his final illness and then his burial on 22 March 1687 in Woburn parish church. Lady Diana wrote that 'Mr Field is dead. I beseech God to comfort the poor widow, for I do really pity her … All my servants are in tears for poor Mr Field'.[390]

poor woman to bury her husband [1663] –

381 Stuart, *Kitchen Garden*, 150.
382 Pepys, *Diary*, 6, 322.
383 Stuart, *Kitchen Garden*, 150.
384 Castelvetro, *Fruit, Herbs & Vegetables*, 127.
385 Evelyn, *Diary*, 393.
386 Stuart, *Kitchen Garden*, 203.
387 Markham, *Well-Kept Kitchen*, 69–70.
388 Stuart, *Kitchen Garden*, 235–37.
389 Evelyn, *Diary*, 336.
390 Scott Thomson, *Life in a Noble Household*, 259.

ye Buriall of your Majesties Postillion [1664] –
ye funerall for one of your Majesties footman [1665] –
One of your Majesties coachmen [1667] –
John Pettoes, your footman's widow, to bury him [1667].[391]
Mistress Le Mar's husband [1668][392]
Charles Eaton, your majesty's footman – yeoman footman to the queen.[393]
Edward Welsh [Welch], ***sumpterman*** [1670] – groom sumpterman to the queen between 1669 and 1674.[394]
Fire maker of the queen's guard chamber [1671] –
Mr Maginis to Bury John Gordon your Majesties footman [1677] – Constantine MacGinnis was yeoman footman to the queen from 1665 to 1674, and the post was vacant by 1682.[395]
Roger Hastright [Hastrik], ***footman*** [1674] – yeoman footman.[396]
Mr Miller, one of the queen's footmen [1680] – footman.[397]

furnishings – most of the furnishings supplied to Catherine were ordered from the Great Wardrobe.
Portugal mats – the Restoration saw the rush matting favoured by the Tudors and early Stuarts, replaced with finer, more colourful mats from the Low Countries, North Africa and Portugal.[398]

furniture – moveable articles, often made of wood, used to furnish a room.
billiard tables – Evelyn noted that there was a billiards table amongst the entertainments at Euston House in 1677.[399] An example of an extant 1670s billiards table of grained oak, with twelve legs, but with a later top, can be seen at Knole, Kent.[400] When Celia Fiennes visited Euston House, she was shown a billiards table in a room that was 'hung with outlandish pictures of Heroes'.[401]
boxes to put handkerchiefs in – storage boxes of this type were popular.

391 Not listed amongst Catherine's staff, Sainty, Wassmann and Bucholz, *Household officers*.

392 Not listed amongst Catherine's staff, Sainty, Wassmann and Bucholz, *Household officers*.

393 Sainty, Wassmann and Bucholz, *Household officers*, 24.

394 Sainty, Wassmann and Bucholz, *Household officers*, 78.

395 Sainty, Wassmann and Bucholz, *Household officers*, but John Gordon not listed.

396 Sainty, Wassmann and Bucholz, *Household officers*, 36, listed 1667 to 1674, post listed as vacant 1682.

397 Not listed amongst Catherine's staff, Sainty, Wassmann and Bucholz, *Household officers*.

398 Joanna Banham (ed.), *Encyclopedia of Interior Design* (London and New York: Routledge, 2015), 435.

399 Evelyn, *Diary*, 639.

400 National Trust, Knole, Kent, NT 129451.

401 Fiennes, *Through England on a Side Saddle*, 123.

On 25 February 1668 Samuel Pepys collected a dressing box 'and other things for her chamber and table' for his wife from the New Exchange.[402]

chairs – in April 1667 Pepys's friend Mrs Martin bought some expensive Turkey work chairs.[403] Turkey work is an embroidered technique using Ghiordes knots, which create a fluffy surface.

comb box – a container to store combs and other hair-dressing accessories.

iron chest – probably a strongbox. Facing the threat of the Great Fire of London in 1666 Samuel Pepys recorded that he 'did remove my money and Iron-chests into my cellar'.[404]

looking glasses and cases – Randle Holme gave an interesting insight into how he perceived women using mirrors when he observed that 'these sort of glasses are mostly used by lady's to look at their faces in, and to see how to dress their heads, and sett their top knots on their fore heads upright'.[405] In 1676, Evelyn visited the duke of Buckingham's glassworks in Lambeth, which made 'Looking-glasses far larger & better than any that came from Venice'.[406]

screens – they were used to divide rooms or provide privacy in the corner of a room. On 30 July 1682, Evelyn visited the home of Mr Bohun 'whose whole house is a Cabinet of all elegancies, especially Indian, and the Contrivement of the (Japan) Skreenes instead of Wainscot'.[407]

staircases – a reference either to integral staircases in the queen's apartments (from the mid-seventeenth century straight flights of stairs were popular) or to a set of moveable library steps with three or four steps.

stands, a pair of – a pair of small tables/trestles or other supports to stand something on.[408] For an example of a contemporary walnut stand for a coffer or trunk, see the support for a coffer associated with Catherine of Braganza. It has barley-twist legs and a carved decorative border of leaves and flowers.[409]

tables and stands – a separate tabletop and a pair of trestles, see above.

402 Pepys, *Diary*, 9, 91.

403 Pepys, *Diary*, 8, 167.

404 Pepys, *Diary*, 7, 272.

405 Holme, *An Accademie of Armorie*, Book 3, ch. 14, sect. Id, nos. 58–59.

406 Evelyn, *Diary*, 629.

407 Evelyn, *Diary*, 728.

408 https://www-oed-com.soton.idm.oclc.org/view/Entry/188958?rskey=c0Gf3C&result=1#eid [accessed 3/9/22].

409 Coffer on a stand, 1650–1700, leather, iron and walnut, Great Gallery, Palace of Holyroodhouse, RCIN 31154: https://www.rct.uk/collection/search#/1/collection/31154/coffer-on-stand [accessed 31/10/22].

Pepys mentioned various types of tables in his diary including side tables, dining tables and inlaid tables.[410]

gambling, money for – On 17 February 1667, Pepys went to the queen's apartments at Whitehall where he saw the queen playing cards 'which I was amazed at to see on a Sunday, having not believed it'.[411]

games and pastimes – games, whether games of chance or sporting activities, were very popular at the Restoration court. On 19 February 1666, Pepys watched 'the Queene at Cards with many ladies, but none of our beauties were there'.[412]

archery – Catherine enjoyed archery. In addition, in 1676 Sir William Wood was presented with a silver badge engraved 'Reginae Catharinae Sagittarii' as the leader of the queen's archers.[413]

bows and arrows – On 12 May 1667, Pepys reminisced about 'when I boarded at Kingsland and used to shoot my bow and arrows in these fields'.[414] Samuel's copy of *Ayme for Finsburie archers* (London, 1601) has his book plate and the binding is stamped with his arms.[415]

butts, a pair of – this term can refer to the archery field, the earth mounds the targets were rested against or the targets themselves.

case of arrows – a rigid case to store and carry arrows.

a press – a bow press flexes the limbs of the bow making it possible to take the tension off the cables and bowstring for repairs and maintenance.

billiards [billyards] – According to Cotgraves' *Dictionary of the French and English Tongues,* a billiard was 'a short and thicke trunchion, or cudgell: hence … the sticke wherewith we touch the ball at billyards'.[416] Pepys played billiards on several occasions including on 17 July 1665 when he noted 'to Billiards – my Lady Wright, Mr Carter[e]t, myself and everybody'.[417]

bowls [boulls], ***bowling*** – a game played on grass, with each player aiming to get their ball as close as possible to the smaller ball or jack. On

410 Pepys, *Diary*, 2, 110; 4, 6; 8, 128–29.

411 Pepys, *Diary*, 8, 70.

412 Pepys, *Diary*, 7, 48.

413 https://www.british-history.ac.uk/vch/middx/vol2/pp283-292#fnn36 [accessed 4/9/22].

414 Pepys, *Diary*, 8, 211.

415 https://magdlibs.com/2015/03/20/pepys-and-archery [accessed 6/8/22].

416 https://www.oed.com/view/Entry/19017?redirectedFrom=billiards#eid [accessed 27/4/22].

417 Pepys, *Diary*, 6, 160. Also 6, 179; 6, 190; 6, 220.

26 July 1662, Pepys went to Whitehall gardens 'and the bowling ally (where lords and ladies are now at bowles)'.[418] On 14 April 1667, he went to Jamaica House with his wife and two maids 'and there the girls did run for wagers over the bowling green'.[419]

cards, card games – gambling at cards was very popular at court where Pepys went to see 'the manner of the gaming at the Groom porter's' while at the Inner and Middle Temple Inns where he saw 'the dirty prentices and idle people playing.[420]

Cuba – a seventeenth century French card game.[421]

here [oheare] – *here* or *coucou*, was a late fifteenth century card game that was popular in the late seventeenth century.[422]

Lodom – *Losing Lodam* was a card game for three or more players and the aim was to lose tricks that contain penalty cards, or loaders, which were worth penalty points (10, Jack, Queen, King and the ace). It was described in William Willughby's *A Volume of Plaies* (*c.*1665–70).[423]

Loo, lanterloo [Lantrelew, Lanterlid] – a card game from the French, *lanturlu*.[424] The aim was to win a trick, with the player being 'looed', i.e. without a trick, losing.

ombre – a Spanish card game for three players using a short pack of forty cards (AKQJ765432), or a Spanish pack, that was very popular with women.[425] In July 1665 Pepys referred to the Lord Treasurer as a man who 'minds his ease' and if he had his salary 'and a game of Lombre, he is well'.[426]

chess [chase] ***board*** – Cornelis de Man's painting *The Chess Players* (*c.* 1670) depicts a man and woman playing.[427] However, it went into a decline during the Restoration and into the eighteenth century when gambling and games of chance increased in popularity. Charles Cotton

418 Pepys, *Diary*, 3, 146.

419 Pepys, *Diary*, 8, 167.

420 Pepys, *Diary*, 9, 2–3.

421 David Parlett, *A History of Card Games* (Oxford: Oxford University Press, 1991), 185.

422 https://www.pagat.com/cuckoo/cuckoo.html [accessed 6/8/22].

423 University of Nottingham library, MS Li 113. It has been published as Jeff Forgeng, Dorothy Johnston and David Cram, *Francis Willughby's Book of Games* (Aldershot: Ashgate, 2003).

424 https://www.parlettgames.uk/histocs/loo.html [accessed 19/1/22].

425 David Parlett, *The Penguin Book of Card Games* (Harmondsworth: Penguin, 1979), 104–12.

426 Pepys, *Diary*, 6, 218.

427 Cornelis de Man, *The Chess Players*, oil on canvas, c.1670, Museum of Fine Arts, Budapest, inv. no. 320.

(1630–87) observed in *The Complete Gamester* that 'the tediousness of the Game hath caus'd the practice thereof to be so little used'.[428]

goose – the *Game of Goose* or the *Royal Game of Goose* was a fifteenth century board game, which is still played.[429] In the seventeenth century it was the inspiration for *The Game of Cupid*, with both games having a spiral drawn on the board and divided into 63 spaces. It is played with two dice.[430]

lotteries – a competition reliant on chance, where numbered tickets are sold and prizes are given to the holders of winning numbers, which are drawn at random.[431] Lotteries were a popular means of raising money, as Evelyn noted on 7 July 1664, when he went 'To Court, where I subscribed to Sir Arthyr Slingsbys loterey, a desperate debt owing me long since in Paris'.[432] The lottery was drawn on 19 July in the banqueting house with Evelyn 'gaining onely a trifle, as well as did the King, Queene Consort & Q: Mother for neere 30 lotts: which was thought to be contriv'd very un-hand-somely by the master of it, who was in truth a meer shark'.[433] Pepys made several references to lotteries including those at court[434] and the Virginia lottery.[435]

ninepins [ninpins] – the game developed in the Middle Ages and consisted of nine pins or skittles arranged in a diamond shape. The central pin is often a different colour, and the aim is to knock as many of the pins over with each roll of the ball. On 27 May 1663 Pepys played ninepins 'where I won a shilling – Creed and I playing against my Lord and Cooke'.[436]

raffles [reifell] – a type of lottery where the prize is given to one of several players, who have bought tickets worth part of the real or presumed value. The winner is selected by drawing a ticket at random or by casting lots.[437]

428 Tim Harding, *British Chess Literature up to 1914: A Handbook for Historians* (Jefferson, NC: McFarland & Company, Inc., 2018), 233.

429 https://www.mastersofgames.com/rules/goose-game-rules.htm [accessed 19/1/22].

430 https://www.bl.uk/picturing-places/articles/the-royal-game-of-cupid-a-17th-century-board-game [accessed 19/1/22].

431 https://www.oed.com/view/Entry/110457?redirectedFrom=lottery#eid [accessed 26/2/22].

432 Evelyn, *Diary*, 461.

433 Evelyn, *Diary*, 462.

434 Pepys, *Diary*, 5, 214–15.

435 Pepys, *Diary*, 5, 323.

436 Pepys, *Diary*, 4, 160.

437 https://www.oed.com/view/Entry/157380?rskey=EalJ3p&result=1#eid [accessed 2/5/22].

tennis, tennis court – this was real or royal tennis, a racquet game, which was played in an indoor, closed court.[438] On 28 November 1663, Pepys recorded how 'walking through White-hall I heard the King was gone to play at Tennis, so I down to the new Tennis Court'.[439] Several years later, on 2 September 1667, Pepys went 'to see a great match at tennis between Prince Rupert and one Captain Cooke against Bab. May and the elder Chichly [Chicheley] where the King was and Court, and it seems are the best players at tennis in the nation'.[440]

gardeners – people who tended a garden for a living or as a hobby. John Evelyn was a very keen gardener and Pepys recorded seeing his *Hortus hyemalis* in November 1665, which consisted of 'leaves laid up in a book of several plants, kept dry, which preserve Colour however, and look very finely, better than any herball'.[441]

from Chiswick –

Hampton Court –

Kensington –

Lady Northumberland's, Mr Gibbs –

Lord Bristol's –

Lord Cornbury's –

Lord Craven –

St James's –

Wimbledon –

Winwood, Mr –

garrison, the – soldiers at a castle or palace to provide protection or defence.

Gascoigne [Gaskins, Jaskyns]**, Sir Bernard** (Bernardino Guasconi) – an army officer and Italian diplomat (1614–87), he was the son of Giovanni Batista di Bernardo Guasconi and Clemenza di Lorenzo Altoviti. He spent his early life as a soldier and in 1643–44 he met Henry Neville who was travelling in Italy, undertaking a Grand Tour, and came to England. Sir Bernard stayed until 1664, when he returned to Italy, coming back to London in 1667 when he was made a member of the Royal Society.[442]

438 Alexis Tadié, 'The uses and transformations of early modern tennis', in Sharron Harrow (ed.), *British Sporting Literature and Culture in the Long Eighteenth Century* (London and New York: Routledge, 2016), 85.

439 Pepys, *Diary*, 4, 435.

440 Pepys, *Diary*, 8, 418–19.

441 Pepys, *Diary*, 6, 289.

442 Roderick Clayton, 'Gascoigne, Sir Bernard [Bernardo Guasconi] (1614–1687), royalist army officer and diplomat', *ODNB*, 3 January 2008, https://doi-org.soton.idm.oclc.org/10.1093/ref:odnb/10420 [accessed 17/4/22].

Evelyn travelled with him on 19 October 1671 and dined with him on 17 September 1681.[443]

man –

gazettes – a newspaper or journal. On 4 July 1663, Pepys was present when Sir Allan Apsly showed a copy of the Lisbon gazette to the duke of York which provided an account of the battle of Ameixial 'to the great honour of the English', which he had first heard about on 29 June.[444] Shortly after saw the advent of an English gazette. It began as the *Oxford Gazette* which first appeared on 7 November 1665 (issue 1) when the court moved to Oxford because of plague in London. However, when Charles moved back to the capital, from issue 24, which was published on 1 February 1666, it became the *London Gazette*.[445]

Gerard [Garrets, Gerrarde]**, lady** – there were two in this period. 1) Jane de Civelle (d.1671), baroness Gerard, was the daughter of Pierre de Civelle, who was an equerry in the household of Henrietta Maria. She told Catherine that Barbara Villiers was the king's mistress and therefore she lost her post within Catherine's household as a lady in waiting. Pepys noted that she was snubbed by Charles.[446] She married Charles Gerard, 1st earl of Macclesfield, on 1 December 1656, and they had two sons and three daughters.[447] 2) Lady Jane Gerard, lady of the queen's bedchamber, from 1669 to 1672, with a possible death date of 1703.[448]

man –

Gerard, lord – Charles Gerard, first earl of Macclesfield (*c.*1618–94), was the eldest son of Sir Charles Gerard of Halsall and Penelope Fitton. He was a royalist supporter during the Civil War, and linked his fortunes to those of Prince Rupert, so spending the 1650s in exile. He commanded the Lifeguard until 1668 when he surrendered the role to the duke of Monmouth. He was made earl of Macclesfield in 1679.[449]

Gibbs [Gibs], **Mr** – lady Northumberland's gardener.

gifts – the queen received and gave gifts on a regular basis.

443 Evelyn, *Diary*, 563, 713.

444 Pepys, *Diary*, 4, 215; 4, 203.

445 https://www.thegazette.co.uk/history/timeline [accessed 16/1/23].

446 Pepys, *Diary*, 4, 68.

447 Ronald Hutton, 'Gerard, Charles, first earl of Macclesfield (c.1618–1694), royalist army officer', *ODNB*, 9 December 2021, https://doi-org.soton.idm.oclc.org/10.1093/ref:odnb/10550 [accessed 19/2/22].

448 Sainty, Wassmann and Bucholz, *Household officers*, 30.

449 Ronald Hutton, 'Gerard, Charles, first earl of Macclesfield (c.1618–1694), royalist army officer', *ODNB*, 9 December 2021, https://doi-org.soton.idm.oclc.org/10.1093/ref:odnb/10550 [accessed 19/2/22].

New Year's gifts – Pepys made several references to New Year's gifts in his diary, including on 2 January 1668, when he 'took my wife and her girl to the New Exchange, and there my wife bought herself a lace for a handkercher, which I do give her, of about 3*l*, for a <new> year's gift'.[450] On 30 December 1663, Pepys noted that Christopher Pett gave the earl of Sandwich 'a Modell, and endeed it is a pretty one, for a New Year's gift'.[451]

arrears of New Year's gifts –

presents – another term for a gift.

Gloud, Monsieur – for his bill.

Goldsborow [Goldsbrough], **Mr** – George Goldsborow, groom of the queen's Great Chamber, from 1671 to 1678.[452]

Gonzone, Monsieur – for his bill.

Goodricke [Goodrich], **Sir Francis** – Sir Francis (d.1673) was son of Sir Henry Goodricke and his wife Jane, and he married Hester Warburton.[453]

man –

Gordon, John – the queen's footman.

Gourlaw, Thomas – things for the dogs.

Grafton [Grafans], **lady** – Isabella Bennet (1667–1723), duchess of Grafton, was the daughter of Henry, earl of Arlington, and Isabella van Nassau-Beverweert. In 1672, she married Henry Fitzroy (1663–90), 1st duke of Grafton, and the son of Charles II and Barbara, countess of Castlemaine.[454] At the time of her marriage, John Evelyn described her as the 'sweetest, hopefullest, most beautifull child, & most vertuous too', who 'was Sacrific'd to a boy that had been rudely bred … [she] will in a few yeares be such a paragon, as were fit to make the Wife of the greatest Prince in Europe'.[455] Fitzroy died at the siege of Cork in 1690. Eight years later she remarried Sir Thomas Hanmer, 4th baronet of Hanmer.[456]

coachman –

Gramont [de Gramontts], **countess de** – Elizabeth Hamilton (1641–1708) was born in Ireland. She was the daughter of George Hamilton and Mary

450 Pepys, *Diary*, 9, 6.

451 Pepys, *Diary*, 4, 437.

452 Sainty, Wassmann and Bucholz, *Household officers*, 32.

453 https://www.geni.com/people/Sir-Francis-Goodricke/6000000005598958612 [accessed 30/1/22].

454 J. D. Davies, 'Fitzroy [formerly Palmer], Henry, first duke of Grafton (1663–1690), naval officer', *ODNB*, 3 January 2008, https://doi-org/10.1093/ref:odnb/9636 [accessed 16/2/22]; MacLeod, *Painted Ladies*, 240.

455 Evelyn, *Diary*, 674.

456 D. W. Hayton, 'Hanmer, Sir Thomas, fourth baronet (1677–1746), speaker of the House of Commons', *ODNB*, 26 May 2005, https://doi-org/10.1093/ref:odnb/12205 [accessed 27/1/22].

Butler, and she was a Catholic. In 1651, she went into exile in France with her father and later she joined the court of Henrietta Maria. By 1661, she was at court in Whitehall and in 1663 she met Philbert, chevalier de Gramont, and they married in 1663 or 1664. She was painted by Lely as one of the Windsor Beauties and in 1667 she went to France with her husband and was made a lady in waiting to Maria Theresa of Spain, Louis XIV's queen.[457]

Gregory, Mrs – a lame woman.

Greenfield, Mr – for sending grapes.

man –

Greeting, Thomas – the duke of Cambridge's violin.

Griffith, Mr – for a screen.

Grill, Mr – going to Newmarket.

Groome, Thorpe – the queen's shoemaker.

Guidat, Mrs – for lace. Possibly one of Agatha, Anne, Catherine, Deborah, Elizabeth and Eve Guidott, all of whom were listed as servants of the queen in November 1674, along with Baltazar, who was a page of the chamber.[458]

guides – a necessary aspect of the queen's travel arrangements. The alternative was getting lost, as Pepys experienced on 16 June 1668 when he noted 'so out and lost our way which made me vexed'.[459]

from Sir John Hubbard's –

from Richmond to Windsor –

to Euston – Euston Hall, Suffolk.

to Gravesend –

to Newmarket –

to Sir Robert Paston's –

to Windsor –

Guildford [Gillford]**, lady** – Elizabeth Boyle, countess Guildford (d.1667), was the daughter of Sir William Feilding and Susan Villiers. In 1639, she married Lewis, 1st viscount Boyle of Kinalmeaky, but she was widowed in 1642. At the Restoration, Charles II made her countess Guildford. She was a Royalist, a Catholic and was in exile with Henrietta Maria. She was lady of the bedchamber and groom of the stool to Henrietta Maria.[460]

man

gum [gome] – possibly a reference to gum sandarac, a resin gathered from a

457 Edward Corp, 'Hamilton, Elizabeth, Countess de Gramont [*called* La Belle Hamilton] (1641–1708), courtier', *ODNB*, 23 September 2004, https://doi.org/10.1093/ref:odnb/12061 [accessed 15/4/22]; MacLeod, *Painted Ladies*, 242.

458 Sainty, Wassmann and Bucholz, *Household officers*, 33.

459 Pepys, *Diary*, 7, 121.

460 No ODNB entry. http://www.thepeerage.com/p14765.htm [accessed 3/9/22].

tree from north Africa (*tetraclinis articulata*). The resin was ground into a powder and placed in a small bag of fine cloth and rubbed over the surface of a sheet of paper or sprinkled over the paper before writing.[461]

gunners [guiners] – for firing salutes for court events.

Gwyn, Mr Richard – litter/chairman.

Hailes, Mr – box keeper.

hair dressing – women wore their hair in a range of styles: 1660–70 – the front hair was taken back over the forehead, the hair above the ears arranged in tight corkscrew curls and held in place with wire and the hair at the back pulled into a bun; 1670–80 – the curls were not wired out but hung down more naturally on either side of the face and possibly with a few small curls on the forehead or tight curls over the head with the hair at the back hanging in ringlets.[462] Women could vary their style according to the time of day and circumstances. According to Pepys, during the 1660s, Princess Henrietta Maria had her hair 'frized short up to her ears', Catherine wore her hair dressed 'à la negligence', while Elizabeth Knepp's hair was 'only tied up in a knot behind'.[463]

combs – often made from bone or ivory, seventeenth century combs, like those from earlier periods had teeth on both long sides of different widths. One side was used to comb head and facial hair and the other to remove lice and fleas. Combs could be very ornate, such as a pair of late seventeenth century tortoiseshell combs made by Paul Bennett (?) in Port Royal, Jamaica, and sent to Lady Arlington in 1682 as a gift along with a quantity of sugar and vanilla.[464]

crine – a term for hair, for example, William Averell, in his *Life & Death of Charles and Iulia*, described 'Her curled crine dyd farre surpasse, the glorious glistering gold'.[465]

curling irons – these were essential for creating the fashionable hairstyles

[461] https://www.patricialovett.com/sand-sanders-and-writing [accessed 1/5/22].

[462] Willett Cunnington and Cunnington, *Handbook*, 181–84.

[463] Pepys, *Diary*, 1, 299; 4, 229–30; 8, 388–89.

[464] Lot 37, *The Collector: Objects to Clocks*, Chiswick Auctions, 30/3/21 https://www.chiswickauctions.co.uk/auction/lot/37-tw0-rare-and-important-late-17th-century-jamaican-colonial-engraved-tortoiseshell-wig-combs/?lot=144484&sd=1 [accessed 20/12/21].

[465] William Averell, *An excellent historie bothe pithy and pleasant, discoursing on the Life and Death of Charles and Iulia* (London: [By J. Charlewood?] for Edward White, dwelling at the little north doore of S. Paules Church, at the signe of the Gun, 1581), sig. Bvi, https://www.oed.com/view/Entry/44480?rskey=83HDxV&result=1#eid [accessed 28/3/22].

of the day. Alternatives to irons included rags or pipe clay curlers of the types used for wigs.

filleting [filliting], ***broad*** [Brad] – a ribbon or narrow band used to bind hair or worn round the head to keep a headdress in position, or to be purely decorative.[466]

periwigs – two possible meanings: 1) women wore false hair as Pepys noted on 24 March 1662 when La Belle Pierce came 'to see my wife and to bring her a pair of peruques of hair, as the fashion now is for ladies to wear'.[467] 2) a wig, especially a peruke, worn by men with curls on the side and the long hair at the back taken back at the nape of the neck.

pins – hair pins, also known as bodkins, could be decorative with a small jewel at one end and were stuck into the hair. They could also be used to secure coifs and caps. Examples of bodkins – thirteen in total – have been found at Jamestown, and were made from copper alloy, silver and bone. The silver example is decorated with a simple chased design and the initials E S. It may have belonged to Elizabeth Southey who arrived in Jamestown in 1623 on *The Southampton*.[468]

ribbon – some of Catherine's ribbon purchases could have been used to decorate her hair because the styles of *c.* 1660 to *c.* 1680 often included ribbon loops above the ears and ribbon bows or knots in the 1680s and 1690s.[469]

Haliard, Mr – the king's barber.

Hall, Mr – payment at Hampton Court.

Hallsall [Halsey], **Edward** – equerry to the queen from 1662 to 1678.[470]

Hamden [Hemden], **Mrs** – possibly Sarah Hampden, seamstress, but she was only present in the queen's household lists in 1680.[471]

Hamilton, lady – Mary Butler (*c.*1605–80), daughter of Thomas Butler, viscount Thurles and Elizabeth Poyntz. In 1629, she married Sir George Hamilton (1607–79), 1st baronet of Donalong, and they had at least twelve sons and five daughters, including Elizabeth Hamilton, 'la belle Hamilton'.[472]

man –

Hamilton, Mr – possibly one of the three Hamiltons at court: James (d.1679), George and Anthony (?1646–1720) Hamilton. They were three of the

466 https://www.oed.com/view/Entry/70228#eid4472739 [accessed 28/3/22].

467 Pepys, *Diary*, 2, 51.

468 https://historicjamestowne.org/collections/artifacts/bodkin [accessed 16/1/23].

469 Willett Cunnington and Cunnington, *Handbook*, 185.

470 Sainty, Wassmann and Bucholz, *Household officers*, 34.

471 Sainty, Wassmann and Bucholz, *Household officers*, 35.

472 https://www.geni.com/people/Mary-Hamilton/6000000006763270214 [accessed15/1/22].

six sons of Sir George Hamilton of Donalong, all of whom served either Charles or his brother James.[473] They were mentioned by Pepys – for instance he noted that a 'Mr Hamilton' was present at the queen's birthday ball in November 1666.[474]

man –

Hamond – delivering cherries.

Hampot, Captain – upon petition.

Harcourt [Harcoat]**, Mr** – Abraham Harcourt, the queen's cook, from 1663 to 1674.[475]

Harris [Haris], **Mr** – as per bill.

Harvey [Heruys], **lady** – Elizabeth, lady Harvey, wife of Sir Daniel Harvey. In association with Arlington and Buckingham, she sought to undermine Castlemaine in 1668 and 1669, ending with Castlemaine arranging for Lady Harvey to be ridiculed by Doll Common during a performance of Ben Jonson's *Cataline*.[476]

footman –

Harwood, Major – paying bills.

Hastright [hastrik], **Roger** – yeoman footman, *also see funerals.*

Hawley [Hally], **lord** – Francis Hawley, 1st baron Hawley (1608–84), was the second son of Sir Henry Hawley of Wiveliscombe and Elizabeth Poulett. He was a royalist and at the Restoration he was made captain of the Horse Guards from 1661 to 1676 and governor of Deal Castle from 1672 to 1674. He was also a gentleman of the bedchamber to James, duke of York, from 1669 to his death.[477]

Hayfield [Hayfeild], **Mrs** – for her bill.

Heames, Mr/Mrs (?) – for hoods and scarves.

Hegeson, Mrs – for her bill.

Henrietta Maria, *see queen dowager*

Herbert, Mr – watch and clock maker.

Heriot, Mr – under-housekeeper.

473 Éamonn Ó Ciardha, 'Hamilton, Sir George', *Dictionary of Irish Biography*, October 2009, https://www.dib.ie/biography/hamilton-sir-george-a3739 [accessed 15/1/22].

474 Pepys, *Diary*, 7, 372.

475 Sainty, Wassmann and Bucholz, *Household officers*, 35.

476 Sonia Wynne, 'Palmer [*née* Villiers], Barbara, countess of Castlemaine, and *suo jure* duchess of Cleveland (bap.1640–1709), royal mistress', *ODNB*, 24 October 2019, https://doi.org/10.1093/ref:odnb/28285 [accessed 16/2/22].; Pepys, *Diary*, 9, 415.

477 Eveline Cruickshanks, 'Hawley, Francis, 1st baron Hawley of Duncannnon [1] (1608–84), of Buckland Sororum, Som. and Scotland Yard, Westminster', https://www.historyofparliamentonline.org/volume/1660-1690/member/hawley-francis-1608-84 [accessed 5/2/22].

Hervey [Heruey], **Mr** – John Hervey, the queen's treasurer, and receiver general, from 1662 to 1679.[478]

High Sheriff – this was probably a reference to the High Sheriff of Wiltshire as the queen had dined at Marlborough and Lacock in June 1676. Sir Matthew Andrews of Mere held this office from 15 November 1675 to 10 November 1676.[479]

trumpets –

Highness [Heighnes], **her** – mentioned on 29 April 1670. This was possibly a reference to Anne Hyde (d.1671), even though she was usually referred to as the duchess of York.

coach hire –

coachmen –

Highness, his – mentioned in 1668, 1669 and 1670 and possibly a reference to James, duke of York.

bargemen –

trumpets –

watermen –

Hill, Mr – box keeper at the duke of York's theatre.

Hill, Mrs – for a coif.

Hill, Robert – assistant bargeman to the queen from 1662 to 1667 and her chief bargeman from 1667 to 1686.[480]

Hilliar, Mr – by his bill.

Hobart [Huberd], **Sir John** – John (1628–83), 3rd baronet, was the son of Miles Hobart of Intwood and Frances Peyton. He was an important figure in Norfolk, where he was a JP and a MP. His house was searched after the Rye House plot and weapons were seized. His family home was Blickling Hall.[481]

Holland – the United Provinces.

gifts –

Homerston [Humerston], **Edward** – trumpeter.[482]

Hoseley, Mr – litterman.

Hosey, Mr – to the sumptermen.

Houlder, Mrs – payment to her servant.

household documents – *also see accounts, letters.*

[478] Sainty, Wassmann and Bucholz, *Household officers*, 37.

[479] https://www.thegazette.co.uk/London/issue/1042/page/2 – *The London Gazette* 1042 (15 November 1675), 2 [accessed 28/4/22].

[480] Sainty, Wassmann and Bucholz, *Household officers*, 38.

[481] Stuart Handley, 'Hobart, Sir John, third baronet (bap.1628–d.1683), politician', *ODNB*, 23 September 2004, https://doi-org.soton.idm.oclc.org/10.1093/ref:odnb/66634 [accessed 22/10/22].

[482] Ashbee, *Records*, 11, 22, 49, 50, 177, 216, 223, 230, 233.

acquittance – a document recording that a debt has been paid.[483]

bills – a record of charges for goods delivered or services rendered, with the cost of each item listed separately.[484]

warrants – several meanings but those relevant here are 1) 'a writing issued by the sovereign, an officer of state, or an administrative body, authorizing those to whom it is addressed to perform some act' and 2) 'a writing which authorizes one person to pay or deliver, and another to receive, a sum of money'.[485]

household items – the types of good sold by hardware men.

andirons – sometimes called firedogs, andirons consist of a horizontal bar and a pair of feet. They were used to support logs in an open fireplace, so allowing good airflow. A sumptuous pair of silver firedogs dating from 1680–81 are decorated with the figures of Lucretia and Cleopatra, and the arms of Lord Edward Russell and his second wife Margaret.[486]

baskets – a container, usually with one or two handles, made of wicker, straw or willow that could be coiled, twined, or woven and used to collect and carry items.

bodkins [bodgins], ***steel*** – a blunt needle with a large eye. They could be used for sewing coarse or thick fabrics, and to insert cords and lacing into the eyelet holes of bodices and bodies, while versions without an eye were also used to decorate a woman's hair or secure her cap or coif (see below).

brushes – either for sweeping floors or for brushing clothing and furnishings to remove dust and dirt.

candlesticks – made from a range of materials, candlesticks were a very important part of domestic lighting.

crystal –

great –

keys – for use with lockable chests and boxes as well as door locks ranging from the front door of a property or individual rooms.

needles – finer than a bodkin, see above, needles have an eye at one end and a point at the other and could be used for embroidery and plain sewing.

mouse traps – these were very important for keeping the mouse population

483 https://www.oed.com/view/Entry/1754?redirectedFrom=aquitance#eid [accessed 23/3/22].

484 https://www.oed.com/view/Entry/18987 [accessed 23/3/22].

485 https://www.oed.com/view/Entry/225837?rskey=TDVicD&result=1#eid [accessed 23/3/22].

486 This pair of firedogs were bought for the National Museum of Wales (Amgueddfa Cymru) in 2016. https://www.nhmf.org.uk/news/pair-charles-ii-silver-andirons-saved-nation [accessed 12/12/21].

under control and on 19 January 1661 Pepys 'bought two mousetrapps of Tho. Pepys the Turner'.[487]

rat traps [Ratt Trape] – these might have been used by the queen's rat killer. In 1694, the queen's rat killer at Somerset House received wages of £5 per year.[488]

shovels – a tool with a broad blade and upturned sides and in a domestic context could be used when removing ash from a fireplace or to add coal to a fire.

sockets – 'The part of a candlestick or chandelier in which the candle is placed'.[489]

sponges [spunges] – natural sponges are the dried remains of simple aquatic animals of the *Porifera* phylum and historically they had been used in a variety of ways, including washing the body, applying cosmetics and as a simple contraceptive.

sugar trenchers – a flat circular, oval or other shaped dish or plate for serving sugar. It was one of a range of sugar utensils. In 1664, Pepys bought a silver sugar box along with spoons and forks costing £22 18s.[490]

tongs – fire implement for gripping and moving logs or coals. On 7 September 1663, after attending a play, Pepys 'hied home, buying several things at the Ironmongers: dogs, tongs, and Shovells for my wife's closet and the rest of my house'.[491]

trunks – a chest or box, often with a domed lid, lined with paper and covered with leather and used for storing and transporting personal possessions.[492] Trunks and chests could also be very decorative as was the case with the lacquer chests that Pepys saw in the duke of York's closet: 'two very fine chests covered with gold and Indian varnish given him by the East India Company of Holland'.[493]

household textiles – also see *textiles*; most of the queen's domestic textiles of this type were supplied by the Great Wardrobe.

blankets –

sheets –

487 Pepys, *Diary*, 2, 19.

488 Bucholz, Sainty and Wassmann, *Household of Queen*, 32.

489 https://www.oed.com/view/Entry/183813?rskey=JBavI0&result=1#eid [accessed 16/1/22].

490 Pepys, *Diary*, 5, 358.

491 Pepys, *Diary*, 4, 301.

492 https://www.oed.com/view/Entry/206968?rskey=VZd9ds&result=1#eid [accessed 28/4/22].

493 Pepys, *Diary*, 2, 79.

Howard, Father – Augustine (?), dean of the queen's chapel, from 1665 to 1675.[494]

Howard, Sir Philip – Philip (*c.*1631–86) was the third son of Sir William Howard and Elizabeth Newton. He was the captain of the Lifeguards from 1660 until his death and governor of Jamaica from 1685 to 1686.[495] Pepys noted that Sir Philip kept an actress, Betty Hall, as his mistress.[496]

coachman –

Howard, Sir Robert – Sir Robert Howard (1626–98), was a playwright and a politician. He was the son of Thomas Howard, 1st earl of Berkshire and Elizabeth Cecil, daughter of William Cecil, 2nd earl of Exeter.[497] He married three times, most notable being his unhappy second marriage to Lady Honoria O'Brien. He was the model for Sir Positive At-all in Shadwell's 1668 play *The Sullen Lovers*.[498] In 1675, he was appointed as deputy lieutenant of Wiltshire and given the office of keeper of the royal game.

gardener –

Howard, Lord – James Howard, 3rd earl of Suffolk (1607–88), was the son of Theophilus Howard, 2nd earl of Suffolk, and Lady Elizabeth Howard.[499]

Hughes, Henry – lost his horse.

Hutton [Huton], **Mr** – for chains and a collar for the pet monkey.

Ingram, lady – Frances, daughter of Thomas Belasyse, 1st viscount Fauconberg, and wife of Sir Thomas Ingram (1614–72). He was a gentleman of the king's privy chamber from 1660 to 1664, and chancellor of the duchy of Lancaster and a privy councillor from 1664.[500]

man –

inns [ind] – there was a hierarchy of places to eat and drink in London and

494 Sainty, Wassmann and Bucholz, *Household officers*, 39.

495 M. W. Helms/Eveline Cruickshanks, 'Howard, Philip (c.1631–86), of Leicester Fields, Westminster and Sissinghurst, Kent', https://www.historyofparliamentonline.org/volume/1660-1690/member/howard-philip-1631-86 [accessed 17/1/22].

496 Pepys, *Diary*, 8, 395.

497 J. P. Vander Motten, 'Howard, Sir Robert (1626–1698), playwright and politician', *ODNB*, 19 May 2011, https://doi-org.soton.idm.oclc.org/10.1093/ref:odnb/13935 [accessed 20/12/21].

498 Wilson, *Court Satires*, 129.

499 Richard Minta Dunn, 'Howard, James, third earl of Suffolk (1619–1689), nobleman', *ODNB*, 23 September 2004, https://doi-org.soton.idm.oclc.org/10.1093/ref:odnb/13919 [accessed 26/4/22].

500 P. A. Bolton/Paula Watson, 'Ingram, Sir Thomas (1614–72), of Sheriff Hutton, Yorks. and Isleworth, Mdx.', https://www.historyofparliamentonline.org/volume/1660-1690/member/ingram-sir-thomas-1614-72 [accessed 10/12/21].

elsewhere: inns, taverns and eating houses. Inns, such as the Sun in Threadneedle Street or the Mitre in Fenchurch Street, were the largest and most expensive.[501]

Irish – probably a reference to the sizeable Catholic Irish population in London.

Irish children –

Irish footmen –

Jermyn [Germin, Jermin]**, Mr** – possibly Henry Jermyn (bap.1636–d.1708), third Baron Jermyn and Jacobite earl of Dover, was the second son of Thomas Jermyn and Rebecca Rodway.[502] As a catholic, he spent time at Henrietta Maria's court in the 1650s and later joined the household of the duke of York, serving as his master of the horse. Henry had a reputation as a great lover and Castlemaine was thought to be in love with him in 1667. He was made baron Dover in 1685.

jewellery – jewellery was popular with men and women at the Restoration court and in 1666 Pepys took great interest in the diamonds and pearls on display at the queen's birthday ball.[503] Gemstones were much admired, as is made clear in the *Mundus Muliebris* (1690) with fashionable women wanting:

The Turquoise, Ruby, emerald Rings,
For fingers, and such pretty things
As Diamond Pendants for the Ears,
Must needs be had, or two Pearl Pears,
Pearl Necklace, large and Oriental,
And Diamond and of Amber pale.[504]

bodkin – a long pin used to secure and decorate women's hair. Three jewelled examples were found in the Cheapside Hoard.[505] *See also under hair accessories.*

diamond watch – small timepieces were popular and two slightly earlier watches formed part of the Cheapside Hoard: the emerald-cased

501 Pepys, *Diary*, 10, 416–17.

502 John Miller, 'Jermyn, Henry, third Baron Jermyn and Jacobite earl of Dover (bap.1636–d.1708), courtier and army officer', *ODNB*, 3 January 2008, https://doi-org.soton.idm.oclc.org/10.1093/ref:odnb/14781 [accessed 13/11/21].

503 Pepys, *Diary*, 7, 371–72.

504 Evelyn, *Mundus Muliebris*, 4; https://quod.lib.umich.edu/e/eebo/A38815.0001.001/1:3?rgn=div1;submit=Go;subview=detail;type=simple;view=fulltext;q1=ruby [accessed 1/5/22].

505 Forsyth, *Cheapside Hoard*, 61–62, 156.

watch and the Ferlite watch, made by Gaultier Ferlite in Geneva, *c.*1610–20.[506]

pearls – pearl necklaces were very desirable, as Pepys noted in April 1666 when he was 'asking in two or three places the worth of pearl – I being now come to the time that I have long ago promised my wife a necklace'.[507]

rings – rings were popular in Stuart England. Some were traditionally associated with love, marriage and ongoing gifts to a spouse and, in August 1665, Pepys gave Elizabeth a diamond ring.[508] Rings could also serve as souvenirs of the royal marriage. In July 1662 Pepys dined with friends who discussed 'Portugall rings' adding that 'Captain Ferrers offered five or six to sell; and I seeming to like a ring made of Coconutt, with a stone done in it, he did offer and would give it me'.[509]

Johns, Mr – supplying essence, as per bill.

Johnston [Jonson], **– William/Will** – porter to the backstairs from 1665 to 1705.[510]

Jordan, Mrs – for a bill.

Kerr [Ker], **Sir Edward –** Edward (d.1680) was appointed as an equerry to the queen in 1662 and remained in office until his death.[511]

Killigrew, mistress – Charlotte, daughter of Johan van Hesse, in Holland, was keeper of the queen's sweet coffers. She was described in *Signior Dildo* as 'Tom Killigrew's wife, North Holland's fine flower'.[512] She was the second wife of Thomas Killigrew (d.1683), who was a page of honour to Charles II. They are named on the white marble monument in the north aisle of the nave of Westminster Abbey to their son, Robert (bap.1660–1707).[513]

Killigrew, Sir William – William (1606–95) was the son of Sir Robert Killigrew and Mary Woodhouse. He was a dramatist and courtier and he married Mary Hill. He was the queen's vice-chamberlain until 27 July 1682 and between 1664 and 1679 he was MP for Richmond, Yorkshire.[514]

506 Forsyth, *Cheapside Hoard*, 136–37, 212–13, 215.

507 Pepys, *Diary*, 7, 108.

508 Pepys, *Diary*, 6, 190.

509 Pepys, *Diary*, 3, 139.

510 Sainty, Wassmann and Bucholz, *Household officers*, 42.

511 Sainty, Wassmann and Bucholz, *Household officers*, 43.

512 Wilson, *Court Satire*, 17.

513 Sainty, Wassmann and Bucholz, *Household officers*, 44; https://www.westminster-abbey.org/abbey-commemorations/commemorations/killigrew-family [accessed 16/1/23].

514 J. P. Vander Motten, 'Killigrew, Sir William (bap.1606–1695), courtier and

King, the – Charles II (1630–85), king of England, Scotland and Ireland, and eldest surviving son of Charles I and Henrietta Maria.[515] After the Civil War he went into exile but was restored to the throne in 1660. He married Catherine in 1662. While he had fourteen children with his mistresses, their marriage was childless. He died in February 1685 and was succeeded by his brother James.

barber –

Mr Halliard

coachmen –

cook –

footmen –

music –

running horse grooms –

trumpets –

Kirkton, Mr – for the yeomen of the Guard.

Kytlys, Lady Frances – for a christening.

lace – a range of Baroque laces were available to someone of Catherine's status, including white, black and coloured laces, as well as lace made from metal thread.[516] While some English-made lace was available, most was imported from Italy, Flanders and France. It was very popular for decorating outer garments and linens and Pepys recorded many purchases in his diary, including on 12 June 1665 when he bought 'some gold lace for my sleeve hands at paternoster Row'.[517] It was especially important for weddings and in May 1674 the duchess of Cleveland spent £646 8s 6d on 'sev'ral parcells of gold and silver lace' purchased from William Gostling and partners for the wedding clothes of her daughter Lady Sussex and Lichfield.[518]

Colbertine, point Colbert – this was another name for *point de France*, a French needle lace with designs of flowers, leaves and scrolls.[519] It was modelled on *point de Venice* and made in France after Louis XIV issued a royal proclamation at the instigation of Colbert supporting the

playwright', *ODNB*, 3 January 2008, https://doi.org/10.1093/ref:odnb/15541 [accessed 30/4/22].

515 Paul Seaward, 'Charles II (1630–1685), king of England, Scotland and Ireland', *ODNB*, 19 May 2011, https://doi.org/10.1093/ref:odnb/5144 [accessed 2/5/22].

516 Santina Levey, *Lace: A History* (Leeds: Victoria and Albert Museum, with W. S. Maney and Sons, 1983), 31–39.

517 Pepys, *Diary*, 6, 125.

518 Akerman, *Secret Services*, 87.

519 Isabel Wingate, *Fairchild's Dictionary of Textiles* (New York: Fairchild Publications, 6th edition, 1979), 138, 465.

French lace industry on 5 August 1665.[520] Officially known as *Point de France*, Evelyn described it as 'A Lace resembling Net-work of the Fabrick of Mons'eur Colbert, Superintendent of the French Kings Manufactures'.[521]

Colbertine sleeves and ruffles –

point – short for *point de Venice*, a needlemade lace produced in a variety of weights with the heaviest being *gros point de Venise* (*punto Venezia a relievi*), a lighter more decorative version known as *rose point* (*punto rosaline*) and the most decorative and delicate *point de neige* (*punto in aria*).[522] In April 1665, Pepys described his wife dressed 'in her new light-coloured silk gown, which is, with her new point very noble'.[523] It was highly prized, as Evelyn noted:

Twice twelve day Smocks of Holland fine,
With Cambric Sleeves, rich Point to joyn,
(For she despises Colbertine).[524]

point to her majesties sleeves –

point de Venice – a very high-quality needle lace and so highly prized.[525]

ladder – in this context, this is likely to be a wooden ladder, which could have been used for a variety of purposes including in the garden to pick fruit or in the queen's apartments to access high shelves.

Lafauer, Peter – duke of York's trumpets.

Lamb/Lambe, Mr – Patrick was appointed as child of the queen's kitchen in 1672, a groom of the queen's kitchen in 1674, and as master cook in 1677. In 1683, he was appointed as master cook of the king's kitchen.[526]

man –

Lands, Mr – to the grooms of the stables.

Lane, Richard – yeoman of the queen's wagons.

Langrishe, Mr – for a muff.

Lapy, Mr – of the standing wardrobe.

Late Queen, *see Queen Mother*

520 Levey, *Lace*, 36.

521 Evelyn, *Mundus Muliebris*, 16: https://quod.lib.umich.edu/e/eebo/A38815.0001.001/1:5?rgn=div1;submit=Go;subview=detail;type=simple;view=fulltext;q1=Colbert [accessed 1/5/22].

522 Levey, *Lace*, 32.

523 Pepys, *Diary*, 6, 76.

524 Evelyn, *Mundus Muliebris*, 3: https://quod.lib.umich.edu/e/eebo/A38815.0001.001/1:3?rgn=div1;submit=Go;subview=detail;type=simple;view=fulltext;q1=point [accessed 1/5/22].

525 *Fairchild's Dictionary*, 468.

526 Sainty, Wassmann and Bucholz, *Household officers*, 45.

Lauderdale, duchess of – Elizabeth Maitland (1626–98), daughter of William Murray, 1st earl of Dysart, and Catherine Bruce, countess of Dysart. Between 1648 and 1669 she was married to Sir Lionel Tollemache and they had 11 children. After her marriage in 1672 to John Maitland she became the duchess of Lauderdale.[527]

chairmen –

Lauderdale [Lawtherdale], **1st duke of** – John Maitland (1616–82), 2nd earl of Lauderdale, was the eldest son of John Maitland, 2nd lord Maitland of Thirlestane, and Lady Isobel Seton. He married twice, first to Lady Anne Home (1612–71) and then in 1672 to Elizabeth (1626–98), countess of Dysart. During his career he held several offices and honours: he was a Knight of the Garter, a privy councillor, Lord High Commissioner, Secretary of State for Scotland and a member of the Cabal Ministry.[528]

Le Noire, Monsieur – furrier.

leather – the skin, often of cows, sheep or goats, prepared by tanning to preserve it. It was used for furnishings and for fashionable accessories such as gloves and shoes.

cut leather –

Legg [Leg], **colonel** – Colonel William Legg, was the son of Edward Henry Legge and Mary Legge Walsh. He fought in the Thirty Years War and was wounded at the battle of Worcester. After the Restoration he was made lieutenant general and treasurer of the Ordnance. He was rumoured to be Catholic, and he was noted as a friend of James, duke of York. His home was at Stoke Court, Stoke Poges, Buckinghamshire.[529]

man –

Leg, Mr – payment to his servant.

man –

Legard, mistress – received a New Year's gift in 1663.

Legate, the – met the queen in 1667.

Leicester, the earl of – either 1) Robert Sidney, 2nd earl of Leicester (1595–1677), who was the son of Robert Sidney, 1st earl of Leicester, and his wife, Barbara Gamage. In 1615, he married Lady Dorothy Percy in secret. He spent much of his time at Penshurst from 1644 until his death.[530] Or

527 Rosalind Marshall, 'Murray [*married names* Tollemache, Maitland], Elizabeth, duchess of Lauderdale, and *suo jure* countess of Dysart (bap.1626–1698), noblewoman', *ODNB*, 23 September 2004, https://doi.org/10.1093/ref:odnb/19601 [accessed 3/4/22].

528 Ronald Hutton, 'Maitland, John, duke of Lauderdale (1616–1682), politician', *ODNB*, 25 May 2006, https://doi.org/10.1093/ref:odnb/17827 [accessed 3/4/22].

529 https://www.geni.com/people/Colonel-William-Legge-MP/6000000001443718220 [accessed 30/3/22].

530 Ian Atherton, 'Sidney, Robert, second earl of Leicester (1595–1677), diplomat

2) Philip Sidney, 3rd earl of Leicester (1619–98), eldest son of Robert Sidney, 2nd earl of Leicester, and Dorothy Percy[531] He used the title viscount Lisle until he succeeded to the title in 1677.

Leigh [Lee], **William/Will** – yeoman footman, 1667–88.[532]

Lenthall, Mrs – possibly the wife of Philip Lenthall, physician in ordinary, who was in office in 1673.[533]

letters – letters were very important for business and for creating and maintaining friendships and increasing numbers of female letter writers speak to growing levels of women's literacy.[534]

Lewis, Tertullian – drummer.

Lightfoot, Mr – possibly Robert Lightfoot, who was the queen's apothecary from 3 September 1680 to 1693, and may have travelled with the queen to Portugal.[535]

lighting – when the queen travelled in the evening and at night her way was lit with torches or lanterns. However, it was not always effective. When the king's coach overturned on 8 March 1669, Pepys noted that 'it was dark and the torches did not, they say, light the coach as they should do'.[536]

Lincoln [Linkhorn], **lady** – a*lso see Lady Clinton*. Probably a reference to Elizabeth Gorges (d.1675), the second wife of the puritan, Theophilus Clinton, 4th earl of Lincoln (1599–1667), whose family estate was at Sempringham, Lincolnshire.[537]

cook –

linens, also see *accessories, clothing*

aprons – a garment, often of linen, worn to protect the wearer' clothes but they could also be worn as a fashionable accessory. On 19 May 1669, Pepys saw the queen dining 'in her white pinner and apern, like a woman with child'.[538]

---

and landowner', *ODNB*, 3 January 2008, https://doi-org.soton.idm.oclc.org/10.1093/ref:odnb/25525 [accessed 28/3/22].

531 C. H. Firth, revised by Sean Kelsey, 'Sidney, Philip, third earl of Leicester (1619–1698), parliamentarian army officer and politician', *ODNB*, 25 September 2014, https://doi-org.soton.idm.oclc.org/10.1093/ref:odnb/25523 [accessed 28/3/22].

532 Sainty, Wassmann and Bucholz, *Household officers*, 46.

533 Sainty, Wassmann and Bucholz, *Household officers*, 47.

534 See Rosemary O'Day, 'Tudor and Stuart women: their lives through their letters', in James Daybell (ed.), *Early Modern Women's Letter Writing, 1450–1700* (Basingstoke: Palgrave Macmillan, 2001), 127–42. For the materials and mechanics of letter writing and posting, see James Daybell, *The Material Letter in Early Modern England* (Basingstoke: Palgrave Macmillan, 2012).

535 Sainty, Wassmann and Bucholz, *Household officers*, 47.

536 Pepys, *Diary*, 9, 474.

537 Francis Hill, *Tudor and Stuart Lincoln* (Cambridge: Cambridge University Press, 1956), 115.

538 Pepys, *Diary*, 9, 557.

band strings – strings, made by loop manipulation, often with highly decorative tassels, which fastened ruffs, and standing and falling bands.[539]

bands – rectangular linen bands, which men and women wore, that could be plain or decorated, with cutwork, embroidery, or bobbin lace.[540] Pepys saw the young women of the court in July 1665 wearing 'laced bands just like men'.[541]

coifs – a close fitting linen cap.

cornets – part of a woman's headdress with lace lappets hanging down on either side of the face. In 1682, a copy of the *London Gazette* mentioned lost property including 'a Point Cornet for the Head' while Evelyn's *Mundus Muliebris* referred to it as having 'the upper pinner dangling about the cheeks like a hound's ears'.[542]

cuffs – a separate band of linen worn round the wrist. On 20 August 1667, Pepys complained that Elizabeth was 'mighty pressing for a new pair of cuffs'.[543]

half shirts – half shirts were worn by men and women and were an undershirt or vest. These shirts were ordered in large numbers, as indicated by Charles II's first bill for linens after the Restoration, which included 108 shirts and 54 half-shirts.[544]

handkerchiefs – a square of linen to wipe the nose or face. On 2 January 1668 Pepys bought Elizabeth 'a lace for a handkercher, which I do give her, of about 3l., for a <new> year's gift'.[545] According to Evelyn 'It was Rude, Vulgar and Uncourtly to call it Handkerchief'.[546] According to the *Mundus Muliebris*,

Of Pocket Mouchoirs Nose to drain
A dozen lac'd, a dozen plain.[547]

539 Janet Arnold with Jenny Tiramani and Santina Levey, *Patterns of Fashion 4: The cut and Construction of Linen Shirts, Smocks, Neckwear, Headwear, and Accessories for Men and Women, c.1540–1660* (London: Macmillan, 2008), 29 (fig. 20), 39 (fig. 36) and 42 (fig. 41).

540 Arnold, *Patterns of Fashion 4*, 11.

541 Pepys, *Diary*, 6, 172.

542 https://www.oed.com/view/Entry/41651 [accessed 23/3/22].

543 Pepys, *Diary*, 8, 392.

544 Patricia Wardle, 'Divers necessaries for his Majesty's use and service': Seamstresses to the Stuart Kings', *Costume* 31 (1997), 24.

545 Pepys, *Diary*, 9, 6.

546 Evelyn, *Mundus Muliebris*, 19: https://quod.lib.umich.edu/e/eebo/A38815.0001.001/1:5?rgn=div1;submit=Go;subview=detail;type=simple;view=fulltext;q1=handkerchief [accessed 1/5/22].

547 Evelyn, *Mundus Muliebris*, 3: https://quod.lib.umich.edu/e/eebo/A38815.0001.001/1:3?rgn=div1;submit=Go;subview=detail;type=simple;view=fulltext;q1=nose [accessed 1/5/22]. Willett Cunnington and Cunnington, *Handbook*, 191.

Moutton hankercher – uncertain meaning.

hoods – a covering for the head, also see *accessories*.

petticoats – also see *clothing*. A reference to linen petticoats worn as underwear. In 1662, Pepys admired the sight of Castlemaine's 'linen petticoats … laced with rich lace at the bottomes'.[548]

ruffles – a strip of linen, often edged with lace, and gathered to form a decorative frill and worn around the neck, wrist or down the front of a garment and according to Evelyn, 'By our Fore-fathers call'd Cuffs'.[549]

tape – a narrow woven strip, in this context, of linen, used to form strings to fasten garments, bind edges or used as a means of securing parcels and bundles.

thread [thred] – possibly linen thread for sewing and repairs or silk thread for embroidery.

Littlemore [Litlemor], **Mr** – of the queen's ewery.

lodgings – a single room or a suite given to members of the royal household. The right to accommodation was a key element of the remuneration of the queen's servants.

the bedchamber women [1663] –

the maids of honour [1663] –

whitening lodgings [1669] –

for Lady Eyvis Lodgins by Mr Slaughter [1674] –

the fathers Lodging at winsor in 1674 [1676] –

to Mr Mead for Lodgings [1677]

to doctor peirce for Lodging [1677] –

the womane that Lookes to the Lodgings at somersethouse [1677] –

for the maids of honoure and Mrs Ropers Lodgings [1678] –

the fathers Lodgings [1678] –

Lodging as per bill [1679] –

Lodging as per bill [1679] –

Lodgings as per bill [1680] –

Lodgings for your Majesties seruants at Newmarkitt [1680] –

John Teughs Lodging [1680] –

Lodging of your Majesties seruants at Newmarkitt [1680] –

the secretaris Clarke for his Lodging at Windsor [1680] –

Loft, Mr – who was tried for his life in 1676.

Long, Mr – at the tennis court.

Lorene, Margaret – for a petticoat.

548 Pepys, *Diary*, 3, 87.

549 Evelyn, *Mundus Muliebris*, 20: https://quod.lib.umich.edu/e/eebo/A38815.0001.001/1:5?rgn=div1;submit=Go;subview=detail;type=simple;view=fulltext;q1=cuffs [accessed 1/5/22].

Loring [Louring], **Mr** – the duchess of York's footman.

Lovelace [Loules, Lovles], **lady** – Martha Pye, the daughter of Sir Edmund Pye, 1st baronet of Bradenham, and Catherine Lucas. In 1662, she married John Lovelace, 3rd baron Lovelace (1641–93). They had four children – three daughters and a son who died young.[550] In the *Satire on Both Whigs and Tories* (1683) her husband was described as a 'sot'.[551]

Low, Mr – possibly William Low, groom of the Great Chamber, 1671–78.[552]

Low, Mrs – for her bill.

MacCarthie [Makerty, Makartan], **Mr** – possibly Charles MacCarthie, gentleman usher, quarter waiter, from 1667 to 1677.[553]

MacGinnis [Maginis], **Mr** – possibly Constantine MacGinnis, yeoman footman to the queen, from 1665 to 1674.[554]

Mackinney, Father Patrick – also known as Dom Patricio, he arrived in 1662, and was the queen's Portuguese almoner in 1665 and almoner in 1669. He had vacated his post by 1682.[555] He was listed as having rooms on the 1670 plan of Whitehall palace.[556]

Madame – Henrietta Anne (1644–70), the youngest daughter of Charles I and Henrietta Maria. She went to France in 1646 where she was brought up by her mother as a Catholic. She returned to England briefly after the Restoration but returned to France in 1661 to marry her cousin, Philip de France (1640–1701), younger brother of Louis XIV and the duke of Orleans.[557] As such she was known as the duchess of Orleans. She was called Minette by her brother Charles II who wrote to her regularly.[558] She was in England between 26 May and 1 June 1670 and took part in

550 Leonard Naylor/Geoffrey Jagger, 'Lovelace, Hon. John (c.1642–93), of Water Eaton, Oxon. and Hurley, Berks.', http://www.historyofparliamentonline.org/volume/1660-1690/member/lovelace-hon-john-1642-93 [accessed 5/3/22].

551 Wilson, *Court Satire*, 122.

552 Sainty, Wassmann and Bucholz, *Household officers*, 48.

553 Sainty, Wassmann and Bucholz, *Household officers*, 49.

554 Sainty, Wassmann and Bucholz, *Household officers*, 49.

555 Sainty, Wassmann and Bucholz, *Household officers*, 49.

556 Simon Thurley, *The Whitehall Palace Plan of 1670* (London: London Topographical Society, 1998), 50.

557 John Miller, 'Henriette Anne [formerly Henrietta], Princess, duchess of Orléans (1644–1670)', *ODNB*, 23 September 2004, https://doi.org/10.1093/ref:odnb/12946 [accessed 1/4/22].

558 For their letters, see Ruth Norrington (ed.), *My Dearest Minette: Letters Between Charles II and His Sister the Duchesse d'Orléans* (London: Peter Owens Publisher, 1996).

the negotiations for the Secret Treaty of Dover. She died shortly after her return to France.

chairmen –

footmen –

Malbury, Lady – uncertain. Not listed as a member of Catherine's household but possibly Judith Edwards (d. in or after 1670) second wife of Sir John Strangways (1584–1666). The family lands were at Chirk castle and Melbury Sampford in Dorset.[559]

Maldon, Lady – Lady Elizabeth Percy, daughter of Algernon Percy, 10th earl of Northumberland and Lady Anne Cecil. She married Arthur Capel (1631–83), viscount Maldon, 1st earl of Essex.[560]

page –

Maley, Richard – one of the queen's postilions.

Manchester, lady – Anne Yelverton (b. after 1630, d.1698), the daughter of Sir Christopher Yelverton, 1st baronet of Easton Maudit, and Anne Twisden. In 1655, she married Ralph Montagu, 3rd earl of Manchester (1634–83), and they had five sons and four daughters.[561] After her husband's death, Anne married Charles Montagu (1661–1715), 1st earl of Halifax.[562]

footmen –

man –

page –

Manchester, lord – Two men held this title. 1) Edward Montagu, 2nd earl of Manchester (1602–71), the son of Henry Montagu, 1st earl of Manchester, and Catherine Spencer. He went to Spain with Prince Charles in 1623, and he was Master of the horse to Henrietta Maria. He married five times: his fourth wife was Eleanor, countess dowager of Warwick (d.1666), and his last wife was Margaret, dowager countess Carlisle who he married on 31 July 1667.[563] He was elected as a member of the Royal Society.

559 David L. Smith, 'Strangways, Sir John (1584–1666), politician', *ODNB*, 3 January 2008, https://doi-org.soton.idm.oclc.org/10.1093/ref:odnb/39725 [accessed 22/10/22].

560 Richard Greaves, 'Capel, Arthur, first earl of Essex (bap. 1632–1683), politician and conspirator', *ODNB*, 27 May 2010, https://doi-org.soton.idm.oclc.org/10.1093/ref:odnb/4584 [accessed 17/7/22].

561 Bertha Porter, 'Montagu, Edward, third earl of Manchester (1602–1671)', *ODNB*, 3 January 2008, https://doi-org.soton.idm.oclc.org/10.1093/odnb/9780192683120.013.19009 [accessed 5/3/22].

562 Stuart Handley, 'Montagu, Charles, earl of Halifax (1661–1715), politician', *ODNB*, 22 September 2005, https://doi-org.soton.idm.oclc.org/10.1093/ref:odnb/19004 [accessed 5/3/22].

563 Ian J. Gentles, 'Montagu, Edward, second earl of Manchester (1602–1671), politician and parliamentarian army officer', *ODNB*, 3 January 2008, https://doi.org/10.1093/ref:odnb/19009 [accessed 5/3/22].

Or 2) Robert Montagu, 3rd earl of Manchester (1634–83), the only son of Edward Montagu, 2nd earl of Manchester, and his second wife Lady Anne Rich. In 1655, he married Anne Yelverton and they had five sons and four daughters. In 1666, he was a gentleman of the bedchamber to the king. In 1677, he became high steward of Cambridge University.[564] The timing of the entry suggests it was the first.

man –

Manuel [Mannell, Manwell], **father** – *see Periera, father.*

maps – Charles II had an interest in maps. In early November 1660 Evelyn visited the king's cabinet of curiosities where he saw 'a vast book of Mapps in a volume of neere 4 yards large', while on 2 September Evelyn saw an 'Aboundance of Mapps & Sea<Charts>' in the king's private library at Whitehall.[565]

map of London –

marble – polished white, coloured, or mottled recrystallized limestone used for decorative sculpture and fireplaces.

Mardan, lady – uncertain, possibly another spelling of Lady Mordaunt, see below.

man –

Marsh, Mr – possibly Alphonso Marsh, court musician, gentleman of the chapel, lutes and violins.[566]

man –

Marischal [Marshall], **lady** – Anne Douglas, countess Marischal, lady of the bedchamber, 1662–79.[567] She was the second wife of William Keith, 6th earl Marischal.

footman –

man –

Masters, Mr – Uncertain, possibly either surgeon or sergeant of the Bath.

Maudlin – supplying brushes.

Maugridge [Mawgridge], **William** – drummer. Not mentioned in Ashbee, unlike John Maugridge, drum major and Richard Maugridge, drummer and Robert Maugridge, drummer.[568]

Maugride [Mawgridge], **William** – yeoman footman from 1667 to 1695.[569]

[564] No ODNB entry of his own, see Ian J. Gentles, 'Montagu, Edward, second earl of Manchester (1602–1671), politician and parliamentarian army officer', *ODNB*, 3 January 2008, https://doi.org/10.1093/ref:odnb/19009 [accessed 5/3/22].

[565] Evelyn, *Diary*, 413, 691.

[566] Ashbee, *Records*, 310.

[567] Sainty, Wassmann and Bucholz, *Household officers*, 49.

[568] Multiple references in Ashbee, *Records*, including for John, 21, 30, 154, 230; Richard 11, 36, 51, 224 and Robert 66, 85, 96, 233.

[569] Sainty, Wassmann and Bucholz, *Household officers*, 51.

May, lord Algernon [Allgornon] – (d.1704), was the son of Sir Humphrey May, and in 1662 he married Dorothy Reynolds, the widow of James Calthorpe. He was equerry to Catherine of Braganza from 1662 to 1668 and he entertained her at his home in 1675.[570] In 1670, he was appointed as Keeper of the Records, a post he held until 1686. He was elected as the MP for New Windsor in 1689.

May, Mr [Mayes] – Baptist or Bab May (1628–97), was the sixth and youngest son of Sir Humphrey May and Judith Poley. In 1648, he was appointed as a page to the duke of York and between 1662 and 1665 he was a groom in the duke's bedchamber. Baptist was appointed as keeper of the king's privy purse in 1665, an office he held until Charles II's death. He was also a close friend of the king and a courtier.[571]

dairy maid –

man –

Maynard [Mamard], **lord** – Sir John Maynard (1604–90), was the son of Alexander Maynard and Honoria, daughter of Arthur Arscott of Tetcott, Devon.[572] In 1667, he defended Clarendon and from 1679 to 1681 he represented Plymouth as MP. He was convinced by Titus Oates' claims relating to the Popish plot and sought to prosecute the viscount Stafford.

man –

Mayor, lord, of London – the Mayors of London were elected annually on Michaelmas, 29 September, and they were in office by second week of November.

To the Lords maires man in gold [1633] – Sir Anthony Bateman (d.1687) was the son of Robert Bateman. He was a London merchant, a member of the worshipful company of Skinners, and he was elected as Lord Mayor in 1663.[573]

Lord Mayor presenting gift [June 1672] – this would have been the mayor elected in 1671, Sir George Waterman, skinner.

570 Leonard Naylor/Geoffrey Jagger, 'May, Sir Algernon (c. 1625–1704), of Old Windsor, Berks. and Ampton, Suff.', http://www.histparl.ac.uk/volume/1660-1690/member/may-sir-algernon-1625-1704 [5/3/22].

571 Andrew Barclay, 'May, Baptist [Bab] (bap.1628–d.1697), courtier', *ODNB*, 3 January 2008, https://doi-org.soton.idm.oclc.org/10.1093/ref:odnb/18418 [accessed 30/3/22].

572 Paul D. Halliday, 'Sir John Maynard (1604–1690), lawyer and politician', *ODNB*, 25 May 2006, https://doi-org.soton.idm.oclc.org/10.1093/ref:odnb/18439 [accessed 2/5/22].

573 Alfred P. Beaven, 'Notes on the aldermen, 1502–1700', in Alfred P. Beaven, The Aldermen of the City of London Temp. Henry III – 1912 (London: Corporation of the City of London, 1908), 168–95: British History Online http://www.british-history.ac.uk/no-series/london-aldermen/hen3-1912/pp168-195 [accessed 20/8/22].

Meade, Mr – possibly David Meade, a gentleman usher daily waiter, from 1662 to 1692 or George Meade, groom of the great chamber in extraordinary, in 1669.[574]

meals – the main meals were breakfast, dinner and supper.

collations – an informal, small, or light meal.

treats – surprise gifts or outings, an enjoyable event or activity.

meat – Gervase Markham divided meat into two groups: pale or white roasted meats, which included 'mutton, veal, lamb, kid, capon, pullet, pheasant, partridge, quail and all sorts of middle and small land or waterfowl and all small birds', while brown roasted meats included 'beef, venison, pork, swan, geese, pigs, crane, bustards, and any large fowl'.[575]

bucks – a buck is the term for male roe and fallow deer, which can weigh between 10 to 25 kg and 46 to 93 kg respectively.[576] On 2 July 1662 Evelyn and his brother 'hunted and killed a buck in the park'.[577]

stags [staig] – male red deer are called stags and weigh between 90 and 190 kg.[578]

venison – the meat of deer was highly prized. Charles II often gave a gift of venison to the Royal Society for their anniversary dinner, including on 30 November 1683, when 'the King sent us two does'.[579] Gervase Markham recommended roasting venison and seasoning the gravy with 'sugar, cinnamon, ginger and salt'.[580] Venison pasties were popular, as was stewed venison. Hannah Wolley suggested in *The Accomplisht Lady's Delight* (1675) cooking the meat with claret, a sprig of rosemary, six cloves, some breadcrumbs, sugar, and vinegar and when it was nearly done to add some grated nutmeg.[581]

medical attendants – the queen and her household were treated by several medical specialists. One of the best known, although he was not mentioned in the privy purse accounts, was Sir George Wakeman (d.1688), the son of Edward Wakeman and Mary Cotton. He was royal physician to Catherine of Braganza. He was also a Catholic. Consequently, he was implicated in the Popish Plot, indicted for high treason, tried, acquitted, and then left the country.[582]

[574] Sainty, Wassmann and Bucholz, *Household officers*, 51.

[575] Markham, *Well-Kept Kitchen*, 32.

[576] https://www.bds.org.uk/information-advice/about-deer/deer-species/red-deer [accessed 20/12/21].

[577] Evelyn, *Diary*, 440.

[578] https://bds.org.uk/information-advice/about-deer/deer-species/red-deer [accessed 20/8/22].

[579] Evelyn, *Diary*, 760.

[580] Markham, *Well-Kept Kitchen*, 38.

[581] Driver and Berriedale-Johnson, *Pepys at Table*, 56.

[582] Thomas Seccombe, revised Michael Bevan, 'Wakeman, Sir George, baronet

apothecary – several men held the office of the queen's apothecary: William Rosewell from 1661, Alexander Rosewell by 1669, John Gaunt in 1672, John Pomfret in 1676 and Robert Lightfoot in 1680. Their careers can be compared with that of John Chase, the royal apothecary.[583]

Bochar [Bosher, Booscher], ***Mr*** – Alexander Bochar, the queen's surgeon from 1662 to 1679.[584]

Bochar [Bocher], ***Mrs*** – possibly the wife of Alexander Bochar.

Chasmary man – uncertain meaning. Possibly a misspelling of chirurgery, for surgery.[585]

nurse – 'to nurse flecher'. Uncertain as to whether this refers to nurse Fletcher or to nurse an individual called Fletcher.

Pearse [Pierce], ***Dr*** – James Pearse, surgeon, and groom of the privy chamber to the queen.[586] However, he was not listed as one of her surgeons by Sainty.[587]

Percival [percivall], ***John*** – he was listed as a bone setter and paid for treating 'Craig the footman being hurte'.

surgeons – the queen's surgeons feature in the documents sporadically: they were Alexander Bochar in 1663, W. Jerman in November 1671, T. Green in March 1672, E. Langford in December 1672, G. Smith in June 1673, P. Savuigner in December 1679, and I. Aime in February 1682.[588]

tooth drawer – on 28 December 1663, Elizabeth Pepys went out to have a tooth removed 'she having it seems been in great pain all day; and at night came home with it drawn, and pretty well'.[589] Pepys did not record who she visited but potentially someone like Peter de la Roche 'operator for the teeth' to Charles II, who lived near Fleet Bridge.[590]

a womane gave your Majestie physique –

medicine, medical treatments – for Catherine and her pet dogs

balm for the dogs – a soothing liquid or cream applied to treat skin conditions such as mange, irritation caused by fleas and ticks, ringworm and food allergies.

(b.1627), physician', *ODNB*, 23 September 2004, https://doi-org.soton.idm.oclc.org/10.1093/ref:odnb/28422 [accessed 24/2/22].

583 Henry Connor, 'By royal appointment: the Chase family of apothecaries', *Journal of Medical Biography* 26.3 (2018), 148–50.

584 Sainty, Wassmann and Bucholz, *Household officers*, 7–8.

585 https://www.oed.com/view/Entry/31911#eid9523400 [accessed 24/3/22].

586 Pepys, *Diary*, 5, 188, n. 2.

587 Sainty, Wassmann and Bucholz, *Household officers*.

588 Bucholz, Sainty and Wassmann, *Household of Queen*, 26.

589 Pepys, *Diary*, 4, 435–36.

590 Pepys, *Diary*, 10, 356.

blood, blood-letting – bleeding, opening a vein, or the process of taking blood from a vein for health-giving reasons, for restoring balance to the body. Evelyn recorded being bled on multiple occasions in his diary.[591] The earl of Bedford paid for his servants to be bled regularly – for instance on 1 March 1675, 'Ann Johnson a vein opened' costing 2s 6d. The treatment was repeated on 5 April.[592]

bottle of oil for the dogs – fish and plant-based oils, along with essential oils, have been used to treat canine dry skin conditions.

leeches [leaches] – a segmented worm, either predatory or parasitic (*Hirudinea*), that sucks the blood of animals or humans and were used by early modern doctors to bleed people to restore balance between the four humours (blood, phlegm, black bile and yellow bile). On 7 September 1669 Evelyn noted 'I let bloud, purged, drew blisters, but Leeches did me most good'.[593]

physic – a term for medicine or medicinal drugs, such as the eye lotion supplied by John Chase, royal apothecary, in April 1669.[594] A few years earlier Samuel recorded that 'The Queen I hear, doth not yet hear of the death of her mother, she being in the course of physic, that they dare not tell her'.[595]

water – as in taking the waters, also see *beverages*.

men – several unidentified men feature in the accounts. For example,

a man who presented carp –

old man –

poor men –

a poore man with a petition –

messengers – messengers, royal and otherwise, delivered many letters, orders and warrants. Royal messengers could also be sent with orders for the arrest of individuals, as was the case with John Potts and Nicholas Copley, who were sent to implement the apprehension of John Beardwell and other musicians for 'taking on themselves to teach, practice and exercise music in companies'.[596] An alternative was offered by the post office, whose offices in Threadneedle Street were destroyed in the Great Fire.[597]

591 Evelyn, *Diary*, 243, 271, 278, 300, 304, 319, 326, 335, 354, 376, 389, 393, 409, 453, 506, 534, 630, 777.

592 Scott Thomson, *Life in a Noble Household*, 309.

593 Evelyn, *Diary*, 534.

594 Pepys, *Diary*, 9, 507.

595 Pepys, *Diary*, 7, 87.

596 TNA LC5/188, f. 116r; Ashbee, *Records*, 104.

597 Pepys, *Diary*, 7, 275.

Capell [Capelle, Caple], ***Mr*** – Matthew Capell, messenger of the chamber, from 1665 to 1686.[598]

Winwood Mr – a royal messenger.

Woodward, Mr – Edward Woodward, messenger of the chapter to the queen, noted in the accounts as in service in June 1680, and 1683 to 1687.[599]

Metlan, Mr – associated with the delivery a gift from the duchess of Castlemaine from France.

man –

Mompesson [Momper] – George Mompesson, groom of the queen's privy chamber, from 1672 to 1677.[600]

money – coinage.

Angels – an angel was a gold coin worth 6s 8d with St Michael on the front and the ship of state on the reverse. Angels were given as touch pieces to individuals who were touched by the monarch to cure them from the King's Evil. From the reign of Edward IV to that of Charles I, angels were legal tender. After the Restoration, Charles II had angels minted for when he touched individuals to cure them of scrofula.[601]

bags and charges – bags, probably made of canvas, were used to carry coins, while the charges relate to the handling of the money and the costs necessary for exchanging foreign currency into sterling.

exchange – Pepys noted the rate of exchange in 1666 when he recorded Mr Slingsby's view that 'the heightening or lowering of money is only a cheat, and doth good to some perticuler men'.[602]

gold – Pepys commented on the price of gold in January 1667 when he recorded that his goldsmith 'tells me gold holds its price still, and did desire me to let him have what old 20s pieces I have, and he would give me 3s -2d change for each'.[603]

gold, Genoa [genny gold] – gold coinage from Genoa, a port city on the Ligurian coast, which during this period included the gold genovino issued by Doge Antoniotto Adorno in 1672.[604]

gratuities – money given in reward for tasks performed.

old gold – possibly a reference to coins produced prior to Charles II's

598 Sainty, Wassmann and Bucholz, *Household officers*, 11.

599 Sainty, Wassmann and Bucholz, *Household officers*, 81.

600 Sainty, Wassmann and Bucholz, *Household officers*, 52.

601 For an example of a Charles II gold touchpiece c. 1660, see RCIN 443149, https://www.rct.uk/collection/443149/charles-ii-touchpiece [accessed 4/9/22].

602 Pepys, *Diary*, 7, 304.

603 Pepys, *Diary*, 8, 35.

604 There is an example of this coin in Museo Bottacin e Museo Civico, Padua, Italy.

accession, including coins from his father's reign, or to coins that were excessively rubbed or damaged.

running money – money given in reward to footmen.

Monmouth, duchess of – Anne Scott (1651–1732), born in Dundee, was the daughter of Francis Scott, 2nd earl of Buccleuch, and Margaret Leslie. In 1661, she became an heiress and on her marriage in 1663 to James Scott (also known as Crofts and Fitzroy) (1649–85), 1st duke of Monmouth, and illegitimate son of Charles II and Lucy Walter, she became duchess of Monmouth and Buccleuch. In 1685, the duke of Monmouth was executed for treason and in 1688 Anne married Charles Cornwallis (1655–98), 3rd baron Cornwallis.[605]

coachman –

postilion –

Montagu, lady [Montagus, Monteagus] – Jemima (1602–75), was the daughter of John Crew, 1st baron Crew and Jemima Waldegrave. She was countess of Sandwich and wife of Sir Edward Montagu, 1st earl of Sandwich.[606] Pepys described her as 'so good and discreet a woman I know not in the world'.[607]

man –

Montagu [Mongroos (?), Montagus, Monteagus]**, lord** – Edward Montagu (1625–72), 1st earl of Sandwich, was the son of Sir Sidney Montagu and Paulina Pepys. He fought for Parliament in the first phase of the war of Three Kingdoms and during the Anglo-Spanish war he, along with Robert Blake, held the office of General at Sea. He was the English ambassador extra-ordinary to Portugal 1661–62 and accompanied Catherine from Portugal.[608] She gave him a gift of gold for bringing her to England.[609]

keeper –

man –

Montagu [Montagus, Monteagus]**, lord** – Edward Montagu (1648–88),

[605] Eirwen E. C. Nicholson, 'Scott, Anna [Anne] duchess of Monmouth and suo jure duchess of Buccleuch (1651–1732), noblewoman', *ODNB*, 23 September 2004, https://doi.org/10.1093/ref:odnb/67531 [accessed 15/4/22]; MacLeod, *Painted Ladies*, 244–45.

[606] Brief mention in J. M. Rigg, revised by Sean Kelsey, 'Crew, John, first Baron Crew (1597/8–1679), politician', *ODNB*, 3 January 2008, https://doi.org/10.1093/ref:odnb/6682 [accessed 2/5/22].

[607] Pepys, *Diary*, 5, 257. Also see 2, 49, 6, 119, 8, 469.

[608] J. D. Davies, 'Montagu [Mountagu], Edward, first earl of Sandwich (1625–1672), army and navy officer and diplomat', *ODNB*, 3 January 2008, https://doi.org/10.1093/ref:odnb/19010 [accessed 2/5/22].

[609] Pepys, *Diary*, 3, 90. Pepys considered it to be 'no honourable present'.

viscount Hinchingbrooke, eldest son of Edward Montagu, 1st earl of Sandwich and Jemima Crew.[610] He married Lady Anne Boyle, daughter of Richard Boyle, 2nd earl of Cork. He was MP for Dover in 1670 and succeeded to his father's title in 1672.

Montagu [Montagus, Monteagus]**, Mr** – Ralph Montagu (1638–1709) was the son of Edward Montagu, 2nd baron Montagu of Boughton.[611] He served in the household of Anne, duchess of York as an equerry from 1662 to 1665 and then as master of the horse to Catherine of Braganza from 1665 to 1678.[612] He was sent as ambassador to France 1669 to 1672 and 1676 to 1678. He married for the first time in 1673 to Lady Elizabeth Wriothesley (d.1690).

for ye Coatchmen and Gromes and others –

Mordaunt, lady – Elizabeth Mordaunt, lady Mordaunt (1645–87), was the daughter of Sir Nicholas Johnson, of St Gregory's, London. She married Sir Charles Mordaunt, 4th baronet Mordaunt (d.1665), in 1663 and, after his death, she married Francis Godolphin of Wiltshire in 1669. She and her sister were cousins of Samuel Pepys and friends of John Evelyn and Thomas Hill.[613]

man –

page –

Mordneat, Mrs – for her bill.

Morgan, Mr – William Morgan (1675 fl.–d.1690) was publisher of maps and the Royal Cartographer and he was the step-grandson of John Ogilby.[614] He was known for his map of London, which went on sale on 25 January 1677 and was made up of four rows of five sheets.[615]

morris dancers [morisdancours] – references in the late fifteenth and early sixteenth centuries suggest morris dancing took place in a court context, moving into urban churches in the mid-sixteenth century and rural

610 Basil Duke Henning, 'Montagu, Edward, Visct. Hinchingbrooke (1648–88)', http://www.historyofparliamentonline.org/volume/1660-1690/member/montagu-edward-1648-88 [accessed 25/6/23].

611 E. R. Edwards, 'Montagu, Hon. Ralph (1638–1709) of Montagu House, Bloomsbury, Mdx. and Boughton, Northants.', https://www.historyofparliamentonline.org/volume/1660-1690/member/montagu-ralph-1638-1709 [accessed 12/6/23].

612 Sainty, Wassmann and Bucholz, *Household officers*, 53.

613 Pepys, *Diary*, 10, 249.

614 For Morgan, see Sarah Tyacke, *London Map Sellers 1660–1720* (London: Map Collector Publications, Ltd, 1978), 124. For Ogilby, see Charles W. J. Withers, 'Ogilby, John (1600–1676), publisher and geographer', *ODNB*, 4 October 2007, https://doi.org/10.1093/ref:odnb/20583 [accessed 3/3/22].

615 Ogilby and Morgan's Large Scale Map of the City As Rebuilt By 1676 ([s.l.], 1676), British History Online http://www.british-history.ac.uk/no-series/london-map-ogilby-morgan/1676/map [accessed 27/12/21].

society in the seventeenth century.[616] These dancers often performed at Whitsun, a tradition that was ended by Cromwell, and reinstated by Charles II. On May Day 1663, Pepys noted that 'in my way in Leadenhall street there was morris dancing, which I have not seen a great while'.[617]

Mors [More], **Mrs Anne** – for a bill.

Murray [Muray], **Mr** – box keeper.

Murray [Murry], **Mr** – the king's coachman.

music/musicians – the accounts demonstrate the importance of music for entertainment, as part of religious services and as part of court ceremonial.[618] Musicians were drawn from across Europe to play at Charles II's court and, on 20 February 1667, Pepys recorded that 'the King's viallin, Bannister, is mad that the King hath a Frenchman come to be chief of some part of the King's music'.[619] Pepys was a great lover of music and played regularly, yet on occasion he worried that he was 'too much taken by musique'.[620]

bagpipe boy – a composite reedpipe, with a chanter, one or more drones and a bag to supply the air, which is compressed by the player's arm.[621] In 1661, while at the Exchange for dinner, Pepys 'had a fellow play well on the bagpipes'.[622] However, when Pepys heard Lord Brounker's piper play, while he admired the instrument 'with pipes of ebony tipped with silver', he added that 'at the best, it is mighty barbaric music'.[623]

country music – music to accompany country dance, which was popular in seventeenth century England and spread to Europe.[624] On New Year's Eve 1662, Pepys observed that the court engaged in country

616 See John Forrest, *The History of Morris Dancing, 1458–1700* (Cambridge: James Clarke, 1999).

617 Pepys, *Diary*, 4, 120.

618 For Catherine's engagement with devotional music, see Peter Leech, 'Musicians in the Catholic Chapel of Catherine of Braganza, 1662–92', *Early Music* 29.4 (2001), 571–87.

619 Pepys, *Diary*, 8, 73. Louis Grabu replaced John Bannister as director of the 24 violins on 4 August 1667.

620 Pepys, *Diary*, 4, 48.

621 William A. Cocks, revised by Anthony C. Baines and Roderick D. Cannon, 'Bagpipe (Fr. *cornemuse*; Ger. *Dudelsack*, *Sackpfeife*; It. *cornamusa*, *piva*, *zampogna*; Port. *gaita*; Sp. *cornamusa*, *gaita*, *zampoña*)', Grove Music online, 2001, https://doi-org.soton.idm.oclc.org/10.1093/gmo/9781561592630.article.01773 [accessed 15/3/22].

622 Pepys, *Diary*, 2, 101.

623 Pepys, *Diary*, 9, 131.

624 'Country dance', Grove Music online, 2001, https://doi-org.soton.idm.oclc.org/10.1093/gmo/9781561592630.article.06695 [accessed 15/3/22].

dancing with 'the King leading the first which he called for; which was – says he, *Cuckolds all a-row*'.[625]

harpers – players of the harp, a term which encompasses a variety of instruments of different forms but all of which can be described as 'chordophones in which … the plane of the strings is perpendicular to the soundboard'.[626] In May 1667 Pepys heard a harp being played in the Spring Garden at Vauxhall.[627]

hautboys [Hoboys, Hoyboys] – a hautboy or *hautbois*, was also the term used from the mid-seventeenth century for the oboe, a double-reed musical instrument.[628] The term could also apply to a group of wind instrument players, often made up of three oboes or hautboys and a bass oboe or bassoon, that might be accompanied by snare drums. They were popular in the late seventeenth century, especially in association with military regiments.[629]

the duchess of York's music – musicians in the pay of Anne Hyde (d.1671) and then Mary of Moderna. In this case, the former.

the duke of Cambridge's music – musicians in the pay of James, duke of Cambridge, son of James, duke of York and Anne Hyde.

the king's music – the name for the king's twenty four violins. Pepys heard them on 23 April 1661.[630]

the queen's music – musicians retained by Catherine. Shortly after her arrival, on 9 June 1662, Evelyn 'heard the Q: Portugals Musique, consisting of Pipes, harps & very ill voices'.[631]

set of music – a probable reference to Catherine obtaining music in parts, which was the standard way of transmitting polyphonic (multi-voice) music in this period. You would have, for example, a Superius, Altus, Tenor and Bassus parts, each separately printed, for a four-voice piece (which might also be played by four instruments, or a mix of voices and instruments on different parts). Catherine's payments could be

625 Pepys, *Diary*, 3, 300–01.

626 Sue Carole DeVale, Bo Lawergren, Joan Rimmer, Robert Evans, William Taylor, Cristina Bordas, Cheryl Ann Fulton, John M. Schechter, Nancy Thym-Hochrein, Hannelore Devaere and Mary McMaster, 'Harp (Fr. *harpe*; Ger. *Harfe*; It., Sp. *arpa*)', Grove Music online, 2001, https://doi-org.soton.idm.oclc.org/10.1093/gmo/9781561592630.article.45738 [accessed 15/3/22].

627 Pepys, *Diary*, 8, 240.

628 'Hautboy(i)', Grove Music online, 2001, https://doi-org.soton.idm.oclc.org/10.1093/gmo/9781561592630.article.12578 [accessed 15/3/22].

629 'Hautboys', Grove Music online, 22 September 2015, https://doi-org.soton.idm.oclc.org/10.1093/gmo/9781561592630.article.A2284595 [accessed 15/3/22].

630 Pepys, *Diary*, 2, 86.

631 Evelyn, *Diary*, 439.

either for printed partbooks or manuscript ones (the partbook format was the same for both formats).[632] Or a group of musicians.

the university's music – a group of musicians retained/employed by the university of Oxford.

trumpeters – a trumpet is a 'lip-vibrated aerophone' and the royal trumpeters were very important for ceremonial events at Charles II's court.[633] The king's trumpeters were supplied with livery and trumpet banners.

violins, bands of – groups of violinists, with those linked to the royal households being much admired. On 28 August 1667 Pepys 'saw the King and Queen at dinner and heard a little of their viallins music'.[634]

violin in ordinary – a violin player who was in regular attendance upon the royal household and so would be eligible for a salary and other benefits of royal service.

waits – a group of musicians who played and sang.

wind music – music produced by players of wind instruments.

musical instruments – a range of instruments were popular with amateur and professional musicians in the seventeenth century, including the guitar, harpsichord, recorder, viola and violin.

drums – drums are membranophones with a resonating cavity, which is sounded by percussion, and were often used to call troops and the militia together.[635] On 26 March 1664 Pepys described how drummers 'drum all up and down the City was beat to raise the train-bands for to quiet the town'.[636] A number of payments for kettle drums and for the kettle drummer's livery feature in the accounts of the Great Wardrobe.[637]

hornpipe – a hornpipe could be one of two things. Either a 'single-reed Aerophone, incorporating animal horn, either around the reed or forming a bell, or both; some are played with a bag'.[638] Or a dance,

632 I am most grateful to Professor Jeanice Brooks for this definition. Also see 'Partbooks', Grove Music online, 20 January 2001, https://doi-org.soton.idm.oclc.org/10.1093/gmo/9781561592630.article.20966 [accessed 20/1/23].

633 Margaret Sarkissian and Edward H. Tarr, 'Trumpet (Fr. *trompette*; Ger. *Trompete*; It. *tromba*)', Grove Music online, 2001, https://doi-org.soton.idm.oclc.org/10.1093/gmo/9781561592630.article.49912 [accessed 15/3/22].

634 Pepys, *Diary*, 8, 404.

635 James Blades, Janet K. Page, Edmund A. Bowles, Anthony King, Mervyn McLean, Mary Riemer-Weller, Robert Anderson and James Holland, 'Drum', Grove Music online, 2001, https://doi-org.soton.idm.oclc.org/10.1093/gmo/9781561592630.article.51410 [accessed 15/3/22].

636 Pepys, *Diary*, 5, 99.

637 Ashbee, *Records*, 27, 122, 146.

638 Anthony C. Baines, 'Hornpipe(i)', Grove Music online, 2001, https://doi-org.soton.idm.oclc.org/10.1093/gmo/9781561592630.article.13366 [accessed 15/3/22].

usually performed by one person, often accompanied by a wind instrument or pipe.[639]

recorders – a woodwind instrument with seven finger holes (usually) and a thumb hole.[640] They were popular in the early modern period and on 8 April 1668 Pepys bought a recorder because 'the sound of it being of all sounds in the world most pleasing to me' and eight days later he began learning how to play it.[641]

trumpet marine – the trumpet marine is a bowed monochord with a vibrating bridge that was played from the fifteenth to mid-eighteenth centuries.[642] On 24 October 1667, Pepys recalled hearing 'one Monsieur Prin, play on the trump-marine, which he do beyond belief'.[643]

virginals – a smaller form of harpsichord, usually with one keyboard, and one set of strings and jacks.[644] On 8 December 1660, Pepys dined at the home of Mr and Mrs Pierce and 'her daughter played after dinner upon the virginalls'.[645]

Muskerry [Muscary], **Lady** – Margaret Bourke (d.1698), was the daughter of Ulick Burke, 1st marquis of Clanricarde, and Lady Anne Compton, who in 1660 or 1661 married Charles MacCarty, viscount Muskerry (1634/5–65). He was killed at the battle of Lowestoft on 3 June 1665. Margaret later remarried: first to Robert Villiers and then to Robert Fielding.[646]

Newcastle [Newcassells], **earl** – William Cavendish, duke of (1593–1676), was the son of Sir Charles Cavendish and Catherine Ogle. He married Elizabeth Howard in 1618 and Margaret Lucas in 1645. He was appointed governor to Prince Charles in 1638 and gentleman of the robes to Charles I in 1641.[647] After the royalist defeat at Marston Moor in July 1644 he went into exile, returning at the Restoration to Bolsover castle where

639 https://www.oed.com/view/Entry/88514?redirectedFrom=hornpipe#eid [accessed 27/4/22].

640 David Lasocki, 'Recorder', Grove Music online, 2001, https://doi-org.soton.idm.oclc.org/10.1093/gmo/9781561592630.article.23022 [accessed 15/3/22].

641 Pepys, *Diary*, 9, 157; 9, 164.

642 Cecil Adkins, 'Trumpet marine (Fr. *trompette marine*; Ger. *Trumscheit, Nonnengeige, Marien Trompet, Trompetengeige*; It. *tromba marina*)', Grove Music Online, 2001, https://doi-org.soton.idm.oclc.org/10.1093/gmo/9781561592630.article.28494 [accessed 15/3/22].

643 Pepys, *Diary*, 8, 500.

644 Edwin M. Ripin, Denzil Wraight and Darryl Martin, 'Virginal [virginals] (Fr. *virginale, épinette*; Ger. *Virginal, Instrument*; It. *arpicordo, spinetta, spinettina*)', Grove Music online, 2001, https://doi-org.soton.idm.oclc.org/10.1093/gmo/9781561592630.article.43136 [accessed 15/3/22].

645 Pepys, *Diary*, 1, 313.

646 http://www.thepeerage.com/p21663.htm [accessed 24/4/22].

647 Lynn Hulse, 'Cavendish, William, first duke of Newcastle upon Tyne

he built a riding house and published on dressage. He was buried in Westminster Abbey with Margaret.[648]

man –

Newport, lady – Diana Russell was the youngest daughter of Francis Russell, 4th earl of Bedford. She married Francis Newport in 1642. Later he became 1st earl of Bradford, and they had four sons and five daughters.[649] In *An Heroic Poem* of 1681 Diana and her husband were described in less than flattering terms:

But this vile cur's a scandal to your kind,
Who never missed the crust for which he whined;
With a she wolf of Bedford falsely joined,
And whelps begot, destined to many a kick:[650]

man –

servant –

Newport, lord – Francis Newport (1620–1708), 1st earl of Bradford (1620–1708), was the eldest son of Richard Newport, 1st baron Newport, and Rachel Leveson. He was comptroller of the king's household 1668–72, and he was treasurer of the king's household under James II and VII and William III. In addition, he was a member of the privy council from 1669–79 and in 1675 he was made viscount Newport.[651]

man –

Norris [Noris], **Mr** – possibly 1) Henry Norris, groom of the queen's great chamber, 1662–63 to 1677.[652] Or 2) Henry Norris, frame maker to the king (fl. 1647–84). He lived in Long Acre where Pepys visited in April 1669 noting that Norris 'showed me several forms of frames … in little bits of mouldings to choose by'.[653]

Northumberland, lady – Elizabeth Percy (1646–90), was the daughter of Thomas Wriothesley, 4th earl of Southampton, and Elizabeth Leigh. She married Jocelyn Percy, 11th earl of Northumberland (1644–70) in 1662 and she was painted by Sir Peter Lely as one of the Windsor Beauties.[654]

gardener –

(bap.1593–1676), writer, patron and royalist army officer', *ODNB*, 6 January 2011, https://doi.org/10.1093/ref:odnb/4946 [accessed 23/1/22].

648 https://www.westminster-abbey.org/abbey-commemorations/commemorations/william-margaret-cavendish [accessed 17/1/23].

649 See Victor Stater, 'Newport, Francis, first earl of Bradford (1619–1708), politician', *ODNB*, 23 September 2004, https://doi.org/10.1093/ref:odnb/20033 [accessed 24/4/22].

650 Wilson, *Court Satire*, 70.

651 Victor Stater, 'Newport, Francis, first earl of Bradford (1619–1708), politician', *ODNB*, 23 September 2004, https://doi.org/10.1093/ref:odnb/20033 [accessed 24/4/22].

652 Sainty, Wassmann and Bucholz, *Household officers*, 54.

653 Pepys, *Diary*, 9, 538; Pepys, *Diary*, 10, 303.

654 No *ODNB* entry; see Lewis Melville, *The Windsor Beauties: Ladies of the Court of Charles II* (Ann Arbor, MI: Modern History Press, 2005), 159–64.

Nuborke, lord – possibly James Livingston (*c.*1622–70), 1st earl of Newburgh, who was the son of Sir John Livingston, 1st baronet of Kinnaird and Jane Sproxton. He married twice: first to Lady Catherine Howard (d.1650) in 1648 and secondly to Anne Poole (d.1692) in 1660. He was created earl of Newburgh in 1660. He was captain of the Scottish Bodyguard from 1661 to 1670 and a gentleman of the king's privy chamber from 1668 until his death.[655]

Nun [Nunn], **mistress** – Elizabeth Nunn was the queen's laundress and starcher, 1662–78, and then laundress of the body, 1671–78.[656] According to Pepys, she was William Chiffinch's sister-in-law.[657]

man –

Nunes [Nons] **mistress –** Mary Nune, was a Portuguese woman of the queen's bedchamber, from 1665 to 1671.[658]

O'Dally [odaly]**, Father** – as per bill.[659]

old, the elderly – as Steven Smith has noted there were three ways early modern people thought about ageing: as a progression through a sequence of seven ages, as becoming either increasingly dignified or not, and that death was either in God's hands or could be delayed though medical care.[660]

to an old man presented Sparagrese –
to the old footman presented Sparegrase –
to the Late Queens old footman –
to the Late Queens old footman presented Sparagras –
to old Georg Bar as per bill –
to old Mr Bure as per bill –
to a poore old man –
to a poore old womane –

Oldfield [old feild], **Mr** – William was a groom of the hobby stable in 1669, and in 1674 he was listed in the queen's establishment books.[661]

Orange Anne [Nan] – she was an orange seller, one of many in the London theatres, the most notable being Nell Gwyn, and Orange Moll.[662] Orange

655 Basil Duke Henning, 'Livingston, James, 1st earl Newburgh [S] (c.1622–70), of Cirencester, Glos.', https://www.historyofparliamentonline.org/volume/1660-1690/member/livingston-james-1622-70 [accessed 28/12/21].

656 Sainty, Wassmann and Bucholz, *Household officers*, 54.

657 Pepys, *Diary*, 10, 305.

658 Sainty, Wassmann and Bucholz, *Household officers*, 55.

659 Not listed in Sainty, Wassmann and Bucholz, *Household officers*.

660 Steven Smith, 'Growing old in early Stuart England', *Albion*, 8.2 (1976), 125.

661 Sainty, Wassmann and Bucholz, *Household officers*, 55.

662 Peter Cunningham, *The Story of Nell Gwyn and the Sayings of Charles II*

women were not above seeking to extract money from those at the theatre as Pepys found to his cost on 11 May 1668 when one seller tried to make him pay for oranges that he had allegedly had eaten but not paid for. He refused to pay but 'for quiet [I] did buy 4s worth of oranges of her – at 6d a piece'.[663]

Orange, prince of – William, later William III (1650–1702), was the son of William II, prince of Orange and Mary, daughter of Charles I and so nephew of Charles II and James II and VII. He was born in the Binnenhof Palace, in the Hague and from 1668 he came to take an important role in Orangist politics and from 1672 to 1688 he was the stadholder. In 1677, he married Mary, the elder daughter of James, duke of York and Charles II's niece.[664] He landed with troops in England on 5 November 1688, initiating what has been referred to as the Glorious Revolution and, in the following year, William and Mary were offered the throne jointly. Their power was limited by the Declaration of Rights, which was drawn up by Parliament.

cook –

trumpets –

Ormond, duchess – Elizabeth Butler (1615–84) (née Preston) was the daughter of Richard Preston and Elizabeth Butler. In 1629, she married her cousin, James. She became a duchess in 1661 and the following year, vicereine of Ireland.[665]

man –

Ormond, duke – James Butler (1610–88), 1st duke of Ormond, was the son of Thomas Butler and Elizabeth Pointz. He married Elizabeth Preston in 1629 and after the Restoration he was appointed lord lieutenant of Ireland from 1662 to 1669 and again from 1677 to 1685.[666]

coachman –

Orrery, lord – Roger Boyle, 1st earl of Orrery (1621–79), was the son of Richard Boyle, 1st earl of Cork, and Catherine Fenton. In 1641, he married Lady Margaret Howard (1623–89), daughter of Theophilus Howard, 2nd

(London: Hutchinson & Co, 1892), 85.

663 Pepys, *Diary*, 9, 195.

664 Tony Claydon, 'William III and II (1650–1702), king of England, Scotland and Ireland and prince of Orange', *ODNB*, 24 May 2008, https://doi.org/10.1093/ref:odnb/29450 [accessed 2/5/22].

665 M. Perceval-Maxwell, 'Butler [*née* Preston], Elizabeth, duchess of Ormond and *suo jure* Lady Dingwall (1615–1684), noblewoman', *ODNB*, 23 September 2004, https://doi.org/10.1093/ref:odnb/67044 [accessed 1/3/22].

666 Toby Barnard, 'Butler, James, first duke of Ormond (1610–1688), lord lieutenant of Ireland', *ODNB*, 3 January 2008, https://doi.org/10.1093/ref:odnb/4191 [accessed 15/3/22].

earl of Suffolk. He was a politician and dramatist. He held the title of baron Broghill until 1660 when he was created earl of Orrery.[667]

Osborne [Osbourn], **Robert** – sumpterman.

Ossory [Orseris, Orseries], **lady** – Emilia van Nassau.

Ossory, lord – Thomas Butler (1634–80), was the eldest son of James Butler, 1st duke of Ormond, and Elizabeth Preston. He was 6th earl of Ossory.[668] In 1659, he married Emilia van Nassau and they attended the queen's birthday ball in 1666.[669] He was Lord Chamberlain from 1676 to 1680 and he died at Arlington House.[670]

footman –

man –

Oswell, Mr – apothecary.

Oxford, countess – this title was contested by the actress Hester Davenport (1642–1717), whom Aubrey de Vere, earl of Oxford, married in 1662 or 1663, and Diana Kirke (d.1719), the daughter of George Kirke, a groom of the bedchamber to the king, whom he married in 1672. When Hester accused de Vere of bigamy, he claimed that the first marriage had been a sham. Hester's claim was not upheld but she continued to use the title.[671]

Oxford, lord – Aubrey de Vere, 20th earl of Oxford (1627–1703), was the son of Robert de Vere, 19th earl of Oxford, and Beatrix van Hemmend. He was a royalist. His relationship with Hester Davenport shocked Pepys, who recorded on 4 January 1665 that 'his lordship was in bed past ten o'clock: and Lord help us, so rude a dirty family I never saw in my life'.[672] In April 1673 he married Diana Kirke, daughter of George Kirke, groom of the bedchamber and keeper of the palace of Whitehall.[673] He was made a member of the privy council in 1670, a gentleman of the bedchamber in 1678 and in 1680 he was an ambassador-extraordinary to Louis XIV.[674]

servant –

667 Toby Barnard, 'Boyle, Roger, first earl of Orrery (1621–1679), politician and writer', *ODNB*, 24 May 2012, https://doi.org/10.1093/ref:odnb/3138 [accessed 15/3/22].

668 J. D. Davies, 'Butler, Thomas, sixth earl of Ossory (1634–1680), politician and naval officer', *ODNB*, 27 May 2010, https://doi.org/10.1093/ref:odnb/4210 [accessed 15/3/22].

669 Pepys, *Diary*, 7, 372.

670 Sainty, Wassmann and Bucholz, *Household officers*, 55.

671 V. E. Chancellor, 'Davenport [*married name* Hoet], Hester, [*known as* Roxalana], styled countess of Oxford (1642–1717), actress', *ODNB*, 3 January 2008, https://doi.org/10.1093/ref:odnb/70999 [accessed 1/6/22].

672 Pepys, *Diary*, 6, 3.

673 MacLeod, *Painted Ladies*, 243.

674 Victor Stater, 'Vere, Aubrey de, twentieth earl of Oxford (1627–1703)', *ODNB*, 24 May 2008, https://doi.org/10.1093/ref:odnb/28206 [accessed 18/3/22].

Pall, Father – for a bill.[675]

Palles, Mr – gallery keeper.

Papphames, colonel – possibly Colonel Alexander Popham (1605–69), who fought for Parliament as commander of the Bath regiment. After the Restoration he entertained Charles II at his home, Littlecote House, Wiltshire.[676] He married twice, first to Dorothy Cole (d.1643) and then to Letitia Carre, with whom he had eight children.

servants –

passementerie – trimmings for clothing and furnishings.[677]

ribbon, French – either ribbon from France or in the French style.

ribbon, garnitures – a decorative set of ribbons, often in a several colours, widths and textures, to trim clothes, in particular men's doublets and breeches.

ribbon, satin – woven using a satin weave, which would give the front face of the ribbon a smooth, shiny surface.

ribbon, silver – incorporating silver metal wrapped thread, flat strip, or silver wire.

scallop – a decorative edging, or lace, with a scalloped edge. On 7 December 1661, Pepys noted 'My wife and I were talking about buying a fine scallop, which is to cost her 45s'.[678]

Paston, Sir Robert – Robert (1631–81) was the eldest son of Sir William Paston and Lady Katherine.[679] In 1650, he married Rebecca Clayton. He was knighted in 1660 and became the 2nd baronet in 1663. His home was at Oxnead, one of the most important country houses in Norfolk and he added a banqueting house in 1671 to entertain Charles II and Catherine when they visited. Only one wing remains now.[680]

Patrick, father – see *Mackinney*.

Paulet [pawlett], **Mr** – submitting a bill.

pavilion – a large, round, decorative tent, usually coming to a central point, rather than having a ridge poll.[681] The royal tents were cared for by the office of the Tents and when Evelyn visited Hampton Court on 8 June

675 Not listed in Sainty, Wassmann and Bucholz, *Household officers*.

676 https://royalarmouries.org/stories/our-collection/the-king-and-the-colonel [accessed 19/2/22].

677 Annabel Westman, *Fringe, Frog and Tassel: The Art of the Trimmings Maker in Interior Decoration* (London: National Trust, 2019).

678 Pepys, *Diary*, 2, 228.

679 John Miller, 'Paston, Robert, first earl of Yarmouth (1631–1683), politician', *ODNB*, 9 December 2021, https://doi.org/10.1093/ref:odnb/21513 [accessed 28/4/22].

680 Wilhelmine Howard, *Norfolk: A Shell Guide* (London: Faber and Faber, 1958, 1982), 135.

681 https://www.oed.com/view/Entry/139098?redirectedFrom=pavillion#eid [accessed 24/4/22].

1662 he was 'curious to visite the Wardrobe, & Tents, & other furniture of State'.[682]

Pavy [Pauy], **Mr** – box keeper.

Pelham [Pellames], **Sir John** – Sir John Pelham (*c*.1623–1703), 3rd baronet Pelham, was the first son of Sir Thomas Pelham, 2nd baronet, and Mary Wilbraham. He married Lady Lucy Sydney. He was a landowner in Suffolk and an MP for the county. He was involved in searching for suspects after the Rye house plot of 1683.[683]

Pembroke [Pemprocke]**, earl of** – Philip Herbert, 5th earl of Pembroke and 2nd earl of Montgomery (1621–69), the son of Philip Herbert, 4th earl of Pembroke, and Susan de Vere. He married Penelope Naunton in 1639 and after her death, Catherine Villiers in 1649.[684]

bowling green keeper –

Penalva [Peneluas], **countess of** – she was one of Catherine's Portuguese ladies in waiting, from 1662 to 1680. She died at Windsor in 1680.[685]

perfumes and cosmetics – Evelyn described cosmetics in the *Fop-Dictionary* as 'any Effeminate Ornament, also Complections and Perfumes'.[686]

essence – a contemporary term for perfume, meaning 'an extract obtained by distillation or otherwise from a plant, or from a medicinal, odoriferous or alimentary substance, and containing its characteristic properties in a concentrated form'.[687]

patches [pachies] – on 30 August 1660 Pepys noted 'this the first day that ever I saw my wife wear black patches since we were married'.[688] In November of that year, Samuel added that 'my wife seemed very pretty today, it being the first time that I have given her leave to weare

682 Evelyn, *Diary*, 439.

683 B. M. Crook, 'Pelham, Sir John, 3rd Bt. (c.1623–1703), of Halland, Laughton, Suss.', https://www.historyofparliamentonline.org/volume/1660-1690/member/pelham-sir-john-1623-1703 [accessed 15/3/22].

684 See David L. Smith, 'Herbert, Philip, first earl of Montgomery and fourth earl of Pembroke (1584–1650), courtier and politician', *ODNB*, 26 May 2016, https://doi-org.soton.idm.oclc.org/10.1093/ref:odnb/13042 [accessed 2/5/22].

685 Sainty, Wassmann and Bucholz, *Household officers*, 57.

686 Evelyn, *Mundus Muliebris*, 17: https://quod.lib.umich.edu/e/eebo/A38815.0001.001/1:5?rgn=div1;submit=Go;subview=detail;type=simple;view=fulltext;q1=cosmeticks [accessed 1/5/22].

687 https://www.oed.com/view/Entry/64494?rskey=8WwWlx&result=1#eid [accessed 24/4/22].

688 Pepys, *Diary*, 1, 234.

a black patch'.[689] According to the *Fop-Dictionary*, mouches were described as 'Flies, or, Black Patches, by the Vulgar'.[690]

sweet powder – a sweet smelling, fine powder that was very popular. In 1682, Mary Doggett included the following recipe for 'A sweet powder for linen' in her receipt book: 'Take some ambergris and musk beat it small and mingle it with the juice of lemon and orange flower water then dip some cloves in the liquor take some damask rose buds and put into every bud a clove and tie it close and dry it then beat it into powder and mingle with some orris roots beaten to powder'.[691] These perfumed powers were often placed in embroidered sweet bags and used to scent chest of stored linens, or to scent hair or wigs.[692] The *Fop-Dictionary* defined 'Polvil' as 'The Portugal term for the most exquisite Powders'.[693]

sweet water – a liquid scent or perfume. Gervase Markham's recipe for sweet water stated: 'Take of bay leaves one handful, of red roses two handfuls, of damask roses three handful, of lavender four handfuls, of basil one handful, marjoram two handfuls, of camomile one handful, the young tops of sweet briar, two handfuls of dandelion [and] tansy two handfuls, of orange peels six or seven ounces, of cloves and mace a groat's worth'.[694]

sweet water pot – a vessel for storing and sprinkling perfumed water, often made of silver amongst the elite.

Periera [Perera], **Father Manuel** [Manwell] – arriving in 1662, he was the queen's Portuguese almoner in 1665, her almoner from 1669 to 1679, and had vacated the office by 1682.[695]

Periera [Perera], **Mr** – John was a page of the backstairs to the chapel from 1672 to 1692, and he appears to have travelled to Portugal with the queen.[696]

Person, Mr – yeoman hanger.

689 Pepys, *Diary*, 1, 283, also see 1, 299. For more on patches, see Karen Hearn, 'Revising the visage: patches and beauty spots in seventeenth-century British and Dutch painted portraits', *Huntingdon Library Quarterly* 78.4 (2015), 809–23.

690 Evelyn, *Mundus Muliebris*, 19: https://quod.lib.umich.edu/e/eebo/A38815.0001.001/1:5?rgn=div1;submit=Go;subview=detail;type=simple;view=fulltext;q1=mouches [accessed 1/5/22].

691 BL Additional MS 27466, p. 33.

692 See Jacqui Carey, *Sweet Bags* (Devon, Carey Company, 2010).

693 Evelyn, *Mundus Muliebris*, 20: https://quod.lib.umich.edu/e/eebo/A38815.0001.001/1:5?rgn=div1;submit=Go;subview=detail;type=simple;view=fulltext;q1=Portugal [accessed 1/5/22].

694 Markham, *Well-Kept Kitchen*, 95–96.

695 Sainty, Wassmann and Bucholz, *Household officers*, 57.

696 Sainty, Wassmann and Bucholz, *Household officers*, 57.

Peterborough, Lady – Penelope (d.1702), was the daughter of Barnabas O'Brien, 6th earl of Thomond, and Anne Fermor. She married Henry Mordaunt (1621–97), 2nd earl of Peterborough, in 1644 and they had two daughters. Later she was groom of the stool to Mary of Modena. Her husband was made Governor of Tangier, arriving in 1662 to take up office but he was replaced at the end of the year. He fought in the Second Anglo-Dutch war and in 1670 was appointed as groom of the stool to James, duke of York. In 1674, he was made a privy councillor and he was implicated in the Popish Plot in 1680 when he lost his post. He carried the sceptre at James II and VII's coronation and converted to Catholicism in 1687.[697]

coachmen and footmen –

page –

petition – there is a subtle distinction from the entry below. Here the implication is that the individuals made their case verbally to the queen in relation to a matter of interest to themselves.

to yor Maties footmen vpon petition [1670]

to Captane Hampot vpon petition [1678]

petitions – a written or formal request, which could be either formal, as in the case of the petitions presented by Parliament to the monarch, or more general, with one or more signatories appealing to an individual or a group with influence.[698] This form of legitimate political expression could be satirised, as was the case with *The Poor Whores* petition, which circulated in 1668 during the Bawdy House riots and was addressed to Lady Castlemaine by Madame Cresswell and Damaris Page, London brothel owners.[699]

a poore man with a petition [1677]

a poore womane with a petition [1678]

pets, *also see birds*

dancing dog – teaching dogs (and other animals including bears) to dance as a form of entertainment was popular in the seventeenth century as indicated by Pieter de Hooch's painting, *A Lady and a Gentleman making Music with Dancing Dogs*.[700]

697 See Victor Stater, 'Mordaunt, Henry, second earl of Peterborough (bap.1623–d.1697), nobleman', *ODNB*, 23 September 2004, https://doi-org.soton.idm.oclc.org/10.1093/ref:odnb/19163 [accessed 1/2/22].

698 https://www.oed.com/view/Entry/141858?rskey=pySsO2&result=1#eid [accessed 17/4/22].

699 See *EEBO* https://quod.lib.umich.edu/e/eebo2/A41738.0001.001?view=toc [accessed 18/1/23].

700 Pieter de Hooch, *A Lady and a Gentleman making Music with Dancing Dogs*,

dogs – a variety of dog breeds were kept for hunting and as companions and lapdogs.

dog collars –

the king's dogs – dogs were much loved by Catherine's husband as Evelyn noted 'he took delight to have a number of little spaniels follow him, & lie in his bed-Chamber'.[701]

monkey [munky] – monkeys were kept as pets, although not always with great success. On 18 January 1661, Pepys returned home to find 'the Monkey loose, which did anger me'.[702] They were also the subject of paintings.[703]

chains and collars –

Pettoes, John – the queen's footman.

Pickering [peckering], **Mr** – possibly 1) Thomas Pickering, groom of the queen's great chamber in 1672, or 2) Thomas Pickering, lay brother, from 1671 to 1679.[704] Or 3) Edward (Ned) Pickering, younger brother of Sir Gilbert Pickering, from Northamptonshire. He held a post in the queen's household from which he was dismissed, and he was generally unpopular, including with Pepys.[705]

Picot, Mr – possibly Henry Pickot, page of the queen's backstairs, from 1662–63 to 1679.[706]

pictures [picktur] – the Stuarts collected paintings and commissioned portraits, with Charles I's collection being very highly regarded.[707] A love of paintings was shared with the middling sort and Pepys took a keen interest. In August 1664 Samuel saw 'some pictures at one Hiseman's, a picture-drawer, a Dutchman, which is said to exceed Lilly … as good pictures I think as ever I saw. The Queene is drawn in one like a shepherdess – in the other like St Katharin, most like and most admirably'.[708]

1680–84, oil on canvas, private collection, see Peter C. Sutton, *Pieter de Hooch* (Oxford: Phaidon, 1980), cat. no. 151.

701 Evelyn, *Diary*, 789.

702 Pepys, *Diary*, 2, 17.

703 Unknown artist, Dutch school, *Monkeys and parrots*, c.1660s, oil on canvas, collection of Glen Dooley, New York. This painting has been attributed to painter of the Paston Treasure.

704 Sainty, Wassmann and Bucholz, *Household officers*, 58.

705 Pepys, *Diary*, 10, 327.

706 Sainty, Wassmann and Bucholz, *Household officers*, 58.

707 See Desmond Shawe-Taylor and Per Rumberg eds., *Charles I: King and Collector* (London: Royal Academy of the Arts, 2018), and for the dispersal of the king's collection, see Jerry Brotton, *The Sale of the Late King's Goods: Charles I and his Art Collection* (London: Macmillan, 2006).

708 Pepys, *Diary*, 5, 254.

picture frames – possibly of the auricular or lobate style, which was fashionable at the time.[709] For a good, slightly earlier example of an auricular frame, see Sir Peter Lely's portrait, *Elizabeth Murray, Lady Tollemach, later Countess of Dysart and Duchess of Lauderdale with a black servant*, at Ham House.[710]

Pigeon [Pigon], **Mrs** – for her bill.

Pinzon [Pingon], **Madame** – for ribbon, for her bills.

places – Catherine travelled regularly, including removing from one royal property to the next and going on summer progresses. Pepys was very interested in royal travel plans, and on 30 September 1663 he recorded that 'tomorrow, the King, Queene, Duke and his Lady, and the whole Court comes to town from their progresse'.[711]

Audley End, Saffron Walden, Essex – built on the site of the abbey of Saffron Walden by Sir Thomas Audley (1488–1544), this house was demolished by Thomas Howard, 1st earl of Suffolk (1561–1626) and he then built a bigger, grander house.[712] In October 1662 William Schellinks saw 'the chamber in which King Charles and his Queen had been staying some time and had been sumptuously entertained'.[713] In 7 March 1666, Charles and James visited and bought the house.[714] Celia Fiennes described Audley End as having 'a noble appearance Like a town, so many towers and buildings of stone within a parke wch is walled round'.[715]

music at Audley End –

servants –

under-housekeeper –

Badminton [Badmenton]***, Gloucester/Badminton House*** – a village in Gloucestershire made up from Great and Little Badminton. It was also the location of Badminton house, a seventeenth century building. The site was bought by Edward Somerset, 4th earl of Worcester, in 1608. After the Restoration, this house became the chief family home with Henry Somerset, 1st duke of Beaufort (1629–1700) undertaking important building work.[716]

709 https://www.npg.org.uk/research/programmes/the-art-of-the-picture-frame/guides-knole [accessed 17/2/22].

710 https://www.nationaltrustcollections.org.uk/object/1139940 [accessed 27/4/22].

711 Pepys, *Diary*, 4, 321.

712 See Pepys, *Diary*, 1, 69–70.

713 Exwood and Lehmann, *Journal of William Schellinks*, 149.

714 Pepys, *Diary*, 7, 68.

715 Fiennes, *Through England on a Side Saddle*, 48.

716 David Verey, *Gloucestershire: The Cotswolds: The Buildings of England* (Harmondsworth: Penguin, 1979), 255.

Barn Elms, Richmond, Surrey – Schellinks described the house of Barn Elms as 'very pleasant as it lies, planted with very tall elm trees, by the river'.[717] Situated between Putney and the small village of Barnes, the house had pleasure gardens where Pepys went walking on several occasions.[718]

Barnet, Hertfordshire – a village north of London, also known as High Barnet or Chipping Barnet, where an important horse market was held in the sixteenth century. In the seventeenth century it was noted for its springs. On 11 July 1664, Pepys went to Barnet 'and there I drank three glasses and went and walked, and came back and drunk two more'.[719]

Bath, Somerset – Bath is a city in valley of the river Avon in Somerset and during the seventeenth century it began developing into a very fashionable spa town. On 25 August 1663, Evelyn noted that he had seen 'her Majestie take leave of the greate-men & Ladies in the Circle, being the next morning to set out towards Bath'.[720] Several days later, on 31 August Pepys recorded that 'The King and Queene and Court at the Bath'.[721] Bath was popular with European visitors, like Schellinks,[722] and the aristocracy, including the earl of Bedford in 1675.[723] Cecil Fiennes described Bath as 'a pretty place full of good houses all for y[e] accomodation of the Company that resort thither to Drink or Bathe in the summer'.[724]

Battersea, Surrey – a village on the south bank of the Thames.

Bramford, Suffolk – a village three miles west of Ipswich.

Bray, Berkshire – a village on the banks of the Thames to the south of Maidenhead. It was the site of Ockwells Manor, a late fifteenth century timber-framed manor house, which Charles I visited for the hunting.

bridge, the, London – probably London bridge, which Celia Fiennes described as 'a stately building all stone wth 18 arches most of them bigg Enough to admit a Large Barge to pass, its so broade that two Coaches drives a breast, and there is on Each side houses and shopps just Like any Large streete in y[e] Citty'.[725]

Bristol – a port with developing trade with the New World and a city on the

717 Exwood and Lehmann, *Journal of William Schellinks*, 78.
718 Pepys, *Diary*, 9, 128, 271.
719 Pepys, *Diary*, 5, 201.
720 Evelyn, *Diary*, 455.
721 Pepys, *Diary*, 4, 292.
722 Exwood and Lehmann, *Journal of William Schellinks*, 105–07.
723 Scott Thomson, *Life in a Noble Household*, 221.
724 Fiennes, *Through England on a Side Saddle*, 199.
725 Fiennes, *Through England on a Side Saddle*, 247.

river Avon. Catherine may have been visiting Hotwells, to the west of Bristol, with hot springs, which were recorded in the fifteenth century. Hotwells developed into a fashionable spa from 1695 onwards.

trumpeters –

Bury [Bery] ***St Edmunds, Suffolk*** – a market town with a cathedral which was an important pilgrimage site associated with the abbey of St Edmund up to the dissolution. In the early seventeenth century Bury was a centre of Puritanism, with families from the town leaving in 1640 for the Massachusetts Bay colony.[726]

gardener –

poor –

Cambridge, Cambridgeshire – a city on the river Cam. In Celia Fienne's opinion, Cambridge architecture was 'old and Indifferent' while 'Trinity Colledg is the ffinest, yet not so Large as Christ-church College in oxford'.[727]

Canterbury, Kent – a cathedral city and pilgrimage site which Celia Fiennes considered to be 'a noble city'. She also noted that there 'is a spring in the town that is dranke by many persons as Tunbridge and approv'd by them, but others find it an ill water'.[728]

Chatham, Kent – a town on the river Medway and on Watling Street, which ran from Dover to London and on to St Albans and Wroxeter. A royal dockyard was established here by Elizabeth I in 1568 with ships moored at Gillingham water. Begun in 1559 and redeveloped in 1599–1601, Upnor castle was an artillery fort intended to protect the dockyards, but it failed to do so during the Dutch raid on the Medway in 1667.

Chelsea, Middlesex – a village on the north bank of the Thames, with pleasure gardens and Neat House gardens, named after the Manor of Nete, near Vauxhall. The gardens produced a range of fruit and vegetables including melons, asparagus and artichokes.[729] Catherine had property at Chelsea.

Chesterton Park [Chesterson] – There are two possibilities. It was probably 1) Chesterton Hall, Chesterton, Cambridge, which is an early to mid-seventeenth century brick-built house with two storeys and

[726] Roger Thompson, *Mobility & Migration, East Anglian Founders of New England, 1629–1640* (Amherst, MA: University of Massachusetts Press, 1994).

[727] Fiennes, *Through England on a Side Saddle*, 49.

[728] Fiennes, *Through England on a Side Saddle*, 101–02.

[729] London's market gardens: the Neat houses https://lostcookbook.wordpress.com/2013/10/25/neat-houses [accessed 18/1/23].

attics.[730] However, 2) there is another Chesterton House and park, in Warwickshire.[731]

Chiswick, Middlesex – a village on the Thames and on Stane Street, the Roman road running from London to Chichester. Sir Stephen Fox had a house there.[732]

Clewer* [Cleworth], *Berkshire – a small village on the Thames, with a place to ford the river. There was also a medieval manor house at Clewer Park. In 1689, John Drummond, 1st earl and later duke of Melfort, was made baron Cleworth, of Clewer, near Windsor.[733]

Cliveden House [Cleuden, Cleuedon], ***Berkshire*** – the house was built by George Villiers, 2nd duke of Buckingham (1628–87), for his mistress, Anna Maria, countess of Shrewsbury (1642-)1702. When their affair was discovered, Buckingham and Shrewsbury fought a duel and Shrewsbury died shortly afterwards. The house was incomplete when Buckingham died in 1687.[734]

Colnbrook [Colbrooke], ***Middlesex*** – a village on the river Colne, on the border of Middlesex and Buckinghamshire. It was a coaching rest stop on the road between Maidenhead and London, and Pepys paused there in June 1668 where his party 'dined and fitted ourselves a little to go through London anon'.[735] When travelling from Windsor to London Celia Fiennes took 'a private road Made for ye kings Coaches and so to Colebrooke'.[736]

Coombe [Combe], ***Kingston upon Thames*** – during the sixteenth century a well at Coombe supplied water to Hampton Court and the conduit room and pipe is still in place.[737]

Cranbourne Lodge [Cranburn Lodg], ***Berkshire*** – the lodge for Cranbourne Chase, next to Windsor Great Park. The house was expanded by Sir George Carteret (*c.*1610–80), treasurer of the navy and chamberlain of the king's household from 1660 to 1667. He was vice-treasurer of

730 https://historicengland.org.uk/listing/the-list/list-entry/1126239 [accessed 20/1/22].

731 https://www.ourwarwickshire.org.uk/content/catalogue_her/chesterton-house-17th-century-park [accessed 20/1/22]. Chesterton House was built for Sir Edward Peyto in 1657 and set in a 17th century designed landscape including avenues as well as a windmill, and a watermill. The house was demolished in 1802.

732 Evelyn, *Diary*, 742.

733 Marquis of Ruvigny and Raineval, *The Jacobite Peerage* (Edinburgh, T. C. and E. C. Jack, 1904), 37.

734 https://www.nationaltrust.org.uk/cliveden/lists/the-history-of-cliveden [accessed 3/9/22].

735 Pepys, *Diary*, 9, 243.

736 Fiennes, *Through England on a Side Saddle*, 241.

737 https://hidden-london.com/gazetteer/coombe – [accessed 21/8/22].

Ireland from 1667 to 1673.[738] On 23 August 1674, Evelyn went 'to a great entertainment at Sir Robert Holmes's at Cranburne Lodge in the forest: There were his Majestie, Queene, Duke, Dutchesse & all the Court'.[739]

Customs House, London – in London, the Customs House was on Wool quay, in the parish of All Hallows, which is an intra-mural parish in the city of London. It was one of several buildings that Schellinks listed as he reviewed the London panorama: 'London Bridge, Lion Quay, Billingsgate, Customs House, Tower Wharf'.[740] In 1666, the Great Fire destroyed the building built by William Paulet, marquis of Winchester. The new building, which was designed by Sir Christopher Wren, was completed in 1671. It was damaged by fire in 1715 and burnt down in 1814.[741]

Dartford, Kent – a town at the point where Watling Street, the Roman road from Dover to London, crossed the river Darent, and which Celia Fiennes described as 'a little neate town'.[742]

Deal [Dalle/Dall], ***Kent*** – while an unusual spelling, this is probably a reference to Deal, a village on the Kent coast, where the English Channel meets the North Sea. Eight miles from Dover, Deal has a Tudor fort and Celia Fiennes noted that it was 'by the sea side wch is Called the Downs' adding that it 'Looks like a good thriveing place ye buildings new and neate Brickwork with gardens'.[743] On 3 May 1672 a barge was hired to carry the queen's bed and necessaries to Deal.[744]

Ditchley Park, near Charlbury, Oxfordshire – the home of Sir Francis Lee, 4th baronet (1639–67), which included a deer park. In 1661, Lee was elected as MP for Malmesbury and he was a member of the Cavalier Parliament. It was also home to Charlotte Lee, countess of Lichfield (1664–1718). She was the illegitimate daughter of Charles II and Barbara Villiers, 1st duchess of Cleveland. The house on this site now dates from the early eighteenth century.[745]

Dover, Kent – a town and port on the south coast of England, and one

738 C. H. Firth, revised by C. S. Knighton, 'Carteret, Sir George, first baronet (1610?–1680), naval officer and administrator', *ODNB*, 3 January 2008, https://doi-org.soton.idm.oclc.org/10.1093/ref:odnb/4803 [accessed 24/4/22].

739 Evelyn, *Diary*, 600.

740 Exwood and Lehmann, *Journal of William Schellinks*, 55–56.

741 Pepys, *Diary*, 10, 84.

742 Fiennes, *Through England on a Side Saddle*, 108.

743 Fiennes, *Through England on a Side Saddle*, 105.

744 TNA LC5/140, p. 53.

745 https://historicengland.org.uk/listing/the-list/list-entry/1000463 [accessed 21/8/22]; https://www.ditchley.com/ditchley-park [accessed 21/8/22].

of the cinque ports, a group consisting of Hastings, New Romney, Hythe, Dover, Sandwich and Rye. Schellinks noted 'the castle, which lies high on the chalk cliffs, [and] which fall off horribly steeply into the sea'.[746]

Epsom Wells, Surrey – sometimes also referred to as Epsom spa because in 1618 the waters at Epson were discovered and became increasingly popular during the seventeenth century. Schellinks recorded that 'Epsom is a very famous and pleasant place, much visited because of the water ... which is much drunk for health reasons, because of its purgative powers and which is being sent in stoneware jars throughout the land'.[747] Proximity to London made Epsom popular with those living there and Pepys visited Epson Wells in late July 1663 where 'we drank each of us two pots'.[748] However, the waters did not suit everyone and in March 1670 Evelyn wrote that his brother was ill 'perhaps by his drinking too excessively of Epsom Waters, when in full health & that he had no neede of them, being all of his lifetime of a sound & healthy constitution'.[749] It was so popular that in 1672 Thomas Shadwell wrote a comedy called *Epsom Wells*.

Erith [Erif], ***Kent*** – a small port on the south bank of the Thames, associated with the royal dockyard developed there by Henry VIII. Schellinks described Erith as a 'hamlet' adding that 'Here the East Indiamen usually discharge some of their cargo to reduce their draught, to enable them to sail up the river to Woolwich'.[750]

Euston [Ewston] ***Hall, West Suffolk*** – bought in 1666 by the earl of Arlington, he spent time and money developing the gardens with advice from Evelyn.[751] Celia Fiennes observed that the house was 'two miles from thetford, it stands in a Large parke 6 miles about. Y^e^ house is a Roman H of brick' while 'in one of the roomes was ye Dutchess of Cleavelands picture in a sultaness dress'.[752]

servants –

Exchange, the, London – either the Royal Exchange or the New Exchange, London's two specialist shopping venues. Celia Fiennes described the Royal Exchange as 'a Large space of Ground Enclosed round wth Cloysters and open arches on wch are built many walkes of Shopps

746 Exwood and Lehmann, *Journal of William Schellinks*, 39.

747 Exwood and Lehmann, *Journal of William Schellinks*, 87.

748 Pepys, *Diary*, 4, 246.

749 Evelyn, *Diary*, 538.

750 Exwood and Lehmann, *Journal of William Schellinks*, 46.

751 Nikolaus Pevsner and Enid Radcliffe, *Suffolk: The Buildings of England* (New Haven and London: Yale University Press, 1975), 202.

752 Fiennes, *Through England on a Side Saddle*, 123.

of all trades…in ye midst of it stands in stone work on a Pedestal ye effigies of King Charles ye second'.[753] The New Exchange was regarded as more fashionable, in terms of its architecture and the goods on sale, as noted in a seventeenth century ballad:

We will go no more to the Old Exchange
There's no good ware at all:
Their bodkins and their thimbles too
Went long since to Guild-hall.
But we will to the new Exchange
Where all things are in fashion
And we will have it hence forth call'd
The Burse of reformation.[754]

Fernhill [fearnhill], ***Berkshire*** – Fernhill Park, on the edge of Cranbourne village, was a mansion which was remodelled in the eighteenth century.[755]

Fulham (foulem), **Middlesex** – a village on the north bank of the Thames and a popular destination by boat for city dwellers. On 14 May 1669, Pepys recorded 'then my wife and I by water, with my brother, as high as Fulham, talking and singing'.[756]

Forest, the – there are two likely locations – 1) Epping Forest, Essex. Queen Elizabeth's hunting lodge was at Chingford and deer were put back after the Restoration but the forest was chiefly used for timber.[757] Or 2) part of Waltham Forest, Essex. On 18 August 1662, Pepys 'rid into Waltham Forrest and there we saw many trees of the King's a-hewing'.[758] On Lady Day 1682, the Earl of Lindsey received £91 14s 2d in part payment of £183 8s 4d for Henry Lowin's wages as under-keeper of New Lodge Walk in Waltham Forest.[759]

Gravesend, Kent – on the south bank of the Thames, just north of Watling Street, and with Tilbury on the opposite bank of the river. Celia Fiennes went 'to Gravesend wch is all by the side of the Cherry grounds … wch is Conveient for to Convey the Cherrys to London … with y^e Kentish Cherrys, a good sort Flemish fruite'.[760]

753 Fiennes, *Through England on a Side Saddle*, 247.

754 Quoted in Will Pritchard, *The Female Exterior in Restoration London* (Lewisburg: Bucknell University Press, 2008), 149.

755 https://www.berkshirehistory.com/castles/fernhill_park.html [accessed 18/1/23].

756 Pepys, *Diary*, 9, 555.

757 William Addison, *Epping Forest: Its Literary and Historical Associations* (London: J. M. Dent & Sons, 1945), 110.

758 Pepys, *Diary*, 3, 169.

759 Akerman, *Secret Services*, 58.

760 Fiennes, *Through England on a Side Saddle*, 107.

Great Park, Windsor, Berkshire – while the park was first laid out in the thirteenth century, Charles II developed the Great Park at Windsor by establishing the tree lined Long Walk in 1680, one of a number of formal avenues which added to the character of the park.[761]

Great Wardrobe, the, London – this was the king's Great Wardrobe, which was located on Puddle dock, London. It was also the London home of earl of Sandwich, who was keeper of the Great Wardrobe. The accommodation included a great chamber, withdrawing chamber and kitchen, as well as a garden. The Great Wardrobe moved to Hatton Garden after the Great Fire of London destroyed the buildings in Blackfriars.[762]

Greenwich, Kent – a village on the Thames. According to Schellinks, Greenwich was 'a fair sized market town with some nice streets and many fine houses. It is renowned for the Queen's House'.[763] There was also the Tudor palace that Charles did some building work on to modernise it and Celia Fiennes admired 'the kings parke att Greenwitch'.[764]

Guernsey [garnsy] – a reference to flowers, coming from the island of Guernsey, one of the Channel Islands. Guernsey flowers were sold at Covent Garden market, which was established in 1670 when Charles II gave a private charter to the earl of Bedford to hold a market. More specifically, it could be a reference to the Guernsey lily (*Nerine sariensis*), a red-flowered bulb, originating in South Africa, which is rumoured to have grown on Guernsey since the early seventeenth century.[765]

Ham/Ham House, Richmond upon Thames, Surrey – Ham was a small village on the bank of the Thames and next to Richmond Park. In 1610, Thomas Vavasour completed Ham House and after it was the family home of Elizabeth Murray. In 1672, she married John Maitland, who became the duke of Lauderdale. Evelyn visited in August 1678 recalling that 'After dinner I walked to Ham, to see the House & Garden of the Duke of Lauderdaile, which is indeed inferiour to few of the best villas in Italy itself, The House furnishd like a greate Princes; The Parterrs flo : Gardens, Orangeries, Groves, Avenues,

761 https://www.windsorgreatpark.co.uk/en/heritage/the-story-of-windsor-great-park [accessed 21/8/22].

762 Pepys, *Diary*, 8, 597.

763 Exwood and Lehmann, *Journal of William Schellinks*, 47.

764 Fiennes, *Through England on a Side Saddle*, 108.

765 Helen Brock (ed.), *A Description of the Guernsey Lily*, by James Douglas (Guernsey: The Clear Vue Publishing Company, 2012), reviewed by Graham Duncan, *Curtis's Botanical Magazine* 32.2 (2015), 162–73.

Courts, Statues, Perspectives, fountains, Aviaries and all this at the banks of the sweetest river in the World'.[766]

Hammersmith, London – Schellinks described Hammersmith as 'a nice market'.[767] Located on the outskirts of London, as Celia Fiennes noted, it was 'to Turnumgreen 2 [miles], thence to Hammersmith 2 to Kensington 2 and London 2 miles'.[768] Catherine had a house at Hammersmith and after she was widowed, she spent a lot of time there. The house had its own staff including a housekeeper, watchman, gardener and porter.[769]

Hampton Court palace, Surrey – An important royal palace for the Tudors and early Stuarts, Evelyn described 'Hampton Court is as noble & uniforme a Pile & as Capacious as any Gotique Architecture can have made it'.[770] Schellinks visited 'the Queen's Chapel, where, on an altar, was a heavy silver ciborium and candlesticks'.[771]

gardener – Evelyn admired the gardens, commenting on 'a rich & notable fountaine, of Syrens & statues &c: cast in Copper by Fanelli, but no plenty of water: The Cradle Walk of horne-beame in the Garden, is for the perplexed twining of the Trees, very observable &c: Another Parterr there is which they call Paradise in which a pretty banqueting house, set over a Cave or Cellar'.[772]

house keeper – the person who oversaw the smooth running of the house.

park keeper – Evelyn noted that 'The Parke formerly a flat, naked piece of Ground, [was] now planted with sweete rows of lime-trees, and the Canale for water now neere perfected: also the hare park'.[773]

wardrobe to – additional items to supplement the wardrobe holdings.

Highgate, Middlesex – a village to the north of London, located on the Great North road, the main road heading out of the capital to the north, with a tollgate owned by the bishop of London. Pepys visited Lauderdale's house on Highgate Hill in 1666, where he found him entertaining some of the Scots in London.[774]

Hoddesdon [Hodsdon], ***Hertfordshire*** – a village 20 miles to the south-west of Audley End.

Hounslow [huntslow], ***Middlesex*** – a small village on the road to Bath and

766 Evelyn, *Diary*, 653.
767 Exwood and Lehmann, *Journal of William Schellinks*, 81.
768 Fiennes, *Through England on a Side Saddle*, 21.
769 Bucholz, Sainty and Wassmann, *Household of Queen*, 33.
770 Evelyn, *Diary*, 439.
771 Exwood and Lehmann, *Journal of William Schellinks*, 92.
772 Evelyn, *Diary*, 439.
773 Evelyn, *Diary*, 439.
774 Pepys, *Diary*, 7, 224.

Schellinks noted how he 'went over Hounslow Heath to Hounslow, a nice market town'.[775] Ceclia Fiennes went via Hounslow Heath on a journey from Windsor to London.[776]

Hyde Park, London – located next to Kensington and established by Henry VIII as a hunting park, Hyde Park would become the largest of the London parks. The public were granted access in 1637 by Charles I but the land was sold during the Interregnum. Charles II recovered the park in 1660, replaced the deer and put a wall round it. Celia Fiennes noted that it was popular 'for Rideing on horseback but mostly for ye Coaches … the rest of ye parke is green and full of deer, there are large ponds with fish and fowle'.[777] According to Schellinks, Hyde Park was the place to be on 1 May when 'all the nobility from the court, town and country present themselves in their best finery, on horseback but mostly in carriages … it is the custom that the King, the Queen, and all of royal blood show themselves every year on this parade'.[778]

keeper –

Ipswich, Suffolk – a town on the river Orwell, which according to Celia Fiennes was 'a very Clean town and much bigger than Colchester is now'.[779]

music –

Isleworth, Middlesex – a village on the Thames and close to the river Crane, which Schellinks described as 'a very pleasant place'.[780] It was home to Syon House, see below.

Kensington, Middlesex – a village on the Bristol road, with ready access by coach, making it popular. On 31 May 1664, Pepys reported that the queen was 'gone by the park to Kensington'.[781] It was home to Nottingham House, a small villa, which William and Mary bought in 1689 and it would later become Kensington Palace.

King's Lynn [Lin], ***Norfolk*** – an important port and town on the Great Ouse river, which is 41 miles west of Norwich. The Customs House was built in 1683 and handled trade from Portugal and Spain.

Lacock [Laycok], ***Wiltshire*** – a small village south of Chippenham and clustered round an Augustinian abbey which was bought by William Sharington in 1540. He transformed the abbey into a country house.

775 Exwood and Lehmann, *Journal of William Schellinks*, 81.
776 Fiennes, *Through England on a Side Saddle*, 241.
777 Fiennes, *Through England on a Side Saddle*, 249.
778 Exwood and Lehmann, *Journal of William Schellinks*, 84.
779 Fiennes, *Through England on a Side Saddle*, 116.
780 Exwood and Lehmann, *Journal of William Schellinks*, 81.
781 Pepys, *Diary*, 5, 163.

Lambeth [Lambet], ***Surrey*** – a large village on the Thames, opposite Westminster. Lambeth Palace was home to the archbishop of Canterbury and and Schellings noted 'three or four royal boathouses and others of the nobility, some still being under construction'.[782]

London – the square mile or city of London on the north bank of the Thames and encompassed by the city walls. Celia Fiennes commented on the organisation of the city noting that it was 'divided into 24 wards to each which there is an alderman, and themselves Consist of Common Council men and all freemen of the Citty, and have power to Choose these aldermen and make their own orders and to maintain their own priviledges'.[783]

Maidenhead, Berkshire – a market town on the south bank of the Thames and five miles from Windsor. It was an important place to cross the Thames, so much so that Celia Fiennes mentioned 'the bridge at Maidenhead'.[784]

Marlborough, Wiltshire – located on the Old Bath Road, this market town sits on the river Kennet, to the north of Salisbury. In June 1654, Evelyn noted that Marlborough 'which having lately ben fired, was now new built'.[785]

Melbury [Malbury] – possibly Melbury House, Melbury Park, Dorset, a sixteenth century house in parkland built for Giles Strangways.[786] It was the home of Sir John Strangways (d.1666) who was succeeded by his son Giles.

Merton College, Oxford – founded in 1264, the college was home to Henrietta Maria from July 1643 during the first Civil War and to Catherine of Braganza after plague broke out in London in 1665. In 1671, Sir Christopher Wren was commissioned to provide a new screen and choir stalls in the chapel.

house cleanser –

Moor Park, Hertfordshire – Moor Park was built in *c.* 1617 by Edward Russell (1572–1627), 3rd earl of Bedford. James Scott, duke of Monmouth rebuilt it in 1678–79 and on his death, it passed to his widow, Anne. In 1686, Sir William Temple bought Moorhouse, Surrey and renamed it Moor Park, after the house of the same name in Hertfordshire.[787]

waterworks –

782 Exwood and Lehmann, *Journal of William Schellinks*, 56.

783 Fiennes, *Through England on a Side Saddle*, 241.

784 Fiennes, *Through England on a Side Saddle*, 21.

785 Evelyn, *Diary*, 337.

786 https://britishlistedbuildings.co.uk/101119248-melbury-house-melbury-sampford#.Y1RVD3bMLIU [accessed 22/10/22].

787 Paul Drury, Sally Jeffrey, and David Wrightson, 'Moor Park in the seventeenth century', *The Antiquaries Journal* 96 (2016), 241–90.

Mulberry garden, Hyde Park, London – a pleasure garden begun by James VI and I on what is now the site of Buckingham palace. According to Evelyn it was 'the best place about the towne for persons of the best quality to be exceeding cheated at', while Pepys described it as 'a silly place with a wilderness, somewhat pretty'.[788] He also added that it was full of 'a rascally, whoring, roguing sort of people'.[789] The gardens closed in the 1670s possible after Goring House, which was bought by Arlington in 1665, burnt down in 1674.[790]

Newbury, Berkshire – a market town on the edge of the Berkshire downs, important for the cloth trade and which Celia Fiennes described as 'a little town famous for makeing the best whipps – it's a good market for Corn and trade'.[791]

house at –

Newmarket, Suffolk – a market town about 65 miles north of London and Celia Fiennes noted that 'New market heath [was] where the Races are'.[792] Charles II and his brother attend the races regularly, for example, on 22 May 1668: 'the King and Duke of York and Court are at this day at Newmarket at a great horse-race'. However, heavy rain spoiled the event.[793]

New Park [Newparke], ***Hampshire*** – located in the New Forest, close to Lyndhurst, Brockenhurst and Lymington, New Park was Charles II's hunting lodge, which Celia Fiennes described in the following terms: 'From Lindhurst about a Mile is a parke called new parke enclosed out of ye fforrest with Pailes, it belongs to ye Kings house; there is a house in it wch was the Lodge – a large old Timber house'.[794]

Newport House, London – the home of Mountjoy Blount, the earl of Newport, until his death in February 1665. It then passed to his widow, Anne Boteler, who was a Catholic, and after her marriage to Thomas Weston, earl of Portland in 1667, she continued to live there until her death in 1669.[795]

Newport, Essex – a village close to Saffron Walden, which had come to overshadow it by the seventeenth century. Pepys visited on 8 October 1667 on his way to Audley End.[796]

Norwich, Norfolk – a market town with a castle and a cathedral on the river

788 Pepys, *Diary*, 9, 207. Davidson, *Catherine*, 181.

789 Pepys, *Diary*, 9, 207.

790 Pepys, *Diary*, 10, 258.

791 Fiennes, *Through England on a Side Saddle*, 21.

792 Fiennes, *Through England on a Side Saddle*, 125.

793 Pepys, *Diary*, 9, 209.

794 Fiennes, *Through England on a Side Saddle*, 40.

795 https://www.british-history.ac.uk/survey-london/vols33-4/pp360-379 [accessed 22/10/22].

796 Pepys, *Diary*, 8, 467.

Wensum. Celia Fiennes described Norwich as 'walled round full of towers Except on the river side wch serves for the wall'.[797]

Nottingham, Nottinghamshire – a city in the valley of the river Trent with a large castle and market; close by is Wollaton Hall. Celia Fiennes described Nottingham as 'the neatest town I have seen, built of stone and delicate, Large and long Streetes much like London, and ye houses Lofty and well built'.[798]

Oatlands, Surrey – a village close to the Thames in north Surrey named after Oatlands palace, which Henry VIII built on the site of Oatlands manor.[799] The palace was demolished *c.* 1650 but a house associated with the palace remained and this was bought by William Boteler and then Sir Edward Herbert.

Old Windsor, Berkshire – on the south bank of the Thames with Windsor Great Park to the west. It is just to the southeast of Windsor.

Oxbridge, Dorset – a hamlet on the river Birt that sits between Beaminster and Bridport.[800]

Oxford, Oxfordshire – county town and university city. Celia Fiennes noted that 'the high Streete is a very Noble one, soe Larg and of a Greate Length'.[801] On 22 September 1663, Pepys recalled that 'this day the King and Queene are to come to Oxford' adding that 'I hear that my Lady Castlemayne is for certain gone to Oxford to meet him'.[802]

Parliament house, Westminster – Ever the keen tourist, Celia Fiennes visited 'the Parliament which in Westminster Hall has apartments, the one for ye house of Lords and Called the Upper House' and one for the Commons.[803] Evelyn offered a little more detail on what happened there when he 'went with his Majestie into the Lobbie behind the house of Lords, where I saw the King & rest of the Lords robe themselves'.[804]

keeper – In October 1666, Pepys made payments to Hughes, house keeper and also to the door keeper.[805]

Queen's engagement with

To ye Man yt keepes ye Parlementt house [5 August 1664]

To ye Keeper of ye parlementt house [4 January 1665]

797 Fiennes, *Through England on a Side Saddle*, 119.

798 Fiennes, *Through England on a Side Saddle*, 55.

799 Simon Thurley, *The Royal Palaces of Tudor England: Architecture and Court Life, 1460–1547* (New Haven and London: Yale University Press, 1993), 60–63.

800 A. D. Mills, *The Place-Names of Dorset, Part 4*, English Place-Name Society 86–87 (2010), 325.

801 Fiennes, *Through England on a Side Saddle*, 24.

802 Pepys, *Diary*, 4, 315.

803 Fiennes, *Through England on a Side Saddle*, 268.

804 Evelyn, *Diary*, 472.

805 Pepys, *Diary*, 7, 305.

To ye Dore Keeper of ye Parlement house [27 September 1666]
To ye Doore Keeper of ye parlement when y^r^ Matie went Incognito [10 December 1666]
To ye Duchess of Mounmouths Coatchman and footemen that weighted one y^r^ Matie that day y^r^ Matie went tto ye parlement house [14 December 1666]
to the door keeper of the parliament [12 April 1678]

Parsons Green, Fulham, Middlesex – a village on the Thames four miles from Hyde Park. On 2 March 1678 Evelyn 'went to P greene to visite my Lady Mordaunt now indisposed'.[806]

Philberts [Filberds], ***Buckinghamshire*** – a house built for Charles II in the manor of Philberts, five miles from Windsor and two from Maidenhead. It was often associated with Thomas Chiffinch and Nell Gwyn.[807]

Physic [Phesike] ***garden*** – There were Physic gardens at St James and in Oxford. On 19 April 1664, Pepys 'walked…in the physique garden in St James park where I first saw Orange trees – and other fine trees'.[808] Schellinks visited the Oxford Physic garden, which is the garden mentioned here, and described it as a place 'in which very many plants and rare trees and herbs are grown'.[809] Celia Fiennes observed that the 'gardens afforded great diversion and pleasure, the variety of flowers and plants would have entertained one a week'.[810]

Portsmouth [Porthmouth], ***Hampshire*** – a port city on the south coast with Stuart connections: Charles I left from Portsmouth to travel to Spain in 1623, and five years later his travelling companion, George Villiers, 1st duke of Buckingham, was fatally stabbed in the Greyhound Pub by John Felton. Catherine of Braganza landed there in 1662 and she was married at the Royal Garrison church. Schellinks considered it to be 'a small but strong and famous town, one of the arsenals of England'.[811] Good diarist that she was, Celia Fiennes described Portsmouth as 'a very Good town, Well built with Stone and brick, its not a large town, there are Walls and Gates about it', adding that she visited the castle and went to the dining room 'where King Charles ye Second met Queen Katherine and was married to her and set the crown on her head'.[812]

Putney, Surrey – a village on the banks of the Thames that was notable

806 Evelyn, *Diary*, 647.

807 Robert O'Byrne, *The Representative History of Great Britain and Ireland* (London: John Ollivier, 1848), 120.

808 Pepys, *Diary*, 5, 127.

809 Exwood and Lehmann, *Journal of William Schellinks*, 96.

810 Fiennes, *Through England on a Side Saddle*, 26.

811 Exwood and Lehmann, *Journal of William Schellinks*, 145.

812 Fiennes, *Through England on a Side Saddle*, 41–42.

because of its ferry crossing mentioned in the household accounts of Edward I. Close by was Putney Heath. In 1649, Evelyn went 'To Putney by Water in barge with divers Ladys to see the Schooles or Colledges of the Young Gentlewomen'.[813] On 7 May 1667 Pepys saw 'the King and Duke of York [go] to Putney-heath to run some horses'.[814] In 1679, John Locke commented upon: 'The sports of England, which, perhaps, a curious stranger would be glad to see, are horse-racing, hawking and hunting. Bowling. At Marebone and Putney he may see several persons of quality bowling two or three times a week, all the summer.'[815]

bowling green keeper –

Reading, Berkshire – a town on the river Kennet and on the Thames. According to Celia Fiennes, Reading was 'a shire town, its pretty Large and accomodated for travellers being a great Road to Gloucester and ye West Country'.[816] Pepys agreed noting that the town was 'a very great one I think bigger then Salisbury'.[817]

Richmond [Richmon], ***Surrey*** – a town on the Thames, which is tidal up to this point, and site of Richmond palace which Schellinks reported was 'razed to the ground in the recent war on the order of the traitor Oliver Cromwell'.[818] In July 1662, Barbara lady Castlemaine moved to Richmond 'which I am apt to think was a design to get out of town, that the King might come at her the better'.[819]

Roehampton [Roe Hampton], ***Surrey*** – a village in the parish of Putney, Surrey. On 8 February 1677, Evelyn commented that he 'Went to Roehampton with my Lady Dutchesse of Ormond. The Garden & perspective is pretty, the Prospect most agreeable'.[820]

Royston, Hertfordshire – a town in north Hertfordshire, 12 miles south-west of Cambridge.

Runnymede [the Meads], ***Surrey*** – named for the meadows or meads which were owned by the Crown or the Church of England.

St James's palace, London – a Tudor royal palace, begun in 1531, located in Westminster, which Celia Fiennes described as 'another pallace St

813 Evelyn, *Diary*, 278. For other river trips, see Pepys, *Diary*, 8, 247 and 9, 552.

814 Pepys, *Diary*, 8, 204.

815 Peter King, Lord King ed., *The Life of John Locke with Extracts from his Correspondence, Journals and Common-Place Books*, vol. 1 (London: Henry Colburn and Richard Bentley, New Burlington Street, 1830), 248.

816 Fiennes, *Through England on a Side Saddle*, 284.

817 Pepys, *Diary*, 9, 242.

818 Exwood and Lehmann, *Journal of William Schellinks*, 78.

819 Pepys, *Diary*, 3, 139.

820 Evelyn, *Diary*, 633.

James wch is very well and was built for ye Royal Family as ye Duke of Yorke or Prince of Wales'.[821]

gardener –

French gardener –

St James's park, London – Acquired by Henry VIII in 1532, the park was developed by Elizabeth I, James VI and I and Charles II, who opened the park to the public and kept his collection of waterfowl and the pelicans he was given by the Russian ambassador there.[822] On 13 July 1663, Pepys 'met the Queene-Mother walking in the pell Mell, led by my Lord St Albans'.[823] On 24 June 1664, 'thence with him [James Pearce] to the park and there met the Queen coming from the chappell'.[824] Celia Fiennes observed that the park was 'full of very fine walkes and rowes of trees, ponds and Curious birds Deer, and some fine Cows'.[825] Schellinks 'saw there the new garden of the duke of York, which is large and long, next to the Pall-Mall court'.[826]

keeper –

train [traino/trenaw] – a term for a bird decoy used to lure wild birds into a trap.[827] Evelyn recorded a visit to St James's park on 9 February 1665 when he saw Charles II's decoy.[828] There is a surviving seventeenth century duck decoy at Boarstall, Buckinghamshire.[829]

Salisbury, Wiltshire – a cathedral city in Wiltshire at the meeting point of the rivers Avon, Bourne and Nadder. Schellinks reported that 'there is a most magnificent cathedral or main church with a very tall pointed spire and two transcepts'.[830] Charles II, Catherine and his court left London for Salisbury on 27 July 1665 and remained there for several months because there was plague in London.[831]

Sevenoaks [Seneck], ***Kent*** – a village in Kent close to the manor of Knole, with its substantial country house.

821 Fiennes, *Through England on a Side Saddle*, 248.

822 https://www.royalparks.org.uk/parks/st-jamess-park/about-st-jamess-park/history-and-architecture [accessed 16/8/22].

823 Pepys, *Diary*, 4, 229.

824 Pepys, *Diary*, 5, 188.

825 Fiennes, *Through England on a Side Saddle*, 248.

826 Exwood and Lehmann, *Journal of William Schellinks*, 84.

827 https://www-oed-com.soton.idm.oclc.org/view/Entry/204408?rskey=nJ1Qox&result=1#eid [accessed 26/1/23].

828 Evelyn, *Diary*, 473.

829 Michael Shrubb, *Feasting, Fowling and Feathers: A History of the Exploitation of Wild Birds* (London: T. and A. D. Poyser, an imprint of Bloomsbury, 2013), 215.

830 Exwood and Lehmann, *Journal of William Schellinks*, 131.

831 Pepys, *Diary*, 6, 172; 6, 189.

Sittingbourne, Kent – located on the river Swale, which separates the Isle of Sheppey from the rest of Kent, and it also sits on the old Roman road, Watling Street. Schellinks described Sittingbourne as 'a very large and long stretched out village, where we refreshed ourselves with new oysters and a cup of sack'.[832] Celia Fiennes felt it 'a very good town for ye Road and travellers as you shall meete wth'.[833]

Somerset Gardens, London – the gardens of Somerset House, which had stairs down to the river Thames.[834] Pepys visited in January 1665 noting that he went 'down the great stone stairs to the garden and tried the brave Eccho upon the stairs – which continues a voice so long as the singing three notes, concords, one after another, they all three shall sound in consort together a good while most pleasantly'.[835]

workmen –

Somerset House, London – the London home of Henrietta Maria from 1625 to 1642. Between 1630 and 1635, Inigo Jones built a Catholic chapel there for her. She resumed ownership in 1661 and began refurbishing the property and from this point the house took on the role of a dower house. Pepys's friend Mr Povy showed him 'the Queene-mother's chamber and closet, the most beautiful places for furniture and pictures'.[836] After Henrietta Maria returned to France in 1665, Catherine of Braganza used Somerset House as one of her London residences.[837] Celia Fiennes commented that 'ye king has a pallace in ye Strand wth fine gardens all to ye Thames river, this appertaines to ye Queen Dowager while she Lives'.[838]

barges to/from –

porters – from 1671 this was H. Beare.[839]

sentries –

wardrobe men –

workmen –

Somerset yard, London – a reference to Somerset House yard, the name given to the area of the Somerset Place site occupied by Worcester Inn.[840]

832 Exwood and Lehmann, *Journal of William Schellinks*, 45.

833 Fiennes, *Through England on a Side Saddle*, 100.

834 See Giovanni Canaletto, *View from Somerset Gardens looking towards London Bridge*, 1746–55, engraving, The Courtauld, London.

835 Pepys, *Diary*, 6, 18.

836 Pepys, *Diary*, 6, 17.

837 Simon Thurley, *Somerset House: The Palace of England's Queens, 1551–1692* (London: London Topographical Society, 2009), 45–56, 60–72.

838 Fiennes, *Through England on a Side Saddle*, 249.

839 Bucholz, Sainty and Wassmann, *Household of Queen*, 21.

840 Thurley, *Somerset House*, 91.

Southampton, Hampshire –a port in Hampshire on England's south coast. According to Pepys 'the towne is one most gallant street – and is walled round with stone … Many old walls of religious houses, and the Keye well worth seeing'.[841]

Southampton House, London – built by Thomas Wriothesley (1607–67), 4th earl of Southampton, on the north side of Southampton Square, London. The square was renamed Bloomsbury Square in *c.* 1723, the house became known as Bedford House and it was demolished in 1800. Southampton Square was the first formally laid out London square.[842] Southampton Row and Southampton Place retain their names and indicate the extent of Southampton's influence in this part of London. Pepys commented on the Lord Treasurer's new market, Southampton market, on 1 August 1666.[843]

Southaris – uncertain meaning. Possibly 'the southaris' could be a designation for 1) Suthrey House (now 119 Mortlake High Street), of which the surviving seventeenth century section was part of the Mortlake Tapestries works, 2) Catherine's house in Hammersmith, or 3) less likely, a reference to South Hayes, just along the road, from Hammersmith.[844]

Stoke Newington [Stoke], ***Middlesex*** – a small village close to the river Lea, with a key road running north going through it, on its way to Cambridge.

Swallowfield Park, Berkshire – near to the village of Swallowfield, which is a few miles south of Reading. The house was built for the Backhouse family at the end of the sixteenth century and it was demolished in 1689. Evelyn described this house in the following terms: it has 'Walks & groves of Elms, Limes, Oake: & other trees: & the Garden so beset with all manner of sweete shrubbs, as perfumes the aire marvelously: The distribution also of the Quarters, Walks, Parterre &tc is excellent. The Nurseries, Kitchin-garden, full of the most desireable plants; two very noble Orangeries well furnish'd; but above all, The Canale & fishponds'.[845] The current house was designed by William Talman, William III's comptroller of the works, for Henry Hyde, 2nd earl of Clarendon and his wife Flower.

Syon [Sion] ***House, Isleworth, Middlesex*** – built on the site of Syon Abbey, Syon House belonged to the Percy family from 1594, when it was

841 Pepys, *Diary*, 3, 71.

842 https://exploring-london.com/tag/southampton-square [accessed 10/1/22].

843 Pepys, *Diary*, 7, 232.

844 B. Weinreb et al., *The London Encyclopedia*, 3rd ed. (London: Macmillan, 2008), 900–01. I am most grateful to Alasdair Hawkyard for his very helpful suggestions.

845 Evelyn, *Diary*, 830.

acquired by Henry Percy, 9th earl of Northumberland. Schellinks described the house as 'a magnificent place, which had previously been a nunnery, which had entirely fallen into ruin because of its great age. It has a magnificent garden with many fruit trees, several remarkable ornamental gardens with very fine, broad avenues, well worth seeing'.[846]

Thetford, Norfolk – a market town at a crossing point on the Little Ouse river. Thetford Abbey was an important pilgrimage site prior to its dissolution in 1540. Over a century later, Celia Fiennes described Thetford as 'formerly a large place but now much decay'd and the ruines only shews it dimensions … Here I Lay wch is still in Norfolk. Next day I went to Euston Hall'.[847]

music –

Tunbridge Wells [Turbrige], ***Kent*** – also referred to as 'the Wells', Tunbridge was made popular by Lord North in 1606 and received royal patronage during the 1630s after Charles I and Henrietta Maria visited in 1630. It began developing as a spa town from the mid-1670s, with purpose-built shops, or Walks, being added in the 1680s. The town became so popular that in 1665 the earl of Bedford rented a house at Southborough, a village to the north of Tunbridge, for a month starting on 3 July at a cost of £4 a week, plus beer, coming to £24 for a month.[848] Tunbridge was popular with the queen and in July 1666 Pepys noted that 'the Queene and Maids of Honour are at Tunbridge'.[849] Celia Fiennes observed that 'they have made the wells very Comodious by the many good buildings all about it and 2 or 3 mile round which are Lodgings for the Company that drinke ye waters'.[850]

Twickenham [Twitnham], ***Middlesex*** – a village on the river Thames, which, from 1659, had a ferry.

Vauxhall [foxhall, fox hall], ***Surrey*** – Vauxhall was famous for its pleasure gardens, most notably the New Spring garden established in *c.* 1661 and the Old Spring garden which Pepys visited with two maids who 'gathered pinks'.[851] Schellinks recorded going 'on to Vauxhall to see the very large and most beautiful and interesting gardens, called the new Spring Gardens'.[852]

846 Exwood and Lehmann, *Journal of William Schellinks*, 81.
847 Fiennes, *Through England on a Side Saddle*, 122–23.
848 Scott Thomson, *Life in a Noble Household*, 222.
849 Pepys, *Diary*, 7, 214.
850 Fiennes, *Through England on a Side Saddle*, 109.
851 Pepys, *Diary*, 3, 95.
852 Exwood and Lehmann, *Journal of William Schellinks*, 58.

Waltham Abbey, Essex – a market town close to the river Lea and home to a bridge and fourteenth century gatehouse, the surviving parts of the Abbey founded in the eleventh century.

bowling green –

Wells, Somerset – a cathedral city, 23 miles south of Bristol. Cecil Fiennes said of Wells that it 'must be Reckoned halfe a Citty this and ye Bath making up but one Bishops See' adding that the cathedral 'has ye greatest Curiosity for Carv'd work in stone, the West front is full of all sorts of ffigures'.[853]

Westminster, Middlesex – In Celia Fiennes's view 'London is y[e] Citty properly for trade, Westminster for y[e] Court'.[854] This was true for events such as the state funeral of the earl of Sandwich on 3 July 1672, 'which was by Water in solemn pomp to Westminster'.[855] However, Westminster was also central to more popular events, such as the frost fair in January 1684, which Evelyn described, noting that 'Coaches now plied from Westminster to the Temple & from severall other stairs too & froo, as in the streets; also on sleds, sliding with skeetes'.[856]

Whitehall gate, Westminster – there were two main gates associated with the palace of Whitehall: the Holbein Gate which was the more northern gate, spanning the Charing Cross to Westminster road, also known as King Street, and the King Street Gate.[857]

porters –

Whitehall palace, Westminster – A large and old-fashioned Tudor palace and so in 1661 John Webb presented ideas for the redevelopment of the site. On 18 February 1666, Samuel 'walked to White-hall, where the Queene and ladies are all come'.[858] Celia Fiennes was impressed when she visited, describing 'y[e] kings pallace' as 'a most magnificent building all of freestone, wth appartments suiteable to y[e] Court of a King, in w[ch] was a Large roome Called the Banqueting-roome w[ch] was fitted for and used in all Publick solemnityes and audiences of ambassadours &c'.[859]

closet –

drawing room –

Wickham – Wickham, Hampshire, a village just north of Fareham.

853 Fiennes, *Through England on a Side Saddle*, 203.

854 Fiennes, *Through England on a Side Saddle*, 241.

855 Evelyn, *Diary*, 576.

856 Evelyn, *Diary*, 765.

857 Simon Thurley, *Whitehall Palace: An Architectural History of the Royal Apartments, 1240–1698* (New Haven and London: Yale University Press, 1999), 60–61.

858 Pepys, *Diary*, 7, 46.

859 Fiennes, *Through England on a Side Saddle*, 248.

Wimbledon, Surrey – a village and royal manor southwest of London. It was granted by Elizabeth I to Sir William Hatton who sold it to Sir Thomas Cecil. Charles I bought Wimbledon manor for Henrietta Maria, in 1638, which she held until 1649 and then she recovered it in 1660. However, she sold it in 1661 in George Digby, 2nd earl of Bristol, who developed the property with John Evelyn's guidance 'to help contrive the Garden after the modern. It is a delicious place for Prospect, & the thicketts, but the soile cold & weeping clay'.[860] The property was sold on the earl's death to Thomas Osborne, earl of Danby and Charles II's Lord High Treasurer. On 18 February 1678 Evelyn went with Osborne to Wimbledon and 'surveied his Gardens & alterations'.[861]

Winchester, Hampshire – a cathedral city in Hampshire, which Celia Fiennes described as 'a large town was once ye metropolis, there is a wall Encompassing it with severall Gates' while also noting 'in this town is a new building begun by K. Charles the Second for a Palace when he Came to hunt and for aire and diversions in the Country. I saw ye Modell of it was very fine and so it would have been if finished; but there is only ye outside shell is set up, ther were designed fine apartments and two Chapples but its never like to be finish'd now'.[862]

Windsor, Berkshire – a village on the river Thames with a royal castle. When Schellinks visited he saw 'the King's and Queen's bedchambers, the state rooms, apartments, and a large number of other places, amongst them one with a balcony, from which one has an overwhelmingly beautiful view'.[863]

housekeeper –

Poor Knights –

Woolwich [Wollige] ***Kent*** – a small village on the south bank of the Thames, located on the road from London to Dover. From the sixteenth century it was home to the oldest royal dockyard on the Thames which was established by Henry VIII.

Worcester House, the Strand – owned by the marquess of Worcester, it was the home of the earl of Clarendon from 1660 to 1666.[864] According to

[860] Evelyn, *Diary*, 436.

[861] Evelyn, *Diary*, 647.

[862] Fiennes, *Through England on a Side Saddle*, 36–37.

[863] Exwood and Lehmann, *Journal of William Schellinks*, 95.

[864] Sidney J. Madge, 'Worcester House in the Strand', *Archaeologia* 91 (1945), 157–80. See also https://www.strandlines.london/2018/11/26/the-lost-mansions-of-the-strand [accessed 9/1/22].

Schellings it was known as 'Salisbury or Worchester House'.[865] This was where Anne Hyde married James, duke of York on 3 September 1660 and their son, Charles Stuart, duke of Cambridge (1660–61), was born there shortly after, on 22 October. From 1682 it was called Beaufort House.[866]

Plancett, mistress – for bringing water.

Plancys, mistress – to her nephew who brought sweet water

her assigns –

plate – much of Catherine's plate was provided by the royal goldsmiths or was given to her as gifts, so only a few smaller items or repairs were paid for from the privy purse.[867] These were mainly objects required for writing or were part of the queen's toilet plate. The latter, as was noted in the *Mundus Muliebris,* could include different elements, according to the owner's taste and wealth:

A new Scene to us next presents,
The Dressing-Room and Implements,
Of Toilet Plate Guilt, and Emboss'd,
And several other things of Cost,
The Table Miroir, one Glue Pot,
One for Pomatum, and whatnot?
Of Washes Unguents and Cosmeticks,
A pair of Silver Candlesticks,
Snuffers and Snuff-dish, Boxes more,
For Powders, Patches, Waters Store,
In silver Flasks, or Bottles, Cups
Covered or open to wash chaps.[868]

gold bottles – most toilet sets were silver but on 20 April 1673 Evelyn saw the toilet set 'all of massie gold' that the king had given to Catherine which was valued at £4,000.[869]

silver box in the standish – a standish or inkstand was an oblong box or casket, with feet, the inside of which was divided into compartments to hold writing equipment: notably ink, seals, sealing wax, pens and pounce or sand.[870]

865 Exwood and Lehmann, *Journal of William Schellinks*, 55.

866 Pepys, *Diary*, 10, 490–91.

867 For the relationship between the monarch and goldsmiths, see Oman, *Caroline Silver*, 6–13.

868 Evelyn, *Mundus Muliebris*, 9: https://quod.lib.umich.edu/e/eebo/A38815.0001.001/1:3?rgn=div1;submit=Go;subview=detail;type=simple;view=fulltext;q1=plate [accessed 1/5/22].

869 Evelyn, *Diary*, 586.

870 Oman, *Caroline Silver*, 56–57.

silver box – this might be another replacement box for a standish or a small box for storing other little items associated with the queen's toilet such as a patch box.

sweet water pot – a pot or bottle, often very decorative, used to hold perfumed waters and scents and a frequent part of a toilet set.

Plessy, Monsieur du – for a bill.

poor, the – giving money to the poor highlights the importance of charitable gifts, either to an individual, as is the case here, or to a married couple. Pepys noted that, Jemima, countess of Sandwich, was left in charge of keeping the poor house while her husband was away in June 1661.[871]

men –

to a poore Man thatt came from Portungall –

to a poore man had his Meare killd –

to a poore man with a petition –

women –

to a Poore woman sent by Lady Gerrarde –

To ye watter fillers and poore women and others at ye wells as per bill –

to a poore womane had her husband killed over the wall –

to a poore womane had her Hog Killed by one of yor Maties Coatches at Chelsy –

to a poore womane with Child –

to a poore womane with a petition –

to the poore at Audley end –

to the poore of Bery – Bury St Edmunds, Suffolk, see above.

to a poore man at heigh park –

to the poore att oxbri<d>ge – Oxbridge, Dorset, see above.

to the poore of Ewston – Euston Hall, West Suffolk, see above.

to the poore by the portingall Embassador –

to the poore of Thetford –

Poor Knights of Windsor – established by Edward III, and numbering 26, to match the number of Garter knights. In return for praying daily for the monarch and his Garter knights in St George's chapel, the Poor Knights of Windsor were given lodgings in the lower ward of Windsor castle. Henry VIII reduced their number to thirteen, while Charles II increased them to eighteen. In March 1660, Pepys' uncle 'came to enquire about the Knights of Windsor, of which he desires to get to

871 Pepys, *Diary*, 2, 122; 5, 316.

be one'.[872] The Secret Service accounts paid £20 in 1682 to William Aldham as bounty 'till a poor Knt's place at Windsor fall void'.[873]

Porter, Mr – possibly Mr George Porter senior, gentleman usher of the privy chamber, from 1662 to 1669 or Mr George Porter junior, gentleman usher of the privy chamber, from 1669 to 1705.[874]

man –

Portland, lady – Anne Boteler, was the daughter of John Boteler, 1st baron Boteler and Elizabeth, daughter of Sir George Villiers. She married Thomas Weston (1609–88), 4th earl of Portland, who inherited the title on the death of Charles Weston (1639–65), 3rd earl of Portland, who was killed at the battle of Lowestoft on 3 June 1665.[875]

footman –

Portsmouth, duchess of – Louise de Kéroualle (1649–1734) was the daughter of Guillaume de Penancoët, count de Kéroualle and his wife, Marie-Anne. In 1668, she was made a maid of honour to the king's sister, Henriette Anne, and came with her to England in 1670. After Henriette's death, Louise was appointed as a lady in waiting to Catherine of Braganza, and not long after she became a mistress of Charles II.[876] In July 1672 she gave birth to a son, called Charles, and in 1675 he was made duke of Richmond and Lennox. In 1673, Louise was made duchess of Portsmouth and a Lady of the Bedchamber. After the king's death she returned to France.

man –

Portugal, Portuguese – Charles II's marriage to Catherine resulted in closer ties with Portugal. In June 1668, Sir Robert Southwell was appointed as envoy-extraordinary to Portugal.[877] At the meeting of the Royal Society on 21 October 1669, Evelyn noted that Sir Robert 'presented Balsomes & other Curiosities out of Portugal'.[878]

baker –

872 Pepys, *Diary*, 1, 78. He was unsuccessful, but in November he did receive a room as an almsman at Winchester cathedral, *CSPD Charles II, 1660–1*, 359.

873 Akerman, *Secret Services*, 61.

874 Sainty, Wassmann and Bucholz, *Household officers*, 59.

875 Mentioned in Sean Kelsey, 'Weston, Jerome, second earl of Portland (1605–1663), politician', *ODNB*, 3 January 2008, https://doi.org.soton.idm.oclc.org/10.1093/ref:odnb/29123 [accessed 15/4/22].

876 Sonia Wynne, 'Kéroualle, Louise Renée de Penancoët de, *suo jure* duchess of Portsmouth and *suo jure* duchess of Aubigny in the French nobility (1649–1734), royal mistress', *ODNB*, 3 January 2008, https://doi.org.soton.idm.oclc.org/10.1093/ref:odnb/15460 [accessed 15/4/22]; MacLeod, *Painted Ladies*, 243.

877 *CSPD Charles II, 1667–8*, 438, 441.

878 Evelyn, *Diary*, 535.

cook – although Catherine employed a Portuguese cook, Evelyn was unimpressed by the food served by the Portuguese ambassador in December 1679: 'besides a good olio, the dishes were trifling, hash'd & Condited after their way, not at all fit for an English stomac, which is for solid meate. There was yet good fowle but roasted to Coale; nor were the sweetemeates good'.[879]

man –

Potts [Pots], **captain** – possibly serving in the garrison at Windsor.

Price, mistress – possibly 1) Mary Price, woman of the queen's Bedchamber, in 1672.[880] Or 2) Goditha Price (1637–93), the daughter of Sir Herbert Price (1605–78), 1st baronet, and master of the king's household. Known as 'fat price', she was a maid of honour to the duchess of York and a mistress of James, duke of York.[881]

Price, Mr – the keeper of the queen's ass.

Proger, Mr – Edward Progers (1621–1713) served as a page at the court of Charles I and then joined the household of Charles, prince of Wales, in 1646 as a groom of the bedchamber. He was appointed in the same role in the king's household at the Restoration.[882]

Queen's majesty – Catherine of Braganza (1638–1705), was the daughter of João de Bragança, eighth duke of Bragança, later King John IV of Portugal, and his wife, Luiza Maria.[883] On 8 May 1661, Charles II informed parliament of his intention to marry Catherine and, on 13 April 1662, she left Lisbon for England. They were married on 21 May and her arrival in London was marked by a river pageant on the Thames on 23 August. She was pregnant in 1666, 1668 and 1669, but none of her pregnancies came to term. During their marriage, Charles maintained multiple mistresses and fathered fourteen children that he acknowledged. Catherine was implicated in the Popish Plot in 1678 but with the king's protection she survived. After Charles died in 1685, she remained in England until 1692 when she travelled back to Portugal. In 1704, she was made regent for her brother Pedro, and she died in office in 1705.

879 Evelyn, *Diary*, 677.

880 Sainty, Wassmann and Bucholz, *Household officers*, 60.

881 Pepys, *Diary*, 7, 159 and fn. 1.

882 Andrew Barclay, 'Progers, Edward (1621–1713), courtier', *ODNB*, 23 September 2004, https://doi-org.soton.idm.oclc.org/10.1093/ref:odnb/58149 [accessed 12/12/21].

883 Sonia Wynne, 'Catherine [Catherine of Braganza, Catarina Henriqueta de Bragança] (1638–1705), queen of England, Scotland and Ireland, consort of Charles II', *ODNB*, 3 January 2008, https://doi.org/10.1093/ref:odnb/4894 [accessed 11/11/21].

baker, Portuguese – possibly the 'Portugal woman', Mary Rotz listed in 1677 with a salary of £60 p.a.[884]

barge men – the rowers of the queen's barge

bedchamber women – women who served the queen within her bedchamber.

bottle men – a term associated with the groom of the bottle horse or groom bottle man. The position within the queen's household was ended in *c.* 1685. Prior to that it was held by M. Ashley by 1669, S. Hadley by 1673 and J. Winch by 1682.[885]

buttery – a term for a storeroom such as a pantry or larder used to house ale and beer and for the staff who worked there.

chairmen – the men who carried the queen's sedan chair.

coachmen – the men who drove the royal coaches and carriages. They were provided with an ornate livery.

cook – the queen's master cook was A. Harcourt from July 1663, P. Lamb from August 1677, and E. Smith from April 1683.[886]

cook, Portuguese – several Portuguese cooks were listed as members of Catherine's household: on 1 October, S. Barioso and M. Laurenco and by 1685 A. Francisco.[887]

cook, Spanish –

dairy maid – a woman who worked in the queen's dairy, involved with milking, making butter, etc. According to Hannah Wolley, in her work *The Complete Servant Maid* (1677), those who aspired to have 'the esteem and reputation of good dairy maids must be very careful that all their vessels be scalded well, and kept very clean, that they milk their cattle in due time, for the kine by custom will expect it though you neglect, which will tend much to their detriment'.[888]

ewery – the office within the household responsible for the care and provision of water for drinking and washing.

footmen – liveried male servants who attended the queen when she travelled by coach as well as admitting guests to her apartments and attending her when she dined.

footmen, Irish –

gallery keepers – individuals who controlled the key, and thereby access, to galleries, which could be used for a variety of reasons including taking exercise, viewing a space below or the display of pictures.

884 Davidson, *Catherine*, 312.

885 Bucholz, Sainty and Wassmann, *Household of Queen*, 62.

886 Bucholz, Sainty and Wassmann, *Household of Queen*, 46.

887 Bucholz, Sainty and Wassmann, *Household of Queen*, 46.

888 Patricia Crawford and Laura Gowing eds., *Women's Worlds in Seventeenth Century England: A Sourcebook* (London: Routledge, 2000), 75.

grooms – members of the queen's household who would undertake a range of tasks.

grooms of the stables – men working within the stables, caring for the queen's horses.

herb woman – a woman who collected fragrant herbs and flowers for strewing in the royal apartments or drying and being used to scent linen. She might also sell herbs.

kitchen – collective term for the kitchen staff headed by the master cook, clerk of the kitchen, yeomen, and grooms of the kitchen and the turnbroaches.[889]

litter men – the men who carried the queen's litter. According to the 1663 household establishment list there were four littermen in service at any time.[890]

maids of honour – unmarried young women in service in the queen's household. On 28 June 1669, Evelyn noted that his wife had 'gon on a journey of Pleasure downe the River as far as the Sea, with Mrs Howard, & her daughters the Maids of Honor, amongst whom, that excellent creature Mrs Blagge'.[891]

mother of the maids – the woman in charge of the maids of honour.

master of the barge – the man in charge of the men rowing the queen's barge. By 1672, he earnt £20 per year plus receiving a New Year's gift of £3 and a pension of £30 per annum. This office was held by W. Jeane from July 1661, R. Hill by 1671, and J. George by 1687.[892]

necessary woman – these women cleaned the royal apartments and their tasks included setting and lighting fires, dusting, and emptying chamber pots. The best-known Stuart necessary woman is Bridget Holmes, who served Charles I, Charles II, James II and William III and was immortalised in a full-length portrait by John Riley.[893] Catherine's necessary women were M. Maget from June 1663, E. Jones by 1678 and A. Gilford by 1685.[894]

pages of the backstairs – the private stairs in a royal palace. In 1663, there were four pages of the backstairs. By 1668, there were eight.[895] A notice in the *London Gazette* during 1682 stated that 'Whoever

889 Bucholz, Sainty and Wassmann, *Household of Queen*, 45–50.

890 Bucholz, Sainty and Wassmann, *Household of Queen*, 62.

891 Evelyn, *Diary*, 539.

892 Bucholz, Sainty and Wassmann, *Household of Queen*, 22.

893 John Riley, *Bridget Holmes*, 1686, oil on canvas, Royal Collection, RCIN 405667. Also see Rufus Bird, Olivia Fryman and Martin Clayton eds., *Charles II: Art and Power* (London: Royal Collection Trust, 2017), 150.

894 Bucholz, Sainty and Wassmann, *Household of Queen*, 39.

895 Bucholz, Sainty and Wassmann, *Household of Queen*, 20.

brings him to her Royal Highnesses Back-stairs, shall have a Guinea Reward'.[896]

pantry – a room or several rooms to store bread and other foodstuffs and the collective term for the staff that worked there.[897]

postillions – the rider of the left, or nearside, horse of a pair of horses pulling a coach.[898]

secretary – an individual who wrote letters, prepared warrants, and other similar tasks.

clerk –

sergeant trumpeter – the officer in charge of the trumpeters.

sumpter men – the men, who were liveried servants, who led the queen's sumpter horses and mules, who had sumpter cloths with the queen's arms and/or initials, and carried the chests and trunks attached to their sumpter saddles.

tennis court man – the keeper of a royal or indoor tennis court.

treasurer – the individual in overall charge of the queen's finances.

clerk –

trumpeters – one who plays or sounds a trumpet.

vice-chamberlain – an important officer in the royal household who served under the chamberlain.

wardrobe men – the officers looking at the queen's wardrobe of the robes, which housed the queen's clothes, and the wardrobe of beds, which cared for her textile furnishings.

watermen – these were the men who rowed small boats or wherries on the Thames, which could carry up to five people. Some were in the employment of the monarch, providing transport on the river or rowing extra barges on ceremonial occasions.[899] They had their own Livery Company, with a grant of arms from Elizabeth I in 1585.

yeomen of the guard – the royal guard, undertaking ceremonial duties and, also, providing protection for Catherine of Braganza.

yeoman of the wagons – the officer in charge of the wagons used to transport the queen's possessions when she removed and went on progress.

Queen dowager – Henrietta Maria (1609–69), the youngest daughter of Henry IV of France and Marie de Medici. She married Charles I in 1625,

896 *London Gazette* (1682), no. 1764/4: https://www.oed.com/view/Entry/14459?redirectedFrom=backstairs#eid [accessed 14/3/22].

897 https://www.oed.com/view/Entry/137062?rskey=7bPINL&result=1&isAdvanced=false#eid [accessed 20/1/23].

898 https://www.oed.com/view/Entry/148549?redirectedFrom=postilion+#eid [accessed 20/1/23].

899 Susan Doran ed., *Royal River: Power, Pageantry and the Thames* (London: Royal Museums Greenwich, 2021), 176.

and Charles II was her first surviving child, who was born in 1630. She returned to France in 1644 and remained there in exile until the Restoration, when she travelled to England in 1660. She went back to France in 1661, came back to England in 1662 and then journeyed to France in 1665. On her death, Henrietta Maria was buried at the Basilica of St Denis in Paris.[900]

chariot men – the men who drove and attended the queen's chariots, a term which could refer to a coach for private use or a cart for transporting goods.[901]

cook –

footmen –

man –

old footman – this was not the only instance of Henrietta Maria's former servants being cared for. On 13 March 1673, a warrant was issued 'to pay £50 to Peter Anthony, trumpeter, late servant to her Majesty the Queen Mother, deceased' for his costs being sent to sea in attendance on Prince Rupert.[902]

Randue, Mr – housekeeper at Windsor.[903]

Ravenicke [Rauerick], **David** – listed as a servant in the queen's chapel and closet in 1665.[904]

Rawson, Mr – bounty to the Chasmary man. Also see Roswan.

Reynolds, Mrs – as per bill.

Richards, Mr – for a boat.

Richmond, duchess of – Mary Villiers (1622–85), the daughter of George Villiers, duke of Buckingham, and Lady Katherine Manners. She married Lord Herbert in 1635 but he died the following year. She remarried in 1637 to James Stuart, 4th duke of Lennox, and from 1641 duke of Richmond. He died in 1655. She married a third time in 1664 to Colonel Thomas Howard (d.1678). She continued to be referred to as the duchess of Richmond until her death in 1685.[905]

footmen –

900 Caroline Hibberd, Henrietta Maria [Princess Henrietta Maria of France] (1609–1669), queen of England, Scotland and Ireland, consort of Charles I, *ODNB*, 3 January 2008, https://doi.org/10.1093/ref:odnb/12947 [accessed 3/1/22].

901 https://www-oed-com.soton.idm.oclc.org/view/Entry/30712?redirectedFrom=chariot+man#eid9603895 [accessed 20/1/23].

902 Ashbee, *Records*, 123.

903 *CTB, 1681–85*, 475.

904 Sainty, Wassmann and Bucholz, *Household officers*, 60.

905 Freda Hast, 'Villiers [married name Stuart], Mary, duchess of Lennox and Richmond (1622–1685), courtier', *ODNB*, 3 January 2008, https://doi-org/10.1093/ref:odnb/56054 [accessed 24/4/22].

Robinson, Mr – John Robinson, groom of the great chamber, from 1662–63 to 1683.[906]

Roche, Mr – her majesty's tailor. Luis Roche, tailor, received 2s a day and had claims worth £13 10s in 1677.[907] He was possibly the Mr Rous of Ashtead, Surrey, who was described as the queen's tailor, who gained denization in 1663 and owned a house in Ashtead in 1664.[908]

Rochester, lady – Elizabeth Wilmot (1651–81), was the daughter of John Malet of Enmore, Somerset (d.1656) and Unton (or Untia) Hawley. Pepys described her as the 'great beauty and fortune of the north'.[909] When she refused to marry John Wilmot, 2nd earl of Rochester, he tried to abduct her on 26 May 1665. He failed, but on 29 January 1667, they were married. They had four children, and she wrote poetry.[910]

servant –

Roe, Mr – for birds; possibly George Rowse, who was listed as a page of the queen's presence chamber, in 1668.[911]

Rogers, Mr – possibly Charles Rogers, gentleman usher quarter waiter, from 1662–63 to 1694.[912]

man –

Roper, Mr – possibly Francis Roper, surveyor of the robes, who received £20 salary in 1677, with an allowance of £80 for livery and all other claims.[913]

Roper, Mrs – possibly the wife of Francis Roper.

Rose, Mr John – John (1619–77) was the son of Stephen Rose, a yeoman farmer, and he was born in Amesbury, Wiltshire. In 1666, he published *The English Vineyard Vindicated*.[914] He was the king's gardener and is traditionally thought to have been painted by Henry Danckerts presenting a pineapple to Charles II.[915] However, this has been doubted.[916]

906 Sainty, Wassmann and Bucholz, *Household officers*, 62.

907 Davidson, *Catherine*, 189–90, 310.

908 Pepys, *Diary*, 10, 356.

909 Pepys, *Diary*, 6, 110.

910 Cited in Frank H. Ellis, 'Wilmot, John, second earl of Rochester (1647–80), poet and courtier', *ODNB*, 3 January 2008, https://doi.org/10.1093/ref:odnb/29623 [26/4/22].

911 Sainty, Wassmann and Bucholz, *Household officers*, 64.

912 Sainty, Wassmann and Bucholz, *Household officers*, 63.

913 Davidson, *Catherine*, p. 310; there is also a Christopher and a Francis Roper, see Sainty, Wassmann and Bucholz, *Household officers*, 63.

914 In addition, in the queen's service were Giles Rose, groom of the queen's kitchen, 1668 to 1674, then groom of the household kitchen in 1674, and Richard Rose, keeper of the council chamber, 1671 to 1678.

915 Sandra Raphael, 'Rose, John (1619–1677), gardener and nurseryman', *ODNB*, 23 September 2004, https://doi.org/10.1093/ref:odnb/37913 [accessed 22/11/21].

916 Margaret Willes, *The Making of the English Gardener: Plants, Books and Inspiration, 1560–1660* (New Haven and London: Yale University Press, 2013), 273.

Roswan, Mr – 'chasmary' man; while this suggests a surgeon, it might be Alexander or William Rosewell, who were apothecaries.

Rowland, Mr – possibly David Rowland, groom of the robes, who was listed in Catherine's household in 1677, with a salary of £39 13s 4d.[917] He became yeoman of the robes in 1682.[918]

Russell, lady – Lady Rachel Russell (*c.*1636–1723), was the daughter of Thomas Wriothesley, 4th earl of Southampton, and Rachel de Massue. She married twice: first to Francis Vaughan (d.1667), lord Vaughan, in 1653 and then William, lord Russell, in 1669. In 1678, they gained the title of lord and lady Russell.[919]

man –

Rutland, Mr – as per bill for the robes feast.

Saints' days – see under *calendar*.

Salmon, Mr – for bounty to the littermen and chairmen.

Sanderson, mistress – Lady Bridget (*c.*1592–1682), was the daughter of Sir Edward Tyrrell, baronet, and wife of Sir William Sanderson (?1586–1676). She was laundress to Henrietta Maria and mother of the maids, from 1662 to 1679, to Catherine of Braganza.[920] On 19 July 1676, Evelyn recorded that he 'went to Sir William Sandersons funerall (husband to the Mother of the Maides, & author of two large, but meane Histories of KK James & Charles the first)'.[921]

Sands, Mr – for making a payment.

Sanford, mistress – presented Catherine with *The History of Portugal*.

Sarsfield [Sarsfeild], **Mrs** – for her bill.

Savingnon [Sauingnon], **Mr** – for holland fabric.

Sayers, Mr – possibly George Sayers, page of honour to the queen, from 1671 to 1676, gentleman usher of the queen's privy chamber in 1679, and her vice-chamberlain from 1682 to 1692.[922]

Scroope [Scrope, Scrup], **lady** – Mary (*c.*1627–85), was the daughter of Sir Robert Carr of Sleaford, Lincolnshire, and widow of Sir Adrian Scroope. She was a member of the queen's household, and she held several posts: as a dresser in 1662 to 1663; as second dresser from 1663 to 1677; as a

917 Davidson, *Catherine*, 310.

918 Sainty, Wassmann and Bucholz, *Household officers*, 64.

919 Lois G. Schwoerer, 'Russell, [*née* Wriothesley; *other married name* Vaughan], Rachel, lady Russell (1637–1723), noblewoman', *ODNB*, 23 September 2004 https://doi.org/10.1093/ref:odnb/24335 [accessed 19/3/22].

920 See D. R. Woolf, Sanderson, Sir William (1586–1676), historian, *ODNB*, 23 September 2004, https://doi-org.soton.idm.oclc.org/10.1093/ref:odnb/24630 [accessed 26/4/22].

921 Evelyn, *Diary*, 627.

922 Sainty, Wassmann and Bucholz, *Household officers*, 66.

chamberer 1665 to 1669 and as first lady dresser 1665 to 1679.[923] She was the mistress of Henry Bennet, earl of Arlington, in 1663, and later to Henry Savile, England's envoy to France. She was mentioned in the satire, *On the Ladies of the Court* (1663):

Scroope, they say, hath no good breath,
But yet, she's well enough beneath,
And hath a good figary;
Or with such ease
She could not please
The King's great secretary.[924]

gardener –
man –
servant –

seaman's wife – one of the challenges Pepys faced in his role with the Navy was the problem of the sailors not being paid on time and their being put on half pay or laid off when they were not required. This had a marked impact on the sailors, their families and national security. On 14 June 1667, Pepys recorded the Dutch attack on the king's ships on the Medway adding that 'the hearts as well as the affections of the seamen are turned away; and in the open streets in Wapping and up and down, the wives have cried publickly "This comes of your not paying our husbands"'.[925]

Sears, Mr – accompanied the queen when fishing.

Semson, Mr – for his bill.

Sentry, sentries – an armed soldier stationed at specific points, such as gateways and doors to particular rooms, to keep guard.

Shore, Mr – for the Guard's trumpets.

Sidney, Mr – possibly Henry Sidney (d.1704), the youngest son of Robert Sidney, 2nd earl of Leicester of Penshurst, and Dorothy Percy. He was a groom of the bedchamber to the duke of York and master of the horse to the duchess of York. He was created viscount of Romney in 1689 and earl in 1694 and was rumoured to have had an affair with the duchess of York.[926] However, he was one of three brothers, all of whom feature in Pepys' *Diary,* and so it might be a reference to either Algernon (1622–83) or Colonel Robert (d.1668).[927]

923 Sainty, Wassmann and Bucholz, *Household officers*, 67.

924 Wilson, *Court Satire*, 6, 9.

925 Pepys, *Diary*, 8, 268.

926 Pepys, *Diary*, 6, 302; David Hosford, 'Sidney, Henry, first earl of Romsey (1641–1704), politician and army officer', *ODNB*, 10 January 2013, https://doi.org/10.1093/ref:odnb/25521 [accessed 26/4/22].

927 Pepys, *Diary*, 10, 397–98.

Slaughter, Mr – possibly George Slaughter, an usher daily waiter, from 1662–63 to 1694.[928]

Smith – keeper of the queen's birds.

Smith, Mr – yeoman of the wagons.

Smith, Mr – Hugh Smith, page of the presence chamber, from 1662–63 to 1702.[929]

soldiers [solger] – while the creation of a royal guard was an important aspect of Charles II's reign, the population was probably more aware of the men wounded fighting in the civil war.[930] The king's secret service accounts for December 1680 included £15 10s for 'one-and-thirty poor decrepit soldjers from Tanger, as of his Ma'ties bounty'.[931]

lame – soldiers with reduced mobility because of injuries to their feet or legs. Payments to a 'poor discharged soldier' and a 'poor wounded soldier' also featured in the accounts of the duke of Bedford.[932]

at Somerset House –

Southampton, lady – Frances Darcy (1618–81), was the daughter of William Seymour, 2nd duke of Somerset, and Lady Frances Devereux. Her second husband was Thomas Wriothesley, 4th earl of Southampton (1607–67), and they married in 1659 (she was his third wife).[933] When Pepys visited the city of Southampton in 1662, he rode 'besides my Lord of Southamptons parks and lands, which in one viewe we could see 6000*l* per annum'.[934] She married a third time in 1676: on this occasion to Conyers Darcy, 2nd earl of Holderness.[935]

footman –

man –

Spencer, Mr – sending gifts. Possibly Mr Robert Spencer, the nephew of the Lord Treasurer and who was put forward for the post of Master of the Horse to the queen.[936]

footman –

man –

page –

928 Sainty, Wassmann and Bucholz, *Household officers*, 68.

929 Sainty, Wassmann and Bucholz, *Household officers*, 69.

930 https://www.civilwarpetitions.ac.uk [accessed 17/8/22].

931 Akerman, *Secret Services*, 22.

932 Scott Thomson, *Life in a Noble Household*, 363.

933 See David Smith, 'Wriothesely, Thomas, fourth earl of Southampton (1608–1667), politician', *ODNB*, 3 January 2008 https://doi.org/10.1093/ref:odnb/30077 [accessed 27/3/22].

934 Pepys, *Diary*, 3, 70.

935 No *ODNB* entry.

936 Davidson, *Catherine*, 210.

spinning – the process of twisting fibres to create yarn using a drop spindle, distaff, or a spinning wheel. A spinning wheel could be used to produce yarn from fleece and from flax.[937]

Staggins [Stagings], **Isaac** – A musician listed in the royal accounts as playing the recorder.[938] Also for payments for violins and wind instruments.

stand, the – the keeper of. A reference to the royal stand, possibly at Datchet Ferry, Windsor. In the print produced by Francis Barlow it was mistakenly referred to as being at Dorsett Ferry but it does record that the last races the king saw at Datchet Ferry was on 24 August 1684.[939]

Stanhope, Mr – possibly 1) Alexander Stanhope (1638–1707), who was a son of Philip, 1st earl of Chesterfield, and his second wife, Anne Pakington. He was a gentleman usher of the queen's privy chamber from 1662–63 to 1686.[940] He received a knighthood in 1683 and he married Catherine Burghill of Hereford.[941] He was mentioned, not overly flatteringly, in *A Ballad to the Tune of Cheviot Races* (1682):

Assist me, Stanhope, while I sing
Of widows great and small;
You best intelligence can bring,
For you debauched 'em all.[942]

Or 2) William Stanhope, a gentleman usher daily waiter, from 1663 to 1689.[943]

Starling [Sterlin], **Mr** – possibly 1) James Starling, the queen's coachman in 1666 or 2) Daniel Starling, senior who was listed as the queen's coachman in 1682.[944]

statue – a three-dimensional representation of a person, animal, or bird, which could be moulded, cast or sculpted. On 9 December 1663, Pepys recalled that Mrs Russell 'did give my wife a very fine St George in Alabaster, which will set out my wife's closet mightily'.[945]

Steward [Stewaards], **mistress** – she received a New Year's gift in 1663, suggesting that this was Frances Teresa Stuart (1647–1702), duchess of

937 James M. Volo and Dorothy Denneen Volo, *Family Life in 17th and 18th Century America* (Westport, CT: Greenwood Press, 2006), 211–12.

938 Ashbee, *Records*, 314.

939 Francis Barlow, *The Last Horse Race run before Charles the Second of Blessed Memory by Doresett Ferry, near Windsor Castle*, 1687, etching, Royal Collection, RCIN 602686.

940 Sainty, Wassmann and Bucholz, *Household officers*, 70.

941 Wilson, *Court Satire*, 109–10.

942 Wilson, *Court Satire*, 105.

943 Sainty, Wassmann and Bucholz, *Household officers*, 70.

944 Sainty, Wassmann and Bucholz, *Household officers*, 70.

945 Pepys, *Diary*, 4, 409.

Richmond and Lennox, daughter of Walter Stuart and Sophia Carew. She was appointed as a maid of honour to the queen in June 1663, a post she held until her marriage in 1667. She was listed as a Lady of the Bedchamber in 1668.[946] Sir Peter Lely painted her as one of the Windsor Beauties. She refused to become Charles II's mistress and in 1667 she married Charles Stuart, 3rd duke of Richmond and 6th duke of Lennox. She had smallpox in 1669, she was widowed in 1672 and remained at court.[947] The Lennox and Richmond titles reverted to the crown as Frances and her husband had no children, and the Richmond title passed to Charles' son with Louise de Kéroualle in 1675. However, Charles II allowed Frances to continue to use the Lennox estate.

Stevens [Steuens], **Mr** – Richard Stevens, junior, a page of the queen's presence chamber in ordinary, in 1666–67, and then page of the back stairs from 1668 to 1692.[948]

stone cutter – supplying a piece of marble.

Story Mrs – Joan Story, the queen's dairy woman, who was listed in 1677 as receiving 4s a day.[949]

Suckley, Mr – for his bill.

Suffolk, countess of – Barbara Howard (1622–81), was daughter of Sir Edward Villliers. She married three times, lastly to James Howard, 3rd earl of Suffolk. In 1662, she was appointed as first lady of the Bedchamber and groom of the stool to Catherine of Braganza.[950] She kept the queen's privy purse accounts until her death. For a fuller discussion of her life, see the Introduction.

footmen –

maid –

my own woman –

my self –

Sunderland, lady – Anne Spencer (*c.*1645–1715) was the daughter of George Digby, 2nd earl of Bristol. Although Robert Spencer (1641–1702), 2nd earl of Sunderland, broke off their engagement in 1665,[951] they reconciled and married later that year. He was secretary of state from 1679 to 1681, and

946 Sainty, Wassmann and Bucholz, *Household officers*, 71.

947 Stuart Handley, 'Stuart [Stewart], Frances Teresa, duchess of Lennox and Richmond, [*called*, La Belle Stuart], courtier', *ODNB*, 3 January 2008, https://doi.org/10.1093/ref:odnb/26703 [accessed 10/5/22].

948 Sainty, Wassmann and Bucholz, *Household officers*, 71.

949 Davidson, *Catherine*, 312.

950 Richard Minta Dunn, 'Howard, James, third earl of Suffolk (1619–1689), nobleman', *ODNB*, 23 September 2004, https://doi-org/10.1093/ref:odnb/13919 [accessed 26/4/22]; Sainty, Wassmann and Bucholz, *Household officers*, 71.

951 Pepys, *Diary*, 4, 208–09.

1683 to 1689.[952] She was a lady of the bedchamber 1673 to 1681. Anne probably lost her office after her husband supported the Exclusion Bill in 1681. Later she was a lady in waiting to Mary of Modena.

footman –

man –

page –

suppliers – the queen's suppliers.

confectioner – makers and sellers of sweetmeats or confections, something Pepys was very fond of.[953] He bought confectionery from Thomas Strudwick, a confectioner based in Snow Hill.[954]

mercer, French – 'The Mercer deals in Silks, Velvets, Brocades. Our Mercer must have a great deal of the Frenchman in his Manners, as well as a large Parcel of French Goods in his shop; he ought to keep close intelligence with the Fashion office at Paris and apply himself with the newest Patterns from that changeable people'.[955]

milliner, Italian – a seller of fancy goods, originally from Milan and often a maker of female accessories and hats. On Sunday 28 February 1669, Pepys went 'to church, where God forgive me! I did most of the time gaze on the fine milliner's wife'.[956]

shoemakers – individuals who made, sold and repaired shoes. Shoemakers often belonged to the cordwainers' livery company and the terms shoemaker and cordwainer (someone who worked with cordovan leather or cordwain) were often interchangeable.

upholsterer, *also see Mr Vernon* – On 10 January 1666, Pepys returned home and 'found my wife busy about making her hangings for her chamber with the Upholsterer'.[957]

Swan, Mrs – Cecilia/Cicilia Swan (d.1698) was the daughter of Sir William Swan, first baronet of Southfleet, Kent, and the third wife of William Bromley (bap.1663–1732), speaker of the House of Commons, who she married by 1692.[958] In December 1675 Sir Richard Bulstrode learnt that

952 See W. A. Speck, 'Spencer, Robert, second earl Sunderland (1641–1702), politician', *ODNB*, 3 January 2008, https://doi-org/10.1093/ref:odnb/26135 [accessed 15/4/22]; MacLeod, *Painted Ladies*, 241.

953 Pepys, *Diary*, 9, 477.

954 Pepys, *Diary*, 2, 8.

955 Robert Campbell, *The London Tradesman: Being a Compendious View of All The Trades, Professions, Arts, both Liberal and Mechanic* (London: printed by T. Gardner, at Cowley Head in the Strand, 1747), quoted in Wardle, *For Our Royal Person*, 110.

956 Pepys, *Diary*, 9, 460.

957 Pepys, *Diary*, 7, 10.

958 A. A. Hanham, 'Bromley, William (bap.1663–1732), speaker of the House of

'One Mrs Swann…who is very young and pretty, is to succeed [Dorothy Howard] and be Maid of Honor', an office she held from 1676 to 1684.[959] In *An Heroic Poem* (1681) she was described as 'widow Swan/For such she is since Ossory is gone'. Ossory died in 1680 but prior to that 'he was deemed not insensible of the charms of a daughter of Sir C [Wm] Swan, with whom he was really in love, and could not help showing it by a chance of counternance or some other mark when she was in company'.[960]

woman –

Swan, Lady – Utricia (or Hester), daughter of Sir John Ogle of Pinchbeck (1569–1640). She married (c. 1657) Sir William Swan (1631–80), created first baronet of Southfleet in 1666.[961]

Symson, John – trumpeter to the duke of York.

Talbot, colonel – Colonel Richard Talbot (1630–91) was the son of Sir William Talbot and Alison Netterville, and later became the earl and then duke of Tyrconnel.[962] He was a gentleman of the duke of York's Bedchamber, and he was sent to Lisbon in 1662 to assist with the marriage arrangements of Charles II and Catherine of Braganza.

gardener –

Talbot, mistress – possibly Richard Talbot's wife. He married twice. First, in 1669, to Katherine Botnton (d.1679) and second, in 1681 to a widow called Frances Jennings.[963]

footman –

Tapham, Mr/sergeant – park keeper.

Taylor [Tailour], **Mr** – possibly Henry Taylor, page of the Presence Chamber, from 1673 to 1677.[964]

Teague, Mr – a footman to the duke of York.

Temple, lady – There are several possibilities. 1) Sarah Draper (d.1699), wife

Commons', *ODNB*, 19 May 2011, https://doi-org/10.1093/ref:odnb/3515 [accessed 20/4/22].

959 Wilson, *Court Satire*, 66; Sainty, Wassmann and Bucholz, *Household officers*, 72.

960 Wilson, *Court Satire*, 71, 74.

961 G. E. Cockayne, *Complete Baronetage*, 6 vols (Exeter: W. Pollard, 1900–09), 4, 26; A. R. Maddison, *Lincolnshire Pedigrees*, Harleian Society 50–52, 55 (1902–06), 3, 732–33.

962 James McGuire, 'Talbot, Richard', *Dictionary of Irish Biography*, https://www.dib.ie/biography/talbot-richard-a8460 [accessed 25/3/22].

963 James McGuire, 'Talbot, Richard', *Dictionary of Irish Biography*, https://www.dib.ie/biography/talbot-richard-a8460 [accessed 25/3/22].

964 Sainty, Wassmann and Bucholz, *Household officers*, 72.

of Sir Purbeck Temple (1623–95).[965] 2) Dorothy Temple (1627–95), daughter of Sir Peter Osborne and Dorothy Danvers who married Sir William Temple (1628–99), 1st baronet, in 1654. She is best known for the letters that she wrote to her husband before their marriage.[966] They lived in Ireland from 1656 to 1660. 3) Philippa Temple, maid of honour (1674 to 1683) and a dresser/woman of the bedchamber (1684/5 to 1705).[967] In *An heroic Poem* (1681), she was described as:

So drunk with lust, she rambles up and down
And bellows out, 'I'm bulling round the town'.
Not Felton's wife was in her youth more lewd.[968]

4) Anne Temple, maid of honour to the duchess of York.[969]

Teynham [Tenham], **lord** – Christopher Roper (d. before 24 July 1689), 5th baron Teynham of Kent, was the son of Christopher Roper, 4th baron Teynham and Philadelphia Knollys. In 1674, he married Elizabeth Browne, daughter of Francis Browne, 3rd viscount Montagu, and Lady Elizabeth Somerset. He succeeded to the title in 1673 and he was Lord-Lieutenant of Kent.[970]

keeper –

man –

tennis court man – for supplying shoes.

Terrey [Tery], **Mr** – Humphrey Terrey, a waterman, from 1662 to 1671.[971]

textiles, *also see household textiles, lace, linens and passementerie*

buckram [Bockrome] – a finer to medium weight linen fabric, which was sometimes stiffened with gum or starch.[972]

calico, yellow – a generic term for cotton textiles imported from India and the east, which could include printed Indian cottons but could also encompass bleached or unbleached plain cottons. On 27 February 1664, Pepys noted 'the dispute between him [Sir Martin Noell], as Farmer of the Addicionall Duty, and the East India Company, whether Callico's be Linnen or no'.[973]

965 No *ODNB* entry. https://www.geni.com/people/Purbeck-Temple/6000000027521246005 [accessed 17/8/22].

966 No *ODNB* entry of her own, see J. D. Davies, 'Temple, Sir William, baronet (1628–1699), diplomat and author', *ODNB*, 21 May 2009, https://doi.org/10.1093/ref:odnb/27122 [accessed 2/5/22].

967 Sainty, Wassmann and Bucholz, *Household officers*, 72.

968 Wilson, *Court Satire*, 72.

969 Pepys, *Diary*, 7, 372.

970 No *ODNB* entry. http://www.thepeerage.com/p3008.htm [accessed 2/2/22].

971 Sainty, Wassmann and Bucholz, *Household officers*, 72.

972 Wardle, *For Our Royal Person*, 136.

973 Pepys, *Diary*, 5, 66. The duty was 5% less on linen than on calicos.

canvas – a heavy weight, strong plain weave material made from flax or hemp often used for tents and sails, as well as a lining/interlining and for hard-wearing clothing. According to Celia Fiennes, light weight canvas was worn for bathing: 'Ladyes goes into the bath with Garments made of a fine yellow canvas, which is stiff and made large with great sleeve like a parsons gown; the water fills it up so that its borne off that your shape is not seen, it does not cling close as other linning, which Lookes sadly in the poorer sort that go in their own linning'.[974]

cloth, brown – cloth was a term usually used to describe a plain weave, woollen fabric. On 28 October 1665, Pepys reported that 'The King and Court, they say, have now finally resolved to spend nothing upon clothes but what is of growth of England – which if observed, will be very pleasing to the people and very good for them'.[975]

crape – a transparent, light weight silk fabric often associated with mourning dress.[976]

diaper – a linen textile, with a small geometric pattern.[977]

gauze [gas, gaus] – a transparent, light, thin silk fabric.

holland – a generic term for plain weave linen cloth, of fine quality.[978] On 26 July 1664 Pepys recorded the advice that he had been given 'of my not getting of children' which included 'Wear cool Holland-drawers'.[979]

silk, Paris – uncertain meaning, but could be a reference to silk thread or a woven textile made in Paris or in a French style.

stuff/stuffs – a generic term for any length of uncut cloth, or for a worsted.[980] It was popular for men's suits, as Pepys noted on 15 June 1665, when he observed that 'up, and put on my new stuff suit with closed knees, which becomes me most nobly as my wife says'.[981]

stuff, French – a woven woollen fabric, either imported from France or made closer to home in a French style.

tiffany, striped – a semi-transparent, very thin, light weight silk from France used for veils.[982]

velvet – a pile fabric with the pile created by the inclusion of a supplementary

974 Fiennes, *Through England on a Side Saddle*, 13.

975 Pepys, *Diary*, 281.

976 Wardle, *For Our Royal Person*, 137.

977 Wardle, *For Our Royal Person*, 137.

978 *Fairchild's Dictionary*, 294.

979 Pepys, *Diary*, 5, 222.

980 *Fairchild's Dictionary*, 589.

981 Pepys, *Diary*, 6, 127–28.

982 *Fairchild's Dictionary*, 619, Willett Cunnington and Cunnington, *Handbook*, 206.

warp. Various types of velvet including ciselé velvet, pile on pile velvets, and voided velvet were available. The desirability of velvet gown is evident from a comment made by Pepys on 29 November 1663: 'I to church alone, my wife not going; and there I find my Lady Batten in a velvet gowne, which vexed me that she should be in it before my wife or that I am able to put her into one'.[983]

wad – a loose, fibrous padding material, made from matted fibres silk or raw cotton and used to line nightgowns.[984]

theatres – the Restoration saw the revival of the theatres with the establishment of the King's company and the duke of York's company.

box keepers – *also see Mr Hailes, Mr Hill, Mr Murray and Mr Pavy* – boxes at the theatre were desirable places to sit but also expensive as Samuel Pepys reveals in several of his diary entries. On 19 October 1667, Pepys arrived at the King's theatre to find 'there was no room in the pit, but we were forced to go into one of the upper-box at 4s apiece, which is the first time I ever sat in a box in my life'.[985] The following year, on 6 January, Pepys went 'to the Duke's house; and the House being full, was forced to carry them to a box which did cost me 20s besides oranges' while later in the same year he went 'to the King's playhouse into a corner of the 18d box'.[986]

Duke's house – the theatre used by the Duke's Company. Initially this was the Salisbury Court theatre, in Whitefriars, then the Lincoln's Inn Field theatre from 1661, and in 1671 they moved to the Dorset Garden theatre.[987] Pepys referred to the chief box at the Duke's House, on 1 January 1663, where he saw 'the old Roxalana [Mrs Hester Davenport] in the chief box, in a velvet gowne as the fashion is'.[988]

plays – as Pepys' diary makes clear, the Theatre Royal and the theatre at Lincoln's Inn Field offered a rich variety of plays by Sir William Davenant, John Dryden and William, duke of Newcastle, to name but a few.[989]

play bills – small, printed bills providing details of the playwright, the actors and the parts they were playing, along with the date, time and venue, were produced once the theatres reopened in 1660. They became larger after 1672, and made use of black and red ink, following

983 Pepys, *Diary*, 4, 400.

984 https://www.oed.com/view/Entry/224935?rskey=OIW47q&result=2#eid [accessed 28/4/22]. Wardle, *For Our Royal Person*, 63.

985 Pepys, *Diary*, 8, 487.

986 Pepys, *Diary*, 9, 12; 9, 164.

987 Pepys, *Diary*, 10, 438–41.

988 Pepys, *Diary*, 4, 2.

989 For example, Pepys, *Diary*, 2, 200; 8, 387; 3, 87–88.

the style of the bills issued by a French company that performed in London that year.[990]

play house – another term for a theatre, such as those used by the King's Company and the Duke's Company. On 27 October 1666, Pepys reported that 'The playhouses begin to play next week'.[991]

thief catcher [thifecatcher] – thief catchers were employed by Charles II's ministers to arrest criminals. For instance, in the late 1660s and early 1670s, Sir William Morton, a judge of King's Bench, and Secretary Williamson used thief catchers to apprehend highwaymen.[992]

Thomas, Mr – for a looking glass.

Tichborne [Tichbornes], **Sir Henry** – third baronet (1624–89). He was the son of Sir Richard Tichborne, 2nd baronet, and Helen, daughter of Robert White of Aldershot.[993] He married the daughter of Charles Arndell, younger brother of Thomas, lord Arundell of Wardour, and with Mary (d.1698) he had four sons and five daughters. Henry served as a gentleman usher of the privy chamber in extraordinary in 1666.[994] He is depicted on the centre left in Gillis van Tilborch, *The Tichborne dole*, 1670, oil on canvas, private collection. As a royalist and a Catholic, Sir Henry was implicated in the Popish plot by Titus Oates in 1678.

man –

Tough, John – he received a New Year's gift 1677.

Townshend, lady – the holder of this title depends on the date. Horatio, 1st viscount Townshend (1630–87), married twice. First, to Mary (d.1673), daughter of Edward Lewkenor, of Denham, Suffolk in 1649 and there were no children from this marriage. Second, he married Mary Ashe (d.1685), daughter of Sir Joseph Ashe, 1st baronet of Twickenham, several months later in November 1673. They had three sons.[995]

transport/travel – Catherine travelled frequently by water and by road, moving from property to property and to attend events. A similar pattern, but on a more modest scale, is evident in Pepys's travel patterns, which

990 https://www.vam.ac.uk/articles/theatre-posters-an-illustrated-history [accessed 20/1/23].

991 Pepys, *Diary*, 7, 344.

992 J. M. Beattie, *Policing and Punishment in London 1660–1750: Urban Crime and Punishment* (Oxford: Oxford University Press, 2001), 229.

993 John Walter, 'Tichborne, Sir Henry, third baronet (1624–1689), landowner', *ODNB*, 23 September 2004, https://doi.org/10.1093/ref:odnb/66939 [accessed 19/12/21].

994 Sainty, Wassmann and Bucholz, *Household officers*, 74.

995 No *ODNB* entry, so see Stuart Handley, 'Townshend, Horatio, first viscount Townshend (bap.1630–1687), politician', *ODNB*, 3 January 2008, https://doi.org/10.1093/ref:odnb/27628 [accessed 22/1/22].

consisted of local travel in and around London as well as his regular journeys to Brampton and Cambridge or his holiday in 1668.[996]

barges – Catherine frequently travelled in her own barge but on occasion borrowed barges from other people. Barges could have decorative barge cloths, such as the surviving cloth belonging to the Pewterers' Company, which is thought to have been made for the queen's official entry in 1662.[997] On 28 September 1668, Pepys reminisced about 'a fine warm evening, the Italians came in a barge under the leads before the Queen's drawing-room, and so the Queen and ladies went out and heard it for almost an hour'.[998]

a hired barge –

boats – boat hire was part of London life, and at times of high demand the price went up, as on 23 August 1662, when Pepys went 'all along Thames streete, but could not get a boat; I offered 8s for one to attend this afternoon and they would not, it being the day of the Queenes coming to town from Hampton Court'.[999]

calash, calèche [challoche, callonch] – a light carriage with a folding and removable hood and low wheels. On 12 April 1665, Evelyn went to 'the Society where were produced several new models of Coaches & Caleches', and a little under two years later, on 13 February 1667 he went to 'Arundel house where Dr Croone produced his Calesh or new invented Charriot, the Carriage a single deale board onely instead of the Pearch: his Majestie was well pleased with it as he told me this Evening'.[1000] In 1667, Pepys saw Sir William Pen's new chariot which was 'plain, but pretty and more fashionable in shape then any coach he hath and yet doth not cost him, harness and all, above 32l'.[1001]

carriages – wheeled vehicles designed for comfort and elegance used for private travel and so the preserve of the elite.[1002]

chairs – sedan chairs were an alternative to coach travel and after the queen's birthday ball in 1666 Samuel's friend Pierce 'hired a chair for my wife'.[1003] In 1660, the accounts of the duke of Bedford included a payment of £6 0s 6d 'paid for a chair or sedan, bought by Mrs

[996] Pepys, *Diary*, 10, 448–56, with the map on 450.

[997] Patricia Wardle, 'A rare survival: the barge cloth of the Worshipful Company of Pewterers and the embroiderer John West', *Textile History* 37.1 (2006), 1–16.

[998] Pepys, *Diary*, 9, 322.

[999] Pepys, *Diary*, 3, 174–75.

[1000] Evelyn, *Diary*, 506.

[1001] Pepys, *Diary*, 8, 289–90.

[1002] https://www.oed.com/view/Entry/28223?redirectedFrom=carriage#eid [accessed 28/4/22].

[1003] Pepys, *Diary*, 7, 372.

Betts for the service of the Countess of Bedford'.[1004] They were also used by men, especially if they were unwell, as was the case on 16 February 1663, when Sir William Wheeler 'was brought down in a sedan-chair from his chamber, being lame of the goute'.[1005]

coach-hire – When Pepys attended a christening in October 1666, coach-hire cost him 5s, in comparison to the 20s he gave to the midwife.[1006]

coaches – a large carriage, and during the sixteenth and seventeenth centuries, they were used by royalty and the elite.[1007] The coach given by Charles II as a gift in 1682 to the Emperor of Morocco cost £212.[1008] However, coach travel was not without risk. On 7 March 1669, the royal coach overturned at the King's Gate in Holborn 'and the King all dirty but no hurt'.[1009]

ferry boats – boats used to carry people or goods across rivers or short stretches of sea. Pepys took ferries when required, for example, from Deptford to the Isle of Dogs, and from Greenwich to the Isle of Dogs.[1010]

galleys [Galy, Gally] – a large open rowboat.[1011] On 18 May 1661 Pepys found 'the Thames full of boats and galleys; and upon enquiry find that there was a wager to be run this morning'.[1012]

The Galley – one of the king's boats.

litters – a means of transport containing a bed, enclosed with curtains, and carried by men on their shoulders, or by animals. While in Bath, Pepys recorded that the sick went to church by litter when he noted that 'two men [were] brought in litters and set down in the chancel to hear'.[1013]

oars, pairs of oars – a rowing boat, and so a pair of oars was a boat rowed by two people.[1014] Pepys made many references to hiring sculls and pairs of oars as well as complaining about the lack of watermen on

1004 Scott Thomson, *Life in a Noble Household*, 210.

1005 Pepys, *Diary*, 4, 43.

1006 Pepys, *Diary*, 7, 330.

1007 https://www.oed.com/view/Entry/34954?rskey=r3sjK6&result=1#eid [accessed 28/4/22].

1008 Akerman, *Secret Services*, 61.

1009 Pepys, *Diary*, 9, 474.

1010 Pepys, *Diary*, 6, 163; 6, 158.

1011 https://www.oed.com/view/Entry/76270?rskey=Rt8Cam&result=1#eid [accessed 28/4/22].

1012 Pepys, *Diary*, 2, 101.

1013 Pepys, *Diary*, 9, 238.

1014 https://www-oed-com.soton.idm.oclc.org/view/Entry/234404?rskey=Q1GTcT&result=1#eid [accessed 21/1/23].

a Sunday.[1015] For instance, on 13 July 1665, Pepys complained that 'there being no oares to carry me, I was fain to call a Sculler'.[1016]

sledges – a carriage with runners rather than wheels, for use on snow and ice, often horse-drawn. During the frost fair of January 1684, Evelyn noted people were riding 'on sleds, sliding with skeetes'.[1017]

wagons – four-wheeled vehicle used to move heavy goods. When Evelyn accompanied the ambassador on 9 November 1675, he recalled that 'we set out [with] 3 Coaches, 3 wagons, and about 40 horses besides my Coach'.[1018]

wherries – light rowing boats with a pointed bow that were used to carry passengers and/or baggage and freight on rivers. They were very popular on the Thames and when there was a lack of wind. When Pepys was in Greenwich on 25 September 1665, he recorded that 'we parted and to our Yacht; but it being calme, we, to make haste, took our Wherry toward Chatham'.[1019] Pepys also used wherries to move his property as in 1666 when he referred to 'My pictures and fine things, that I will bring home in wherrys'.[1020]

Treasurer, Lord – Thomas Wriothesley (1607–67), 4th earl of Southampton, was the son of Henry Wriothesley, 3rd earl of Southampton, and Elizabeth Vernon. He was the king's Lord High Treasurer from 8 September 1660 until his death on 16 May 1667.[1021]

Trevor, Lady – Jane (d.1704) was the daughter of Sir Roger Mostyn, 1st baronet. She married twice. Her first husband was Roger Puleston of Emral, and then on 23 October 1669 she married John Trevor (*c*.1637–1717). He was knighted on 29 January 1671. After a legal career, he was a MP and speaker of the House of Commons from 1685 to 1687 and 1690 to 1695.[1022]

man –

trial [tryall] – this is a reference to the trial of Mr Loft which was noted in the queen's accounts on 30 June 1676.

1015 Pepys, *Diary*, 1, 206; 8, 32.

1016 Pepys, *Diary*, 6, 156.

1017 Evelyn, *Diary*, 765.

1018 Evelyn, *Diary*, 620.

1019 Pepys, *Diary*, 6, 241.

1020 Pepys, *Diary*, 7, 285.

1021 David L. Smith, 'Wriothesley, Thomas, fourth earl of Southampton (1608–1667), politician', *ODNB*, 3 January 2008, https://doi-org.soton.idm.oclc.org/10.1093/ref:odnb/30077 [accessed 26/4/22].

1022 A. M. Mimardière, 'Trevor, Sir John (*c*.1637–1717), of Clement's Lane, Westminster and Pulford, Denb.', http://www.histparl.ac.uk/volume/1690-1715/member/trevor-sir-john-1637-1717 [accessed 15/4/22].

Tuke [Teuk], **lady** – Mary (d.1705) was the daughter of Edward Sheldon of Ditchford. She was the second wife of Sir Samuel Tuke, 1st Baronet (*c*.1615–74), who she married in 1668. He was a royalist and a playwright. He was made a baronet in 1664. Mary was a dresser to the queen, and she exchanged letters with Mary Evelyn. In 1674, her husband died at Somerset House, and he was buried in the chapel. During the Popish Plot Mary was accused of trying to influence one of the witnesses. In 1692, she went to Portugal with Catherine, and she died there in 1705.[1023]

turf – a sod of grass with roots and soil attached.[1024] Lawns developed in popularity during the sixteenth century but comprised of fragrant plants like thyme or camomile. The seventeenth century saw the development of lawns comprised of short cut grass. Kept short either by grazing or cutting, lawns formed an important part of gardens, while also used for bowling greens and for playing golf.

Twist, Mr – payment to the king's violins.

van der Doos, Mr – by his bill.

Vancoe, Mr – by his bill.

Vaughan [Vahan], **Mr** – there are two possibilities. Either 1) Edward Vaughan, the son of Sir John Vaughan (d.1684), or 2) John Vaughan (1603–74), MP for Cardiganshire from 1661 to 1668, and Chief Justice for Common Pleas from 1668 until his death.[1025]

vegetables – a wide variety of vegetables, including root vegetables and salad crops, were available but only a small number were given to Catherine as gifts, or in the case of the leeks, to mark St David's Day.

asparagus [esparagrese] – Castelvetro described asparagus (*Asparagus officinalis*) as a spring vegetable adding that 'some people eat it raw, with salt, pepper and Parmesan cheese but I prefer it cooked and served like hops, with oil, a little vinegar, and salt and pepper'.[1026] He added that 'asparagus is a most health-giving vegetable' that 'is positively helpful to those who find urinating painful'.[1027] When Pepys

1023 No *ODNB* entry of her own, so see C. H. Firth revised by Andrew J. Hopper, 'Tuke, Sir Samuel, first baronet (c.1615–1674), royalist army officer and playwright', *ODNB*, 3 January 2008, https://doi.org/10.1093/ref:odnb/27807 [accessed 12/2/22]; Sainty, Wassmann and Bucholz, *Household officers*, 75.

1024 https://www.oed.com/view/Entry/207586?rskey=9Xugv5&result=1#eid [accessed 19/4/22].

1025 https://biography.wales/article/s-VAUG-JOH-1603 [accessed 19/4/22].

1026 Castelvetro, *Fruit, Herbs & Vegetables*, 53.

1027 Castelvetro, *Fruit, Herbs & Vegetables*, 53.

was at Guildford on 22 April 1662, he spent 'time in the garden cutting of Sparagus for supper'.[1028]

leeks– probably a descendent of the wild leek (*Alium ampeloprasum*), which is native to England, a symbol of Wales, and associated with St David's Day (1 March).[1029] In 1690, John Field, gardener at Woburn Abbey, bought two ounces of leek seeds for 8d from Edward Fuller's seeds and flower shop close to the Strand Bridge.[1030]

peas – Castelvetro described peas (*Pisum sativum*) as 'the noblest of vegetables' that were eaten as part of 'fat' and 'lean' dishes.[1031] They were referred to as 'pease' during Charles I's reign, the short form of 'peas' was in use in the later seventeenth century (but not by Pepys).[1032] Pepys made several references to enjoying the first peas of the year including on 25 May 1662, 22 May 1664 and 21 May 1668.[1033]

Vernon, Mr – upholsterer.

Verrio, Mr – Antonio Verrio (*c.*1635–1707) was an Italian painter born in Naples, who came to England in 1672 with the support of Ralph Montagu. He painted interiors for Charles II, his brother James and nephew William III. He was also gardener at St James's.[1034] In August 1686 Evelyn noted that he 'din'd at Signor Verrios the famous Italian painter & now settled in his Majesties garden of St <James> which he had made now a very delicious Paradise'.[1035]

gardener –

verses – Charles and Catherine were often the subject of fulsome verses written in their honour: for example, at the time of their marriage or when visiting a town for the first time. In this instance it was during their summer travels in June 1677.[1036] However, they were also the topic of scurrilous verses.[1037]

1028 Pepys, *Diary*, 3, 69.

1029 Stuart, *Kitchen Garden*, 146–49.

1030 Scott Thomson, *Life in a Noble Household*, 260.

1031 Castelvetro, *Fruit, Herbs & Vegetables*, 60–61.

1032 Stuart, *Kitchen Garden*, 184.

1033 Pepys, *Diary*, 3, 91; 5, 156; 9, 208.

1034 Kathryn Barron, Verrio, Antonio (c.1639–1707), decorative painter, *ODNB*, 3 January 2008, https://doi.org/10.1093/ref:odnb/28251 [accessed 28/4/22]; Julian Munby, 'Signor Verrio and Monsieur Beaumont, gardeners to James II', *Journal of the British Archaeological Association* 149.1 (1996), 55–71.

1035 Evelyn, *Diary*, 851.

1036 LAO, 1-Worsley 8, fo. 22v. Compare with Sir Thomas Ireland, *Speeches spoken to the King and Queen, Duke and Duchesse of York, in Christ-Church Hall, Oxford, Sept. 29. 1663* (London: printed [by John Grismond] for Richard Royston, bookseller to His most sacred Majesty, 1663).

1037 See Wilson, *Court Satire*, for many examples.

Warwick, earl of – Charles Rich (1623–73), was the son of Robert Rich, 2nd earl of Warwick, and Frances Hatton. He married Lady Mary Boyle, daughter of Richard Boyle, 1st earl of Cork and Catherine Fenton.[1038]

***servant* –**

Watts, Mr – probably William Watts, the king's tailor.

Web, Mr – 'that hooks the birds'. So potentially a man who might also be described as a bird-angler, bird-catcher or bird-snarer.[1039]

Wells, mistress – possibly Winifred Wells, youngest daughter of Gilbert Wells of Twyford, Hampshire. She was a maid of honour to the queen, from 1662/3 to 1673. She was then a dresser or woman of the bedchamber, 1673 to 1705.[1040] According to Gramont she was 'a big splendidly handsome creature who dressed finely [and] had the carriage of a Goddess…[but with] the physiognomy of a dreamy sheep'.[1041] In 1675, she married Thomas Wyndham. She was said to have given birth to a child during a court ball in 1662.[1042] When Pepys dined at Whitehall on 30 May 1669 he admired 'fine Mrs Wells, who is a great beauty and there I had my full gaze upon her, to my great content, she being a women of pretty conversation'.[1043] She was a royal mistress from 1662 to 1673 but she remained a member of the queen's household until 1692.

Welsh [Welch]**, Edward** – the queen's groom sumpterman, from 1669 to 1674.[1044]

Wherwood, Major – as per bill.

Whitock, Mr – as per bill.

Whorwood [Whorewood]**, major** – possibly Willian Whorwood/Howard, equerry, from 1665 to 1684.[1045]

widows – several widows were mentioned in the accounts.

your Matie Gromes widow [1664]
yr Ma:tie footemans widdow [1664]
To one of yr Ma:ties footmen widdows [1665]
Jon Pettoes yor footmans Widdow to bury him [1667]
Mrs Bussy yor Maties grooms wedow [1671]

1038 NO *ODNB* entry.

1039 https://www-oed-com.soton.idm.oclc.org/view/Entry/19327?redirectedFrom=bird+catcher#eid20149191 [accessed 21/1/23].

1040 Sainty, Wassmann and Bucholz, *Household officers*, 78.

1041 Gramont, cited in Pepys, *Diary*, 10, 472.

1042 Wilson, *Court Satire*, 7.

1043 Pepys, *Diary*, 9, 563.

1044 Sainty, Wassmann and Bucholz, *Household officers*, 78.

1045 Sainty, Wassmann and Bucholz, *Household officers*, 79.

William, Mr – sent to Newmarket. Possibly Christopher William, who by 1686–87 served as the queen's surveyor's clerk.[1046]

Winchester, bishop of – George Morley (1598–1684), bishop of Winchester (1662–84), was appointed as Dean of the Chapel Royal in 1663 (a post he held until 1668).[1047]

Winchilsea [winssellies], **countess** – depending on the date this could be either: 1) Mary Seymour (1637–73), countess of Winchilsea, who was the daughter of William Seymour, 2nd duke of Somerset and Lady Frances Devereux – she was the second wife of Sir Heneage Finch, 3rd earl of Winchilsea (1628–89), and they had four children;[1048] or 2) his third wife, Catherine Norcliffe (1649/50–1678), daughter of Sir Thomas Norcliffe and widow of Christopher Lister and Sir John Wentworth who he married in 1673. The date suggests it was the former.

Winchilsea [Winsellsis], **lord** – Sir Heneage Finch, 3rd earl of Winchelsea (1628–89), was the son of Thomas Finch, 2nd earl of Winchilsea, and Cecille Wentworth. In 1660, he was made Lord Warden of the Cinque Ports and Governor of Dover castle. He was Charles II's ambassador to the Ottoman Empire from 1668 to 1672. He married four times: Diana Willoughby in 1645, Mary Seymour in *c.* 1650, Catherine Norcliffe in 1673 and Elizabeth Ayres in 1681.[1049]

Winwood [Winewood], **Mr** – Richard Winwood (1609–88) was the first surviving son of Sir Ralph Winwood and Elizabeth Ball. He owned land in Buckinghamshire including Ditton Park, which was close to Windsor, and he was MP for New Windsor in 1641, 1679, 1680 and 1681.[1050]

gardener –

women – several unnamed women were listed in Catherine's accounts, usually as the recipients of charity.

a womane called Kathrine –

poor –

a woman presented Creame Cheese –

1046 Sainty, Wassmann and Bucholz, *Household officers*, 79.

1047 John Spurr, 'Morley, George (1598?–1684), bishop of Winchester', *ODNB*, 23 September 2004, https://doi.org/10.1093/ref:odnb/19285 [accessed 30/11/21].

1048 Sonia P. Anderson, 'Finch, Heneage, third earl of Winchilsea (1627/8–1689), diplomat', *ODNB*, 3 September 2008, https://doi.org/10.1093/ref:odnb/9434 [accessed 26/11/21].

1049 Sonia P. Anderson, 'Finch, Heneage, third earl of Winchilsea (1627/8–1689), diplomat', *ODNB*, 3 September 2008, https://doi.org/10.1093/ref:odnb/9434 [accessed 24/11/21].

1050 A. W. Helms/Leonard Naylor/Geoffrey Jagger, Winwood, Richard (1609–88), of Quainton, Bucks. https://www.historyofparliamentonline.org/volume/1660-1690/member/winwood-richard-1609-88 [accessed 2/2/22].

a woman presented fruit –
a woman presented Hony –
the womane whair was your Majesties dary –
a womane gave your Majestie physique –
tall – Tall women provoked comment, as was the case with the orange seller at the Theatre Royal, Betty Mackerel, who was described as 'the Gyantess Betty-Mackerela' in John Philip's *The History of Don Quixote* (1687).[1051]
a woman from winsor presented fishe –
a womane from Bramford presented fruite –
a woman that Longd to kisse the Queens hand –
a poore womane had her Hog Killed –
a womane with Eyle pye –

Wood, lady – Mary Wood (d.1665) was the daughter of Sir Thomas Gardiner. She was a Maid of Honour to Henrietta Maria and went into exile with her. While in Paris she married Sir Henry Wood in 1650. When Charles was restored to the throne in 1660, Wood was made clerk of the Board of the Green Cloth. Mary was appointed as first dresser and a woman of the bedchamber to Catherine of Braganza in 1662.[1052] She died in 1665, which caused Pepys to comment that she was 'a good-natured woman and a good wife but for all that it was ever believed she was as others were'.[1053] They had a daughter, also called Mary (d.1680), who married Charles Fitzroy, duke of Southampton.

Woodward, Mr – as per bill.

Worcester, marquis of – Henry Somerset (1629–1700) was the son of Edward Somerset, 6th earl and 2nd marquis of Worcester, and Elizabeth Dormer. He was created duke of Beaufort in 1682, and he was godfather to the duke of Cambridge.[1054]
man –

Wright, Mr – possibly Richard Wright, page of the Presence Chamber, from 1672 to 1677.[1055]

1051 Wilson, *Court Satire*, 264.

1052 No *ODNB* entry; Pepys noted her pregnancy, see Pepys, *Diary*, 4, 348–49. Sainty, Wassmann and Bucholz, *Household officers*.

1053 Pepys, *Diary*, 6, 57–58; Wilson, *Court Satire*, 7.

1054 Molly McClain, 'Somerset, Henry, first duke of Beaufort (1629–1700), nobleman', *ODNB*, 3 October 2013, https://doi.org/10.1093/ref:odnb/26009 [accessed 25/11/21].

1055 Sainty, Wassmann and Bucholz, *Household officers*, 81.

writing materials – *also see accounts.* On 16 July 1662, Pepys bought 'a very neat leather standish to carry papers, pen and ink in when one travels'.[1056]

ink – this was probably black iron gall ink, so-called because it was made from iron galls found on oak trees, iron sulphate, gum Arabic and water. Other ingredients might be added, including honey to improve the consistency and vinegar or alcohol to make it last longer. It could be made at home or bought ready-made.[1057] Ink was also made using carbon (most commonly soot).

To make common inke of wine take a quart
Two ounces of Gumme let that be a part,
Fiue ounces of Gals, of Copres take three,
Long standing doth make it the better to be.
If wine ye do want, raine water is best,
And then as much stuffe as aboue at the least.
If inke be too thicke, put vinegar in:
For water doth make the colour more dim.[1058]

paper – paper made from textile rags (cotton, linen, or hemp) was produced in seventeenth century England, but it was also imported from Europe.[1059]

pens – probably a goose-quill pen, which was trimmed to shape with a penknife, creating a nib.[1060]

sand – sand, a very fine granular substance, was used to absorb wet ink from paper, rather like blotting paper, and it was kept in a shaker or sander. Other very fine absorbent materials, sometimes also referred to as sand, included a variety of other materials such as pounce, a fine powder, frequently made by grinding cuttlefish and gum sandarac.[1061]

Wyche, lady – Elizabeth Jermyn, daughter of Sir Thomas Jermyn, was the first wife of Sir Cyril Wyche (*c.*1632–1707). They married in 1663 and they had four children. She died before 1684, when he married a second time to Susanna, daughter of Sir Francis Norreys.[1062] OR Isabella Wyche,

1056 Pepys, *Diary*, 3, 139.

1057 'Ink', in Kathryn James, *English Palaeography and Manuscript Culture, 1500–1800* (New Haven and London: Yale University Press, 2020), 44–45.

1058 From 'Rules made by E. B. for children to write by', in Anon., *A new booke, containing all sort of hands* (London: by Richard Field, 1611).

1059 'Paper', in James, *English Palaeography*, 32–39.

1060 'Pens and writing implements', in James, *English Palaeography*, 40–41.

1061 B. Reissland, Ineke Joostens, Evi Eis, and Anja Schubert, 'Blotting sand on writing inks: An underestimated source of information' (2006); https://www.researchgate.net/publication/341822306_Blotting_sand_on_writing_inks_as_an_underestimated_source_of_information_extended_abstract [accessed 22/1/22].

1062 No *ODNB* entry of her own, so see C. I. McGrath, 'Wyche, Sir Cyril

dresser to the queen, 1675 to 1695, who may have travelled to Portugal with the queen.[1063]

York, duchess [dutchesse] **of** – 1) Anne Hyde (1637–71), was the daughter of Edward Hyde and 1st earl of Clarendon and Frances Aylesbury. She was a Maid of Honour to Charles II's sister, Mary, princess of Orange. She met James, duke of York, became pregnant, and they married in 1659 (secretly) and in 1660 (officially). She had several children but only two lived to be adult, Mary and Anne, who both became queens regnant. She converted to Catholicism in 1669.[1064]

coachman –

footmen –

music –

2) Mary of Modena/Maria Beatrice Eleonora Anna Margherita Isabella d'Este (1658–1718), was the daughter of Alfonso IV d'Este, duke of Modena, and Laura Martinozzi. She married James, duke of York, in 1673. From 1679 to 1681 they spent time in Brussels and Scotland, when times were very difficult for Catholics in England. She had a number of pregnancies and children who died in their early years. She was crowned queen consort in 1685, and her son James was born on 10 June 1688, leading to the Warming Pan scandal. She went to France with her son in 1688 and her last child, Louise Maria Theresa (1692–1712), was born at St Germain-en-Laye. Mary died in exile.[1065]

coachmen and footmen –

York, duke [duck] **of** – James Stuart (1633–1701), second surviving son of Charles I and Henrietta Maria. He married Anne Hyde in 1659 and only two of their children – Mary and Anne – survived beyond infancy and both ruled as queens regnant. He converted to Catholicism in 1669. Anne died in 1671 and two years later he married Mary of Modena.[1066] As he was Charles II's heir, James became king in 1685. Invited to do

---

(*c*.1632–1707), government official', *ODNB*, 23 September 2004, https://doi.org/10.1093/ref:odnb/30117 [accessed 20/11/21].

1063 Sainty, Wassmann and Bucholz, *Household officers*; *CSPD, William III 1691–92*, 209.

1064 John Miller, 'Anne [née Hyde], duchess of York (1637–1671), first wife of James II', *ODNB*, 3 January 2008, https://doi.org/10.1093/ref:odnb/14325 [accessed 22/11/21].

1065 Andrew Barclay, 'Mary [of Modena] (1658–1718), queen of England, Scotland and Ireland, consort of James II and VII', *ODNB*, 3 January 2008, https://doi.org/10.1093/ref:odnb/18247 [accessed 22/11/21].

1066 W. A. Speck, 'James II and VII, (1633–1701), king of England, Scotland and Ireland', *ODNB*, 8 October 2009, https://doi.org/10.1093/ref:odnb/14593 [accessed 22/11/21].

so, by leading protestants, William of Orange landed on English soil on 5 November 1688 and James left the country shortly after for France. He sought to recover his Stuart kingdoms but after his defeat at the battle of the Boyne in 1690, James returned to France and died in exile in 1701.

footmen –

gardener –

music –

trumpeters –

BIBLIOGRAPHY

Primary sources

Dorset History Centre, Dorchester
D/FSI, box 275, duchess of Monmouth's accounts 1665–67

Folger Shakespeare Library, Washington DC
Folger MS X.d.76.

Lincolnshire Archives, Lincoln
LRO I-Worsley 6
LRO I-Worsley 7
LRO I-Worsley 8
LRO I-Worsley 9

British Library, London
BL Additional MS 27466

Merton College, Oxford
MCR 1.3 College Register

The National Archive, Kew
AO3/910/6
LC5/12
LC5/13
LC5/14
LC5/137
LC5/138
LC5/140
LC5/141
LC5/142
LC5/143
LC5/144
LC5/145
LC5/188
LC5/193

University of Nottingham Library, Nottingham
MS Li 113

Printed primary sources

John Yonge Akerman (ed.), *Moneys Received and Paid for Secret Services of Charles II and James II* old series, 52 (London: The Camden Society, 1851).

Anon., *A full and true relation of the elephant that is brought over into England from the Indies, and landed at London, August 3d. 1675* (London: printed for William Sutten, 1675).

Anon., *The Complete Cook* (London: printed for E. B. for Nath. Brooke, at the Angel in Cornhill, 1658).

Anon., *A new booke, containing all sort of hands* (London: by Richard Field, 1611).

Anon., *The Whole Duty of a Woman Or A Guide to the Female Sex* (London: printed for J. Gwillim against the Great James Tavern in Bishopsgate street, 1696).

Andrew Ashbee (ed.), *Records of English Court Music volume 1 (1660–1685)* (Snodland: T. J. Press (Padstow), Ltd, 1986).

William Averell, *An excellent historie bothe pithy and pleasant, discoursing on the Life and Death of Charles and Iulia* (London: [by J. Charlewood?] for Edward White, dwelling at the little north doore of S. Paules Church, at the signe of the Gun, 1581).

Esmond Samuel de Beer (ed.), *The Diary of John Evelyn* (London: Oxford University Press, 1959).

Andrew Borde, *The Compendious Regiment, or, Dyetary of Health* (London: 1542).

William Bray (ed.), *Diary and Correspondence of John Evelyn*, vol. 2 (London: Henry Colburn, 1850).

Andrew Browning (ed.), *Memoires of Sir John Reresby* (London: Royal Historical Society, 1991).

Robert Campbell, *The London Tradesman: Being a Compendious View of All The Trades, Professions, Arts, both Liberal and Mechanic* (London: printed by T. Gardner, at Cowley Head in the Strand, 1747)

Giacomo Castelvetro, *The Fruit, Herbs & Vegetables of Italy: An Offering to Lucy, Countess of Bedford*, translated by Gilliam Riley (London: British Museum/ Viking, 1989).

Edward Cocker, *The guide to pen-man-ship* (London: printed and are to be sold by John Ruddiard, near the Royal Exchange, 1664).

Patricia Crawford and Laura Gowing eds., *Women's Worlds in Seventeenth Century England: A Sourcebook* (London: Routledge, 2000).

John Dennys, *The Secrets of Angling, 1613* (London: W. Satchell & Co, 1883).

John Dryden, *Absalom and Achitophel* (London: 1681).

Mary Evelyn, *Mundus Muliebris: or, The ladies dressing-room unlock'd, and her toilette spread In burlesque. Together with the fop-dictionary, compiled for the use of the fair sex* (London: printed for R. Bentley, in Russel-Street in Covent-Garden, 1690).

Mary Anne Everett Green et al (eds.), *Calendar of State Papers Domestic, of the reign of Charles II* 28 vols (London: HMSO, 1860–1938).

Maurice Exwood and H. L. Lehmann (eds.), *The Journal of William Schellink's Travels in England, 1661–1663*, Camden Society, 5th Series, 1 (London: Royal Historical Society, 1993).

Celia Fiennes, *Through England on a Side Saddle in the Time of William and Mary* (Cambridge: Cambridge University Press, 2010).

Jeff Forgeng, Dorothy Johnston and David Cram, *Francis Willughby's Book of Games* (Aldershot: Ashgate, 2003).

Anthony Hamilton, *Memoirs of the Court de Grammont* (London: George Allen & Unwin Ltd, 1926).

Brilliana Harley, *Letters of Lady Brilliana Harley* (Cambridge: Cambridge University Press, 1954).

Nicholas Harris Nicolas (ed.), *Privy Purse Expenses of Elizabeth of York, Wardrobe Accounts of Edward the Fourth* (London: William Pickering, 1830).

John Heneage Jesse, *Memoirs of the Court of England, during the Reign of the Stuarts*, vol. 3 (London: Richard Bentley, 1846).

Allen B. Hinds (ed.), *Calendar of State Papers, Venetian* (London: HMSO, 1916–35).

Randle Holme, *An Accademie of Armorie; Or A Store House of Armory and Blazon*, 2 vols (Chester: printed for the author, 1688).

Sir Thomas Ireland, *Speeches spoken to the King and Queen, Duke and Duchesse of York, in Christ-Church Hall, Oxford, Sept. 29. 1663* (London: printed [by John Grismond] for Richard Royston, bookseller to His most sacred Majesty, 1663).

Sarah Kane (ed.), *Pasta for Nightingales: A 17th Century Handbook of Bird-care and Folklore* (London: Royal Collection Trust, 2018).

W. E. Knowles Middleton (ed.), *Lorenzo Magalotti at the Court of Charles II: His Relazione d'Inghilterra of 1668* (Waterloo, ON: Wilfrid Laurier University Press, 1980).

Robert Latham and William Matthews (eds.), *The Diary of Samuel Pepys*, 11 vols (London: Harper Collins, 1978).

Mary Liquorice (ed.), *Mrs Cromwell's Cookery Book: The Court and Kitchen of Elizabeth Wife of Oliver Cromwell* (Peterborough: Cambridgeshire Libraries, 1983).

Alexander Luders, Thomas Edlyne Tomlins, and John. France (eds.), *Statutes of the Realm, 1235–1713*, 12 vols (London: G. Eyre and A. Strahan, 1810–28).

Frederick Madden (ed.), *Privy Purse Expenses of the Princess Mary, Daughter of King Henry the Eighth* (London: William Pickering, 1831).

Gervase Markham, *The English Housewife* (Montreal, QC: McGill-Queens Press, 1994).

Gervase Markham, *The Well-Kept Kitchen* (London: Penguin, 2011).

Robert May, *The Accomplisht Cook, Or The whole art and mystery of cookery, fitted for all degrees and qualities* (London: printed by R. W. for Nath. Brooke at the sign of the Angel in Cornhill, 1660).

Ruth Norrington (ed.), *My Dearest Minette: Letters Between Charles II and His Sister the Duchesse d'Orléans* (London: Peter Owens Publisher, 1996).

John Parkinson, *A Garden of All Sorts of Pleasant Flowers* (London: printed by Humfrey Lownes and Robert Young at the Sign of the Starre on Bread-Street Hill, 1629).

William Penn, *An Address to Protestants upon the present conjunctive* (London: Sowle, 1679).

Caroline Robbins (ed.), *The Diary of John Milward Esq, Member of Parliament for Derbyshire, September 1666 to May 1668* (Cambridge: at the University Press, 1938).

Robert Scott-Moncrieff (ed.), *The Household Book of Lady Grisell Baillie, 1692–1733* (Edinburgh, W. S. 1911).

Dr James Smith, *The Burse of Reformation* (London: 1658).

Margaret Toynbee, 'A further note on the early correspondence of Queen Mary of Modena', *Notes and Queries* 193 (1948), 292–95.

Izaak Walton, *The Complete Angler* (London: printed by T. Maxey for Richard Marriot, 1653).

Patricia Wardle, *For Our Royal Person: Master of the Robes Bills of King-Stadholder William III* (Apeldoorn: Paleis Het Loo National Museum, 2002).

John Harold Wilson, *Court Satires of the Restoration* (Columbus, OH: Ohio State University Press, 1976).

PhD theses

Christopher Plumb, 'Exotic animals in eighteenth century Britain' (unpublished PhD thesis, University of Manchester, 2010).

Databases

The Database of Court Officers: 1660–1837 – https://courtofficers.ctsdh.luc.edu

1. Lists – Robert O. Bucholz, with John C. Sainty and Lydia Wassmann, *Household of Queen (from 1685 Queen Dowager) Catherine 1660–1705* [alphabetical list by office] https://courtofficers.ctsdh.luc.edu/lists/List%2002%20Household%20of%20Catherine%20of%20Braganzab.pdf
2. Indexes – John C. Sainty, Lydia Wassmann and Robert O. Bucholz, *Household of Queen (from 1685 Queen Dowager) Catherine 1660–1705* [alphabetical list by name] https://courtofficers.ctsdh.luc.edu/indices/Index%2002%20Household%20of%20Queen%20Catherine%201662b.pdf

Secondary sources

William Addison, *Epping Forest: Its Literary and Historical Associations* (London: J. M. Dent & Sons, 1945).

Ken Albala, *The Banquet: Dining in the Great Courts of Late Renaissance Europe*,(Urbana and Chicago, IL: University of Illinois Press, 2007).

Julia Marciari Alexander, 'Painting a Life: the case of Barbara Villiers, duchess of Cleveland', in Kevin Sharpe and Steven N. Zwicker (ed.), *Writing Lives: Biography and Textuality, Identity and Representation in Early Modern England* (Oxford: Oxford University Press, 2008) 161–84.

Mea Allan, *The Tradescants: Their Plants, Gardens and Museum* (London: Michael Joseph, 1964).

David Allen, 'The political function of Charles II's Chiffinch', *Huntington Library Quarterly*, 39 (1976), pp. 277–90.

Sonia P. Anderson, 'Finch, Heneage, third earl of Winchilsea, (1627/8–1689), diplomat', *ODNB*, 3 September 2008, https://doi.org/10.1093/ref:odnb/9434.

Robert Armstrong, Bellew, John, *Dictionary of Irish Biography*, https://www.dib.ie/biography/bellew-john-a0559.

Janet Arnold with Jenny Tiramani and Santina Levey, *Patterns of Fashion 4: The cut and Construction of Linen Shirts, Smocks, Neckwear, Headwear, and Accessories for Men and Women, c.1540–1660* (London: Macmillan, 2008).

Jane Ashelford, *The Art of Dress: Clothes and Society, 1500–1914* (London: National Trust, 1996).

Nigel Aston, 'Worsley, Sir Richard, seventh baronet, (1751–1805), antiquary and politician', *ODNB*, 21 May 2009, https://doi-org.soton.idm.oclc.org/10.1093/ref:odnb/29986.

Ian Atherton, 'Sidney, Robert, second earl of Leicester, (1595–1677), diplomat and landowner', *ODNB*, 3 January 2008, https://doi-org.soton.idm.oclc.org/10.1093/ref:odnb/25525.

Rosemary Baird, *Mistress of the House: Great Ladies and Great Houses, 1670–1830* (London: Weidenfeld & Nicolson, 2003).

Vahé Baladouni and Margaret Makepeace, 'Armenian merchants of the seventeenth and early eighteenth centuries: English East India Company sources', *Transactions of the American Philosophical Society* New Series 88.5 (1998), i–xxxvii, 1–294.

Olive Baldwin and Thelma Wilson, 'Davis [Davies; *married name* Paisible], Mary [Moll] (c.1651–1708), actress and royal mistress', *ODNB*, 3 January 2008, https://doi.org/10.1093/ref:odnb/7291.

James Balfour Paul, *The Scots Peerage* (Edinburgh, David Douglas, 1908).

Joanna Banham (ed.), *Encyclopaedia of Interior Design* (London and New York: Routledge, 2015).

Andrew Barclay, 'Mary [of Modena] (1658–1718), queen of England, Scotland and Ireland, consort of James II and VII', *ODNB*, 3 January 2008, https://doi.org/10.1093/ref:odnb/18247.

Andrew Barclay, 'May, Baptist [Bab], (bap.1628–d.1697), courtier', *ODNB*, 3 January 2008, https://doi-org.soton.idm.oclc.org/10.1093/ref:odnb/18418.

Andrew Barclay, 'Progers, Edward, (1621–1713), courtier', *ODBN*, 23 September 2004, https://doi-org.soton.idm.oclc.org/10.1093/ref:odnb/58149.

Toby Barnard, 'Boyle, Roger, first earl of Orrery, (1621–1679), politician and writer', *ODNB*, 24 May 2012, https://doi.org/10.1093/ref:odnb/3138.

Toby Barnard, 'Butler, James, first duke of Ormond, (1610–1688), lord lieutenant of Ireland', *ODNB*, 3 January 2008, https://doi.org/10.1093/ref:odnb/4191.

Kathryn Barron, 'Verrio, Antonio, (c.1639–1707), decorative painter', *ODNB*, 3 January 2008, https://doi.org/10.1093/ref:odnb/28251.

J. M. Beattie, *Policing and Punishment in London 1660–1750: Urban Crime and Punishment* (Oxford: Oxford University Press, 2001).

Alfred P. Beaven, 'Notes on the aldermen, 1502–1700', in Alfred P. Beaven, The Aldermen of the City of London Temp. Henry III – 1912 (London: Corporation of the City of London, 1908).

Gerald Belcher, 'Spain and the Anglo-Portuguese alliance of 1661: a reassessment of Charles II's foreign policy at the Restoration', *Journal of British Studies* 15.1 (1975), 67–88.

Sarah A. Bendall, 'The queen's dressmakers: women's work and the clothing trades in late seventeenth century London', *Women's History Review*, 32.3, 2023, 389–414.

Rufus Bird, Olivia Fryman and Martin Clayton (eds.), *Charles II: Art and Power* (London: Royal Collection Trust, 2017).

P. A. Bolton/Paula Watson, 'Ingram, Sir Thomas (1614–72), of Sheriff Hutton, Yorks. and Isleworth, Mdx.', https://www.historyofparliamentonline.org/volume/1660-1690/member/ingram-sir-thomas-1614-72.

Lindsay Boynton, 'Sir Richard Worsley and the firm of Chippendale', *The Burlington Magazine*, 110, no. 783 (1968), 352–55.

Michael J. Braddick, 'Fox, Sir Stephen (1627–1716), financier and government official', *ODNB*, 23 September 2004, https://doi.org/10.1093/ref:odnb/10043.

Mark Brayshay, 'Royal post-horse routes in England and Wales: the evolution of the network in the late-sixteenth and early-seventeenth century', *Journal of Historical Geography* 17.4 (1991), 373–89.

Charles Brears, *Lincolnshire in the 17th and 18th Centuries* (London: A. Brown and Sons, 1940).

Helen Brock (ed.), *A Description of the Guernsey Lily*, by James Douglas (Guernsey, The Clear Vue Publishing Company, 2012), reviewed by Graham Duncan, *Curtis's Botanical Magazine* 32.2 (2015), 162–73.

Jerry Brotton, *The Sale of the Late King's Goods: Charles I and his Art Collection* (London: Macmillan, 2006).

Jane Brown, *The Art and Architecture of English Gardens: Designs for the Garden from the Collection of the Royal Institute of British Architects 1609 to the Present Day* (London: Weidenfeld and Nicolson, 1989).

Jacqui Carey, *Sweet Bags* (Devon, Carey Company, 2010).

May Anne Caton (ed.), *Fooles and Fricassees: Food in Shakespeare's England* (Washington: Folger Shakespeare Library, 1999).

V. E. Chancellor, 'Davenport [*married name* Hoet], Hester, [*known as* Roxalana], styled countess of Oxford, (1642–1717), actress', *ODNB*, 3 January 2008, https://doi.org/10.1093/ref:odnb/70999.

Christopher R. Cheney, *A Handbook of Dates, for Students of British History* (Cambridge: Cambridge University Press, 2004).

Richard Christen, 'Boundaries between liberal and technical learning: Images of seventeenth century writing masters', *History of Education Quarterly*, 39.1 (1999), 31–50.

Tony Claydon, 'William III and II, (1650–1702), king of England, Scotland and Ireland, and prince of Orange', *ODNB*, 24 May 2008, https://doi.org/10.1093/ref:odnb/29450.

Roderick Clayton, 'Gascoigne, Sir Bernard [Bernardo Guasconi], (1614–87), royalist army officer and diplomat', *ODNB*, 3 January 2008, https://doi-org.soton.idm.oclc.org/10.1093/ref:odnb/10420.

Robin Clifton, 'Monck, Christopher, second duke of Albemarle (1653–88), army officer and colonial governor', *ODNB*, 3 January 2008, https://doi-org.soton.idm.oclc.org/10.1093/ref:odnb/18938.

Howard M. Colvin, J. Mordaunt Crook, K. Downes, J. Newman (eds.), *The History of the King's Works: Volume 5 1660–1782* (London: HMSO, 1976).

Henry Connor, 'By royal appointment: the Chase family of apothecaries', *Journal of Medical Biography* 26.3 (2018), 148–50.

Edward Corp, 'Hamilton, Elizabeth, Countess de Gramont [*called* La Belle Hamilton] (1641–1708), courtier', *ODNB*, 23 September 2004, https://doi.org.soton.idm.oclc.org/10.1093/ref:odnb/12061.

Barry Coward, 'Stanley, James, seventh earl of Derby, (1607–51), royalist army officer', *ODNB*, 3 January 2008, https://doi-org.soton.idm.oclc.org/10.1093/ref:odnb/26274.

Nancy Cox, *Retailing and the Language of Goods, 1550–1820* (London and New York: Routledge, 2016).

Patricia Crawford, 'Attitudes to menstruation in seventeenth-century England', *Past & Present*, 91 (1981), 47–73.

Anne Creighton, 'Plunket, Luke', *Dictionary of Irish Biography*, https://www.dib.ie/biography/plunket-luke-a7370.

David Cressy, *Bonfires and Bells* (Stroud: Sutton Publishing Ltd, 2004).

B. M. Crook, 'Pelham, Sir John, 3rd Bt. (c.1623–1703), of Halland, Laughton, Suss.', https://www.historyofparliamentonline.org/volume/1660-1690/member/pelham-sir-john-1623-1703.

J. S. Crossette, 'Carr, Sir Robert (c.1637–82), of Aswarby, Linc.'. https://www.historyofparliamentonline.org/volume/1660-1690/member/carr-sir-robert-1637-82.

Eveline Cruickshanks, 'Hawley, Francis, 1st baron Hawley of Duncannnon [1] (1608–84), of Buckland Sororum, Som. and Scotland Yard, Westminster', https://www.historyofparliamentonline.org/volume/1660-1690/member/hawley-francis-1608-84.

Peter Cunningham, *The Story of Nell Gwyn and the Sayings of Charles II* (London: Hutchinson & Co, Paternoster Row, 1892).

C. Willett Cunnington and Phillis Cunnington, *Handbook of English Costume in the Seventeenth Century* (London: Faber & Faber, 1972).

Alan Davidson, *The Oxford Companion to Food* (Oxford: Oxford University Press, 2014).

Lillias Campbell Davidson, *Catherine of Braganza, Infanta of Spain and Queen Consort of England* (London: John Murray, 1908).

J. D. Davies, 'Butler, Thomas, sixth earl of Ossory, (1634–1680), politician and naval officer', *ODNB*, 27 May 2010, https://doi.org/10.1093/ref:odnb/4210.

J. D. Davies, 'Fitzroy [formerly Palmer], Henry, first duke of Grafton, (1663–90), naval officer', *ODNB*, 3 January 2008, https://doi-org.soton.idm.oclc.org/10.1093/ref:odnb/9636.

J. D. Davies, 'Montagu [Mountagu], Edward, first earl of Sandwich, (1625–1672), army and naval officer and diplomat', *ODNB*, 3 January 2008, https://doi.org/10.1093/ref:odnb/19010.

J. D. Davies, 'Temple, Sir William, baronet, (1628–1699), diplomat and author', *ODNB*, 21 May 2009, https://doi.org/10.1093/ref:odnb/27122.

James Daybell, *The Material Letter in Early Modern England* (Basingstoke: Palgrave Macmillan, 2012).

Susan Doran (ed.), *Royal River: Power, Pageantry and the Thames* (London: Royal Museums Greenwich, 2021).

Thomas Doyle, 'Capel, Henry, Baron Capel of Tewkesbury, (bap.1638–96), politician and government official', *ODNB*, 3 January 2008, https://doi-org.soton.idm.oclc.org/10.1093/ref:odnb/4585.

Christopher Driver and Michelle Berriedale-Johnson, *Pepys at Table: Seventeenth Century Recipes for the Modern Cook* (London: Bell & Hyman, 1984).

Paul Drury, Sally Jeffrey and David Wrightson, 'Moor Park in the seventeenth century', *The Antiquaries Journal* 96 (2016), 241–90.

Basil Duke Henning, 'Livingston, James, 1st earl Newburgh [S] (c.1622–70), of Cirencester, Glos.', https://www.historyofparliamentonline.org/volume/1660-1690/member/livingston-james-1622-70.

Basil Duke Henning, 'Montagu, Edward, Visct. Hinchingbrooke (1648–88)', http://www.historyofparliamentonline.org/volume/1660-1690/member/montagu-edward-1648-88.

Susan Dunn-Hensley, *Anne of Denmark and Henrietta Maria: Virgins, Witches and Catholic Queens* (London: Palgrave Macmillan, 2017).

Ruth Duthie, 'The planting plans of some seventeenth-century flower gardens', *Garden History* 18.2 (1990), 77–102.

Jacqueline Eales, 'Fairfax [née Vere], Anne, Lady Fairfax, (1617/18–1665), noblewoman', *ODNB*, 23 September 2004 https://doi-org.soton.idm.oclc.org/10.1093/ref:odnb/66848.

E. R. Edwards, 'Cavendish, William, Lord Cavendish (1641–1707), of Chatsworth, Derbys.', https://www.historyofparliamentonline.org/volume/1660-1690/member/cavendish-william-1641-1707.

E. R. Edwards, 'Montagu, Hon. Ralph (1638–1709) of Montagu House, Bloomsbury, Mdx. and Boughton, Northants.', https://www.historyofparliamentonline.org/volume/1660-1690/member/montagu-ralph-1638-1709.

Geoff Egan, *Material Culture in London in an Age of Transition: Tudor and Stuart Period Finds c.1450–c.1700 from Excavations at Riverside Sites in Southwark* (London: Museum of London Archaeology Service, 2005).

Frank H. Ellis, 'Wilmot, John, second earl of Rochester, (1647–80), poet and courtier', *ODNB*, 3 January 2008, https://doi.org/10.1093/ref:odnb/29623.

Ewan Fernie, 'Chiffinch [Cheffin], Thomas, (1600–1666), courtier and royal official', *ODNB*, 23 September 2004, https://doi-org.soton.idm.oclc.org/10.1093/ref:odnb/5280.

Ewan Fernie, 'Chiffinch, William, (1602–1691), courtier and royal official', *ODNB*, 23 September 2004, https://doi-org.soton.idm.oclc.org/10.1093/ref:odnb/5281.

John P. Ferris, 'Bowerman (Boreman), George (c.1646–83), of East Greenwich, Kent', http://www.historyofparliamentonline.org/volume/1660-1690/member/bowerman-(boreman)-george-1646-83.

C. H. Firth revised by Andrew J. Hopper, 'Tuke, Sir Samuel, first baronet, (c.1615–1674), royalist army officer and playwright', *ODNB*, 3 January 2008, https://doi.org/10.1093/ref:odnb/27807.

C. H. Firth, revised by C. S. Knighton, 'Carteret, Sir George, first baronet, (1610?–1680), naval officer and administrator', *ODNB*, 3 January 2008, https://doi-org.soton.idm.oclc.org/10.1093/ref:odnb/4803.

C. H. Firth, revised by Sean Kelsey, 'Sidney, Philip, third earl of Leicester, (1619–98), parliamentarian army officer and politician', *ODNB*, 25 September 2014, https://doi-org.soton.idm.oclc.org/10.1093/ref:odnb/25523.

Celia Fisher, *The Golden Age of Flowers: Botanical Illustration in the Age of Discovery 1600–1800* (London: The British Library, 2011).

James Fitzmaurice et al., *Major Women Writers of Seventeenth Century England* (Ann Arbor, MI: University of Michigan Press, 1997).

John Forrest, *The History of Morris Dancing, 1458–1700* (Cambridge: James Clarke, 1999).

Hazel Forsyth, *The Cheapside Hoard: London's Lost Jewels* (London: Museum of London, 2013).

Michael Foster, 'Digby, Sir Kenelm, (1603–1665), natural philosopher and courtier', *ODNB*, 8 January 2009, https://doi-org.soton.idm.oclc.org/10.1093/ref:odnb/7629.

Antonia Fraser, *King Charles II* (London: Weidenfeld & Nicholson, 2020).

Olivia Fryman, 'Coffer-makers to the late Stuart court, 1660–1714', *Furniture History* 52 (2016), 1–16.

Mireille Galinou (ed.), *City merchants and the Arts, 1670–1720* (London: Oblong for the Corporation of London, 2004).

Ian J. Gentles, 'Montagu, Edward, second earl of Manchester, (1602–1671), politician and parliamentarian army officer', *ODNB*, 3 January 2008, https://doi.org/10.1093/ref:odnb/19009.

Anne Gerritsen & Giorgio Riello, *Writing Material Culture History* (London: Bloomsbury, 2015).

Laura Giannetti, 'Taste of Luxury in Renaissance Italy: In practice and in the literary imagination', in Catherine Kovesi (ed.), *Luxury and the Ethics of Greed in Early Modern Italy* (Turnhout: Brepols, 2018), 73–93.

Darra Goldstein (ed.), *The Oxford Companion to Sugar and Sweets* (Oxford: Oxford University Press, 2015).

Gordon Goodwin, revised by Sean Kelsey, 'Howard, Charles, first earl of Carlisle, (1628–1685), army officer and politician', *ODNB*, 8 October 2009, https://doi-org.soton.idm.oclc.org/10.1093/ref:odnb/13886.

Frans Gooskens, 'Sweden and the Treaty of Breda in 1667: Swedish diplomats help to end naval warfare between the Dutch Republic and England', *Forum Navale: Swedish Society for Naval History* 74 (2018), 54–80.

Laura Gowing, *Common Bodies: Women, Touch and Power in Seventeenth-Century England* (Cambridge: Cambridge University Press, 2003).

Richard Greaves, 'Capel, Arthur, first earl of Essex (bap. 1632–1683), politician and conspirator', *ODNB*, 27 May 2010, https://doi-org.soton.idm.oclc.org/10.1093/ref:odnb/4584.

Richard Griffin-Neville, Lord Braybrooke, *The History of Audley End and Saffron Walden* (London: Samuel Bentley, 1835).

Caroline Grigson, *Menagerie: The History of Exotic Animals in England* (Oxford: Oxford University Press, 2015).

Paul D. Halliday, 'Sir John Maynard (1604–90), lawyer and politician', *ODNB*, 25 May 2006, https://doi-org.soton.idm.oclc.org/10.1093/ref:odnb/18439.

Stuart Handley, 'Duras, Louis, second earl of Feversham, (1641–1709), soldier and diplomat', *ODNB*, 26 May 2016, https://doi.org/10.1093/ref:odnb/8309.

Stuart Handley, 'Hobart, Sir John, third baronet, (bap.1628–d.1683), politician', *ODNB*, 23 September 2004, https://doi-org.soton.idm.oclc.org/10.1093/ref:odnb/66634.

Stuart Handley, 'Montagu, Charles, earl of Halifax, (1661–1715), politician', *ODNB*, 22 September 2005, https://doi-org.soton.idm.oclc.org/10.1093/ref:odnb/19004.

Stuart Handley, 'Stanhope, Philip, second earl of Chesterfield, (1633–1714), courtier and politician', *ODNB*, 23 September 2004, https://doi.org/10.1093/ref:odnb/26253.

Stuart Handley, 'Stuart [Stewart], Frances Teresa, duchess of Lennox and Richmond, [*called*, La Belle Stuart], courtier', *ODNB*, 3 January 2008, https://doi.org/10.1093/ref:odnb/26703.

Stuart Handley, 'Townshend, Horatio, first viscount Townshend, (bap.1630–1687), politician', *ODNB*, 3 January 2008, https://doi.org/10.1093/ref:odnb/27628.

A. A. Hanham, 'Bromley, William, (bap.1663–1732), speaker of the House of Commons', *ODNB*, 19 May 2011, https://doi-org.soton.idm.oclc.org/10.1093/ref:odnb/3515.

Tim Harding, *British Chess Literature up to 1914: A Handbook for Historians* (Jefferson, NC: McFarland & Company, Inc., 2018).

Frances Harris, *Transformations of Love: The Friendship of John Evelyn and Margaret Godolphin* (Oxford: Oxford University Press, 2002).

Tim Harris, 'Cooper, Anthony Ashley, first earl of Shaftsbury, (1621–83), politician', *ODNB*, 3 January 2008, https://doi.org/10.1093/ref:odnb/6208.

Freda Hast, 'Villiers [married name Stuart], Mary, duchess of Lennox and Richmond, (1622–1685), courtier', *ODNB*, 3 January 2008, https://doi-org.soton.idm.oclc.org/10.1093/ref:odnb/56054.

Richard Hawkins, 'Bellew, Sir John', *Dictionary of Irish Biography*, https://www.dib.ie/biography/bellew-sir-john-a0560.

D. W. Hayton, 'Hanmer, Sir Thomas, fourth baronet, (1677–1746), speaker of the House of Commons', *ODNB*, 26 May 2005, https://doi-org.soton.idm.oclc.org/10.1093/ref:odnb/12205.

Maria Hayward, ' "The best of queens, the most obedient wife": Fashioning a place for Catherine of Braganza as consort to Charles II', in Erin Griffey (ed.), *Sartorial Politics in Early Modern Europe: Fashioning Women* (Amsterdam University Press, 2020), 227–52.

Karen Hearn, 'Revising the visage: patches and beauty spots in seventeenth-century British and Dutch painted portraits', *Huntingdon Library Quarterly* 78.4 (2015), 809–23.

M. W. Helms, 'Cornwallis, Charles, (1632–73), of Brome Hall, Suffolk', https://www.historyofparliamentonline.org/volume/1660-1690/member/cornwallis-charles-ii-1632-73.

M. W. Helms/Eveline Cruickshanks, 'Howard, Philip (c.1631–86), of Leicester Fields, Westminster and Sissinghurst, Kent', https://www.historyofparliamentonline.org/volume/1660-1690/member/howard-philip-1631-86.

A. W. Helms/Leonard Naylor/Geoffrey Jagger, 'Winwood, Richard (1609–88), of Quainton, Bucks.', https://www.historyofparliamentonline.org/volume/1660-1690/member/winwood-richard-1609-88.

T. F. Henderson, revised Edward M. Furgol, 'Seton, Charles, second earl of Dunfermline, (1615–1672), politician and army officer', *ODNB*, 23 September 2004, https://doi.org/10.1093/ref:odnb/25117.

John Heneage Jesse, *Memoirs of the Court of England During the Reigns of the Stuarts including the Protectorate of Oliver Cromwell*, vol. 3 (Boston, MA: L. C. Page, 1901).

Caroline Hibberd, 'Henrietta Maria [Princess Henrietta Maria of France], (1609–1669), queen of England, Scotland and Ireland, consort of Charles I', *ODNB*, 3 January 2008, https://doi.org/10.1093/ref:odnb/12947.

Francis Hill, *Tudor and Stuart Lincoln* (Cambridge: Cambridge University Press, 1956).

Mary Hill Cole, *The Portable Queen: Elizabeth I and the Politics of Ceremony* (Amherst, MA: University of Massachusetts Press, reprint 2011).

Clive Holmes, *Seventeenth Century Lincolnshire* (Lincoln: History of Lincolnshire Committee, 1980).

David Hosford, 'Sidney, Henry, first earl of Romsey, (1641–1704), politician and army officer', *ODNB*, 10 January 2013, https://doi.org/10.1093/ref:odnb/25521.

Wilhelmine Howard, *Norfolk: A Shell Guide* (London: Faber and Faber, 1958, 1982).

Lynn Hulse, 'Cavendish, William, first duke of Newcastle upon Tyne, (bap.1593–1676), writer, patron and royalist army officer', *ODNB*, 6 January 2011, https://doi.org/10.1093/ref:odnb/4946.

Paul Hunneyball, 'Killigrew, Sir William II (1606–1695) of Pendennis Castle, Cornw.; later of Lincoln's Inn Fields, London and Kempton Park, Mdx.', http://www.historyofparliamentonline.org/volume/1604-1629/member/killigrew-sir-william-ii-1606-1695.

Ronald Hutton, *The Rise and Fall of Merry England: The Ritual Year1400–1700* (Oxford: Oxford University Press, 1994).

Ronald Hutton, 'Berkeley, Charles, earl of Falmouth, (bap.1630–d.1665), courtier', *ODNB*, 3 January 2008, https://doi-org.soton.idm.oclc.org/10.1093/ref:odnb/37185.

Ronald Hutton, 'Digby, George, second earl of Bristol (1612–77), politician', *ODNB*, 21 May 2009 https://doi.org/10.1093/ref:odnb/7627.

Ronald Hutton, 'Gerard, Charles, first earl of Macclesfield, (c.1618–94), royalist army officer', *ODNB*, 9 December 2021, https://doi-org.soton.idm.oclc.org/10.1093/ref:odnb/10550.

Ronald Hutton, 'Maitland, John, duke of Lauderdale, (1616–1682), politician', *ODNB*, 25 May 2006, https://doi.org/10.1093/ref:odnb/17827.

Ronald Hutton, 'Monck [Monk], George, first duke of Albemarle, (1608–70), army officer and navy officer', *ODNB*, 4 October 2021, https://doi.org/10.1093/ref:odnb/18939.

Claire Jackson, *Devil-Land: England Under Siege, 1588–1688* (London: Penguin, 2022).

Helen Jacobsen, *Luxury and Power: The Material World of the Stuart Diplomat, 1660–1714* (Oxford: Oxford University Press, 2012).

Kathryn James, *English Palaeography and Manuscript Culture, 1500–1800* (New Haven and London: Yale University Press, 2020).

James Johnson, *A Profane Witt: The Life of John Wilmot, Earl of Rochester* (Rochester, NY: University of Rochester Press, 2004).

Sean Kelsey, 'Booth, George, first Baron Delamer [Delamere] (1622–1684), politician', *ODNB*, 5 January 2006, https://doi.org/10.1093/ref:odnb/2877.

Sean Kelsey, 'Weston, Jerome, second earl of Portland, (1605–1663), politician',

ODNB, 3 January 2008, https://doi.org.soton.idm.oclc.org/10.1093/ref:odnb/29123.

John Philipps Kenyon, 'The acquittal of Sir George Wakeman: 18 July 1679', *The Historical Journal* 14.4 (1971), 693–708.

R. W. Ketton-Cremer, 'The visit of King Charles II to Norfolk', in *Norfolk Portraits* (London: Faber and Faber, 1944), 9–21.

Peter King, Lord King (ed.), *The Life of John Locke with Extracts from his Correspondence, Journals and Common-Place Books*, vol. 1 (London: Henry Colburn and Richard Bentley, New Burlington Street, 1830).

Fiona Kisby, 'Kingship and the royal itinerary: a study of the peripatetic household of the early Tudor kings, 1485–1547', *Court Historian* 4.1 (1999), 29–39.

Peter Leech, 'Musicians in the Catholic Chapel of Catherine of Braganza, 1662–92', *Early Music* 29.4 (2001), 571–87.

Prudence Leith-Ross, *The Johns Tradescants: Gardeners to the Rose and Lily Queen* (London and Chester Spring, Peter Edwards, 2006).

Santina Levey, *Lace: A History* (Leeds: Victoria and Albert Museum, with W. S. Maney and Sons, 1983).

Harold Love, 'Sackville, Charles, sixth earl of Dorset and first earl of Middlesex, (1643–1706), poet and politician', *ODNB*, 3 January 2008, https://doi-org.soton.idm.oclc.org/10.1093/ref:odnb/24442.

Susannah Lyon-Whaley, 'Queens at the spa: Catherine of Braganza, Mary of Modena and the politics of display at Bath and Tunbridge Wells', *The Court Historian* 27.1 (2022), 24–41.

Ralph Lytton Bower, 'An early seventeenth century angler', *The Sewanee Review* 10.2 (1902), 199–206.

Catherine MacLeod and Julia Marciari Alexander, *Painted Ladies: Women at the Court of Charles II* (London: National Portrait Gallery Publications, 2001).

Sidney J. Madge, 'Worcester House in the Strand', *Archaeologia* 91 (1945), 157–80.

Nancy K. Maguire, 'The duchess of Portsmouth: English royal consort and French politician, 1670–85', in R. Malcolm Smutts (ed.), *The Stuart Court and Europe: Essays in Politics and Political Culture* (Cambridge: Cambridge University Press, 1996), 247–73.

Gaby Mahlberg, *The English Republican Exiles in Europe during the Restoration* (Cambridge: Cambridge University Press, 2020).

Francis Manley, 'An early seventeenth-century manuscript art of angling', *The Yale University Library Gazette* 35.1 (1960), 1–10.

Joanna Marschner, 'Baths and bathing at the early Georgian court', *Furniture History*, 31 (1995), 23–28.

Alan Marshall, 'Bennet, Henry, first earl of Arlington, (1618–85), politician', *ODNB*, 3 January 2008, https://doi.org/10.1093/ref:odnb/2104.

Rosalind Marshall, 'Murray [*married names* Tollemache, Maitland], Elizabeth, duchess of Lauderdale, and *suo jure* countess of Dysart, (bap.1626–1698), noblewoman', *ODNB*, 23 September 2004, https://doi.org/10.1093/ref:odnb/19601.

William Marshall, 'Croft, Herbert, (1603–1691), bishop of Hereford', *ODNB*, 3 January 2008, https://doi-org.soton.idm.oclc.org/10.1093/ref:odnb/6717.

Molly McClain, 'Somerset, Henry, first duke of Beaufort, (1629–1700), nobleman', *ODNB*, 3 October 2013, https://doi.org/10.1093/ref:odnb/26009.

C. I. McGrath, 'Wyche, Sir Cyril, (c.1632–1707), government official', *ODNB*, 23 September 2004, https://doi.org/10.1093/ref:odnb/30117.

James McGuire, 'Talbot, Richard', *Dictionary of Irish Biography*, https://www.dib.ie/biography/talbot-richard-a8460.

Neil McKendrick, John Brewer and J. H. Plumb, *The Birth of a Consumer Society: The Commercialisation of Eighteenth-century England* (London: Hutchinson & Co, 2007).

Lewis Melville, *The Windsor Beauties: Ladies of the Court of Charles II* (Ann Arbor, MI: Modern History Press, 2005).

John Miller, 'Anne [née Hyde], duchess of York (1637–1671), first wife of James II', *ODNB*, 3 January 2008, https://doi.org/10.1093/ref:odnb/14325.

John Miller, 'Henriette Anne [formerly Henrietta], Princess, duchess of Orléans, (1644–1670)', *ODNB*, 23 September 2004, https://doi.org/10.1093/ref:odnb/12946.

John Miller, 'Jermyn, Henry, third Baron Jermyn and Jacobite earl of Dover, (bap.1636–d.1708), courtier and army officer', *ODNB*, 3 January 2008, https://doi-org.soton.idm.oclc.org/10.1093/ref:odnb/14781.

John Miller, 'Paston, Robert, first earl of Yarmouth, (1631–1683), politician', *ODNB*, 9 December 2021, https://doi.org/10.1093/ref:odnb/21513.

Anthony David Mills, *Oxford Dictionary of English Place-Names* (Oxford: Oxford University Press, 1998).

A. M. Mimardière, 'Trevor, Sir John, (c.1637–1717), of Clement's Lane, Westminster and Pulford, Denb.', http://www.histparl.ac.uk/volume/1690-1715/member/trevor-sir-john-1637-1717.

Richard Minta Dunn, 'Howard, James, third earl of Suffolk, (1619–89), nobleman', *ODNB*, 23 September 2004, https://doi-org.soton.idm.oclc.org/10.1093/ref:odnb/13919.

Rosemary Mitchell, 'Strickland, Agnes, (1796–1874), historian', *ODNB*, 10 October 2019, https://doi.org/10.1093/ref:odnb/26663.

Julian Munby, 'Signor Verrio and Monsieur Beaumont, gardeners to James II', *Journal of the British Archaeological Association* 149.1 (1996), 55–71.

Leonard Naylor, 'Strickland, Sir Thomas, (1621–94), of Sizergh Castle, Westmld.', https://www.historyofparliamentonline.org/volume/1660-1690/member/strickland-sir-thomas-1621-94.

Leonard Naylor/Geoffrey Jagger, 'Chiffinch, William, (d.1691), of Whitehall and Philberts, Bray, Berks.', https://www.historyofparliamentonline.org/volume/1660-1690/member/chiffinch-william-1691.

Leonard Naylor/Geoffrey Jagger, 'Lovelace, Hon. John (c.1642–93), of Water Eaton, Oxon. and Hurley, Berks.', http://www.historyofparliamentonline.org/volume/1660-1690/member/lovelace-hon-john-1642-93.

Leonard Naylor/Geoffrey Jagger, 'May, Sir Algernon (c. 1625–1704), of Old Windsor, Berks. and Ampton, Suff.', http://www.histparl.ac.uk/volume/1660-1690/member/may-sir-algernon-1625-1704.

Eirwen E. C. Nicholson, 'Scott, Anna [Anne] duchess of Monmouth and suo jure

duchess of Buccleuch, (1651–1732), noblewoman', *ODNB*, 23 September 2004, https://doi.org/10.1093/ref:odnb/67531.
Robert O'Byrne, *The Representative History of Great Britain and Ireland* (London: John Ollivier, 1848).
Éamonn Ó Ciardha, 'Hamilton, Sir George', *Dictionary of Irish Biography*, October 2009, https://www.dib.ie/biography/hamilton-sir-george-a3739.
Rosemary O'Day, 'Tudor and Stuart women: their lives through their letters', in James Daybell (ed.), *Early Modern Women's Letter Writing, 1450–1700* (Basingstoke: Palgrave Macmillan, 2001), 127–42.
Tadhg Ó hAnnracháin, 'Bellings, Richard, (c.1603–1677), politician and historian', *ODNB*, 23 September 2004, https://doi-org.soton.idm.oclc.org/10.1093/ref:odnb/2059.
Charles Oman, *Caroline Silver 1625–1688* (London: Faber and Faber, 1970).
David Parlett, *The Penguin Book of Card Games* (Harmondsworth: Penguin, 1979).
David Parlett, *A History of Card Games* (Oxford: Oxford University Press, 1991).
M. Perceval-Maxwell, 'Butler [*née* Preston], Elizabeth, duchess of Ormond and *suo jure* Lady Dingwall, (1615–1684), noblewoman', *ODNB*, 23 September 2004, https://doi.org/10.1093/ref:odnb/67044.
Nikolaus Pevsner and Enid Radcliffe, *Suffolk: The Buildings of England* (Harmondsworth: Penguin, 1975).
Sophie Pitman, 'Prodigal years? Negotiating luxury and fashioning identity in a seventeenth-century account book', *Luxury* 3.1–2 (2016), 7–31.
Lucy Pratt and Linda Woolley, *Shoes* (London: V&A Publications, 2005).
Will Pritchard, *The Female Exterior in Restoration London* (Lewisburg: Bucknell University Press, 2008).
Sandra Raphael, 'Rose, John, (1619–1677), gardener and nurseryman', *ODNB*, 23 September 2004, https://doi.org/10.1093/ref:odnb/37913.
Erika Rappaport, *A Thirst for Empire: How Tea Shaped the Modern World* (New Jersey, Princeton University Press, 2019).
Erik Rath, *Food and Fantasy in Early Modern Japan* (Berkeley, CA: University of California Press, 2010).
Conor Reilly, 'Francis Line, peripatetic', *Osiris*, 14 (1962), 222–53.
Chelsea Reutcke, 'Royal patronage of illicit print: Catherine of Braganza and Catholic books in late seventeenth century London', in Nina Lamal, Jamie Cumby and Helmer J. Helmers (eds.), *Print and Power in Early Modern Europe, 1500–1800* (Leiden: Brill, 2021), 239–56.
Aileen Ribeiro, *Fashion and Fiction: Dress in Art and Literature in Stuart England* (London and New Haven: Yale University Press, 2005).
Catherine Richardson, 'Written texts and the performance of materiality', in Anne Gerritsen and Giorgio Riello (eds.), *Writing Material Culture History* (London: Bloomsbury, 2015) 43–58.
J. M. Rigg, revised by Sean Kelsey, 'Crew, John, first Baron Crew, (1597/8–1679), politician', *ODNB*, 3 January 2008, https://doi.org/10.1093/ref:odnb/6682.
Sandra Riley, *Charlotte de la Trémoïlle, the Notorious Countess of Derby* (Newcastle upon Tyne, Cambridge Scholars Publishing, 2017).
Melville de Ruvigny (comp.), *The Jacobite Peerage* (Edinburgh: T. C. and E. C. Jack, 1904).

Lois G. Schwoerer, 'Russell, [*née* Wriothesley; *other married name* Vaughan], Rachel, lady Russell, (1637–1723), noblewoman', *ODNB*, 23 September 2004, https://doi.org/10.1093/ref:odnb/24335.

Gladys Scott Thomson, *Life in a Noble Household, 1641–1700* (London: Jonathan Cape, 1937).

Jason Scott-Warren, 'Early modern book keeping and life writing revisited: Accounting for Richard Stonley', *Past & Present* 230 (2016), 151–70.

Paul Seaward, 'Hyde, Edward, first earl of Clarendon, (1609–74), politician and historian', *ODNB*, 4 October 2008, https://doi.org/10.1093/ref:odnb/14328.

Paul Seaward, 'Charles II (1630–1685), king of England, Scotland and Ireland', *ODNB*, 19 May 2011, https://doi.org/10.1093/ref:odnb/5144.

Thomas Seccombe, revised Michael Bevan, 'Wakeman, Sir George, baronet, (b.1627), physician', *ODNB*, 23 September 2004, https://doi-org.soton.idm.oclc.org/10.1093/ref:odnb/28422.

R. C. L. Sgroi, 'Piscatorial politics revisited: the language of economic debate and the evolution of fishing policy in Elizabethan England', *Albion*, 35.1 (2003), 1–24.

Henry Shapiro, 'The great Armenian flight: migration and cultural change in the seventeenth-century Ottoman empire', *Journal of Early Modern History* 23.1 (2019), 67–89.

Desmond Shawe-Taylor and Per Rumberg (eds.), *Charles I: King and Collector* (London: Royal Academy of the Arts, 2018).

Alexander Shepard, *Accounting for Oneself: Worth, Status and the Social Order in Early Modern England* (Oxford: Oxford University Press, 2018).

Michael Shrubb, *Feasting, Fowling and Feathers: A History of the Exploitation of Wild Birds* (London: T. and A. D. Poyser, an imprint of Bloomsbury, 2013).

David L. Smith, 'Herbert, Philip, first earl of Montgomery and fourth earl of Pembroke, (1584–1650), courtier and politician', *ODNB*, 26 May 2016, https://doi-org.soton.idm.oclc.org/10.1093/ref:odnb/13042.

David L. Smith, 'Strangways, Sir John, (1584–1666), politician', *ODNB*, 3 January 2008, https://doi-org.soton.idm.oclc.org/10.1093/ref:odnb/39725.

David Smith, 'Wriothesely, Thomas, fourth earl of Southampton, (1608–1667), politician', *ODNB*, 3 January 2008 https://doi.org/10.1093/ref:odnb/30077.

Steven Smith, 'Growing old in early Stuart England', *Albion*, 8.2, (1976), 125–41.

Malcolm Smuts, 'Craven, William, earl of Craven, (bap.1608–d.1697), army officer and royal servant', *ODNB*, 24 May 2007, https://doi.org/10.1093/ref:odnb/6636.

W. A. Speck, 'Hyde, Henry, second earl of Clarendon, (1638–1709), politician', *ODNB*, 5 January 2012, https://doi.org/10.1093/ref:odnb/14329.

W. A. Speck, 'James II and VII, (1633–1701), king of England, Scotland and Ireland', *ODNB*, 8 October 2009, https://doi.org/10.1093/ref:odnb/14593.

W. A. Speck, 'Spencer, Robert, second earl Sunderland, (1641–1702), politician', *ODNB*, 3 January 2008, https://doi-org.soton.idm.oclc.org/10.1093/ref:odnb/26135.

John Spurr, 'Morley, George, (1598?–1684), bishop of Winchester', *ODNB*, 23 September 2004, https://doi.org/10.1093/ref:odnb/19285.

John Spurr, 'Sheldon, Gilbert (1598–1677), archbishop of Canterbury', *ODNB*, 24 May 2008, https://doi.org/10.1093/ref:odnb/25304.

Kay Staniland, 'Samuel Pepys and his wardrobe', *Costume*, 37.1 (2003), 41–50.

Victor Stater, 'Cavendish, William, third earl of Devonshire, (1617–1684), nobleman', *ODNB*, 25 May 2006, https://doi-org.soton.idm.oclc.org/10.1093/ref:odnb/4947.

Victor Stater, 'Cecil, James, third earl of Salisbury, (d.1683), politician', *ODNB*, 23 September 2004, https://doi-org.soton.idm.oclc.org/10.1093/ref:odnb/4976.

Victor Stater, 'Grenville, John, first earl of Bath, (1628–1701), nobleman', *ODNB*, 3 January 2008, https://doi.org/10.1093/ref:odnb/11492.

Victor Stater, 'Mordaunt, Henry, second earl of Peterborough, (bap.1623–d.1697), nobleman', *ODNB*, 23 September 2004, https://doi-org.soton.idm.oclc.org/10.1093/ref:odnb/19163.

Victor Stater, 'Newport, Francis, first earl of Bradford, (1619–1708), politician', *ODNB*, 23 September 2004, https://doi.org/10.1093/ref:odnb/20033.

Victor Stater, 'Vere, Aubrey de, twentieth earl of Oxford, (1627–1703), nobleman', *ODNB*, 24 May 2008, https://doi.org/10.1093/ref:odnb/28206.

Gesa Stedman, *Culture Exchange in Seventeenth-Century France and England* (London: Routledge, 2013).

Agnes Strickland, *Lives of the Queens of England*, vol. 8 (Philadelphia, PA: Lea and Blanchard, 1850).

David Stuart, *The Kitchen Garden: An Historical Guide to Traditional Crops* (Gloucester: Alan Sutton, 1984).

Peter C. Sutton, *Pieter de Hooch* (Oxford: Phaidon, 1980).

Alexis Tadié, 'The uses and transformations of early modern tennis', in Sharron Harrow (ed.), *British Sporting Literature and Culture in the Long Eighteenth Century* (London and New York: Routledge, 2016), 83–104.

Lou Taylor, *Mourning: A Costume and Social History* (Abingdon: Routledge, reprint, 2010).

Roger Thompson, *Mobility & Migration, East Anglian Founders of New England, 1629–1640* (Amherst, MA: University of Massachusetts Press, 1994).

Andrew Thrush, 'Villiers, Sir Edward (c.1585–1626), government official and administrator', ODNB online ed, 24 May 2008, https://doi-org.soton.idm.oclc.org/10.1093/ref:odnb/28288.

Simon Thurley, *The Royal Palaces of Tudor England: Architecture and Court Life, 1460–1547* (New Haven and London: Yale University Press, 1993).

Simon Thurley, *The Whitehall Palace Plan of 1670* (London: London Topographical Society, 1998).

Simon Thurley, *Whitehall Palace: An Architectural History of the Royal Apartments, 1240–1698* (New Haven and London: Yale University Press, 1999).

Simon Thurley, 'A country seat fit for a king: Charles II, Greenwich and Winchester', in Eveline Cruickshanks (ed.), *The Stuart Court* (Stroud: Sutton, 2000), 214–39.

Simon Thurley, 'The Stuart kings, Oliver Cromwell and the Chapel Royal, 1618–1685', *Architectural History* 45 (2002), 238–74.

Simon Thurley, *Somerset House: The Palace of England's Queens, 1551–1692* (London: London Topographical Society, 2009).

Maurice Tucker, 'Quartz replaced anhydrite nodules ('Bristol diamonds') from the Triassic of the Bristol district', *Geological Magazine* 113.6 (1976), 569–74.

Sarah Tyacke, *London Map Sellers 1660–1720* (London: Map Collector Publications, Ltd, 1978).

Albert Valente, *Chronicles of the Dutch Republic, 1566–1702* (Lisbon: Albert Valente, 2022).

J. P. Vander Motten, 'Howard, Sir Robert, (1626–98), playwright and politician', *ODNB*, 19 May 2011, https://doi-org.soton.idm.oclc.org/10.1093/ref:odnb/13935.

J. P. Vander Motten, 'Killigrew, Sir William, (bap.1606–95), courtier and playwright', *ODNB*, 3 January 2008, https://doi.org/10.1093/ref:odnb/15541.

David Verey, *Gloucestershire: The Cotswolds: The Buildings of England* (Harmondsworth: Penguin, 1979).

Amanda Vickery, 'Women and the world of goods: a Lancashire consumer and her possessions, 1751–81' in John Brewer & Roy Porter (eds.), *Consumption and the World of Goods* (London: Routledge, 1993), 274–301.

Amanda Vickery, *The Gentleman's Daughter: Women's Lives in Georgian England* (New Haven and London: Yale University Press, 1998).

James M. Volo and Dorothy Denneen Volo, *Family Life in 17th and 18th Century America* (Westport, CT: Greenwood Press, 2006).

Andrew Walkling, 'Masque and politics at the Restoration Court: John Crowne's "Callisto"', *Early Music* 24.1 (1996), 27–62.

John Walter, 'Tichborne, Sir Henry, third baronet, (1624–1689), landowner', *ODNB*, 23 September 2004, https://doi-org.soton.idm.oclc.org/10.1093/ref:odnb/66939.

Patricia Wardle, ' "Divers necessaries for his Majesty's use and service": Seamstresses to the Stuart Kings', *Costume* 31 (1997), 16–27.

Patricia Wardle, 'A rare survival: the barge cloth of the Worshipful Company of Pewterers and the embroiderer John West', *Textile History* 37.1 (2006), 1–16.

Paula Watson, 'Worsley, Sir Robert, 4th Bt. (?1669–1747), of Appuldurcombe, I.o.W. and Chilton Condover, Hants.', https://www.historyofparliamentonline.org/volume/1715-1754/member/worsley-sir-robert-1669-1747.

Paula Watson and Andrew A Hanham, 'Capel, Sir Henry (1638–96), of Kew, Surr.', https://www.historyofparliamentonline.org/volume/1690-1715/member/capel-hon-sir-henry-1638-96

Donald Watts, *Elsevier's Dictionary of Plant Lore* (Burlington, MA: Elsevier, 2007).

Lorna Weatherill, *Consumer Behaviour and Material Culture in Britain, 1660–1760* (London: Routledge, 2nd edition, 1996).

Rachel Weil, 'Villiers [married name Hamilton], Elizabeth, countess of Orkney, (c.1657–1733), presumed mistress of William III', *ODNB* online ed., 3 October 2013, https://doi-org.soton.idm.oclc.org/10.1093/ref:odnb/28290.

Brian Weiser, *Charles II and the Politics of Access* (Woodbridge: The Boydell Press, 2003).

Annabel Westman, *Fringe, Frog and Tassel: The Art of the Trimmings Maker in Interior Decoration* (London: National Trust, 2019).

Jane Whittle and Elizabeth Griffiths, *Consumption and Gender in the Early Seventeenth-Century Household: The World of Alice Le Strange* (Oxford: Oxford University Press, 2012).

Margaret Willes, *The Making of the English Gardener: Plants, Books and Inspiration, 1560–1660* (New Haven and London: Yale University Press, 2013).

Margaret Willes, *In the Shadow of St Paul's Cathedral: The Churchyard that Shaped London* (New Haven and London: Yale University Press, 2022).

Isabel Wingate, *Fairchild's Dictionary of Textiles* (New York: Fairchild Publications, 6th edition, 1979).

Charles W. J. Withers, 'Ogilby, John, (1600–1676), publisher and geographer', *ODNB*, 4 October 2007, https://doi.org/10.1093/ref:odnb/20583.

Heather Wolfe, 'Women's handwriting', in Laura Lunger Knoppers (ed.), *The Cambridge Companion to Early Modern Women's Writing* (Cambridge: Cambridge University Press, 2009), 21–39.

D. R. Woolf, 'Sanderson, Sir William (1586–1676), historian', *ODNB*, 23 September 2004, https://doi-org.soton.idm.oclc.org/10.1093/ref:odnb/24630.

Sonia Wynne, 'Catherine [Catherine of Braganza, Catarina Henriqueta de Bragança], (1638–1705), queen of England, Scotland and Ireland, consort of Charles II', *ODNB*, 3 January 2008, https://doi.org/10.1093/ref:odnb/4894.

Sonia Wynne, 'Kéroualle, Louise Renée de Penancoët de, *suo jure* duchess of Portsmouth and *suo jure* duchess of Aubigny in the French nobility, (1649–1734), royal mistress', *ODNB*, 3 January 2008, https://doi.org.soton.idm.oclc.org/10.1093/ref:odnb/15460.

Sonia Wynne, 'Palmer [*née* Villiers], Barbara, countess of Castlemaine, and *suo jure* duchess of Cleveland, (bap.1640–1709), royal mistress', *ODNB*, 24 October 2019, https://doi-org.soton.idm.oclc.org/10.1093/ref:odnb/28285 [accessed 14/4/22].

Bruce Yardley, 'Villiers, George, second duke of Buckingham, (1628–1687), politician and wit', *ODNB*, 21 May 2009, https://doi.org/10.1093/ref:odnb/28294.

Websites

The British Deer Society/BRS – https://bds.org.uk

British History Online/BHO – https://www.british-history.ac.uk

The British Library – https://www.bl.uk

British Listed Buildings – https://britishlistedbuildings.co.uk

Chiswick Auctions – https://www.chiswickauctions.co.uk

Civil War Petitions: Conflict, Warfare and Memory during and after the English Civil Wars, 1642–1710, https://www.civilwarpetitions.ac.uk

The Complete Angler: And other meditations on the Art and Philosophy of Fishing, 15th Century to the Present: 17th Century Editions – https://pitt.libguides.com/compleatangler/17thcenturyeditions

The Cookbook of Unknown Ladies – https://lostcookbook.wordpress.com

Cooking in the Archives: Updating Early Modern Recipes (1600–1800) in a Modern Kitchen – https://rarecooking.com

Council of Europe: Recommendation concerning Muscovy Ducks and Hybrids of Muscovy and Domestic Ducks – https://www.coe.int/en/web/cdcj/1999-rec-muscovy-and-domestic-ducks

Dictionary of Irish Biography – https://www.dib.ie

Ditchley – https://www.ditchley.com

Early English Books Online – https://quod.lib.umich.edu/e/eebo

Exploring London – https://exploring-london.com

Family search – https://ancestors.familysearch.org

Fishing Museum – http://www.fishingmuseum.org.uk/rods_overview.html

Folger Shakespeare Library: Shakespeare & Beyond – https://shakespeareandbeyond.

folger.edu/2017/08/08/recipe-salmon-pastry-shakespeare-kitchen-francine-segan
Games and Gamebooks by David Parlett – https://www.parlettgames.uk
The Gazette Official Public Record – https://www.thegazette.co.uk
Geni: A MyHeritage company – https://www.geni.com
Greenwich Peninsula History – https://greenwichpeninsulahistory.wordpress.com
Grove Music Online – https://www.oxfordmusiconline.com/grovemusic
Hidden London – https://hidden-london.com
Historic England – https://historicengland.org.uk
The Historic Foodie's Blog – https://thehistoricfoodie.wordpress.com
The History of Parliament – https://www.historyofparliamentonline.org
Jamestown Rediscovery: Historic Jamestowne – https://historicjamestowne.org
Magdalene College Libraries – https://magdlibs.com/2015/03/20/pepys-and-archery
Many-Headed Monster – https://manyheadedmonster.com/2023/05/18/black-lives-in-the-restoration-household-the-queens-account
Masters Traditional Games – https://www.mastersofgames.com
Medieval Archaeology – https://medievalarchaeology.co.uk
National Gallery of Art, Washington DC – https://www.nga.gov/collection
National Museum of Wales (Amgueddfa Cymru) – https://www.nhmf.org.uk
National Portrait Gallery – https://www.npg.org.uk
National Trust – https://www.nationaltrustcollections.org.uk
OED: Oxford English Dictionary – https://www.oed.com
Our Warwickshire – https://www.ourwarwickshire.org.uk
Pagat.com – Card game rules – https://www.pagat.com
Patricia Lovett – https://www.patricialovett.com
The Peerage – http://www.thepeerage.com
Researchgate – https://www.researchgate.net
Royal Armouries – https://royalarmouries.org
Royal Berkshire History – https://www.berkshirehistory.com
The Royal Collection Trust – https://www.rct.uk
The Royal Parks – https://www.royalparks.org.uk
Strandlines – the Lost Mansions of the Strand – https://www.strandlines.london/2018/11/26/the-lost-mansions-of-the-strand
Twickenham Museum – http://www.twickenham-museum.org.uk/detail.php?aid=301&ctid=1&cid=9
Victoria and Albert Museum – https://www.vam.ac.uk
Victoria & Albert Museum Theatre posters: an illustrated history – https://www.vam.ac.uk/articles/theatre-posters-an-illustrated-history
Virgilio Nogueiro Gomes Gastronomo – https://www.virgiliogomes.com
Westminster Abbey – https://www.westminster-abbey.org
Wild Trout Trust – https://www.wildtrout.org
Windsor Great Park – https://www.windsorgreatpark.co.uk
Y Bywgraffiadur Cymreig/Dictionary of Welsh Biography – https://biography.wales

INDEX